ATL INTERNALS

The Addison-Wesley Object Technology Series

Grady Booch, Ivar Jacobson, and James Rumbaugh, Series Editors
For more information check out the series web site [http://www.awl.com /cseng/otseries/] as well as the pages
on each book [http://www.awl.com/cseng/I-S-B-N/] (I-S-B-N represents the actual ISBN, including dashes).

David Bellin and Susan Suchman Simone, *The CRC Card Book*, ISBN 0-201-89535-8

Grady Booch, *Object Solutions: Managing the Object-Oriented Project*, ISBN 0-8053-0594-7

Grady Booch, *Object-Oriented Analysis and Design with Applications, Second Edition*, ISBN 0-8053-5340-2

Grady Booch, James Rumbaugh, and Ivar Jacobson, *The Unified Modeling Language User Guide*, ISBN 0-201-57168-4

Don Box, *Essential COM*, ISBN 0-201-63446-5

Don Box, Keith Brown, Tim Ewald, and Chris Sells, *Effective COM: 50 Ways to Improve Your COM and MTS-based Applications*, ISBN 0-201-37968-6

Alistair Cockburn, *Surviving Object-Oriented Projects: A Manager's Guide*, ISBN 0-201-49834-0

Dave Collins, *Designing Object-Oriented User Interfaces*, ISBN 0-8053-5350-X

Bruce Powel Douglass, *Doing Hard Time: Designing and Implementing Embedded Systems with UML*, ISBN 0-201-49837-5

Bruce Powel Douglass, *Real-Time UML: Developing Efficient Objects for Embedded Systems*, ISBN 0-201-32579-9

Desmond F. D'Souza and Alan Cameron Wills, *Objects, Components, and Frameworks with UML: The Catalysis Approach*, ISBN 0-201-31012-0

Martin Fowler, *Analysis Patterns: Reusable Object Models*, ISBN 0-201-89542-0

Martin Fowler, *Refactoring: Improving the Design of Existing Code*, ISBN 0-201-48567-2

Martin Fowler with Kendall Scott, *UML Distilled: Applying the Standard Object Modeling Language*, ISBN 0-201-32563-2

Peter Heinckiens, *Building Scalable Database Applications: Object-Oriented Design, Architectures, and Implementations*, ISBN 0-201-31013-9

Ivar Jacobson, Grady Booch, and James Rumbaugh, *The Unified Software Development Process*, ISBN 0-201-57169-2

Ivar Jacobson, Magnus Christerson, Patrik Jonsson, and Gunnar Overgaard, *Object-Oriented Software Engineering: A Use Case Driven Approach*, ISBN 0-201-54435-0

Ivar Jacobson, Maria Ericsson, and Agneta Jacobson, *The Object Advantage: Business Process Reengineering with Object Technology*, ISBN 0-201-42289-1

Ivar Jacobson, Martin Griss, and Patrik Jonsson, *Software Reuse: Architecture, Process and Organization for Business Success*, ISBN 0-201-92476-5

David Jordan, *C++ Object Databases: Programming with the ODMG Standard*, ISBN 0-201-63488-0

Philippe Kruchten, *The Rational Unified Process: An Introduction*, ISBN 0-201-60459-0

Wilf LaLonde, *Discovering Smalltalk*, ISBN 0-8053-2720-7

Lockheed Martin Advanced Concepts Center and Rational Software Corporation, *Succeeding with the Booch and OMT Methods: A Practical Approach*, ISBN 0-8053-2279-5

Thomas Mowbray and William Ruh, *Inside CORBA: Distributed Object Standards and Applications*, ISBN 0-201-89540-4

Bernd Oestereich, *Developing Software with UML: Object-Oriented Analysis and Design in Practice*, ISBN 0-201-39826-5

Ira Pohl, *Object-Oriented Programming Using C++, Second Edition*, ISBN 0-201-89550-1

Rob Pooley and Perdita Stevens, *Using UML: Software Engineering with Objects and Components*, ISBN 0-201-36067-5

Terry Quatrani, *Visual Modeling with Rational Rose and UML*, ISBN 0-201-31016-3

Brent E. Rector and Chris Sells, *ATL Internals*, ISBN 0-201-69589-8

Doug Rosenberg with Kendall Scott, *Use Case Driven Object Modeling with UML: A Practical Approach*, ISBN 0-201-43289-7

Walker Royce, *Software Project Management: A Unified Framework*, ISBN 0-201-30958-0

William Ruh, Thomas Herron, and Paul Klinker, *IIOP Complete: Middleware Interoperability and Distributed Object Standards*, ISBN 0-201-37925-2

James Rumbaugh, Ivar Jacobson, and Grady Booch, *The Unified Modeling Language Reference Manual*, ISBN 0-201-30998-X

Geri Schneider and Jason P. Winters, *Applying Use Cases: A Practical Guide*, ISBN 0-201-30981-5

Yen-Ping Shan and Ralph H. Earle, *Enterprise Computing with Objects: From Client/Server Environments to the Internet*, ISBN 0-201-32566-7

David N. Smith, *IBM Smalltalk: The Language*, ISBN 0-8053-0908-X

Daniel Tkach, Walter Fang, and Andrew So, *Visual Modeling Technique: Object Technology Using Visual Programming*, ISBN 0-8053-2574-3

Daniel Tkach and Richard Puttick, *Object Technology in Application Development, Second Edition*, ISBN 0-201-49833-2

Jos Warmer and Anneke Kleppe, *The Object Constraint Language: Precise Modeling with UML*, ISBN 0-201-37940-6

ATL INTERNALS

Brent Rector
Chris Sells

ADDISON-WESLEY

An imprint of Addison Wesley Longman, Inc.

Reading, Massachusetts · Harlow, England · Menlo Park, California
Berkeley, California · Don Mills, Ontario · Sydney
Bonn · Amsterdam · Tokyo · Mexico City

The publisher offers discounts on this book when ordered in quantity for special sales. For more information, please contact:

AWL Direct Sales
Addison Wesley Longman, Inc.
One Jacob Way
Reading, Massachusetts 01867
Visit AW on the Web: *www.awl.com/cseng/*

Library of Congress Cataloging-in-Publication Data

Rector, Brent.
    ATL internals / Brent Rector, Chris Sells.
      p. cm.
    Includes bibliographical references.
    ISBN 0-201-69589-8
    1. Application software—Development.   2. Active template library.
  I. Sells, Chris. II. Title.
  QA76.76.D47R43   1999
  005.26'8—dc21   99-11448
                                   CIP

Executive Editor: J.Carter Shanklin
Production Coordinator: Jacquelyn Young
Compositor: G&S Typesetters, Inc.
Cover Designer: Jennifer Collins

Text printed on recycled and acid-free paper.

ISBN 0-201-69589-8

2 3 4 5 6 7 MA   02 01 00 99

2nd Printing June 1999

Contents

Foreword

When I first saw the title of this book, I told Chris Sells that it sounded like the book I always wanted to write. Ever since we released ATL, some of us have been saying, "We I've often thought that I should write a book on how ATL works." After reading *ATL Internals*, I don't think there would be much left for me to write about. Actually, this is kind of a relief. At this point, I think most aspects of ATL have been covered, and *ATL Internals* provides an excellent source of information on the inner workings of ATL. So, Chris asked me to provide some information that can't be deduced by looking at the ATL source code.

A Brief History of ATL

I first got into templates in late 1995, while I was a developer on the MFC team. A friend of mine here was evaluating various STL vendors for the Visual C++ product and he talked a lot about templates to me. I played around with templates a bit, but didn't do much with them. Soon after, the VC team split off an enterprise team to focus solely on Visual C++ 4.2 Enterprise Edition (VCEE), our first VC enterprise product. I moved over to head up the libraries work for VCEE. At the time we explored several different ideas. Microsoft Transaction Server was just getting started then and we talked a lot with them about COM, transactions, databases, and middle-tier business objects. Pretty quickly, we realized that we needed a better mechanism for creating COM objects from C++. Jan Falkin and Christian Beaumont were working for me at that time. Jan was working on an automation interface to ODBC data sources, and Christian was working on a template-based access method to ODBC data sources (a forerunner of our current OLEDB consumer templates). I was working on the COM infrastructure, since everything was already pointing to COM back then.

Initially, I was just playing around with COM and templates, but slowly it started to stabilize around a few important concepts. From the beginning I wanted to support all threading models, but I didn't want to pay for it unless it was needed. The same was true for aggregation. I didn't want anyone to have an excuse not to use ATL. (I didn't want to hear, "Well, ATL is cool, but I can save a couple of bytes if I do this myself.") So, performance and flexibility outranked ease of use when that decision had to be made.

ATL 1.0

One of the main concepts that came out of this was that the class that a user writes is not the class that was actually instantiated. This allowed many optimizations that otherwise could not have occurred. Some of the other concepts were multiple inheritance for interfaces, "creator" functions, and a data-driven COM map. We started to show this around and got a lot of good feedback on it. Several people thought we should get this out to customers as soon as possible, so we decided to RTW (release to the web) in the early summer of '96. That was ATL 1.0.

Our working name for our libraries had been MEC (Microsoft Enterprise Classes), but our marketing person thought we should have something that more reflected what we were doing. Because of our COM focus and the fact that at the time, everything was being called "Active" something or other, we selected the name Active Template Library.

ATL 1.1

We got a good reception for ATL and in late summer of '96 we released ATL 1.1. By this time, Jan and Christian had started working directly on ATL. ATL 1.1 had bug fixes and support for a few more features such as connection points, NT services, RGS registry support, and security.

ATL 2.0 and 2.1

After ATL 1.1, we started working on ATL 2.0. Its primary focus was the creation of ActiveX controls. Jan and Christian did much of the work on this, while I still focused on the core stuff (such as rewriting the connection points to make them smaller). Nenad Stefanovic also joined us at that time and started work on the windowing support in ATL, as well as doing the composite control support in VC 6.0. We were originally planning on ATL 2.0 to be shipped on the web targeting VC 4.2. However, our plans changed and we shipped ATL 2.0 in VC 5.0 (12/96), and shipped ATL 2.1 with the Alpha version of Visual C++ 5.0. The only difference between ATL 2.0 and 2.1 were some bug fixes for Alpha, MIPS, and PowerPC. We also simultaneously shipped ATL 2.1 on the web with AppWizard and ObjectWizard support for VC 4.2.

ATL 3.0

After a couple of months of working on ATL 3.0 (called ATL 2.5 at the time), Christian and I were burned out and took some time off from ATL, while Jan took over as ATL lead. After a few months we came back, and Christian became the ATL lead while I moved on to explore some other things for Visual C++, although I do still get into the source code every now and then.

The Future of ATL

We shipped VC 6.0 in June '98 and as I write this, we are currently working on the next release. Expect to see lots of cool new stuff in ATL as well as some new ways of accessing the ATL functionality. I am glad to see ATL continue to evolve, while at the same time maintaining the original goals of generating small, efficient code. So, take a look at this book, learn some new tricks, and gain a deeper understanding of how it all works.

Jim Springfield
Inventor of ATL
Microsoft Corporation

Preface

C is a framework for generating assembly language code (ASM). Most ASM programmers shifting to C spent a lot of time examining and replacing the compiler-generated code because they didn't trust the compiler to create correct code. As time went on and C compilers got better, ASM programmers gradually learned to trust the compiler to generate not only correct code, but also efficient code. Of course, talented C programmers never forget that the compiler is generating ASM. They know that they can still reach into selected areas and dictate the generated code when their needs exceed the capabilities of the language.

Microsoft's Active Template Library (ATL) is a framework for generating C++/COM code. Most C++ programmers shifting to ATL seem to fear examining, let alone replacing, ATL-generated code. They don't trust ATL any more than ASM programmers trusted their C compilers, because the source for ATL is fairly inscrutable to the casual observer. However, ATL is performing the same services for the C++/COM programmer that the C compiler performed for ASM programmers, namely, providing a simpler way to generate boilerplate code correctly and efficiently. Of course, talented ATL programmers never forget that ATL is generating C++/COM code. They know that they can still reach into selected areas and dictate the generated code when their needs exceed the capabilities of ATL. Our goal in writing this book is to turn you into an ATL programmer, unafraid to reach into it and bend it to your will.

This book is for the C++/COM programmer shifting to ATL 3.0, as provided with Visual C++ 6.0. Because ATL was built with a set of assumptions, to be an effective ATL programmer you need to understand not only how ATL is built but also why. Of course, to understand the why of ATL, you'll have to understand the environment in which ATL was developed, that is, COM. Instead of attempting to compress all required COM knowledge into one or two chapters, this book assumes you already know COM and shows you the design, usage, and internals of ATL. Don Box's *Essential COM* (Addison-Wesley, 1998) is a good source of COM knowledge, if you'd like to brush up before diving into ATL.

With the exception of the first chapter, this book was arranged from the lowest levels of ATL to the highest, each chapter building on knowledge in previous chapters. The first chapter is a brief overview of some of the more common uses for ATL, and the wizards (if they exist) that aid in these uses. Whenever things get too detailed in the first chapter, however, we refer you to a subsequent chapter that will provide more in-depth coverage. Chapters 2 through 5 present the core of ATL. Chapter 2 covers the ATL smart types, such as `CComPtr`, `CComQIPtr`, `CComBSTR`, and `CComVariant`. Chapter 3 discusses how objects are implemented in ATL, concentrating on the great range of choices you have when implementing `IUnknown`. Chapter 4 discusses the glue code required to expose COM objects from COM servers. Chapter 5 delves into the implementation of `IUnknown` again, this time concentrating on how to implement `QueryInterface`, showing techniques such as tear-off interfaces and aggregation. Chapters 6, 7, and 8 discuss canned interface implementations that ATL provides to support object persistence, connection points, and COM collections and enumerators, respectively. These services can be used by components that may or may not provide their own user interface. Chapters 9, 10, and 11, on the other hand, concentrate on building both standalone applications and user interface components. These chapters cover the ATL window classes, controls, and control containment, respectively. Because much of what makes the ATL source difficult to read is its advanced use of templates, Appendix A provides a set of examples meant to illustrate how templates are used and built. If you've seen ATL source code before and wondered why you can pass the name of a deriving class to a base class template, you may find Appendix A useful. Appendix B provides a list of the important ATL classes and the header files in which they are declared (and often implemented).

When writing these chapters, it became necessary not only to show diagrams and sample usage code, but also internal ATL implementation code. In fact, this book often becomes your personal tour guide through the ATL source code. So that you may distinguish author-generated code from Microsoft-employee-generated code, we've adopted the following conventions:

```
// This code is author-generated and is an example of what you'd type.
// Bold-faced code requires your particular attention.
CComBSTR bstr = OLESTR("Hello, World.");
```

```
// This code is part of ATL or Windows.
CComBSTR(LPCOLESTR pSrc) { m_str = ::SysAllocString(pSrc); }
```

Because the ATL team didn't write their code to be published in book form, it was often necessary to reformat it or even to abbreviate it. Every effort has been made to retain the essence of the original code, but, as always, the ATL source code is the final arbiter. You might find Appendix B useful when tracking down the actual implementation.

If there are any errors in the sample source or in any part of this book, you may contact Brent Rector at http://www.wiseowl.com and Chris Sells at http://www.sellsbrothers.com. The source code used in this book is available at http://www.wiseowl.com/ATLInternals.htm.

The authors would like to thank all of the following for their contributions to this book. While it may have been possible to complete this book without them, it would have been a pale imitation of what we were able to achieve with their help. Chris would like to thank his wife, Melissa, and his boys, John and Tom, for sparing him the countless evenings and weekends to work on this project. Chris would also like to thank Brent Rector for letting him horn in on his book project.

Brent would like to thank his wife, Lisa, and his children, Carly and Sean, for delaying the delivery of this book significantly. If it weren't for them, he'd never leave the computer some days. Brent would like to thank Chris for his intelligence, patience, and general good looks.[1]

Brent and Chris would like to thank several folks together. Special thanks to Christian Beaumont, Jim Springfield, Walter Sullivan, and Mark Kramer for suffering our nagging questions and taking the time to answer them. More special thanks to Don Box for his *MSJ* ATL feature, which so heavily influenced the course and, in turn, this book. Thanks to the reviewers: Don Box, Keith Brown, Jon Flanders, Mike Francis, Kevin Jones, Stanley Lippman, Dharma Shukla, Jim Springfield, Jeff Stalls, Jaganathan Thangavelu, and Jason Whittington. Special thanks goes to Dharma for his especially thorough, and educational, reviews. Thanks to fellow DevelopMentor instructor Fritz Onion for his groundbreaking work delving into the depths of ATL control containment. Thanks to a former student, Valdan Vidakovic, for inspiring Chris to delve a bit more into the HTML control. Thanks to Tim Ewald, Jim Springfield, and Don Box for their help in developing the forwarding shims trick. Thanks to the members of the ATL and DCOM mailing lists, especially Don Box, Tim Ewald, Charlie Kindel, Valery Pryamikov, Mark Ryland, and Zane Thomas. And last, but not least, thanks to Addison-Wesley, especially J. Carter Shanklin and Krysia Bebick, for providing an environment in which we actually want to write (although not as quickly or as concisely as they might like).

---

[1] You only get one guess as to who wrote this sentence, and he doesn't have my initials or my good looks. BER

1 | Hello, ATL

Welcome to the Active Template Library (hereafter referred to as ATL). In this chapter, I present a few of the tasks that I expect you'll want to perform using ATL and the integrated wizards. This is by no means all of what ATL can accomplish nor is it meant to be exhaustive coverage of the wizards or their output. In fact, the rest of this book is focused on how ATL is implemented to provide the COM (Component Object Model) glue that holds this example together (as well as several others). This chapter is really just a warm-up to get you familiar with the support that the Visual Studio environment provides the ATL programmer.

What Is ATL?

Expanding the acronym really doesn't describe very well what ATL is or why we have it. The *Active* part is really a residue from the marketing age at Microsoft when ActiveX[1] meant all of COM. As of this writing (and it's bound to change again), ActiveX means controls. And while ATL does provide extensive support for building controls, it provides much more than that.

What ATL Provides

1. Class wrappers around high-maintenance data types such as interface pointers, VARIANTs, BSTRs, and HWNDs.

2. Classes that provide implementations of basic COM interfaces such as IUnknown, IClassFactory, IDispatch, IPersistXxx, IConnectionPoint-Container, and IEnumXxx.

3. Classes for managing COM servers, that is, for exposing class objects, self-registration, and server lifetime management.

4. Wizards to save you typing.

---

[1] The original expansion of ATL was the ActiveX Template Library.

What You Provide

ATL was inspired by the current model citizen in the world of C++ class libraries, the Standard Template Library (STL). Like STL, ATL is meant to be a set of small, efficient, and flexible classes. However, with power comes responsibility. So, like STL, ATL can only be used effectively by an experienced C++ programmer (a little STL experience is valuable, too).

Of course, since we're going to be programming COM, experience using and implementing COM objects and servers is absolutely required. For those of you hoping for a COM-knowledge-free way to build your COM objects, ATL is not for you (nor is Visual Basic, Visual J++, or anything else, for that matter). In fact, using ATL means being intimately familiar with COM in C++ as well as with some of the implementation details of ATL itself.

Still, ATL is packaged with several wizards that are helpful for generating the initial code. In the rest of this chapter, I present the various wizards available for ATL programmers as of Visual C++ 6.0. Feel free to follow along.

Creating a COM Server

Running the ATL COM AppWizard

The first step in any Visual C++ development endeavor is building the workspace and the initial project. For ATL programmers, this means choosing the ATL COM AppWizard from the Projects tab of the New dialog, as shown in Figure 1.1. Note that the ATL COM AppWizard is selected by default. That is because it is the most important kind of project you can create using the Visual Studio (it's just a coincidence that it's also alphabetically first). The name of the project (shown in the figure as PiSvr) will be the name of your generated DLL or EXE server.

The job of the ATL COM AppWizard is to build a project for your COM server. A COM server is either a dynamic link library (DLL) or an executable (EXE). Further, the EXE can be a standalone application or an NT service. The ATL COM AppWizard supports all three of these server types, as shown in Figure 1.2.

The ATL COM AppWizard also provides three other options. The first allows you to bundle your custom proxy/stub code with your DLL server. Regardless of the kind of server you choose, ATL will provide a <projectname>ps.mk makefile for use when building your custom proxy/stub. This file is for building a separate proxy/stub DLL to distribute to all client and server machines that need to be able to marshal and unmarshal your custom interfaces. If you'd like to bundle the proxy/stub DLL into the server DLL (and save yourself a separate proxy/stub DLL on the server machine), you may check the "Allow merging of proxy/stub code" op-

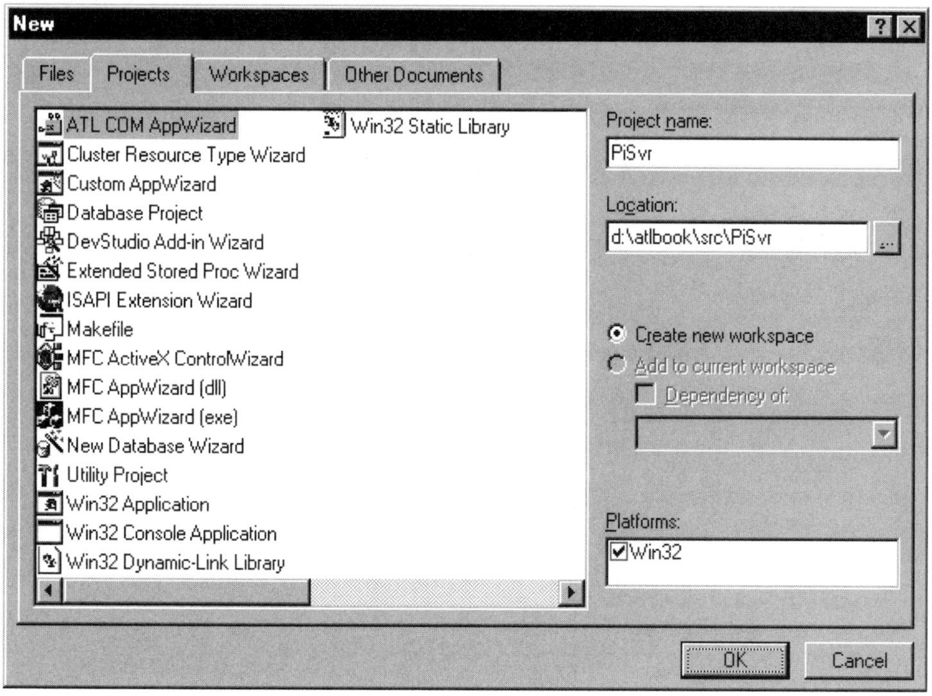

Figure 1.1. Creating a new Visual Studio project

tion. Doing so will put a bunch of conditionally compiled statements into your server code to *allow* merging the proxy/stub code. To actually *merge* the proxy/ stub code, you must also perform the following steps (after the wizard generates the project).

1. Add _MERGE_PROXYSTUB to the preprocessor definitions for all configurations in the Project Settings dialog.
2. Uncheck the "Exclude file from build" option in the settings for dlldatax.c. The dlldatax.c file is really just a wrapper that brings dlldata.c and <projectname>_i.c into the project properly.
3. Change the precompiled header settings for dlldatax.c to "Not using pre-compiled headers."

The second ATL COM AppWizard option allows you to use MFC (Microsoft Foundation Classes). Frankly, you should avoid this option. The following are a few common objections that I have heard about why developers believe that they should use MFC with an ATL server.

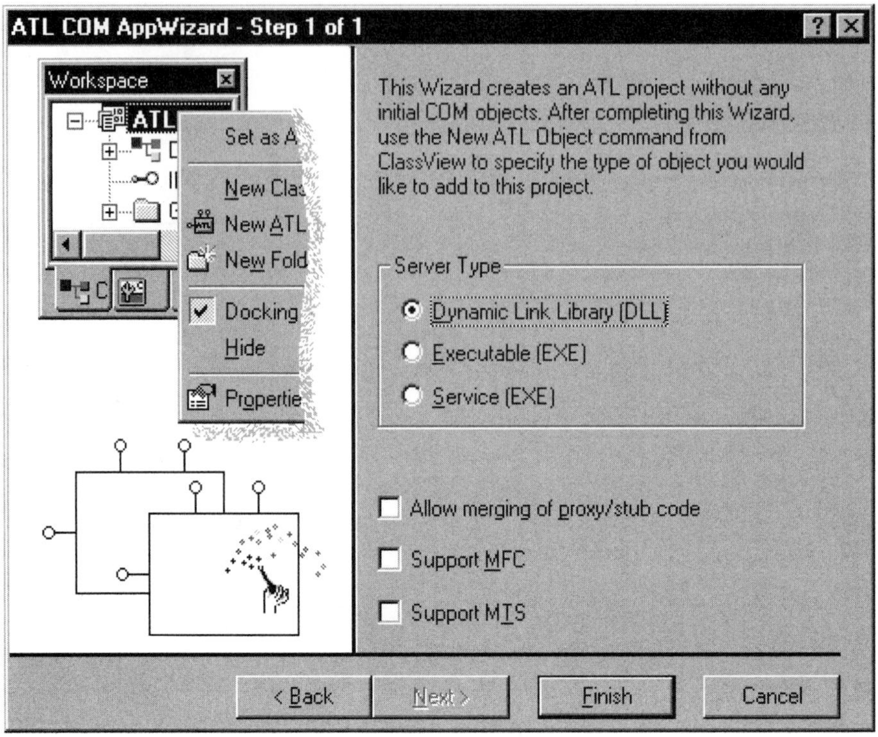

Figure 1.2. Creating a new ATL COM server

1. **"I can't live without CString (or CMap, CList, etc.)."** The MFC utility classes were built as a stopgap until the C++ standards committee defined a standard library. They've done it, so we can stop using the MFC versions. The classes (string, map, list, etc.) provided in STL are more flexible and more robust than their MFC equivalents.

2. **"I can't live without the wizards."** This chapter is all about the wizards provided by the Visual Studio for ATL programmers. As of Visual C++ 6.0, the ATL wizards are nearly as extensive as those that generate MFC code.

3. **"I already know MFC and I can't learn anything new."** Luckily, none of these people are reading this book and they're either perfectly happy with, or blissfully ignorant of, the 973K DLL they're using.[2]

The third ATL COM AppWizard option, Support MTS, does two things. First, it changes some compiler and linker settings so that Microsoft Transaction Server

---

[2]To be fair, it's possible to statically link with MFC, too, but the minimum overhead for such an action still seems high at roughly 250K.

(MTS) has the modifications it needs in the proxy/stub DLL. This saves a bunch of tedious hand tweaking. Second, the wizard adds a custom build option so that when the server is built, `mtxrereg.exe` is run. This will cause MTS to reacquire COM servers and save you from refreshing your MTS packages. Those of you who have ever rebuilt an MTS server and suddenly found it no longer running in MTS will appreciate this feature.

Results of the ATL COM AppWizard

With or without these three options, every COM server generated by the ATL COM AppWizard will support the three jobs of every COM server, namely, self-registration, server lifetime control, and exposing class objects. As an additional convenience, the wizard adds a custom build step that registers the COM server on each successful build. This step will either run `regsvr32.exe <project>.dll` or `<project>.exe /regserver`, depending on whether it is a DLL or EXE server.

For more information about ATL's support for the three jobs of every COM server as well as how you can extend it for more advanced concurrency and lifetime needs, see Chapter 4.

Inserting a COM Class

Running the ATL Object Wizard

Once you have an ATL COM server, you'll probably want to insert a new COM class. This can be done with the New ATL Object item in the Insert menu. I should note that the ATL team got the terminology wrong here. You're not going to be inserting an *object*, that is, an instance of a type—you're going to be inserting a *class*, that is, the definition of a type. Still, while the terminology is wrong, at least they're consistent about it. In future chapters, we'll discuss the object map, which is all about classes.[3]

When inserting an ATL class, you'll first have to choose the type of class you'd like, as shown in Figure 1.3. If you're following along, you may want to take a moment and explore the various types of classes that the ATL Object Wizard knows about. Each of these classes will result in a specific bunch of code being generated, using the ATL base classes to provide the majority of the functionality and then generating the skeleton for your own custom functionality. The ATL Object Wizard is really your chance to decide which interfaces you'd like your COM class

---

[3]Christian Beaumont, the development lead for ATL, assures me that he knows the difference between class and object but that Visual Studio already had a Class Wizard (for generation of MFC code), and he didn't want to confuse things.

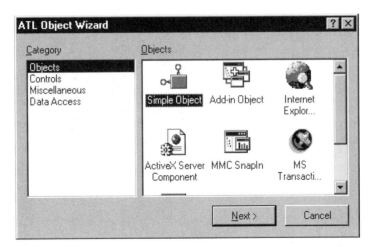

Figure 1.3. Inserting a new ATL COM class

to implement. Of course, the wizard won't provide access to all the functionality of ATL (or even most of it), but the generated code is designed to be easy for you to add or subtract functionality after the wizard has gotten you started. Experimentation is the best way to get familiar with the various wizard-generated class types and their options.

Once you've chosen one of the class types (and pressed OK), the wizard will generally ask for some specific information from you. While some of the classes have more options than the Simple Object (as selected in Figure 1.3), most of the COM classes require at least the information shown in Figures 1.4 and 1.5.

The Names tab of the ATL Object Wizard Properties dialog really only requires you to type in the short name, for example, CalcPi. This short name is used to compose the rest of the information in this dialog (which you may override, if you choose). The information is broken into two categories. The necessary C++ information is the name of the C++ class and the names of the header and implementation files. The necessary COM information is the coclass name (for the Interface Definition Language [IDL]), the name of the default interface (also for the IDL), the friendly name, called the Type (for the IDL and the registration settings), and finally the version-independent programmatic identifier (for the registration settings). The versioned ProgID is just the version-independent ProgID with the ".1" suffix.

The Attributes tab is your chance to make some lower-level COM decisions. The Threading Model setting describes the kind of apartment in which you'd like instances of this new class to live: SingleThreaded Apartment (STA)—which is also known as the Apartment model or a MultiThreaded Apartment (MTA)—known as the Free-Threaded model. The Single model is for the rare class that requires all its objects to share the same apartment, regardless of the client's apartment type. The

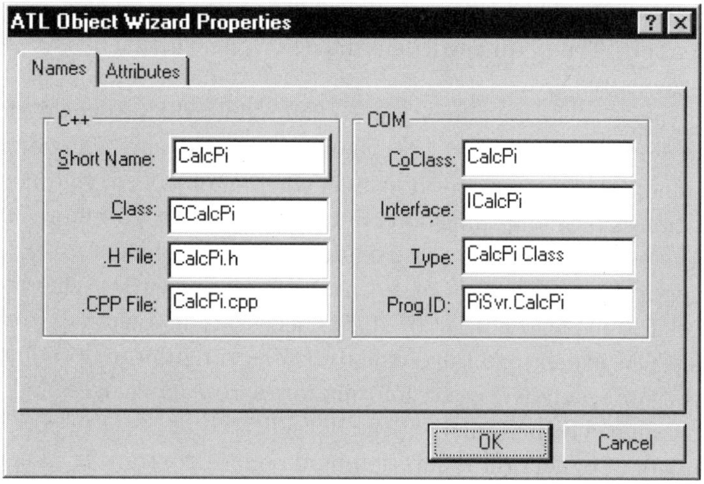

Figure 1.4. Setting COM class names

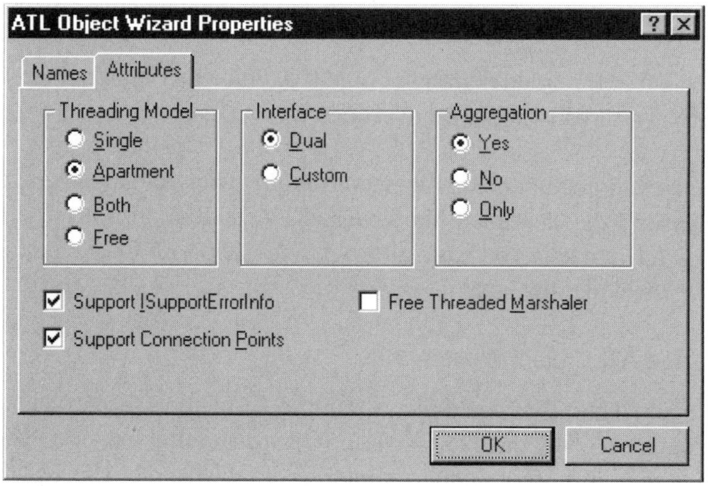

Figure 1.5. Setting COM class attributes

Both model is for objects that you want to live in the same apartment as their clients to avoid the overhead of a proxy/stub pair. The Threading Model setting you choose will determine the value for the `ThreadingModel` named value in your in-process server self-registration settings as well as just how thread safe you need your object's implementation of `AddRef` and `Release` to be.

The Interface setting allows you to determine the kind of interface you'd like the class's default interface to be: custom (it needs a custom proxy/stub and will not derive from `IDispatch`) or dual (it will use the typelib marshaler and will derive from `IDispatch`). This setting will determine how the IDL that defines your default interface is generated.

The Aggregation setting allows you to determine whether you'd like your objects to be aggregatable or not, that is, whether to participate in aggregation as the controlled inner. This setting does not affect whether objects of your new class can use aggregation as the controlling outer or not. See Chapter 3 for more details about being aggregated and Chapter 5 about aggregating other objects.

The Support ISupportErrorInfo setting directs the wizard to generate an implementation of `ISupportErrorInfo`. This is necessary if you'd like to throw COM exceptions. COM exceptions (also called COM Error Information objects) allow you to pass more detailed error information across languages and apartment boundaries than can be provided with an `HRESULT` alone.

The Support Connection Points setting directs the wizard to generate an implementation of `IConnectionPoint`, which allows your object to fire events into scripting environments such as those hosted by Internet Explorer. Connection points are also used by controls to fire events into control containers.

The Help information for the Free Threaded Marshaler setting reads as follows:

> Creates a free threaded marshaler object to efficiently marshal interface pointers between threads in the same process.

With a ringing endorsement like that, who wouldn't want to choose that option? Unfortunately, the Free Threaded Marshaler (FTM) is like an item in an expensive store: If you have to ask, you can't afford it. See Chapter 5 for a description of the FTM *before* checking this box.

Faking out the ATL Object Wizard

Sometimes you'll find that you'd like to run the ATL Object Wizard inside a project that wasn't generated by the ATL COM AppWizard and that may not even be a COM server. For example, it's common to want to insert a Dialog or an OLEDB Data Consumer into a standalone Win32 application. If the Object Wizard doesn't find the pieces of the project that it needs to generate the code, it will let you know with the message box shown in Figure 1.6. If, like me, you take this message as a personal challenge rather than an actual barrier, you're going to want to know how to make it go away. Toward that end, here are the minimum requirements that the ATL Object Wizard, as of Visual C++ 6.0, is looking for.[4]

---

[4]Thanks to the ATL mailing list gang for working together to figure out these requirements. Lord knows they're not documented.

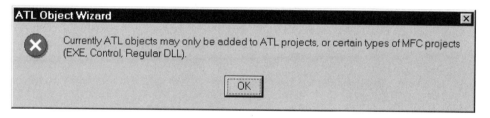

Figure 1.6. ATL Object Wizard error message box

- The project must be a DLL or a Win32 application. It may not be a console application.

- The following code must appear in the <project>.cpp file:

```
BEGIN_OBJECT_MAP(ObjectMap)
END_OBJECT_MAP()
```

- There must be a <project>.idl file as part of the project (although it may be marked "Exclude file from build" in the settings) and the following minimum library block must be present (the comments are not necessary):

```
// Library does not need a [uuid] attribute
library LIB // Library can be named anything, but it does need a name
{
}
```

- If the integrated development environment (IDE) still gives you trouble, close the workspace, remove the .ncb file, reload the workspace, and try again. In the event that this still doesn't help, well, you tried. . . .

  Warning: Please be aware that by faking out the ATL Object Wizard, you are circumventing the problem that the ATL Object Wizard is trying to save you from, namely, that you don't have the right support from the project to actually build the code that the wizard will generate for you. So, if you're going to use this technique, you had better become familiar with the ATL source so you can manually add the appropriate .h and .cpp files to stdafx.h and stdafx.cpp, respectively. Appendix B shows you what ATL header files contain which classes.

Results of the ATL Object Wizard

After you have filled in the necessary options, the ATL Object Wizard will generate a new C++ class, derive it from the appropriate interfaces and ATL interface implementations, and put it into a new header file. It will also give you a C++

implementation file for you to add your custom code. The C++ class will derive from some ATL base classes and your new interface and will provide a COM_MAP that lists all the interfaces that your object exposes. An example follows.

```
// Shaded code generated by ATL wizard
class ATL_NO_VTABLE CCalcPi :
 public CComObjectRootEx<CComSingleThreadModel>,
 public CComCoClass<CCalcPi, &CLSID_CalcPi>,
 public ISupportErrorInfo,
 public IConnectionPointContainerImpl<CCalcPi>,
 public IDispatchImpl<ICalcPi, &IID_ICalcPi, &LIBID_PISVRLib>
{
public:
 CCalcPi()
 {
 }

DECLARE_REGISTRY_RESOURCEID(IDR_CALCPI)

BEGIN_COM_MAP(CCalcPi)
 COM_INTERFACE_ENTRY(ICalcPi)
 COM_INTERFACE_ENTRY(IDispatch)
 COM_INTERFACE_ENTRY(ISupportErrorInfo)
 COM_INTERFACE_ENTRY(IConnectionPointContainer)
END_COM_MAP()

BEGIN_CONNECTION_POINT_MAP(CCalcPi)
END_CONNECTION_POINT_MAP()

 // ISupportsErrorInfo
 STDMETHOD(InterfaceSupportsErrorInfo)(REFIID riid);

 // ICalcPi
public:
};
```

For more information about the base classes that ATL uses to implement basic COM functionality and how you can leverage this implementation for building object hierarchies and properly synchronize multithreaded objects, see Chapter 3. For more information about how to make full use of the COM_MAP, see Chapter 5.

Adding Properties and Methods

One of the things that make a C++ programmer's life hard is the separation of the class declaration (usually in the .h file) and the class definition (usually in the `.cpp` file). The reason that this can be a pain is the maintenance required between the two. Any time a member function is added in one, it has to be replicated to the other. Manually, this can be a tedious process and is made even more tedious if the C++ COM progammer must start the process in the `.idl` file. Don't get me wrong. I love IDL. A language-independent representation of interfaces and classes is the *only* way to go. However, when I'm adding properties and methods to my interfaces, I'd like it if my C++ development environment could translate the IDL into C++ and drop it into my `.h` and `.cpp` files for me, leaving me a nice place to provide my implementation. That's just what Visual C++ provides.

By right-clicking on a COM interface in the ClassView, you can choose to add a new property or method. Figure 1.7 shows the dialog that allows you to add a property to a COM interface. Notice the Implementation box in Figure 1.7. It shows the

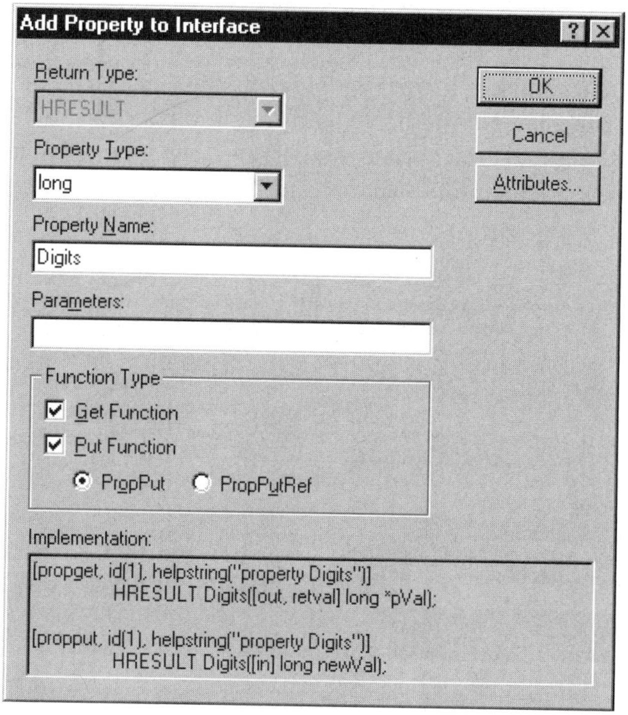

Figure 1.7. Adding a property

resultant IDL based on the options as set in the dialog. The IDL will be updated and the appropriate C++ code will be generated when you click the OK button. The following shaded code shows the implementation skeleton generated by the wizard. We have only to provide the appropriate behavior (shown as nonshaded code).

```
STDMETHODIMP CCalcPi::get_Digits(long *pVal)
{
   *pVal = m_nDigits;
   return S_OK;
}


STDMETHODIMP CCalcPi::put_Digits(long newVal)
{
   if( newVal < 0 )
    return Error(L"Can't calculate negative digits of PI");
   m_nDigits = newVal;

   return S_OK;
}
```

Similarly, we can add a method by right-clicking on an interface in the ClassView and choosing Add Method. Figure 1.8 shows the Add Method to Interface dialog. Again, the wizard will update the IDL file (using the IDL shown in the Implementation box), generate the appropriate C++ code, and place us in the im-

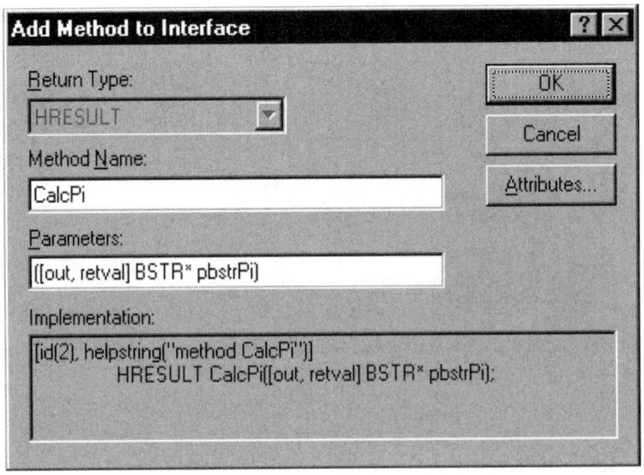

Figure 1.8. Adding a method

plementation skeleton to do our job. The shaded code in the following is what remains of the wizard-generated C++ code after I added the code to implement the method.

```
STDMETHODIMP CCalcPi::CalcPi(BSTR *pbstrPi)
{
    _ASSERTE(m_nDigits >= 0);

  if( m_nDigits )
  {
    *pbstrPi = SysAllocStringLen(L"3.", m_nDigits+2);
    if( *pbstrPi )
    {
      for( int i = 0; i < m_nDigits; i += 9 )
      {
        long nNineDigits = NineDigitsOfPiStartingAt(i+1);
        swprintf(*pbstrPi + i+2, L"%09d", nNineDigits);
      }

      // Truncate to number of digits
      (*pbstrPi)[m_nDigits+2] = 0;
    }
  }
  else
  {
    *pbstrPi = SysAllocString(L"3");
  }

  return *pbstrPi ? S_OK : E_OUTOFMEMORY;
}
```

For a description of COM exceptions and the ATL `Error` function (used in the `put_Digits` member function), see Chapter 4.

Implementing Additional Interfaces

Interfaces are the core of COM, and most COM objects implement more than one. Even the wizard-generated Simple Object shown earlier implements four interfaces (one custom interface and three standard interfaces). If you want your ATL-based

COM class to implement another interface, you must first have a definition of it. For example:

```
interface IAdvertiseMyself : IUnknown
{
 [helpstring("method ShowAd")] HRESULT ShowAd(BSTR bstrClient);
};
```

If you're going to implement it, you're going to need a C++ header file that describes the interface and you're going to have to do a little bit of typing to add the interface and its methods to your class:

```
class ATL_NO_VTABLE CCalcPi :
 public CComObjectRootEx<CComSingleThreadModel>,
 public CComCoClass<CCalcPi, &CLSID_CalcPi>,
 ...
 public IAdvertiseMyself
{
...
BEGIN_COM_MAP(CCalcPi)
  ...
  COM_INTERFACE_ENTRY(IAdvertiseMyself)
END_COM_MAP()
...
// IAdvertiseMyself
    STDMETHOD(ShowAd)(BSTR bstrClient);
};
```

Of course, once you've added these lines, you still have to implement the methods.

```
STDMETHODIMP CCalcPi::ShowAd(BSTR bstrClient)
{
 CComBSTR  bstrCaption = OLESTR("CalcPi hosted by ");
 bstrCaption += (bstrClient && *bstrClient ? bstrClient : "no one");
 CComBSTR  bstrText = OLESTR("These digits of pi brought to you by
    CalcPi!");

 USES_CONVERSION;
 MessageBox(0, OLE2CT(bstrText), OLE2CT(bstrCaption),
   MB_SETFOREGROUND);

 return S_OK;
}
```

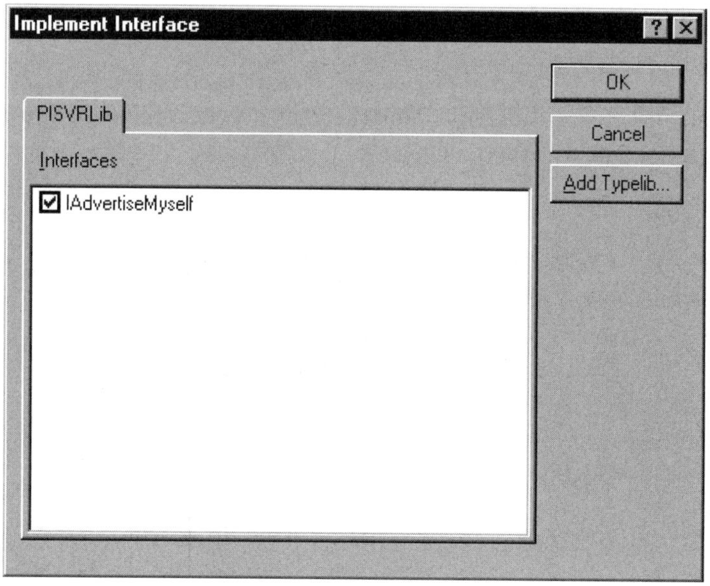

Figure 1.9. Implement Interface dialog

If you happen to have the interface you'd like to implement defined in a Type-Lib, you can use the Implement Interface wizard to insert the skeleton code for you. You can access the Implement Interface wizard by right-clicking on the class and choosing Implement Interface. The Implement Interface dialog (Figure 1.9) shows all the custom or dual interfaces in the currently selected TypeLib that aren't already implemented by the class in question. By default, the wizard shows the TypeLib associated with the current project,[5] but you can choose any TypeLib by pressing the Add TypeLib button. Unfortunately, as of this writing, the Implement Interface dialog does not support interfaces that don't exist in TypeLibs, which leaves out most of the standard COM interfaces, such as IPersist, IMarshal, and IoleItemContainer. One hopes that future versions will address this deficiency.

After you've chosen to implement an interface, the wizard derives the class from the interface, adds the interface to the COM_MAP, and puts the method signatures into the class (as well as some helpful skeleton code).

For more information about the various ways that ATL allows your COM classes to implement interfaces, see Chapter 5. For more information about CComBSTR and the string conversion routines used in the ShowAd method, see Chapter 2.

---

[5] If you're going to implement an interface newly declared in your project's IDL, make sure to rebuild the TypeLib before using the Implement Interface wizard.

Support for Scripting

Any time you run the ATL Object Wizard and choose Dual as the interface type, ATL will generate IDL for the default interface that derives from IDispatch and is marked with the dual attribute, like so:

```
[
    object,
    uuid(DEC22F36-DD78-11D1-97FD-006008243C8C),
    dual,
    helpstring("ICalcPi Interface"),
    pointer_default(unique)
]
interface ICalcPi : IDispatch
{
 ...
};
```

Because it derives from IDispatch, our dual interface can be used by scripting clients, for example, Active Server Pages (ASP) and Internet Explorer (IE). ATL provides an implementation of the four IDispatch methods in the IDispatch-Impl base class:

```
template <class T,
          const IID* piid,
          const GUID* plibid = &CComModule::m_libid,
          WORD wMajor = 1,
          WORD wMinor = 0,
          class tihclass = CComTypeInfoHolder>
class ATL_NO_VTABLE IDispatchImpl : public T
{...};
```

To support scripting environments, our ATL COM class derives from IDispatchImpl and adds IDispatch to the COM_MAP, as shown here.

```
class ATL_NO_VTABLE CCalcPi : ...
  public IDispatchImpl<ICalcPi, &IID_ICalcPi, &LIBID_PISVRLib>
{
public:
BEGIN_COM_MAP(CCalcPi)
  COM_INTERFACE_ENTRY(ICalcPi)
```

```
    COM_INTERFACE_ENTRY(IDispatch)
    COM_INTERFACE_ENTRY(ISupportErrorInfo)
    COM_INTERFACE_ENTRY(IConnectionPointContainer)
END_COM_MAP()
...
};
```

As you have no doubt already noticed, by simply choosing Dual as the interface type in the ATL Object Wizard, the wizard will provide all the implementation code just shown as well as the interface definition. Once our COM class supports `IDispatch`, we can use objects of that class from scripting environments. Here's an example HTML page that uses an instance of the `CalcPi` object:

```
<object classid="clsid:DEC22F37-DD78-11D1-97FD-006008243C8C"
        id=objPiCalculator>
</object>

<script language=vbscript>
 ' Set the digits property
 objPiCalculator.digits = 5

 ' Calculate pi
 dim pi
 pi = objPiCalculator.CalcPi

 ' Tell the world!
 document.write "Pi to " & objPiCalculator.digits & " digits is " & pi
</script>
```

For more information about how to handle the inconvenient data types associated with scripting, namely, BSTRs and VARIANTs, see Chapter 2.

Adding Persistence

ATL provides base classes for objects that wish to be persistent, that is, saved to some persistent medium (like a disk) and then restored later. COM objects expose this support by implementing one of the COM persistence interfaces, such as `IPersistStreamInit`, `IPersistStorage`, `IPersistPropertyBag`. ATL provides implementation of these three persistence interfaces, namely, `IPersistStreamInitImpl`, `IPersistStorageImpl`, and `IPersistPropertyBagImpl`. By deriving from any of these base classes, adding a data member called `m_bRequiresSave` expected by each of these base classes, and adding the name of the interface to the COM_MAP, your COM object will support persistence.

```
class ATL_NO_VTABLE CCalcPi :
 public CComObjectRootEx<CComSingleThreadModel>,
 public CComCoClass<CCalcPi, &CLSID_CalcPi>,
 public IDispatchImpl<ICalcPi, &IID_ICalcPi, &LIBID_PISVRLib>,
 public IPersistPropertyBagImpl<CCalcPi>
{
public:
 ...

BEGIN_COM_MAP(CCalcPi)
  COM_INTERFACE_ENTRY(ICalcPi)
  COM_INTERFACE_ENTRY(IDispatch)
  COM_INTERFACE_ENTRY(IPersistPropertyBag)
END_COM_MAP()

 // ICalcPi
public:
 STDMETHOD(CalcPi)(/*[out, retval]*/ BSTR* pbstrPi);
 STDMETHOD(get_Digits)(/*[out, retval]*/ long *pVal);
 STDMETHOD(put_Digits)(/*[in]*/ long newVal);

 public:
 BOOL m_bRequiresSave; // Used by persistence base classes

private:
 long m_nDigits;
};
```

However, that's not quite all there is to it. ATL's implementation of persistence needs to know which parts of your object need to be saved and restored. For that information, ATL's implementations of the persistent interfaces rely on a table of object properties that you wish to persist between sessions. This table is called a PROP_MAP and contains a mapping of property names and dispatch identifiers (as defined in the IDL). So, given the following interface,

```
interface ICalcPi : IDispatch
{
   [propget, id(1)] HRESULT Digits([out, retval] long *pVal);
```

```
  [propput, id(1)] HRESULT Digits([in] long newVal);
  [id(2)] HRESULT CalcPi([out, retval] BSTR* pbstrPi);
};
```

The PROP_MAP would be contained inside our implementation of ICalcPi like so:

```
class ATL_NO_VTABLE CCalcPi : ...
{
 ...
public:
BEGIN_PROP_MAP(CCalcPi)
 PROP_ENTRY("Digits", 1, CLSID_NULL)
END_PROP_MAP()
};
```

Given an implementation of IPersistPropertyBag, our IE sample code can be expanded to support initialization of object properties via persistence using the <param> tag like so:

```
<object classid="clsid:DEC22F37-DD78-11D1-97FD-006008243C8C"
        id=objPiCalculator>
        <param name=digits value=5>
</object>

<script language=vbscript>
 ' Calculate pi
 dim pi
 pi = objPiCalculator.CalcPi

 ' Tell the world!
 document.write "Pi to " & objPiCalculator.digits & " digits is " & pi
</script>
```

For more information about ATL's implementation of persistence, see Chapter 6.

Adding and Firing Events

When something interesting happens in a COM object, we'd like to be able to spontaneously notify its client without the client polling the object. COM provides a standard mechanism for sending these notifications to clients (normally called *firing an event*) using the connection point architecture.

Connection point events are really just methods on an interface. To support the widest variety of clients, an event interface is often defined as a dispinterface. Choosing Supports Connection Points in the ATL Object Wizard will generate an event interface and publish it as the default source interface in your class. The following is an example of the wizard-generated code augmented with a single event method (shown in bold):

```
dispinterface _ICalcPiEvents
{
 properties:
 methods:
     [id(1)] void OnDigit([in] short nIndex, [in] short nDigit);
};

coclass CalcPi
{
    [default] interface ICalcPi;
    [default, source] dispinterface _ICalcPiEvents;
};
```

Once the event interface has been defined, and the server's <project>.tlb has been built, right-clicking on the class in the ClassView and choosing Implement Connection Point will display the dialog shown in Figure 1.10. Selecting an event interface in this dialog (and pressing OK) will cause the wizard to generate a wrapper class (called a connection point proxy) for firing methods to interested clients:

```
template <class T>
class CProxy_ICalcPiEvents :
 public IConnectionPointImpl<T, &DIID__ICalcPiEvents,
                            CComDynamicUnkArray>
{
 //Warning this class may be recreated by the wizard.
public:
   VOID Fire_OnDigit(SHORT nIndex, SHORT nDigit);
};
```

Because the wizard will also generate code so that the class of objects firing these events derives from the Proxy class, the class is free to use the Fire methods anytime something interesting happens. For example:

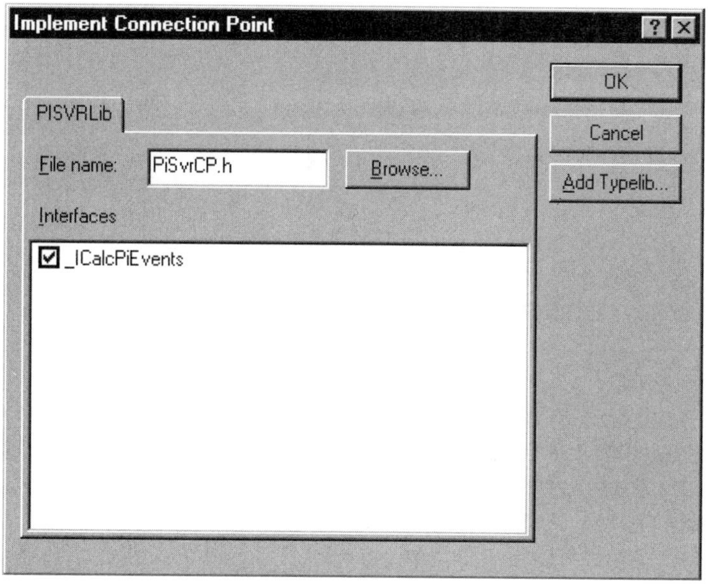

Figure 1.10. Implementing a connection point

```
STDMETHODIMP CCalcPi::CalcPi(BSTR *pbstrPi) {
 // (code to calculate pi removed for clarity)
 ...

 // Fire each digit
 for( short j = 0; j != m_nDigits; ++j ) {
   Fire_OnDigit(j, (*pbstrPi)[j+2]-L'0');
 }

 ...
 }
```

For a scripting client to receive events, an object must support the IProvide-ClassInfo2 interface. This interface allows the client to inquire as to the object's default interface identifier, which is then used to establish contact via IConnectionPointContainer. ATL provides an implementation of IProvideClassInfo2 that is used like so:

```
class ATL_NO_VTABLE CCalcPi :
 public CComObjectRootEx<CComSingleThreadModel>,
 public CComCoClass<CCalcPi, &CLSID_CalcPi>,
```

```
public IConnectionPointContainerImpl<CCalcPi>,
public CProxy_ICalcPiEvents<CCalcPi>,
public IProvideClassInfo2Impl<&CLSID_CalcPi, &DIID__ICalcPiEvents>,
... {
public:
BEGIN_COM_MAP(CCalcPi)
  COM_INTERFACE_ENTRY(IConnectionPointContainer)
  COM_INTERFACE_ENTRY(IProvideClassInfo)
  COM_INTERFACE_ENTRY(IProvideClassInfo2)
  ...
END_COM_MAP()

BEGIN_CONNECTION_POINT_MAP(CCalcPi)
 CONNECTION_POINT_ENTRY(DIID__ICalcPiEvents)
END_CONNECTION_POINT_MAP()
 ...
};
```

This object is now able to send events that can be handled in a page of HTML,
like so:

```
<object classid="clsid:DEC22F37-DD78-11D1-97FD-006008243C8C"
        id=objPiCalculator>
        <param name=digits value=50>
</object>

<input type=button name=cmdCalcPi value="Pi to 50 Digits:">
<span id=spanPi>unknown</span>

<p>Distribution of first 50 digits in pi:
<table border cellpadding=4>
... <!- table code removed for clarity -->
</table>

<script language=vbscript>
 ' Handle button click event
 sub cmdCalcPi_onClick
   spanPi.innerText = objPiCalculator.CalcPi
 end sub

 ' Handle calculator digit event
 sub objPiCalculator_onDigit(index, digit)
```

```
    select case digit
    case 0: span0.innerText = span0.innerText + 1
    case 1: span1.innerText = span1.innerText + 1
    ... <!- etc --->
    end select
    spanTotal.innerText = spanTotal.innerText + 1
  end sub
</script>
```

The sample HTML page handles these events to provide the first 50 digits of pi and their distribution, as shown in Figure 1.11.

For more information about ATL's support for connection points, see Chapter 8.

Using a Window

Because this is Microsoft Windows we're developing for, sometimes it's handy to be able to put up a window or a dialog box. For example, the MessageBox call we made earlier yielded a somewhat boring advertisement, as shown in Figure 1.12. Normally, putting up a custom dialog is kind of a pain. For the average C++ programmer, it either involves lots of procedural code, which we don't like, or it involves building a bunch of forwarding code to map Windows messages to member

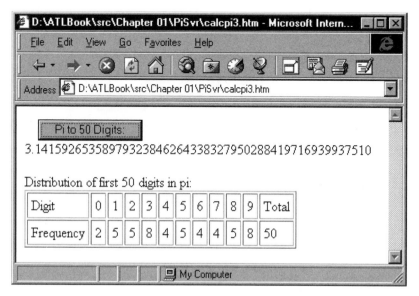

Figure 1.11. Pi to 50 digits

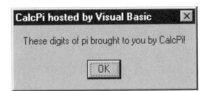

Figure 1.12.   Boring message box

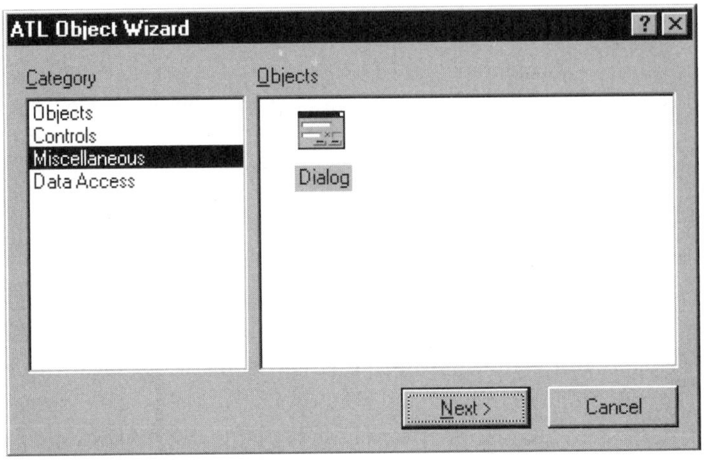

Figure 1.13.   Inserting a dialog box class

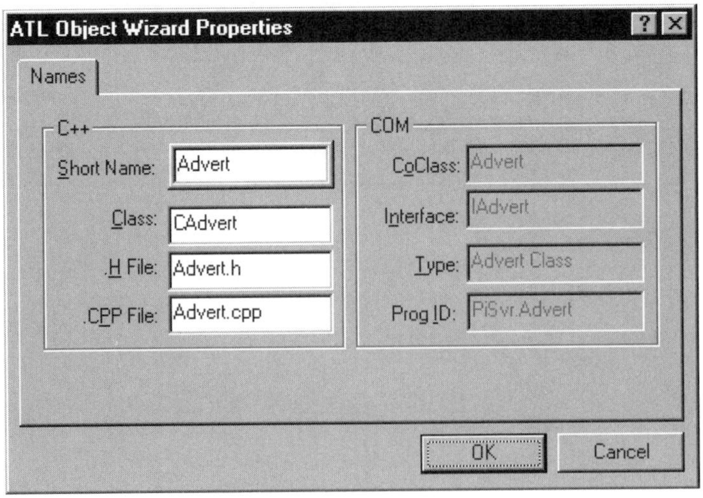

Figure 1.14.   Dialog-special ATL Object Wizard properties

functions (a dialog is an object, after all). Like MFC, ATL has a great deal of functionality for building windows and dialogs. To add a new dialog, the ATL Object Wizard provides the Dialog object as part of the Miscellaneous category, shown in Figure 1.13. The Dialog-specific part of the ATL Object Wizard (Figure 1.14) is much simpler than other parts and only allows you to enter C++ name information, because a dialog is a Win32 object, not a COM object.

The generated code creates a class that derives from CAxDialogImpl and uses a new dialog box template, also provided by the wizard. The derived class routes messages to handlers using the MSG_MAP macros, as shown here:

```
class CAdvert : public CAxDialogImpl<CAdvert>
{
public:
 CAdvert() {}
 ~CAdvert() {}
 enum { IDD = IDD_ADVERT };

BEGIN_MSG_MAP(CAdvert)
 MESSAGE_HANDLER(WM_INITDIALOG, OnInitDialog)
 COMMAND_ID_HANDLER(IDOK, OnOK)
 COMMAND_ID_HANDLER(IDCANCEL, OnCancel)
END_MSG_MAP()

 LRESULT OnInitDialog(UINT uMsg, WPARAM wParam, LPARAM lParam,
                      BOOL& bHandled) {
    if( m_bstrClient.Length() ) {
    CComBSTR  bstrCaption = OLESTR("CalcPi sponsored by ");
    bstrCaption += m_bstrClient;

    USES_CONVERSION;
    SetWindowText(OLE2CT(bstrCaption));
   }

   return 1;  // Let the system set the focus
 }

 LRESULT OnOK(WORD wNotifyCode, WORD wID, HWND hWndCtl,
              BOOL& bHandled) {
   EndDialog(wID);
   return 0;
 }
```

```
LRESULT OnCancel(WORD wNotifyCode, WORD wID, HWND hWndCtl,
                 BOOL& bHandled) {
  EndDialog(wID);
  return 0;
}
```

```
CComBSTR  m_bstrClient;
};
```

If you'd like to handle another message, you can add the appropriate entries to the message map and add the handler member functions by hand. If you prefer, you can also run the Message Handler wizard, accessible by right-clicking on the name of the `CWindowImpl` or `CDialogImpl`-based class in the ClassView and choosing Add Windows Message Handler. The Message Handler dialog is shown in Figure 1.15.

For more information on ATL's extensive support for windowing, including building standalone Windows applications, see Chapter 9.

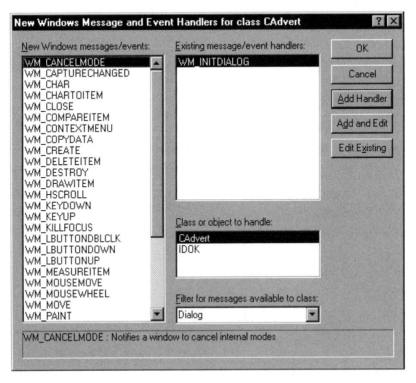

Figure 1.15. Adding a windows message handler

Implementing Component Categories

If you've been following along, or if you've tried to run your COM objects inside of Internet Explorer before, you may have noticed the really annoying dialog shown in Figure 1.16. This is Internet Explorer's way of telling you that the CalcPi object has not promised to be safe in the paranoid world of the Internet. Since calculating pi can never really do any harm, we'd like IE to stop bothering our users (or at least us) with this accusatory dialog. To let IE know we promise to behave, we have to list our class in the registry as implementing the proper component categories. A component category is a way of listing a class as behaving in a certain way. For example, the Embedded component category says that an object of the class can be embedded using the OLE protocols.

To promise to do nothing bad, no matter the initialization data or the script that is run against us (the worse we could do is crash a single process), our CalcPi class needs to implement the Safe For Scripting and Safe For Initialization component categories. We can do that using the ATL CATEGORY_MAP and the appropriate component category unique IDs (CATIDs):

```
class ATL_NO_VTABLE CCalcPi : ... {
...

public:
BEGIN_CATEGORY_MAP(CCalcPi)
 IMPLEMENTED_CATEGORY(CATID_SafeForScripting)
 IMPLEMENTED_CATEGORY(CATID_SafeForInitializing)
END_CATEGORY_MAP()

...
};
```

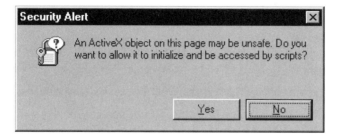

Figure 1.16. Internet Explorer Security Alert dialog

Not only are component categories good for making promises to Internet Explorer, they're also good for publishing classes to arbitrary clients, as well as requiring functionality of clients before they bother to create instances. For more information on ATL's support for component categories, see Chapter 4.

Adding a User Interface

COM controls are objects that provide their own user interface (UI), which is closely integrated with that of their clients. ATL provides extensive support for COM controls via the CComControl base class as well as various other base IXxxImpl classes. These base classes handle most of the details of being a basic control (although there's plenty of room for advanced features, as shown in Chapter 10). Had you chosen Full Control or Lite Control from the Controls section of the ATL Object Wizard when generating the CalcPi class, you could have provided the UI merely by implementing the OnDraw function:

```
HRESULT CCalcPi::OnDraw(ATL_DRAWINFO& di) {
 CComBSTR  bstrPi;
 if( SUCCEEDED(this->CalcPi(&bstrPi)) ) {
   USES_CONVERSION;
   DrawText(di.hdcDraw, OLE2CT(bstrPi), -1, (RECT*)di.prcBounds,
           DT_SINGLELINE | DT_CENTER | DT_VCENTER);
 }

 return S_OK;
}
```

The wizard would also have generated a sample HTML page, which I've augmented to take up the entire browser window and to set the initial number of digits to 50:

```
<HTML>
<HEAD>
<TITLE>ATL 3.0 test page for object CalcPi</TITLE>
</HEAD>
<BODY>
<OBJECT CLASSID="CLSID:DEC22F37-DD78-11D1-97FD-006008243C8C"
        ID="CalcPi"
        height=100% width=100%>
```

```
    <param name=digits value=50>
</OBJECT>
</BODY>
</HTML>
```

Displaying this sample page in Internet Explorer yields a view of a control (Figure 1.17).

For more information about building controls in ATL, see Chapter 10.

Hosting a Control

If you'd like to host a control, you can do so with ATL's control hosting support. For example, the Ax in CAxDialogImpl stands for ActiveX control and indicates that the dialog is able to host controls. To host a control in a dialog, right-click on the dialog box resource and choose Insert ActiveX Control. This will produce a dialog listing the controls installed on your system, as shown in Figure 1.18. Once you've inserted the control, you can right-click on it and set its properties, as shown in Figure 1.19. Also by right-clicking, you can choose to handle a control's events, as shown in Figure 1.20.

When the dialog box is shown, the control will be created and initialized based on the properties set at development time. An example of a dialog box hosting a control is shown in Figure 1.21.

ATL provides support for hosting ATL controls not only in dialogs, but also in other windows, in controls that have a UI declared as a dialog box resource (called composite controls), and in controls that have a UI declared as an HTML resource (called HTML controls). For more information about control containment, see Chapter 11.

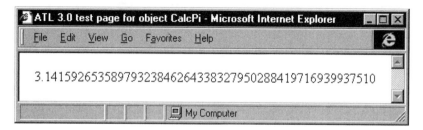

Figure 1.17. The CalcPi control hosted in Internet Explorer

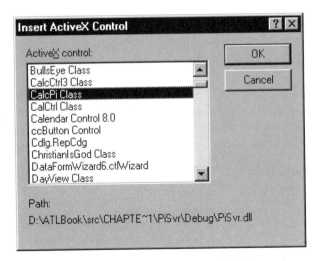

Figure 1.18. Insert ActiveX Control dialog

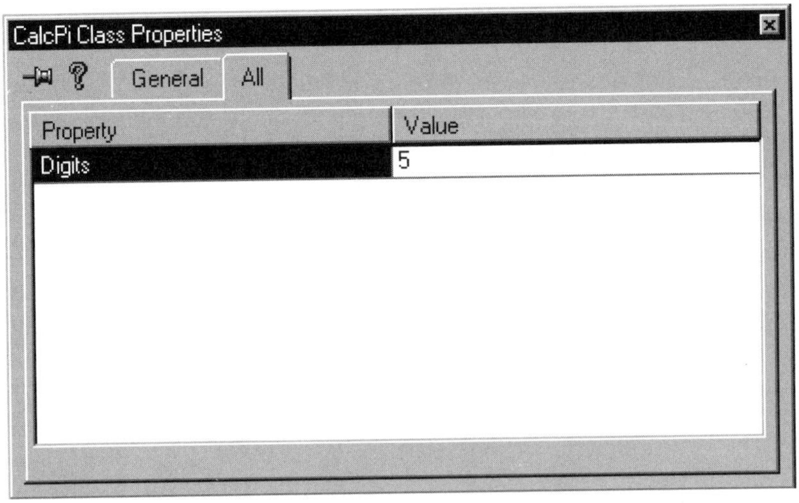

Figure 1.19. Control Properties dialog

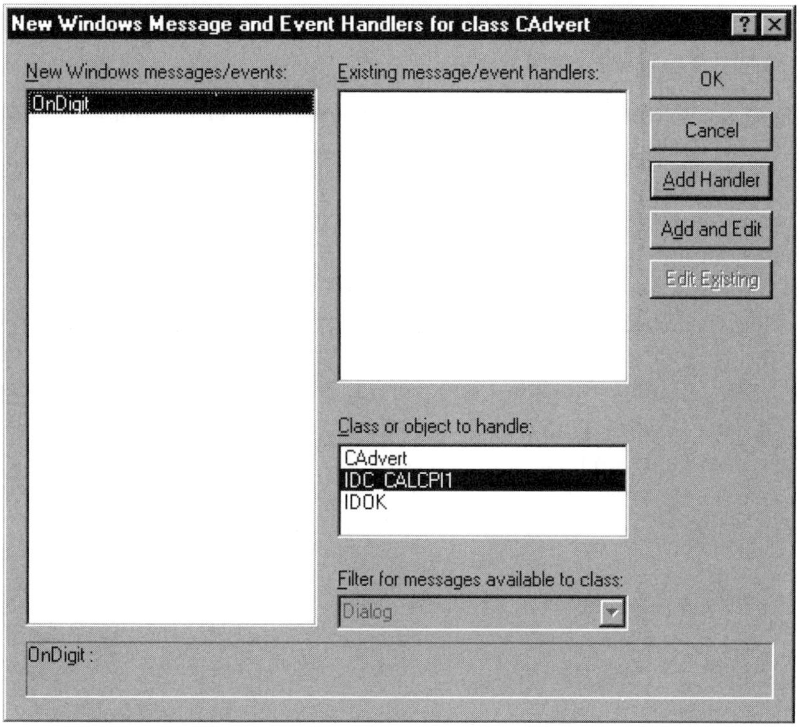

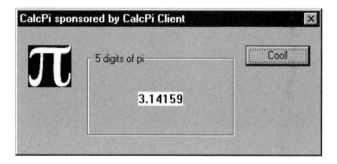

Figure 1.20. Choosing which control events to handle

Figure 1.21. A dialog hosting a COM control

Summary

This chapter has been a whirlwind tour through some of the functionality of ATL that the wizards expose, as well as some of the basic interface implementations of ATL. Even with the wizards, it should be clear that ATL is no substitute for solid COM knowledge. You still have to know how to design and implement your interfaces. As you'll see throughout the rest of this book, you still have to know about interface pointers, reference counting, runtime type discovery, threading, persistence . . . the list goes on. ATL can help, but you still have to know COM.

It should also be clear that the wizard is not a substitute for intimate ATL knowledge. For every tidbit of ATL information I've shown in this chapter, there are ten more salient details, extensions, and pitfalls. And although the wizard saves you typing, it can't do everything. It can't make sure your design and implementation goals are met: That's up to you.

ATL Smart Types
Strings, BSTRs, VARIANTs, and Interface Pointers

COM has a number of data types beyond the numeric types available in the C language. Three such data types are text strings (especially in the form of a BSTR), the VARIANT data type, and interface pointers. ATL provides useful classes that encapsulate each of these data types and their special idiosyncrasies.

Strings come in a number of different character sets. COM components often need to use multiple character sets and occasionally need to convert from one set to another. ATL provides a number of string conversion macros (which it inherited from the MFC source code base), for example, A2W, OLE2CT, and others, that convert from one character set to another, if necessary, and do nothing when they are not needed.

The CComBSTR class is a smart string class. This class properly allocates, copies, and frees a string according to the BSTR string semantics. CComBSTR instances can be used in most, but not all, of the places you would use a BSTR.

The CComVariant class is a smart VARIANT class. The class implements the special initialization, copy, and destruction semantics of the COM VARIANT data type. CComVariant instances can be used in most, but not all, of the places you would use a VARIANT.

The CComPtr and CComQIPtr classes are smart pointer classes. Smart pointer classes are definitions of objects that *act* like a pointer, specifically, a pointer with extra semantics. One example, in the case of smart interface pointers, is that the destructor can release the interface pointer any time the smart pointer goes out of scope, including unusual situations like exception handling.

String Data Types, Conversion Macros, and Helper Functions

A Review of Text Data Types

The text data type is rather a pain to deal with in C++ programming. The main problem is that there isn't *one, single* text data type. There are too many of them. I'm using the term *text data type* here in the general sense of an array of characters. Often, different operating systems and programming languages introduce additional semantics on an array of characters (for example, NUL character termination or a length prefix) before they consider an array of characters a text string.

When you select a text data type, there are a number of decisions to make. First, there is the issue of what type of characters constitute the array. Some operating systems require you to use ANSI characters when you pass a string (for example, a file name) to the operating system. Some operating systems prefer you to use Unicode characters but will accept ANSI characters. Other operating systems require you to use EBCDIC characters. There are stranger character sets in use as well, such as the Multi/Double Byte Character Sets (MBCS/DBCS), the details of which this book largely doesn't discuss.

Second, there is the question of what character set you use when writing a program. There is no requirement that your source code use the same character set as the one preferred by the operating system running your program. Clearly, it's more convenient when both use the same character set. Nevertheless, a program and the operating system can use different character sets. You "simply" have to convert all text strings going to and coming from the operating system.

Third, there is the issue of determining the length of a text string. Some languages, such as C and C++, and some operating systems, such as Windows 9x/NT and UNIX, use a terminating NUL character to delimit the end of a text string. Other languages, such as Microsoft's Visual Basic interpreter, Microsoft's Java virtual machine, and Pascal, prefer an explicit length prefix specifying the number of characters in the text string.

Fourth, in practice, a text string presents a resource management issue. Text strings typically vary in length. Therefore, for efficient memory usage, a text string is often dynamically allocated. Of course, this means a text string must be freed eventually. Resource management introduces the idea of an owner of a text string. The owner of the string, and only the owner, frees the string and only frees it once. Ownership becomes quite important when you pass a text string between components distributed across multiple heterogeneous computers.

Two COM objects, however, may reside on two different computers running two different operating systems that prefer two different character sets for a text string. For example, you can write one COM object in Visual Basic and run it on the Windows NT operating system. You might pass a text string to another COM object written in C++ running on an IBM mainframe. Clearly, we need some standard text data type that all COM objects in a heterogeneous environment can understand.

COM uses the OLECHAR character data type. A COM text string is a NUL-character-terminated array of OLECHAR characters, and a pointer to such a string is an LPOLESTR.[1] As a rule, a text string parameter to a COM interface method should

---

[1] Note that the actual underlying character data type for OLECHAR on one operating system (for example, Windows NT) can be different from the underlying character data type for OLECHAR on a different

be of type LPOLESTR. When a method doesn't change the string, the parameter should be of type LPCOLESTR, that is, a constant pointer to an array of OLECHAR characters.

Frequently, though not always, the OLECHAR type isn't the same as the characters you use when writing your code. Sometimes, though not always, the OLECHAR type isn't the same as the characters you must provide when passing a text string to the operating system. This means that, *depending on context*, sometimes you'll need to convert a text string from one character set to another and sometimes you won't.

Unfortunately, a change in compiler options (for example, a Windows NT Unicode build or a Windows CE build) can change this context, resulting in code that previously didn't need to convert a string now needing conversion and vice versa. You don't want to rewrite all string manipulation code each time you change a compiler option. Therefore, ATL provides a number of string conversion macros that convert a text string from one character set to another and *are sensitive to the context in which you invoke the conversion.*

Windows Character Data Types

Now, let's focus specifically on the Windows platform. Windows-based COM components typically use a mix of four text data types.

- **Unicode:** A specification for representing a character as a "wide-character," 16-bit multilingual character code. The Windows NT operating system uses the Unicode character set internally. All characters used in modern computing worldwide, including technical symbols and special publishing characters, can be represented uniquely in Unicode. The fixed character size simplifies programming using international character sets. In C/C++, you represent a wide-character string as a wchar_t array; a pointer to such a string is a wchar_t* pointer.

- **MBCS/DBCS:** The Multi-Byte Character Set is a mixed-width character set, in which some characters consist of more than one byte. The Windows 9x operating systems, in general, use the MBCS to represent characters. The DBCS (Double-Byte Character Set) is a specific type of multibyte character set. It includes some characters that consist of one byte and some characters that consist of two bytes to represent the symbols for one specific locale, such as the Japanese, the Chinese, and the Korean languages.

---

operating system (for example, OS/390). The COM remoting infrastructure performs any necessary character set conversion during marshaling and unmarshaling. Therefore, a COM component always receives text in its expected OLECHAR format.

In C/C++, you represent an MBCS/DBCS string as an `unsigned char` array; a pointer to such a string is an `unsigned char*` pointer. Sometimes a character is one `unsigned char` in length. Sometimes it's more than one. This is loads of fun to deal with, especially when trying to back up through a string. In Visual C++, MBCS always means DBCS. Character sets wider than two bytes are not supported.

- **ANSI:** You can represent all characters used by the English language, as well as many western European languages, using only eight bits. Versions of Windows supporting such languages use a degenerate case of MBCS, called the Microsoft Windows ANSI character set, in which no multibyte characters are present. The Microsoft Windows ANSI character set, which is essentially ISO 8859/x plus additional characters, was originally based on an ANSI draft standard.

  The ANSI character set maps the letters and numerals in the same manner as ASCII. However, ANSI does not support control characters and it maps many symbols, including accented letters, that are not mapped in standard ASCII. All Windows fonts are defined in the ANSI character set. This is also called the SBCS (Single-Byte Character Set) for symmetry.

  In C/C++, you represent an ANSI string as a `char` array; a pointer to such a string is a `char*` pointer. A character is always one `char` in length. By default, a `char` is a `signed char` in Visual C++. Because MBCS characters are `unsigned` and ANSI characters are, by default, `signed` characters, expressions can evaluate differently when using ANSI characters as compared with using MBCS characters.

- **TCHAR/_TCHAR:** A Microsoft-specific generic-text data type that you can map to a Unicode character, an MBCS character, or an ANSI character using compile-time options. You use this character type to write generic code that can be compiled for any of the three character sets. This simplifies code development for international markets. The C runtime library defines the _TCHAR type, and the Windows operating system defines the TCHAR type. They are synonymous.

  Note: `tchar.h`, a Microsoft-specific C runtime library header file, defines the generic-text data type _TCHAR. ANSI C/C++ compiler compliance requires implementor-defined names to be underscore prefixed. When you do not define the __STDC__ preprocessor symbol (the default setting in Visual C++), you indicate you don't require ANSI compliance. In this case, the `tchar.h` header file also defines the symbol TCHAR as another alias for the generic-text data type if it isn't already defined. `winnt.h`, a Microsoft-specific Win32 operating system header file, defines the generic-text data type TCHAR. This header file is operating system specific, so the symbol names don't need to have the underscore prefix.

Win32 APIs and Strings

Each Win32 API that requires a string has two versions: one that requires a Unicode argument and another that requires an MBCS argument. On a non-MBCS-enabled version of Windows, the MBCS version of an API expects an ANSI argument. For example, the SetWindowText API doesn't really exist. There are actually two functions: SetWindowTextW, which expects a Unicode string argument, and Set-WindowTextA, which expects an MBCS/ANSI string argument.

The Windows NT operating system internally uses only Unicode strings. Therefore, when you call SetWindowTextA on Windows NT, the function translates the specified string to Unicode, then calls SetWindowTextW. The Windows 9x operating systems do not support Unicode. The SetWindowTextA function on the Windows 9x operating systems does the work, whereas SetWindowTextW returns an error.

This gives you a difficult choice. You can write a performance-optimized component using Unicode character strings that runs on Windows NT but not on Windows 9x. You can write a more general component using MBCS/ANSI character strings that runs on both operating systems, but not optimally on Windows NT. Alternatively, you can hedge your bets by writing source code in such a way that you can decide at compile time what character set to support.

A little coding discipline and some preprocessor magic lets you code as if there were a single API called SetWindowText that expects a TCHAR string argument. You specify at compile time which kind of component you wish to build. For example, you write code that calls SetWindowText and specifies a TCHAR buffer. When compiling a component as Unicode, you actually call SetWindowTextW and the argument is a wchar_t buffer. When compiling an MBCS/ANSI component, you actually call SetWindowTextA and the argument is a char buffer.

When you write a Windows-based COM component, you should typically use the TCHAR character type to represent characters used by the component internally. Additionally, use it for all characters used in interactions with the operating system. Similarly, you should use the TEXT or __TEXT macro to surround every literal character or string. tchar.h defines the functionally equivalent macros _T, __T, and _TEXT, which all compile a character or string literal as a generic-text character or literal. winnt.h also defines the functionally equivalent macros TEXT and __TEXT, which both do exactly the same thing as _T, __T, and _TEXT. There's nothing like five ways to do exactly the same thing. The examples in this chapter use __TEXT because it's defined in winnt.h. I actually prefer _T because it's less clutter in my source code.

An operating-system-agnostic coding approach would favor including tchar.h and using the _TCHAR generic-text data type because that's somewhat less tied to the Windows operating systems. However, we're discussing building components with text handling optimized at compile time for specific versions of the Windows operating systems. This argues we should use TCHAR, the type defined in winnt.h. Plus, TCHAR isn't as jarring to the eyes as _TCHAR. It's less to type. Most code already implicitly includes the winnt.h. header file, and you must explicitly include tchar.h. There are all sorts of good reasons to prefer TCHAR, so the examples in this book use TCHAR as the generic-text data type.

This allows you to compile specialized versions of the component for different markets or for performance reasons. These types and macros are defined in the winnt.h header file.

You also must use a different set of string runtime library functions when manipulating strings of TCHAR characters. The familiar functions strlen, strcpy, and so on only operate on char characters. The less familar functions wcslen, wcscpy, and so on work on wchar_t characters. Moreover, the totally strange functions _mbslen, _mbscpy, and so on work on multibyte characters. Because TCHAR characters are sometimes wchar_t and sometimes char-holding ANSI characters and sometimes char-holding (nominally unsigned) multibyte characters, you need an equivalent set of runtime library functions that work with TCHAR characters.

The tchar.h header file defines a number of useful generic-text mappings for string handling functions. These functions expect TCHAR parameters, so all their function names use the _tcs (the _t character set) prefix. For example, _tcslen is equivalent to the C runtime library strlen function. The _tcslen function expects TCHAR characters, whereas the strlen function expects char characters.

Controlling Generic-Text Mapping Using the Preprocessor

Two preprocessor symbols and two macros control the mapping of the TCHAR data type to the underlying character type used by the application.

- UNICODE/_UNICODE: The header files for the Windows operating system APIs use the UNICODE preprocessor symbol. The C/C++ runtime library header files use the _UNICODE preprocessor symbol. Typically, you'll either define both symbols or define neither of them. When you compile with the symbol _UNICODE defined, tchar.h maps all TCHAR characters to wchar_t characters. The _T, __T, and _TEXT macros prefix each character or string literal with a capital L (creating a Unicode character or literal, respectively). When you compile with the symbol UNICODE defined, winnt.h maps all TCHAR characters to wchar_t characters. The TEXT and __TEXT macros prefix each character or string literal with a capital L (creating a Unicode character or literal, respectively).

- _MBCS: When you compile with the symbol _MBCS defined, all TCHAR characters map to char characters and the preprocessor removes all the _T and __TEXT macro variations, leaving the character or literal unchanged (creating an MBCS character or literal, respectively).

- When you compile with neither symbol defined, all TCHAR characters map to char characters and the preprocessor removes all the _T and __TEXT macro variations, leaving the character or literal unchanged (creating an ANSI character or literal, respectively).

You write generic-text-compatible code by using the generic-text data types and functions. Some generic-text code that reverses the order of the characters in a string and then appends a string literal as follows:

```
TCHAR *reversedString, *sourceString, *completeString;
reversedString = _tcsrev (sourceString);
completeString = _tcscat (reversedString, __TEXT("suffix"));
```

When you compile the code without defining any preprocessor symbols, the preprocessor produces this output:

```
char *reversedString, *sourceString, *completeString;
reversedString = _strrev (sourceString);
completeString = strcat (reversedString, "suffix");
```

When you compile the code after defining the _UNICODE preprocessor symbol, the preprocessor produces this output:

```
_wchar_t *reversedString, *sourceString, *completeString;
reversedString = _wcsrev (sourceString);
completeString = wcscat (reversedString, L"suffix");
```

When you compile the code after defining the _MBCS preprocessor symbol, the preprocessor produces this output:

```
char *reversedString, *sourceString, *completeString;
reversedString = _mbsrev (sourceString);
completeString = _mbscat (reversedString, "suffix");
```

COM Character Data Types

COM uses two character types.

- OLECHAR: The character type used by COM on the operating system for which you compile your source code. For Win32 operating systems, this is the wchar_t character type.

  Note: Actually, you can change the Win32 OLECHAR data type from the default wchar_t (which is what COM uses internally) to char by defining the preprocessor symbol OLE2ANSI. This lets you pretend that COM uses ANSI. MFC used this feature at one time. Don't give in to the dark side, Luke. Using this "convenience" feature requires that you then link your components with the OLE2ANSI thunking library. This library converts all ANSI string parameters back to wchar_t on every API and COM interface method call. Similarly, it converts output strings from wchar_t to char. This adds needless overhead in many cases. MFC's performance improved roughly 10 percent when Microsoft rewrote it without using OLE2ANSI and used the string conversion macros where necessary.

  For Win16 operating systems, this is the char character type. For the Mac OS, this is the char character type. For the Solaris OS, this is the wchar_t character type. For the as yet unknown operating system, this is who knows what. Let's just pretend there is an abstract data type called OLECHAR. COM uses it. Don't rely on it mapping to any specific underlying data type.

- BSTR: A specialized string type used by some COM components. A BSTR is a length-prefixed array of OLECHAR characters with numerous special semantics.

Now let's complicate things a bit. You want to write code for which you can select, at compile time, the type of characters it uses. Therefore, you're manipulating strictly TCHAR strings internally. You also want to call a COM method and pass it the same strings. You'll have to pass the method either an OLECHAR string or a BSTR string, depending on its signature. The strings used by your component may or may not be in the correct character format, depending on your compilation options. This is a job for supermacro.

ATL String Conversion Macros

ATL provides a number of string conversion macros that convert, when necessary, between the various character types described previously. The macros perform no conversion, and, in fact, do nothing, when the compilation options cause the source and destination character types to be identical.

The macro names use a number of abbreviations for the various character data types:

- **T** represents a pointer to the Win32 `TCHAR` character type—a `LPTSTR` parameter.

- **W** represents a pointer to the Unicode `wchar_t` character type—a `LPWSTR` parameter.

- **A** represents a pointer to the MBCS/ANSI `char` character type—a `LPSTR` parameter.

- **OLE** represents a pointer to the COM `OLECHAR` character type—a `LPOLESTR` parameter.

- **C** represents the C/C++ `const` modifier.

All macro names use the form "<source-abbreviation>2<destination-abbreviation>"; for example, the A2W macro converts a `LPSTR` to a `LPWSTR`. When there is a C in the macro name, add a `const` modification to the following abbreviation; for example, the T2COLE macro converts a `LPTSTR` to a `LPCOLESTR`.

The actual macro behavior depends on which preprocessor symbols you define (Table 2.1). Table 2.2 lists the ATL string conversion macros.

All macros accept one argument, which is a pointer to a string in the source character set. Each macro acts like a function call that returns a pointer to a string

Table 2.1. Character Set Preprocessor Symbols

Preprocessor symbol defined	T becomes	OLE becomes
None	A	W
_UNICODE	W	W
OLE2ANSI	A	A
_UNICODE and OLE2ANSI	W	A

Table 2.2. ATL String Conversion Macros

A2BSTR	A2W	OLE2CW	T2COLE	W2CA
A2COLE	A2WBSTR	OLE2T	T2CW	W2COLE
A2CT	OLE2A	OLE2W	T2OLE	W2CT
A2CW	OLE2BSTR	T2A	T2W	W2OLE
A2OLE	OLE2CA	T2BSTR	W2A	W2T
A2T	OLE2CT	T2CA	W2BSTR	

in the destination character set. When the source and destination character sets are the same, the macro simply returns the specified argument as the destination.

When the source and destination character sets are different *and the destination type is not* BSTR, the macro allocates the destination string using the _alloca runtime library function. The _alloca function allocates memory on the stack (that is, it grows the stack pointer). The conversion macros allocate the destination string on the stack so that when your function (the one using the conversion macro) returns, the memory is automatically reclaimed. However, it's important to realize what is happening with the memory so you don't use the conversion macros within a loop. Repeated invocations of these conversion macros within a loop grow the stack larger and larger. Eventually, you will run out of stack space.

The conversion macros use local variables. You must allocate these variables by specifying the USES_CONVERSION macro once at the beginning of any function that uses a string conversion macro. The following code converts a TCHAR string to an OLECHAR string and calls a COM method that expects a constant pointer to an OLECHAR string. You don't need to free the OLECHAR string because it will be freed automatically when the function returns.

```
STDMETHODIMP put_Name (/* [in] */ const OLECHAR* pName);

void SetName (LPTSTR lpsz)
{
    USES_CONVERSION;
    . . .
    pObj->put_Name (T2COLE(lpsz));
}
```

When the source and destination character sets are different *and the destination type is* BSTR, the macro allocates the destination string using the SysAlloc-String or SysAllocStringLen function. You must explicitly free this BSTR using SysFreeString. The following code converts a TCHAR string to a BSTR, calls a COM method that expects a BSTR string, and then frees the BSTR.

```
void SetName (LPTSTR lpsz)
{
    USES_CONVERSION;
    . . .
    BSTR bstr = T2BSTR(lpsz);
    pObj->put_Name (bstr);
    ::SysFreeString (bstr) ;
}
```

ATL String Helper Functions

Sometimes you want to copy a string of OLECHAR characters. You also happen to know that OLECHAR characters are wide characters on the Win32 operating system. When writing a Win32 version of your component, you might call the Win32 operating system function lstrcpyW, which copies wide characters. Unfortunately, Windows NT, which supports Unicode, implements lstrcpyW, but Windows 95 does not. A component that uses the lstrcpyW API doesn't work correctly on Windows 95.

Instead of lstrcpyW, use the ATL string helper function ocscpy to copy an OLECHAR character string. It works properly on both Windows NT and Windows 95. There is an ATL string helper function ocslen that returns the length of an OLECHAR string. This is nice for symmetry, though the lstrlenW function it replaces does work on both operating systems.

```
OLECHAR* ocscpy(LPOLESTR dest, LPCOLESTR src);
size_t ocslen(LPCOLESTR s);
```

Similarly, the Win32 CharNextW operating system function doesn't work on Windows 95, so ATL provides a CharNextO string helper function that increments an OLECHAR* by one character and returns the next character pointer. It will not increment the pointer beyond a NUL termination character.

```
LPOLESTR CharNextO(LPCOLESTR lp);
```

The CComBSTR Smart BSTR Class

A Review of the COM String Data Type—BSTR

COM is a language-neutral, hardware-architecture-neutral model. Therefore, it needs a language-neutral, hardware-architecture-neutral text data type. Unfortunately, there is no single text data type that is universally available on all hardware and usable by all languages. Some platforms use the ASCII/ANSI character set, which consists of 8-bit characters. Some use the EBCDIC character set, which consists of a different 8-bit character set. Some use the MBCS (Multi-Byte Character Set), which consists of intermingled 8-bit and 16-bit characters. Some use the Unicode character set, which consists of 16-bit characters. There are other, less frequently used, character sets in use as well.

COM defines a generic text data type, OLECHAR, which represents the text data used by COM on a specific platform. On most platforms, including all 32-bit Windows platforms, the OLECHAR data type is a typedef for the wchar_t data type. That is, on most platforms, the COM text data type is equivalent to the C/C++ wide-character data type, which contains Unicode characters. On some platforms, such as the 16-bit Windows operating system and the Macintosh OS, OLECHAR is a `typedef` for the standard C `char` data type, which contains ANSI characters. Generally, you'll want to define all string parameters used in a COM interface as OLECHAR* arguments.

COM also defines an additional text data type called BSTR. A BSTR is a length-prefixed string of OLECHAR characters. Most interpretive environments prefer length-prefixed strings for performance reasons. For example, a length-prefixed string requires no time-consuming scanning for a NUL character terminator to determine the length of a string. Actually, the NUL-character-terminated string is a language-specific concept originally unique to the C/C++ language. The Microsoft Visual Basic interpreter, the Microsoft Java virtual machine, and most scripting languages, such as VBScript and JScript, internally represent a string as a BSTR.

Therefore, you'll find that when you pass or receive a string to or from a method parameter to an interface defined by a C/C++ component, you'll often use the OLECHAR* data type. However, if you need to use an interface defined by another language, frequently string parameters will be the BSTR data type. The BSTR data type has a number of poorly documented semantics, which makes using BSTRs a tedious and error-prone task for C++ developers.

A BSTR has the following attributes:

- A BSTR is a pointer to a length-prefixed array of OLECHAR characters.
- A BSTR is a pointer data type. It points at the first character in the array. The length prefix is stored as an integer immediately preceding the first character in the array.
- The array of characters is NUL character terminated.
- The length prefix is in bytes, not characters, and does not include the terminating NUL character.
- The array of characters may contain embedded NUL characters.
- It must be allocated and freed using the `SysAllocString` and `SysFree String` family of functions.
- A NULL BSTR pointer implies an empty string.
- A BSTR is not reference counted; therefore, two references to the same string content must refer to separate BSTRs. In other words, copying a BSTR implies making a duplicate string, not simply copying the pointer.

With all these special semantics, it would be useful to encapsulate these details in a reusable class. ATL provides such a class: CComBSTR.

The CComBSTR Class

The CComBSTR class is an ATL utility class that is a useful encapsulation for the COM string data type, BSTR. The `atlbase.h` file contains the definition of the CComBSTR class. The only state maintained by the class is a single public member variable, m_str, of type BSTR.

```
/////////////////////////////////////////////////////////////
// CComBSTR

class CComBSTR
{
public:
  BSTR m_str;
  . . .
} ;
```

Constructors and Destructor

There are eight constructors available for CComBSTR objects. The default constructor simply initializes the m_str variable to NULL, which is equivalent to a BSTR that represents an empty string. The destructor destroys any BSTR contained in the m_str variable by calling SysFreeString. The SysFreeString function explicitly documents that the function simply returns when the input parameter is NULL so the destructor can run on an empty object without problem.

```
CComBSTR() { m_str = NULL; }
~CComBSTR() { ::SysFreeString(m_str); }
```

You will see, later in this section, numerous convenience methods provided by the CComBSTR class. However, I'd argue that one of the most compelling reasons for using the class is so the destructor frees the internal BSTR at the appropriate time, so you don't have to free a BSTR explicitly. This is exceptionally convenient during times like stack frame unwinding, when locating an exception handler.

Probably the most frequently used constructor initializes a CComBSTR object from a pointer to a NUL character-terminated array of OLECHAR characters, or, as it's more commonly known, a LPCOLESTR.

```
CComBSTR(LPCOLESTR pSrc) { m_str = ::SysAllocString(pSrc);}
```

You invoke the preceding constructor when you write code such as the following:

```
CComBSTR str1 (OLESTR ("This is a string of OLECHARs")) ;
```

The previous constructor copies characters until it finds the end-of-string NUL character terminator. When you want some lesser number of characters copied, such as the prefix to a string, or when you want to copy from a string containing embedded NUL characters, you must explicitly specify the number of characters to copy. In this case, use the following constructor:

```
CComBSTR(int nSize, LPCOLESTR sz) { m_str = ::SysAllocStringLen
  (sz, nSize); }
```

This constructor creates a BSTR with room for the number of characters specified by nSize, copies the specified number of characters, including any embedded NUL characters, from sz, then appends a terminating NUL character. When sz is NULL, SysAllocStringLen skips the copy step, which creates an uninitialized BSTR of the specified size. You invoke the preceding constructor when you write code such as the following:

```
CComBSTR str2 (16, OLESTR ("This is a string of OLECHARs"));
// str2 contains "This is a string"

CComBSTR str3 (64, (LPCOLESTR) NULL);
// Allocates an uninitialized BSTR with room for 64 characters

CComBSTR str4 (64);
// Allocates an uninitialized BSTR with room for 64 characters
```

The CComBSTR class provides a special constructor for the str3 example in the preceding code, which doesn't require you to provide the NULL argument. The preceding str4 example shows its usage. Here's the constructor:

```
CComBSTR(int nSize) { m_str = ::SysAllocStringLen(NULL, nSize); }
```

One odd semantic feature of a BSTR is that a NULL pointer is a valid value for an empty BSTR string. Visual Basic, for example, considers a NULL BSTR to be equivalent to a pointer to an empty string, that is, a string of zero length where the first character is the terminating NUL character. Or to put it symbolically, Visual Basic considers IF "" = p, where p is a BSTR set to NULL, to be true.

Unfortunately, not all the APIs dealing with BSTRs recognize this fact. Specifically, the documentation for the SysStringLen function explicitly specifies that the argument must be non-NULL. This means to obtain the length of a BSTR correctly (according to the documentation), you need to write code such as this:

```
UINT length = bstrInput ? SysStringLen (bstrInput) : 0 ;
```

After you have a BSTR encapsulated in a CComBSTR object, you can simply call the Length member function which does the same thing:

```
unsigned int Length() const
  { return (m_str == NULL) ? 0 : SysStringLen(m_str); }
```

Testing under Windows NT 4.0 Service Pack 3 shows that SysStringLen doesn't really care whether its argument is NULL. When its argument is non-NULL, SysStringLen returns the proper length. When its argument is NULL, SysStringLen returns zero. However, this may not hold true under older versions of Windows NT, or on other operating systems that support COM (Solaris, OS/390, etc.). SysStringLen may have been implemented according to the documentation on other operating systems.

You can also use the following copy constructor to create and initialize a CComBSTR object to be equivalent to an already initialized CComBSTR object.

```
CComBSTR(const CComBSTR& src) { m_str = src.Copy(); }
```

In the following code, creating the str5 variable invokes the preceding copy constructor to initialize their respective objects:

```
CComBSTR str1 (OLESTR("This is a string of OLECHARs")) ;
CComBSTR str5 = str1 ;
```

Note that the preceding copy constructor called the Copy method on the source CComBSTR object. The Copy method makes a copy of its string and returns the new BSTR. Because the Copy method allocates the new BSTR using the length of the existing BSTR and copies the string contents for the specified length, the Copy method properly copies a BSTR that contains embedded NUL characters.

```
BSTR Copy() const
  { return ::SysAllocStringLen(m_str, ::SysStringLen(m_str)); }
```

Two constructors initialize a CComBSTR object from a LPCSTR string. The single argument constructor expects a NUL-terminated LPCSTR string. The two-argument constructor permits you to specify the length of the LPCSTR string. These two constructors are functionally equivalent to the two previously discussed constructors that accept a LPCOLESTR parameter. The following two constructors expect ANSI characters and create a BSTR containing the equivalent string in OLECHAR characters.

```
#ifndef OLE2ANSI
CComBSTR(LPCSTR pSrc) { m_str = A2WBSTR(pSrc);}
CComBSTR(int nSize, LPCSTR sz) { m_str = A2WBSTR(sz, nSize);}
#endif
```

These two constructors are only present when the OLE2ANSI compiler symbol is not defined during compilation. When you define the OLE2ANSI compiler symbol, the LPCOLESTR data type becomes identical to the LPCSTR data type, so these constructors have already been defined.

The final constructor is an odd one. It takes an argument that is a GUID and produces a string containing the string representation of the GUID.

```
CComBSTR(REFGUID src) { . . . }
```

This constructor is quite useful when building strings used during component registration. There are a number of situations when you need to write the string representation of a GUID to the registry. Some code that uses this constructor follows:

```
// Define a GUID as a binary constant
static const GUID GUID_Sample = { 0x8a44e110, 0xf134, 0x11d1,
    { 0x96, 0xb1, 0xBA, 0xDB, 0xAD, 0xBA, 0xDB, 0xAD } };
// Convert the binary GUID to its string representation
CComBSTR str6 (GUID_Sample) ;
// str6 contains "{8A44E110-F134-11d1-96B1-BADBADBADBAD}"
```

Initialization

The CComBSTR class defines three assignment operators. The first one initializes a CComBSTR object using a different CComBSTR object. The second one initializes a CComBSTR object using a LPCOLESTR pointer. The third one initializes the object

using a LPCSTR pointer. The following `operator=()` method initializes one CCom-
BSTR object from another CComBSTR object.

```
CComBSTR& operator=(const CComBSTR& src)
{
    if (m_str != src.m_str) {
        if (m_str)
            ::SysFreeString(m_str);
        m_str = src.Copy();
    }
    return *this;
}
```

Note that this assignment operator uses the Copy method, discussed a little later in
this section, to make an exact copy of the specified CComBSTR instance. You invoke
this operator when you write code such as the following:

```
CComBSTR str1 (OLESTR("This is a string of OLECHARs"));
CComBSTR str7 ;

str7 = str1; // str7 contains "This is a string of OLECHARs"
str7 = str7; // This is a NOP. Assignment operator detects this case
```

The second `operator=()` method initializes one CComBSTR object from a
LPCOLESTR pointer to a NUL character-terminated string.

```
CComBSTR& operator=(LPCOLESTR pSrc)
{
    ::SysFreeString(m_str);
    m_str = ::SysAllocString(pSrc);
    return *this;
}
```

Note that this assignment operator uses the SysAllocString function to allocate
a BSTR copy of the specified LPCOLESTR argument. You invoke this operator when
you write code such as the following:

```
CComBSTR str8 ;

str8 = OLESTR ("This is a string of OLECHARs");
```

It's quite easy to misuse this assignment operator when you're dealing with strings containing embedded NUL characters. For example, the following code demonstrates how to use and misuse this method.

```
CComBSTR str9 ;
str9 = OLESTR ("This works as expected");

// BSTR bstrInput contains "This is part one\0and here's part two"
CComBSTR str10 ;
str10 = bstrInput; // str10 now contains "This is part one"!!!
```

The third `operator=()` method initializes one CComBSTR object using a LPC-STR pointer to a NUL character-terminated string. The operator converts the input string, which is in ANSI characters, to a UNICODE string, then creates a BSTR containing the UNICODE string. Again, when you define the (deprecated) preprocessor symbol OLE2ANSI, the LPCSTR and LPCOLESTR data types are equivalent, so this method has already been defined and must not be redefined.

```
#ifndef OLE2ANSI
CComBSTR& operator=(LPCSTR pSrc)
{
    ::SysFreeString(m_str);
    m_str = A2WBSTR(pSrc);
    return *this;
}
#endif
```

The final initialization methods are two overloaded methods called Load-String.

```
bool LoadString(HINSTANCE hInst, UINT nID) ;
bool LoadString(UINT nID) ;
```

The first loads the specified string resource nID from the specified module hInst (using the instance handle). The second loads the specified string resource nID from the current module using the global variable _pModule.

The _pModule global variable points to this module's CComModule-derived instance variable. You initialize the variable when you call the CComModule::Init method. You typically call CComModule::Init in DllMain (for DLLs) or WinMain (for EXEs). Watch out though. The other CComBSTR methods work quite well in a module that has no global CComModule object. However, using the LoadString (UINT nID) method requires not only that you have a global instance of CComModule but that you've also initialized it. Ask me how I know . . .

CComBSTR Operations

There are four methods which give you access, in varying ways, to the internal BSTR string that is encapsulated by the CComBSTR class. The operator BSTR() method allows you to use a CComBSTR object where a raw BSTR pointer is required. You invoke this method any time you cast, implicitly or explicitly, a CComBSTR object to a BSTR.

```
operator BSTR() const { return m_str; }
```

Frequently, you'll invoke this operator implicitly when you pass a CComBSTR object as a parameter to a function that expects a BSTR. The following code demonstrates this:

```
HRESULT put_Name (/* [in] */ BSTR pNewValue) ;

CComBSTR bstrName = OLESTR ("Frodo Baggins");
pObj->put_Name (bstrName); // Implicit cast to BSTR
```

The operator&() method returns the address of the internal m_str variable when you take the address of a CComBSTR object. Use care when taking the address of a CComBSTR object. Because the operator&() method returns the address of the internal BSTR variable, you can overwrite the internal variable without first freeing the string. This causes a memory leak.

```
BSTR* operator&() { return &m_str; }
```

This operator is quite useful when you are receiving a BSTR pointer as the output of some method call. You can store the returned BSTR directly into a CComBSTR object so the object manages the lifetime of the string as follows:

```
HRESULT get_Name (/* [out] */ BSTR* pName);

CComBSTR bstrName ;
get_Name (&bstrName); // bstrName empty so no memory leak
```

The CopyTo method makes a duplicate of the string encapsulated by a CCom-BSTR object and copies the duplicate's BSTR pointer to the specified location. You will need to free the returned BSTR explicitly by calling SysFreeString.

```
HRESULT CopyTo(BSTR* pbstr) { . . . }
```

This method is handy when you need to return a copy of an existing BSTR property to a caller. For example:

```
STDMETHODIMP SomeClass::get_Name (/* [out] */ BSTR* pName)
{
 // Name is maintained in variable m_strName of type CComBSTR
 return m_strName.CopyTo (pName);
}
```

The Detach method returns the BSTR contained by a CComBSTR object. It empties the object so the destructor will not attempt to release the internal BSTR. You will need to free the returned BSTR explicitly by called SysFreeString.

```
BSTR Detach() { BSTR s = m_str; m_str = NULL; return s; }
```

You would use this method when you have a string in a CComBSTR object that you wish to return to a caller and you no longer need to keep the string. In this situation, using the CopyTo method would be less efficient because you would make a copy of a string, return the copy, then discard the original string. Use Detach as follows to return the original string directly:

```
STDMETHODIMP SomeClass::get_Label (/* [out] */ BSTR* pName)
{
 CComBSTR strLabel;
 // Generate the returned string in strLabel here
 *pName = strLabel.Detach ();
 return S_OK;
}
```

The Attach method performs the inverse operation. It takes a BSTR and attaches it to an empty CComBSTR object. Ownership of the BSTR now resides with the CComBSTR object and the object's destructor will eventually free the string. Note that you should not attach a BSTR to a non-empty CComBSTR object. If you do, you'll receive an assertion at runtime when running a debug build. However, a release build will silently leak memory.

```
void Attach(BSTR src) { ATLASSERT(m_str == NULL); m_str = src; }
```

Use care when using the `Attach` method. You must have ownership of the BSTR you are attaching to a CComBSTR object because eventually the object will attempt to destroy the BSTR. For example, *the following code is incorrect:*

```
STDMETHODIMP SomeClass::put_Name (/* [in] */ BSTR bstrName)
{
// Name is maintained in variable m_strName of type CComBSTR
m_strName.Empty();
m_strName.Attach (bstrName); // Wrong! We don't own bstrName
return E_BONEHEAD;
}
```

More often, you'll use `Attach` when you're given ownership of a BSTR and you wish a CComBSTR object to manage the lifetime of the string.

```
STDMETHODIMP SomeClass::get_Name (/* [out] */ BSTR* pName);
. . .
BSTR bstrName;
pObj->get_Name (&bstrName); // We own and must free the raw BSTR

CComBSTR strName;
strName.Attach(bstrName); // Attach raw BSTR to the object
```

When a CComBSTR object to which you wish to attach a BSTR might already contain a BSTR, call the `Empty` method first. The `Empty` method releases any internal BSTR and sets the `m_str` member variable to NULL. The `SysFreeString` function explicitly documents that the function simply returns when the input parameter is NULL so you can call `Empty` on an empty object without problem.

```
void Empty() { ::SysFreeString(m_str); m_str = NULL; }
```

String Concatenation Using CComBSTR

Six methods concatenate a specified string with a CComBSTR object: four overloaded Append methods, one AppendBSTR method and the `operator+=()` method.

```
HRESULT Append(LPCOLESTR lpsz, int nLen);
HRESULT Append(LPCOLESTR lpsz);
#ifndef OLE2ANSI
```

```
HRESULT Append(LPCSTR);
#endif

HRESULT Append(const CComBSTR& bstrSrc);
CComBSTR& operator+=(const CComBSTR& bstrSrc);

HRESULT AppendBSTR(BSTR p);
```

The Append(LPCOLESTR lpsz, int nLen) method computes the sum of the length of the current string plus the specified nLen value and allocates an empty BSTR of the correct size. It copies the original string into the new BSTR, then concatenates nLen characters of the lpsz string onto the end of the new BSTR. Finally, it frees the original string and replaces it with the new BSTR.

```
CComBSTR strSentence = OLESTR("Now is ");
strSentence.Append(OLESTR("the time of day is 03:00 PM", 9);
// strSentence contains "Now is the time "
```

The remaining three overloaded Append methods all use the first method to perform the real work. They differ only in the manner in which the method obtains the string and its length. The Append(LPCOLESTR lpsz) method appends the contents of a NUL character-terminated string of OLECHAR characters. The Append (LPCSTR lpsz) method appends the contents of a NUL character-terminated string of ANSI characters. The Append(const CComBSTR& bstrSrc) method appends the contents of another CComBSTR object. For notational and syntactical convenience, the operator+=() method also appends the specified CComBSTR to the current string.

```
CComBSTR str11 (OLESTR("for all good men ");
strSentence.Append(str11); // calls Append(const CComBSTR& bstrSrc);
// strSentence contains "Now is the time for all good men "

strSentence.Append((OLESTR("to come ")); // calls Append (LPCOLESTR
                                                             lpsz);
// strSentence contains "Now is the time for all good men to come"

strSentence.Append("to the aid "); // calls Append (LPCSTR lpsz);
// strSentence contains
```

```
// "Now is the time for all good men to come to the aid "

CComBSTR str12 (OLESTR("of their country"));
StrSentence += str12; // calls operator+=()
// "Now is the time for all good men to come to the aid of their
// country"
```

When you call Append using a BSTR parameter, you are actually calling the Append(LPCOLESTR lpsz) method, because, to the compiler, the BSTR argument *is* an OLECHAR* argument. Therefore, the method appends characters from the BSTR until the first NUL character is encountered. When you want to append the contents of a BSTR that possibly contains embedded NUL characters, you must explicitly call the AppendBSTR method. You can't go wrong following these guidelines:

- When the parameter is a BSTR, use the AppendBSTR method to append the entire BSTR regardless of whether it contains embedded NUL characters.

- When the parameter is a LPCOLESTR or a LPCSTR, use the Append method to append the NUL character-terminated string.

- So much for function overloading . . .

Character Case Conversion

The two character case conversion methods, ToLower and ToUpper, convert the internal string to lower case or upper case, respectively. Both methods use the ATL string conversion macro OLE2T to convert, if necessary, a pointer to a string of OLECHAR characters to a pointer to a string of TCHAR characters. The Win32 functions CharLower and CharUpper are used to convert the case of a TCHAR string. Finally, the methods use the ATL string conversion macro T2BSTR to convert the case-converted string back into a BSTR. When everything works, the new string replaces the original string as the contents of the CComBSTR object.

```
HRESULT ToLower()
{
    USES_CONVERSION;
    if (m_str != NULL) {
        LPTSTR psz = CharLower(OLE2T(m_str));
        if (psz == NULL) return E_OUTOFMEMORY;
        BSTR b = T2BSTR(psz);
        if (psz == NULL) return E_OUTOFMEMORY;
        SysFreeString(m_str);
```

```
        m_str = b;
    }
    return S_OK;
}
```

Note that the conversion, from OLECHAR characters to TCHAR characters, stops at the first embedded NUL character regardless of the actual length of the string. These methods produce a case-converted BSTR that is truncated at the first embedded NUL character in the original string. Also, the conversion is potentially lossy in the sense that it cannot convert a character when the local code page doesn't contain a character equivalent to the original UNICODE character.

CComBSTR Comparison Operators

The simplest comparison operator is operator!(). It returns true when the CComBSTR object is empty and false otherwise.

```
bool operator!() const { return (m_str == NULL); }
```

There are two overloaded versions of both the operator<() and the operator==() methods. As the code in both methods is nearly the same, I'll discuss only the operator<() methods. The comments apply equally to the operator==() methods.

All these comparison operators are arguably broken to a slight degree. The basic problem is that they do not support comparing two CComBSTR objects that contain strings with embedded NUL characters. These comparison operators use the ANSI C runtime library function wcscmp to perform the comparison. The wcscmp function expects NUL character-terminated strings. Therefore, it stops comparing at the first NUL character it encounters.

In addition, the wcscmp function compares strings using comparison rules according to the C runtime locale setting. By default, it is the "C" locale that handles only the 52 non-accented alpha characters. To have your string comparisons performed using the locale used by the operating system, call setlocale like this:

```
setlocale (LC_ALL, "");
```

In the first overloaded version of the operator<() method, the operator compares against a provided BSTR argument. The function prototype specifies (therefore also implies) that this function should compare against a BSTR, not simply an OLECHAR*. Therefore, I think it should handle embedded NUL characters. However, it doesn't because it uses the wcscmp function.

```
bool operator<(BSTR bstrSrc) const
{
    if (bstrSrc == NULL && m_str == NULL) return false;
    if (bstrSrc != NULL && m_str != NULL) return wcscmp
      (m_str, bstrSrc) < 0;
    return m_str == NULL;
}
```

In the second overloaded version of the operator<() method, the operator compares against a provided LPCSTR argument. A LPCSTR isn't the same character type as the internal BSTR string, which contains wide characters. Therefore, the method uses the A2W ATL helper macro to convert the ANSI string to wide characters before performing the comparison.

```
bool operator<(LPCSTR pszSrc) const
{
  if (pszSrc == NULL && m_str == NULL) return false;
  USES_CONVERSION;
  if (pszSrc != NULL && m_str != NULL) return wcscmp(m_str, A2W
    (pszSrc)) < 0;
  return m_str == NULL;
}
```

Strangely, there are no other comparison operators. The CComBSTR class defines no operator>() or operator!=() methods. They aren't necessary, of course, but they would be convenient and are simple to implement.

CComBSTR Persistence Support

The last two methods of the CComBSTR class read and write a BSTR string to and from a stream. The WriteToStream method writes an ULONG count containing the numbers of bytes in the BSTR to a stream. It writes the BSTR characters to the stream immediately following the count. Note that the method does not tag the stream with an indication of the byte-order used to write the data. Therefore, as is frequently the case for stream data, a CComBSTR object writes its string to the stream in a hardware-architecture specific format.

```
HRESULT WriteToStream(IStream* pStream)
{
    ATLASSERT(pStream != NULL);
    ULONG cb;
```

```
    ULONG cbStrLen = m_str ? SysStringByteLen(m_str)+sizeof
      (OLECHAR) : 0;
    HRESULT hr = pStream->Write((void*) &cbStrLen, sizeof (cbStrLen),
      &cb);
    if (FAILED(hr)) return hr;
    return cbStrLen ? pStream->Write((void*) m_str, cbStrLen, &cb) :
      S_OK;
}
```

The ReadFromStream method reads an ULONG count of bytes from the specified stream, allocates a BSTR of the correct size, then reads the characters directly into the BSTR string. The CComBSTR object must be empty when you call Read-FromStream, otherwise you'll receive an assertion from a debug build or will leak memory in a release build.

```
HRESULT ReadFromStream(IStream* pStream)
{
    ATLASSERT(pStream != NULL);
    ATLASSERT(m_str == NULL); // should be empty
    ULONG cbStrLen = 0;
    HRESULT hr = pStream->Read((void*) &cbStrLen, sizeof (cbStrLen),
      NULL);
    if ((hr == S_OK) && (cbStrLen != 0)) {
        //subtract size for terminating NULL that we wrote out
        //since SysAllocStringByteLen overallocates for the NULL
        m_str = SysAllocStringByteLen(NULL, cbStrLen-sizeof(OLECHAR));
        if (m_str == NULL) hr = E_OUTOFMEMORY;
        else hr = pStream->Read((void*) m_str, cbStrLen, NULL);
    }
    if (hr == S_FALSE) hr = E_FAIL;
    return hr;
}
```

Minor Rant on BSTRs, Embedded NUL Characters in Strings and Life in General

The compiler considers the types BSTR and OLECHAR* as synonymous. In fact, the BSTR symbol is simply a typedef for OLECHAR*. For example, from wtypes.h:

```
typedef /* [wire_marshal] */ OLECHAR __RPC_FAR *BSTR;
```

This is more than somewhat brain-damaged. An arbitrary BSTR is not an OLE-CHAR* and an arbitrary OLECHAR* is not a BSTR. One is often misled on this regard because in frequently occurring situations, a BSTR works just fine as an OLECHAR*.

```
STDMETHODIMP SomeClass::put_Name (LPCOLESTR pName) ;


BSTR bstrInput =  . . .
pObj->put_Name (bstrInput) ; // This works just fine... usually
SysFreeString (bstrInput) ;
```

In the previous example, the `bstrInput` argument, as it's defined to be a BSTR, can contain embedded NUL characters within the string. The `put_Name` method, which is expecting a LPCOLESTR (a NUL character-terminated string), will probably save only the characters preceding the first embedded NUL character. In other words, it will cut the string short.

You also cannot use a BSTR where an [out] OLECHAR* parameter is required. For example:

```
STDMETHODIMP SomeClass::get_Name (/* [out] */ OLECHAR** ppName)
{
 BSTR bstrOutput =. . . // Produce BSTR string to return
 *ppName = bstrOutput ; // This compiles just fine
 return S_OK ;        // but leaks memory as caller doesn't release BSTR
}
```

Conversely, you cannot use an OLECHAR* where a BSTR is required. When it does happen to work, it's a latent bug. For example, *the following code is incorrect:*

```
STDMETHODIMP SomeClass::put_Name (BSTR bstrName) ;

pObj->put_Name (OLECHAR("This is not a BSTR!")) ; // Wrong! Wrong!
```

Should the `put_Name` method call `SysStringLen` to obtain the length of the BSTR, it's going to be quite surprised as it will try to get the length from the integer preceding the string and there is no such integer. Things get worse should the `put_Name` method be remoted, that is, live out of process. In this case, the marshaling code *will* call SysStringLen to obtain the number of characters to place in the ORPC request packet. This is usually a huge number (4 bytes from the preceding string in the literal pool in this example) and often causes a GPF while trying to copy the string.

Because the compiler cannot tell the difference between a BSTR and an OLECHAR*, it's quite easy to accidentally call a method in CComBSTR that doesn't work correctly when you are using a BSTR containing embedded NUL characters. So the following discussion shows exactly which methods you must use for these kinds of BSTRs.

To construct a CComBSTR, you must specify the length of the string:

```
BSTR bstrInput =
 SysAllocStringLen (OLESTR ("This is part one\0and here's part two"),
    36) ;


CComBSTR str8 (bstrInput) ; // Wrong! Unexpected behavior here
                            // Note: str2 contains only "This is part one"


CComBSTR str9 (::SysStringLen (bstrInput), bstrInput); // Correct!
// str9 contains "This is part one\0and here's part two"
```

Assigning a BSTR containing embedded NUL characters to a CComBSTR object never works. For example:

```
// BSTR bstrInput contains "This is part one\0and here's part two"
CComBSTR str10 ;
str10 = bstrInput; // Wrong! Unexpected behavior here
                   // str10 now contains "This is part one"!!!
```

The easiest way to perform an assignment of a BSTR is to use the Empty and AppendBSTR methods:

```
str10.Empty ();              // Insure object is initially empty
str10.AppendBSTR (bstrInput); // This works!
```

Be careful using the ToLower and ToUpper methods. They truncate the case-converted string at the first embedded NUL character. Also, the comparison operators, operator<() and operator==(), only compare characters up to the first embedded NUL character.

In practice, while a BSTR can potentially contain zero or more embedded NUL characters, most of the time it doesn't. This, of course, means that most of the time, you don't see the latent bugs caused by incorrect BSTR usage.

The ComVariant Smart VARIANT Class

A Review of the COM VARIANT Data Type

Occasionally, while using COM, you'll want to pass parameters to a method without any knowledge of the data types the method requires. For the method to be able to interpret its received parameters, the caller must specify the format of the data as well as its value.

Alternatively, you may call a method that returns a result consisting of varying data types depending on context. Sometimes it returns a string, sometimes a long, or even an interface pointer. This requires the method to return data in a self-describing data format. For each value transmitted, you would send two fields: a code specifying a data type and a value represented in the specified data type. Clearly, for this to work, the sender and receiver must agree on the set of possible formats.

COM specifies one such set of possible formats (the VARTYPE enumeration) and specifies the structure that contains both the format and an associated value (the VARIANT structure). The VARIANT structure looks like this:

```
typedef struct FARSTRUCT tagVARIANT VARIANT;
typedef struct FARSTRUCT tagVARIANT VARIANTARG;

typedef struct tagVARIANT {
    VARTYPE vt;
    unsigned short wReserved1;
    unsigned short wReserved2;
    unsigned short wReserved3;
    union {
        unsigned char        bVal;        // VT_UI1
        short                iVal;        // VT_I2
        long                 lVal;        // VT_I4
        float                fltVal;      // VT_R4
        double               dblVal;      // VT_R8
        VARIANT_BOOL         boolVal;     // VT_BOOL
        SCODE                scode;       // VT_ERROR
        CY                   cyVal;       // VT_CY
        DATE                 date;        // VT_DATE
        BSTR                 bstrVal;     // VT_BSTR
        IUnknown        FAR* punkVal;     // VT_UNKNOWN
        IDispatch       FAR* pdispVal;    // VT_DISPATCH
        SAFEARRAY       FAR* parray;      // VT_ARRAY|*
        unsigned char   FAR* pbVal;       // VT_BYREF|VT_UI1
```

```
        short              FAR* piVal;        // VT_BYREF|VT_I2
        long               FAR* plVal;        // VT_BYREF|VT_I4
        float              FAR* pfltVal;      // VT_BYREF|VT_R4
        double             FAR* pdblVal;      // VT_BYREF|VT_R8
        VARIANT_BOOL       FAR* pboolVal;     // VT_BYREF|VT_BOOL
        SCODE              FAR* pscode;       // VT_BYREF|VT_ERROR
        CY                 FAR* pcyVal;       // VT_BYREF|VT_CY
        DATE               FAR* pdate;        // VT_BYREF|VT_DATE
        BSTR               FAR* pbstrVal;     // VT_BYREF|VT_BSTR
        IUnknown FAR*      FAR* ppunkVal;     // VT_BYREF|VT_UNKNOWN
        IDispatch FAR*     FAR* ppdispVal;    // VT_BYREF|VT_DISPATCH
        SAFEARRAY FAR*     FAR* pparray;      // VT_ARRAY|*
        VARIANT            FAR* pvarVal;      // VT_BYREF|VT_VARIANT
        void               FAR* byref;        // Generic ByRef
    };
};
```

You initialize the VARIANT structure by storing a value into one of the fields of the tagged union and then storing the corresponding type code for the value into the vt member of the VARIANT structure. The VARIANT data type has a number of semantics that make using it tedious and error-prone for C++ developers.

A VARIANT has the following attributes.

- A VARIANT must be initialized before use by calling the VariantInit function on it. Alternatively, you can initialize the type and associated value field to a valid state.

- A VARIANT must be copied by calling the VariantCopy function on it. This performs the proper shallow or deep copy, as appropriate for the data type stored in the VARIANT.

- A VARIANT must be destroyed by calling the VariantClear function on it. This performs the proper shallow or deep destroy, as appropriate for the data type stored in the VARIANT. For example, when you destroy a VARIANT containing a SAFEARRAY of BSTRs, VariantClear frees each BSTR element in the array, then frees the array itself.

- A VARIANT can optionally represent, at most, one level of indirection, which is specified by the addition of the VT_ARRAY bit setting to the type code. You can call VariantCopyInd to remove a single level of indirection from a VARIANT.

- You can attempt to change the data type of a VARIANT by calling Variant-ChangeType[Ex].

With all these special semantics, it would be useful to encapsulate these details in a reusable class. ATL provides such a class: CComVariant.

The CComVariant Class

The CComVariant class is an ATL utility class that is a useful encapsulation for the COM self-describing data type, VARIANT. The atlbase.h file contains the definition of the CComVariant class. The only state maintained by the class is an instance of the VARIANT structure, which the class obtains by inheritance from the tag-VARIANT structure. This, conveniently, means a CComVariant instance is a VARIANT structure, so you can pass a CComVariant instance to any function expecting a VARIANT structure.

```
class CComVariant: public tagVARIANT
{
. . .
} ;
```

You'll often use a CComVariant instance when you need to pass a VARIANT argument to a COM method. The following code passes a string argument to a method that expects a VARIANT. The code uses the CComVariant class, so it doesn't need to deal with the messy semantics of a BSTR.

```
STDMETHODIMP put_Name(/* [in] const VARIANT* name);

HRESULT SetName (LPTSTR pszName)
{
    // Initializes the VARIANT structure
    // Allocates a BSTR copy of pszName
    // Sets the VARIANT to the BSTR
    CComVariant v (pszName);

    // Pass the raw VARIANT to the method
    Return pObj->put_Name(&v);

    // Destructor clears v, freeing the BSTR
}
```

Constructors and Destructor

There are 16 constructors available for CComVariant objects. The default constructor simply initializes the VARIANT to EMPTY, which says the VARIANT contains no information. The destructor calls the Clear member function to release any resources potentially held in the VARIANT.

```
CComVariant()  { vt = VT_EMPTY; }
~CComBSTR() { Clear (); }
```

The other 15 constructors initialize the VARIANT structure appropriately, based on the type of the constructor argument.

Many of the constructors simply set the vt member of the VARIANT structure to the value representing the type of the constructor argument and store the value of the argument into the appropriate member of the union.

```
CComVariant(int nSrc)       { vt = VT_I4;  lVal = nSrc; }
CComVariant(BYTE nSrc)      { vt = VT_UI1; bVal = nSrc; }
CComVariant(short nSrc)     { vt = VT_I2;  iVal = nSrc; }
CComVariant(float fltSrc)   { vt = VT_R4;  fltVal = fltSrc; }
CComVariant(double dblSrc)  { vt = VT_R8;  dblVal = dblSrc; }
CComVariant(CY cySrc)       { vt = VT_CY;  cyVal.Hi = cySrc.Hi ;
                                           cyVal.Lo = cySrc.Lo ; }
```

A few of the constructors are more complex. An SCODE looks like a long to the compiler. Therefore, constructing a CComVariant specifying an SCODE or a long initialization value invokes the constructor accepting a long. To permit you to distinguish these two cases, this constructor also takes an optional argument allowing you to specify whether the long should be placed in the VARIANT as a long or as an SCODE. When you specify a variant type other than VT_I4 or VT_ERROR, this constructor asserts in a debug build.

Windows 16-bit COM defined an HRESULT (a handle to a result code) as a data type that contained an SCODE (a status code). Therefore, you'll occasionally see older legacy code that considers the two data types to be different. In fact, there are obsolete macros that convert an SCODE to an HRESULT and that extract the SCODE from an HRESULT. However, the SCODE and HRESULT data types are identical in 32-bit COM applications. The VARIANT data structure contains an SCODE field, rather than an HRESULT, because that's the way it was originally declared.

```
CComVariant(long nSrc, VARTYPE vtSrc = VT_I4);
```

The constructor accepting a bool initialization value sets the contents of the VARIANT to VARIANT_TRUE or VARIANT_FALSE, as appropriate, not to the bool value specified. A logical TRUE value, as represented in a VARIANT, must be VARIANT_TRUE (-1 as a 16-bit value), and logical FALSE is VARIANT_FALSE (0 as a 16-bit value). The C++ language defines the bool data type as an 8-bit (0 or 1) value. This constructor provides the conversion between the two representations of a Boolean value.

```
CComVariant(bool bSrc)
    { vt = VT_BOOL; boolVal = bSrc ? VARIANT_TRUE : VARIANT_FALSE ; }
```

Two constructors accept an interface pointer as an initialization value and produce a CComVariant instance that contains an AddRef'ed copy of the interface pointer. The first constructor accepts an IDispatch* argument. The second accepts an IUnknown* argument.

```
CComVariant(IDispatch* pSrc);
CComVariant(IUnknown* pSrc);
```

Two constructors allow you to initialize a CComVariant instance from another VARIANT structure or CComVariant instance.

```
CComVariant(const VARIANT& varSrc) { vt = VT_EMPTY; InternalCopy
                                      (&varSrc); }
CComVariant(const CComVariant& varSrc); { Same as above }
```

They both have identical implementations, which have a subtle side effect, so let's look at the InternalCopy helper function used by both constructors.

```
void InternalCopy(const VARIANT* pSrc)
{
    HRESULT hr = Copy(pSrc);
    if (FAILED(hr)) { vt = VT_ERROR; scode = hr; }
}
```

Notice how InternalCopy attempts to copy the specified VARIANT into the instance being constructed; when the copy fails, InternalCopy initializes the CComVariant instance as holding an error code (VT_ERROR). The actual error code is that returned by the Copy method used to attempt the copy. This seems like an odd approach until you realize that a constructor cannot return an error, short of throwing an exception. ATL doesn't require support for exceptions, so this constructor must initialize the instance even when the Copy method fails.

I once had a CComVariant instance that always seemed to have a VT_ERROR code in it, even when I thought it shouldn't. As it turned out, I was constructing the CComVariant instance from an uninitialized VARIANT structure that resided on the stack. Watch out for code like this:

```
void func ()
{                        // The following code is incorrect
    VARIANT v;           // Uninitialized stack garbage in vt member
    CComVariant vv (v);  // Indeterminate state - with luck, VT_ERROR
}
```

Three constructors accept a string initialization value and produce a CCom-Variant instance that contains a BSTR. The first constructor accepts a BSTR argument and creates a CComVariant containing a BSTR that is a copy of the specified BSTR. The second accepts a LPCOLESTR argument and creates a CComVariant containing a BSTR that is a copy of the specified string of OLECHAR characters. The third accepts a LPCSTR argument and creates a CComVariant containing a BSTR that is a converted-to-OLECHAR copy of the specified ANSI character string. When you define the symbol OLE2ANSI, the LPCOLESTR type is the same as the LPCSTR type. In that case, ATL must not define the constructor again. These three constructors also have the possibility of "failing." In all three constructors, when the constructor cannot allocate memory for the new BSTR, it initializes the CComVariant instance to VT_ERROR with SCODE E_OUTOFMEMORY.

```
CComVariant(BSTR bstrSrc);
CComVariant(LPCOLESTR lpszSrc);
#ifndef OLE2ANSI
CComVariant(LPCSTR lpszSrc);
#endif
```

It's somewhat strange that there is a separate constructor for a BSTR argument and for a LPCOLESTR argument. Because of a brain-damaged typedef, ranted about previously in the chapter, the only difference between the two data types is a const type specifier. That is, a BSTR is an OLECHAR*, whereas a LPCOLESTR is a const OLECHAR*. This means that you usually aren't calling the constructor you might think you're calling.

```
void func ()
{
 BSTR bstrInput = ::SysAllocString (OLESTR ("This is a BSTR string")) ;

 CComVariant v1 (bstrInput); // calls CComVariant (BSTR)

 // calls CComVariant (BSTR)
 CComVariant v2 (OLESTR("This is an OLECHAR string")) ;

 OLECHAR* ps = OLESTR("This is another OLECHAR string") ;
 CComVariant v3 (ps); // calls CComVariant (BSTR)

 const OLECHAR* pcs = OLESTR("This is another OLECHAR string") ;
 CComVariant v4 (pcs); // Only this calls CComVariant (LPCOLESTR)

 ::SysFreeString (bstrInput) ;
}
```

The ComVariant (BSTR) constructor also doesn't properly handle a BSTR containing embedded NUL characters. It produces a CComVariant initialized with a BSTR that contains only the character preceding the first embedded NUL. In summary, this constructor provides no functionality beyond what is already available in the ComVariant (LPCOLESTR) constructor.

Initialization

The CComVariant class defines 15 assignment operators. All the assignment operators

- Clear the VARIANT of its current contents.
- Set the vt member of the VARIANT structure to the value representing the type of the assignment operator argument.
- Store the value of the argument into the appropriate member of the union.

```
CComVariant& operator=(int nSrc);       // Creates VT_I4 variant
CComVariant& operator=(BYTE nSrc);      // Creates VT_UI1 variant
CComVariant& operator=(short nSrc);     // Creates VT_U2 variant
CComVariant& operator=(long nSrc);      // Creates VT_I4 variant
CComVariant& operator=(float fltSrc);   // Creates VT_R4 variant
CComVariant& operator=(double dblSrc);  // Creates VT_R8 variant
CComVariant& operator=(CY cySrc);       // Creates VT_CY variant
```

The remaining operator= methods have additional semantics. Like the equivalent constructor, the assignment operator accepting a bool initialization value sets the contents of the VARIANT to VARIANT_TRUE or VARIANT_FALSE, as appropriate, not to the bool value specified.

```
CComVariant& operator=(bool bSrc);
```

Two assignment operators accept an interface pointer and produce a CComVariant instance that contains an AddRef'ed copy of the interface pointer. One assignment operator accepts an IDispatch* argument. Another accepts an IUnknown* argument.

```
CComVariant& operator=(IDispatch* pSrc);
CComVariant& operator=(IUnknown* pSrc);
```

Two assignment operators allow you to initialize a CComVariant instance from another VARIANT structure or CComVariant instance. They both use the InternalCopy method, described previously, to make a copy of the provided argument.

Therefore these constructors can "fail" and produce an instance initialized to the VT_ERROR type.

```
CComVariant& operator=(const CComVariant& varSrc);
CComVariant& operator=(const VARIANT& varSrc);
```

The remaining three assignment operators accept a string initialization value and produce a CComVariant instance that contains a BSTR. The first constructor accepts a BSTR argument and creates a CComVariant containing a BSTR that is a copy of the specified BSTR. The second accepts an LPCOLESTR argument and creates a CComVariant containing a BSTR that is a copy of the specified string of OLECHAR characters. The third accepts an LPCSTR argument and creates a CCom-Variant containing a BSTR that is a converted-to-OLECHAR copy of the specified ANSI character string.

```
CComVariant& operator=(BSTR bstrSrc);
CComVariant& operator=(LPCOLESTR lpszSrc);
#ifndef OLE2ANSI
CComVariant& operator=(LPCSTR lpszSrc);
#endif
```

The remarks made previously about the constructors with a string initialization value apply equally here to the assignment operators with a string initialization value. In fact, the constructors actually use these assignment operators to perform their initialization.

- These assignment operators can "fail," producing a CComVariant instance initialized to the VT_ERROR type.
- There is no meaningful distinction between the operator=(BSTR) method and the operator=(LPCOLESTR) method.
- The operator=(BSTR) method expects a NUL-character-terminated string. Therefore, it only copies the characters preceding the first embedded NUL character.

CComVariant Operations

It's important to realize that a VARIANT is a resource that must be managed properly. Just as memory from the heap must be allocated and freed, a VARIANT must be initialized and cleared. Just as the ownership of a memory block must be explicitly managed so it's freed only once, the ownership of the contents of a VARIANT must also be explicitly managed so it's cleared only once. Four methods give you control over any resources owned by a CComVariant instance.

The Clear method releases any resources the instance may contain by calling the VariantClear function. For an instance containing, for example, a long or similar scalar value, this method does nothing. However, for an instance containing a BSTR, the method releases the string. For an instance containing an interface pointer, the method releases the interface pointer. For an instance containing a SAFEARRAY, this method iterates over each element in the array, releasing each element, and then releases the SAFEARRAY itself.

```
HRESULT Clear() { return ::VariantClear(this); }
```

When you no longer need the resource contained in a CComVariant instance, you should call the Clear method to release it. The destructor does this automatically for you. So, if an instance will quickly go out of scope after you're finished using its resources, let the destructor take care of the cleanup. However, a CComVariant instance as a global or static variable doesn't leave scope for a potentially long time. The Clear method is useful in this case.

The Copy method makes a unique copy of the specified VARIANT. The Copy method produces a CComVariant instance that has a lifetime separate from the lifetime of the VARIANT that it copies.

```
HRESULT Copy(const VARIANT* pSrc)
        { return ::VariantCopy(this,const_cast<VARIANT*>(pSrc)); }
```

Often you'll use the Copy method to copy a VARIANT that you receive as an [in] parameter. The caller providing an [in] parameter is loaning the resource to you. When you want to hold the parameter longer than the scope of the method call, you'll need to copy the VARIANT.

```
STDMETHODIMP SomeClass::put_Option (/* [in] */ const VARIANT* pOption)
{
    // Option saved in member m_Option of type CComVariant
    return m_varOption.Copy (pOption) ;
}
```

When you want to transfer ownership of the resources in a CComVariant instance from the instance to a VARIANT structure, use the Detach method. It clears the destination VARIANT structure, does a memcpy of the CComVariant instance into the specified VARIANT structure, and then sets the instance to VT_EMPTY. Note that this technique avoids extraneous memory allocations and AddRef/Release calls.

```
HRESULT Detach(VARIANT* pDest);
```

Do not use the Detach *method to update an* [out] VARIANT *argument without special care!* An [out] parameter is uninitialized on input to a method. The Detach method clears the specified VARIANT before overwriting it. Clearing a VARIANT filled with random bits produces random behavior.

```
STDMETHODIMP SomeClass::get_Option (/* [out] */ VARIANT* pOption)
{
   CComVariant varOption ;
   . . . Initialize the variant with the output data

   // Wrong! The following code can generate an exception, corrupt
   // your heap, and give at least seven years' bad luck!
   return varOption.Detach (pOption);
}
```

Before detaching into an [out] VARIANT argument, be sure to initialize the output argument.

```
// Special care taken to initialize [out] VARIANT
::VariantInit (pOption) ;    |or|    pOption->vt = VT_EMPTY ;
return vOption.Detach (pOption); // Now we can Detach safely.
```

When you want to transfer ownership of the resources in a VARIANT structure from the structure to a CComVariant instance, use the Attach method. It clears the current instance, does a memcpy of the specified VARIANT into the current instance, and then sets the specified VARIANT to VT_EMPTY. Note that this technique avoids extraneous memory allocations and AddRef/Release calls.

```
HRESULT Attach(VARIANT* pSrc);
```

Client code can use the Attach method to assume ownership of a VARIANT that it receives as an [out] parameter. The function providing an [out] parameter is transferring ownership of the resource to the caller.

```
STDMETHODIMP SomeClass::get_Option (/* [out] */ VARIANT* pOption);

void VerboseGetOption () {
```

```
    VARIANT v;
    pObj->get_Option (&v) ;

    CComVariant cv;
    cv.Attach (&v);    // Destructor now releases the VARIANT
}
```

You could, somewhat more efficiently, but potentially more dangerously, code this differently:

```
void FragileGetOption() {
  CComVariant v;              // This is fragile code!!
  pObj->get_Option (&v) ; // Directly update the contained VARIANT
                          // Destructor now releases the VARIANT
}
```

Note that in this case, the get_Option method overwrites the VARIANT structure contained in the CComVariant instance. Because the method expects an [out] parameter, the get_Option method will not release any resources contained in the provided argument. In the preceding example, the instance was freshly constructed, so it is empty when overwritten. The following code, however, causes a memory leak.

```
void LeakyGetOption() {
  CComVariant v (OLESTR ("This string leaks!")) ;
  pObj->get_Option (&v) ;// Directly updates the contained VARIANT
                          // Destructor now releases the VARIANT
}
```

When you use a CComVariant instance as an [out] parameter to a method expecting a VARIANT, you must first clear the instance if there is any possibility the instance is not empty.

```
void NiceGetOption() {
  CComVariant v (OLESTR ("This string doesn't leak!")) ;
  . . .
  v.Clear ();
  pObj->get_Option (&v) ;// Directly updates the contained VARIANT
                          // Destructor now releases the VARIANT
}
```

The ChangeType method converts a CComVariant instance to the new type specified by the vtNew parameter. When you specify a second argument, ChangeType uses it as the source for the conversion. Otherwise, ChangeType uses the CComVariant instance as the source for the conversion and performs the conversion in place.

```
HRESULT ChangeType(VARTYPE vtNew, const VARIANT* pSrc = NULL);
```

ChangeType converts between the fundamental types (including numeric-to-string and string-to-numeric coercions). ChangeType coerces a source that contains a reference to a type (that is, the VT_BYREF bit is set) to a value by retrieving the referenced value. ChangeType always coerces an object reference to a value by retrieving the object's Value property. This is the property with the DISPID_VALUE DISPID.

CComVariant Comparison Operators

The operator==() method compares a CComVariant instance for equality with the specified VARIANT structure.

```
bool operator==(const VARIANT& varSrc) const;
bool operator!=(const VARIANT& varSrc) const;
```

When the two operands have differing types, the operator returns false. For the basic types, the operator compares the two values for equality. The operator compares two BSTR operands by comparing their lengths. When both BSTRs have equal lengths, the operator compares all characters for the specified length. This means, unlike the CComBSTR class, that the CComVariant operator==() method correctly compares two BSTRs that contain embedded NUL characters.

The comparison of interface pointers is somewhat unusual and of questionable usefulness. The operator directly compares the binary values of the interface pointers. This means the comparison is *not* determining that the two interface pointers reference the same object identity.

COM permits an object to hand out different binary values each time a client queries it for a specific interface pointer (with the exception of a query for the IUnknown interface). Therefore, two VARIANTs containing IDispatch pointers referencing the same object might not compare for equality. Even two VARIANTs containing IUnknown pointers referencing the same object might not compare for equality. There is no requirement that the canonical IUnknown (the one returned by a QueryInterface (IID_IUnknown, ...) call) be placed in a VARIANT with type VT_UNKNOWN. The VARIANT with type VT_UNKNOWN can contain any interface pointer cast to an IUnknown interface pointer.

The `operator!=()` method returns the negation of the `operator==()` method, so all the above comments apply equally to `operator!=()`.

Both the `operator<()` and `operator>()` methods perform their respective comparisons using the Variant Math API function `VarCmp`.[2]

```
bool operator<(const VARIANT& varSrc) const;
bool operator>(const VARIANT& varSrc) const;
```

CComVariant Persistence Support

The last two methods of the `CComVariant` class read and write a VARIANT to and from a stream.

```
HRESULT WriteToStream(IStream* pStream);
HRESULT ReadFromStream(IStream* pStream);
```

The `WriteToStream` method writes the vt type code to the stream. For the simple types, such as VT_I4, VT_R8, and similar scalar values, it writes the value of the VARIANT to the stream immediately following the type code. For an interface pointer, `WriteToStream` writes the GUID CLSID.NULL to the stream when the pointer is NULL. When the interface pointer is not NULL, `WriteToStream` queries the referenced object for its `IPersistStream` interface. When the object supports this interface, `WriteToStream` calls the COM `OleSaveToStream` function to save the object to the stream. When the interface pointer is not NULL and the object does not support the `IPersistStream` interface, `WriteToStream` fails.

Note: In ATL 3.0, `WriteToStream` does not attempt to use the `IPersistStreamInit` interface, which many objects implement in preference to `IPersistStream`.

For complex types, including VT_BSTR, all by-reference types, and all arrays, `WriteToStream` attempts to convert the value, if necessary, to a BSTR and writes the string to the stream using `CComBSTR::WriteToStream`.

The `ReadFromStream` method performs the inverse operation. First, it clears the current `CComVariant` instance. Then it reads the variant type code from the stream. For the simple types, such as VT_I4, VT_R8, and similar scalar values, it reads the value of the VARIANT from the stream. For an interface pointer, it calls the COM `OleLoadFromStream` function to read the object from the stream, requesting

---

[2] A number of operating system functions manipulate VARIANTs. The functions VarAbs, VarAdd, VarAnd, VarCat, VarCmp, VarDiv, VarEqv, VarFix, VarIdiv, VarImp, VarInt, VarMod, VarMul, VarNeg, VarNot, VarOr, VarPow, VarRound, VarSub, and VarXor collectively comprise the Variant Math API. The only documentation I've found for these functions is the function prototypes defined in `oleauto.h`.

the IUnknown or IDispatch interface, as appropriate. When OleLoadFrom-Stream returns REGDB_E_CLASSNOTREG (usually due to reading CLSID.NULL), ReadFromStream silently returns an S_OK status.

For all other types, including VT_BSTR, all by-reference types, and all arrays, ReadFromStream calls CComBSTR::ReadFromStream to read the previously written string from the stream. The method then coerces the string back to the original type.

The CComPtr, CComQIPtr, and CComDispatchDriver Smart Pointer Classes

A Review of Smart Pointers

A *smart pointer* is an object that behaves like a pointer. That is, you can use an instance of a smart pointer class in many of the places you normally use a pointer. However, using a smart pointer provides some advantages over using a raw pointer. For example, a smart interface pointer class can

- Release the encapsulated interface pointer when the class destructor executes.
- Automatically release its interface pointer during exception handling when you allocate the smart interface pointer on the stack, thus reducing the need to write explicit exception handling code.
- Release the encapsulated interface pointer before overwriting it during an assignment operation.
- Call AddRef on the interface pointer received during an assignment operation.
- Provide different constructors to initialize a new smart pointer through convenient mechanisms.
- Be used in many, *but not all*, of the places where you would conventionally use a raw interface pointer.

ATL provides three smart pointer classes: CComPtr, CComQIPtr, and CComDispatchDriver.

The CComPtr class is a smart COM interface pointer class. You create instances tailored for a specific type of interface pointer. For example, the first line of the following code creates a smart IUnknown interface pointer. The second line creates a smart INamedObject custom interface pointer.

```
CComPtr<IUnknown>      punk;
CComPtr<INamedObject>  pno;
```

The `CComQIPtr` class is a smarter COM interface pointer class, which does everything `CComPtr` does and more. When you assign to a `CComQIPtr` instance an interface pointer of a different type than the smart pointer, the class calls `Query-Interface` on the provided interface pointer.

```
CComPtr<IUnknown>        punk = /* Init to some IUnknown* */ ;
CComQIPtr<INamedObject>  pno = punk;
  // Calls punk->QI (IID_INamedObject, ...)
```

The `CComDispatchDriver` class is a smart `IDispatch` interface pointer. You use instances of this class to retrieve and set an object's properties using an `IDispatch` interface.

```
CComVariant            v;
CComDispatchDriver     pdisp = /* Init to object's IDispatch* */ ;

HRESULT hr = pdisp->GetProperty (DISPID_COUNT, &v); // Get the
  Count property
```

The CComPtr and CComQIPtr Classes

The `CComPtr` and `CComQIPtr` classes are very similar, with the exception of initialization and assignment. Therefore, all the following comments about the `CComPtr` class apply equally to the `CComQIPtr` class unless I specifically state otherwise.

The `atlbase.h` file contains the definition of both classes. The only state maintained by each class is a single public member variable, `T* p`.

```
template <class T>     template <class T, const IID* piid =
                                &__uuidof(T)>
class CComPtr          class CComQIPtr
{                      {
public:                public:
    T* p;                  T* p;
. . .                  . . .
} ;                    } ;
```

The first template parameter specifies the type of the smart interface pointer. The second template parameter to the `CComQIPtr` class specifies the interface ID for the smart pointer. By default, it is the globally unique identifier (GUID) associated with the class of the first parameter. Here are a few examples that use these smart pointer classes. The middle three examples are all equivalent.

```
CComPtr<IUnknown> punk;    // Smart IUnknown*
CComPtr<INamedObject> pno; // Smart INamedObject*

CComQIPtr<INamedObject> pno;
CComQIPtr<INamedObject, &__uuidof(INamedObject)> pno;
CComQIPtr<INamedObject, &IID_INamedObject> pno;

CComQIPtr<IDispatch, &IID_ISomeDual> pdisp;
```

Constructors and Destructor

A CComPtr object can be initialized with an interface pointer of the appropriate type. That is, a CComPtr<IFoo> object can be initialized using an IFoo* or another CComPtr<IFoo> object. Using any other type produces a compiler error. The default constructor initializes the internal interface pointer to NULL. The other constructors initialize the internal interface pointer to the specified interface pointer. When the specified value is non-NULL, the constructor calls the AddRef method. The destructor calls the Release method on a non-NULL interface pointer

```
CComPtr()                          { p = NULL; }
CComPtr(T* lp)                     { if ((p = lp) != NULL) p-> AddRef(); }
CComPtr(const CComPtr<T>& lp)
  { if ((p = lp.p) != NULL) p-> AddRef(); }
~CComPtr()                         { if (p) p->Release(); }
```

A CComQIPtr object can be initialized with an interface pointer of any type. When the initialization value is the same type as the smart pointer, the constructor simply AddRef's the provided pointer, like the CComPtr class. However, specifying a different type invokes the following constructor, which queries the provided interface pointer for the appropriate interface:

```
CComQIPtr(IUnknown* lp)
  { p= NULL; if (lp != NULL) lp->QueryInterface(*piid, (void **)&p); }
```

A constructor can never fail. Nevertheless, the QueryInterface call may not succeed. The CComQIPtr class sets the internal pointer to NULL when it cannot obtain the required interface. Therefore, you'll use code such as the following to test whether the object initializes:

```
void func (IUnknown* punk)
{
    CComQIPtr<INamedObject> pno (punk);
    if (pno) {
        // Can call SomeMethod because the QI worked
        pno->SomeMethod ();
    }
}
```

You can tell whether the query failed by checking for a NULL pointer, but you cannot determine why it fails. The constructor doesn't save the HRESULT from a failed `QueryInterface` call.

Initialization

The `CComPtr` class defines two assignment operators, the `CComQIPtr` class defines the same two plus a third. All the assignment operators

- `Release` the current interface pointer when it's non-NULL.
- `AddRef` the source interface pointer when it's non-NULL.
- Save the source interface pointer as the current interface pointer.

The additional `CComQIPtr` assignment operator queries a non-NULL source interface pointer for the appropriate interface to save. You receive a NULL pointer when the `QueryInterface` calls fails. Like the equivalent constructor, the HRESULT for a failed query is not available.

```
// CComPtr assignment operators      // CComQIPtr assignment ops.
T* operator=(T* lp);                 T* operator=(T* lp);
T* operator=(const CComPtr<T>& lp);  T* operator=
                                       (const CComQIPtr<T>& lp);
                                     T* operator=(IUnknown* lp);
```

Typically, you'll use the `CComQIPtr` assignment operator to perform a `QueryInterface` call. You'll immediately follow the assignment with a NULL pointer test, as follows:

```
CComQIPtr<IExpectedInterface> m_object;  // Member variable holding
    object

STDMETHODIMP put_Object (IUnknown* punk)
```

```
{                         // Releases current object, if any, and
    m_object = punk; // queries for the expected interface
    if (!m_object)
        return E_UNEXPECTED;
    return S_OK;
}
```

Object Instantiation Methods

The smart interface pointer classes provide an overloaded method, called `CoCre-ateInstance`, that you can use to instantiate an object and retrieve an interface pointer on the object. There are two forms of the method. The first requires the class identifier (`CLSID`) of the class to instantiate. The second requires the programmatic identifier (`ProgID`) of the class to instantiate. Both overloaded methods accept optional parameters for the controlling unknown and class context for the instantiation. The controlling unknown parameter defaults to NULL—the normal case, indicating no aggregation. The class context parameter defaults to CLSCTX_ALL, indicating that any available server can service the request.

```
HRESULT CoCreateInstance (REFCLSID rclsid,
                          LPUNKNOWN pUnkOuter = NULL,
                          DWORD dwClsContext = CLSCTX_ALL)
{
    ATLASSERT(p == NULL);
    return ::CoCreateInstance(rclsid, pUnkOuter, dwClsContext,
                              __uuidof(T), (void**)&p);
}

HRESULT CoCreateInstance (LPCOLESTR szProgID,
                          LPUNKNOWN pUnkOuter = NULL,
                          DWORD dwClsContext = CLSCTX_ALL);
```

Notice how the preceding code for the first `CoCreateInstance` method creates an instance of the specified class. It passes the parameters of the method to the `CoCreateInstance` COM API and, additionally, requests that the initial interface be the interface supported by the smart pointer class. (This is the purpose of the `__uuidof(T)` expression.) The second overloaded `CoCreateInstance` method translates the provided `ProgID` to a `CLSID`, then creates the instance in the same manner as the first method.

Therefore, the following code is equivalent (though the smart pointer code is easier to read, in my opinion). The first instantiation request explicitly uses the

CoCreateInstance COM API. The second uses the smart pointer CoCreateInstance method.

```
ISpeaker* pSpeaker;
HRESULT hr =
::CoCreateInstance (__uuidof (Demagogue), NULL, CLSCTX_ALL,
                    __uuidof (ISpeaker_, (void**) &pSpeaker);
. . . Use the interface
pSpeaker->Release () ;

CComPtr<ISpeaker> pSpeaker;
HRESULT hr = pSpeaker.CoCreateInstance (__uuidof (Demogogue));
. . . Use the interface. It releases when pSpeaker leaves scope
```

CComPtr and CComQIPtr Operations

Because a smart interface pointer should behave as much as possible like a raw interface pointer, the CComPtr class defines some operators to make the CComPtr object act like a pointer. For example, when you dereference a pointer using operator*(), you expect to receive a reference to whatever the pointer points. So dereferencing a smart interface pointer should produce a reference to whatever the underlying interface pointer points. And it does:

```
T& operator*() const { ATLASSERT(p!=NULL); return *p; }
```

Note that the operator*() method kindly asserts when you attempt to dereference a NULL smart interface pointer in a debug build of your component. Of course, I've always considered the General Protection Fault message box to be an equivalent assertion. However, the ATLASSERT macro produces a more programmer-friendly indication of the error location.

To maintain the semblance of a pointer, taking the address of a smart pointer object (i.e., invoking operator&()) should actually return the address of the underlying raw pointer. Note that the issue here isn't the actual binary value returned. A smart pointer contains only the underlying raw interface pointer as its state. Therefore, a smart pointer occupies exactly the same amount of storage as a raw interface pointer. The address of a smart pointer object and the address of its internal member variable will be the same binary value.

Without overriding CComPtr<T>::operator&(), taking the address of an instance would return a CComPtr<T>*. In order to have a smart pointer class maintain the same pointer semantics as a pointer of type T*, the operator&() method for the class must return a T**.

```
T** operator&() { ATLASSERT(p==NULL); return &p; }
```

Note that this operator asserts when you take the address of a non-NULL smart interface pointer because you might dereference the returned address and overwrite the internal member variable without properly releasing the interface pointer. It asserts to protect the semantics of the pointer and keep you from accidentally stomping on the pointer. This behavior, however, keeps you from using a smart interface pointer as an [in,out] function parameter.

```
STDMETHODIMP SomeClass::UpdateObject (/* [in, out] */ IExpected**
  ppExpected);

CComPtr<IExpected> pE = /* Initialize to some value */ ;

pobj->UpdateObject (&pE); // Asserts in debug build: pE is non-NULL
```

When you really want to use a smart interface pointer in this way, take the address of the member variable:

```
pobj->UpdateObject (&pE.p);
```

CComPtr and CComQIPtr Resource Management Operations.   A smart interface pointer represents a resource, albeit one that tries to manage itself properly. Sometimes, though, you want to manage the resource explicitly. For example, you must release all interface pointers before calling the CoUninitialize method. This means that you can't wait for the destructor of a CComPtr object to release the interface pointer when you allocate the object as a global or static variable (or even a local variable in main()). The destructor for global and static variables only executes after the main function exits, long after CoUninitialize runs. (That is, if it runs at all. You must link with the C++ runtime library for the constructors and destructors of global and static variable to run. ATL itself doesn't use the C/C++ runtime library; thus, by default, ATL components don't link with the library.)

You can release the internal interface pointer by assigning NULL to the smart pointer. Alternatively and more explicitly, you can call the Release method.

```
int main ()
{
   HRESULT hr = CoInitialize (NULL);
```

```
    If (FAILED (hr)) return -1;   // Something is seriously wrong

    CComPtr<IUnknown> punk = /* Initialize to some object */ ;
    . . .
    punk.Release ();              // Must Release before CoUninitialize!

    CoUninitialize();
}
```

Note that this code *calls the smart pointer object's* CComPtr<T>::Release *method* because it uses the dot operator to reference the object. *It does not directly call the underlying interface pointer's* IUnknown::Release *method as you might expect.* The smart pointer's CComPtr<T>::Release method calls the underlying interface pointer's IUnknown::Release method and sets the internal interface pointer to NULL. This prevents the destructor from releasing the interface again. Here is the smart pointer's Release method:

```
template <class T> void CComPtr<T>::Release()
{
    IUnknown* pTemp = p;
    if (pTemp) { p = NULL; pTemp->Release(); }
}
```

It's not immediately obvious why the CComPtr<T>::Release method doesn't simply call IUnknown::Release using its p member variable. Instead, it copies the interface pointer member variable into the local variable, sets the member variable to NULL, then releases the interface using the temporary variable. This approach avoids a situation in which the interface held by the smart pointer is released twice.

For example, assume the smart pointer is a member variable of class A and the smart pointer holds a reference to object B. You call the smart pointer's .Release method. The smart pointer releases its reference to object B. Object B in turn holds a reference to the class A instance containing the smart pointer. Object B decides to release its reference to the class A instance. The class A instance decides to destruct, which invokes the destructor for the smart pointer member variable. The destructor detects that the interface pointer is non-NULL, so it releases the interface again.[3]

---

[3] Thanks go to Jim Springfield for pointing this out.

In releases of ATL prior to version 3.0, the following code would compile successfully and would release the interface pointer twice. Note the use of the arrow operator.

```
punk->Release ();          // Wrong! Wrong! Wrong!
```

In those releases of ATL, the arrow operator returned the underlying interface pointer. Therefore, the previous line actually called the IUnknown::Release function, not the CComPtr<T>::Release method as expected. This leaves the smart pointer's interface pointer member variable non-NULL, so the destructor will eventually release the interface a second time.

This was a nasty bug to find. A smart pointer class encourages you to think about an instance as if it were an interface pointer. However, in this particular case, you shouldn't use the arrow operator (which you would if it really were a pointer) but must use the dot operator because it's really an object. What's worse, the compiler wouldn't tell you when you got it wrong.

This changed in version 3.0 of ATL. Note that the current definition of the arrow operator returns a _NoAddRefReleaseOnCComPtr<T>* value.

```
_NoAddRefReleaseOnCComPtr<T>* operator->() const
{
    ATLASSERT(p!=NULL); return (_NoAddRefReleaseOnCComPtr<T>*)p;
}
```

This is a simple template class whose only purpose is to make the AddRef and Release methods inaccessible.

```
template <class T>
class _NoAddRefReleaseOnCComPtr : public T
{
    private:
        STDMETHOD_(ULONG, AddRef)()=0;
        STDMETHOD_(ULONG, Release)()=0;
};
```

The _NoAddRefReleaseOnCComPtr<T> template class derives from the interface being returned. Therefore, it inherits all the methods of the interface. The class then overrides the AddRef and Release methods, making them private and pure virtual.

Now you get the following compiler error when you use the arrow operator to call either of these methods:

```
error C2248: 'Release' : cannot access private member declared in
   class 'ATL::_NoAddRefReleaseOnCComPtr<T>'
```

The CopyTo Method.   The CopyTo method makes an AddRef'ed copy of the interface pointer and places it in the specified location. Therefore, the CopyTo method produces an interface pointer that has a lifetime separate from the lifetime of the smart pointer that it copies.

```
HRESULT CopyTo(T** ppT)
{
   ATLASSERT(ppT != NULL);
   if (ppT == NULL) return E_POINTER;
   *ppT = p;
   if (p) p->AddRef();
   return S_OK;
}
```

Often, you'll use the CopyTo method to copy a smart pointer to an [out] parameter. An [out] interface pointer must be AddRef'ed by the code returning the pointer.

```
STDMETHODIMP SomeClass::get_Object (/* [out] */ IExpected** ppExpected)
{
   // Interface saved in member m_object of type CComPtr<IExpected>
   return m_object.CopyTo (ppExpected) ; // Correctly AddRefs pointer
}
```

Watch out for the following code. It probably doesn't do what you expect and isn't correct.

```
STDMETHODIMP SomeClass::get_Object (/* [out] */ IExpected** ppExpected)
{
   // Interface saved in member m_object of type CComPtr<IExpected>
   *pExpected = m_object ;   // Wrong! Does not AddRef pointer!
}
```

The Type-Cast Operator. When you assign a smart pointer to a raw pointer, you are implicitly invoking the operator T() method. In other words, you are casting the smart pointer to its underlying type. Notice that operator T() doesn't AddRef the pointer it returns:

```
operator T*() const { return (T*) p; }
```

That's because you don't want the AddRef in the following case:

```
STDMETHODIMP SomeClass::put_Object (/* [in] */ IExpected* pExpected);

// Interface saved in member m_object of type CComPtr<IExpected>
pObj->put_Object (m_object); // Correctly does not AddRef pointer!
```

The Detach and Attach Methods. When you want to transfer ownership of the interface pointer in a CComPtr instance from the instance to an equivalent raw pointer, use the Detach method. It returns the underlying interface pointer and sets the smart pointer to NULL, ensuring that the destructor doesn't release the interface. The client calling Detach becomes responsible for releasing the interface.

```
T* Detach() { T* pt = p; p = NULL; return pt; }
```

You often use Detach when you need to return to a caller an interface pointer that you no longer need. Rather than provide the caller an AddRef'ed copy of the interface, then immediately releasing your held interface pointer, you can simply transfer the reference to the caller, thus avoiding extraneous AddRef/Release calls. Yes, it's a minor optimization, but it's also simple.

```
STDMETHODIMP SomeClass::get_Object (/* [out] */ IExpected** ppExpected)
{
    CComPtr<IExpected> pobj = /* Initialize the smart pointer */ ;
    *ppExpected = pobj->Detach(); // Destructor no longer Releases
    return S_OK;
}
```

When you want to transfer ownership of a raw interface pointer to a smart pointer, use the Attach method. It releases the interface pointer held by the smart pointer, then sets the smart pointer to use the raw pointer. Note that, again, this technique avoids extraneous AddRef/Release calls and is a useful minor optimization.

```
void Attach(T* p2) { if (p) p->Release(); p = p2; }
```

Client code can use the `Attach` method to assume ownership of a raw interface pointer that it receives as an `[out]` parameter. The function providing an `[out]` parameter is transferring ownership of the interface pointer to the caller.

```
STDMETHODIMP SomeClass::get_Object (/* [out] */ IExpected** ppObject);

void VerboseGetOption () {
    IExpected* p;
    pObj->get_Object (&p) ;

    CComPtr<IExpected> pE;
    pE.Attach (p);    // Destructor now releases the interface pointer
    // Let the exceptions fall where they may now!!!
    CallSomeFunctionWhichThrowsExceptions();
}
```

Miscellaneous Smart Pointer Methods. The smart pointer classes also provide useful shorthand syntax for querying for a new interface: the `QueryInterface` method. It takes one parameter—the address of a variable that is of the type of the desired interface.

```
template <class Q>
HRESULT QueryInterface(Q** pp) const
{
    ATLASSERT(pp != NULL && *pp == NULL);
    return p->QueryInterface(__uuidof(Q), (void**)pp);
}
```

Using this method reduces the chance of making the common mistake of querying for one interface (e.g., `IID_IBar`) but specifying a different type of pointer for the returned value (e.g., `IFoo*`).

```
CComPtr<IFoo> pfoo = /* Initialize to some IFoo */
IBar* pbar;

// We specify an IBar variable so the method queries for IID_IBar
HRESULT hr = pfoo.QueryInterface(&IBar);
```

Use the `IsEqualObject` method to determine if two interface pointers refer to the same object.

```
bool IsEqualObject(IUnknown* pOther);
```

It performs the test for COM identity: Query each interface for `IID_IUnknown` and compare the results. A COM object must always return the same pointer value when asked for its `IUnknown` interface. The `IsEqualObject` method expands a little on the COM identity test. It considers two `NULL` interface pointers equal objects.

```
bool SameObjects(IUnknown* punk1, IUnknown* punk2)
{
    CComPtr<IUnknown> p (punk1);
    return p.IsEqualObject (punk2);
}

IUnknown* punk1 = NULL;
IUnknown* punk2 = NULL;
ATLASSERT (SameObjects(punk1, punk2); // true
```

The `SetSite` method associates a site object (specified by the `punkParent` parameter) with the object referenced by the internal pointer. The smart pointer must point to an object that implements the `IObjectWithSite` interface.

```
HRESULT SetSite(IUnknown* punkParent);
```

The `Advise` method associates a connection point sink object with the object referenced by the smart interface pointer (which is the event source object). The first parameter is the sink interface. You specify the sink interface ID as the second parameter. The third parameter is an output parameter. The `Advise` method returns a token through this parameter that uniquely identifies this connection.

```
HRESULT Advise(IUnknown* pUnk, const IID& iid, LPDWORD pdw);
```

```
CComPtr<ISource> ps /* Initialized via some mechanism */ ;
ISomeSink* psink = /* Initialized via some mechanism */ ;
DWORD dwCookie;

ps->Advise (psink, __uuidof(IsomeSink), &dwCookie);
```

There is no `Unadvise` smart pointer method to end the connection because the pointer is not needed for the `Unadvise`. To break the connection, you need only the cookie, the sink interface identifier (IID), and an event source reference.

CComPtr Comparison Operators

Three operators provide comparison operations on a smart pointer. The `operator!()` method returns `true` when the interface pointer is `NULL`. The `operator==()` method returns `true` when the comparison operand is equal to the interface pointer. The `operator<()` method is rather useless, in general, because it compares two interface pointers using their binary values. However, a class needs these comparison operators so that STL collections of class instances work properly.

```
bool operator!() const        { return (p == NULL); }
bool operator< (T* pT) const  { return p <  pT; }
bool operator==(T* pT) const  { return p == pT; }
```

Note that you might have to change your coding style for comparisons when using smart pointers. Some programmers prefer to write equality comparisons to a literal value with the literal on the left side of the expression. This doesn't work with the ATL smart interface classes. For example:

```
CComPtr<IFoo> pFoo;
if (!pFoo)            // Tests for pFoo.p == NULL using operator!
if (pFoo == NULL)     // Tests for pFoo.p == NULL using operator==
if (NULL == pFoo)     // Does not compile!
```

The CComDispatchDriver Class

In ATL 3.0, the `CComDispatchDriver` class is more or less a specialization of `CComQIPtr<IDispatch>`, except it's not quite as good as it could be. First, it's an independent class. It doesn't actually derive from `CComQIPtr`, Therefore, all the `CComQIPtr` smart pointer functionality is implemented independently in the `CComDispatchDriver` class. Unfortunately, some of the improvements made to the `CComQIPtr` class weren't propagated to this class. In the next release of ATL, `CComDispatchDriver` is `typedef`'ed as a specialization of `CComQIPtr<IDispatch>`.

Note that the state consists of a single member variable, `IDispatch* p`.

```
class CComDispatchDriver
{
public:
    IDispatch* p;
```

This class contains typical smart pointer methods, so I'll only examine the ones significantly different from those discussed for the CComPtr and CComQIPtr classes.

Strange Implementation Quirks

You can initialize an instance of the CComDispatchDriver class from an IDispatch pointer and from an IUnknown pointer. In the latter case, the constructor will query the specified pointer for the IDispatch interface. Unlike the CComPtr and CComQIPtr classes, you cannot initialize a CComDispatchDriver instance from another CComDispatchDriver instance.

```
CComDispatchDriver();
CComDispatchDriver(IDispatch* lp);
CComDispatchDriver(IUnknown* lp);
```

Note that the operator->() method returns an IDispatch*.

```
IDispatch* operator->() {ATLASSERT(p!= NULL); return p; }
```

It should return a _NoAddRefReleaseOnCComPtr<IDispatch> pointer, like the other smart pointer classes do. This means you can still use the operator arrow method and call Release on the underlying interface pointer without clearing the p member variable. The destructor later will release the interface pointer again.

It's sort of minor, but the operator!() method returns a BOOL, not a bool like the other smart pointer classes return. A BOOL value is a Windows typedef for an int (a 32-bit value on Win32 systems), typically considered to have the semantics of nonzero being TRUE, and zero FALSE. A bool value is an intrinsic C++ type that is a byte value with intrinsic true and false values.

```
BOOL operator!() {return (p == NULL) ? TRUE : FALSE;}
```

Property Accessor and Mutator Methods

A few of the methods make it lots easier to get and set properties on an object using the object's IDispatch interface. First, you can get the DISPID for a property, given its string name, by calling the GetIDOfName method.

```
HRESULT GetIDOfName(LPCOLESTR lpsz, DISPID* pdispid);
```

Once you have the DISPID for a property, you can get and set the property's value using the GetProperty and PutProperty methods. You specify the DISPID of the property to get or set and send or receive the new value in a VARIANT structure.

```
HRESULT GetProperty(DISPID dwDispID, VARIANT* pVar);
HRESULT PutProperty(DISPID dwDispID, VARIANT* pVar);
```

You can skip the initial step and get and set a property given only its name using the well-named GetPropertyByName and PutPropertyByName methods.

```
HRESULT GetPropertyByName(LPCOLESTR lpsz, VARIANT* pVar);
HRESULT PutPropertyByName(LPCOLESTR lpsz, VARIANT* pVar);
```

Method Invocation Helper Functions

It's a royal pain to call an object's methods using the IDispatch::Invoke method. You have to package up all the arguments into VARIANT structures, build an array of those VARIANTs, and translate the name of the method to a DISPID. Nothing extremely difficult, but it's all tedious and error-prone coding.

The CComDispatchDriver class has a number of methods that are customized for the frequent cases for calling an object's method(s) using IDispatch. There are four basic variations:

- Call a method by DISPID or name, passing zero parameters.
- Call a method by DISPID or name, passing one parameter.
- Call a method by DISPID or name, passing two parameters.
- Call a method by DISPID or name, passing an array of N parameters.

Each variation expects the DISPID or name of the method to invoke, the arguments, and an optional return value.

```
HRESULT Invoke0(DISPID dispid, VARIANT* pvarRet = NULL)
HRESULT Invoke0(LPCOLESTR lpszName, VARIANT* pvarRet = NULL)
HRESULT Invoke1(DISPID dispid, VARIANT* pvarParam1,
                VARIANT* pvarRet = NULL)
HRESULT Invoke1(LPCOLESTR lpszName,
         VARIANT* pvarParam1, VARIANT* pvarRet = NULL)
```

```
HRESULT Invoke2(DISPID dispid,
        VARIANT* pvarParam1, VARIANT* pvarParam2,
        VARIANT* pvarRet = NULL)
HRESULT Invoke2(LPCOLESTR lpszName,
        VARIANT* pvarParam1, VARIANT* pvarParam2,
        VARIANT* pvarRet = NULL)
HRESULT InvokeN(DISPID dispid,
        VARIANT* pvarParams, int nParams, VARIANT* pvarRet = NULL)
HRESULT InvokeN(LPCOLESTR lpszName,
        VARIANT* pvarParams, int nParams, VARIANT* pvarRet = NULL)
```

Finally, there are two static member functions, `GetProperty` and `SetProperty`. You can use these methods to get and set a property using its `DISPID` without first attaching an `IDispatch` pointer to a `CComDispatchDriver` object.

```
static HRESULT GetProperty(IDispatch* pDisp, DISPID dwDispID,
                           VARIANT* pVar);
static HRESULT PutProperty(IDispatch* pDisp, DISPID dwDispID,
                           VARIANT* pVar);
```

Here's an example:

```
HRESULT GetCount (IDispatch* pdisp, long* pCount)
{
    *pCount = 0;
    const int DISPID_COUNT = 1;

    CComVariant v;
    CComDispatchDriver::GetProperty (pdisp, DISPID_COUNT, &v);

    HRESULT hr = v.ChangeType (VT_I4);
    If (SUCCEEDED (hr))
        *pCount = V_I4(&v) ;
    return hr;
}
```

Summary

ATL provides a rich set of classes for manipulating the data types frequently used by COM programmers. The string conversion macros provide efficient conversion between the various text types, but you must be careful not to use them in a loop.

You must be especially careful when using the BSTR string type because it has numerous special semantics. The ATL CComBSTR class manages many of the special semantics for you and is quite useful. However, the class cannot compensate for the poor decision that, to the C++ compiler, equates the OLECHAR* and BSTR types. You will always need to use care when using the BSTR type because the compiler will not warn you of many pitfalls.

The CComVariant class provides practically the same benefits as the CCom-BSTR class, only for VARIANT structures. If you use a VARIANT structure, and you will need to use one sooner or later, you should instead use the ATL CComVariant smart VARIANT class. You'll have far fewer problems with resource leaks.

The CComPtr, CComQIPtr, and CComDispatchDriver smart pointer classes ease, but do not totally alleviate, the resource management needed for interface pointers. These classes have numerous useful methods that let you write more application code and deal less with the low-level resource management details. You'll find smart pointers most useful when you're using interface pointers with code that can throw exceptions.

CHAPTER 3 | Objects in ATL

ATL's fundamental support for COM can be split into two pieces: objects and servers. This chapter covers classes and concentrates on how IUnknown is implemented as related to threading and various COM identity issues, for example, standalone versus aggregated objects. The next chapter focuses on how to expose classes from COM servers.

Recall: COM Apartments

COM supports two kinds of objects, multithreaded and single threaded. Multithreaded objects are those that perform their own synchronization, whereas single-threaded objects are objects that prefer to let COM handle the synchronization. Single-threaded objects are easier to implement, although multithreaded objects may have a higher degree of concurrency.

An object is known to COM as single threaded or multithreaded based on the apartment in which it lives. A COM *apartment* is a group of one or more threads marked as either single threaded or multithreaded. A thread is marked with a call to CoInitializeEx:

```
HRESULT CoInitializeEx(void* pvReserved, DWORD dwCoInit);
```

The dwCoInit parameter is either COINIT_APARTMENTTHREADED or COINIT_ MULTITHREADED, based on whether objects created on that thread are to be single threaded or multithreaded, respectively. Calls to CoInitialize map to a call to CoInitializeEx, passing COINIT_APARTMENTTHREADED. By calling CoInitializeEx, a thread is said to be *joining* an apartment.

In the case of a single-threaded apartment (STA), COM creates an invisible window to queue requests for objects in that apartment. To service these requests, the thread must pump a Windows message loop. For example:

```
int WINAPI WinMain(HINSTANCE, HINSTANCE, LPSTR, int) {
  CoInitializeEx(0, COINIT_APARTMENTTHREADED); // or CoInitialize(0);
  ...
```

```
MSG msg;
while( GetMessage(&msg, 0, 0, 0) ) DispatchMessage(&msg);
CoUninitialize();
}
```

Since the requests can only be serviced one at a time, each call to an object created in a single-threaded apartment must complete before another can be serviced. This is how COM provides synchronization for single-threaded objects.

On the other hand, objects created in a multithreaded apartment (MTA) must be prepared to receive calls from any number of threads simultaneously. Multithreaded objects are responsible for synchronizing their own state.

In-process Server Considerations

Although clients and executable servers manage all their own threads, and therefore are responsible for creating their own apartments, in-process servers have no such luxury. When an in-process server is first loaded, it will be in the context of a thread that has already joined an apartment. Any thread that calls `CoGetClass-Object` or `CoCreateInstance` must already have joined an apartment, or the call will fail immediately.[1] So, does that mean that all objects exposed from in-process servers must be equally at home in single-threaded and multithreaded apartments so that random clients can't cause harm? Fortunately, no.

When, in the process of accessing a class object, COM notices that the threading model of the calling apartment is incompatible with that of the class being activated, it will call the class object from the context of another, compatible, apartment, even creating a new apartment if necessary. To allow communication between any two apartments while maintaining the synchronization and concurrency requirements of both apartments, COM will load proxy/stubs on demand, that is, when an interface pointer is passed between two apartments.

To notify COM to provide the appropriate protection, a class will be marked in the registry using the `ThreadingModel` named value under the `InProcServer32` key. Using the `.reg` file format, an apartment model in-process class would mark itself thusly:

```
REGEDIT4
[HKEY_CLASSES_ROOT\CLSID\{44EBF751-...}\InProcServer32]
@=bworsvr.dll
ThreadingModel=Apartment
```

---

[1]COM requires that `CoInitializeEx` be called before any "interesting" COM calls are allowed.

The ThreadingModel named value has the following possible values.

- (none): If there is no ThreadingModel given in the registry, COM will assume a legacy single-threaded class and access the class object from the process's first STA, creating a new STA if necessary. This protects objects from having to synchronize access to global, static, or instance data.

- Apartment: This protects objects from having to synchronize access to instance data; however, objects of this class could be created in different STAs, so static and global data must still be synchronized.

- Free: This value indicates that the objects of this class would like to live only in the MTA. Objects living in the MTA must synchronize access to instance as well as static and global data.

- Both: Objects that want to share the same apartment as the client will mark their class as Both, which means that there is no incompatible client threading model. This value is used when you want to avoid the overhead of a proxy/stub pair between the initial client and the object.

Implementing IUnknown

A COM object has one responsibility: implementing the methods of IUnknown. Those methods perform two services, lifetime management and runtime type discovery, as follows:

```
interface IUnknown {
 // runtime type discovery
 HRESULT QueryInterface([in] REFIID riid,
                        [out, iid_is(riid)] void **ppv);

 // lifetime management
 ULONG AddRef();
 ULONG Release();
}
```

COM allows every object to implement these methods as it chooses (within certain restrictions, as described in Chapter 5). The canonical implementation is as follows:

```
// Server lifetime management
extern void ServerLock();
extern void ServerUnlock();
```

```
class CPenguin : public IBird, public ISnappyDresser {
public:
 CPenguin() : m_cRef(0) { ServerLock(); }
 virtual ~CPenguin()    { ServerUnlock(); }

 // IUnknown methods
 STDMETHODIMP QueryInterface(REFIID riid, void **ppv) {
   if( riid == IID_IBird || riid == IID_IUnknown )
     *ppv = static_cast<IBird*>(this);
   else if( riid == IID_ISnappyDresser )
     *ppv = static_cast<ISnappyDresser*>(this);
   else *ppv = 0;

   if( *ppv ) {
     reinterpret_cast<IUnknown*>(*ppv)->AddRef();
     return S_OK;
   }
   return E_NOINTERFACE;
 }

 STDMETHODIMP_(ULONG) AddRef()
 { return InterlockedIncrement(&m_cRef); }

 STDMETHODIMP_(ULONG) Release() {
   ULONG l = InterlockedDecrement(&m_cRef);
   if( l == 0 ) delete this;
   return l;
 }

 // IBird and ISnappyDresser methods...
private:
 ULONG m_cRef;
};
```

This implementation of IUnknown is based on several assumptions:

- The object is heap based because it removes itself using the delete operator. Further, the object's lifetime is completely governed by its outstanding references. When it has no more references, it deletes itself.

- The object is able to live in a multithreaded apartment because it manipulates the reference count in a thread-safe manner. Of course, the other methods must be implemented in a thread-safe manner as well for the object to be fully thread safe.

- The object is standalone and cannot be aggregated because it does not cache a reference to a controlling outer nor does it forward the methods of IUnknown to a controlling outer.

- The object exposes its interfaces using multiple inheritance.

- The existence of the object keeps the server running. The constructor and the destructor are used to lock and unlock the server, respectively.

While these are common assumptions, they are not the only possibilities. Common variations include the following:

- An object may be global and live for the life of the server. Such objects have no need of a reference count because they never delete themselves.

- An object may not need to be thread safe because it may only be meant to live in single-threaded apartments.

- An object may choose to allow itself to be aggregated as well as, or instead of, supporting standalone activation.

- An object may expose interfaces using other techniques besides multiple inheritance, including nested composition, tear-offs, and aggregation.

- You may not want the existence of an object to force the server to keep running. This is common for global objects, because their mere existence would prohibit the server from unloading.

Changing any of these assumptions will result in a different implementation of IUnknown, although the rest of the object's implementation is unlikely to change much (with the notable exception of thread safety). Because these implementation details of IUnknown, while important, tend to take a very regular form, they can be encapsulated into C++ classes. Frankly, we'd really like to use someone else's tested code and to be able to change our minds later without a great deal of effort. We'd also like this boilerplate code to be easily separable from the actual behavior of our objects so that we can focus on our domain-specific implementation. ATL was designed from the ground up to provide just this kind of functionality and flexibility.

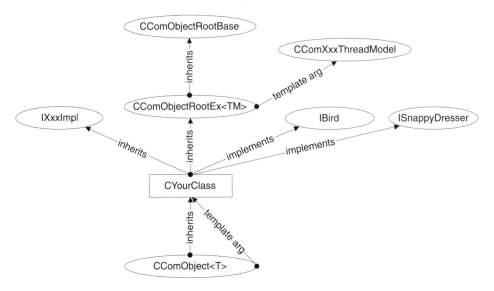

Figure 3.1. The layers of ATL

The Layers of ATL

ATL's support for building COM objects is separated into several layers, as shown in Figure 3.1. These layers break down into services exposed by ATL for building objects.

1. A `CComXxxThreadModel` is used by `CComObjectRootEx` to provide just-thread-safe-enough object lifetime management and object locking.

2. `CComObjectRootBase` and `CComObjectRootEx` provide helper functions used in implementing `IUnknown`.

3. Your class derives from `CComObjectRootEx`. Your class must also derive from any interfaces it wants to implement as well as providing the method implementations. Method implementations may be provided by you or by one of the ATL `IXxxImpl` classes.

4. `CComObject` et al. provide the actual implementation of the methods of `IUnknown` in a way consistent with your desires for object and server lifetime management requirements. This final layer will actually derive from your class.

Your choice of base classes and the most derived class will determine the way in which the methods of `IUnknown` are implemented. Should your choices change, using different classes at compile time (or runtime) will change how ATL implements IUnknown, independently of the rest of the behavior of your object. The following sections explore each of the layers of ATL.

Threading Model Support

Just Enough Thread Safety

The thread-safe implementation of AddRef and Release shown previously may be overkill for our COM objects. For example, if instances of a specific class will only live in a single-threaded apartment, there's no reason to use the thread-safe Win32 functions InterlockedIncrement and InterlockedDecrement. For single-threaded objects, the following implementation of AddRef and Release is more efficient:

```
class Penguin {
...
 ULONG AddRef()
 { return ++m_cRef; }

 ULONG Release() {
   ULONG l = --m_cRef;
   if( l == 0 ) delete this;
   return l;
 }
...
};
```

Although using the thread-safe Win32 functions will also work for single-threaded objects, unnecessary thread safety requires extra overhead that we'd like to avoid if we can. For this reason, ATL provides three classes, CComSingleThreadModel, CComMultiThreadModel, and CComMultiThreadModelNoCS. These classes provide two static member functions, Increment and Decrement, for abstracting away the differences between managing an object's lifetime count in a multithreaded or single-threaded manner. The two versions of these functions are as follows (notice that both CComMultiThreadModel and CComMultiThreadModelNoCS have identical implementations of these functions).

```
class CComSingleThreadModel {
 static ULONG WINAPI Increment(LPLONG p) { return ++(*p); }
```

```
  static ULONG WINAPI Decrement(LPLONG p) { return --(*p); }
  ...
};

class CComMultiThreadModel {
  static ULONG WINAPI Increment(LPLONG p)
    { return InterlockedIncrement(p); }
  static ULONG WINAPI Decrement(LPLONG p)
    { return InterlockedDecrement(p); }
  ...
};

class CComMultiThreadModelNoCS {
  static ULONG WINAPI Increment(LPLONG p)
    { return InterlockedIncrement(p); }
  static ULONG WINAPI Decrement(LPLONG p)
    { return InterlockedDecrement(p); }
  ...
};
```

Using these classes, we can parameterize[2] our class to give a just-thread-safe-enough AddRef and Release implementation, like so:

```
template <typename ThreadModel>
class Penguin {
...
 ULONG AddRef()
 { return ThreadModel::Increment(&m_cRef); }

 ULONG Release() {
   ULONG l = ThreadModel::Decrement(&m_cRef);
   if( l == 0 ) delete this;
   return l;
 }
...
};
```

_____

[2] For an introduction to C++ templates and how they're used in ATL, see Appendix A.

Now, based on our requirements for the CPenguin class, we can make it just thread-safe enough by supplying the threading model class as a template parameter.

```
// Let's make a thread-safe CPenguin
CPenguin* pobj = new CPenguin<CComMultiThreadModel>;
```

Instance Data Synchronization

When you create a thread-safe object, protecting the object's reference count isn't enough. We'll also have to protect the member data from multithreaded access. One popular method for protecting data accessible from multiple threads is to use a Win32 critical section object, as shown here:

```
template <typename ThreadModel>
class CPenguin {
public:
 CPenguin()  { ServerLock();   InitializeCriticalSection(&m_cs); }
 ~CPenguin() { ServerUnlock(); DeleteCriticalSection(&m_cs); }

 // IBird
 STDMETHODIMP get_Wingspan(long* pnWingspan) {
   Lock(); // Lock out other threads during data write
   *pnWingSpan = m_nWingspan;
   Unlock();
   return S_OK;
 }

 STDMETHODIMP put_Wingspan(long nWingspan) {
   Lock(); // Lock out other threads during data read
   m_nWingspan = nWingspan;
   Unlock();
   return S_OK;
 }
 ...
private:
 CRITICALSECTION m_cs;

 void Lock()   { EnterCriticalSection(&m_cs); }
 void Unlock() { LeaveCriticalSection(&m_cs); }
};
```

Notice that before reading or writing any member data, the CPenguin object enters the critical section, locking out access by other threads. This course-grained, object-level locking keeps the scheduler from swapping in another thread that may corrupt the data members during a read or a write on the original thread.

However, object-level locking doesn't give us as much concurrency as we may like. If we have only one critical section per object, one thread may be blocked trying to increment the reference count while another is updating an unrelated member variable. A greater degree of concurrency would require more critical sections, allowing one thread to access one data member while a second thread accessed another. Be careful using this kind of finer-grained synchronization, however, as it often leads to deadlock. For example:

```
class CSneech : public ISneech {
public:
 ...
 // ISneech
 STDMETHODIMP GoNorth() {
    EnterCriticalSection(&m_cs1); // Enter cs1...
    EnterCriticalSection(&m_cs2); // ...then enter cs2
    // Go north...
    LeaveCriticalSection(&m_cs2);
    LeaveCriticalSection(&m_cs1);
 }

 STDMETHODIMP GoSouth() {
    EnterCriticalSection(&m_cs2); // Enter cs2...
    EnterCriticalSection(&m_cs1); // ...then enter cs1
    // Go south...
    LeaveCriticalSection(&m_cs1);
    LeaveCriticalSection(&m_cs2);
 }
 ...
private:
 CRITICAL_SECTION  m_cs1;
 CRITICAL_SECTION  m_cs2;
};
```

Imagine that the scheduler let a thread executing the GoNorth method enter the first critical section and then swapped in a thread executing the GoSouth method that enters the second critical section. If this happens, neither thread can enter the other critical section and therefore neither thread will be able to proceed, leaving them deadlocked. This situation should be avoided.[3]

Whether you decide to use object-level locking or finer-grained locking, critical sections are handy. ATL provides two class wrappers that simplify their use: CCom-CriticalSection and CComAutoCriticalSection.

```
class CComCriticalSection {
public:
 void Lock()    { EnterCriticalSection(&m_sec); }
 void Unlock() { LeaveCriticalSection(&m_sec); }
 void Init()    { InitializeCriticalSection(&m_sec); }
 void Term()    { DeleteCriticalSection(&m_sec); }
 CRITICAL_SECTION m_sec;
};

class CComAutoCriticalSection {
public:
 void Lock()                    { EnterCriticalSection(&m_sec); }
 void Unlock()                  { LeaveCriticalSection(&m_sec); }
 CComAutoCriticalSection()     { InitializeCriticalSection(&m_sec); }
 ~CComAutoCriticalSection()    { DeleteCriticalSection(&m_sec); }
 CRITICAL_SECTION m_sec;
};
```

Notice that CComCriticalSection has no constructor or destructor, but rather has Init and Term functions. This makes CComCriticalSection useful when a global or static critical section is required and the C runtime library (CRT) is not available to perform automatic construction and destruction. CComAuto-CriticalSection, on the other hand, is easier to use, both in the presence of the CRT as well as when created as an instance data member. For example, using a CComAutoCriticalSection in our CPenguin class simplifies the code a bit:

```
template <typename ThreadModel>
class CPenguin {
public:
  // IBird methods call Lock() and Unlock() as before...
```

---

[3]For quite a bit more guidance on what to do about deadlocks, read *Win32 Multithreaded Programming*, by Mike Woodring and Aaron Cohen (O'Reilly & Associates, 1997).

```
...
private:
  CComAutoCriticalSection m_cs;

  void Lock() { m_cs.Lock(); }
  void Unlock() { m_cs.Unlock(); }
};
```

However, notice that our `CPenguin` is still parameterized by the threading model. There's no sense in protecting our member variables in the single-threaded case. In this case, it would be handy to have another critical section class that could be used in place of `CComCriticalSection` or `CComAutoCriticalSection`. ATL provides the `CComFakeCriticalSection` class for this purpose.

```
class CComFakeCriticalSection {
public:
    void Lock()   {}
    void Unlock() {}
    void Init()   {}
    void Term()   {}
};
```

Given `CComFakeCriticalSection`, we could further parameterize the `CPenguin` class by adding another template parameter, but this is unnecessary. The ATL threading model classes already contain type definitions that map to a real or a fake critical section, based on whether we're doing single or multithreading:

```
class CComSingleThreadModel {
public:
  static ULONG WINAPI Increment(LPLONG p) { return ++(*p); }
  static ULONG WINAPI Decrement(LPLONG p) { return --(*p); }
  typedef CComFakeCriticalSection AutoCriticalSection;
  typedef CComFakeCriticalSection CriticalSection;
  typedef CComSingleThreadModel ThreadModelNoCS;
};

class CComMultiThreadModel {
public:
  static ULONG WINAPI Increment(LPLONG p)
    { return InterlockedIncrement(p); }
```

```
    static ULONG WINAPI Decrement(LPLONG p)
      { return InterlockedDecrement(p); }
    typedef CComAutoCriticalSection AutoCriticalSection;
    typedef CComCriticalSection CriticalSection;
    typedef CComMultiThreadModelNoCS ThreadModelNoCS;
};

class CComMultiThreadModelNoCS {
public:
    static ULONG WINAPI Increment(LPLONG p)
      { return InterlockedIncrement(p); }
    static ULONG WINAPI Decrement(LPLONG p)
      { return InterlockedDecrement(p); }
    typedef CComFakeCriticalSection AutoCriticalSection;
    typedef CComFakeCriticalSection CriticalSection;
    typedef CComMultiThreadModelNoCS ThreadModelNoCS;
};
```

Using these type definitions allows us to make the CPenguin class just thread-safe enough both for the object's reference count and for coarse-grained object synchronization:

```
template <typename ThreadingModel>
class CPenguin {
public:
 // IBird methods as before...
 ...
private:
 ThreadingModel::AutoCriticalSection m_cs;

 void Lock() { m_cs.Lock(); }
 void Unlock() { m_cs.Unlock(); }
};
```

This technique allows us to provide the compiler with operations that are just thread-safe enough. When the threading model is CComSingleThreadModel, the calls to Increment and Decrement resolve to operator++ and operator--, and the Lock and Unlock calls resolve to empty inline functions.

When the threading model is CComMultiThreadModel, the calls to Increment and Decrement resolve to calls to InterlockedIncrement and

Table 3.1. Expanded Code Based on Threading Model Class

	CcomSingle-ThreadModel	CComMultiThreadModel	CComMulti-ThreadModelNoCS
TM::Increment	++	InterlockedIncrement	InterlockedIncrement
TM::Decrement	--	InterlockedDecrement	InterlockedDecrement
TM::AutoCriticalSection:: Lock	(nothing)	EnterCriticalSection	(nothing)
TM::AutoCriticalSection:: Unlock	(nothing)	LeaveCriticalSection	(nothing)

InterlockedDecrement, and the Lock and Unlock calls resolve to calls to EnterCriticalSection and LeaveCriticalSection.

Finally, when the model is CComMultiThreadModelNoCS, the calls to Increment and Decrement are thread safe, but the critical section is fake, just like CComSingleThreadModel. CComMultiThreadModelNoCS is designed for multithreaded objects that eschew object-level locking in favor of a more fine-grained scheme. Table 3.1 shows how the code is expanded based on the threading model class you use.

The Server's Default Threading Model

ATL-based servers have a concept of what is the server's "default" threading model. This is used for things that you don't specify directly. To set the server's default threading model, you define one of the following symbols: _ATL_SINGLE_ THREADED, _ATL_APARTMENT_THREADED, or _ATL_FREE_THREADED. If you don't specify one of these symbols, ATL will assume _ATL_FREE_THREADED. However, the ATL COM AppWizard will define _ATL_APARTMENT_THREADED in the generated stdafx.h file. ATL uses these symbols to define two type definitions:

```
#if defined(_ATL_SINGLE_THREADED)
    typedef CComSingleThreadModel CComObjectThreadModel;
    typedef CComSingleThreadModel CComGlobalsThreadModel;
#elif defined(_ATL_APARTMENT_THREADED)
    typedef CComSingleThreadModel CComObjectThreadModel;
    typedef CComMultiThreadModel CComGlobalsThreadModel;
#else // _ATL_FREE_THREADED
    typedef CComMultiThreadModel CComObjectThreadModel;
    typedef CComMultiThreadModel CComGlobalsThreadModel;
#endif
```

Internally, ATL uses `CComObjectThreadModel` to protect instance data and `CComGlobalsThreadModel` to protect global and static data. Because the usage is difficult to override in some cases, you should make sure that ATL is compiled using the most protective threading model of any of the classes in your server. In practice, this means you should change the wizard-generated _ATL_APARTMENT_ THREADED symbol to _ATL_FREE_THREADED if you have even one multithreaded class in your server.

The Core of IUnknown

Standalone Reference Counting

To encapsulate the `Lock` and `Unlock` methods as well as the just thread-safe enough reference counting, ATL provides the `CComObjectRootEx` base class, parameterized by the desired threading model.[4]

```
template <class ThreadModel>
class CComObjectRootEx : public CComObjectRootBase {
public:
    typedef ThreadModel _ThreadModel;
    typedef _ThreadModel::AutoCriticalSection _CritSec;
    typedef CComObjectLockT<_ThreadModel> ObjectLock;

    ULONG InternalAddRef() {
        ATLASSERT(m_dwRef != -1L);
        return _ThreadModel::Increment(&m_dwRef);
    }

    ULONG InternalRelease() {
        ATLASSERT(m_dwRef > 0);
        return _ThreadModel::Decrement(&m_dwRef);
    }

    void Lock()   { m_critsec.Lock(); }
    void Unlock() { m_critsec.Unlock(); }
private:
    _CritSec m_critsec;
};
```

---

[4]As an optimization, ATL provides a specialization of `CComObjectRootEx<CComSingleThread-Model>` that does not have a `_CritSec` object, sidestepping minimum object size requirements imposed by the compiler.

ATL classes derive from CComObjectRootEx and forward AddRef and Release calls to the InternalAddRef and InternalRelease methods when the object is created standalone (that is, not aggregated).

With the Lock and Unlock methods so readily available in the base class, we may be tempted to write the following *incorrect* code:

```
class CPenguin : public CComObjectRootEx<CComMultiThreadModel>, ... {
STDMETHODIMP get_Wingspan(long* pnWingspan) {
  Lock();
  if( !pnWingspan ) return E_POINTER; // Forgot to Unlock
  *pnWingSpan = m_nWingspan;
  Unlock();
  return S_OK;
}
...
};
```

To help us avoid this kind of mistake, CComObjectRootEx provides a type definition for a class called ObjectLock, based on CComObjectLockT parameterized by the threading model, as shown:

```
template <class ThreadModel>
class CComObjectLockT {
public:
 CComObjectLockT(CComObjectRootEx<ThreadModel>* p) {
   if (p) p->Lock();
   m_p = p;
 }
 ~CComObjectLockT() {
   if (m_p) m_p->Unlock();
 }
 CComObjectRootEx<ThreadModel>* m_p;
};
```

Instances of CComObjectLockT will Lock the object passed to the constructor and Unlock it upon destruction. The ObjectLock type definition provides a convenient way to write code that will properly release the lock regardless of the return path:

```
Class CPenguin : public CComObjectRootEx<CComMultiThreadModel>, ... {
STDMETHODIMP get_Wingspan(long* pnWingspan) {
```

```
    ObjectLock lock(this);
    if( !pnWingspan ) return E_POINTER; // Stack unwind invokes Unlock
    *pnWingSpan = m_nWingspan;
    return S_OK;
  }
  ...
};
```

Table-Driven QueryInterface

In addition to just-thread-safe-enough implementations of AddRef and Release for standalone COM objects, CComObjectRootEx, via its base class, CComObject-RootBase, provides a static, table-driven implementation of QueryInterface called InternalQueryInterface.

```
static HRESULT WINAPI
CComObjectRootBase::InternalQueryInterface(
  void*                   pThis,
  const _ATL_INTMAP_ENTRY* pEntries,
  REFIID                  iid,
  void**                  ppvObject);
```

This static member function uses the this pointer of the object, provided as the pThis parameter, and the requested interface to fill the ppvObject parameter with a pointer to the appropriate virtual function table pointer (vptr). It does this using the pEntries parameter, a zero-terminated array of _ATL_INTMAP_ENTRY structures:

```
struct _ATL_INTMAP_ENTRY {
  const IID*          piid;
  DWORD               dw;
  _ATL_CREATORARGFUNC* pFunc;
};
```

Each interface exposed from a COM object will be one entry in the interface map, which is a class-static array of _ATL_INTMAP_ENTRY structures. Each entry will consist of an interface identifier (IID), a function pointer, and an argument for the function represented as a DWORD. This provides a flexible, extensible mechanism for implementing QueryInterface that supports multiple inheritance, aggregation, tear-offs, nested composition, debugging, chaining, and just about any

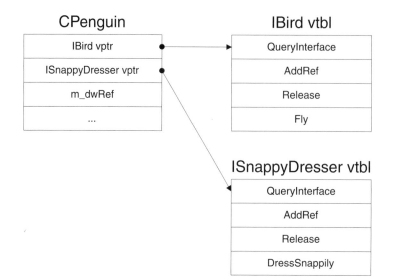

Figure 3.2. CPenguin object layout including vptrs to vtbls

other wacky COM identity tricks currently in use by C++ programmers.[5] However, since most interfaces are implemented using multiple inheritance, we don't often need this much flexibility. For example, consider one possible object layout for instances of the CPenguin class, as shown in Figure 3.2.

```
class CPenguin : public IBird, public ISnappyDresser {...};
```

The typical implementation of QueryInterface for a class using multiple inheritance consists of a series of if statements and static_cast operations, the purpose of which is to adjust the this pointer by some fixed offset to point to the appropriate vptr. Because the offsets are known at compile time, a table that matched interface identifiers to offsets would provide an appropriate data structure for adjusting the this pointer at runtime. To support this common case, the InternalQueryInterface function treats the _ATL_INTMAP_ENTRY as a simple IID/offset pair if the pFunc member has the special value _ATL_SIMPLEMAPENTRY:

```
#define _ATL_SIMPLEMAPENTRY ((_ATL_CREATORARGFUNC*)1)
```

To be able to use the InternalQueryInterface function, each implementation populates a static interface map. To facilitate populating this data structure,

---

[5] All these uses of the interface map are described in Chapter 5.

and to provide some other methods used internally, ATL provides the following macros (as well as others described in Chapter 5):

```
#define BEGIN_COM_MAP(class) ...
#define COM_INTERFACE_ENTRY(itf) ...
#define END_COM_MAP() ...
```

For example, our CPenguin class would declare its interface map like so:

```
class CPenguin :
 public CComObjectRootEx<CComMultiThreadModel>,
 public IBird,
 public ISnappyDresser {
...
public:
BEGIN_COM_MAP(CPenguin)
 COM_INTERFACE_ENTRY(IBird)
 COM_INTERFACE_ENTRY(ISnappyDresser)
END_COM_MAP()
...
};
```

In an abbreviated form, this would expand to the following:

```
class CPenguin :
 public CComObjectRootEx<CComMultiThreadModel>,
 public IBird,
 public ISnappyDresser {
...
public:
  IUnknown* GetUnknown() {
    ATLASSERT(_GetEntries()[0].pFunc == _ATL_SIMPLEMAPENTRY);
    return (IUnknown*)((int)this+_GetEntries()->dw); }
 }
  HRESULT _InternalQueryInterface(REFIID iid, void** ppvObject) {
    return InternalQueryInterface(this, _GetEntries(), iid, ppvObject);
 }
  const static _ATL_INTMAP_ENTRY* WINAPI _GetEntries() {
    static const _ATL_INTMAP_ENTRY _entries[] = {
      { &IID_IBird,          0, _ATL_SIMPLEMAPENTRY },
      { &IID_ISnappyDresser, 4, _ATL_SIMPLEMAPENTRY },
```

```
      { 0, 0, 0 }
    };
    return _entries;
  }
  ...
};
```

Figure 3.3 shows how this interface map relates to an instance of a CPenguin object in memory.

Something else worth mentioning is the GetUnknown member function that the BEGIN_COM_MAP provides. Although this is used internally by ATL, it's also useful when passing your this pointer to a function that requires an IUnknown*. Because your class derives from potentially more than one interface, each of which derives from IUnknown, passing your own this pointer as an IUnknown* is considered ambiguous by the compiler. For example:

```
HRESULT FlyInAnAirplane(IUnknown* punkPassenger);
```

```
// Penguin.cpp
STDMETHODIMP CPenguin::Fly() {
 return FlyInAnAirplane(this); // ambiguous
}
```

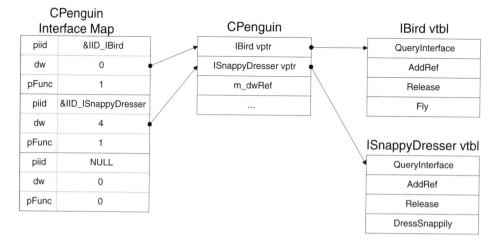

Figure 3.3. CPenguin interface map, CPenguin object, and vtbls

For these situations, GetUnknown is your friend:

```
STDMETHODIMP CPenguin::Fly() {
  return FlyInAnAirplane(this->GetUnknown()); // unambiguous
}
```

As we'll see later, GetUnknown is implemented by handing out the first entry in the interface map.

Support for Aggregation: The Controlled Inner

So far, we've discussed the implementation of IUnknown for standalone COM objects. However, when our object is to participate in aggregation as a controlled inner, our job is not to think for ourselves but rather to be subsumed by the thoughts and desires of another. A controlled inner does this by blindly forwarding all calls on the publicly available implementation of IUnknown to the controlling outer's implementation. The controlling outer's implementation is provided as the pUnk-Outer argument to the CreateInstance method of IClassFactory. When our ATL-based COM object is used as a controlled inner, it simply forwards all calls to IUnknown methods to the OuterQueryInterface, OuterAddRef, and Outer-Release functions provided in CComObjectRootBase, which, in turn, forward to the controlling outer. The relevant functions of CComObjectRootBase are shown here.

```
class CComObjectRootBase {
public:
  CComObjectRootBase() { m_dwRef = 0L; }
  ...
  ULONG OuterAddRef() {
    return m_pOuterUnknown->AddRef();
  }
  ULONG OuterRelease() {
    return m_pOuterUnknown->Release();
  }
  HRESULT OuterQueryInterface(REFIID iid, void ** ppvObject) {
    return m_pOuterUnknown->QueryInterface(iid, ppvObject);
  }
  ...
  union {
    long      m_dwRef;
```

```
    IUnknown* m_pOuterUnknown;
  };
};
```

Notice that `CComObjectRootBase` keeps the object's reference count and a pointer to a controlling unknown as a union. This implies that an object can either maintain its own reference count *or* be aggregated, but not both at the same time. This implication is not true. When the object is being aggregated, it must maintain a reference count *and* a pointer to a controlling unknown. In this case, as I'll discuss later, ATL keeps the `m_pUnkOuter` in one instance of the `CComObjectBase` and then derives from `CComObjectBase` again to keep the object's reference count.

While it's possible to implement the methods of `IUnknown` directly in your class using the methods of the base class `CComObjectRootEx`, most ATL classes don't. Instead, the actual implementations of the `IUnknown` methods will be left to a class that derives from your class, for example, `CComObject`. I'll discuss this after I've talked about the responsibilities of your class.

Your Class

Because ATL provides the behavior for `IUnknown` in the `CComObjectRootEx` class and will provide the actual implementation in the `CComObject` (and friends) class, the job your class performs is pretty simple: derive from interfaces and implement their methods. Besides making sure that the interface map lists all the interfaces you're implementing, you can pretty much leave implementing `IUnknown` to ATL and concentrate on your custom functionality. This is, after all, the whole point of ATL in the first place.

ATL's Implementation Classes

Many standard interfaces have common implementations. ATL provides implementation classes of many standard interfaces; for example, `IPersistStreamInitImpl`, `IConnectionPointContainerImpl`, and `IViewObjectExImpl` implement `IPersistStreamInit`, `IConnectionPointContainer`, and `IViewObjectEx`, respectively. Some of these interfaces are common enough that many objects may implement them, for example, persistence, eventing, or enumeration. Some are more special purpose and related only to a particular framework, for example, controls, Internet-enabled components, or Microsoft Management Console extensions. Most of the general-purpose interface implementations will be discussed in Chapters 6, 7, and 8. The interface implementations related to the controls framework will be discussed in Chapters 10 and 11. One implementation is general purpose enough to discuss right here: `IDispatchImpl`.

Scripting Support

For a scripting environment to access functionality from a COM object, the COM object must implement IDispatch, as shown here.

```
interface IDispatch : IUnknown {
 HRESULT GetTypeInfoCount([out] UINT * pctinfo);

 HRESULT GetTypeInfo([in] UINT iTInfo,
                     [in] LCID lcid,
                     [out] ITypeInfo ** ppTInfo);

 HRESULT GetIDsOfNames([in] REFIID riid,
                       [in, size_is(cNames)] LPOLESTR * rgszNames,
                       [in] UINT cNames,
                       [in] LCID lcid,
                       [out, size_is(cNames)] DISPID * rgDispId);

 HRESULT Invoke([in] DISPID dispIdMember,
                [in] REFIID riid,
                [in] LCID lcid,
                [in] WORD wFlags,
                [in, out] DISPPARAMS * pDispParams,
                [out] VARIANT * pVarResult,
                [out] EXCEPINFO * pExcepInfo,
                [out] UINT * puArgErr);
}
```

The most important methods of IDispatch are GetIDsOfNames and Invoke. Imagine the following line of scripting code:

```
penguin.wingspan = 102
```

This will translate into two calls on IDispatch. The first will be GetIDsOfNames, which will ask the object if it supports the wingspan property. When the answer is yes, the second call to IDispatch will be to Invoke. This call will include an identifier (called a DISPID) that uniquely identifies the name of the property or method the client is interested in (as retrieved from GetIDsOfNames), the type of operation to perform (calling a method or getting or setting a property), a list of arguments, and a place to put the result (if any). The object's implementation of Invoke must then interpret the request made by the scripting client. This typically involves unpacking the list of arguments (which is passed as an array of VARIANT structures), converting them to the appropriate types (if possible), pushing them onto the stack, and calling some other implemented method that deals in real data types, not VARIANTs.

In theory, the object's implementation could take any number of interesting, dynamic steps to parse and interpret the client's request. In practice, most objects forward the request to a helper, whose job it is to build a stack and call a method on an interface implemented by the object to do the real work. The helper makes use of type information held in a type library typically bundled with the server. COM type libraries hold just enough information to allow an instance of a TypeInfo object (that is, an object that implements ITypeInfo) to perform this service. The Type-Info object used to implement IDispatch is usually based on a dual interface, defined in IDL like so:

```
[ dual, uuid(44EBF74E-116D-11D2-9828-00600823CFFB) ]
interface IPenguin : IDispatch {
 [propput] HRESULT Wingspan([in] long nWingspan);
 [propget] HRESULT Wingspan([out, retval] long* pnWingspan);
         HRESULT Fly();
}
```

Using a TypeInfo object as a helper allows an object to implement IDispatch like this (code in bold indicates differences between one implementation and another):

```
class CPenguin :
 public CComObectRootEx<CComSingleThreadModel>,
 public IBird,
 public ISnappyDresser,
 public IPenguin {
public:
 CPenguin() : m_pTypeInfo(0) {
    IID*      pIID   = &IID_IPenguin;
    GUID*     pLIBID = &LIBID_BIRDSERVERLib;
    WORD      wMajor = 1;
    WORD      wMinor = 0;
    ITypeLib* ptl = 0;
    HRESULT hr = LoadRegTypeLib(*pLIBID, wMajor, wMinor, 0, &ptl);
    if( SUCCEEDED(hr) ) {
      hr = ptl->GetTypeInfoOfGuid(*pIID, &m_pTypeInfo);
      ptl->Release();
    }
 }
```

```
  virtual ~Penguin() {
    if( m_pTypeInfo ) m_pTypeInfo->Release();
  }

BEGIN_COM_MAP(CPenguin)
 COM_INTERFACE_ENTRY(IBird)
 COM_INTERFACE_ENTRY(ISnappyDresser)
 COM_INTERFACE_ENTRY(IDispatch)
 COM_INTERFACE_ENTRY(IPenguin)
END_COM_MAP()

 // IDispatch methods
 STDMETHODIMP GetTypeInfoCount(UINT *pctinfo) {
    return (*pctinfo = 1), S_OK;
 }

 STDMETHODIMP GetTypeInfo(UINT ctinfo, LCID lcid, ITypeInfo **ppti) {
    if( ctinfo != 0 ) return (*ppti = 0), DISP_E_BADINDEX;
    return (*ppti = m_pTypeInfo)->AddRef(), S_OK;
 }

 STDMETHODIMP GetIDsOfNames(REFIID riid,
                            OLECHAR **rgszNames,
                            UINT cNames,
                            LCID lcid,
                            DISPID *rgdispid) {
    return m_pTypeInfo->GetIDsOfNames(rgszNames, cNames, rgdispid);
 }

 STDMETHODIMP Invoke(DISPID dispidMember,
                     REFIID riid,
                     LCID lcid,
                     WORD wFlags,
                     DISPPARAMS *pdispparams,
                     VARIANT *pvarResult,
                     EXCEPINFO *pexcepinfo,
                     UINT *puArgErr) {
    return m_pTypeInfo->Invoke(static_cast<IPenguin*>(this),
                               dispidMember, wFlags,
                               pdispparams, pvarResult,
                               pexcepinfo, puArgErr);
  }
```

```
// IBird, ISnappyDresser, and IPenguin methods...
private:
 ITypeInfo*  m_pTypeInfo;
};
```

Since this implementation is so boilerplate (it only varies by the dual interface type, the interface identifier, the type library identifier, and the major and minor version numbers), it can be easily implemented in a template base class. ATL's parameterized implementation of IDispatch is IDispatchImpl.

```
template <class T,
         const IID* piid,
         const GUID* plibid = &CComModule::m_libid,
         WORD wMajor = 1,
         WORD wMinor = 0,
         class tihclass = CComTypeInfoHolder>
class ATL_NO_VTBL IDispatchImpl : public T {...};
```

Given IDispatchImpl, our IPenguin implementation gets quite a bit simpler:

```
class CPenguin :
 public CComObjectRootEx<CComMultiThreadModel>,
 public IBird,
 public ISnappyDresser,
 public IDispatchImpl<IPenguin, &IID_IPenguin> {
public:
BEGIN_COM_MAP(CPenguin)
 COM_INTERFACE_ENTRY(IBird)
 COM_INTERFACE_ENTRY(ISnappyDresser)
 COM_INTERFACE_ENTRY(IDispatch)
 COM_INTERFACE_ENTRY(IPenguin)
END_COM_MAP()
// IBird, ISnappyDresser and IPenguin methods...
};
```

Supporting Multiple Dual Interfaces

I wish it didn't, but this question always comes up: "How do I support multiple dual interfaces in my COM objects?" My answer is always, "Why would you want to?"

The problem is that, of the scripting environments I'm familiar with that require an object to implement IDispatch, not one supports QueryInterface. So, while it's possible to use ATL to implement multiple dual interfaces, you have to choose which implementation to hand out as the "default," that is, the one the client gets when it asks for IDispatch. For example, let's say that instead of having a special IPenguin interface that represented the full functionality of my object to scripting clients, I decided to make *all* the interfaces dual interfaces.

```
[ dual, uuid(...) ] interface IBird : IDispatch {...}
[ dual, uuid(...) ] interface ISnappyDresser : IDispatch { ... };
```

You may implement both of these dual interfaces using ATL's IDispatchImpl:

```
class CPenguin :
    public CComObjectRootEx<CComSingleThreadModel>,
    public IDispatchImpl<IBird, &IID_IBird>,
    public IDispatchImpl<ISnappyDresser, &IID_ISnappyDresser> {
public:
BEGIN_COM_MAP(CPenguin)
 COM_INTERFACE_ENTRY(IBird)
 COM_INTERFACE_ENTRY(ISnappyDresser)
 COM_INTERFACE_ENTRY(IDispatch) // ambiguous
END_COM_MAP()
...
};
```

However, when you fill in the interface map in this way, the compiler gets upset. Remember that the COM_INTERFACE_ENTRY macro essentially boils down to a static_cast to the interface in question. Since there are two different interfaces that derive from IDispatch, the compiler is not able to resolve the one to which you're trying to cast. To resolve this difficulty, ATL provides another macro:

```
#define COM_INTERFACE_ENTRY2(itf, branch)
```

This macro allows us to tell the compiler which branch to follow up the inheritance hierarchy to the IDispatch base. Using this macro allows us to choose the default IDispatch interface:

```
class CPenguin :
    public CComObjectRootEx<CComSingleThreadModel>,
    public IDispatchImpl<IBird, &IID_IBird>,
    public IDispatchImpl<ISnappyDresser, &IID_ISnappyDresser> {
public:
```

```
BEGIN_COM_MAP(CPenguin)
 COM_INTERFACE_ENTRY(IBird)
 COM_INTERFACE_ENTRY(ISnappyDresser)
 COM_INTERFACE_ENTRY2(IDispatch, IBird) // Compiles (unfortunately)
END_COM_MAP()
...
};
```

Which brings me to my objection. Just because ATL and the compiler conspire to allow this usage doesn't mean that it's a good one. *There is no good reason to support multiple dual interfaces on a single implementation.* Any client that supports QueryInterface will not need to use GetIDsOfNames or Invoke. These kinds of clients are perfectly happy using a custom interface as long as it matches their argument type requirements. On the other hands, scripting clients that don't support QueryInterface will only be able to get to methods and properties on the default dual interface. For example, the following will not work:

```
// Since IBird is the default, its operations are available
penguin.fly
// Since ISnappyDresser is not the default, its operations aren't
available
penguin.straightenTie // runtime error
```

So, here's my advice. Don't design your reusable, polymorphic COM interfaces as dual interfaces. Instead, if you're going to support scripting clients, define a single dual interface that exposes the entire functionality of the class, as I did when defining IPenguin in the first place. As an added benefit, this means that you only have to define one interface that supports scripting clients instead of mandating that all of them do.

CComObject et al.

Consider the following C++ class:

```
class CPenguin :
 public CComObjectRootEx<CComMultiThreadModel>,
 public IBird,
 public ISnappyDresser {
public:
BEGIN_COM_MAP(CPenguin)
```

```
 COM_INTERFACE_ENTRY(IBird)
 COM_INTERFACE_ENTRY(ISnappyDresser)
END_COM_MAP()
// IBird and ISnappyDresser methods...
// IUnknown methods not implemented here
};
```

Because this class doesn't implement the methods of IUnknown, the following code will fail at compile time:

```
STDMETHODIMP
CPenguinCO::CreateInstance(IUnknown* pUnkOuter,
                           REFIID riid, void** ppv) {
   ...
   CPenguin* pobj = new CPenguin; // IUnknown not implemented
   ...
}
```

Given CComObjectRootBase, we can easily implement the methods of IUnknown. For example:

```
// Server lifetime management
extern void ServerLock();
extern void ServerUnlock();

class CPenguin :
 public CComObjectRootEx<CComMultiThreadModel>,
 public IBird,
 public ISnappyDresser {
public:
 CPenguin()  { ServerLock(); }
 ~CPenguin() { ServerUnlock(); }
BEGIN_COM_MAP(CPenguin)
 COM_INTERFACE_ENTRY(IBird)
 COM_INTERFACE_ENTRY(ISnappyDresser)
END_COM_MAP()
// IBird and ISnappyDresser methods...
// IUnknown methods for standalone, heap-based objects
 STDMETHODIMP QueryInterface(REFIID riid, void** ppv)
 { return _InternalQueryInterface(riid, ppv); }
```

```
STDMETHODIMP_(ULONG) AddRef()
{ return InternalAddRef(); }

STDMETHODIMP_(ULONG) Release() {
  ULONG l = InternalRelease();
  if( l == 0 ) delete this;
  return cRef;
}
};
```

Unfortunately, although this implementation does leverage the base class behavior, it has hard-coded assumptions about the lifetime and identity of our objects. For example, instances of this class can't be created as an aggregate. Just as we're able to encapsulate decisions about thread safety into the base class, we'd like to encapsulate decisions about lifetime and identity. However, unlike thread-safety decisions, which are made on a per-class basis and are therefore safe to encode into a base class, lifetime and identity decisions can be made on a per-instance basis. Therefore, we'll want to encapsulate lifetime and identity behavior into classes meant to derive from our class.

Standalone Activation

To encapsulate the standalone, heap-based object implementation of IUnknown I just showed you, ATL provides CComObject, shown in a slightly abbreviated form here.

```
template <class Base>
class CComObject : public Base {
public:
 typedef Base _BaseClass;

CComObject(void* = NULL)
{ _Module.Lock(); } // Keeps server loaded

~CComObject() {
  m_dwRef = 1L;
  FinalRelease();
  _Module.Unlock(); // Allows server to unload
}
```

```
STDMETHOD(QueryInterface)(REFIID iid, void ** ppvObject)
{ return _InternalQueryInterface(iid, ppvObject); }

STDMETHOD_(ULONG, AddRef)()
{ return InternalAddRef(); }

STDMETHOD_(ULONG, Release)() {
  ULONG l = InternalRelease();
  if (l == 0) delete this;
  return l;
}

template <class Q>
HRESULT STDMETHODCALLTYPE QueryInterface(Q** pp)
{ return QueryInterface(__uuidof(Q), (void**)pp); }

static HRESULT WINAPI CreateInstance(CComObject<Base>** pp);
};
```

Notice that CComObject takes a template parameter called Base. This is the base class from which CComObject derives to obtain the functionality of CComObjectRootEx as well as whatever custom functionality we'd like to include in our objects. Given the implementation of CPenguin that did not include the implementation of the IUnknown methods, the compiler would be happy with CComObject used as follows (although I'll describe later why new shouldn't be used directly when creating ATL-based COM objects):

```
STDMETHODIMP
CPenguinCO::CreateInstance(IUnknown* pUnkOuter,
                          REFIID riid, void** ppv) {
 *ppv = 0;
 if( pUnkOuter ) return CLASS_E_NOAGGREGATION;
 // Read on for why not to use new like this!
 CComObject<CPenguin>* pobj = new CComObject<CPenguin>;
 if( pobj ) {
  pobj->AddRef();
  HRESULT hr = pobj->QueryInterface(riid, ppv);
  pobj->Release();
```

```
    return hr;
  }
  return E_OUTOFMEMORY;
}
```

Besides the call to `FinalRelease` and the static member function `Create-Instance` (which are both described in the "ATL Creators" section of this chapter), `CComObject` provides one additional item of note, the `QueryInterface` member function template.[6]

```
template <class Q>
HRESULT STDMETHODCALLTYPE QueryInterface(Q** pp)
{ return QueryInterface(__uuidof(Q), (void**)pp); }
```

This member function template uses the new capability of the Visual C++ (VC++) compiler to tag a type with a universally unique identifier (UUID). This capability has been available since VC++ 5.0 and takes the form of a declarative specifier (`declspec`), for example:

```
struct __declspec(uuid("00000000-0000-0000-C000-000000000046")) IUnknown
    {...};
```

These `declspecs` are output by the Microsoft IDL compiler and are available for both standard and custom interfaces. You can retrieve the UUID of a type using the `__uuidof` operator, allowing the following syntax:

```
void TryToFly(IUnknown* punk) {
  IBird* pbird = 0;
  if( SUCCEEDED(punk->QueryInterface(__uuidof(pbird), (void**)&pbird) ){
    pbird->Fly();
    pbird->Release();
  }
}
```

Using the `QueryInterface` member function template provided in `CComObject` allows us a bit more syntactic convenience, given a `CComObject`-based object reference. For example:

---

[6] For a brief description of member function templates, see Appendix A.

```
void TryToFly(CComObject<CPenguin>* pPenguin) {
 IBird* pbird = 0;
 if( SUCCEEDED(pPenguin->QueryInterface(&pbird) ) {
   pbird->Fly();
   pbird->Release();
 }
}
```

Aggregated Activation

Notice that the CPenguin class object implementation shown previously disallowed aggregation by checking for a nonzero pUnkOuter and returning CLASS_E_NOAGGREGATION. If we want to support aggregation as well as, or instead of, standalone activation, we're going to need another class to implement the forwarding behavior of aggregated instances. For this, ATL provides CComAggObject.

CComAggObject performs the chief service of being a controlled inner, that is, providing two implementations of IUnknown. One implementation forwards calls to the controlling outer, subsumed by its lifetime and identity. The other implementation is for private use of the controlling outer for actually maintaining the lifetime of and querying interfaces from the inner. To obtain the two implementations of IUnknown, CComAggObject derives from CComObjectRootEx twice, once directly and once indirectly via a contained instance of your class derived from CComContainedObject, as shown here.

```
template <class contained>
class CComAggObject :
 public IUnknown,
 public CComObjectRootEx<contained::_ThreadModel::ThreadModelNoCS> {
public:
 typedef contained _BaseClass;
 CComAggObject(void* pv) : m_contained(pv)
 { _Module.Lock(); }

 ~CComAggObject() {
   m_dwRef = 1L;
   FinalRelease();
   _Module.Unlock();
 }

 STDMETHOD(QueryInterface)(REFIID iid, void ** ppvObject) {
   HRESULT hRes = S_OK;
```

```
  if (InlineIsEqualUnknown(iid)) {
    if (ppvObject == NULL) return E_POINTER;
    *ppvObject = (void*)(IUnknown*)this;
    AddRef();
  }
  else
    hRes = m_contained._InternalQueryInterface(iid, ppvObject);
  return hRes;
}

STDMETHOD_(ULONG, AddRef)()
{ return InternalAddRef(); }

STDMETHOD_(ULONG, Release)() {
  ULONG l = InternalRelease();
  if (l == 0) delete this;
  return l;
}

template <class Q>
HRESULT STDMETHODCALLTYPE QueryInterface(Q** pp)
{ return QueryInterface(__uuidof(Q), (void**)pp); }

static HRESULT WINAPI CreateInstance(LPUNKNOWN pUnkOuter,
  CComAggObject<contained>** pp);

CComContainedObject<contained> m_contained;
};
```

You can see that instead of deriving from your class (passed as the template argument), CComAggObject derives directly from CComObjectRootEx. Its implementation of QueryInterface relies on the interface map you've built in your class, but its implementations of AddRef and Release rely on the second instance of CComObjectRootBase it gets by deriving from CComObjectRootEx. This second instance of CComObjectRootBase uses the m_dwRef member of the union.

The first instance of CComObjectRootBase, the one that manages the m_pOuterUnknown member of the union, is the one that CComAggObject gets by creating an instance of your class derived from CComContainedObject as the m_contained data member. CComContainedObject implements QueryInterface, AddRef, and Release by delegating to the m_pOuterUnknown passed to the constructor as shown:

```
template <class Base>
class CComContainedObject : public Base {
public:
  typedef Base _BaseClass;
  CComContainedObject(void* pv) { m_pOuterUnknown = (IUnknown*)pv; }

  STDMETHOD(QueryInterface)(REFIID iid, void ** ppvObject) {
    HRESULT hr = OuterQueryInterface(iid, ppvObject);
    if (FAILED(hr) && _GetRawUnknown() != m_pOuterUnknown)
      hr = _InternalQueryInterface(iid, ppvObject);
    return hr;
  }

  STDMETHOD_(ULONG, AddRef)()
  { return OuterAddRef(); }

  STDMETHOD_(ULONG, Release)()
  { return OuterRelease(); }

  template <class Q>
  HRESULT STDMETHODCALLTYPE QueryInterface(Q** pp)
  { return QueryInterface(__uuidof(Q), (void**)pp); }

  IUnknown* GetControllingUnknown()
  { return m_pOuterUnknown; }
};
```

Being the Controlled Inner

Using CComAggObject and its two implementations of IUnknown, our CPenguin class object implementation can support either standalone or aggregation activation without touching the CPenguin source:

```
STDMETHODIMP
CPenguinCO::CreateInstance(IUnknown* pUnkOuter,
                           REFIID riid, void** ppv) {
  *ppv = 0;
  if( pUnkOuter ) {
    CComAggObject<CPenguin>* pobj =
```

```
                  new CComAggObject<CPenguin>(pUnkOuter);
      ...
   }
   else {
      CComObject<CPenguin>* pobj = new CComObject<CPenguin>;
      ...
   }
}
```

This usage provides the most efficient runtime decision making. When the object is standalone, it pays the price of one reference count and one implementation of IUnknown. When it is aggregated, it pays the price of one reference count, one pointer to the controlling outer, and two implementations of IUnknown. However, one additional price we're paying is one extra set of vtbls. By using both CComAggObject<CPenguin> and CComObject<CPenguin>, we've created two classes and therefore two sets of vtbls.

When you have a small number of instances or nearly all your instances are aggregated, you may want a single class that can handle both aggregated and standalone activation, thereby eliminating one set of vtbls. You do this by using CComPolyObject in place of both CComObject and CComAggObject, like so:

```
STDMETHODIMP
CPenguinCO::CreateInstance(IUnknown* pUnkOuter,
                           REFIID riid, void** ppv) {
  *ppv = 0;
  CComPolyObject<CPenguin>* pobj =
    new CComPolyObject<CPenguin>(pUnkOuter);
  ...
}
```

CComPolyObject is nearly identical to CComAggObject, except that in its constructor, if the pUnkOuter is zero, it will use its second implementation of IUnknown as the outer for the first to forward to, as shown:

```
class CComPolyObject :
  public IUnknown,
  public CComObjectRootEx<contained::_ThreadModel::ThreadModelNoCS> {
public:
  ...
  CComPolyObject(void* pv) : m_contained(pv ? pv : this) {...}
  ...
};
```

The use of CComPolyObject saves a set of vtbls, so the module size is smaller, but the price you pay for standalone objects is getting an extra implementation of IUnknown as well as an extra pointer to that implementation.

Alternative Activation Techniques

Besides standalone operation, CComObject makes certain assumptions about where the object's memory has been allocated from (the heap) and whether the existence of the object should keep the server loaded (it does). For other needs, ATL provides four more classes meant to be the most derived class in your implementation hierarchy: CComObjectCached, CComObjectNoLock, CComObjectGlobal, and CComObjectStack.

CComObjectCached

CComObjectCached objects implement reference counting with the assumption that you're going to create an instance and then hold it for the life of the server, handing out references to it as requested. To avoid keeping the server running forever after the cached instance is created, the boundary for keeping the server running is a reference count of 1, although the lifetime of the object is still managed on a boundary of 0, like so:

```
template <class Base>
class CComObjectCached : public Base {
public:
  ...
  STDMETHOD_(ULONG, AddRef)() {
    m_csCached.Lock();
    ULONG l = InternalAddRef();
    if (m_dwRef == 2) _Module.Lock();
    m_csCached.Unlock();
    return l;
  }
  STDMETHOD_(ULONG, Release)() {
    m_csCached.Lock();
    InternalRelease();
    ULONG l = m_dwRef;
    m_csCached.Unlock();
    if (l == 0) delete this;
    else if (l == 1) _Module.Unlock();
    return l;
  }
}
```

```
...
CComGlobalsThreadModel::AutoCriticalSection m_csCached;
};
```

Cached objects are useful for in-process class objects:

```
static CComObjectCached<CPenguinCO>* g_pPenguinCO = 0;

BOOL WINAPI DllMain(HINSTANCE, DWORD dwReason, void*) {
  switch( dwReason ) {
  case DLL_PROCESS_ATTACH:
    g_pPenguinCO = new CComObjectCached<CPenguinCO>;

    // 1st ref. doesn't keep server alive
    if( g_pPenguinCO ) g_pPenguinCO->AddRef();
  break;

  case DLL_PROCESS_DETACH:
    if( g_pPenguinCO ) g_pPenguinCO->Release();
  break;
  }
  return TRUE;
}

STDAPI DllGetClassObject(REFCLSID clsid, REFIID riid, void** ppv) {
  // Subsequent references do keep server alive
  if( clsid == CLSID_Penguin && g_pPenguinCO )
    return g_pPenguinCO->QueryInterface(riid, ppv);
  return CLASS_E_CLASSNOTAVAILABLE;
}
```

CComObjectNoLock

Sometimes you don't want outstanding references on your object to keep the server alive at all. For example, class objects in an out-of-process server are cached in a table maintained in ole32.dll *some number of times* (not necessarily just one time). For this reason, COM itself manages how the lifetime of a class object affects the lifetime of its out-of-process server using the LockServer method of the IClassFactory interface. For this usage, ATL provides CComObjectNoLock, whose implementation does not affect the lifetime of the server.

```
template <class Base>
class CComObjectNoLock : public Base {
public:
 ...
 STDMETHOD_(ULONG, AddRef)()
 { return InternalAddRef(); }

 STDMETHOD_(ULONG, Release)() {
   ULONG l = InternalRelease();
   if (l == 0) delete this;
   return l;
 }
 ...
};
```

No-lock objects are useful for out-of-process class objects:

```
int WINAPI WinMain(HINSTANCE, HINSTANCE, LPSTR, int) {
  CoInitialize(0);

  CComObjectNoLock<CPenguinCO>* pPenguinCO =
    new CComObjectNoLock<CPenguinCO>;
  if( !pPenguinCO ) return E_OUTOFMEMORY;
  pPenguinCO->AddRef();

  DWORD   dwReg;
  HRESULT hr;

  // Reference(s) cached by ole32.dll
  // won't keep server from shutting down
  hr = CoRegisterClassObject(CLSID_Penguin, pPenguinCO, ..., &dwReg);
  if( SUCCEEDED(hr) ) {
    MSG msg; while( GetMessage(&msg, 0, 0, 0) ) DispatchMessage(&msg);
    CoRevokeClassObject(dwReg);
    pPenguinCO->Release();
  }

  CoUninitialize();
  return hr;
}
```

CComObjectGlobal

Just as it's handy to have an object whose existence or outstanding references don't keep the server alive, sometimes it's handy to have an object whose lifetime matches that of the server. For example, a global or static object is constructed once when the server is loaded and is not destroyed until after `WinMain` or `DllMain` has completed. Clearly, the mere existence of a global object cannot keep the server running or the server would never be able to shut down. On the other hand, we'd like to be able to keep the server running if there are outstanding references to a global object. For this, we have `CComObjectGlobal`.

```
template <class Base>
class CComObjectGlobal : public Base {
public:
  ...
  STDMETHOD_(ULONG, AddRef)()  { return _Module.Lock(); }
  STDMETHOD_(ULONG, Release)() { return _Module.Unlock(); }
  ...
};
```

Global objects could be used instead of cached objects for implementing in-process class objects, but they're useful for any global or static object:

```
// No references yet, so server not forced to stay alive
static CComObjectGlobal<CPenguinCO> g_penguinCO;

STDAPI DllGetClassObject(REFCLSID clsid, REFIID riid, void** ppv) {
  // All references keep the server alive
  if( clsid == CLSID_Penguin )
    return g_penguinCO.QueryInterface(riid, ppv);
  return CLASS_E_CLASSNOTAVAILABLE;
}
```

Notice that the global object usage is simpler than the cached object because we're relying on the C runtime library to properly construct and destroy our object. Automatic construction and destruction of global and static objects requires linking with the CRT, however—something that is often avoided when building ATL-based COM servers (as discussed in Chapter 4).

CComObjectStack

Instead of using a global or static object, you may find yourself with the urge to allocate a COM object on the stack. ATL supports this technique with CComObject-Stack.

```
template <class Base>
class CComObjectStack : public Base {
public:
  ...
  STDMETHOD_(ULONG, AddRef)()
  { ATLASSERT(FALSE); return 0; }

  STDMETHOD_(ULONG, Release)()
  { ATLASSERT(FALSE); return 0; }

  STDMETHOD(QueryInterface)(REFIID iid, void** ppvObject)
  { ATLASSERT(FALSE); return E_NOINTERFACE; }
  ...
};
```

Based on the implementation, it should be pretty clear you're no longer doing COM. CComObjectStack will shut the compiler up, but you still cannot use any of the methods of IUnknown, which means you cannot pass out an interface reference from an object on the stack. This is good, because like a reference to anything on the stack, as soon as the stack goes away, the reference points at garbage. The nice thing about ATL's implementation of CComObjectStack is that it will warn you at runtime (in a debug build) that you're doing something bad. For example:

```
void DoABadThing(IBird** ppbird) {
  CComObjectStack<CPenguin> penguin;
  penguin.Fly();          // Using IBird method is OK
  penguin.StraightenTie(); // Using ISnappyDresser method also OK

  // This will trigger an assert at runtime
  penguin.QueryInterface(IID_IBird, (void**)ppbird);
}
```

One from Column A, Two from Column B...

Table 3.2 shows the various identity and lifetime options ATL provides.

Table 3.2. ATL's Identity and Lifetime Options

Class	Standalone or aggregated	Heap or stack	Existence keeps server alive	Extent refs keep server alive
CcomObject	Standalone	Heap	Yes	Yes
CcomAggObject	Aggregated	Heap	Yes	Yes
CcomPolyObject	Standalone or aggregated	Heap	Yes	Yes
CcomObjectCached	Standalone	Heap	No	Second reference
CcomObjectNoLock	Standalone	Heap	No	No
CcomObjectGlobal	Standalone	Data segment	No	Yes
CcomObjectStack	Standalone	Stack	No	No

ATL Creators

Multiphase Construction

As I've mentioned (and as you'll hear more about in Chapter 4), ATL servers don't often link with the CRT. However, living without the CRT can be a pain. Among other things, if we don't have the CRT, we also don't get C++ exceptions. That doesn't leave us much to do in the following scenario:

```
// CPenguin constructor
CPenguin::CPenguin() {
 HRESULT hr = CoCreateInstance(CLSID_EarthAtmosphere, 0, CLSCTX_ALL,
                          IID_IAir, (void**)&m_pAir);
 if( FAILED(hr) ) {
   return hr; // Can't return an error from a ctor
   throw hr;  // Can't throw an error without the CRT
   // This won't help much
   OutputDebugString(__T("Help! Can't bre...\n"));
 }
}
```

The OutputDebugString isn't going to notify the client that the object it just created doesn't have the resources it needs to survive; that is, there's no way to return the failure result back to the client. This hardly seems fair since the IClassFactory method CreateInstance that's creating our objects certainly can return an HRESULT. The problem is having a way to hand a failure from the instance to the class object so that it can be returned to the client. By convention, ATL classes provide a public member function called FinalConstruct for objects to participate in multiphase construction:

```
HRESULT FinalConstruct();
```

An empty implementation of the FinalConstruct member function is provided in CComObjectRootBase, so all ATL objects have one. Because FinalConstruct returns an HRESULT, now we have a nice clean way to obtain the result of any nontrivial construction.

```
HRESULT CPenguin::FinalConstruct() {
  return CoCreateInstance(CLSID_EarthAtmosphere, 0, CLSCTX_ALL,
                          IID_IAir, (void**)&m_pAir);
}


STDMETHODIMP
CPenguinCO::CreateInstance(IUnknown* pUnkOuter,
                              REFIID riid, void** ppv) {
  *ppv = 0;
  if( !pUnkOuter ) {
    CComObject<CPenguin>* pobj = new CComObject<CPenguin>;
    if( FAILED(hr) ) return E_OUTOFMEMORY;
    hr = pobj->FinalConstruct();
    if( SUCCEEDED(hr) ) ...
    return hr;
  }
  ...
}
```

We do have something else to consider, though. Notice that when CreateInstance calls FinalConstruct, it has not yet increased the reference count of the object. This causes a problem if, during the FinalConstruct implementation, the object handed a reference to itself to another object. If you think this

uncommon, remember the pUnkOuter parameter to the IClassFactory method
CreateInstance. However, even without aggregation, it's possible to run into this
problem. Imagine the following somewhat contrived, but perfectly legal, code:

```
// CPenguin implementation
HRESULT CPenguin::FinalConstruct() {
  HRESULT hr;
  hr = CoCreateInstance(CLSID_EarthAtmosphere, 0, CLSCTX_ALL,
                        IID_IAir, (void**)&m_pAir);
  if( SUCCEEDED(hr) ) {
    // Pass reference to object with reference count of 0
    hr = m_pAir->CheckSuitability(GetUnknown());
  }
  return hr;
}


// CEarthAtmosphere implementation in separate server
STDMETHODIMP CEarthAtmosphere::CheckSuitability(IUnknown* punk) {
  IBreatheO2* pbo2 = 0;
  HRESULT     hr = E_FAIL;

  // CPenguin's lifetime increased to 1 via QI
  hr = punk->QueryInterface(IID_IBreatheO2, (void**)&pbo2);
  if( SUCCEEDED(hr) ) {
    pbo2->Release(); // During this call, lifetime decreases to 0 and
                     // destruction sequence begins...
  }

  return (SUCCEEDED(hr) ? S_OK : E_FAIL);
}
```

To avoid the problem of premature destruction, we need to artificially increase
the object's reference count before FinalConstruct is called and then decrease
its reference count afterward, like so:

```
STDMETHODIMP
CPenguinCO::CreateInstance(IUnknown* pUnkOuter,
                           REFIID riid, void** ppv) {
  *ppv = 0;
  if( !pUnkOuter ) {
```

```
        CComObject<CPenguin>* pobj = new CComObject<CPenguin>;
        if( FAILED(hr) ) return E_OUTOFMEMORY;

        // Protect object from premature destruction
        pobj->InternalAddRef();
        hr = pobj->FinalConstruct();
        pobj->InternalRelease();

      if( SUCCEEDED(hr) ) ...
      return hr;
    }
    ...
  }
```

Just Enough Reference Count Safety

Arguably, not all objects need their reference count artificially managed in the way I've just described. In fact, for multithreaded objects that don't require this kind of protection, extra calls to InterlockedIncrement and InterlockedDecrement represent unnecessary overhead. Toward that end, CComObjectRootBase provides a pair of functions just for bracketing the call to FinalConstruct in a just-reference-count-safe-enough way:

```
    STDMETHODIMP
    CPenguinCO::CreateInstance(IUnknown* pUnkOuter,
                               REFIID riid, void** ppv) {
      *ppv = 0;
      if( !pUnkOuter ) {
        CComObject<CPenguin>* pobj = new CComObject<CPenguin>;
        if( FAILED(hr) ) return E_OUTOFMEMORY;

        // Protect object from premature destruction (maybe)
        pobj->InternalFinalConstructAddRef();
        hr = pobj->FinalConstruct();
        pobj->InternalFinalConstructRelease();

      if( SUCCEEDED(hr) ) ...
      return hr;
    }
    ...
  }
```

By default, `InternalFinalConstructAddRef` and `InternalFinalConstructRelease` incur no release-build runtime overhead.

```
class CComObjectRootBase {
public:
  ...
  void InternalFinalConstructAddRef() {}
  void InternalFinalConstructRelease() { ATLASSERT(m_dwRef == 0); }
  ...
};
```

To change the implementation of `InternalFinalConstructAddRef` and `InternalFinalConstructRelease` to provide reference count safety, ATL provides the following macro:

```
#define DECLARE_PROTECT_FINAL_CONSTRUCT() \
  void InternalFinalConstructAddRef() { InternalAddRef(); } \
  void InternalFinalConstructRelease() { InternalRelease(); }
```

The DECLARE_PROTECT_FINAL_CONSTRUCT macro is used on a per-class basis to turn on reference count safety as required. Our `CPenguin` would use it thusly:

```
class CPenguin : ... {
public:
  HRESULT FinalConstruct();
  DECLARE_PROTECT_FINAL_CONSTRUCT()
  ...
};
```

In my opinion, DECLARE_PROTECT_FINAL_CONSTRUCT is one ATL optimization too many. Using it requires not only a great deal of COM and ATL internals knowledge, but also a great deal of knowledge of the implementation of the objects we create in our `FinalConstruct` methods. Because we often don't have that knowledge, the only safe thing to do is to always use DECLARE_PROTECT_FINAL_CONSTRUCT if we're handing out references to our instances in our `FinalConstruct` calls. And since that rule is too complicated, I imagine most folks will forget it. So, I'll give you a simpler one:

Wherever you have a `FinalConstruct` *member function, you should also have a* DECLARE_PROTECT_FINAL_CONSTRUCT *macro instantiation.*

Luckily, the wizard will generate DECLARE_PROTECT_FINAL_CONSTRUCT when it generates a new class, so your FinalConstruct code will be safe by default. If you decide you don't want it, you may remove it.[7]

Another Reason for Multiphase Construction

Imagine a plain-vanilla C++ class that wishes to call a virtual member function during its construction and another C++ class that overrides that function:

```
class Base {
public:
 Base() { Init(); }
 virtual void Init() {}
};

class Derived : public Base {
public:
 virtual void Init() {}
};
```

Because it's fairly uncommon to call virtual member functions as part of the construction sequence, it's not widely known that the Init function during the construction for Base will not be Derived::Init, but Base::Init. While this may seem counterintuitive, the reason it works this way is a good one: It doesn't make sense to call a virtual member function in a derived class until the derived class has been properly constructed. However, the derived class won't be properly constructed until after the base class has been constructed. To make sure that only functions of properly constructed classes are called during construction, the C++ compiler will lay out two vtbls, one for Base and one for Derived. The C++ runtime library will then adjust the vptr to point to the appropriate vtbl during the construction sequence.

While this is all part of the official C++ standard, it's not exactly intuitive, especially because it is so rarely used (or maybe it's so rarely used because it's unintuitive). Because it's rarely used, Microsoft introduced __declspec(novtbl) in Visual C++ 5.0 to turn off the adjustment of vptrs during construction. When the base class is an abstract base class, this will often result in vtbls that are generated by the compiler but not used, so the linker can remove them from the final image.

---

[7] As my friend Tim Ewald always said, "Subtractive coding is easier than additive coding."

This optimization is used in ATL whenever a class is declared using the ATL_NO_VTBL macro:

```
#ifdef _ATL_DISABLE_NO_VTBL
#define ATL_NO_VTBL
#else
#define ATL_NO_VTBL __declspec(novtbl)
#endif
```

Unless the _ATL_DISABLE_NO_VTBL is defined, a class defined using _ATL_NO_VTBL will have its constructor behavior adjusted with __declspec(novtbl):

```
class ATL_NO_VTBL CPenguin ... {};
```

While this is a good and true optimization, classes that use it must not call virtual member functions in their constructors.[8] Rather than calling virtual member functions during construction, call them in FinalConstruct, which ATL calls after the most derived class's constructor executes and after the compiler adjusts the vptrs to the correct values.

There is one last thing to mention about __declspec(novtbl). Just as it turns off adjustment of vptrs during construction, so does it turn off adjustment of vptrs during destruction. Therefore, avoid calling virtual functions in the destruction as well; instead, call them in the object's FinalRelease member function.

FinalRelease

ATL will call the object's FinalRelease function after the object's final interface reference is released and before your ATL-based object's destructor is called:

```
void FinalRelease();
```

The FinalRelease member function is useful for calling virtual member functions and when releasing interfaces to another object that also has pointers back to you. Because that other object may wish to query for an interface during its shutdown sequence, it's just as important to protect the object against double destruction as it was to protect against premature destruction in FinalConstruct. Even though the FinalRelease member function will be called after the object's reference

---

[8]Strictly speaking, the compiler will statically bind to virtual calls made in the constructor or the destructor, but if a statically bound function calls a dynamically bound function, you're still in big trouble.

count has been decreased to 0 (which is why the object is being destroyed), the caller of FinalRelease will artificially set the reference count to 1 to avoid double deletion. The caller of FinalRelease will be the destructor of the most derived class. For example:

```
CComObject::~CComObject() {
  m_dwRef = 1L;
  FinalRelease();
  _Module.Unlock();
}
```

ATL Creators

Because the extra steps to manage the multiphase construction process are easy to forget, ATL encapsulates this algorithm into several C++ classes called creators, each of which performs the appropriate multiphase construction. Each creator class is really just a way to wrap a scope around a single static member function called CreateInstance:

```
static HRESULT WINAPI CreateInstance(void* pv,
                                     REFIID riid, LPVOID* ppv);
```

The name of the creator class is used in a type definition associated with the class, as I'll discuss later.

CComCreator

CComCreator is a creator that creates either standalone or aggregated instances and is parameterized by the C++ class being created, for example, CCom-Object<CPenguin>. CComCreator is declared as follows:

```
template <class T1> class CComCreator {
public:
  static HRESULT WINAPI CreateInstance(void* pv,
                                       REFIID riid, LPVOID* ppv) {
    ATLASSERT(*ppv == NULL);
    HRESULT hRes = E_OUTOFMEMORY;
    T1* p = NULL;
    ATLTRY(p = new T1(pv))
    if (p != NULL) {
      p->SetVoid(pv);
```

```
    p->InternalFinalConstructAddRef();
    hRes = p->FinalConstruct();
    p->InternalFinalConstructRelease();
    if (hRes == S_OK) hRes = p->QueryInterface(riid, ppv);
    if (hRes != S_OK) delete p;
  }
  return hRes;
 }
};
```

Using CComCreator simplifies our class object implementation quite a bit:

```
STDMETHODIMP
CPenguinCO::CreateInstance(IUnknown* pUnkOuter,
                          REFIID riid, void** ppv) {
  typedef CComCreator< CComPolyObject<CPenguin> > PenguinPolyCreator;
  return PenguinPolyCreator::CreateInstance(pUnkOuter, riid, ppv);
}
```

Notice the use of the type definition to define a new creator type. If we were to create penguins other places in our server, we'd have to rebuild the type definition. For example:

```
STDMETHODIMP CAviary::CreatePenguin(IBird** ppbird) {
  typedef CComCreator< CComObject<CPenguin> > PenguinCreator;
  return PenguinCreator::CreateInstance(0, IID_IBird, (void**)ppbird);
}
```

Defining a creator like this outside of the class being created has two problems. First, it duplicates the type definition code. Second, and more important, we've taken away the right of the CPenguin class to decide for itself whether it wants to support aggregation or not, since the type definition is making this decision now. By convention in ATL, to reduce code and to let the class designer make the decision about standalone versus aggregate activation, we place the type definition inside the class declaration and give it the well-known name _CreatorClass:

```
class CPenguin : ... {
public:
  ...
```

```
    typedef CComCreator< CComPolyObject<CPenguin> > _CreatorClass;
};
```

Using the creator type definition, creating an instance and obtaining an initial interface actually takes fewer lines of code than when using operator new and Query-Interface:

```
STDMETHODIMP CAviary::CreatePenguin(IBird** ppbird) {
    return CPenguin::_CreatorClass::CreateInstance(0,
                                                   IID_IBird,
                                                   (void**)ppbird);
}
```

In Chapter 4, I'll discuss one other base class that your class will often derive from: CComCoClass. For example:

```
class CPenguin : ..., public CComCoClass<CPenguin, &CLSID_Penguin>, ...
    {...};
```

CComCoClass provides two static member functions, each called CreateInstance, that make use of the class's creators like so:

```
template <class T, const CLSID* pclsid = &CLSID_NULL>
class CComCoClass {
public:
  ...
  template <class Q>
  static HRESULT CreateInstance(IUnknown* punkOuter, Q** pp)
  {
    return T::_CreatorClass::CreateInstance(punkOuter, __uuidof(Q),
                                            (void**) pp);
  }

  template <class Q>
  static HRESULT CreateInstance(Q** pp)
  {
    return T::_CreatorClass::CreateInstance(NULL, __uuidof(Q),
                                            (void**) pp);
  }
};
```

This simplifies our creation code still further:

```
STDMETHODIMP CAviary::CreatePenguin(IBird** ppbird) {
  return CPenguin::CreateInstance(ppbird);
}
```

CComCreator2

It may be that we'd like to support both standalone and aggregate activation using CComObject and CComAggObject instead of CComPolyObject because of the overhead associated with CComPolyObject in the standalone case. To avoid putting the logic of choosing the appropriate creator back into the class object's CreateInstance method based on whether we have a NULL pUnkOuter or not, ATL provides CComCreator2:

```
template <class T1, class T2> class CComCreator2 {
public:
  static HRESULT WINAPI CreateInstance(void* pv,
                                       REFIID riid, LPVOID* ppv) {
    ATLASSERT(*ppv == NULL);
    return (pv == NULL) ? T1::CreateInstance(NULL, riid, ppv)
                        : T2::CreateInstance(pv, riid, ppv);
  }
};
```

Notice that CComCreator2 is parameterized by the types of two other creators. All CComCreator2 does is check for a NULL pUnkOuter and forward the call to one of two other creators. So, if we'd like to use CComObject and CComAggObject instead of CComPolyObject, we can do so like this:

```
class CPenguin : ... {
public:
  ...
  typedef CComCreator2< CComCreator< CComObject<CPenguin> >,
                        CComCreator< CComAggObject<CPenguin> > >
          _CreatorClass;
};
```

Of course, the beauty of this scheme is that, because all the creators have the same function, CreateInstance, and are exposed via a type definition of the same name, _CreatorClass, none of the server code that creates penguins needs to change if the designer of the class changes his or her mind about how penguins should be created.

CComFailCreator

One of the changes we may want to make to our creation scheme is to support either standalone or aggregate activation only, not both. To make this happen, we need a special creator to return an error code to use in place of one of the creators passed as template arguments to CComCreator2. That's what CComFailCreator is for:

```
template <HRESULT hr> class CComFailCreator {
public:
 static HRESULT WINAPI CreateInstance(void*, REFIID, LPVOID*)
    { return hr; }
};
```

If we'd like standalone activation only, we can use CComFailCreator like this:

```
class CPenguin : ... {
public:
  ...
  typedef CComCreator2< CComCreator< CComObject<CPenguin> >,
                    CComFailCreator<CLASS_E_NOAGGREGATION> >
         _CreatorClass;

  };
```

If we'd like aggregate activation only, we can use CComFailCreator like this:

```
class CPenguin : ... {
public:
  ...
  typedef CComCreator2< CComFailCreator<E_FAIL>,
                    CComCreator< CComAggObject<CPenguin> > >
         _CreatorClass;
};
```

Convenience Macros

As a convenience, ATL provides the following macros in place of manually specifying the _CreatorClass type definition for each class.

```
#define DECLARE_POLY_AGGREGATABLE(x) public:\
 typedef CComCreator< CComPolyObject< x > > _CreatorClass;

#define DECLARE_AGGREGATABLE(x) public:\
 typedef CComCreator2< CComCreator< CComObject< x > >,
                       CComCreator< CComAggObject< x > > >
        _CreatorClass;

#define DECLARE_NOT_AGGREGATABLE(x) public:\
 typedef CComCreator2< CComCreator< CComObject< x > >,
                       CComFailCreator<CLASS_E_NOAGGREGATION> >
        _CreatorClass;

#define DECLARE_ONLY_AGGREGATABLE(x) public:\
 typedef CComCreator2< CComFailCreator<E_FAIL>,
                       CComCreator< CComAggObject< x > > >
        _CreatorClass;
```

Using these macros, I can declare that CPenguin may be activated both standalone and aggregated as follows:

```
class CPenguin : ... {
public:
  ...
  DECLARE_AGGREGATABLE(CPenguin)
};
```

Table 3.3 summarizes the classes that the creators use to derive from your class.

Table 3.3. Creator Type Definition Macros

Macro	Standalone	Aggregation
DECLARE_AGGREGATABLE	CComObject	CComAggObject
DECLARE_NOT_AGGREGATABLE	CComObject	N/A
DECLARE_ONLY_AGGREGATABLE	N/A	CComAggObject
DECLARE_POLY_AGGREGATABLE	CComPolyObject	CComPolyObject

Private Initialization

Creators are handy because they follow the multiphase construction sequence used by ATL-based objects. However, creators only return an interface pointer, not a pointer to the implementing class (that is, `IBird*` instead of `CPenguin*`). This can be a problem if the class exposes public member functions or member data that is not available via a COM interface. Your first instinct as a former C programmer may be to simply cast the resultant interface pointer to the type you'd like:

```
STDMETHODIMP
CAviary::CreatePenguin(BSTR bstrName, long nWingspan, IBird** ppbird) {
 HRESULT hr;
 hr = CPenguin::_CreatorClass::CreateInstance(0,
                                              IID_IBird,
                                              (void**)ppbird);
 if( SUCCEEDED(hr) ) {
    CPenguin* pPenguin = (CPenguin*)(*ppbird); // Resist this instinct!
    pPenguin->Init(bstrName, nWingspan);
 }
 return hr;
}
```

Unfortunately, because `QueryInterface` allows interfaces of a single COM identity to be implemented on multiple C++ objects or even multiple COM objects, in many cases a cast won't work. Instead, you should use the `CreateInstance` static member functions of `CComObject`, `CComAggObject`, and `CComPolyObject`:

```
static HRESULT WINAPI
CComObject::CreateInstance(CComObject<Base>** pp);


static HRESULT WINAPI
CComAggObject::CreateInstance(IUnknown* puo,
                             CComAggObject<contained>** pp);


static HRESULT WINAPI
CComPolyObject::CreateInstance(IUnknown* puo,
                              CComPolyObject<contained>** pp);
```

These static member functions do not make creators out of `CComObject`, `CComAggObject`, or `CComPolyObject`, but they each perform the additional work required to call the object's `FinalConstruct` member function. The reason to use them, however, is that each of them returns a pointer to the most derived class. For example:

```
STDMETHODIMP
CAviary::CreatePenguin(BSTR bstrName, long nWingspan, IBird** ppbird) {
  HRESULT hr;
  CComObject<CPenguin>* pPenguin = 0;
  hr = CComObject<CPenguin>::CreateInstance(&pPenguin);
  if( SUCCEEDED(hr) ) {
    pPenguin->AddRef();
    pPenguin->Init(bstrName, nWingspan);
    hr = pPenguin->QueryInterface(IID_IBird, (void**)ppbird);
    pPenguin->Release();
  }
  return hr;
}
```

The class you use for creation in this manner depends on the kind of activation you want. For standalone activation, use `CComObject::CreateInstance`. For aggregated activation, use `CComAggObject::CreateInstance`. For either standalone or aggregated activation that saves a set of vtbls at the expense of per-instance overhead, use `CComPolyObject::CreateInstance`.

Multiphase Construction on the Stack

When creating an instance of an ATL-based COM object, you should always use a creator (or the static `CreateInstance` member function of `CComObject` and friends) instead of the C++ operator `new`. However, if you have a global or a static object or an object that's allocated on the stack, you can't use a creator, because you're not calling `new`. As I discussed earlier, ATL provides two classes for creating instances that are not from the heap: `CComObjectGlobal` and `CComObjectStack`. However, instead of requiring you to call `FinalConstruct` (and `FinalRelease`) manually, both these classes will perform the proper initialization and shutdown in their constructors and destructors, as shown here in `CComObjectGlobal`.

```
template <class Base>
class CComObjectGlobal : public Base {
public:
  typedef Base _BaseClass;
```

```
   CComObjectGlobal(void* = NULL)
   { m_hResFinalConstruct = FinalConstruct(); }

   ~CComObjectGlobal()
   { FinalRelease(); }
   ...
   HRESULT m_hResFinalConstruct;
};
```

Because there is no return code from a constructor, if you're interested in the result from FinalConstruct, you must check the cached result in the public member variable m_hResFinalConstruct.

Debugging

ATL provides a number of helpful debugging facilities, including both a normal and a categorized wrapper for producing debug output, a macro for making assertions, and debug output for tracing calls to QueryInterface, AddRef, and Release on an interface-by-interface basis. Of course, during a release build, all these debugging facilities fall away to produce the smallest, fastest binary image possible.

Making Assertions

Potentially the best debugging technique is the use of assertions. Assertions allow you to make assumptions in your code and to be notified immediately when those assumptions are invalidated. While ATL doesn't exactly support assertions, it does provide the ATLASSERT macro. However, it's really just another name for the Microsoft CRT macro _ASSERTE.

```
#ifndef ATLASSERT
#define ATLASSERT(expr) _ASSERTE(expr)
#endif
```

Flexible Debug Output

OutputDebugString is handy as the Win32 equivalent of printf, but it only takes a single string argument. What we want is a printf that outputs to debug output instead of standard output, and that's what AtlTrace is for:

```
void AtlTrace(LPCTSTR lpszFormat, ...);
```

However, instead of using `AtlTrace` directly, ATL provides ATLTRACE, a macro that either expands to a call to `AtlTrace` or expands to nothing, depending on whether the _DEBUG symbol is defined or not. Typical usage is as follows:

```
HRESULT CPenguin::FinalConstruct() {
  ATLTRACE(__T("%d+%d= %d\n"), 2, 2, 2+2);
}
```

If you'd like to be even more selective about what makes it to debug output, ATL provides a second trace function, `AtlTrace2`, also with its own macro, ATL-TRACE2.

```
void AtlTrace2(DWORD category, UINT level, LPCTSTR lpszFormat, ...);
```

In addition to the format string and the variable arguments, `AtlTrace2` takes a trace category and a trace level. The trace category is one or more of the following:

```
enum atlTraceFlags {
// Application-defined categories
atlTraceUser        = 0x00000001,
atlTraceUser2       = 0x00000002,
atlTraceUser3       = 0x00000004,
atlTraceUser4       = 0x00000008,

// ATL-defined categories
atlTraceGeneral     = 0x00000020,
atlTraceCOM         = 0x00000040,
atlTraceQI          = 0x00000080,
atlTraceRegistrar   = 0x00000100,
atlTraceRefcount    = 0x00000200,
atlTraceWindowing   = 0x00000400,
atlTraceControls    = 0x00000800,
atlTraceHosting     = 0x00001000,
atlTraceDBClient    = 0x00002000,
atlTraceDBProvider  = 0x00004000,
atlTraceSnapin      = 0x00008000,
atlTraceNotImpl     = 0x00010000,
};
```

The trace level is a measure of severity, with 0 the most severe. ATL itself uses only levels 0 and 2, and the documentation recommends that you stay between 0 and 4, but you can use any level up to 4,294,967,295 (although that may be a little too fine-grained to be useful). AtlTrace2 matches the category and the level against server-wide definitions of ATL_TRACE_CATEGORY and ATL_TRACE_LEVEL:

```
void AtlTrace2(DWORD category, UINT level, LPCWSTR lpszFormat, ...) {
  if (category & ATL_TRACE_CATEGORY && level <= ATL_TRACE_LEVEL) {
    ... // ouput code removed for brevity
  }
}
```

If ATL finds ATL_TRACE_CATEGORY or ATL_TRACE_LEVEL undefined, it will provide its own defaults:

```
#ifndef ATL_TRACE_CATEGORY
#define ATL_TRACE_CATEGORY 0xFFFFFFFF   // Output all categories
#endif

#ifndef ATL_TRACE_LEVEL
#define ATL_TRACE_LEVEL 0               // Output most severe only
#endif
```

Typical usage allows fine-grained control of debug output:

```
STDMETHODIMP CPenguin::Fly() {
  ATLTRACE2(atlTraceUser,   2, _T("IBird::Fly\n"));
  ATLTRACE2(atlTraceUser,  42, _T("Hmmm... Penguins can't fly...\n"));
  ATLTRACE2(atlTraceNotImpl, 0, _T("IBird::Fly not implemented!\n"));
  return E_NOTIMPL;
}
```

In fact, because ATL uses the category atlTraceNotImpl so often, there's even a special macro for it:

```
#define ATLTRACENOTIMPL(funcname) \
 ATLTRACE2(atlTraceNotImpl, 2, _T("ATL: %s not implemented.\n"), \
   funcname); \
 return E_NOTIMPL
```

This macro is used a lot in the implementations of the OLE interfaces:

```
STDMETHOD(SetMoniker)(DWORD, IMoniker*) {
  ATLTRACENOTIMPL(_T("IOleObjectImpl::SetMoniker"));
}
```

When you're interested in the interaction between the client and your object's implementation of standard interfaces, you will want to define ATL_TRACE_LEVEL to 2 before compiling. ATL's interface implementation classes make heavy use of level 2 to provide tracing of individual method calls.

Tracing Calls to QueryInterface

ATL's implementation of QueryInterface is especially well instrumented for debugging. When you define the _ATL_DEBUG_QI symbol before compiling, your objects will output their class name, the interface being queried for (by name,[9] if available), and whether the query succeeded or failed. This is extremely useful for reverse engineering clients' interface requirements. For example, here's a sample of the _ATL_DEBUG_QI output when hosting a control in Internet Explorer (IE) 4:

```
CComClassFactory - IUnknown
CComClassFactory - IClassFactory
CPenguin - IUnknown
CPenguin - IOleControl
CPenguin - IClientSecurity - failed
CPenguin - IQuickActivate - failed
CPenguin - IOleObject
CPenguin - IOleObject
CPenguin - IPersistPropertyBag2 - failed
CPenguin - IPersistPropertyBag - failed
CPenguin - IPersistStreamInit
CPenguin - IID_IViewObjectEx
CPenguin - IConnectionPointContainer - failed
CPenguin - IActiveScript - failed
CPenguin - {6D5140D3-7436-11CE-8034-00AA006009FA} - failed
CPenguin - IOleControl
CPenguin - IOleCommandTarget - failed
CPenguin - IDispatchEx - failed
```

---

[9]Interface names for remotable interfaces are available in the registry as the default value of the HKEY_CLASSES_ROOT\Interfaces\{IID} key.

```
CPenguin - IDispatch
CPenguin - IOleObject
CPenguin - IOleObject
CPenguin - IRunnableObject - failed
CPenguin - IOleControl
CPenguin - IOleObject
CPenguin - IOleInPlaceObject
CPenguin - IID_IOleInPlaceObjectWindowless
CPenguin - IOleInPlaceActiveObject
CPenguin - IOleControl
CPenguin - IClientSecurity - failed
CPenguin - IClientSecurity - failed
```

Tracing Calls to AddRef and Release

The only calls more heavily instrumented for debugging than `QueryInterface` are `AddRef` and `Release`. ATL 3.0 introduced quite an elaborate scheme for tracking calls to `AddRef` and `Release` on individual interfaces. The reason it is elaborate is that each ATL-based C++ class has a single implementation of `AddRef` and `Release`, implemented in the most derived class, for example, `CComObject`. To overcome this limitation, when `_ATL_DEBUG_INTERFACES` is defined, ATL wraps each new interface [10] handed out via `QueryInterface` in another C++ object that implements a single interface. Each of these *thunk objects* keeps track of the real interface pointer as well as the name of the interface and the name of the class that has implemented the interface. The thunk object also keeps an interface-pointer-specific reference count, in addition to the object's reference count, that the thunk object's implementation of `AddRef` and `Release` manages. As calls to `AddRef` and `Release` are made, each thunk object knows exactly which interface is being used and dumps reference count information to the debug output. For example, here's the same interaction between a control and IE4, but using _ATL_DEBUG_INTER-FACES instead of _ATL_DEBUG_QI:

```
1> CComClassFactory - IUnknown
1> CComClassFactory - IClassFactory
1> CPenguin - IUnknown
1> CPenguin - IOleControl
0< CPenguin - IOleControl
1> CPenguin - IOleObject
```

---

[10] ATL makes sure to always hand out the same thunk for each object's `IUnknown*` to observe the rules of COM identity, as discussed in Chapter 5.

```
1> CPenguin - IOleObject
0< CPenguin - IOleObject
0< CPenguin - IOleObject
1> CPenguin - IPersistStreamInit
0< CPenguin - IPersistStreamInit
1> CPenguin - IID_IViewObjectEx
1> CPenguin - IOleControl
0< CPenguin - IOleControl
1> CPenguin - IDispatch
1> CPenguin - IOleObject
1> CPenguin - IOleObject
0< CPenguin - IOleObject
0< CPenguin - IOleObject
1> CPenguin - IOleControl
0< CPenguin - IOleControl
0< CComClassFactory - IClassFactory
1> CPenguin - IOleObject
1> CPenguin - IOleInPlaceObject
1> CPenguin - IID_IOleInPlaceObjectWindowless
1> CPenguin - IOleInPlaceActiveObject
0< CPenguin - IOleInPlaceActiveObject
0< CPenguin - IOleInPlaceObject
0< CPenguin - IOleObject
1> CPenguin - IOleControl
0< CPenguin - IOleControl
```

ATL maintains a list of outstanding thunk objects. This list is used at server shutdown to detect any leaks, that is, any interfaces that have not been released by the client. When using _ATL_DEBUG_INTERFACES, watch your debug output for the string INTERFACE LEAK, which is an indication that someone has mismanaged an interface reference. For example:

```
INTERFACE LEAK: RefCount = 1, MaxRefCount = 1, {Allocation = 4}
    CPenguin - ISnappyDresser
```

The most useful part of this notification is the Allocation number. You can use this to track when the leaked interface is acquired by setting the m_nIndexBreakAt member of the CComModule at server start-up time. For example:

```
extern "C"
BOOL WINAPI DllMain(HINSTANCE hInstance, DWORD dwReason, LPVOID) {
    if (dwReason == DLL_PROCESS_ATTACH) {
```

```
    _Module.Init(ObjectMap, hInstance, &LIBID_PISVRLib);
    DisableThreadLibraryCalls(hInstance);

    // Track down interface leak
    _Module.m_nIndexBreakAt = 4;
    }
    else if (dwReason == DLL_PROCESS_DETACH)
      _Module.Term();
    return TRUE;      // ok
  }
```

When that interface thunk is allocated, the _Module will call DebugBreak, handing control over to the debugger and allowing you to examine the call stack and plug the leak.

_ATL_DEBUG_REFCOUNT

Versions of ATL prior to 3.0 used the _ATL_DEBUG_REFCOUNT symbol to track interface reference counts for ATL IXxxImpl classes only. Since _ATL_DEBUG_INTERFACES is so much more general, it has replaced _ATL_DEBUG_REFCOUNT, although _ATL_DEBUG_REFCOUNT is still supported for backward compatibility.

```
#ifdef _ATL_DEBUG_REFCOUNT
#ifndef _ATL_DEBUG_INTERFACES
#define _ATL_DEBUG_INTERFACES
#endif
#endif
```

Summary

ATL provides a layered approach to implementing IUnknown. The top layer, represented by the CComXxxThreadModel classes, provides helper functions and type definitions for the synchronization required by objects residing in both STAs and MTAs. The second level, CComObjectRootEx, uses the threading model classes to support just-thread-safe-enough AddRef and Release implementations and object-level locking. CComObjectRootEx also provides a table-driven implementation of QueryInterface, using an interface map provided by your class. Your class derives from CComObjectRootEx and any number of interfaces, providing the interface member function implementations. The final level is provided by CComObject or one of its friends, which provides the implementation of Query-Interface, AddRef, and Release based on the lifetime and identity requirements of the object.

To allow each class to define its one lifetime and its identity requirements, each class defines its own `_CreatorClass`, which defines the appropriate creator. The creator is responsible for properly creating an instance of your ATL-based class and should be used in place of the C++ operator `new`.

Finally, to debug your objects, ATL provides a number of debugging facilities, including tracing and interface usage and leak tracking.

4 | **COM Servers**

A Review of COM Servers

Once you've created one or more COM classes, you need to package all the classes together and install them on a system. The package is called a *COM server*. A COM server is a dynamically activated collection of the implementations of one or more COM classes. Modern Win32 versions of COM allow you to create a COM server as an in-process (inproc) server (a dynamic link library), an out-of-process server (an executable), or, on the Windows NT operating system, as a system service executable.[1] Some people mean a COM server when they refer to a COM component. (Others mean a COM class when they refer to a COM component, so I'll use COM server.)

A COM server has three jobs, in addition to hosting the implementations of its classes:

1. Register and unregister all classes in the server and, potentially, the server itself.

2. Provide the COM Service Control Manager (SCM) access to all COM *class objects* implemented by the server (often called *exposing* the class objects). Class objects are frequently called *class factory objects* because they generally implement the `IClassFactory` interface.

3. Manage the server's lifetime. This typically means allowing the SCM to unload an inproc server from memory when it's no longer used. A local server often terminates when there are no more references to objects managed by the server.

Although technically the first and third items are optional, all COM servers should implement this functionality. How, exactly, a server does this depends on the type of server.

---

[1] Here "Modern Win32 versions of COM" refers to Windows NT 4.0 and greater, Windows 98, and Windows 95 with the DCOM95 upgrade.

Inproc Servers

An inproc server is a dynamic link library (DLL) containing five well-known entry points—one used by the Win32 operating systems and the other four used by COM:

```
BOOL WINAPI DllMain(HINSTANCE hInstance, DWORD dwReason,
                    LPVOID lpReserved);

STDAPI DllRegisterServer(void);
STDAPI DllUnregisterServer(void);
STDAPI DllGetClassObject(REFCLSID rclsid, REFIID riid, LPVOID* ppv);
STDAPI DllCanUnloadNow(void);
```

Each of the Win32 operating systems calls a dynamic link library's `DllMain` function when it loads a DLL into a process and removes a DLL from a process. The operating system also calls `DllMain` each time the current process creates a new thread and when a thread terminates cleanly. This function is optional but present in all ATL inproc servers.

The `DllRegisterServer` and `DllUnregisterServer` functions create and remove, respectively, all entries in the Windows registry that are necessary for the correct operation of the server and its classes. When you use the REGSVR32 utility to register or unregister an inproc server, the utility loads the DLL and calls the appropriate one of these functions in the DLL. Technically, both of these functions are optional, but, in practice, you want to have them in your server.

The SCM calls a server's `DllGetClassObject` function when it requires a class object exposed by the server. The server should return the requested interface, `riid`, on the specified class object, `rclsid`.

When you call the `CoFreeUnusedLibraries` API, COM asks each inproc server in your process if COM should unload the DLL by calling the `DllCanUnloadNow` function. An S_OK return value means that the server permits COM to unload the server. An S_FALSE return value indicates that the server is busy at the moment and COM cannot unload it.

Local Servers and Service-Based Servers

A local server or NT service is an executable image (EXE) server containing one well-known entry point:

```
extern "C"
int WINAPI _tWinMain(HINSTANCE hInstance, HINSTANCE hPrevInstance,
                     LPTSTR lpCmdLine, int nShowCmd);
```

Executables cannot provide multiple specialized entry points, unlike DLLs, so a local server must use a different technique to implement the three requirements of a COM server: registration, exposing class objects, and lifetime management.

A local server registers or unregisters itself and then immediately terminates when the server parses its command line and finds the well-known (case-insensitive) command-line switches `Regserver` or `UnregServer`, respectively.

A local server exposes its class objects by calling the `CoRegisterClass-Object` API and handing an `IUnknown` interface pointer to each of the server's class objects to the SCM. A local server must call this API after the SCM starts the server process.[2] When the server is ready to shut down, it must first call `CoRevokeClass-Object` to notify the SCM that each of the server's class objects is no longer available for use.

A local server manages its own lifetime. When a server detects that there are no references to any of the objects managed by the server, the server can shut down (or not) as it wishes. As you'll see later in this chapter, detecting that there are no references is a little trickier than you might think.

COM Createable and Noncreateable Classes

A *COM createable class* is a COM object class that supports a client creating instances of the class using the `CoCreateInstance` API. This implies that the class must provide a class object and that the class object implements the `IClassFactory` interface.

A noncreateable class typically provides no class object, so calling `CoCreate-Instance` using the class's class identifier (CLSID) fails.[3] In many designs, there are far more noncreateable classes than there are createable ones. For example, in one version of Microsoft Excel, there were roughly 130 classes, only 3 of which were createable.

The Object Map and the CComModule Class

ATL uses two constructs to support the functionality required by all types of servers: the *object map* and the `CComModule` class. The object map (more properly entitled a class map) is a table of all classes implemented in the server.

---

[2] As of this writing, a local server must register its class objects within 120 seconds. The time was less in previous software releases. It might change again in the future, so simply register your class objects as quickly as possible.

[3] I don't know how many times people have told me "Noncreateable classes do not have CLSIDs." Sometimes they do. When you want to describe a noncreateable class in a type library, you must assign the `coclass` a CLSID. MIDL won't compile a `coclass` statement, even one with the `noncreatable` attribute, unless the class has the `uuid` attribute. (Note also that MIDL uses a different spelling—"noncreatable"—than other areas of COM.)

Various methods of the CComModule class use the object map to

- Find each class and ask it to register and unregister itself.
- Create the class object, if any, for each createable class.
- Register and unregister the class objects with the SCM.
- Find a table of implemented and required component categories for a class.
- Call each class's static initialization and termination member function.

The basic idea is that you describe the classes that you are implementing in a server using the object map. Whenever you need basic server functionality, there is probably a method of the CComModule class that implements much, if not all, of the required functionality.

Many CComModule methods iterate over the entries in the object map and either ask each class to perform the required function or ask each class to provide the information needed to allow the CComModule method to do it.

The Object Map

Here's an example of an object map called ObjectMap that defines three classes. You start defining the object map using the BEGIN_OBJECT_MAP macro, populate the table using the OBJECT_ENTRY and the OBJECT_ENTRY_NON_CREATEABLE macros, and end the definition using the END_OBJECT_MAP macro.

In the following example, the object map describes three classes. Clients can call CoCreateInstance to create instances of the CDemagogue and CEarPolitic classes (that is, they are COM createable classes) but cannot for the CSoapBox class.[4]

```
BEGIN_OBJECT_MAP(ObjectMap)
OBJECT_ENTRY(CLSID_Demagogue, CDemagogue)
OBJECT_ENTRY(CLSID_EarPolitic, CEarPolitic)
OBJECT_ENTRY_NON_CREATEABLE(CSoapBox)
END_OBJECT_MAP()
```

You define a COM createable class using the OBJECT_ENTRY macro. You define a noncreateable class using the OBJECT_ENTRY_NON_CREATEABLE macro. (Big

---

[4]For those curious, I decided that we needed a new term for something or someone that listens to the Body Politic, and clearly this should be an Ear Politic.

surprise there, I bet!) The ATL infrastructure starts with the assumption that you'll always have an instance class (you create instances of this class). An instance class may or may not have an associated class object class. The first assumption supports noncreateable objects. An instance class that has an associated class object can be a createable class.

However, the ATL object map currently has no support for a standalone class object, that is, a class object that never creates any instances of its class. In ATL you must first define an instance class; then, within the instance class declaration, you can define the class of its class object. At runtime, you can fail requests for `IClass-Factory` or, preferably, support `IClassFactory` and fail all instance creation requests.[5]

The Object Map Macros

BEGIN_OBJECT_MAP Macro

The `BEGIN_OBJECT_MAP` macro begins the array definition. The macro parameter specifies the name of the array.

```
#define BEGIN_OBJECT_MAP(x)     static _ATL_OBJMAP_ENTRY x[] = {
```

_ATL_OBJMAP_ENTRY Structure

The object map is an array of _ATL_OBJMAP_ENTRY structures that looks like this:

```
struct _ATL_OBJMAP_ENTRY
{
    const CLSID* pclsid;
    HRESULT (WINAPI *pfnUpdateRegistry)(BOOL bRegister);
    _ATL_CREATORFUNC* pfnGetClassObject;
    _ATL_CREATORFUNC* pfnCreateInstance;
    IUnknown* pCF;
    DWORD dwRegister;
    _ATL_DESCRIPTIONFUNC* pfnGetObjectDescription;
    _ATL_CATMAPFUNC* pfnGetCategoryMap;
    void (WINAPI *pfnObjectMain)(bool bStarting);
};
```

---

[5] You should implement `IClassFactory` even when you want to fail instantiation requests so that the stub can call `LockServer` when remoting references to the class object.

The structure contains the following fields, many of which are pointers to functions:

`pclsid`	Pointer to CLSID for this class entry.
`pfnUpdateRegistry`	The function that registers and unregisters the class.
`pfnGetClassObject`	The creator function that creates an instance of the class object.
`pfnCreateInstance`	The creator function that creates an instance of the class.
`pCF`	Pointer to the inproc class object instance; NULL if not yet created.
`dwRegister`	Registration cookie returned by `CoRegister-ClassObject`.
`pfnGetObjectDescription`	The function that returns the object description for the class.
`pfnGetCategoryMap`	The function that returns the component category map.
`pfnObjectMain`	The class initialization/termination function.

END_OBJECT_MAP Macro

You use the `END_OBJECT_MAP` macro to add a terminating entry to the array and end the array definition.

```
#define END_OBJECT_MAP() \
    {NULL, NULL, NULL, NULL, NULL, NULL, NULL, NULL}};
```

Each `OBJECT_ENTRY` and `OBJECT_ENTRY_NON_CREATEABLE` macro adds one `_ATL_OBJMAP_ENTRY` structure to the array.

OBJECT_ENTRY Macro

You use the `OBJECT_ENTRY` macro to specify a COM createable class. Typically, this means the specified class derives from the `CComCoClass` base class. Often these are top-level objects in an object model. Clients typically create such top-level objects using `CoCreateInstance`.

```
#define OBJECT_ENTRY(clsid, class) \
    {&clsid, class::UpdateRegistry, \
    class::_ClassFactoryCreatorClass::CreateInstance, \
```

```
    class::_CreatorClass::CreateInstance, NULL, 0, \
    class::GetObjectDescription, class::GetCategoryMap, \
      class::ObjectMain },
```

OBJECT_ENTRY_NON_CREATEABLE Macro

You use the OBJECT_ENTRY_NON_CREATEABLE macro to specify a class that does not have an associated class object. Often these are non-top-level objects in an object model. Clients typically must call a method on a higher-level object in the object hierarchy to obtain an instance of this class. Because the specified class does not have an associated class object, clients cannot create an instance by calling CoCreateInstance.

```
#define OBJECT_ENTRY_NON_CREATEABLE(class) \
    {&CLSID_NULL, class::UpdateRegistry, \
    NULL, NULL, NULL, 0, NULL, class::GetCategoryMap, \
      class::ObjectMain },
```

You will use the OBJECT_ENTRY_NON_CREATEABLE macro primarily for non-createable classes that need class-level initialization and uninitialization. Occasionally, you might want to have a noncreateable class maintain registry entries and possibly persistent class configuration information and/or component categories.

Methods Required of an Object Map Class

The CComModule class registers, unregisters, initializes, and uninitializes noncreateable object map entries. It does all that plus creates class objects and class instances for createable object map entries.

A class listed in the object map using the OBJECT_ENTRY_NON_CREATEABLE macro must provide the first three well-known static methods listed in Table 4.1. A class listed in the object map using the OBJECT_ENTRY macro must provide the same three methods as a noncreateable class plus the last three well-known static methods and two typedefs listed in Table 4.1.

All classes listed in the object map must define an UpdateRegistry method. It's the only method not provided by any base class. As you'll see soon, ATL contains various macros that expand to different implementations of this method, so the method is not difficult to provide.

All ATL objects derive from CComObjectRootBase and therefore already have a default implementation of the ObjectMain method.

Table 4.1. Object Map Class Methods

Static member function	Description
UpdateRegistry	Registers and unregisters the class. The DECLARE_REGISTRY macros provide various implementations of this method.
ObjectMain	Initializes and uninitializes the class. CComObjectRootBase provides a default implementation of this method.
GetCategoryMap	Returns a pointer to a component category map. Use the BEGIN_CATEGORY_MAP macros to provide a specialized implementation. CComCoClass provides a default implementation of this method.
_CreatorClass:: CreateInstance	The DECLARE_AGGREGATABLE macros set the _CreatorClass typedef to the name of the class that creates instances. CComCoClass provides a default definition of this typedef.
_ClassFactoryCreatorClass:: CreateInstance	The DECLARE_CLASSFACTORY macros set the _ClassFactoryCreatorClass typedef to the name of the class that creates class objects. CComCoClass provides a default definition of this typedef.
GetObjectDescription	Returns the object description text string. CComCoClass provides a default implementation of this method.

Most createable ATL classes derive from CComCoClass, which provides the implementation of the remaining four methods required by an object map entry as well as both the required typedefs. A noncreateable class must implement the GetCategoryMap method. ATL contains a set of macros that define and implement this method as well.

Class Registration Support Methods

When ATL registers all the classes in a server, ATL iterates over the object map looking for entries containing a NULL GetObjectDescription function pointer and entries where the function returns a NULL description. The latter case is the typical one because `CComCoClass` provides the following implementation of `GetObject-Description`, and the object map stores a pointer to this method:

```
static LPCTSTR WINAPI GetObjectDescription() {return NULL;}
```

For every such entry, ATL calls the `UpdateRegistry` method to register or unregister the class, then registers or unregisters the component categories for the class using the table of required and implemented categories provided by `GetCategory-Map` method.

The GetObjectDescription Method

The `GetObjectDescription` static method retrieves the text description for your class object, as shown previously, the default implementation returns NULL. You can override this method with the `DECLARE_OBJECT_DESCRIPTION` macro. For example:

```
class CMyClass : public CComCoClass< ... >, ...
{
public:
  DECLARE_OBJECT_DESCRIPTION("MyClass Object Description")

  ...
};
```

When you ask a COM server to register its classes, it registers all of them. You can't ask a server to register just one, or some subset, of its classes.

A Component Registrar Object.   To register or unregister a subset of the classes in a server, you need to provide a Component Registrar object. This is a COM createable class that implements the `IComponentRegistrar` interface.

```
[
    object, dual, pointer_default(unique)
    uuid(a817e7a2-43fa-11d0-9e44-00aa00b6770a)
]
interface IComponentRegistrar : IDispatch
{
    [id(1)] HRESULT Attach([in] BSTR bstrPath);
    [id(2)] HRESULT RegisterAll();
    [id(3)] HRESULT UnregisterAll();
```

```
    [id(4)] HRESULT GetComponents([out] SAFEARRAY(BSTR)* pbstrCLSIDs,
                        [out] SAFEARRAY(BSTR)* bstrDescriptions);
    [id(5)] HRESULT RegisterComponent([in] BSTR bstrCLSID);
    [id(6)] HRESULT UnregisterComponent([in] BSTR bstrCLSID);
};
```

A Component Registrar object registers all objects in your server that declare the DECLARE_OBJECT_DESCRIPTION macro. Using the Component Registrar object, you can register and unregister objects individually, unlike DllRegisterServer and DllUnregisterServer, which register and unregister all objects in your server.

You may also get a list of objects in the server and their descriptions with the IComponentRegistrar::GetComponents method. Normally, GetObject-Description is called by IComponentRegistrar::GetComponents. When you create a Component Registrar object with the ATL Object Wizard, the wizard will automatically implement the IComponentRegistrar interface.

It's important to realize that when ATL registers all classes in a server, it does not register any class that provides a non-NULL object description. ATL expects some other software to use the Component Registrar object in the server to register the classes with an object description. At one time, Microsoft Transaction Server (MTS) was going to use the Component Registrar object to register and unregister individual classes in a server. However, I can find no references describing if, when, or how MTS uses the Component Registrar object. Basically, as of this writing, the Component Registrar object and class object descriptions seem to be unused features, and you shouldn't use them.

The UpdateRegistry Method

Every class that you list in the object map, createable and noncreateable, must provide an UpdateRegistry static member function. The ATL server implementation calls this method to ask the class to register and unregister itself depending on the value of bRegister.

```
static HRESULT WINAPI UpdateRegistry(BOOL bRegister) ;
```

The DECLARE_REGISTRY Macros.   You can provide a custom implementation of UpdateRegistry (that is, write it yourself) or use an ATL-provided implementation. ATL provides an implementation of this method when you use one of the following macros in your class declaration:

```
#define DECLARE_NO_REGISTRY()\
    static HRESULT WINAPI UpdateRegistry(BOOL /*bRegister*/)\
    {return S_OK;}

#define DECLARE_REGISTRY(class, pid, vpid, nid, flags)\
    static HRESULT WINAPI UpdateRegistry(BOOL bRegister) {\
        return _Module.UpdateRegistryClass(GetObjectCLSID(), pid, \
            vpid, nid, flags, bRegister);\
    }

#define DECLARE_REGISTRY_RESOURCE(x)\
    static HRESULT WINAPI UpdateRegistry(BOOL bRegister) {\
        return _Module.UpdateRegistryFromResource(_T(#x), bRegister);\
    }

#define DECLARE_REGISTRY_RESOURCEID(x)\
    static HRESULT WINAPI UpdateRegistry(BOOL bRegister) {\
    return _Module.UpdateRegistryFromResource(x, bRegister);\
    }
```

The DECLARE_NO_REGISTRY macro provides an UpdateRegistry method that simply returns S_OK. You commonly use this macro when declaring a non-createable class. For example, here is the CSoapBox noncreateable object class declaration:

```
BEGIN_OBJECT_MAP(ObjectMap)
. . .
OBJECT_ENTRY_NON_CREATEABLE(CSoapBox)
END_OBJECT_MAP()

class ATL_NO_VTABLE CSoapBox :
    public CComObjectRootEx<CComSingleThreadModel>,
    ...          // No CComCoClass derivation
{
public:
    DECLARE_NO_REGISTRY()
    . . .
};
```

The DECLARE_REGISTRY macro provides an implementation that registers the standard class information for an object: the class, the path to the server module, the programmatic identifier (ProgID), the version-independent ProgID, the description, and the threading model. This macro uses the GetObjectCLSID function to obtain the CLSID to register. Normally, your CComCoClass base class provides the GetObjectCLSID implementation. The DECLARE_REGISTRY macro isn't generally useful for modern components because many servers need more than the standard registry entries it provides.

The preferred registration technique for ATL servers is to use registry scripts, which are far more flexible than DECLARE_REGISTRY. When asked to register or unregister, a server using registry scripts uses an interpreter object to parse the script and make the appropriate registry changes. The interpreter object implements the IRegistrar interface. ATL provides such an object, which can be either statically linked to reduce dependencies or dynamically loaded using CoCreateInstance for the smallest code size.

The DECLARE_REGISTRY_RESOURCE and DECLARE_REGISTRY_RESOURCEID macros provide an implementation of UpdateRegistry that delegates the call to the CComModule::UpdateRegistryFromResource method. You specify a string resource name when you use the first macro. The second macro expects an integer resource identifier. The UpdateRegistryFromResource runs the script contained in the specified resource. When bRegister is TRUE, this method adds the script entries to the system registry; otherwise, it removes the entries.

Registry Script Files.   Registry scripts are text files that specify what registry changes must be made for a given CLSID. Wizard-generated code uses an RGS extension by default for registry script files. Your server contains the script file as a custom resource of type REGISTRY in your executable or DLL.

Registry script syntax isn't complicated, and can be summarized as follows:

```
[NoRemove | ForceRemove | val] Name |
  [ = s 'Value' | d 'Value' | b 'Value']
{
 ... optional script entries for subkeys
}
```

The NoRemove prefix specifies that the parser should not remove the key when unregistering. The ForceRemove prefix specifies that the parser should remove the current key and any subkeys prior to writing the key. The val prefix specifies that the entry is a named value and not a key. The s, d, and b value prefixes indicate REG_SZ, REG_DWORD, and REG_BINARY, respectively. The Name token is the string for the named value or key. It must be surrounded by apostrophes when the string contains spaces; otherwise, the apostrophes are optional. ATL's parser recognizes the standard registry key names, for example, HKEY_CLASSES_ROOT, as well as their four-character abbreviations (HKCR).

As an example demonstrating the flexibility (and improved readability) of registry scripts, I present two techniques for registering a class. First, here's a REGEDIT4 sample for the nontrivial Demagogue class registration. Watch out, because a few lines are too long to list on the page and have wrapped.

```
REGEDIT4
[HKEY_CLASSES_ROOT\ATLInternals.Demagogue.1]
@="Demagogue Class"
[HKEY_CLASSES_ROOT\ATLInternals.Demagogue.1\CLSID]
@="{95CD3731-FC5C-11D1-8CC3-00A0C9C8E50D}"
[HKEY_CLASSES_ROOT\ATLInternals.Demagogue]
@="Demagogue Class"
[HKEY_CLASSES_ROOT\ATLInternals.Demagogue\CLSID]
@="{95CD3731-FC5C-11D1-8CC3-00A0C9C8E50D}"
[HKEY_CLASSES_ROOT\ATLInternals.Demagogue\CurVer]
@="ATLInternals.Demagogue.1"
[HKEY_CLASSES_ROOT\CLSID\{95CD3731-FC5C-11D1-8CC3-00A0C9C8E50D}]
@="Demagogue Class"
[HKEY_CLASSES_ROOT\CLSID\{95CD3731-FC5C-11D1-8CC3-00A0C9C8E50D}\ProgID]
@="ATLInternals.Demagogue.1"
[HKEY_CLASSES_ROOT\CLSID\{95CD3731-FC5C-11D1-8CC3-
   00A0C9C8E50D}\VersionIndependentProgID]
@="ATLInternals.Demagogue"
[HKEY_CLASSES_ROOT\CLSID\{95CD3731-FC5C-11D1-8CC3-
   00A0C9C8E50D}\Programmable]
[HKEY_CLASSES_ROOT\CLSID\{95CD3731-FC5C-11D1-8CC3-
   00A0C9C8E50D}\InprocServer32]
@="C:\\ATLINT~1\\Debug\\ATLINT~1.DLL"
"ThreadingModel"="Apartment"
[HKEY_CLASSES_ROOT\\CLSID\\{95CD3731-FC5C-11D1-8CC3-
   00A0C9C8E50D}\TypeLib]
@="{95CD3721-FC5C-11D1-8CC3-00A0C9C8E50D}"
[HKEY_CLASSES_ROOT\CLSID\{95CD3731-FC5C-11D1-8CC3-
   00A0C9C8E50D}\Implemented Categories]
[HKEY_CLASSES_ROOT\CLSID\{95CD3731-FC5C-11D1-8CC3-
   00A0C9C8E50D}\Implemented Categories\{0D22FF22-28CC-11D2-ABDD-
   00A0C9C8E50D}]
```

The corresponding registry script would look like this:

```
HKCR
{
 ATLInternals.Demagogue.1 = s 'Demagogue Class'
 {
    CLSID = s '{95CD3731-FC5C-11D1-8CC3-00A0C9C8E50D}'
 }
 ATLInternals.Demagogue = s 'Demagogue Class'
 {
    CLSID = s '{95CD3731-FC5C-11D1-8CC3-00A0C9C8E50D}'
    CurVer = s 'ATLInternals.Demagogue.1'
 }
 NoRemove CLSID
 {
    ForceRemove {95CD3731-FC5C-11D1-8CC3-00A0C9C8E50D} = s 'Demagogue
      Class'
    {
      ProgID = s 'ATLInternals.Demagogue.1'
      VersionIndependentProgID = s 'ATLInternals.Demagogue'
      ForceRemove 'Programmable'
      InprocServer32 = s '%MODULE%'
      {
        val ThreadingModel = s 'Apartment'
      }
      'TypeLib' = s '{95CD3721-FC5C-11D1-8CC3-00A0C9C8E50D}'
      'Implemented Categories'
      {
        {0D22FF22-28CC-11D2-ABDD-00A0C9C8E50D}
      }
    }
  }
 }
}
```

After you have the resource script file, you reference the file in your server's re-source (.rc) file. You can either reference it using an integer identifier or a string identifier. In a typical ATL project, each class can have a registry script file, and the server as a whole typically has its own unique registry script file.

In the following examples, the Demagogue script file uses the integer identifier IDR_DEMAGOGUE, whereas the EarPolitic script file uses EARPOLITIC as its string identifier. ATL wizard-created classes use the DECLARE_REGISTRY_RESOURCEID

macro to specify a resource by its integer identifier. You can use the DECLARE_
REGISTRY_RESOURCE macro to identify a resource by its name.

```
// resource.h file
#define IDR_DEMAGOGUE                  102


// Server.rc file
IDR_DEMAGOGUE            REGISTRY DISCARDABLE    "Demagogue.rgs"
EARPOLITIC              REGISTRY DISCARDABLE    "EarPolitic.rgs"


// Demagogue.h file
class ATL_NO_VTABLE CDemagogue :
    public CComObjectRootEx<CComSingleThreadModel>,
    public CComCoClass<CDemagogue, &CLSID_Demagogue>,
. . .
public:
DECLARE_REGISTRY_RESOURCEID(IDR_DEMAGOGUE)
. . .
};


// EarPolitic.h file
class ATL_NO_VTABLE CEarPolitic :
    public CComObjectRootEx<CComSingleThreadModel>,
    public CComCoClass<CEarPolitic, &CLSID_EarPolitic>,
. . .
{
public:
DECLARE_REGISTRY_RESOURCE(EARPOLITIC)
. . .
};
```

Registry Script Variables.   Note that in the registry script one of the lines referenced a symbol called %MODULE%:

```
InprocServer32 = s '%MODULE%'
```

When the parser evaluates the script, it replaces all occurrences of the registry
script variable %MODULE% with the actual results of a call to GetModuleFileName.
So what the parser actually registered looked like this:

```
InprocServer32 = s 'C:\\ATLInternals\\Debug\\ATLInternals.dll'
```

You can use additional, custom registry script variables in your scripts. Your server must provide the registry script parser with a table that maps variable names to replacement values when you ask the parser to parse the script. The parser will substitute the replacement values for the variable names prior to registration.

To use custom registry script variables, first select the registry script variable name, using percent signs to delimit the name. Here is a sample line from a registry script:

```
DateInstalled = s '%INSTALLDATE%'
```

Then, instead of using the DECLARE_REGISTRY_RESOURCEID macro, define a custom UpdateRegistry method. In the method, build a table of replacement name/value pairs. Finally, call the CComModule::UpdateRegistryFromResource method specifying the resource identifier, a register/unregister flag, and a pointer to the replacement name/value table. Note that ATL uses the provided table entries *in addition to* the default replacement map (which, as of this writing, only contains %MODULE%).

Here is an example from the Demagogue class that substitutes the variable %INSTALLDATE% with a string containing the current date:

```
static HRESULT WINAPI UpdateRegistry(BOOL b) {
    OLECHAR wszDate [16]; SYSTEMTIME st;
    GetLocalTime(&st);
    wsprintfW(wszDate, L"%.4d/%.2d/%.2d", st.wYear, st.wMonth, st.wDay);
    _ATL_REGMAP_ENTRY rm[] =
        { { OLESTR("INSTALLDATE"), wszDate}, { 0, 0 } };
    return _Module.UpdateRegistryFromResource(IDR_DEMAGOGUE, b, rm);
}
```

After registration of the class, the registry key DateInstalled will contain the year, month, and day, in the form "yyyy/mm/dd," at the time of install.

The GetCategoryMap Method

The last step in the registration process for each class in the object map is to register the component categories for the class. The ATL server registration code calls each class's GetCategoryMap method to ask the class for its list of required and implemented component categories. The method looks like this:

```
static const struct _ATL_CATMAP_ENTRY* GetCategoryMap()
    { return NULL; }
```

The ATL server registration code uses the standard component category manager object (CLSID_StdComponentCategoriesMgr) to register your class's required and implemented categories. Older versions of Win32 operating systems do not have this component installed. When the category manager is not installed, your class's registration of its component categories silently fails. Typically, this is not good.

Microsoft permits you to redistribute the standard component category manager (comcat.dll) with your application. However, it's really easier simply to define the component categories in your class's registry script file. As it turns out, you might want to use the script file anyway because, at the time of this writing, ATL 3.0 has a bug involving the category map and noncreateable classes. I'll discuss the bug shortly.

The Component Category Map

Typically, you will use ATL-provided category map macros for the implementation of this method. Here's a typical category map:

```
// {0D22FF22-28CC-11d2-ABDD-00A0C9C8E50D}
static const GUID CATID_ATLINTERNALS_SAMPLES =
{0xd22ff22, 0x28cc, 0x11d2, {0xab, 0xdd, 0x0, 0xa0, 0xc9, 0xc8, 0xe5,
   0xd}};

BEGIN_CATEGORY_MAP(CDemagogue)
IMPLEMENTED_CATEGORY(CATID_ATLINTERNALS_EXAMPLE)
END_CATEGORY_MAP()
```

This example defines a component category called CATID_ATLINTERNALS_SAMPLES. All examples in this book register themselves as a member of this category.

The Category Map Macros. The BEGIN_CATEGORY_MAP macro declares the GetCategoryMap static member function, which returns a pointer to an array of _ATL_CATMAP_ENTRY entries, each of which describes one component category that is either required or implemented by your class.

```
#define BEGIN_CATEGORY_MAP(x)\
   static const struct _ATL_CATMAP_ENTRY* GetCategoryMap() {\
   static const struct _ATL_CATMAP_ENTRY pMap[] = {
```

The IMPLEMENTED_CATEGORY and REQUIRED_CATEGORY macros populate the table with the appropriate entries.

```
#define IMPLEMENTED_CATEGORY(catid)\
  { _ATL_CATMAP_ENTRY_IMPLEMENTED, &catid },
#define REQUIRED_CATEGORY(catid)\
  { _ATL_CATMAP_ENTRY_REQUIRED, &catid },
```

The END_CATEGORY_MAP adds a delimiting entry to the table and completes the GetCategoryMap function.

```
#define END_CATEGORY_MAP()\
  { _ATL_CATMAP_ENTRY_END, NULL } };\
  return( pMap ); }
```

Each table entry contains a flag (indicating whether the entry describes a required category, an implemented category, or is the end-of-table entry) and a pointer to the category identifier (CATID).

```
struct _ATL_CATMAP_ENTRY {
  int iType;
  const CATID* pcatid;
};


#define _ATL_CATMAP_ENTRY_END          0
#define _ATL_CATMAP_ENTRY_IMPLEMENTED 1
#define _ATL_CATMAP_ENTRY_REQUIRED     2
```

The ATL helper function AtlRegisterClassCategoriesHelper iterates through the table and uses COM's standard component category manager to register each CATID as a required or implemented category for your class. The ATL server registration code uses this helper function to register the component categories for each class in the object map.

Unfortunately, the category map logic does not add a category to a system before trying to enroll a class as a member of the (nonexistent) category. The component category manager silently fails to add a category to a class when the category isn't already defined on the system.

This means that you must enhance the registration of the server itself so that it registers any custom component categories used by your classes. For example, the following registry script registers the application identifier (AppID) for an inproc server and it also adds a component category to the list of component categories on the system.

```
HKCR
{
    NoRemove AppID
    {
        {A11552A2-28DF-11d2-ABDD-00A0C9C8E50D} = s 'ATLInternals'
        'ATLInternals.DLL'
        {
            val AppID = s {A11552A2-28DF-11d2-ABDD-00A0C9C8E50D}
        }
    }
    NoRemove 'Component Categories'
    {
        {0D22FF22-28CC-11d2-ABDD-00A0C9C8E50D}
        {
            val 409 = s 'ATL Internals Example Components'
        }
    }
}
```

This technique defines all categories (just one in the above example) used by the classes implemented in this server in the system registry. Separately, each class will register itself as a member of one or more of these categories.

Category Map Bug for Noncreateable Classes. You must supply an empty category map to be able to add a noncreateable class to the object map at all using the OBJECT_ENTRY_NON_CREATEABLE macro. Once you have the empty category map in place, you might want to add a few implemented or required categories to the noncreateable class's map. The ATL 3.0 implementation of the category map processing has a bug when you have a nonempty category map in a noncreateable class.

The problem is that the category map registration code registers the categories in the map using information from the object map entry for the class containing the category map, specifically, the CLSID entry. Unfortunately, you cannot specify a CLSID using the OBJECT_ENTRY_NON_CREATEABLE macro. The macro sets the CLSID to GUID_NULL. Thus, all implemented and required categories in a noncreateable class's category map end up registered under the HKCR/CLSID/{GUID_NULL} registry key rather than the correct HKCR/CLSID/{Your CLSID}.

You can easily work around this bug, however. I've defined a new macro, OBJECT_ENTRY_NON_CREATEABLE_EX. It looks like this:

```
#define OBJECT_ENTRY_NON_CREATEABLE_EX(clsid, class) \
{&clsid, class::UpdateRegistry, \
NULL, NULL, NULL, 0, NULL, class::GetCategoryMap, class::ObjectMain },
```

You should use this version of the macro in preference to the one ATL provides until the bug is fixed. In the meantime, I expect GUID_NULL to join a lot of component categories.

Server, not Class, Registration

Often, you need registry entries for the server (inproc, local, or service) as a whole. For example, the HKCR/AppID registry entries for a server apply to the entire DLL or EXE, and not to a specific class implemented in the DLL or EXE. As mentioned previously, you have to register a new component category with the system before you can enroll a class as a member of the category. Up till now, we've seen only support for registration of class-specific information.

This is simple enough. Write a registry script that adds the entries required by the server, such as its AppID and component categories used by the server's classes. Then register the server's script before registering all the classes implemented in the server. The wizard-generated code for a local server and a service does this for you. Unfortunately, at present, the wizard-generated code for an inproc server does not.

Local Server and Service Registration

The ATL wizard-generated code for a local server creates a registry script file for your *server* registration in addition to any registry script files for your classes. By default, the server registry script defines only an AppID for the local server. Here are the entries for an ATL project called ATLLocal.

```
// In the resource.h file
#define IDR_ATLLocal                    100

// In the ATLLocal.rc file
IDR_ATLLocal REGISTRY "ATLLocal.rgs"

// ATLLocal.rgs file
HKCR
{
```

```
    NoRemove AppID
    {
        {006859E6-2EF2-11D2-ABEA-00A0C9C8E50D} = s 'ATLLocal'
        'ATLLocal.EXE'
        {
            val AppID = s {006859E6-2EF2-11D2-ABEA-00A0C9C8E50D}
        }
    }
}
```

A wizard-generated local server's `WinMain` code registers or unregisters the server's resource script entries, then calls the _Module object's `RegisterServer` method to do the same for each class in the object map.

```
if (lstrcmpi(lpszToken, _T("UnregServer"))==0) {
        _Module.UpdateRegistryFromResource(IDR_ATLLocal, FALSE);
        nRet = _Module.UnregisterServer(TRUE);
        . . .
        break;
}
if (lstrcmpi(lpszToken, _T("RegServer"))==0) {
        _Module.UpdateRegistryFromResource(IDR_ATLLocal, TRUE);
        nRet = _Module.RegisterServer(TRUE);
        . . .
        break;
}
```

A service specializes the `CComModule` class with a derivation called `CSer-viceModule`. `CServiceModule` provides an overloaded `RegisterServer` method, which performs server registration before calling `CComModule::RegisterServer` to register the classes in the object map.

```
inline HRESULT CServiceModule::RegisterServer(BOOL bRegTypeLib,
                                              BOOL bService)
{
    HRESULT hr = CoInitialize(NULL);
    if (FAILED(hr)) return hr;

    ...
    // Add service entries
    UpdateRegistryFromResource(IDR_ATLService, TRUE);
```

```
    . . .
    // Add object entries
    hr = CComModule::RegisterServer(bRegTypeLib);

    CoUninitialize();
    return hr;
}
```

Inproc Server Registration

Unfortunately, the wizard-generated code for an inproc server doesn't provide equivalent code, even though an inproc server may need an AppID key, as well as other server-specific, rather than class-specific, registration. Fortunately, it's easy to provide this functionality for an inproc server.

```
// In the resource.h file
#define IDR_ATLInProc          100

// In the ATLInProc.rc file
IDR_ATLInProc REGISTRY "ATLInProc.rgs"

// ATLInProc.rgs file
HKCR
{
    NoRemove AppID
    {
        {A11552A2-28DF-11d2-ABDD-00A0C9C8E50D} = s 'ATLInProc'
        'ATLInProc.DLL'
        {
            val AppID = s {A11552A2-28DF-11d2-ABDD-00A0C9C8E50D}
        }
    }
}
```

You then need to add an UpdateRegistryFromResource function call to the DllRegisterServer and DllUnregisterServer methods of the inproc server.

```
//////////////////////////////////////////////
// DllRegisterServer-Adds entries to the system registry
```

```
STDAPI DllRegisterServer(void)
{
   HRESULT hr =
     _Module.UpdateRegistryFromResource(IDR_ATLInProc, TRUE);
   if (FAILED (hr)) return hr ;

   // registers object, typelib, and all interfaces in typelib
   return _Module.RegisterServer(TRUE);
}


/////////////////////////////////////////////
// DllUnregisterServer–Removes entries from the system registry

STDAPI DllUnregisterServer(void)
{
   HRESULT hr =
     _Module.UpdateRegistryFromResource(IDR_ATLInProc, FALSE);
   if (FAILED (hr)) return hr ;

   return _Module.UnregisterServer(TRUE);
}
```

Class Initialization and Uninitialization

The ObjectMain Method

Typically, in an ATL project, you don't want to use global or static objects for class-level initialization because the C runtime library (CRT) calls the constructors of static and global objects. Linking with the CRT increases the size of your server considerably for such little benefit. ATL supports class-level initialization for all classes listed in the object map, createable and noncreateable. In fact, frequently you'll add a noncreateable class entry to the object map solely because the noncreateable class needs class-level initialization. (A createable class must always be in the object map and therefore will always receive class-level initialization.)

When an ATL server initializes, it iterates over the object map and calls the ObjectMain static member function (with the bStarting parameter set to true) of each class in the map. When an ATL server terminates, it calls the ObjectMain function (with the bStarting parameter set to false) of each class in the map. You always have a default implementation, provided by CComObjectRootBase, that does nothing and looks like this:

```
static void WINAPI  ObjectMain(bool bStarting ) {};
```

When you have class initialization and termination logic (as opposed to instance initialization and termination logic), define an `ObjectMain` static member function in your class and place the logic there.[6]

```
BEGIN_OBJECT_MAP(ObjectMap)
. . .
OBJECT_ENTRY_NON_CREATEABLE(CSoapBox)
END_OBJECT_MAP()

class ATL_NO_VTABLE CSoapBox :
    public CComObjectRootEx<CComSingleThreadModel>,
    . . .
{
public:
   DECLARE_NO_REGISTRY()
   . . .
   static void WINAPI ObjectMain(bool bStarting) ;
};
```

Instantiation Requests

Class Object Registration

ATL creates the class objects for an inproc server slightly differently than it does the class objects for a local server or service. For an inproc server, ATL defers creating each class object until the SCM actually requests the class object via `DllGet-ClassObject`. For a local server or service, ATL creates all class objects during server initialization, then registers the objects with the SCM.

For an inproc server, ATL uses the `AtlModuleGetClassObject` helper function to scan the object map, create, if necessary, the class object, and return the requested interface on the class object.

```
ATLINLINE ATLAPI AtlModuleGetClassObject(_ATL_MODULE* pM,
                                         REFCLSID rclsid,
                                         REFIID riid, LPVOID* ppv)
{
   . . .
   _ATL_OBJMAP_ENTRY* pEntry = pM->m_pObjMap;
   . . .
```

---

[6]Instance initialization and termination logic should go in the `FinalConstruct` and `FinalRelease` methods, as Chapter 3 describes.

```
    while (pEntry->pclsid != NULL) {
        if ((pEntry->pfnGetClassObject != NULL) &&
            InlineIsEqualGUID(rclsid, *pEntry->pclsid)) {
            if (pEntry->pCF == NULL) {
                EnterCriticalSection(&pM->m_csObjMap);
                if (pEntry->pCF == NULL)
                    hRes = pEntry->pfnGetClassObject(
                                        pEntry->pfnCreateInstance,
                                        IID_IUnknown,
                                        (LPVOID*)&pEntry->pCF);
                LeaveCriticalSection(&pM->m_csObjMap);
            }
            if (pEntry->pCF != NULL)
                hRes = pEntry->pCF->QueryInterface(riid, ppv);
            break;
        }
        pEntry = _NextObjectMapEntry(pM, pEntry);
    }
    if (*ppv == NULL && hRes == S_OK)
        hRes = CLASS_E_CLASSNOTAVAILABLE;
    return hRes;
}
```

Notice how the logic checks to see if the class object has not already been created
(pEntry->pCF == NULL), then acquires the critical section that guards access to
the object map, then checks once more that pCF is still NULL. What might not be
obvious is why ATL checks twice. This is to maximize concurrency by avoiding
grabbing the critical section in the normal case (when the class factory has already
been created).

Also notice that ATL caches the IUnknown interface for the class object in the
object map entry's pCF member variable. Because the SCM may well make subsequent requests for the same class object, ATL caches the IUnknown pointer to the
object in the pCF field of the object map entry for the class. Subsequent requests for
the same class object reuse the cached interface pointer.

There is a helper method, called GetClassObject, in your _Module global object (discussed in detail later in this chapter) that you can use to retrieve a previously registered class object. However, it only works for inproc servers.

```
// Obtain a Class Factory (DLL only)
HRESULT GetClassObject(REFCLSID rclsid, REFIID riid, LPVOID* ppv);
```

You would use it like this:

```
ISpeaker* pSpeaker;
HRESULT hr = _Module.GetClassObject (CLSID_Demagogue, IID_ISpeaker,
                               reinterpret_case <void**> (&pSpeaker);
```

A local server must register all its class objects during the server's initialization. ATL uses the `AtlModuleRegisterClassObjects` helper function to register all the class objects in a local server. This helper function iterates over the object map, calling `RegisterClassObject` for each object map entry.

```
ATLINLINE ATLAPI AtlModuleRegisterClassObjects (_ATL_MODULE* pM,
                                          DWORD dwClsContext,
                                          DWORD dwFlags)
{
    . . .
    _ATL_OBJMAP_ENTRY* pEntry = pM->m_pObjMap;
    HRESULT hRes = S_OK;
    while (pEntry->pclsid != NULL && hRes == S_OK) {
        hRes = pEntry->RegisterClassObject(dwClsContext, dwFlags);
        pEntry = _NextObjectMapEntry(pM, pEntry);
    }
    return hRes;
}
```

`RegisterClassObject` is a method of the _ATL_OBJMAP_ENTRY structure. It basically encapsulates the process of creating, then registering a class object from an object map entry. First, it ignores entries with a NULL `pfnGetClassObject` function pointer. This skips the noncreateable class entries in the map. Then, `RegisterClassObject` creates the instance of the class object and registers it.

```
struct _ATL_OBJMAP_ENTRY {
 HRESULT WINAPI RegisterClassObject(DWORD dwClsContext,
                                DWORD dwFlags)
 {
   IUnknown* p = NULL;
   if (pfnGetClassObject == NULL) return S_OK;
   HRESULT hRes = pfnGetClassObject(pfnCreateInstance,
                              IID_IUnknown, (LPVOID*) &p);
   if (SUCCEEDED(hRes))
       hRes = CoRegisterClassObject(*pclsid, p,
```

```
                                     dwClsContext, dwFlags, &dwRegister);
    if (p != NULL) p->Release();
    return hRes;
  }
};
```

Notice that the function does not cache the IUnknown interface pointer to the class object it creates. It hands the interface to the SCM (which caches the pointer), stores the registration code in the object map, and releases the interface pointer. Because ATL does not cache any class object interface pointers in an out-of-process server, the simplest method for obtaining your own class object from within the server is to ask the SCM for it by calling CoGetClassObject.

The _ClassFactoryCreatorClass and _CreatorClass typedefs

When ATL created a class object in the prior examples, it asked your class to instantiate the class object by calling indirectly through the function pointer pfnGet-ClassObject, which ATL stores in the object map entry for the class.

```
struct _ATL_OBJMAP_ENTRY
{
    . . .
    _ATL_CREATORFUNC* pfnGetClassObject;   // Creates a class object
    _ATL_CREATORFUNC* pfnCreateInstance;   // Creates a class instance
    . . .
};
```

This member variable is of type _ATL_CREATORFUNC* and is a creator function.[7] Notice that the pfnCreateInstance member variable is also a creator function pointer.

```
typedef HRESULT (WINAPI _ATL_CREATORFUNC)(void* pv,
                                     REFIID riid, LPVOID* ppv);
```

These function pointers are non-NULL only when you describe a COM createable class using the OBJECT_ENTRY macro.

---

[7]Although there are logically two types of creator functions, instance creator functions and class creator functions, all creator functions used by the object map have a static member function with the example function signature. Chapter 3 discusses the various types of instance creator functions in depth. This chapter discusses the various class creator classes.

```
#define OBJECT_ENTRY(clsid, class) \
    {&clsid, class::UpdateRegistry, \
    class::_ClassFactoryCreatorClass::CreateInstance, \
    class::_CreatorClass::CreateInstance, NULL, 0, \
    class::GetObjectDescription, class::GetCategoryMap, \
    class::ObjectMain },
```

A createable class must define a `typedef`, called `_ClassFactoryCreator-Class`, which ATL uses as the name of the *class object's creator class*. The `OBJECT_ENTRY` macro expects this creator class to have a static member function called `CreateInstance` and stores the address of this static member function in the `pfnGetClassObject` object map entry.

A createable class also must define a `typedef`, called `_CreatorClass`, which ATL uses as the name of the *class instance's creator class*. The `OBJECT_ENTRY` macro expects this creator class to have a static member function called `Create-Instance` and stores the address of this static member function in the `pfnCreateInstance` object map entry.

DECLARE_CLASSFACTORY

Typically, your createable class will inherit a definition of the `_ClassFactory-CreatorClass` `typedef` from its `CComCoClass` base class. `CComCoClass` uses the `DECLARE_CLASSFACTORY` macro to define an appropriate default class object creator class, based on the type of server.

```
template <class T, const CLSID* pclsid = &CLSID_NULL>
class CComCoClass
{
public:
      DECLARE_CLASSFACTORY()
      DECLARE_AGGREGATABLE(T)
   . . .
};
```

The _ClassFactoryCreatorClass typedef

The `DECLARE_CLASSFACTORY` macro evaluates to the `DECLARE_CLASSFACTORY_EX` macro with `CComClassFactory` as the `cf` argument. The `DECLARE_CLASS-FACTORY_EX` macro produces a `typedef` for the symbol `_ClassFactory-CreatorClass`. This `typedef` is the name of a creator class that ATL uses to create the class object for a class.

```
#define DECLARE_CLASSFACTORY() \
 DECLARE_CLASSFACTORY_EX (CComClassFactory)

#if defined(_WINDLL) | defined(_USRDLL)
#define DECLARE_CLASSFACTORY_EX(cf) \
 typedef CComCreator< CComObjectCached< cf > > \
   _ClassFactoryCreatorClass;
#else
// don't let class factory refcount influence lock count
#define DECLARE_CLASSFACTORY_EX(cf) \
 typedef CComCreator< CComObjectNoLock< cf > > \
   _ClassFactoryCreatorClass;
#endif
```

When you build an inproc server, ATL standard build options define the
_USRDLL preprocessor symbol. This causes the `_ClassFactoryCreatorClass`
`typedef` to evaluate to a `CComCreator` class that creates a `CComObject-`
`Cached<cf>` version of your class object class `cf`. Out-of-process servers evaluate
the `typedef` as a `CComCreator` class that creates a `CComObjectNoLock<cf>` version of the class object class `cf`.

Class Object Usage of CComObjectCached and CComObjectNoLock

As described in Chapter 3, the `CComObjectCached::AddRef` method does not increment the server's lock count until the cached object's reference count changes
from 1 to 2. Similarly, `Release` doesn't decrement the server's lock count until the
cached object's reference count changes from 2 to 1.

ATL caches the `IUnknown` interface pointer to an inproc server's class object in
the object map. This cached interface pointer represents a reference. If this cached
reference affected the server's lock count, the DLL could not unload until the server
released this interface pointer. However, the server doesn't release the interface
pointer until the server is unloading. In other words, the server would never unload.
By waiting to adjust the server's reference count until there is a second reference
to the class object, the reference in the object map isn't sufficient to keep the DLL
loaded.

Also described in Chapter 3, `CComObjectNoLock` never adjusts the server's
lock count. This means an instance of `CComObjectNoLock` does not keep a server
loaded. This is exactly what we need for a class object in a local server.

When ATL creates a class object for an out-of-process server, it registers the
class object with the SCM, then ATL releases its reference. However, the SCM will
keep an unknown number of references to the class object, where "unknown"

means one or more. Therefore, the CComObjectCached class won't work correctly for an out-of-process class object. ATL uses the CComObjectNoLock class for out-of-process class objects because references to such objects don't affect the server's lifetime in any way. However, in modern versions of COM, the marshaling stub will call the class object's LockServer method when it marshals an interface pointer to a remote client. This keeps the server loaded when out-of-apartment clients have a reference to the class object.

Class Object Instantiation—CComCreator::CreateInstance Revisited

Earlier in this chapter, you saw the ATL class object registration helper functions AtlModuleGetClassObject and RegisterClassObject. When they create a class object, they call the class object's creator class's CreateInstance method like this:

```
// Inproc server class object instantiation
ATLINLINE ATLAPI AtlModuleGetClassObject(_ATL_MODULE* pM,
                                          REFCLSID rclsid,
                                          REFIID riid, LPVOID* ppv)
{
  . . .
  hRes = pEntry->pfnGetClassObject(pEntry->pfnCreateInstance,
                         IID_IUnknown,
                         (LPVOID*)&pEntry->pCF);
  . . .
};


// Out-of-process server class object instantiation
struct _ATL_OBJMAP_ENTRY {
 HRESULT WINAPI RegisterClassObject(DWORD dwClsContext,
                                    DWORD dwFlags)
 {
   . . .
   HRESULT hRes = pfnGetClassObject(pfnCreateInstance,
                            IID_IUnknown, (LPVOID*) &p);
   . . .
 }
};
```

Recall that the pfnGetClassObject member variable is set by the OBJECT_ENTRY macro and contains a pointer to the CreateInstance method of the _ClassFactoryCreatorClass.

```
class::_ClassFactoryCreatorClass::CreateInstance
```

For an inproc server, this evaluates to the following (assuming you're using the default class factory class, which is CComClassFactory):

```
class::CComCreator< CComObjectCached< CComClassFactory > >
  ::CreateInstance
```

For an out-of-process server, this evaluates to

```
class::CComCreator< CComObjectNoLock< CComClassFactory > >
  ::CreateInstance
```

This means the pfnGetClassObject member points to the CreateInstance method of the appropriate parameterized CComCreator class. When ATL calls this CreateInstance method, the creator class creates the appropriate type of the CComClassFactory instance (cached or no lock) for the server. You saw the definition of the CComCreator class in Chapter 3, but let's examine part of the code in depth.

```
template <class T1>
class CComCreator
{
public:
    static HRESULT WINAPI CreateInstance(void* pv,
                                          REFIID riid, LPVOID* ppv)
    {
        . . .
        ATLTRY(p = new T1(pv))
        if (p != NULL) {
            p->SetVoid(pv);
            . . .
        }
        return hRes;
    }
};
```

After the creator class's CreateInstance method creates the appropriate class object, the method calls the class object's SetVoid method, passing it the pv parameter of the CreateInstance call. Note that ATL uses a creator class both to create instances of class objects (sometimes called class factories) and to create instances of a class (often called *COM objects*). For regular ol' COM objects, ATL defines the SetVoid method in CComObjectRootBase as a do-nothing method, so this creator class call to SetVoid has no effect on an instance of a class.

```
class CComObjectRootBase
{
    . . .
    void SetVoid(void*) {}
};
```

However, when a creator class creates an instance of a class object, it's typically creating a CComClassFactory instance. CComClassFactory overrides the Set-Void method. When a creator class calls the SetVoid method while creating a class factory instance, the method saves the pv parameter in its m_pfnCreateInstance member variable.

```
class CComClassFactory :
    public IClassFactory,
    public CComObjectRootEx<CComGlobalsThreadModel>
{
public:
    . . .
 void SetVoid(void* pv)
  { m_pfnCreateInstance = (_ATL_CREATORFUNC*)pv;}
 _ATL_CREATORFUNC* m_pfnCreateInstance;
};
```

Let's look at the class object creation code in the ATL helper function once again:

```
HRESULT hRes = pfnGetClassObject( pfnCreateInstance,
                                  IID_IUnknown, (LPVOID*) &p);
```

The pfnGetClassObject variable points to the CreateInstance creator function that creates the appropriate instance of the *class object* for the server. The pfnCreateInstance variable points to the CreateInstance creator function that creates an instance of the *class*.

When ATL calls the pfnGetClassObject function, it passes the pfnCreate-Instance object map entry member variable as the pv parameter to the CCom-ClassFactory::CreateInstance method. The class object saves this pointer in its `m_pfnCreateInstance` member variable and calls the `m_pfnCreate-Instance` function whenever a client requests the class object to create an instance of the class. Whew!

You must be wondering why ATL goes to all this trouble. Holding a function pointer to an instance creation function increases the size of every class object by four bytes (the size of the `m_pfnCreateInstance` variable). Nearly everywhere else, ATL uses templates for this kind of feature. For example, we could define the `CComClassFactory` class to accept a template parameter that is the instance class to create. Then each instance of the class object wouldn't need the extra four-byte function pointer. The code would look something like this:

```
template <class T>
class CComClassFactory :
  . . .
{
  . . .
  STDMETHOD(CreateInstance)(LPUNKNOWN pUnkOuter,
                            REFIID riid, void** ppvObj)
  {
      . . .
      ATLTRY(p = new T ());
      . . .
  }
};
```

The problem with this alternative approach is that it actually takes more memory to implement. For example, let's assume you have a server that implements three classes: A, B, and C.

ATL's current approach takes 12 bytes per class object (4-byte vptr, 4-byte unused reference count, and 4-byte function pointer) times three class objects (A, B, and C) plus 20 bytes for a single `CComClassFactory` vtable (five entries of 4 bytes each). All three classes' objects are actually unique instances of the same `CComClassFactory` class, so all three share a single vtable. Each instance maintains unique state—a function pointer—which creates different instance classes when called. This is a total of 56 bytes for the three class objects. (Recall that ATL never creates more than one instance of a class object.)

The template approach takes 8 bytes per class object (4-byte vptr and 4-byte unused reference count) times three class objects (A, B, and C) plus 20 bytes each for three `CComClassFactory` vtables (one for `CComClassFactory<A>`, one for `CComClassFactory<B>`, and one for `CComClassFactory<C>`). In this case, the class object doesn't maintain state to tell it what instance class to create. Therefore, each class must have its own unique vtable that points to a unique Create-Instance method that calls new on the appropriate class. This is a total of 84 bytes.

The above is mostly a theoretical calculation, though. Most heap managers round allocations up to a multiple of 16 bytes, which makes the instance sizes the same. This more or less makes moot the issue that class objects carry around a reference count member variable that they never use.

However, the memory savings are real, mainly due to the single required vtable. The function pointer implementation requires only a single copy of the IClass-Factory methods, therefore only one vtable, regardless of the number of classes implemented by a server. The template approach requires one copy of the IClass-Factory methods per class, therefore one vtable per class. The memory savings increase as you have more classes in a server.

I know. That's more detail than you wanted to know. Think of all the character and moral fiber you're building. You're welcome. That's why I'm here. Now, let's look at how CComClassFactory and related classes actually work.

CComClassFactory and Friends

DECLARE_CLASSFACTORY and CComClassFactory.   Typically, ATL objects acquire a class factory by deriving from CComCoClass. This class includes the macro DECLARE_CLASSFACTORY, which declares CComClassFactory as the default class factory class.

The CComClassFactory class is the most frequently used of the ATL-supplied class object implementations. It implements the IClassFactory interface and also explicitly specifies that the class object needs the same level of thread safety, CComGlobalsThreadModel, that globally available objects require. This is because a class object can be accessed by multiple threads when the server's threading model is Apartment, Free, or Both. Only when the server's threading model is Single does the class object not need to be thread safe.

```
class CComClassFactory :
    public IClassFactory,
    public CComObjectRootEx<CComGlobalsThreadModel>
public:
    BEGIN_COM_MAP(CComClassFactory)
        COM_INTERFACE_ENTRY(IClassFactory)
    END_COM_MAP()

// IClassFactory
STDMETHOD(CreateInstance)(LPUNKNOWN pUnkOuter,
                          REFIID riid, void** ppvObj);
STDMETHOD(LockServer)(BOOL flock);
```

```
// helper
void SetVoid(void* pv);

_ATL_CREATORFUNC* m_pfnCreateInstance;
};
```

Your class object must implement a `CreateInstance` method that creates an instance of your class. The `CComClassFactory` implementation of this method does some error checking, then calls the `m_pfnCreateInstance` function pointer to create the appropriate instance.

```
STDMETHOD(CreateInstance)(LPUNKNOWN pUnkOuter,
                          REFIID riid, void** ppvObj)
{
    . . .
        else hRes = m_pfnCreateInstance(pUnkOuter, riid, ppvObj);
    }
    return hRes;
}
```

As described earlier, the object map entry for your class contains the original value for this function pointer. It points to an instance creator class, as described in Chapter 3, and is set by the following part of the `OBJECT_ENTRY` macro:

```
class::_CreatorClass::CreateInstance, NULL, 0, \
```

When your class derives from `CComCoClass`, you inherit a `typedef` for `_CreatorClass`, which will be used unless you override it with a new definition.

```
template <class T, const CLSID* pclsid = &CLSID_NULL>
class CComCoClass
{
public:
        DECLARE_AGGREGATABLE(T)
    . . .
};
```

The default `DECLARE_AGGREGATABLE` macro defines the `CreatorClass` typedef to reference the `CComCreator2` class. This creator class creates instances of your class using one or two other creator classes, depending on whether or not the instance is aggregated. It uses a `CComCreator` to create instances of

`CComObject<YourClass>` type when asked to create a nonaggregated instance. It uses a `CComCreator` to create instances of `CComAggObject<YourClass>` type when asked to create an aggregated instance.

```
#define DECLARE_AGGREGATABLE(x) public:\
    typedef CComCreator2< CComCreator< CComObject< x > >, \
      CComCreator< CComAggObject< x > > > \
    _CreatorClass;
```

DECLARE_CLASSFACTORY_EX.   You can specify a custom class factory class for ATL to use when creating instances of your object class. To override the default specification of `CComClassFactory`, add the DECLARE_CLASSFACTORY_EX macro to your object class and, as the macro parameter, specify the name of your custom class factory class. This class should derive from `CComClassFactory` and override its `CreateInstance` method. For example:

```
class CMyClass : ..., public CComCoClass< ... >
{
public:
  DECLARE_CLASSFACTORY_EX(CMyClassFactory)

  ...
};

class CMyClassFactory : public CComClassFactory
{
 . . .
  STDMETHOD(CreateInstance)(LPUNKNOWN pUnkOuter,
                            REFIID riid, void** ppvObj);
};
```

ATL also provides three other macros that declare a class factory:

- DECLARE_CLASSFACTORY2 uses `CComClassFactory2` to control creation through a license.

```
#define DECLARE_CLASSFACTORY2(lic) \
    DECLARE_CLASSFACTORY_EX(CComClassFactory2<lic>)
```

- DECLARE_CLASSFACTORY_SINGLETON uses CComClassFactorySingleton to construct a single CComObjectGlobal object and return the object in response to all instantiation requests.

```
#define DECLARE_CLASSFACTORY_SINGLETON(obj) \
    DECLARE_CLASSFACTORY_EX(CComClassFactorySingleton<obj>)
```

- DECLARE_CLASSFACTORY_AUTO_THREAD uses CComClassFactoryAuto-Thread to create new instances in a round-robin manner in multiple apartments.

```
#define DECLARE_CLASSFACTORY_AUTO_THREAD() \
    DECLARE_CLASSFACTORY_EX(CComClassFactoryAutoThread)
```

DECLARE_CLASSFACTORY2 and CComClassFactory2<lic>. The DECLARE_ CLASSFACTORY2 macro defines CComClassFactory2 as your object's class factory implementation. CComClassFactory2 implements the IClassFactory2 interface, which controls object instantiation using a license. A CComClassFactory2 class object running on a licensed system can provide a runtime license key that a client can save. Later, when the client runs on a nonlicensed system, it can only use the class object by providing the previously saved license key.

```
template <class license>
class CComClassFactory2 :
    public IClassFactory2,
    public CComObjectRootEx<CComGlobalsThreadModel>,
    public license
public:
    . . .

 STDMETHOD(CreateInstance)(LPUNKNOWN pUnkOuter,
                           REFIID riid, void** ppvObj)
 {
    . . .
    if (!IsLicenseValid()) return CLASS_E_NOTLICENSED;
    . . .
        return m_pfnCreateInstance(pUnkOuter, riid, ppvObj);
 }
 STDMETHOD(CreateInstanceLic)(IUnknown* pUnkOuter,
                              IUnknown* pUnkReserved,
                           REFIID riid, BSTR bstrKey, void** ppvObject);
```

```
STDMETHOD(RequestLicKey)(DWORD dwReserved, BSTR* pbstrKey);
STDMETHOD(GetLicInfo)(LICINFO* pLicInfo);
. . .
};
```

Note that the main difference between CComClassFactory and CComClassFactory2 is that the latter class's CreateInstance method only creates the instance on a licensed system, that is, when IsLicenseValid returns TRUE. The additional CreateInstanceLic method will always create an instance on a licensed system but only create an instance on an unlicensed system when the caller provides the correct license key.

The template parameter to CComClassFactory2<license> is a class that implements the following static functions:

VerifyLicenseKey	Returns TRUE if the argument is a valid license key.
GetLicenseKey	Returns a license key as a BSTR.
IsLicenseValid	Returns TRUE if the current system is licensed.

The following is an example of a simple license class:

```
const OLECHAR rlk[] = OLESTR("Some runtime license key") ;

class CMyLicense
{
protected:

 static BOOL VerifyLicenseKey(BSTR bstr) {
   return wcscmp (bstr, rlk) == 0;
 }

 static BOOL GetLicenseKey(DWORD dwReserved, BSTR* pBstr) {
   *pBstr = SysAllocString(rlk);
   return TRUE;
 }

 static BOOL IsLicenseValid() { return TRUE; }
};
```

You specify this license class as the parameter to the DECLARE_CLASSFACTORY2 macro in your object class. It overrides the _ClassFactoryCreatorClass type-def inherited from CComCoClass.

```
class ATL_NO_VTABLE CEarPolitic :
     public CComObjectRootEx<CComSingleThreadModel>,
     public CComCoClass<CEarPolitic, &CLSID_EarPolitic>,
     . . .
{
public:
   DECLARE_CLASSFACTORY2 (CMyLicense);
   . . .
};
```

DECLARE_CLASSFACTORY_SINGLETON and CComClassFactorySingleton. The DECLARE_CLASSFACTORY_SINGLETON macro defines CComClassFactory-Singleton as your object's class factory implementation. This class factory only creates a single instance of your class. All instantiation requests return the requested interface pointer on this one (singleton) instance.

The template parameter specifies the class of the singleton. The class factory creates this singleton object as a member variable, m_Obj, of the class factory.

```
template <class T>
class CComClassFactorySingleton : public CComClassFactory
{
public:
 void FinalRelease() { CoDisconnectObject(m_Obj.GetUnknown(), 0); }

 // IClassFactory
 STDMETHOD(CreateInstance)(LPUNKNOWN pUnkOuter,
                           REFIID riid, void** ppvObj)
 {
   . . .
   hRes = m_Obj.QueryInterface(riid, ppvObj);
   . . .
   return hRes;
 }
 CComObjectGlobal<T> m_Obj;
};
```

The following is an example of a simple singleton class:

```
class CMyClass : ..., public CComCoClass< ... >
{
public:
  DECLARE_CLASSFACTORY_SINGLETON(CMySingletonClass)

  ...
};
```

You should avoid using singletons if possible. A singleton in a DLL is only unique per process. A singleton in an out-of-process server is only unique per system at best, and often not even then due to security and multiuse settings. Typically, most uses of a singleton would be better modeled as multiple instances sharing state, rather than as one shared instance. Also, you should realize that singletons do not work under MTS.

Most surprising to many people is that an ATL-based inproc singleton that runs in a single-thread apartment (STA) must not require thread affinity, must be thread safe, and must be apartment neutral! This is because the singleton class object will hand out a direct pointer to every STA-based client. Only a multithreaded-apartment-based client receives the (expected) proxy pointer in this case.

DECLARE_CLASSFACTORY_AUTO_THREAD and CComClassFactoryAuto-Thread. The DECLARE_CLASSFACTORY_AUTO_THREAD macro defines CCom-ClassFactoryAutoThread as your object's class factory implementation. This class factory creates each instance in one of a number of apartments. You can only use this class in an out-of-process server. Basically, this class factory passes every instantiation request to your server's global _Module instance (discussed later in this chapter), which does all the real work:

```
class CComClassFactoryAutoThread :
  . . .
  STDMETHODIMP CreateInstance(LPUNKNOWN pUnkOuter,
                             REFIID riid, void** ppvObj)
  {
    . . .
    hRes = _Module.CreateInstance(m_pfnCreateInstance, riid, ppvObj);
    . . .
  }
};
```

The server's _MODULE global instance must derive from CComAutoThreadModule, not simply CExeModule. CComAutoThreadModule derives from CComModule to implement a pool of single-thread apartments in an out-of-process server. By default, the server creates four STAs per processor on the system. The class factory forwards each instantiation request, in a round-robin basis, to one of the STAs. This allocates the class instances in multiple apartments, which can, in certain situations, provide greater concurrent execution without the complexity of writing a thread-safe object.

The following is an example of a class that uses this class factory:

```
class CMyClass : ..., public CComCoClass< ... >
{
public:
  DECLARE_CLASSFACTORY_AUTO_THREAD()

  ...
};
```

You've seen the object map, which is a fundamental data structure in an ATL server. You've seen the various requirements and options for classes, both createable and noncreateable, to be listed in the object map. Now, let's look at the part of ATL that actually uses the object map: the CComModule class, its derived classes, and the global variable of that type called _Module.

The CComModule Class

All COM servers need to support registration, class object management, and lifetime management. Each type of server provides these functions slightly differently, but the basic required functionality is the same for all types of servers.

ATL defines the CComModule class, which provides numerous helper methods supporting server registration, class object management, and lifetime management. Many of these methods simply iterate over the entries in the object map and ask each class in the map to perform the real work.

When you create an ATL COM server project using the Visual C++ ATL project wizard, it generates relatively boilerplate code that uses CComModule functionality to implement the server. An ATL server contains one global instance of the CComModule (or derived) class, which you must name _Module. The _Module instance also holds state global to the entire server.

The _Module Global Variable

An ATL inproc server uses the CComModule class directly by declaring a global in-stance of the class in the server's project.cpp file.

```
CComModule _Module;
```

A local server defines a specialized version of CComModule, called CExe-Module, in the server's project.h file and creates an instance of the derived class in the server's project.cpp file.

```
// <project>.h
class CExeModule : public CComModule
{
// Code deleted for clarity
};

// <project>.cpp
CExeModule _Module;
```

A service-based server also defines a specialized version of CComModule, called CServiceModule, in the server's project.h file and creates an instance of the derived class in the server's project.cpp file.

```
// <project>.h
class CServiceModule : public CComModule
{
// Code deleted for clarity
};

// <project>.cpp
CServiceModule _Module;
```

A server containing any classes using the auto-threading class object (DECLARE _CLASSFACTORY_AUTO_THREAD) needs to define a specialized version of CCom-AutoThreadModule (which derives from the wizard-generated CExeModule) in the server's project.h file and create an instance of the derived class in the server's project.cpp file. It must override the Unlock method to call the base class's Unlock method and, when the server's lock count reaches zero, set the bActivity flag to true and signal a shutdown event.

```
// <project>.h
class CAutoModule : public
CComAutoThreadModule<CComSimpleThreadAllocator>
{
public:
  LONG Unlock( )
  {
    LONG l = CComAutoThreadModule<ComSimpleThreadAllocator>::Unlock( );
    if (l == 0) {
      bActivity = true;
      // tell monitor that we transitioned to zero
      SetEvent(hEventShutdown);
    }
    return l;
  }
};

// <project>.cpp
CAutoModule _Module;
```

CComAutoThreadModule itself derives from CComModule to implement an out-of-process server that contains a pool of single-threaded apartments. CComAutoThreadModule uses CComApartment to manage an apartment for each thread in the module. The template parameter defaults to CComSimpleThreadAllocator, which manages thread selection for CComAutoThreadModule.

```
class CComSimpleThreadAllocator
{
public:
    CComSimpleThreadAllocator() { m_nThread = 0; }
    int GetThread(CComApartment* /*pApt*/, int nThreads)
    {
        if (++m_nThread == nThreads) m_nThread = 0;
        return m_nThread;
    }
    int m_nThread;
};
```

CComSimpleThreadAllocator provides one method, GetThread, which selects the thread on which CComAutoThreadModule will create the next object instance.

You can write your own apartment-selection algorithm by creating a thread alloca-tor class and specifying it as the parameter to CComAutoThreadModule.

For example, the following code selects the thread (apartment) for the next ob-ject instantiation randomly (though it has the downside of using a C runtime library function to get the random number).

```
class CRandomThreadAllocator
{
public:
    int GetThread(CComApartment* /*pApt*/, int nThreads)
    {
        return rand () % nThreads;
        }
};
```

Then you need to derive your _Module instance class from CComAutoThread-Module and specify your new thread selection class as the template parameter.

```
class CAutoModule : public CComAutoThreadModule<CRandomThreadAllocator>
{
public:
    . . .
};
```

The _Module Instance Initialization

Before you can use a CComModule instance, you must initialize it, and, when done with it, uninitialize it. Normally you'd initialize an object in its constructor and uninitialize it in its destructor. However, the _Module instance is a global variable. The C++ runtime library calls the constructors and destructors of global and static object instances. ATL, *by default*, does not use or link with the C++ runtime library. This means that, *by default*, the constructors and destructors of global and static objects are never called in an ATL project.

Therefore, the CComModule class defines Init and Term methods that you must explicitly call to initialize and uninitialize the _Module global instance.[8] When you call the Init method, you specify the *object map* for the server, the *instance handle* for the module (DLL or EXE), and the *globally unique identifier* (GUID) of a type library that describes the classes and interfaces used by the server. Many of the methods of the CComModule class operate on all classes defined in the object map.

---

[8]An initialization method would have to be called even if ATL used global constructors because the in-stance handle isn't available at the time the CRT runs constructors of global objects.

```
HRESULT Init(_ATL_OBJMAP_ENTRY* p, HINSTANCE h,
             const GUID* plibid = NULL);

void Term();
```

An inproc server initializes and uninitializes its `_Module` object in its `DllMain` function.

```
extern "C" BOOL
WINAPI DllMain(HINSTANCE hInstance, DWORD dwReason,
               LPVOID /*lpReserved*/)
{
    if (dwReason == DLL_PROCESS_ATTACH) {
        _Module.Init(ObjectMap, hInstance, &LIBID_ATLINPROCLib);
        DisableThreadLibraryCalls(hInstance);
    }
    else if (dwReason == DLL_PROCESS_DETACH)
        _Module.Term();
    return TRUE;      // ok
}
```

Both local servers and service-based servers initialize and uninitialize their respective `_Module` objects in their `WinMain` functions. Here's an example for a local server. A service calls the Windows NT Service Control Manager from `WinMain` rather than running a message loop, but otherwise operates the same.

```
extern "C" int
WINAPI _tWinMain(HINSTANCE hInstance, HINSTANCE /*hPrevInstance*/,
                 LPTSTR lpCmdLine, int /*nShowCmd*/)
{
    . . .
    _Module.Init(ObjectMap, hInstance, &LIBID_ATLLOCALLib);
    . . .
    MSG msg;
    while (GetMessage(&msg, 0, 0, 0)) DispatchMessage(&msg);
    . . .
    _Module.Term();
    . . .
}
```

When you call the `Init` method on the `_Module` instance ATL not only initializes the `CComModule` instance but also iterates over the object map and calls the

ObjectMain static member function of each class in the map with the bStarting parameter set to true. When you call the Term method, ATL releases any references to class objects that it has cached in the object map, then calls the Object-Main function of each class in the map with the bStarting parameter set to false.

The CComModule Registration Support

The CComModule class has extensive support for registration and unregistration of COM objects and servers.

The UpdateRegistryClass Method

The UpdateRegistryClass method enters or removes an object's standard class registration information (ProgID, version-independent ProgID, class description, and threading model) into or from the system registry. It calls on the Register-ClassHelper and UnregisterClassHelper methods to perform the actual task.

```
// Standard registration entries method
HRESULT WINAPI
UpdateRegistryClass(const CLSID& clsid, LPCTSTR lp szProgID,
 LPCTSTR lpszVerIndProgID, UINT nDescID,
 DWORD dwFlags, BOOL bRegister);

// Helper methods
HRESULT WINAPI
RegisterClassHelper(const CLSID& clsid, LPCTSTR lpszProgID,
 LPCTSTR lpszVerIndProgID, UINT nDescID, DWORD dwFlags);

HRESULT WINAPI
UnregisterClassHelper(const CLSID& clsid, LPCTSTR lpszProgID,
 LPCTSTR lpszVerIndProgID);
```

The UpdateRegistryClass method and its helper methods typically aren't used that often because they're limited in the registration entries they support.

The RegisterServer and UnregisterServer Methods

More often, you'll use the RegisterServer or UnregisterServer methods.

```
HRESULT RegisterServer(BOOL bRegTypeLib = FALSE,
                       const CLSID* pCLSID = NULL);
HRESULT UnregisterServer(const CLSID* pCLSID = NULL);
```

```
HRESULT UnregisterServer(BOOL bUnRegTypeLib,
                const CLSID* pCLSID = NULL);
```

The `RegisterServer` method updates the system registry for a single class object when the `pCLSID` parameter is non-NULL. When the parameter is NULL, the method calls the `UpdateRegistry` method for all classes listed in the object map. When the `bRegTypeLib` parameter is TRUE, the method also registers the type library.

The `UnregisterServer` method removes the registry entries for a single class when the `pCLSID` parameter is non-NULL. When the parameter is NULL, the method calls the `UpdateRegistry` method for all classes listed in the object map. The overloaded method accepting a `bUnRegTypeLib` parameter will also unregister the type library when the parameter is TRUE.

Inproc servers call on this support from their `DllRegisterServer` and `DllUnregisterServer` functions:

```
STDAPI DllRegisterServer(void)
{
    return _Module.RegisterServer(TRUE);
}

STDAPI DllUnregisterServer(void)
{
    return _Module.UnregisterServer(TRUE);
}
```

A local server's `WinMain` code registers or unregisters the server's resource script entries and then calls the `_Module` object's `RegisterServer` method to do the same for each class in the object map.

```
if (lstrcmpi(lpszToken, _T("UnregServer"))==0) {
    _Module.UpdateRegistryFromResource(IDR_ATLLocal, FALSE);
    nRet = _Module.UnregisterServer(TRUE);

    . . .

    break;
}
if (lstrcmpi(lpszToken, _T("RegServer"))==0) {
    _Module.UpdateRegistryFromResource(IDR_ATLLocal, TRUE);
    nRet = _Module.RegisterServer(TRUE);

    . . .

    break;
}
```

The UpdateRegistryFromResource Methods

Notice that a local server first calls the `UpdateRegistryFromResource` member function to register and unregister the server-specific entries before registering the class-specific entries. The `UpdateRegistryFromResource` method is the same method that your class uses when you specify the DECLARE_REGISTRY_RESOURCE or DECLARE_REGISTRY_RESOURCEID macros, discussed previously in this chapter.

Note that when you define the preprocessor symbol _ATL_STATIC_REGISTRY, the `UpdateRegistryFromResource` method maps to `UpdateRegistryFromResourceS`, which is a function that is statically linked into your server. When you do not define this preprocessor symbol, the method maps to `UpdateRegistryFromResourceD`, which is a function in `atl.dll` to which your server dynamically links. When you don't define the preprocessor symbol, you must distribute `atl.dll` along with your server.

```
#ifdef _ATL_STATIC_REGISTRY
#define UpdateRegistryFromResource UpdateRegistryFromResourceS
#else
#define UpdateRegistryFromResource UpdateRegistryFromResourceD
#endif


// Resource-based registration
HRESULT WINAPI UpdateRegistryFromResourceD(LPCTSTR lpszRes,
  BOOL bRegister, struct _ATL_REGMAP_ENTRY* pMapEntries = NULL);
HRESULT WINAPI UpdateRegistryFromResourceD(UINT nResID,
  BOOL bRegister, struct _ATL_REGMAP_ENTRY* pMapEntries = NULL);


#ifdef _ATL_STATIC_REGISTRY
// Statically linking to Registry COM Ponent
HRESULT WINAPI UpdateRegistryFromResourceS(LPCTSTR lpszRes,
  BOOL bRegister, struct _ATL_REGMAP_ENTRY* pMapEntries = NULL);
HRESULT WINAPI UpdateRegistryFromResourceS(UINT nResID,
  BOOL bRegister, struct _ATL_REGMAP_ENTRY* pMapEntries = NULL);
#endif
```

The Type Library Registration Methods

There are a few other registration helper methods provided by `CComModule`.

```
// Registry support (helpers)
HRESULT RegisterTypeLib();
HRESULT RegisterTypeLib(LPCTSTR lpszIndex);
```

```
HRESULT UnRegisterTypeLib();
HRESULT UnRegisterTypeLib(LPCTSTR lpszIndex);
```

RegisterTypeLib, as you might expect, registers the type library contained in your server's resources. UnRegisterTypeLib unregisters it, of course. These two methods expect the type library to be present in your server's resources as a custom resource of type TYPELIB with integer resource identifier 1, by default. You create such a resource by adding the following line to your server's .rc file:

```
1 TYPELIB "ATLInternals.tlb"
```

You can embed multiple type libraries in a server, though it's an unusual thing to do. You simply need to give them unique integer resource identifiers.

```
1 TYPELIB "ATLInternals.tlb"
2 TYPELIB "ATLInternalsEx.tlb"
```

To register or unregister the second type library, you must call the RegisterType-Lib or UnRegisterTypeLib method, respectively, and specify a string in the form "\\N", where N is the integer index of the TYPELIB resource. The following lines register both type libraries from the previous resource script example:

```
_Module.RegisterTypeLib ()
_Module.RegisterTypeLib (_T ("\\2))
```

The RegisterProgID Method

The last registration helper method is RegisterProgID. It does what you might expect. It creates the specified ProgID entry under HKEY_CLASSES_ROOT with the specified description. Additionally, it creates the CLSID named value for the ProgID, which points at the specified CLSID. It requires the string version of the CLSID.

```
static HRESULT RegisterProgID(LPCTSTR lpszCLSID, LPCTSTR lpszProgID,
                              LPCTSTR lpszUserDesc);
```

Basically, it sets up these registry entries:

```
HKEY_CLASSES_ROOT\lpszProgID = lpszUserDesc
HKEY_CLASSES_ROOT\lpszProgID\CLSID = lpszCLSID
```

CComCoClass Revisited

Earlier in this chapter, you saw how deriving from CComCoClass provided your class with a default implementation of support for aggregation as well as a default implementation of a class factory.

CComCoClass provides aggregation support via inheritance of the DECLARE_ AGGREGATABLE macro's typedef of _CreatorClass. It also provides the default implementation of a class factory via inheritance of the DECLARE_CLASS_FACTORY macro's _ClassFactoryCreatorClass typedef.

The Error Methods

CComCoClass also provides a number of other useful static methods. Six of the methods are overloaded and call Error. They set up the COM Error object, using its IErrorInfo interface to provide rich error information to the client. In order to call Error, your object should also implement the ISupportErrorInfo interface.

When the hRes parameter is nonzero, Error returns the value of hRes. When hRes is zero, the first four versions of Error return DISP_E_EXCEPTION. The last two versions return the result of the macro MAKE_HRESULT(1, FACILITY_ITF, nID), creating a custom failure HRESULT.

```
static HRESULT WINAPI
Error(LPCOLESTR lpszDesc, const IID& iid = GUID_NULL,
      HRESULT hRes = 0);
static HRESULT WINAPI
Error(LPCOLESTR lpszDesc, DWORD dwHelpID, LPCOLESTR lpszHelpFile,
      const IID& iid = GUID_NULL, HRESULT hRes = 0);

#ifndef OLE2ANSI
static HRESULT WINAPI
Error(LPCSTR lpszDesc, const IID& iid = GUID_NULL, HRESULT hRes = 0);

static HRESULT WINAPI
Error(LPCSTR lpszDesc, DWORD dwHelpID, LPCSTR lpszHelpFile,
      const IID& iid = GUID_NULL, HRESULT hRes = 0);
#endif

static HRESULT WINAPI
Error(UINT nID, const IID& iid = GUID_NULL, HRESULT hRes = 0,
      HINSTANCE hInst = _Module.GetResourceInstance());
```

```
static HRESULT WINAPI
Error(UINT nID, DWORD dwHelpID, LPCOLESTR lpszHelpFile,
      const IID& iid = GUID_NULL, HRESULT hRes = 0,
      HINSTANCE hInst = _Module.GetResourceInstance());
```

It seems odd to me that ATL includes the `Error` functionality in `CComCoClass` rather than in a more widely applicable place, such as `CComObjectRootEx`. Should you need to generate rich error information when your class isn't derived from `CComCoClass`, you can always call the ATL helper function `AtlReportError`. The `CComCoClass::Error` methods all use this helper function.

```
HRESULT WINAPI AtlReportError(const CLSID& clsid, UINT nID,
    const IID& iid,HRESULT hRes, HINSTANCE hInst);
HRESULT WINAPI AtlReportError
  (const CLSID& clsid, UINT nID, DWORD dwHelpID,
   LPCOLESTR lpszHelpFile, const IID& iid, HRESULT hRes, HINSTANCE
     hInst);

HRESULT WINAPI AtlReportError(const CLSID& clsid, LPCSTR lpszDesc,
    DWORD dwHelpID, LPCSTR lpszHelpFile, const IID& iid, HRESULT hRes)

HRESULT WINAPI AtlReportError(const CLSID& clsid, LPCSTR lpszDesc,
    const IID& iid, HRESULT hRes);

HRESULT WINAPI AtlReportError(const CLSID& clsid, LPCOLESTR lpszDesc,
    const IID& iid, HRESULT hRes);

HRESULT WINAPI AtlReportError(const CLSID& clsid, LPCOLESTR lpszDesc,
    DWORD dwHelpID, LPCOLESTR lpszHelpFile, const IID& iid,
      HRESULT hRes);
```

The Instantiation Methods

`CComCoClass` also provides two useful overloaded `CreateInstance` methods that create an instance of your class: one for creating an aggregated instance of your class and one that creates a nonaggregated instance.

```
template <class Q>
static HRESULT CreateInstance(IUnknown* punkOuter, Q** pp)
{
```

```
return T::_CreatorClass::CreateInstance(punkOuter, __uuidof(Q),
                                        (void**) pp);
}


template <class Q>
static HRESULT CreateInstance(Q** pp)
{
return T::_CreatorClass::CreateInstance(NULL, __uuidof(Q),
                                        (void**) pp);
}
```

You use these two methods like this:

```
ISpeaker* pSpeaker;
// Creates nonaggregated instance
HRESULT hr = CDemagogue::CreateInstance (&pSpeaker);

// Creates aggregated instance (assuming the class supports
// aggregation)
HRESULT hr = CDemagogue::CreateInstance (punkOuter, &pSpeaker);
```

Note that the use of the __uuidof operator in the template functions means you do not have to specify the interface ID for the interface that you want on the newly instantiated object. The compiler gets the ID from the type of the interface pointer variable you pass as an argument to the CreateInstance method.

Server Optimization Compilation Options

ATL supports building a server optimized for minimum size or minimum dependencies. There are three preprocessor symbols you define to affect the server optimization.

_ATL_MIN_CRT	The server doesn't link with the standard C/C++ runtime library.
_ATL_DLL	The server dynamically links to the atl.dll utility function library.
_ATL_STATIC_REGISTRY	The server statically links to the component registrar support.

When you define the _ATL_MIN_CRT preprocessor symbol, your server does not link with the C/C++ runtime library, and ATL provides an implementation of the `malloc`, `realloc`, `free`, `new`, and `delete` functions. You should not call any other C/C++ runtime library functions when you define this symbol.[9] If you do, you will receive the following (unintuitive) error message:

```
LIBC.lib(crt0.obj) : error LNK2001: unresolved external symbol _main
```

This error means you've called one or more functions in the C runtime library implementation in the CRT but, because you defined the _ATL_MIN_CRT preprocessor symbol, you didn't link with the library. Either eliminate the call(s) to the runtime library functions or remove the preprocessor symbol definition. Wizard-generated ATL projects define _ATL_MIN_CRT for all release builds and do not define the symbol for all debug builds.

Note that a server also requires the CRT when it uses exception handling or needs to run the constructors and destructors of objects declared as global or static variables.

ATL provides a few utility functions commonly used by servers plus the Component Registrar object (used to parse registry scripts) in `atl.dll`. When you define the _ATL_DLL preprocessor symbol, your server dynamically links to the utility functions in `atl.dll`, which means your server now requires `atl.dll` to be present. The absence of this symbol causes your server to link to the utility functions statically, which doesn't require `atl.dll` but increases the size of your server. Note also that ATL provides two versions of `atl.dll`—a Unicode version that only works on Windows NT and an ANSI version for Windows 9x.

When you define the _ATL_STATIC_REGISTRY preprocessor symbol, your server statically links with the component registrar, which increases the size of your server when the server uses registry scripts (the default). The absence of this symbol causes your server to link dynamically to the component registrar in `atl.dll`.

A wizard-generated project generates various build configurations using these symbols. The `Debug` build configurations do not define any of these three symbols. The `RelMinSize` build configurations define _ATL_MIN_CRT and _ATL_DLL. The `RelMinDependency` build configurations define _ATL_MIN_CRT and _ATL_STATIC_REGISTRY.

---

[9]This isn't strictly true. You can request that the Microsoft C/C++ compiler generate inline code for some runtime library functions by specifying the `#pragma intrinsic` compiler directive. For example, you can generate inline code for the `memcmp` and `strcmp` functions in this manner. Other "runtime library functions," such as `alloca` and `setjmp`, always generate inline code regardless of the setting of the intrinsic `pragma`. References to such functions in this case do not require the C/C++ runtime library.

Summary

The object map is the primary data table used by the CComModule-derived _Module object to register and unregister the classes in the server. CComModule provides numerous helper methods you can use to register and unregister your server, the classes in the server, and the component categories in the classes.

An ATL server creates a class factory for a class, as needed, using the class creator function entry in the object map. This class factory then creates instances of the class using the instance creator function entry in the object map. Typically, you inherit a default specification for the implementation of these two creator classes when you derive your class from CComCoClass. However, with the appropriate macro entries in your class, you can override these defaults and provide a custom class factory and/or custom instance creator function.

CComCoClass has some useful utility functions for reporting rich errors to a client using the COM ErrorInfo protocol. The class also has convenient instantiation methods that create an instance and query for the proper interface based on the type of the provided interface pointer variable.

Additionally, ATL provides three preprocessor symbols that allow you to build a server tailored for the smallest size or external dependencies.

CHAPTER 5

Interface Maps

While Chapter 3 discussed how ATL implements IUnknown, only AddRef and Release were covered completely. This chapter takes a look first at the requirements that COM makes on an object's implementation of QueryInterface and second on how ATL supports those requirements while still providing flexibility and extensibility.

Recall: COM Identity

From a client perspective, the rules of AddRef and Release are fairly stringent. Unless the client is careful about their use, objects could go away before expected or stay around too long. The object, however, is allowed to implement AddRef and Release in any number of ways, depending on how it would like to manage its own lifetime, for example, as a heap based, stack based, or cached object.

On the other hand, QueryInterface is pretty easy to get right on the client side. Any client can ask an object if it supports any other functionality with a simple call. However, clients expect certain relationships between the interfaces on a COM object. These expectations form the laws of COM identity.

The Laws of COM Identity

The laws of COM identity say the following things about how an object must expose its interfaces via QueryInterface.

- A client must be able to get directly to any interface implemented by the object via QueryInterface.
- An object's interfaces must be static for its life.
- QueryInterface for IUnknown must always succeed and must always return the same pointer value.

Direct Access to All Interfaces

The COM specification states that an implementation of QueryInterface must be "reflexive, symmetric and transitive." What this means is that, given an interface, a client must be able to use it to get directly to *any interface* implemented on the object, including the interface the client is using to perform the query. These relationships are mandated to maintain an object's identity in the face of multiple references to the same object. If these relationships are not upheld, a client could find itself with some code that doesn't work just because it has asked for the interfaces in the wrong order. Given a properly implemented `QueryInterface`, query order will not matter.

Static Types

Each object may decide for itself whether it wants to expose an interface via `QueryInterface`, regardless of the class to which it belongs. However, once it has been asked and has answered either "Yes, I support that interface" or "No, I don't support that interface," it must stick to that answer. The reason for this is simple: Once an object answers the query, it may never be asked again. For example, a client may pass a resultant interface pointer to another client, who never has to ask the object at all.

The potential for clients "talking amongst themselves" means that an object cannot use `QueryInterface` to make client-specific decisions, for example, decisions based on security constraints. The object also may not use `QueryInterface` to make context decisions that may change during the life of an object, for example, the time of day. If a client caches an interface pointer returned when the context is favorable, it may not ask again when the context has changed.

An Object's Apartment-Specific Identifier

The remoting layer of COM uses the four-byte pointer returned when querying for `IUnknown` as an object's unique identifier in that apartment. Clients may also compare `IUnknown*`s as an identity test. For example:

```
bool AreEqualObjects(IUnknown* punk1, IUnknown* punk2) {
  if( !punk1 || !punk2 ) return false;
  IUnknown* punka = 0;
  punk1->QueryInterface(IID_IUnknown, (void**)&punka);
  IUnknown* punkb = 0;
  punk2->QueryInterface(IID_IUnknown, (void**)&punkb);
  bool b = (punka == punkb);
  punka->Release(); punkb->Release();
  return b;
}
```

In fact, the ATL smart pointer classes have a method called `IsEqualObject` for performing just this comparison:

```
STDMETHODIMP CBall::SetPlaySurface(IRollSurface* prsNew) {
  if( m_sprs.IsEqualObject(prsNew) ) return S_OK;
  ...
}
```

However, while COM dictates that the pointer value of IUnknown must always be the same, it places no such restrictions on any other interface. This particular loophole leads to such techniques as tear-off interfaces, discussed later in this chapter.

Nothing Else

As long as the three laws of COM identity are upheld, an implementation of Query-Interface can be developed using scenes from your most vivid fever dreams. Frankly, I doubt you'll be able to come up with any techniques wackier than those already known, which I'll present during the rest of this chapter. However, if you do, ATL's implementation of QueryInterface is fully extensible, as you'll see.

Table-Driven QueryInterface

The Raw Interface Map

Remember from Chapter 3 that ATL's implementation of QueryInterface is called InternalQueryInterface and is provided as a static member function of CComObjectRootBase (shown here with debugging extensions removed):

```
static HRESULT WINAPI
CComObjectRootBase::InternalQueryInterface(
  void*                   pThis,
  const _ATL_INTMAP_ENTRY* pEntries,
  REFIID                  iid,
  void**                  ppvObject)
{
  // First entry in the com map should be a simple map entry
  ATLASSERT(pEntries->pFunc == _ATL_SIMPLEMAPENTRY);
  HRESULT hRes =
    AtlInternalQueryInterface(pThis, pEntries, iid, ppvObject);
  return hRes;
}
```

I'll show you the implementation of internal function, AtlInternalQuery-Interface, later. First, let's discuss the ATL_INTMAP_ENTRY structure, an array that is passed to InternalQueryInterface:

```
struct _ATL_INTMAP_ENTRY {
 const IID*          piid;
 DWORD               dw;
 _ATL_CREATORARGFUNC* pFunc;
};
```

Each entry provides a pointer to an interface identifier (IID), a pointer to a function to retrieve the requested interface, and a user-defined parameter to pass to the function. Functions that fit into this table must have the following signature:

```
HRESULT WINAPI InterfaceMapFunction(
 void*   pvThis, // Object's this pointer
 REFIID  riid,   // Interface requested
 LPVOID* ppv,    // Storage for requested interface
 DWORD   dw);    // dw from the interface map entry
```

The job of the interface map function is to take the object's this pointer, the interface being requested by the client, and the dw argument and to return the appropriate interface pointer in the ppv argument. The function is free to do whatever it likes, within the laws of COM identity, to perform this magic. For example, the following function assumes that the dw member is the offset of the vptr from the this pointer, that is, that we're using multiple inheritance (MI) to implement the interface:

```
HRESULT WINAPI _MI(void* pvThis, REFIID riid, LPVOID* ppv, DWORD dw) {
 *ppv = (BYTE*)pvThis + dw;
 reinterpret_cast<IUnknown*>(*ppv)->AddRef();
 return S_OK;
}
```

To fill in the _ATL_INTMAP_ENTRY for use with this function, we need to be able to calculate the offset of a vptr from the base, preferably at compile time. To help with this chore, ATL provides an interesting macro:

```
#define _ATL_PACKING 8
#define offsetofclass(base, derived) \
 ((DWORD)(static_cast<base*>((derived*)_ATL_PACKING))-_ATL_PACKING)
```

The offsetofclass macro makes it look as if we're asking the compiler to de-reference a pointer with the value 8, which is not such a great value for a pointer.[1] Instead, what we're doing is asking the compiler to imagine a pointer to an object and to calculate the difference between that and a member inside that object, that is, a vptr associated with a specific base class. The offsetofclass macro performs the same offset calculation the compiler does whenever it needs to perform a static_cast to a base class. Using offsetofclass allows us to fill the entry in an interface map like so:

```
class CBeachBall :
 public CComObjectRootEx<CBeachBall>,
 public ISphere,
 public IRollableObject,
 public IPlaything {
public:
const static _ATL_INTMAP_ENTRY* WINAPI
_GetEntries() {
 static const _ATL_INTMAP_ENTRY _entries[] = {
 { &IID_IUnknown, offsetofclass(ISphere, CBeachBall),
    _ATL_SIMPLEMAPENTRY },
 { &IID_ISphere, offsetofclass(ISphere, CBeachBall), _MI },
 { &IID_IRollableObject,  offsetofclass(IRollableObject,
    CBeachBall), _MI },
 { &IID_IPlaything, offsetofclass(IPlaything, CBeachBall),  _MI },
 };
return _entries;
};

HRESULT _InternalQueryInterface(REFIID iid, void** ppvObject)
{ return InternalQueryInterface(this, _GetEntries(), iid, ppvObject); }
...
};
```

Besides the population of the interface map, there are a couple of interesting things to notice about this code snippet. First, the _InternalQueryInterface function calls _GetEntries to retrieve the static interface map and forwards it to the InternalQueryInterface static member function in CComObjectRoot-Base. The _InternalQueryInterface function is required by CComObject et al. to implement QueryInterface.

---

[1] Microsoft didn't invent this particular oddity. The standard C runtime library comes with a macro very much like offsetofclass called offsetof.

Second, notice that IUnknown is the initial entry in the list and uses _ATL_ SIMPLEMAPENTRY instead of _MI. As I discussed in Chapter 3, the first entry is the one used for IUnknown and is required to be a *simple entry*. A simple entry is a special case that indicates that the interface is being exposed using multiple inheritance and that an offset is all that is needed to calculate the requested interface pointer. _ATL_SIMPLEMAPENTRY is a special value used in the pFunc field of the _ATL_INTMAP_ENTRY structure to indicate this case:

```
#define _ATL_SIMPLEMAPENTRY ((_ATL_CREATORARGFUNC*)1)
```

When AtlInternalQueryInterface encounters this special value, it knows how to perform the offset calculation just like the example function, _MI. Since _ATL_SIMPLEMAPENTRY completely replaces the need for a function that performs the offset calculation, ATL provides no interface map functions like _MI, although it provides others, as I'll discuss later.

Convenience Macros

You may enjoy writing the required _InternalQueryInterface and _Get-Entries methods, as well as the GetUnknown method discussed in Chapter 3, but I do not. To write these functions and to begin the static definition of the interface map, ATL provides BEGIN_COM_MAP.

```
#define BEGIN_COM_MAP(x) public: \
 typedef x _ComMapClass; \
 ... 
 IUnknown* _GetRawUnknown() { \
   ATLASSERT(_GetEntries()[0].pFunc == _ATL_SIMPLEMAPENTRY); \
   return (IUnknown*)((int)this+_GetEntries()->dw); \
 } \
 IUnknown* GetUnknown() { return _GetRawUnknown(); } \
 \
 HRESULT _InternalQueryInterface(REFIID iid, void** ppvObject) \
 { return InternalQueryInterface(this, _GetEntries(), iid, \
     ppvObject); } \
 \
 const static _ATL_INTMAP_ENTRY* WINAPI _GetEntries() { \
 static const _ATL_INTMAP_ENTRY _entries[] = {
```

To zero-terminate the interface map and to round out the _GetEntries implementation, ATL provides END_COM_MAP.

```
#define END_COM_MAP() { NULL, 0, 0 }}; return _entries; } \
virtual ULONG STDMETHODCALLTYPE AddRef( void) = 0; \
virtual ULONG STDMETHODCALLTYPE Release( void) = 0; \
STDMETHOD(QueryInterface)(REFIID, void**) = 0;
```

One other interesting thing that END_COM_MAP does is to provide another set of pure virtual member function definitions for QueryInterface, AddRef, and Release. This makes calls to IUnknown member functions unambiguous while calling them in the member functions of your ATL-based classes.

To populate each entry in the interface map, ATL provides a set of macros beginning with the COM_INTERFACE_ENTRY prefix, the simplest and most useful being COM_INTERFACE_ENTRY itself:

```
#define COM_INTERFACE_ENTRY(x)\
 {&_ATL_IIDOF(x), offsetofclass(x, _ComMapClass), \
   _ATL_SIMPLEMAPENTRY },
```

Notice the use of _ComMapClass as the name of the class associated with the static interface map. This type is provided by BEGIN_COM_MAP. The _ATL_IIDOF macro, on the other hand, is ATL's way of turning an interface type name into the corresponding globally unique identifier (GUID). Based on the presence or absence of the _ATL_NO_UUIDOF symbol, ATL will either use the VC++-specific __uuidof operator[2] or it will use the C preprocessor's token pasting operator:

```
#ifndef _ATL_NO_UUIDOF
#define _ATL_IIDOF(x) __uuidof(x)
#else
#define _ATL_IIDOF(x) IID_##x
#endif
```

Using these macros, the interface map can be defined much more simply than the previous example:

```
class CBeachBall :
 public CComObjectRootEx<CBeachBall>,
 public ISphere,
 public IRollableObject,
 public IPlaything {
```

---

[2]The __declspec(uuid()) and __uuidof operators are discussed in Chapter 3.

```
public:
BEGIN_COM_MAP(CBeachBall)
  COM_INTERFACE_ENTRY(ISphere)
  COM_INTERFACE_ENTRY(IRollableObject)
  COM_INTERFACE_ENTRY(IPlaything)
END_COM_MAP()
  ...
};
```

AtlInternalQueryInterface

Checking for IUnknown

`InternalQueryInterface` delegates to a global function, `AtlInternalQuery-Interface`, to provide its implementation. Before walking the table of interface entries, `AtlInternalQueryInterface` checks the IID of the request. If IUnknown is requested, the first entry is pulled from the table and handed back immediately, without walking the rest of the table. This is a welcome optimization, but it's more than that. It's absolutely necessary that IUnknown not be calculated by calling a function. Functions can fail and functions can return different values for the same interface identifier, both of which actions violate the laws of COM identity. The practical meaning for your classes is that the first entry must always be a simple one. Luckily, ATL is laden with assertions to this effect, so as long as you test your implementations at least once in debug mode before shipping them to your customers, you should be safe (on this note, anyway).

Walking the Table

At each entry in the table, a decision is made based on whether the `piid` member, a pointer to the interface identifier for that entry, is NULL or not. When it is not NULL, then the IID of the entry is compared with the IID of the request. When a match is found, the function referenced by `pFunc` is called and the result is returned to the client. When there is no match, the search advances to the next entry in the table.

On the other hand, when the `piid` member *is* NULL, the `pFunc` is called, no matter what the IID of the request is. If the result is S_OK, the result is returned to the client. Otherwise, the search continues with the next entry. This behavior is used for any of the COM_INTERFACE_ENTRY_XXX_BLIND macros, for example, COM_INTERFACE_ENTRY_AGGREGATE_BLIND.

Implementation

The following is the implementation of `AtlInternalQueryInterface`.

```
ATLINLINE ATLAPI AtlInternalQueryInterface(
 void*                    pThis,
 const _ATL_INTMAP_ENTRY* pEntries,
 REFIID                   iid,
 void**                   ppvObject)
{

 ATLASSERT(pThis != NULL);
 ATLASSERT(pEntries->pFunc == _ATL_SIMPLEMAPENTRY);
 if (ppvObject == NULL) return E_POINTER;
 *ppvObject = NULL;

 if (InlineIsEqualUnknown(iid)) {
   IUnknown* pUnk = (IUnknown*)((int)pThis+pEntries->dw);
   pUnk->AddRef();
   *ppvObject = pUnk;
   return S_OK;
 }

 while (pEntries->pFunc != NULL) {
   BOOL bBlind = (pEntries->piid == NULL);
   if (bBlind || InlineIsEqualGUID(*(pEntries->piid), iid)) {
     if (pEntries->pFunc == _ATL_SIMPLEMAPENTRY) {
       ATLASSERT(!bBlind);
       IUnknown* pUnk = (IUnknown*)((int)pThis+pEntries->dw);
       pUnk->AddRef();
       *ppvObject = pUnk;
       return S_OK;
     }
     else {
       HRESULT hRes = pEntries->pFunc(pThis, iid, ppvObject,
         pEntries->dw);
       if (hRes == S_OK || (!bBlind && FAILED(hRes)))
         return hRes;
     }
   }
   pEntries++;
 }
 return E_NOINTERFACE;
}
```

Multiple Inheritance

To support multiple inheritance of interfaces, ATL provides four separate interface entry macros. Two are for straight casts and two are for branching casts. A *straight cast* is a static_cast that the compiler needs no extra information to perform; that is, there are no ambiguities. On the other hand, a *branching cast* is used when a class has several base classes that all derive from the same base class themselves. Since a straight cast to the common base class would be ambiguous, the compiler needs to be provided with the inheritance branch to follow to resolve the ambiguity.

Straight Casting

COM_INTERFACE_ENTRY and COM_INTERFACE_ENTRY_IID

As I mentioned, COM_INTERFACE_ENTRY is the macro you're going to use most of the time. Its close cousin is COM_INTERFACE_ENTRY_IID:

```
#define COM_INTERFACE_ENTRY_IID(iid, x) \
  { &iid, offsetofclass(x, _ComMapClass), _ATL_SIMPLEMAPENTRY},
```

This latter macro allows you to specify the IID separately from the name of the interface. The classic usage of this macro is to avoid ambiguity. Imagine you have two interfaces that derive from the same base interface. For example,

```
interface IGlobe : ISphere {};
interface IPlanet : ISphere {};
```

If you have a class that derives from both of these interfaces, the compiler won't know which base class to cast to if you use COM_INTERFACE_ENTRY for ISphere:

```
class CDesktopGlobe :
 public CComObjectRootEx<CDesktopGlobe>,
 public IGlobe,
 public IPlanet {
public:
 ...
BEGIN_COM_MAP(CDesktopGlobe)
 COM_INTERFACE_ENTRY(ISphere) // ambiguous
 COM_INTERFACE_ENTRY(IGlobe)
 COM_INTERFACE_ENTRY(IPlanet)
END_COM_MAP()
 // ISphere methods
```

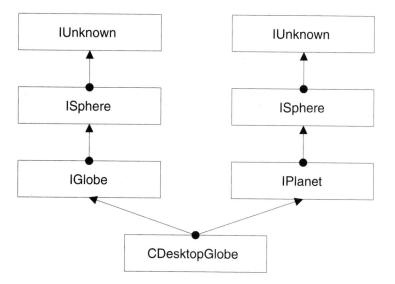

Figure 5.1. CDesktopGlobe inheritance hierarchy

```
...
// IGlobe methods
...
// IPlanet methods
...
};
```

The problem is more easily seen by looking at the inheritance hierarchy, as shown in Figure 5.1. The figure shows that we have two interfaces that CDesktop-Globe has inherited from more than once, IUnknown and ISphere. IUnknown is not a problem because ATL handles it specially by choosing the first entry in the interface map (as I discussed earlier). ISphere is a problem, though, because we have two of them, IGlobe and IPlanet. Each base interface has a separate vptr that points to a separate vtbl. Even though we have a shared implementation of all the methods of ISphere, and therefore duplicate entries in both the IGlobe and the IPlanet vtbls, the compiler still needs us to pick one. COM_INTERFACE_ENTRY_IID allows us to resolve this ambiguity:

```
class CDesktopGlobe :
  public CComObjectRootEx<CDesktopGlobe>,
  public IGlobe,
  public IPlanet {
public:
```

```
  ...
BEGIN_COM_MAP(CDesktopGlobe)
  COM_INTERFACE_ENTRY_IID(IID_ISphere, IGlobe) // unambiguous
  COM_INTERFACE_ENTRY(IGlobe)
  COM_INTERFACE_ENTRY(IPlanet)
END_COM_MAP()
  ...
};
```

In this case, because we have shared implementations of the ISphere methods in our implementation of IGlobe and IPlanet, it doesn't really matter which one we hand out. Sometimes it matters very much. As I mentioned in Chapter 3, COM_INTERFACE_ENTRY_IID is often used when exposing multiple dual interfaces, each of which derives from IDispatch. Using IDispatchImpl, we provide base class implementations of IDispatch that are different based on the dual interface we're implementing. In fact, any time you have multiple implementations of the same interface in the base classes, you must decide which implementation is the "default." Imagine another example of a base class interface implementation that has nothing to do with scripting:

```
template <typename Base> class ISphereImpl : public Base {...};
```

Using ISphereImpl would look like this:

```
class CDesktopGlobe :
  public CComObjectRootEx<CDesktopGlobe>,
  public ISphereImpl<IGlobe>,
  public ISphereImpl<IPlanet> {
public:
  ...
BEGIN_COM_MAP(CDesktopGlobe)
  COM_INTERFACE_ENTRY_ENTRY(IID_ISphere, IGlobe) // Default ISphere
  COM_INTERFACE_ENTRY(IGlobe)
  COM_INTERFACE_ENTRY(IPlanet)
END_COM_MAP()
  ...
};
```

Here's the problem: if the client queries for IGlobe (or ISphere) and calls ISphere methods, it will get different behavior than if it were to query for IPlanet and call ISphere methods. Now the client has just the kind of order-of-query problem that the laws of COM identity were built to prohibit. Multiple implementations of the same base interface clearly violate the spirit of the laws of COM identity, if not the letter.

Branch Casting

COM_INTERFACE_ENTRY2 and COM_INTERFACE_ENTRY2_IID

Both COM_INTERFACE_ENTRY2 and COM_INTERFACE_ENTRY2_IID are also simple entries meant for use with multiple inheritance:

```
#define COM_INTERFACE_ENTRY2(x, x2) \
  { &_ATL_IIDOF(x), \
    (DWORD)((x*)(x2*)((_ComMapClass*)8))-8, \
    _ATL_SIMPLEMAPENTRY},
```

```
#define COM_INTERFACE_ENTRY2_IID(iid, x, x2) \
  { &iid, \
    (DWORD)((x*)(x2*)((_ComMapClass*)8))-8, \
    _ATL_SIMPLEMAPENTRY},
```

COM_INTERFACE_ENTRY2 is very much like COM_INTERFACE_ENTRY_IID because it allows you to resolve the multiple bases problem. For example:

```
class CDesktopGlobe :
  public CComObjectRootEx<CDesktopGlobe>,
  public IGlobe,
  public IPlanet {
public:
  ...
BEGIN_COM_MAP(CDesktopGlobe)
  COM_INTERFACE_ENTRY2(ISphere, IGlobe) // Use the IGlobal branch
  COM_INTERFACE_ENTRY(IGlobe)
  COM_INTERFACE_ENTRY(IPlanet)
END_COM_MAP()
  ...
};
```

This macro performs its magic by allowing you to specify two things: the interface to expose (e.g., ISphere), and the branch of the inheritance hierarchy to follow to get to the implementation of that interface to use (e.g., IGlobe). This macro is slightly different from COM_INTERFACE_ENTRY_IID in that the interface is specified by name instead of by IID. If you'd like to be very explicit about both, use COM_INTERFACE_ENTRY2_IID:

```
class CDesktopGlobe :
  public CComObjectRootEx<CDesktopGlobe>,
  public IGlobe,
  public IPlanet {
public:
  ...
BEGIN_COM_MAP(CDesktopGlobe)
  COM_INTERFACE_ENTRY2_IID(&IID_ISphere, ISphere, IGlobe)
  COM_INTERFACE_ENTRY(IGlobe)
  COM_INTERFACE_ENTRY(IPlanet)
END_COM_MAP()
  ...
};
```

Since COM_INTERFACE_ENTRY2[_IID] provides no extra functionality beyond that provided by COM_INTERFACE_ENTRY[_IID], I tend to always use the latter and forget the former.

Handling Name Conflicts

One of the problems with multiple inheritance is that of name collisions. Imagine the following interfaces:

```
interface ICowboy : IUnknown {
    HRESULT Draw();
};

interface IArtist : IUnknown {
    HRESULT Draw();
};
```

Because both Draw methods have the same signature, using straight multiple inheritance requires a single shared implementation:

```
// Ace Powell was a cowboy/artist who lived in the western US from 1912
// to his death in 1978. I'd like to thank Tim Ewald for this fabulous
// example, which I have used to death for years.
class CAcePowell :
```

```
    public CComObjectRootEx<CComSingleThreadModel>,
    public ICowboy,
    public IArtist {
public:
BEGIN_COM_MAP(CAcePowell)
  COM_INTERFACE_ENTRY(ICowboy)
  COM_INTERFACE_ENTRY(IArtist)
END_COM_MAP()
...
    STDMETHODIMP Draw() { /* Act as a cowboy or an artist? */ }
};
```

Since the implied meaning of Draw is very different for an artist than it is for a cowboy, we'd like to be able to provide two Draw implementations. For that, we use a technique long known to the C++ community that I'll call "forwarding shims."[3]

The problem is that C++ has no syntax to be able to distinguish methods with the same signature from different bases in the derived class. For example, the following is not legal C++.

```
class CAcePowell :
    public CComObjectRootEx<CComSingleThreadModel>,
    public ICowboy,
    public IArtist {
public:
BEGIN_COM_MAP(CAcePowell)
 COM_INTERFACE_ENTRY(ICowboy)
 COM_INTERFACE_ENTRY(IArtist)
END_COM_MAP()
...
    STDMETHODIMP IArtist::Draw(); // error
    STDMETHODIMP ICowboy::Draw(); // error
};
```

However, we can certainly distinguish the methods in individual base classes, for example:

```
struct _IArtist : public IArtist {
 STDMETHODIMP Draw() { return ArtistDraw(); }
 STDMETHOD(ArtistDraw)() =0;
};
```

---

[3] Tim Ewald showed me this technique originally, and Jim Springfield made me see its relevance to ATL.

```
struct _ICowboy : public ICowboy {
 STDMETHODIMP Draw() { return CowboyDraw(); }
 STDMETHOD(CowboyDraw)() =0;
};
```

Both _IArtist and _ICowboy are shim classes that implement the method with the conflicting name and forward to another pure virtual member function with a *unique name*. Since both shims derive from the interface in question, the interfaces IArtist and ICowboy can still appear in the interface map without difficulty:

```
class CAcePowell :
    public CComObjectRootEx<CComSingleThreadModel>,
    public _ICowboy,
    public _IArtist {
public:
BEGIN_COM_MAP(CAcePowell)
  COM_INTERFACE_ENTRY(ICowboy)
  COM_INTERFACE_ENTRY(IArtist)
END_COM_MAP()
...
  STDMETHODIMP ArtistDraw();
  STDMETHODIMP CowboyDraw();
};
```

This trick fills the vtbls for IArtist and ICowboy with _IArtist::Draw and _ICowboy::Draw. These functions, in turn, forward to the more derived class's implementation of the ArtistDraw and CowboyDraw. The forwarding shims remove our name conflict at the cost of an extra vtable per shim class, an extra entry per method per vtable, and an extra virtual function invocation per call. If this extra cost bothers you, remove it using the standard ATL tricks:[4]

```
template <typename Deriving>
struct ATL_NO_VTABLE _IArtist : public IArtist {
 STDMETHODIMP Draw()
   { return static_cast<Deriving*>(this) ->ArtistDraw(); }
};

template <typename Deriving>
struct ATL_NO_VTABLE _ICowboy : public ICowboy {
```

---

[4]Don Box suggested the final efficiency trick, the use of ATL_NO_VTABLE.

```
STDMETHODIMP Draw()
  { return static_cast<Deriving*>(this) ->CowboyDraw(); }
};

class ATL_NO_VTABLE CAcePowell :
    public CComObjectRootEx<CComSingleThreadModel>,
    public _ICowboy<CAcePowell>,
    public _IArtist<CAcePowell> {
public:
BEGIN_COM_MAP(CAcePowell)
 COM_INTERFACE_ENTRY(ICowboy)
 COM_INTERFACE_ENTRY(IArtist)
END_COM_MAP()
...
 HRESULT ArtistDraw();
 HRESULT CowboyDraw();
};
```

Don't Go Off Half-Cocked...

You may think it would be enough to change one of the names by only using one forwarding shim:

```
template <typename Deriving>
struct ATL_NO_VTABLE _ICowboy : public ICowboy {
 STDMETHODIMP Draw()
   { return static_cast<Deriving*>(this) ->CowboyDraw(); }
};

class ATL_NO_VTABLE CAcePowell :
    public CComObjectRootEx<CComSingleThreadModel>,
    public _ICowboy<CAcePowell>,
    public IArtist {
public:
BEGIN_COM_MAP(CAcePowell)
 COM_INTERFACE_ENTRY(ICowboy)
 COM_INTERFACE_ENTRY(IArtist)
END_COM_MAP()
...
  HRESULT Draw();       // Use for both IArtist::Draw and ICowboy::Draw
  HRESULT CowboyDraw(); // Never called!
};
```

Don't be tempted to try this. Remember that forwarding shims depend on overriding the behavior for the same member function name in the base classes. If you provide an implementation of the function in question with the same name as the function we're implementing in the forwarding shim in the base, *the forwarding shim function will never be called.* By implementing one of the functions in the deriving class, you've effectively provided an implementation of both, putting you right back where you were in the first place.

Interface Coloring

In the same "sneaky C++ trick" way that forwarding shims lets you fill the appropriate vtbl entries even if the compiler won't cooperate, ATL supports another technique called *interface coloring.* Interface coloring is based on the idea that two classes can be *layout compatible* but not *type compatible.* For example, the following two classes are layout compatible, because they each result in a vtbl with the same number of methods and every method at the same offset has the same signature:

```
struct ISphere : IUnknown {
  STDMETHOD(Rotate)(long nDegrees, long* pnOrientation) =0;
  STDMETHOD(Twirl)(long nVelocity) =0;
};


struct IRedSphere {
  // Colored IUnknown methods
  STDMETHOD(RedQueryInterface)( REFIID riid, void** ppv) =0;
  STDMETHOD_(ULONG, RedAddRef)() =0;
  STDMETHOD_(ULONG, RedRelease)() =0;

  // Uncolored ISphere methods
  STDMETHOD(Rotate)(long nDegrees, long* pnOrientation) =0;
  STDMETHOD(Twirl)(long nVelocity) =0;
};
```

However, because IRedSphere does not derive from ISphere, IRedSphere is not type compatible; that is, the compiler won't let you pass IRedSphere where ISphere is expected (without coercion).

Cloning the layout of an interface is known as *interface coloring.* The layout-compatible interface is said to be *colored* because it is identical to the original except for the names, a feature not important to the runtime behavior of your object, just as a color is unimportant to the runtime behavior of your car. The names are used at compile time, though, and allow you to implement multiple versions of the same interface. For example:

```
class CDesktopGlobe :
  public CComObjectRootEx<CDesktopGlobe>,
  public IRedSphere,
  public IGlobe,
  public IPlanet {
public:
 ...
BEGIN_COM_MAP(CDesktopGlobe)
  // Expose IRedShere when ISphere is requested
  COM_INTERFACE_ENTRY_IID(IID_ISphere, IRedSphere)
  COM_INTERFACE_ENTRY(IGlobe)
  COM_INTERFACE_ENTRY(IPlanet)
END_COM_MAP()
  ...
  // Colored method implementations
  STDMETHODIMP RedQueryInterface(REFIID riid, void** ppv)
  { return GetUnknown()->QueryInterface(riid, ppv); }

  STDMETHODIMP_(ULONG) RedAddRef() {
    _ThreadModel::Increment(&m_cRefSphere);
    return GetUnknown()->AddRef();
  }

  STDMETHODIMP_(ULONG) RedRelease() {
    _ThreadModel::Decrement(&m_cRefSphere);
    return GetUnknown()->Release();
  }

private:
  long  m_cRefSphere;
};
```

By deriving from IRedSphere, we can provide an implementation of all of the colored methods separately from the uncolored ones. By coloring the IUnknown methods of IRedSphere, we can handle IUnknown calls on ISphere separately from the other implementations of IUnknown by the other interfaces. In this case, we're using RedAddRef and RedRelease to keep track of an ISphere-specific reference count. And even though we expose IRedSphere to the client when it asks for

ISphere, as far as it's concerned it just received an ISphere interface pointer. Since IRedSphere and ISphere are layout compatible, as far as COM is concerned, the client is right.

```
void TryRotate(IUnknown* punk) {
 ISphere* ps = 0;

 // Implicit AddRef really a call to RedAddRef
 if( SUCCEEDED(punk->QueryInterface(IID_ISphere, (void**)&ps) {
   // ps actually points to an IRedSphere*

   ps->Rotate();
   ps->Release();  // Really a call to RedRelease
 }
}
```

COM_INTERFACE_ENTRY_IMPL and COM_INTERFACE_ENTRY_IMPL_IID

While interface coloring is somewhat interesting in the same way that a car wreck on the side of the road is interesting, it can also be disconcerting and may well slow down traffic. Beginning with ATL 3.0, interface coloring is no longer used by the vast majority of IXxxImpl classes.[5] In ATL 2.x, interface coloring was used for some, but not all, of the IXxxImpl classes to perform interface-specific reference counting. These implementation classes took the following form:

```
template <typename Deriving> class IXxxImpl {...};
```

Instead of deriving from the interface the class implemented, the implementation class used interface coloring to make itself layout compatible with the implemented interface. This allowed each class to implement its own reference counting but prohibited the use of the simple COM_INTERFACE_ENTRY macro. Instead, additional macros were provided to make the necessary entries in the interface map:

```
#define COM_INTERFACE_ENTRY_IMPL(x) \
COM_INTERFACE_ENTRY_IID(IID_##x, x##Impl<_ComMapClass>)
```

```
#define COM_INTERFACE_ENTRY_IMPL_IID(iid, x) \
COM_INTERFACE_ENTRY_IID(iid, x##Impl<_ComMapClass>)
```

---

[5]To my knowledge, only IPropertyPage2Impl still uses it. However, since it uses interface coloring to return E_NOTIMPL, it doesn't seem too important.

The interface coloring technique was only useful if you wanted to track references on some of the ATL-implemented interfaces. Beginning with ATL 3.0, ATL uses a more generic mechanism[6] that tracks reference counts on all interfaces. Toward that end, all the ATL implementation classes actually derive from the interface in question, making the use of COM_INTERFACE_ENTRY_IMPL and COM_INTER-FACE_ENTRY_IMPL_IID macros unnecessary.[7] All new and ported code should use COM_INTERFACE_ENTRY or COM_INTERFACE_ENTRY_IID instead. Old code that used the IMPL forms of the macros will still compile under the new ATL and will act appropriately.

Tear-off Interfaces

While multiple inheritance is preferred when implementing multiple interfaces, it's not perfect. One of the problems is something called *vptr bloat*. For each interface a class derives from, there is another vptr per instance of that class. Beefing up our beach ball implementation can lead to some significant overhead:

```
class CBeachBall :
  public CComObjectRootEx<CBeachBall>,
  public ISphere,
  public IRollableObject,
  public IPlaything,
  public ILethalObject,
  public ITakeUpSpace,
  public IWishIWereMoreUseful,
  public ITryToBeHelpful,
  public IAmDepressed {...};
```

Because each beach ball implements eight interfaces, each instance has 32 bytes of overhead before the reference count or any useful state. If clients actually made heavy use of these interfaces, that wouldn't be too high a price to pay. However, my guess is that most clients are going to use beach balls for their rollable and plaything abilities. Since the other interfaces will only be used infrequently, we'd rather not pay the overhead until they are used. For this, Crispin Goswell invented the tear-off interface, which he described in the "COM Programmer's Cookbook," available in the Microsoft Developer Network documentation.[8]

---

[6]The _ALT_DEBUG_INTERFACES macro provides this service and is discussed in Chapter 3.
[7]Except for IPropertyPage2Impl, as I mentioned earlier.
[8]As of this writing, Crispin's article is also available online at http://www.microsoft.com/oledev/olecom/com_co.htm.

Standard Tear-offs

A tear-off interface is an interface that we'd like to expose on demand, but not actually inherit from in the main class. Instead, an auxiliary class inherits from the tear-off interface and instances of that class are created any time a client queries for that interface. For example, assuming that few clients will think to turn a beach ball into a lethal weapon, ILethalObject would make an excellent tear-off interface for the CBeachBall class. Instead of using CComObjectRootEx as the base class, ATL classes implementing tear-off interfaces use the CComTearOffObjectBase as their base class.

```
template <class Owner, class ThreadModel = CComObjectThreadModel>
class CComTearOffObjectBase : public CComObjectRootEx<ThreadModel> {
public:
    typedef Owner _OwnerClass;
    // BUG: The owner must be a CComObject.
    CComObject<Owner>* m_pOwner;
    CComTearOffObjectBase() { m_pOwner = NULL; }
};
```

CComTearOffObjectBase provides one additional service, which is the caching of the *owner* of the tear-off interface. Each tear-off belongs to an owner object that has torn it off to satisfy a client's request. The owner is useful so that the tear-off instance can access member data or member functions of the owner class. For example:

```
class CBeachBallLethalness :
  public CComTearOffObjectBase<CBeachBall, CComSingleThreadModel>,
  public ILethalObject {
public:
BEGIN_COM_MAP(CBeachBallLethalness)
  COM_INTERFACE_ENTRY(ILethalObject)
END_COM_MAP()

  // ILethalObject methods
  STDMETHODIMP Kill() {
    m_pOwner->m_gasFill = GAS_HYDROGEN;
    m_pOwner->HoldNearOpenFlame();
    return S_OK;
  }
};
```

COM_INTERFACE_ENTRY_TEAR_OFF

To make use of this tear-off implementation, the owner class uses the COM_INTER-FACE_ENTRY_TEAR_OFF macro:

```
#define COM_INTERFACE_ENTRY_TEAR_OFF(iid, x) \
 { &iid, \
   (DWORD)&_CComCreatorData< \
          CComInternalCreator< CComTearOffObject< x > > >::data, \
 _Creator },
```

The _CComCreatorData is just a sneaky trick to fill in the dw entry of the interface entry with a function pointer to the appropriate creator function. The creator function will be provided by CComInternalCreator, which is similar to CComCreator except that it calls _InternalQueryInterface to get the initial interface instead of QueryInterface. This is necessary because, as I'll show you soon, Query-Interface on a tear-off instance forwards to the owner, but we want the initial interface on a new tear-off to come from the tear-off itself. That is, after all, why we're creating the tear-off: to expose that interface.

The pFunc entry made by COM_INTERFACE_ENTRY_TEAR_OFF is the first instance of a nonsimple entry so far in this chapter. The _Creator function is a static member of the CComObjectRootBase class that simply calls the creator function pointer held in the dw parameter:

```
static HRESULT WINAPI
CComObjectRootBase::_Creator(void* pv, REFIID iid,
                            void** ppv, DWORD dw) {
 _ATL_CREATORDATA* pcd = (_ATL_CREATORDATA*)dw;
 return pcd->pFunc(pv, iid, ppv);
}
```

The most derived class of a tear-off implementation is not CComObject, but rather CComTearOffObject. CComTearOffObject knows about the m_pOwner member of the base and will fill it during construction. Because each tear-off instance is a separate C++ object, each will maintain its own lifetime. However, to live up to the laws of COM identity, each tear-off will forward requests for new interfaces to the owner:

```
template <class Base> class CComTearOffObject : public Base {
public:
 CComTearOffObject(void* pv) {
```

```
      ATLASSERT(m_pOwner == NULL);
      m_pOwner = reinterpret_cast<CComObject<Base::_OwnerClass>*>(pv);
      m_pOwner->AddRef();
    }

  ~CComTearOffObject() {
      m_dwRef = 1L;
      FinalRelease();
      m_pOwner->Release();
    }

  STDMETHOD(QueryInterface)(REFIID iid, void ** ppvObject)
  { return m_pOwner->QueryInterface(iid, ppvObject); }

  STDMETHOD_(ULONG, AddRef)()
  { return InternalAddRef(); }

  STDMETHOD_(ULONG, Release)() {
    ULONG l = InternalRelease();
    if (l == 0) delete this;
    return l;
  }
};
```

To make use of a tear-off, the owner class adds an entry to its interface map:

```
class CBeachBall :
  public CComObjectRootEx<CBeachBall>,
  public ISphere,
  public IRollableObject,
  public IPlaything,
  //public ILethalObject, // Implemented by the tear-off
  public ITakeUpSpace,
  public IWishIWereMoreUseful,
  public ITryToBeHelpful,
  public IAmDepressed {
public:
BEGIN_COM_MAP(CBeachBall)
  COM_INTERFACE_ENTRY(ISphere)
  COM_INTERFACE_ENTRY(IRollableObject)
  COM_INTERFACE_ENTRY(IPlaything)
  COM_INTERFACE_ENTRY_TEAR_OFF(IID_ILethalObject, CBeachBallLethalness)
```

```
    COM_INTERFACE_ENTRY(ITakeUpSpace)
    COM_INTERFACE_ENTRY(IWishIWereMoreUseful)
    COM_INTERFACE_ENTRY(ITryToBeHelpful)
    COM_INTERFACE_ENTRY(IAmDepressed)
  END_COM_MAP()
  ...
  private:
   GAS_TYPE m_gasFill;
   void      HoldNearOpenFlame();
   friend class CBeachBallLethalness; // Tear-offs are generally friends
  };
```

Since the owner class is no longer deriving from ILethalObject, each instance is 4 bytes lighter. However, when the client queries for ILethalObject, we're spending 4 bytes for the ILethalObject vptr in CBeachBallLethalness, 4 bytes for the CBeachBallLethalness reference count, and 4 bytes for the m_pOwner back pointer. You may wonder how spending 12 bytes to save 4 actually results in a savings. I'll tell you: volume! Or rather, the lack thereof. Since we're only paying the 12 bytes during the lifetime of the tear-off instance and we've used extensive profiling to determine that ILethalObject is rarely used, the overall object footprint should be smaller. Be careful with that extensive profiling, though. You do need it if you're going to be sure that you're not paying more than you're saving when using tear-offs.

Tear-off Caveats

Before wrapping yourself in the perceived efficiency of tear-offs, there are some things of which you should be aware.

- **Tear-offs are only for rarely used interfaces.** Tear-off interfaces are an implementation trick to be used to reduce vptr bloat after extensive prototyping has revealed this to be a problem. If you don't have this problem, save yourself the trouble and avoid tear-offs.

- **Tear-offs are for intra-apartment use only.** The stub will cache a tear-off interface for the life of an object. In fact, the current implementation of the stub manager will cache each interface twice, sending the overhead of that particular interface from 4 bytes to 24 bytes.

- **Tear-offs should contain no state of their own.** When a tear-off contains its own state, there will be one copy of that state per tear-off instance, breaking the spirit if not the laws of COM identity. If you have per-interface state, especially large state that you would like to be released when no client is using the interface, use a cached tear-off.

Cached Tear-offs

You may have noticed that every query for ILethalObject will result in a new tear-off instance, even if the client already holds an ILethalObject interface pointer. This may be fine for a single interface tear-off, but what about a related group of interfaces that will be used together?[9] For example, imagine moving the other rarely used interfaces of CBeachBall to a single tear-off implementation:

```
class CBeachBallAttitude :
    public CComTearOffObjectBase<CBeachBall, CComSingleThreadModel>,
    public ITakeUpSpace,
    public IWishIWereMoreUseful,
    public ITryToBeHelpful,
    public IAmDepressed {
public:
BEGIN_COM_MAP(CBeachBallAttitude)
    COM_INTERFACE_ENTRY(ITakeUpSpace)
    COM_INTERFACE_ENTRY(IWishIWereMoreUseful)
    COM_INTERFACE_ENTRY(ITryToBeHelpful)
    COM_INTERFACE_ENTRY(IAmDepressed)
END_COM_MAP()
...
};
```

Although the following usage of this tear-off implementation will compile and exhibit the appropriate behavior, the overhead of even a single tear-off will be exorbitant:

```
class CBeachBall :
    public CComObjectRootEx<CBeachBall>,
    public ISphere,
    public IRollableObject,
    public IPlaything {
public:
BEGIN_COM_MAP(CBeachBall)
    COM_INTERFACE_ENTRY(ISphere)
    COM_INTERFACE_ENTRY(IRollableObject)
    COM_INTERFACE_ENTRY(IPlaything)
```

---

[9]The control interfaces fit into this category for objects that also support nonvisual use.

```
    COM_INTERFACE_ENTRY_TEAR_OFF(IID_ILethalObject, CBeachBallLethalness)
    COM_INTERFACE_ENTRY_TEAR_OFF(IID_ITakeUpSpace, CBeachBallAttitude)
    COM_INTERFACE_ENTRY_TEAR_OFF(IID_IWishIWereMoreUseful,
      CBeachBallAttitude)
    COM_INTERFACE_ENTRY_TEAR_OFF(IID_ITryToBeHelpful, CBeachBallAttitude)
    COM_INTERFACE_ENTRY_TEAR_OFF(IID_IAmDepressed, CBeachBallAttitude)
  END_COM_MAP()
  ...
  };
```

Because we've grouped the "attitude" interfaces together into a single tear-off implementation, every time the client queries for *any* of them, it pays the overhead of *all* of them. To allow this kind of grouping but avoid the overhead of creating a new instance for every query, ATL provides an implementation of a *cached tear-off*. A cached tear-off is held by the owner if there is even one outstanding interface to the tear-off. The initial query will create the tear-off and cache it. Subsequent queries will use the cached tear-off. The final release will delete the tear-off instance.

COM_INTERFACE_ENTRY_CACHED_TEAR_OFF

To support caching tear-offs, ATL provides another interface macro:

```
#define COM_INTERFACE_ENTRY_CACHED_TEAR_OFF(iid, x, punk) \
  { &iid, \
    (DWORD)&_CComCacheData< \
      CComCreator< CComCachedTearOffObject < x > >, \
      (DWORD)offsetof(_ComMapClass, punk) >::data, \
    _Cache },
```

The _CComCacheData class is used to stuff a pointer into an _ATL_CACHEDATA structure:

```
struct _ATL_CACHEDATA {
  DWORD              dwOffsetVar;
  _ATL_CREATORFUNC* pFunc;
};
```

The use of this structure allows the dw to point to a creator function pointer as well as another member, an offset. The offset is from the base of the owner class to the member data that is used to cache the pointer to the tear-off. The _Cache function, another static member function of CComObjectRootBase, uses the offset to calculate the address of the pointer and checks the pointer to determine whether to create a new instance of the cached tear-off:

```
static HRESULT WINAPI
CComObjectRootBase::_Cache(void* pv, REFIID iid,
                          void** ppvObject, DWORD dw) {
 HRESULT hRes = E_NOINTERFACE;
 _ATL_CACHEDATA* pcd = (_ATL_CACHEDATA*)dw;
 IUnknown** pp = (IUnknown**)((DWORD)pv + pcd->dwOffsetVar);
 if (*pp == NULL) hRes = pcd->pFunc(pv, IID_IUnknown, (void**)pp);
 if (*pp != NULL) hRes = (*pp)->QueryInterface(iid, ppvObject);
 return hRes;
}
```

Just as an instance of a tear-off uses CComTearOffObject instead of CCom-Object to provide the implementation of IUnknown, cached tear-offs use CCom-CachedTearOffObject. CComCachedTearOffObject is nearly identical to CComAggObject[10] because of the way that the lifetime and identity of the tear-off are subsumed by that of the owner. The only difference is that the cached tear-off, like the tear-off, will initialize the m_pOwner member.

Replacing the inefficient use of COM_INTERFACE_ENTRY_TEAR_OFF with COM_INTERFACE_ENTRY_CACHED_TEAR_OFF looks like this:

```
class CBeachBall :
 public CComObjectRootEx<CBeachBall>,
 public ISphere,
 public IRollableObject,
 public IPlaything {
public:
BEGIN_COM_MAP(CBeachBall)
  COM_INTERFACE_ENTRY(ISphere)
  COM_INTERFACE_ENTRY(IRollableObject)
  COM_INTERFACE_ENTRY(IPlaything)
  COM_INTERFACE_ENTRY_TEAR_OFF(IID_ILethalObject, CBeachBallLethalness)
  COM_INTERFACE_ENTRY_CACHED_TEAR_OFF(IID_ITakeUpSpace,
                                CBeachBallAttitude,
                                m_spunkAttitude.p)
  COM_INTERFACE_ENTRY_CACHED_TEAR_OFF(IID_IWishIWereMoreUseful,
                                CBeachBallAttitude,
                                m_spunkAttitude.p)
```

---

[10] Discussed in Chapter 3.

```
     COM_INTERFACE_ENTRY_CACHED_TEAR_OFF(IID_ITryToBeHelpful,
                                         CBeachBallAttitude,
                                         m_spunkAttitude.p)
     COM_INTERFACE_ENTRY_CACHED_TEAR_OFF(IID_IAmDepressed,
                                         CBeachBallAttitude,
                                         m_spunkAttitude.p)
END_COM_MAP()
DECLARE_GET_CONTROLLING_UNKNOWN() // See the Aggregation section
...
public:
  CComPtr<IUnknown> m_spunkAttitude;
};
```

Another Use for Cached Tear-offs

Cached tear-offs have another use that is in direct opposition to standard tear-offs: caching per-interface resources. For example, imagine a rarely used IHyphena-tion interface:

```
interface IHyphenation : public IUnknown {
 HRESULT Hyphenate([in] BSTR bstrUnhyphed,
                   [out, retval] BSTR* pbstrHyphed);
};
```

Performing hyphenation is a matter of consulting a giant lookup table. If a CDictionary object were to implement the IHyphenation interface, it would likely do so as a cached tear-off to manage the resources associated with the lookup table. When the hyphenation cached tear-off was first created, it would acquire the lookup table. Since the tear-off is cached, subsequent queries would use the same lookup table. Once all references to the IHyphenation interface were released, the lookup table could be released. If we had used a standard tear-off for this same functionality, a naïve implementation would have acquired the resources for the lookup table for each tear-off.

Aggregation: The Controlling Outer

Like tear-offs, aggregation allows you to separate the code for a single identity into multiple objects. However, whereas using tear-offs requires shared source code between the owner and the tear-off class, aggregation does not. The controlling outer and the controlling inner do not have to share the same server or even the same implementation language (although they do have to share the same apartment). If you like, you can consider an aggregated object a kind of "binary cached tear-off." Just like a cached tear-off, an aggregated instance's lifetime and identity are subsumed by that of the controlling outer. Just like a cached tear-off, an aggregated instance must have a way to obtain the interface pointer of the controlling outer. In a tear-off, we pass the owner as a constructor argument. In aggregation, we do the same thing, but using the COM constructor that accepts a single, optional constructor argument, that is, the pUnkOuter parameter of IClassFactory::CreateInstance and its wrapper, CoCreateInstance.

```
interface IClassFactory : IUnknown {
 HRESULT CreateInstance([in, unique] IUnknown* pUnkOuter,
                               [in] REFIID riid,
                 [out, iid_is(riid)] void **ppvObject);
 HRESULT LockServer([in] BOOL flock);
};
```

```
WINOLEAPI CoCreateInstance([in] REFCLSID rclsid,
                   [in, unique] LPUNKNOWN pUnkOuter,
                           [in] DWORD dwClsContext,
                           [in] REFIID riid,
             [out, iid_is(riid)] LPVOID FAR* ppv);
```

In Chapter 3, I discussed how ATL supports aggregation as a controlled inner using CComAggObject (or CComPolyObject). In this chapter, I'll show you the four macros that ATL provides to allow you to be the controlling outer in the aggregation relationship.

Planned versus Blind Aggregation

Once an aggregate is created, the controlling outer has two choices about how to expose the interface(s) of the aggregate as its own. The first choice is *planned aggregation* (Figure 5.2). Planned aggregation means that the controlling outer only wants the inner to expose one of a set of interfaces known by the outer. The downside to this technique is that, if the inner's functionality grows, clients using the outer will not gain access to the additional functionality. The upside is that this may well be exactly what the outer had in mind. For example, consider the standard interface IPersist:

```
interface IPersist : IUnknown {
 HRESULT GetClassID([out] CLSID *pClassID);
}
```

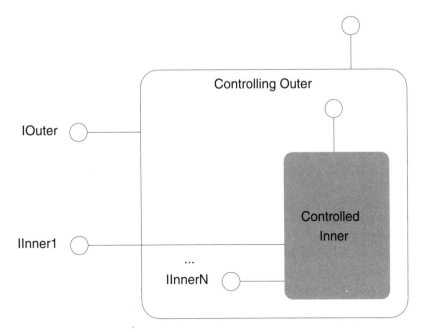

Figure 5.2. Planned aggregation

If the outer were to blindly expose the inner's implementation of IPersist, when the client called GetClassID, it would get the class identifier (CLSID) of the inner, not the outer. Since the client is after the outer object's CLSID, we have yet again broken the spirit of the COM identity laws. Planned aggregation helps us to prevent this breach.

Blind aggregation, on the other hand, allows the outer's functionality to grow with the inner's but provides the potential for exposing identity information from the inner (Figure 5.3). For this reason, blind aggregation should be avoided.

Manual versus Automatic Creation

COM_INTERFACE_ENTRY_AGGREGATE and
COM_INTERFACE_ENTRY_AGGREGATE_BLIND

ATL provides support for both planned and blind aggregation via the following two macros:

```
#define COM_INTERFACE_ENTRY_AGGREGATE(iid, punk) \
  { &iid, (DWORD)offsetof(_ComMapClass, punk), _Delegate },


#define COM_INTERFACE_ENTRY_AGGREGATE_BLIND(punk) \
  { NULL, (DWORD)offsetof(_ComMapClass, punk), _Delegate},
```

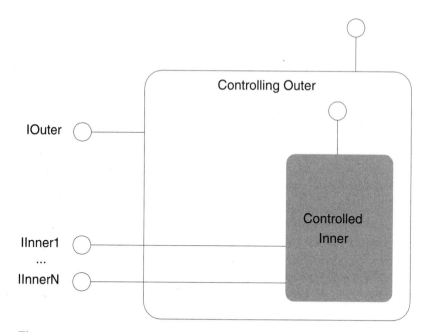

Figure 5.3. Blind aggregation

These macros assume that the aggregate has already been created manually and that the interface pointer is stored in the punk parameter to the macro. The _Delegate function forwards the QueryInterface request to that pointer:

```
static HRESULT WINAPI
CComObjectRootBase::_Delegate(void* pv, REFIID iid,
                              void** ppv, DWORD dw) {
 HRESULT hRes = E_NOINTERFACE;
  IUnknown* p = *(IUnknown**)((DWORD)pv + dw);
  if (p != NULL) hRes = p->QueryInterface(iid, ppv);
  return hRes;
}
```

To aggregate an inner that has been manually created, a classes uses COM_INTER-FACE_ENTRY_AGGREGATE or COM_INTERFACE_ENTRY_AGGREGATE_BLIND in the interface map:

```
class CBeachBall :
  public CComObjectRootEx<CBeachBall>,
  public ISphere,
```

```
    public IRollableObject,
    public IPlaything {
public:
BEGIN_COM_MAP(CBeachBall)
  COM_INTERFACE_ENTRY(ISphere)
  COM_INTERFACE_ENTRY(IRollableObject)
  COM_INTERFACE_ENTRY(IPlaything)
  COM_INTERFACE_ENTRY_AGGREGATE(IID_ILethalObject, m_spunkLethalness)
  COM_INTERFACE_ENTRY_AGGREGATE_BLIND(m_spunkAttitude)
END_COM_MAP()

DECLARE_GET_CONTROLLING_UNKNOWN()
DECLARE_PROTECT_FINAL_CONSTRUCT()

  HRESULT FinalConstruct() {
   HESULT hr;
   hr = CoCreateInstance(CLSID_Lethalness,
                         GetControllingUnknown(),
                         CLSCTX_INPROC_SERVER,
                         IID_IUnknown,
                         (void**)&m_spunkLethalness);
   if( SUCCEEDED(hr) ) {
     hr = CoCreateInstance(CLSID_Attitude,
                         GetControllingUnknown(),
                         CLSCTX_INPROC_SERVER,
                         IID_IUnknown,
                         (void**)&m_spunkAttitude);
   }

   return hr;
 }
  void FinalRelease() {
   m_spunkLethalness.Release();
   m_spunkAttitude.Release();
 }
...
public:
  CComPtr<IUnknown> m_spunkLethalness;
  CComPtr<IUnknown> m_spunkAttitude;
};
```

Notice that I have used the FinalConstruct method to create the aggregates so that failure will stop the creation process. Notice also that because I have a Final-Construct that hands out interface pointers to the object being created, I'm using DECLARE_PROTECT_FINAL_CONSTRUCT to protect against premature destruction. And because the aggregates have pointers to the outer, I have a FinalRelease method to manually release the aggregate interface pointers to protect against double destruction. Aggregation was one of the chief motivations behind the multi-phase construction of ATL base COM objects, so it's not surprising to see all of the pieces used in this example.

However, one thing I have not yet mentioned is the DECLARE_GET_CONTROL-LING_UNKNOWN macro. The controlling unknown is a pointer to the most outer controlling outer. Because aggregation can go arbitrarily deep, the outer needs to pass the pUnkOuter of the most outer when aggregating. To support this, ATL provides the GET_CONTROLLING_UNKNOWN macro, which gives an object the definition of a GetControllingUnknown function:

```
#define DECLARE_GET_CONTROLLING_UNKNOWN() public: \
  virtual IUnknown* GetControllingUnknown() { return GetUnknown(); }
```

You may question the value of this function, since it simply forwards to Get-Unknown, but notice that it's virtual. When the object is actually being created as an aggregate while it is aggregating, GetControllingUnknown will be overridden in CComContainedObject like so:

```
template <class Base> class CComContainedObject : public Base {
...
  IUnknown* CComContainedObject::GetControllingUnknown()
  { return m_pOuterUnknown; }
...
};
```

So, if the object is standalone, GetControllingUnknown will return the IUn-known* of the object, but if the object is itself being aggregated, GetControl-lingUnknown will return the IUnknown* of the outermost outer.

COM_INTERFACE_ENTRY_AUTOAGGREGATE and COM_INTERFACE_ENTRY_AUTOAGGREGATE_BLIND

When you're not initializing any of the aggregates, it seems a waste to create them until, or unless, they're needed. For automatic creation of aggregates on demand, ATL provides the following two macros:

```
#define COM_INTERFACE_ENTRY_AUTOAGGREGATE(iid, punk, clsid) \
 { &iid, \
   (DWORD)&_CComCacheData< \
     CComAggregateCreator<_ComMapClass, &clsid>, \
                         (DWORD)offsetof(_ComMapClass, punk)>::data,\
   _Cache },
```

```
#define COM_INTERFACE_ENTRY_AUTOAGGREGATE_BLIND(punk, clsid) \
 { NULL, \
   (DWORD)&_CComCacheData< \
     CComAggregateCreator<_ComMapClass, &clsid>, \
                         (DWORD)offsetof(_ComMapClass, punk)>::data,\
   _Cache },
```

The only new thing in these macros is the CComAggregateCreator, which simply performs the CoCreateInstance for us the first time the interface is requested:

```
template <class T, const CLSID* pclsid> class CComAggregateCreator {
public:
 static HRESULT WINAPI CreateInstance(void* pv,
                                      REFIID, LPVOID* ppv) {
   ATLASSERT(*ppv == NULL);
   ATLASSERT(pv != NULL);
   T* p = (T*)pv;
   return CoCreateInstance(*pclsid, p->GetControllingUnknown(),
                      CLSCTX_INPROC, IID_IUnknown, ppv);
 }
};
```

Using automatic creation simplifies the outer's code somewhat:

```
class CBeachBall :
 public CComObjectRootEx<CBeachBall>,
 public ISphere,
 public IRollableObject,
 public IPlaything {
public:
BEGIN_COM_MAP(CBeachBall)
 COM_INTERFACE_ENTRY(ISphere)
```

```
        COM_INTERFACE_ENTRY(IRollableObject)
        COM_INTERFACE_ENTRY(IPlaything)
        COM_INTERFACE_ENTRY_AUTOAGGREGATE(IID_ILethalObject,
                                  m_spunkLethalness, CLSID_Lethalness)
        COM_INTERFACE_ENTRY_AGGREGATE_BLIND(m_spunkAttitude, CLSID_Attitude)
    END_COM_MAP()

    DECLARE_GET_CONTROLLING_UNKNOWN()

     void FinalRelease() {
       m_spunkLethalness.Release();
       m_spunkAttitude.Release();
     }
     ...
    public:
     CComPtr<IUnknown> m_spunkLethalness;
     CComPtr<IUnknown> m_spunkAttitude;
    };
```

Although we no longer need to perform the creation in FinalConstruct, we're still required to use DECLARE_GET_CONTROLLING_UNKNOWN and to provide storage for the aggregated interfaces. We should still release the interfaces manually in FinalRelease, as well, if we're interested in avoiding double destruction.

Aggregating the Free-Threaded Marshaler

One particularly interesting use of aggregation is supported directly by the ATL Object Wizard: aggregating the implementation of IMarshal provided by the Free-Threaded Marshaler (FTM). Any object that aggregates the FTM is said to be an *apartment-neutral* object. Normally, passing an interface pointer between apartments, even in the same process, results in a proxy/stub pair. While the proxy/stub pair maintains the concurrency and synchronization requirements of both the object and the client, it also adds overhead. In-process objects that provide their own synchronization and prefer to snuggle up to the client without the overhead of the proxy/stub can aggregate the FTM. By aggregating the FTM, an object is short-circuiting the creation of the proxy/stub, and therefore the object can be passed between apartments in the same address space without the overhead of a proxy/stub.

The following code is generated by the wizard when the Free-Threaded Marshaler option is checked in the ATL Object Wizard:

```
class ATL_NO_VTABLE CBowlingBall :
 public CComObjectRootEx<CComMultiThreadModel>,
```

```
  public CComCoClass<CBowlingBall, &CLSID_BowlingBall>,
  public IBowlingBall
{
public:
  CBowlingBall() { m_pUnkMarshaler = NULL; }

DECLARE_REGISTRY_RESOURCEID(IDR_BOWLINGBALL)
DECLARE_NOT_AGGREGATABLE(CBowlingBall)
DECLARE_GET_CONTROLLING_UNKNOWN()
DECLARE_PROTECT_FINAL_CONSTRUCT()

BEGIN_COM_MAP(CBowlingBall)
  COM_INTERFACE_ENTRY(IBowlingBall)
  COM_INTERFACE_ENTRY_AGGREGATE(IID_IMarshal, m_pUnkMarshaler.p)
END_COM_MAP()

  HRESULT FinalConstruct() {
    return CoCreateFreeThreadedMarshaler(GetControllingUnknown(),
                                         &m_pUnkMarshaler.p);
  }
  void FinalRelease() {
    m_pUnkMarshaler.Release();
  }

  CComPtr<IUnknown> m_pUnkMarshaler;
  ...
};
```

Because the CLSID of the FTM is not available, instead of using auto-creation, ATL uses `CoCreateFreeThreadMarshaler` to create an instance of the FTM in the `FinalConstruct` method.

FTM Danger, Will Robinson! Danger! Danger!

Since aggregating the FTM is so easy, I should mention a couple of big responsibilities that you, the developer, have accepted by aggregating the FTM.

- **Apartment-neutral objects must be thread safe.** You can mark your class `ThreadingModel=Apartment` all day long, but because your object can be passed freely between apartments in the same process and therefore used simultaneously by multiple threads, you had better use `CComMultiThread-Model` and at least object-level locking. Unfortunately, the same wizard that makes it so easy to use the FTM is also perfectly willing to let you choose the Single or the Apartment threading models. I suggest using Both to avoid the spurious creation of an extra apartment.

- **Apartment-neutral objects are not aggregatable.** Aggregating the FTM depends on being able to implement `IMarshal`. If the outer decides to implement `IMarshal` and doesn't ask the inner object, the inner can no longer be apartment neutral.

- **Apartment-neutral objects may not cache interface pointers.** An apartment-neutral object is said to be apartment neutral because it doesn't care from which apartment it is accessed. However, other objects used by an apartment-neutral object may or may not also be apartment neutral. Interface pointers to objects that aren't apartment neutral can only be used in the apartment to which they belong. If you're lucky, the apartment-neutral object attempting to cache and use an interface pointer from another apartment will have a pointer to a proxy. Proxies know when they are being accessed outside of their apartments and will return `RPC_E_WRONG_THREAD` for all such method calls. If you're not so lucky, the apartment-neutral object will obtain a raw interface pointer. Imagine the poor single-threaded object accessed simultaneously from multiple apartments as part of its duty to the apartment-neutral object. It's not going to last long.

    The only safe way to cache interface pointers in an apartment-neutral object is as cookies obtained from the Global Interface Table (GIT). The GIT is a process-global object provided to map apartment-specific interface pointers to apartment-neutral cookies and back. The GIT was invented after the FTM and is provided in the third service pack to NT 4.0, the DCOM upgrade for Windows 95, and out of the box with Windows 98. If you're aggregating the FTM and caching interface pointers, you must use the GIT.

For an in-depth discussion of the FTM, the GIT, and their use, read *Essential COM* by Don Box (Addison-Wesley, 1998).

Interface Map Tricks

Interface Map Chaining

C++ programmers are accustomed to code reuse via inheritance of implementation. For example, inheritance is how we reuse the implementation provided in `CComObjectRootEx` as well as the various ATL implementation classes, for example, `IDispatchImpl`. For each implementation class used, one or more corresponding entries must be made in the interface map. However, what about deriving from a class that already provides an interface map? For example:

```
class CBigBeachBall :
 public CBeachBall,
 public IBigObject {
public:
BEGIN_COM_MAP(CBigBeachBall)
 COM_INTERFACE_ENTRY(IBigObject)
 // All entries from CBeachBall base?
END_COM_MAP()
...
};
```

COM_INTERFACE_ENTRY_CHAIN

What we'd like to avoid, when inheriting from a base class that provides its own interface map, is duplicating all the entries in the deriving class's interface map. The reason is maintenance. If the base class decides to change how it supports an interface or to add or remove support for an interface, we have to change the deriving classes, too. It would be much nicer to be able to "inherit" the interface map along with the interface implementations. That's what COM_INTERFACE_ENTRY_ CHAIN is for.

```
#define COM_INTERFACE_ENTRY_CHAIN(classname) \
  { NULL, (DWORD)&_CComChainData<classname, _ComMapClass>::data, \
    _Chain },
```

The _CComChainData template simply fills the dw member of the interface entry with a pointer to the base class's interface map so that the _Chain function can walk that list when evaluating a query request:

```
static HRESULT WINAPI
CComObjectRootBase::_Chain(void* pv, REFIID iid,
                          void** ppvObject, DWORD dw) {
  _ATL_CHAINDATA* pcd = (_ATL_CHAINDATA*)dw;
  void* p = (void*)((DWORD)pv + pcd->dwOffset);
  return InternalQueryInterface(p, pcd->pFunc(), iid, ppvObject);
}
```

When the _Chain function returns a failure—for example, the base class doesn't support the requested interface—the search continues with the next entry in the table. For example:

```
class CBigBadBeachBall :
  public CBeachBall,
  public IBigObject,
  public IBadObject {
public:
BEGIN_COM_MAP(CBigBadBeachBall)
  COM_INTERFACE_ENTRY(IBigObject)
  COM_INTERFACE_ENTRY_CHAIN(CBeachBall)
  COM_INTERFACE_ENTRY(IBadObject)
END_COM_MAP()
...
};
```

It may seem natural to make the chaining entries first in the interface map. However, remember that the first entry must be a simple entry, so put at least one of the derived class's interfaces first. If the derived class has no additional interfaces, use IUnknown as the first entry:

```
class CBetterBeachBall :
  public CBeachBall {
public:
BEGIN_COM_MAP(CBetterBeachBall)
  COM_INTERFACE_ENTRY(IUnknown)
  COM_INTERFACE_ENTRY_CHAIN(CBeachBall)
END_COM_MAP()
...
};
```

Just Say "No"

COM_INTERFACE_ENTRY_NOINTERFACE

Sometimes you'd like to short-circuit the interface request by explicitly returning E_NOINTERFACE when a specific interface is requested. For this, ATL provides COM_INTERFACE_ENTRY_NOINTERFACE:

```
#define COM_INTERFACE_ENTRY_NOINTERFACE(x) \
  { &_ATL_IIDOF(x), NULL, _NoInterface },
```

The _NoInterface function does pretty much what you'd expect:

```
static HRESULT WINAPI
CComObjectRootBase::_NoInterface(void*, REFIID, void**, DWORD)
{ return E_NOINTERFACE; }
```

This interface map macro is handy when you have blind entries in the interface map (for example, blind aggregation or chaining) and you'd like to remove functionality provided by the inner object or the base class. For example:

```
class CBigNiceBeachBall :
  public CBeachBall,
  public IBigObject {
public:
BEGIN_COM_MAP(CBigBeachBall)
  COM_INTERFACE_ENTRY(IBigObject)
  COM_INTERFACE_ENTRY_NOINTERFACE(ILethalObject)
  COM_INTERFACE_ENTRY_CHAIN(CBeachBall)
END_COM_MAP()
...
};
```

Debugging

COM_INTERFACE_ENTRY_BREAK

Imagine that you're building an in-process server and a client as two projects. You'd like to debug both the client side and the server side. One way is to set the client as the Executable for Debug in the project settings, set a breakpoint, and go. Another way is to add the server dynamic link library (DLL) to the list of Additional DLLs to debug in the project settings of the client, set the breakpoints, and go. Both of these methods mean futzing with the project settings. A third way that doesn't involve the project settings in either the client or the server is COM_INTERFACE_ENTRY_BREAK:

```
#define COM_INTERFACE_ENTRY_BREAK(x) \
  { &_ATL_IIDOF(x), NULL, _Break },
```

The _Break function outputs some helpful debugging information and calls DebugBreak:

```
static HRESULT WINAPI
CComObjectRootbase::_Break(void*, REFIID iid, void**, DWORD) {
```

```
_ATLDUMPIID(iid, _T("Break due to QI for interface "), S_OK);
DebugBreak();
return S_FALSE;
}
```

The call to DebugBreak is just like a breakpoint set in your debugger. It gives the active debugger the chance of taking control of the process. Once you're debugging, you can set other breakpoints and continue executing.

Extensibility

COM_INTERFACE_ENTRY_FUNC and COM_INTERFACE_ENTRY_FUNC_BLIND

ATL provides two macros for putting raw entries into the interface map:

```
#define COM_INTERFACE_ENTRY_FUNC(iid, dw, func) \
{ &iid, dw, func },
```

```
#define COM_INTERFACE_ENTRY_FUNC_BLIND(dw, func) \
{ NULL, dw, func },
```

These macros are the universal backdoor to ATL's implementation of Query-Interface. If you come up with another way of exposing COM interfaces, you can use these macros to achieve it, as long as it lives up to the laws of COM identity.

Direct Access to the this Pointer

One identity trick you can perform using COM_INTERFACE_ENTRY_FUNC was kicked around the ATL mailing list for quite a while, but was recently perfected by Don Box (a slightly modified version of his solution is provided below). In Chapter 3, as you may recall, I presented the CreateInstance static member functions of CComObject, CComAggObject, and CComPolyObject when using private initialization. The CreateInstance method performed the same job as a creator would, but returned a pointer to the this pointer of the object instead of only to one of the interfaces. This was useful for calling member functions or setting member data not exposed via interfaces. We used this technique because it was unsafe to perform a cast. However, why not make QueryInterface perform the cast safely? In other words, why not add an entry to the interface map that returns the object's this pointer? Imagine a global function with the following implementation:

```
inline
HRESULT WINAPI _This(void* pv, REFIID iid, void** ppvObject, DWORD) {
  ATLASSERT(iid == IID_NULL);
  *ppvObject = pv;
  return S_OK;
}
```

This function takes the first parameter, pv, which points to the object's this pointer and hands it out directly in ppvObject. Notice also that this function does not AddRef the resultant interface pointer. Since it's returning an object pointer, not an interface pointer, it's not subject to the laws of COM. Remember, the this pointer is only useful within the server. To make sure that any out-of-apartment calls to QueryInterface fail, be sure to pick an interface ID without a proxy/stub, for example, IID_NULL.

For example, imagine implementations of the following interfaces, creating a simple object model:

```
interface IBalloonMan : IUnknown {
   HRESULT CreateBalloon(long rgbColor, IBalloon** ppBalloon);
   HRESULT SwitchColor(IBalloon* pBalloon, long rgbColor);
};

interface IBalloon : IUnknown {
   [propget] HRESULT Color([out, retval] long *pVal);
};
```

Notice that the balloon's color can't be changed via IBalloon, but the implementation of IBalloonMan is able to give you a balloon of the color you're after. If the implementations of IBalloonMan and IBalloon share the same server, the implementation of IBalloon can expose its this pointer via the _This function like so:

```
class ATL_NO_VTABLE CBalloon :
 public CComObjectRootEx<CComSingleThreadModel>,
 public CComCoClass<CBalloon>,
 public IBalloon {
public:
DECLARE_REGISTRY_RESOURCEID(IDR_BALLOON)
DECLARE_NOT_AGGREGATABLE(CBalloon)
```

```
DECLARE_PROTECT_FINAL_CONSTRUCT()

BEGIN_COM_MAP(CBalloon)
  COM_INTERFACE_ENTRY(IBalloon)
  COM_INTERFACE_ENTRY_FUNC(IID_NULL, 0, _This)
END_COM_MAP()

  // IBalloon
public:
  STDMETHOD(get_Color)(/*[out, retval]*/ long *pVal);

private:
  COLORREF  m_rgbColor;
  friend class CBalloonMan;
};
```

Because CBalloonMan is a friend of CBalloon, CBalloonMan can set the private color data member of CBalloon, assuming it can obtain the object's this pointer. CBalloon's special entry for IID_NULL lets CBalloonMan do just that:

```
STDMETHODIMP CBalloonMan::CreateBalloon(long rgbColor,
                                        IBalloon** ppBalloon) {
  // Create balloon
  HRESULT     hr = CBalloon::CreateInstance(0, ppBalloon);

  if( SUCCEEDED(hr) ) {
    // Use backdoor to acquire CBalloon's this pointer
    CBalloon*   pBalloonThis = 0;
    hr = (*ppBalloon)->QueryInterface(IID_NULL, (void**)&pBalloonThis);
    if( SUCCEEDED(hr) ) {
      // Use CBalloon's this pointer for private initialization
      pBalloonThis->m_rgbColor = rgbColor;
    }
  }

  if( FAILED(hr) ) {
    (*ppBalloon)->Release();
    *ppBalloon = 0;
  }
  return hr;
}
```

The benefit of this technique over the private initialization technique exposed by the `CreateInstance` member function of `CComObject` et al. is that the `this` pointer can be obtained after creation. For example:

```
STDMETHODIMP CBalloonMan::SwitchColor(IBalloon* pBalloon,
                                      long rgbColor) {
  // Use backdoor to acquire CBalloon's this pointer
  CBalloon*    pBalloonThis = 0;
  HRESULT hr =
    pBalloon->QueryInterface(IID_NULL, (void**)&pBalloonThis);
  if( SUCCEEDED(hr) ) {
   hr = pBalloonThis->m_rgbColor = rgbColor;
  }
  return hr;
}
```

Clearly, this technique is a backdoor hack with limited usefulness. It should not be used to subvert the binary boundary between client and object. However, it does have its own special charm. For objects that share the same apartment in the same server, it's a valid way to discover just who is who. If you find yourself using this technique, you may find the following macro to be a useful shortcut:

```
#define COM_INTERFACE_ENTRY_THIS() \
        COM_INTERFACE_ENTRY_FUNC(IID_NULL, 0, _This)
```

Per-Object Interfaces

Sometimes it's useful to handle interfaces on a per-object basis instead of a per-class basis. Another friend of mine, Martin Gudgin, provided the following example. If you'd like to implement something known as a "smart proxy," you're going to have to keep track of the list of interfaces each object supports, and you may not know what those are until runtime. Each smart proxy object has its own list of interfaces, which can easily be managed by a member function. Unfortunately, interface maps can't hold member functions (believe me, I tried). However, you can use a combination of COM_INTERFACE_ENTRY_FUNC_BLIND and a static member function to perform the forwarding to a member function. For example:

```
class ATL_NO_VTABLE CSmartProxy :
 public CComObjectRootEx<CComSingleThreadModel>,
 public CComCoClass<CSmartProxy, &CLSID_SmartProxy>,
 public IUnknown
{
```

```
public:
DECLARE_REGISTRY_RESOURCEID(IDR_SMARTPROXY)
DECLARE_PROTECT_FINAL_CONSTRUCT()

BEGIN_COM_MAP(CSmartProxy)
  COM_INTERFACE_ENTRY(IUnknown)
  COM_INTERFACE_ENTRY_FUNC_BLIND(0, _QI)
END_COM_MAP()

public:
  static HRESULT WINAPI _QI(void* pv,
                            REFIID iid, void** ppvObject, DWORD) {
    // Forward to QI member function
    return ((CSmartProxy*)pv)->QI(iid, ppvObject);
  }

  // Per-object implementation of QI
  HRESULT QI(REFIID riid, void** ppv);
};
```

Of course, you may wonder why you'd go to all this trouble to get back to the per-object implementation of QueryInterface that you've come to know and love, but that's ATL.

Summary

Even after you understand and commit to the laws of COM identity, you'll find that they aren't very restrictive. Prefer multiple inheritance, but do not feel that ATL limits you to that technique. And for any identity trick that ATL doesn't support directly, the interface map can be extended to support it.

6 | Persistence in ATL

A Review of COM Persistence

Objects that have a persistent state of any kind should implement at least one persistence interface, and preferably multiple interfaces, in order to provide the container with the most flexible choice of how it wishes to save the object's state. Persistent state is that data (typically properties and instance variables) that an object needs preserved before a container destroys the object. The container provides the saved state to the object after recreating the object so the object can reinitialize itself to its previous state.

COM itself doesn't require an object to support persistence, nor does COM use such support if it's present in an object. COM simply documents a protocol by which clients may use any persistence support provided by an object. Often, we refer to this persistence model as *client-managed persistence* because it is the client that determines where the persistent data (the medium) is saved and when the save occurs.

COM defines some interfaces that model a persistence medium and, for some media, an implementation of the interfaces. Such interfaces typically use the naming convention I*Medium*, where *Medium* is Stream, Storage, PropertyBag, and so on. The medium interface has methods such as Read and Write, which an object uses when loading and saving its state.

COM also documents interfaces that an object implements when it wishes to support persistence into various media. Such interfaces typically use the naming convention IPersist*Medium*. The persist interface has methods such as Load and Save, which the client calls to request the object to restore or save its state. The client provides the appropriate medium interface to the object as an argument to the Load or Save request. Figure 6.1 illustrates this model.

All IPersist*Medium* interfaces derive from the IPersist interface, which looks like this:

```
interface IPersist : IUnknown
{ HRESULT GetClassID([out] CLSID* pclsid); }
```

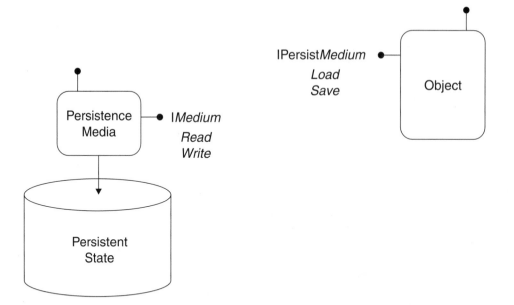

Figure 6.1. The client-managed persistence model

A client uses the `GetClassID` method when it wishes to save the state of an object. Typically, the client queries for `IPersistMedium`, calls the `GetClassID` method to obtain the class identifier (CLSID) for the object the client wishes to save, then writes the CLSID to the persistence medium. The client then requests the object to save its state into the medium. Restoring the object is the inverse operation: Read the CLSID from the medium. Create an instance of the class. Query for the `IPersistMedium` interface on that object. Request the object to load its state from the medium.

There are two basic forms in which a client might ask an object to save its state: a self-describing set of named properties or an opaque binary stream of bytes. When an object provides its state as a self-describing set of named properties, it provides each property as a name/type/value tuple to its client. The client then stores the properties in the form most convenient to the client, for example, text on HTML pages. The benefit of self-describing data, for example, <param> tags and XML, is that one entity can write it and another can read it without tight coupling between the two.

It is more efficient for an object to provide its state as a binary stream of bytes because the object doesn't need to provide a property name or translate each property into the name/type/value tuple. Also, the client doesn't need to translate the property to and from text. However, opaque streams will contain machine dependencies, such as byte order and floating point/character set representations, unless specifically addressed by the object writing the stream.

ATL provides support for both forms of persistence, but before we explore ATL's persistence implementation, let's look at how you might implement COM persistence directly.

IPropertyBag and IPersistPropertyBag

ActiveX control containers that implement a *save as text* mechanism typically use IPropertyBag and IPersistPropertyBag. A container implements IPropertyBag and a control implements IPersistPropertyBag to indicate that it can persist its state as a self-describing set of named properties.

```
interface IPropertyBag : public IUnknown {
 HRESULT Read ([in]        LPCOLESTR  pszPropName,
              [out][in] VARIANT*  pVar, [in] IErrorLog* pErrorLog);

 HRESULT Write ([in] LPCOLESTR pszPropName, [in] VARIANT*  pVar);
};


interface IPersistPropertyBag : public IPersist {
 HRESULT InitNew ();
 HRESULT Load ([in] IPropertyBag* pPropBag,
              [in] IErrorLog* pErrorLog);
 HRESULT Save ([in] IPropertyBag* pPropBag, [in] BOOL fClearDirty,
              [in] BOOL fSaveAllProperties);
};
```

When a client (container) wishes to have exact control over how individually named properties of an object are saved, it attempts to use an object's IPersistPropertyBag interface as the persistence mechanism. The client supplies a property bag to the object in the form of an IPropertyBag interface.

When the object wishes to read a property in IPersistPropertyBag::Load, it will call IPropertyBag::Read. When the object is saving properties in IPersistPropertyBag::Save, it will call IPropertyBag::Write. Each property is described with a name in pszPropName whose value is exchanged in a VARIANT. For read operations, the property bag provides the named property from the bag in the form specified by the input VARIANT, unless the type is VT_EMPTY, in which case, the property bag provides the property as any VARIANT type convenient to the bag.

The information provided by the object for each property (name/type/value) during a save operation allows a client to save the property values as text, for instance, which is the primary reason why a client might choose to support IPersistPropertyBag. The client records errors that occur during reading into the supplied error log.

IPropertyBag2 and IPersistPropertyBag2

The IPropertyBag interface doesn't give an object much information about the properties contained in the bag. Therefore, there is a newer interface, IPropertyBag2, which allows an object much greater access to information about the properties in a bag. Objects that support persistence using IPropertyBag2 naturally implement the IPersistPropertyBag2 interface.

```
interface IPropertyBag2 : public IUnknown {
  HRESULT Read  ([in]  ULONG cProperties, [in] PROPBAG2*  pPropBag,
                 [in]  IErrorLog* pErrLog, [out] VARIANT* pvarValue,
                 [out] HRESULT*   phrError);
  HRESULT Write ([in]  ULONG cProperties, [in] PROPBAG2*  pPropBag,
                 [in]  VARIANT*   pvarValue);
  HRESULT CountProperties ([out] ULONG* pcProperties);
  HRESULT GetPropertyInfo ([in]  ULONG iProperty,
                           [in] ULONG cProperties,
                           [out] PROPBAG2* pPropBag,
                           [out] ULONG* pcProperties);
  HRESULT LoadObject ([in] LPCOLESTR pstrName, [in] DWORD dwHint,
                      [in] IUnknown* pUnkObject, [in] IErrorLog*
    pErrLog);
};

interface IPersistPropertyBag2 : public IPersist {
  HRESULT InitNew ();
  HRESULT Load ([in] IPropertyBag2* pPropBag,
               [in] IErrorLog* pErrLog);
  HRESULT Save ([in] IPropertyBag2* pPropBag, [in] BOOL fClearDirty,
               [in] BOOL fSaveAllProperties);
  HRESULT IsDirty();
};
```

IPropertyBag2 is an enhancement of the IPropertyBag interface. IProperty-Bag2 allows the object to obtain the number of properties in the bag and the type information for each property through the use of the CountProperties and Get-PropertyInfo methods. A property bag that implements IPropertyBag2 must also support IPropertyBag so that objects that only support IPropertyBag can access their properties. Likewise, an object that supports IPersistProperty-Bag2 must also support IPersistPropertyBag so that it can communicate with property bags that only support IPropertyBag.

When the object wants to read a property in IPersistPropertyBag2::Load, it will call IPropertyBag2::Read. When the object is saving properties in IPer-sistPropertyBag2::Save, it will call IPropertyBag2::Write. The client records errors that occur during Read with the supplied IErrorLog interface.

Implementing IPersistPropertyBag

Clients will only ask an object to initialize itself once. When the client has no initial values to give the object, the client calls the object's IPersistPropertyBag ::InitNew method. In this case, the object should initialize itself to default values. When the client has initial values to give the object, it will load the properties into a property bag and call the object's IPersistPropertyBag::Load method. When the client wishes to save the state of an object, it creates a property bag and calls the object's IPersistPropertyBag::Save method.

This is pretty straightforward to implement in an object. For example, the Demagogue object has three properties: its name, speech, and volume. Here's an example of an implementation to save and restore these three properties from a property bag:

```
class ATL_NO_VTABLE CDemagogue : public IPersistPropertyBag,
 . . .
{
   BEGIN_COM_MAP(CDemagogue)
     . . .
     COM_INTERFACE_ENTRY(IPersistPropertyBag)
     COM_INTERFACE_ENTRY2(IPersist, IPersistPropertyBag)
   END_COM_MAP()
   . . .
   CComBSTR m_name;
   long     m_volume;
   CComBSTR m_speech;

   STDMETHODIMP Load (IPropertyBag *pBag, IErrorLog *pLog)
   {
```

```
                CComVariant v ((BSTR) NULL);   // Initialize the VARIANT to VT_BSTR
                HRESULT hr = pBag->Read(OLESTR("Name"), &v, pLog);
                if (FAILED (hr)) return hr;
                m_name = v.bstrVal;

                v = 0L;                        // Initialize the VARIANT to VT_I4
                hr = pBag->Read(OLESTR("Volume"), &v, pLog);
                if (FAILED (hr)) return hr;
                m_volume = v.lVal;

                v = (BSTR) NULL;               // Initialize the VARIANT to VT_BSTR
                hr = pBag->Read(OLESTR("Speech"), &v, pLog);
                if (FAILED (hr)) return hr;
                m_speech = v.bstrVal;

                return S_OK;
            }
            STDMETHODIMP Save (IPropertyBag *pBag,
                               BOOL fClearDirty, BOOL /* fSaveAllProperties */)
            {
                CComVariant v = m_name;
                HRESULT hr = pBag->Write(OLESTR("Name"), &v);
                if (FAILED(hr)) return hr;

                v = m_volume;
                hr = pBag->Write(OLESTR("Volume"), &v);
                if (FAILED(hr)) return hr;

                v = m_speech;
                hr = pBag->Write(OLESTR("Speech"), &v);
                if (FAILED(hr)) return hr;

                if (fClearDirty) m_fDirty = FALSE;
                return hr;
            }
        };
```

The IStream, IPersistStreamInit, and IPersistStream Interfaces

COM objects that wish to save their state efficiently as a binary stream of bytes typically implement IPersistStream or IPersistStreamInit. An *ActiveX control* that has persistent state must, as a minimum, implement either IPersistStream or IPersistStreamInit. The two interfaces are mutually exclusive and shouldn't be implemented together, generally speaking. A control implements IPersist-StreamInit when it wishes to know when it is newly created as opposed to created and reinitialized from an existing persistent state. The IPersistStream interface does not provide a means to inform the control that it is newly created. The existence of either interface indicates that the control can save and load its persistent state into a stream, that is, an instance of IStream

The IStream interface closely models the Win32 file API, and you can easily implement the interface on any byte-oriented media. COM provides two implementations of IStream, one that maps to a file and another that maps to a memory buffer.

```
interface IStream : IUnknown {
 HRESULT Read([out] void *pv, [in] ULONG cb,
              [out] ULONG *pcbRead);
 HRESULT Write([in] const void *pv, [in] ULONG cb,
               [out] ULONG *pcb);
 HRESULT Seek([in] LARGE_INTEGER dlibMove,
              [in] DWORD dwOrigin,
              [out] ULARGE_INTEGER *plibNewPosition);
 //...
}

interface IPersistStreamInit : public IPersist {
       HRESULT IsDirty();
       HRESULT Load([in] LPSTREAM pStm);
       HRESULT Save([in] LPSTREAM pStm, [in] BOOL fClearDirty);
       HRESULT GetSizeMax([out] ULARGE_INTEGER*pCbSize);
       HRESULT InitNew();
};

interface IPersistStream : public IPersist {
       HRESULT IsDirty();
       HRESULT Load([in] LPSTREAM pStm);
       HRESULT Save([in] LPSTREAM pStm, [in] BOOL fClearDirty);
       HRESULT GetSizeMax([out] ULARGE_INTEGER*pCbSize);
};
```

When a client wants an object to save its state as an opaque stream of bytes, it typically attempts to use the object's IPersistStreamInit interface as the persistence mechanism. The client supplies the stream into which the object saves in the form of an IStream interface.

When the client calls `IPersistStreamInit::Load`, the object reads its properties from the stream by calling `IStream::Read`. When the client calls `IPersistStreamInit::Save`, the object writes its properties by calling `IStream::Write`. Note that unless the object goes to the extra effort of handling the situation, the stream contains values in an architecture-specific byte order.

Most recent clients prefer to use an object's `IPersistStreamInit` interface, and, if it's not present, fall back and try to use `IPersistStream`. However, older client code only attempt to use an object's `IPersistStream` implementation.[1] To be compatible with both types of clients, your object needs to implement `IPersistStream`. However there are other containers that ask only for `IPersistStreamInit`, so to be compatible with them, you need to implement that interface.[2] But you're not supposed to implement both interface, because then it's unclear to the container whether the object needs to be informed when it's newly created. Pragmatically, the best solution to this dilemma is to support both interfaces when your object doesn't care to be notified when it's newly created—even though this violates the specification for controls.

Although `IPersistStreamInit` doesn't derive from `IPersistStream` (it can't, because of the mutual exclusion aspect of the interfaces), they have identical vtables for all methods except the last—the `InitNew` method. Due to COM's binary compatibility, when your object doesn't need an `InitNew` call, your object can hand out an `IPersistStreamInit` interface when asked for an `IPersistStream` interface. So with a single implementation of `IPersistStreamInit` and an extra COM interface map entry, your object becomes compatible with a larger number of clients.

```
class ATL_NO_VTABLE CDemagogue : public IPersistStreamInit,
. . .
{
    . . .
    BEGIN_COM_MAP(CDemagogue)
    . . .
    COM_INTERFACE_ENTRY(IPersistStreamInit)
    COM_INTERFACE_ENTRY2(IPersistStream, IPersistStreamInit)
    COM_INTERFACE_ENTRY2(IPersist, IPersistStreamInit)
    END_COM_MAP()
    . . .
};
```

---

[1] ATL 3.0's implementation of CComVARIANT's ReadFromStream and WriteToStream methods only attempts to use IPersistStream when asked to read/write a VARIANT containing an interface pointer. The next version of ATL will also attempt to use IPersistStreamInit.

[2] ATL 3.0's implementation of CAxHostWindow::ActivateAx only uses IPersistStreamInit.

Implementing IPersistStreamInit

Clients will only ask an object to initialize itself once. When the client has no initial values to give the object, the client calls the object's `IPersistSteamInit::Init-New` method. In this case, the object should initialize itself to default values. When the client has initial values to give the object, the client will open the stream and call the object's `IPersistStreamInit::Load` method. When the client wishes to save the state of an object, it creates a stream and calls the object's `IPersist-StreamInit::Save` method.

Like the property bag implementation, this is pretty straightforward to implement in an object. Here's an example of an implementation for the Demagogue object to save and restore its three properties to and from a stream.

```
Class CDemagogue : public IPersistStreamInit,
   . . .
   CComBSTR m_name;
   long     m_volume;
   CComBSTR m_speech;

   STDMETHODIMP IsDirty () { return m_fDirty ? S_OK : S_FALSE; }
   STDMETHODIMP Load (IStream* pStream)
   {
     HRESULT hr = m_name.ReadFromStream(pStream);
     if (FAILED (hr)) return hr;

     ULONG cb;
     hr = pStream->Read (&m_volume, sizeof (m_volume), &cb);
     if (FAILED (hr)) return hr;
     hr = m_speech.ReadFromStream(pStream);
     if (FAILED (hr)) return hr;
     m_fDirty = FALSE ;
     return S_OK;
   }
   STDMETHODIMP Save (IStream* pStream)
   {
     HRESULT hr = m_name.WriteToStream (pStream);
     if (FAILED(hr)) return hr;

     ULONG cb;
     hr = pStream->Write(&m_volume, sizeof (m_volume), &cb);
     if (FAILED(hr)) return hr;
```

```
        hr = m_speech.WriteToStream (pStream);
        return hr;
    }
    STDMETHODIMP GetSizeMax(ULARGE_INTEGER*pCbSize)
    {
        if (NULL == pCbSize) return E_POINTER;
            pCbSize->QuadPart = sizeof (ULONG);   // length of m_name
        pCbSize->QuadPart +=
          m_name ? SysStringByteLen(m_name) + sizeof(OLECHAR) : 0;
        pCbSize->QuadPart += sizeof (m_volume);
        pCbSize->QuadPart += sizeof (ULONG);   // length of m_speech
        pCbSize->QuadPart +=
          m_speech ? SysStringByteLen(m_speech) + sizeof(OLECHAR) : 0;
        return S_OK;
    }
    STDMETHODIMP InitNew() { return S_OK; }
};
```

IStorage and IPersistStorage

An embeddable object—an object that you can store in a OLE linking and embedding container such as Microsoft Word and Microsoft Excel—must implement IPersistStorage. The container provides the object an IStorage interface pointer. The IStorage interface pointer references a structured storage medium. The storage object (the object implementing the IStorage interface) acts much like a directory object in a traditional file system. An object can use the IStorage interface to create new and open existing substorages and streams within the storage medium provided by the container.

```
interface IStorage : public IUnknown {
    HRESULT CreateStream([string,in] const OLECHAR* pwcsName,
            [in] DWORD grfMode, [in] DWORD reserved1,
            [in] DWORD reserved2, [out] IStream** ppstm);
    HRESULT OpenStream([string,in] const OLECHAR* pwcsName,
            [unique][in] void* reserved1, [in] DWORD grfMode,
            [in] DWORD reserved2, [out] IStream** ppstm);
    HRESULT CreateStorage([string,in] const OLECHAR* pwcsName,
            [in] DWORD grfMode, [in] DWORD reserved1,
            [in] DWORD reserved2, [out] IStorage** ppstg);
    HRESULT OpenStorage([string,unique,in] const OLECHAR* pwcsName,
```

```
            [unique,in] IStorage* pstgPriority,
            [in] DWORD grfMode, [unique,in] SNB snbExclude,
            [in] DWORD reserved, [out] IStorage** ppstg);
    // Following methods abbreviated for clarity...
    HRESULT CopyTo( . . . );
    HRESULT MoveElementTo( . . . )
    HRESULT Commit( . . . )
    HRESULT Revert(void);
    HRESULT EnumElements( . . . );
    HRESULT DestroyElement( . . , );
    HRESULT RenameElement( . . . );
    HRESULT SetElementTimes( . . . );
    HRESULT SetClass( . . . );
    HRESULT SetStateBits( . . . );
    HRESULT Stat( . . . );
};


interface IPersistStorage : public IPersist {
    HRESULT IsDirty ();
    HRESULT InitNew ([unique,in] IStorage* pStg);
    HRESULT Load ([unique,in] IStorage* pStg);
    HRESULT Save ([unique,in] IStorage* pStgSave,
                  [in] BOOL fSameAsLoad);
    HRESULT SaveCompleted ([unique,in] IStorage* pStgNew);
    HRESULT HandsOffStorage ();
};
```

The IsDirty, InitNew, Load, and Save methods work much as the similarly named methods in the persistence interfaces you've seen previously. However, unlike streams, when a container hands an object an IStorage during the Init-New or Load call, the object can hold onto the interface pointer (after AddRef'ing it, of course). This permits the object to read and write its state incrementally, rather than all at once as do the other persistence mechanisms. A container uses the HandsOffStorage and SaveCompleted methods to instruct the object to release the held interface and to give the object a new IStorage interface, respectively.

Typically, a container of embedded objects will create a storage to hold the objects. In this storage, the container will create one or more streams to hold the container's own state. In addition, the container, for each embedded object, creates a sub-storage in which the container asks the embedded object to save its state.

This is a pretty heavyweight persistence technique for many objects. Simple objects, like the Demagogue example used so far, don't really need this flexibility. Often, such objects simply create a stream in their given storage and save their state into the stream using `IPersistStreamInit`. As this is exactly what the ATL implementation of `IPersistStorage` does, I'll defer creating a custom example here; you'll see the ATL implementation shortly.

ATL Persistence Implementation Classes

ATL provides implementations of the `IPersistPropertyBag`, `IPersistStream`, and `IPersistStorage` interfaces called `IPersistPropertyBagImpl`, `IPersistStreamImpl`, and `IPersistStorageImpl`, respectively. Each template class takes one parameter, the name of the deriving class. You add support for these three persistence interfaces to your object like this:

```
class ATL_NO_VTABLE CDemagogue :
    public IPersistPropertyBagImpl<CDemagogue>,
    public IPersistStreamInitImpl<CDemagogue>,
    public IPersistStorageImpl<CDemagogue>
    { . . .
      BEGIN_COM_MAP(CDemagogue)
      . . .
      COM_INTERFACE_ENTRY2(IPersist, IPersistPropertyBag)
      COM_INTERFACE_ENTRY(IPersistPropertyBag)
      COM_INTERFACE_ENTRY(IPersistStreamInit)
      COM_INTERFACE_ENTRY(IPersistStorage)
      END_COM_MAP()
      . . .
};
```

Don't forget to add the COM MAP entry for `IPersist`. All three persistence interfaces derive from `IPersist`, not `IUnknown`, so you need to respond affirmatively to queries for `IPersist`. Note also that you need to use the `COM_INTERFACE_ENTRY2` (or `COM_INTERFACE_ENTRY_IID`) macro because there are multiple base classes deriving from `IPersist`.

The Property Map

The ATL implementation of these three persistence interfaces requires that your object provide a table describing all the properties that should be saved and loaded during a persistence operation. This table is called the *property map*. ATL uses the property map of a class for two independent purposes: persistence support and control property page support (discussed in Chapter 10).

The various property map entries allow you to

- Define the properties of the COM object that the ATL persistence implementation classes save and restore during a persistence request.
- Define the member variables of the C++ class that the ATL persistence implementation classes save and restore during a persistence request.
- Define the property pages used by a class.
- Associate a property with its property page.

The CDemagogue class's property map looks like this:

```
BEGIN_PROP_MAP(CDemagogue)
  PROP_ENTRY_EX("Speech", DISPID_SPEECH, CLSID_NULL, IID_ISpeaker)
  PROP_ENTRY_EX("Volume", DISPID_VOLUME, CLSID_NULL, IID_ISpeaker)
  PROP_ENTRY_EX("Name",   DISPID_NAME,   CLSID_NULL, IID_INamedObject)
END_PROP_MAP()
```

The BEGIN_PROP_MAP and END_PROP_MAP macros define a class's property map. When you create an object with the ATL Object Wizard, the wizard will create an empty property map by specifying BEGIN_PROP_MAP followed by END_PROP_MAP.

You list the persistent properties of an object in the property map using the PROP_ENTRY and PROP_ENTRY_EX macros. The PROP_ENTRY macro describes a property that the persistence implementation can access via the default dispatch interface, or, in other words, the interface retrieved when you query for IID_IDispatch. You use the PROP_ENTRY_EX macro to describe a property that the persistence implementation must access using some other specified dispatch interface. Both macros require the name of the property, the property's DISPID, and the CLSID of the property's associated property page (discussed in Chapter 10). The PROP_ENTRY_EX macro also requires the IID of the dispatch interface that supports the specified property, whereas the PROP_ENTRY macro uses IID_IDispatch:

```
    PROP_ENTRY (szDesc, dispid, clsid)
    PROP_ENTRY_EX (szDesc, dispid, clsid, iidDispatch)

    PROP_DATA_ENTRY (szDesc, member, vt)
```

You may also want to load and save member variables of your object that are not accessible via a dispatch interface. The PROP_DATA_ENTRY macro also allows you to specify the name of a property, the member variable containing the value, and the VARIANT type of the variable.

```
BEGIN_PROP_MAP(CBullsEye)
 PROP_DATA_ENTRY("_cx", m_sizeExtent.cx, VT_UI4)
 PROP_DATA_ENTRY("_cy", m_sizeExtent.cy, VT_UI4)
 . . .
END_PROP_MAP()
```

Effectively, the PROP_DATA_ENTRY macro causes the persistence implementation to reach into your object, access the specified member variable for the length implied by the VARIANT type, place the data into a VARIANT, and write the VARIANT to the persistent medium. This is quite handy when you have a member variable that is a VARIANT-compatible type. However, it doesn't work for noncompatible types such as indexed properties. Note: There is also a PROP_PAGE macro used to associate a property to a property page. I discuss its use in Chapter 10. The persistence implementations skip entries in the property map made with the PROP_PAGE macro.

One caution: Don't add a PROP_ENTRY, PROP_ENTRY_EX, or PROP_DATA_ ENTRY macro that has a property name containing an embedded space character. Some relatively popular containers, for example Visual Basic, provide an implementation of IPropertyBag that cannot handle names with embedded spaces. This is a bug in the current version of Visual Basic, as other containers allow space-separated property names.

When you have a member variable you want to load and save during a persistence operation and that variable is not a VARIANT-compatible type (for example, an indexed or array variable), the property map mechanism doesn't help. You have to override the appropriate member functions of the persistence implementation classes and read and write the variable explicitly. To do this, you need to know the basic structure of the ATL persistence implementation.

The Persistence Implementations

Let's look at how the persistence implementations work. As you'll see shortly, the ATL 3.0 property bag persistence implementation has a bug I'd like to fix, so I'll use it as the example. However, all persistence implementations are similar.

The Property Map

The property map macros basically add a static member function called GetProp- ertyMap to your class. GetPropertyMap returns a pointer to an array of ATL_ PROPMAP_ENTRY structures. This structure looks like this:

```
struct ATL_PROPMAP_ENTRY
{
    LPCOLESTR szDesc;
    DISPID dispid;
    const CLSID* pclsidPropPage;
    const IID* piidDispatch;
    DWORD dwOffsetData;
    DWORD dwSizeData;
    VARTYPE vt;
};
```

For example, here's a property map and the resulting macro expansion. The property map

```
BEGIN_PROP_MAP(CDemagogue)
 PROP_ENTRY     ("Speech", DISPID_SPEECH, CLSID_NULL)
 PROP_ENTRY_EX  ("Name",   DISPID_NAME,   CLSID_NULL, IID_INamedObject)
 PROP_DATA_ENTRY("_cx",    m_sizeExtent.cx, VT_UI4)
END_PROP_MAP()
```

expands to this:

```
typedef _ATL_PROP_NOTIFY_EVENT_CLASS __ATL_PROP_NOTIFY_EVENT_CLASS; \
typedef CDemagogue _PropMapClass;
static ATL_PROPMAP_ENTRY* GetPropertyMap() {
 static ATL_PROPMAP_ENTRY pPropMap[] = {
 {OLESTR(("Speech"), DISPID_SPEECH, &CLSID_NULL, &IID_IDispatch,
    0, 0, 0},
 {OLESTR("Name"),    DISPID_ NAME, &CLSID_NULL, &IID_INamedObject,
    0, 0, 0},
 {OLESTR("_cx"),     0,            &CLSID_NULL, NULL,
    offsetof(_PropMapClass, m_sizeExtent.cx),
    sizeof(((_PropMapClass*)0)-> m_sizeExtent.cx), VT_UI4},
 {NULL, 0, NULL, &IID_NULL, 0, 0, 0}
```

The szDesc field of the structure holds the name of the property. It's only used by the property bag persistence implementation. The other common persistence mechanisms don't require a textual name for a property.

The dispid field contains the property's dispatch identifier. All the persistence implementations need this so they can access the property via one of the object's IDispatch implementations by calling the Invoke method.

The `pclsidPropPage` field contains a pointer to the CLSID for the property page associated with the object. It's not used during persistence.

The `piidDispatch` field contains a pointer to the IID of the dispatch interface that supports this property. The specified `dispid` is unique to this interface.

The last three fields are used only by PROP_DATA_ENTRY macros. The `dwOffsetData` field contains the offset of the specified member variable from the beginning of a class instance. The `dwSizeData` field contains the size of the variable in bytes, and the `vt` field contains the variable's VARTYPE (VARIANT type enumeration code).

The various persistence implementations basically iterate over this map and load or save the properties listed. For properties listed using PROP_ENTRY and PROP_ENTRY_EX, the implementations call `IDispatch::Invoke` with the specified `dispid` to get or put the property.

`Invoke` transfers all properties via a VARIANT. The stream persistence implementation simply wraps the variant in a `CComVARIANT` instance and uses its `ReadFromStream` and `WriteToStream` methods to do all the hard work. Therefore stream persistence supports all VARIANT types supported by the `CComVARIANT` persistence implementation (discussed in Chapter 2). The property bag implementation has it even easier because property bags deal directly in VARIANTs.

For properties listed using the PROP_DATA_ENTRY macro, things aren't quite so simple. The `IPersistStreamInit` implementation directly accesses the object instance at the specified offset for the specified length. The implementation reads or writes the specified number of bytes directly to or from the object. The VARIANT type is completed ignored.

However, the `IPersistPropertyBag` implementation must read and write properties held in a VARIANT. Therefore, this implementation copies the member variable of the object to a VARIANT before writing the property to the bag and copies a VARIANT to the member variable after reading the property from the bag. The current implementation of `IPersistPropertyBag` persistence only supports a limited set of VARIANT types; what's worse is that it silently fails to load and save properties with any VARTYPEs other than these:

VT_UI1, VT_I1	Reads and writes the variable as a BYTE.
VT_BOOL	Reads and write the variable as a VARIANT_BOOL.
VT_UI2	Reads and writes the variable as a short.
VT_UI4, VT_INT, VT_UINT	Reads and writes the variable as a long.

Strangely, commonly used VARIANT types, such as VT_I2 (signed short) and VT_I4 (signed long) aren't supported, though it's simply a matter of adding a few more `case` statements to the code. I expect this to be corrected in the next ATL release.

IPersistPropertyBagImpl

The `IPersistPropertyBagImpl<T>` class implements the `IPersistProperty-Bag` interface methods. `IPersistPropertyBag`, like all the persistence interfaces, derives from `IPersist`, which has one method—`GetClassID`.

```
interface IPersist : IUnknown
{ HRESULT GetClassID([out] CLSID* pclsid); }
```

All the persistence implementation classes have the same implementation of `Get-ClassID`. They call a static member function called `GetObjectCLSID` method to retrieve the CLSID. This method must be in the deriving class (your object's class) or one of its base classes.

```
template <class T>
class ATL_NO_VTABLE IPersistPropertyBagImpl :
  public IPersistPropertyBag
{
public:
  . . .
  STDMETHOD(GetClassID)(CLSID *pClassID)
  {
    ATLTRACE2(atlTraceCOM, 0,
      _T("IPersistPropertyBagImpl::GetClassID\n"));
    *pClassID = T::GetObjectCLSID();
    return S_OK;
  }
};
```

Normally, your class obtains its `GetObjectCLSID` static member function from `CComCoClass`.

```
template <class T, const CLSID* pclsid = &CLSID_NULL>
class CComCoClass
{
public:
  . . .
  static const CLSID& WINAPI GetObjectCLSID() {return *pclsid;}
};
```

This implies that a class must be createable in order for it to use the persistence classes. This is reasonable because it doesn't do much good to save a class to some persistent medium and then be unable to create a new instance when loading the object from that medium.

The `IPersistPropertyBagImpl<T>` class also implements the remaining `IPersistPropertyBag` methods, including, for example, the Load method. `IPersistPropertyBagImpl<T>::Load` call `T::IPersistPropertyBag_Load` to do most of the work. This allows your class to provide this method when it needs a custom implementation of Load. Normally, your object (`class T`) doesn't provide an `IPersistPropertyBag_Load` method, so this call vectors to a default implementation provided by the base-class `IPersistPropertyBagImpl<T>:: IPersistPropertyBag_Load` method. The default implementation calls the global function `AtlIPersistPropertyBag_Load`. This global function iterates over the property map and, for each entry in the map, loads the property from the property bag.

```
template <class T>
class ATL_NO_VTABLE IPersistPropertyBagImpl :
  public IPersistPropertyBag
{
public:
 . . .
 // IPersistPropertyBag
 //
 STDMETHOD(Load)(LPPROPERTYBAG pPropBag, LPERRORLOG pErrorLog)
 {
   ATLTRACE2(atlTraceCOM, 0, _T("IPersistPropertyBagImpl::Load\n"));
   T* pT = static_cast<T*>(this);
   ATL_PROPMAP_ENTRY* pMap = T::GetPropertyMap();
   ATLASSERT(pMap != NULL);
   return pT->IPersistPropertyBag_Load(pPropBag, pErrorLog, pMap);
 }
 HRESULT IPersistPropertyBag_Load(LPPROPERTYBAG pPropBag,
                     LPERRORLOG pErrorLog, ATL_PROPMAP_ENTRY* pMap)
 {
   T* pT = static_cast<T*>(this);
   HRESULT hr = AtlIPersistPropertyBag_Load(pPropBag, pErrorLog,
                                     pMap, pT, pT->GetUnknown());
   if (SUCCEEDED(hr)) pT->m_bRequiresSave = FALSE;
```

```
    return hr;
    }
    . . .
};
```

This implementation structure provides three places where we can override methods and provide custom persistence support for a non-VARIANT-compatible property. We could override the `Load (LPPROPERTYBAG pPropBag, LPERRORLOG pErrorLog)` method itself, in effect directly implementing the `IPersistProperyBag` method. Alternatively, we can let ATL implement `Load` while our object implements `IPersistPropertyBag_Load`. Finally, we can let ATL implement `Load` and `IPersistPropertyBag_Load` while we provide a replacement global function called `AtlIPersistPropertyBag_Load` and play some linker tricks so our object uses our global function rather than the ATL-provided one.

The most natural method is to implement `Load`. Normally, in this implementation you'd call the base-class `Load` method to read all properties described in the property map, then read any custom, non-VARIANT-compatible properties. For example:

```
HRESULT CMyObject::Load(LPPROPERTYBAG pPropBag, LPERRORLOG pErrorLog)
{
  HRESULT hr =
   IPersistPropertyBagImpl<CMyObject>::Load(pPropBag, pErrorLog);
  If (FAILED (hr)) return hr;

  // Read an array of VT_I4
  // This requires us to create a "name" for each array element
  // Read each element as a VARIANT, then recreate the array
  . . .
}
```

This approach has a few disadvantages. It's a minor point, but the object now requires four methods for its persistence implementation—its `Load`, the base-class `Load`, the base-class `IPersistPropertyBag_Load`, and `AtlIPersistPropertyBag_Load`. I could copy the base-class `Load` implementation into the object's `Load` method, but that makes the object more fragile because future versions of ATL might change its persistence implementation technique.

Another slight disadvantage to this approach is that it is clear from the ATL implementation that the ATL designers intended for your object to override `IPersistPropertyBag_Load`. Note the following code fragment from the default implementation of `Load`:

```
STDMETHOD(Load)(LPPROPERTYBAG pPropBag, LPERRORLOG pErrorLog)
{
    . . .
    T* pT = static_cast<T*>(this);
    . . .
    return pT->IPersistPropertyBag_Load(pPropBag, pErrorLog, pMap);
}
```

Rather than directly calling IPersistPropertyBag_Load, which is present in the same class as the Load method, the code calls the method using a pointer to the deriving class—your object's class. This provides the same functionality as making the method virtual without the overhead of a virtual function.

A more significant disadvantage is that calling the base-class Load method in turn calls the base class IPersistPropertyBagImpl<T>::IPersistPropertyBag_Load method. That function in turn calls the AtlIPersistPropertyBag_Load function, which has a bug. The ATL 3.0 implementation of AtlIPersistPropertyBag_Load for properties described using PROP_DATA_ENTRY macro is slightly flawed. Here's a code fragment from that function:

```
CComVariant var;

if (pMap[i].dwSizeData != 0) {
    void* pData = (void*) (pMap[i].dwOffsetData + (DWORD)pThis);
    var.vt = pMap[i].vt;     // BUG FIX line added
    HRESULT hr = pPropBag->Read(pMap[i].szDesc, &var, pErrorLog);
    if (SUCCEEDED(hr)) {
        switch (pMap[i].vt) {
        case VT_UI4:
        *((long*)pData) = var.lVal;
        break;
    }
}
```

The CComVariant constructor initializes var to VT_EMPTY. An empty input VARIANT permits the IPropertyBag::Read method to coerce the value read to any appropriate type. Note, however, that the code copies the VARIANT's value into the member variable of the control based on the type specified in the property map entry, regardless of the type contained in the VARIANT.

When the _cx and _cy extents (described in a property map using PROP_DATA_ENTRY macros previously) are small enough, the Read method initializes the variant to contain a VT_I2 (short) value. However, the property map entry specifies that the member variable is VT_UI4 type. In other words, the data source is 16 bits, the destination is 32 bits, and the code copies 32 bits. In this case, this code sets the high-order 16 bits of the control's extents to bogus values. Initializing the VARIANT type to the type contained in the property map, as shown in the "BUG FIX line added" statement in the code fragment, fixes the problem.

I could play some linker tricks and provide a custom AtlIPersistProperty-Bag function that gets linked in preference to the one ATL provides. This approach fixes the problem for all classes that use the property bag persistence implementation. However, it's easier (and less fragile) to have the object provide an IPersist-PropertyBag_Load method that simply calls a fixed version of AtlIPersist-PropertyBag_Load. (Of course, you can always simply go correct the header file, but that leads to its own set of maintenance issues.)

It seems the best solution is to let the object provide its own implementation of the IPersistPropertyBag_Load method. In this implementation, the object can call a corrected version of AtlIPersistProperyBag_Load *and* save any non-VARIANT-compatible properties it possesses. Here's an example from the BullsEye control described in Chapter 10. It contains a property that is an array of long integers. This can't be described as a VARIANT-compatible type as it's not a SAFE-ARRAY, so I can't list the property in the property map.

```
HRESULT CBullsEye::IPersistPropertyBag_Load(LPPROPERTYBAG pPropBag,
    LPERRORLOG pErrorLog, ATL_PROPMAP_ENTRY* pMap)
{
    if (NULL == pPropBag) return E_POINTER;

    // Load the properties described in the PROP_MAP
    // Work around ATL 3.0 bug in AtlIPersistPropertyBag_Load
    HRESULT hr =
        FixedAtlIPersistPropertyBag_Load(pPropBag, pErrorLog, pMap,
                    this, GetUnknown());
        if (SUCCEEDED(hr)) m_bRequiresSave = FALSE;

    if (FAILED (hr)) return hr;

    // Load the indexed property-RingValues
    // Get the number of rings
    short sRingCount;
    get_RingCount (&sRingCount);

    // For each ring, read its value
    for (short nIndex = 1; nIndex <= sRingCount; nIndex++) {
```

```
        // Create the base property name
        CComBSTR bstrName = OLESTR("RingValue");

        // Create ring number as a string
        CComVariant vRingNumber = nIndex;
        hr = vRingNumber.ChangeType (VT_BSTR);
        ATLASSERT (SUCCEEDED (hr));

        // Concatenate the two strings to form property name
        bstrName += vRingNumber.bstrVal;

        // Read ring value from the property bag
        CComVariant vValue = 0L;
        hr = pPropBag->Read(bstrName, &vValue, pErrorLog);
        ATLASSERT (SUCCEEDED (hr));
        ATLASSERT (VT_I4 == vValue.vt);

        if (FAILED (hr)) {
            hr = E_UNEXPECTED;
            break;
        }

        // Set the ring value
        put_RingValue (nIndex, vValue.lVal);
         }

    if (SUCCEEDED(hr)) m_bRequiresSave = FALSE;
    return hr;
}
```

The Save method works symmetrically. The IPersistPropertyBagImpl<T> class implements the Save method. IPersistPropertyBagImpl<T>::Save calls T::IPersistPropertyBag_Save to do the work. Again, your object (class T) doesn't normally provide an IPersistPropertyBag_Save method, so this call vectors to a default implementation provided by the base-class IPersistProper-tyBagImpl<T>::IPersistPropertyBag_Save method. The default implementation calls the global function AtlIPersistPropertyBag_Save. This global function iterates over the property map and, for each entry in the map, saves the property to the property bag.

```
template <class T>
class ATL_NO_VTABLE IPersistPropertyBagImpl :
  public IPersistPropertyBag
{
public:
  . . .
 // IPersistPropertyBag
 //
 STDMETHOD(Save)(LPPROPERTYBAG pPropBag, BOOL fClearDirty,
               BOOL fSaveAllProperties)
 {
   ATLTRACE2(atlTraceCOM, 0, _T("IPersistPropertyBagImpl::Save\n"));
   T* pT = static_cast<T*>(this);
   ATL_PROPMAP_ENTRY* pMap = T::GetPropertyMap();
   ATLASSERT(pMap != NULL);
   return pT->IPersistPropertyBag_Save(pPropBag, fClearDirty,
                                      fSaveAllProperties, pMap);
 }
 HRESULT IPersistPropertyBag_Save(LPPROPERTYBAG pPropBag,
         BOOL fClearDirty,
         BOOL fSaveAllProperties, ATL_PROPMAP_ENTRY* pMap)
 {
   T* pT = static_cast<T*>(this);
   return AtlIPersistPropertyBag_Save(pPropBag, fClearDirty,
         fSaveAllProperties, pMap, pT, pT->GetUnknown());
 }
};
```

Finally, `IPersistPropertyBagImpl` implements the `InitNew` method this way:

```
STDMETHOD(InitNew)()
{
 ATLTRACE2(atlTraceCOM, 0, _T("IPersistPropertyBagImpl::InitNew\n"));
 return S_OK;
}
```

Therefore, you'll need to override `InitNew` directly when you have any initialization to perform when there are no properties to load.

IPersistStreamInitImpl

The implementation contained in `IPersistStreamInitImpl` is quite similar to the one just described. The `Load` and `Save` methods call the `IPersistStreamInit_Load` and `IPersistStreamInit_Save` methods, respectively, potentially provided by the deriving object but typically provided by the default implementation in `IPersistStreamInitImpl`. These implementations call the global helper functions `AtlIPersistStreamInit_Load` and `AtlIPersistStreamInit_Save`.

```
template <class T>
class ATL_NO_VTABLE IPersistStreamInitImpl :
  public IPersistStreamInit
{
public:
. . .
 // IPersistStream
 STDMETHOD(Load)(LPSTREAM pStm)
 {
   ATLTRACE2(atlTraceCOM, 0, _T("IPersistStreamInitImpl::Load\n"));
   T* pT = static_cast<T*>(this);
   return pT->IPersistStreamInit_Load(pStm, T::GetPropertyMap());
 }
 HRESULT IPersistStreamInit_Load(LPSTREAM pStm,
                                 ATL_PROPMAP_ENTRY* pMap)
 {
   T* pT = static_cast<T*>(this);
   HRESULT hr = AtlIPersistStreamInit_Load(pStm, pMap,
                                           pT, pT->GetUnknown());
   if (SUCCEEDED(hr)) pT->m_bRequiresSave = FALSE;
   return hr;
 }
 STDMETHOD(Save)(LPSTREAM pStm, BOOL fClearDirty)
 {
   T* pT = static_cast<T*>(this);
   ATLTRACE2(atlTraceCOM, 0, _T("IPersistStreamInitImpl::Save\n"));
   return pT->IPersistStreamInit_Save(pStm, fClearDirty,
                                      T::GetPropertyMap());
 }
 HRESULT IPersistStreamInit_Save(LPSTREAM pStm, BOOL fClearDirty,
                                 ATL_PROPMAP_ENTRY* pMap)
 {
```

```
    T* pT = static_cast<T*>(this);
    return AtlIPersistStreamInit_Save(pStm, fClearDirty, pMap, pT,
                                      pT->GetUnknown());
  }
};
```

`IPersistStreamInitImpl` also implements the `InitNew` method this way:

```
STDMETHOD(InitNew)()
{
  ATLTRACE2(atlTraceCOM, 0, _T("IPersistStreamInitImpl::InitNew\n"));
  return S_OK;
}
```

Therefore, as with property bags, you'll need to override `InitNew` directly when you have any initialization to perform when there are no properties to load.

The implementation of the `IsDirty` method assumes the presence of a member variable called `m_bRequiresSave` somewhere in your class hierarchy.

```
STDMETHOD(IsDirty)()
{
  ATLTRACE2(atlTraceCOM, 0, _T("IPersistStreamInitImpl::IsDirty\n"));
  T* pT = static_cast<T*>(this);
  return (pT->m_bRequiresSave) ? S_OK : S_FALSE;
}
```

The persistence implementations originally assumed that they would only be used by ActiveX controls—as if controls were the only objects that needed a persistence implementation. While the coupling between the control classes and the persistence implementation is greatly reduced in ATL 3.0, it is the `CComControlBase` class that normally provides the `m_bRequiresSave` variable and the `SetDirty` and `GetDirty` helper functions usually used to access the variable:

```
class ATL_NO_VTABLE CComControlBase
{
public:
  void SetDirty(BOOL bDirty) { m_bRequiresSave = bDirty; }
  // Obtain the dirty state for the control
  BOOL GetDirty() { return m_bRequiresSave ? TRUE : FALSE; }
  . . .
  unsigned m_bRequiresSave:1;
};
```

To use the persistence implementation classes in an object that doesn't derive from CComControlBase, you'll need to define the m_bRequiresSave variable in your class hierarchy somewhere. Typically, for convenience, you'll also define the Set-Dirty and GetDirty helper methods as well. So here's a class that noncontrols can use to provide this persistence support:

```
class ATL_NO_VTABLE CSupportDirtyBit
{
public:
 CSupportDirtyBit() : m_bRequiresSave(FALSE) {}
 void SetDirty(BOOL bDirty) { m_bRequiresSave = bDirty ? TRUE : FALSE;}
 BOOL GetDirty() { return m_bRequiresSave ? TRUE : FALSE; }
 BOOL m_bRequiresSave;
};
```

Finally, the IPersistStreamInitImpl class provides the following implementation of GetSizeMax:

```
STDMETHOD(GetSizeMax)(ULARGE_INTEGER FAR* /* pcbSize */)
{
 ATLTRACENOTIMPL(_T("IPersistStreamInitImpl::GetSizeMax"));
}
```

One could argue that this is an invalid implementation of GetSizeMax. The Platform SDK even warns that GetSizeMax should always return a value equal to or greater than the number of bytes in the stream that the object requires in order to save its state. This is due to the fact that a caller may allocate a nongrowable stream based on the size returned by GetSizeMax. Regardless, the lack of support for this method causes it to be difficult, though not impossible, to use the stream persistence implementation provided by ATL when adding marshal-by-value support to the object. You'll see how to do that at the end of this chapter.

IPersistStorageImpl

The ATL implementation of IPersistStorage is very simplistic. The Save method creates a stream called "Contents" within the provided storage and depends on an IPersistStreamInit implementation to write the contents of the stream.

```
template <class T>
class ATL_NO_VTABLE IPersistStorageImpl : public IPersistStorage
{
```

```
public:
 STDMETHOD(Save)(IStorage* pStorage, BOOL fSameAsLoad)
 {
   ATLTRACE2(atlTraceCOM, 0, _T("IPersistStorageImpl::Save\n"));
   CComPtr<IPersistStreamInit> p;
   p.p = IPSI_GetIPersistStreamInit();
   HRESULT hr = E_FAIL;
   if (p != NULL) {
     CComPtr<IStream> spStream;
     static LPCOLESTR vszContents = OLESTR("Contents");
     hr = pStorage->CreateStream(vszContents,
       STGM_READWRITE | STGM_SHARE_EXCLUSIVE | STGM_CREATE,
       0, 0, &spStream);
     if (SUCCEEDED(hr)) hr = p->Save(spStream, fSameAsLoad);
   }
   return hr;
 }
 . . .
};
```

Similarly, the `Load` method opens the "Contents" stream and uses the `IPersistStreamInit` implementation to read the contents of the stream.

```
STDMETHOD(Load)(IStorage* pStorage)
{
 ATLTRACE2(atlTraceCOM, 0, _T("IPersistStorageImpl::Load\n"));
 CComPtr<IPersistStreamInit> p;
 p.p = IPSI_GetIPersistStreamInit();
 HRESULT hr = E_FAIL;
 if (p != NULL) {
   CComPtr<IStream> spStream;
   hr = pStorage->OpenStream(OLESTR("Contents"), NULL,
     STGM_DIRECT | STGM_SHARE_EXCLUSIVE, 0, &spStream);
   if (SUCCEEDED(hr)) hr = p->Load(spStream);
 }
 return hr;
}
```

The `InitNew` and `IsDirty` implementations retrieve the object's `IPersistStreamInit` interface pointer (using a helper function to get the interface) and delegate to the same named method in that interface.

```
STDMETHOD(IsDirty)(void)
{
 ATLTRACE2(atlTraceCOM, 0, _T("IPersistStorageImpl::IsDirty\n"));
 CComPtr<IPersistStreamInit> p;
 p.p = IPSI_GetIPersistStreamInit();
 return (p != NULL) ? p->IsDirty() : E_FAIL;
}
STDMETHOD(InitNew)(IStorage*)
{
 ATLTRACE2(atlTraceCOM, 0, _T("IPersistStorageImpl::InitNew\n"));
 CComPtr<IPersistStreamInit> p;
 p.p = IPSI_GetIPersistStreamInit();
 return (p != NULL) ? p->InitNew() : E_FAIL;
}
```

One of the main reasons an object supports `IPersistStorage` is so the object can incrementally read and write its state. Unfortunately, the ATL implementation doesn't support this. The implementation does not cache the `IStorage` interface provided during the `Load` and `Save` calls, so it's not available for later incremental reads and writes. Not caching the `IStorage` interface makes implementing the last two methods trivial, however.

```
STDMETHOD(SaveCompleted)(IStorage* /* pStorage */)
{
 ATLTRACE2(atlTraceCOM, 0,
   _T("IPersistStorageImpl::SaveCompleted\n"));
 return S_OK;
 }
STDMETHOD(HandsOffStorage)(void)
{
 ATLTRACE2(atlTraceCOM, 0,
   _T("IPersistStorageImpl::HandsOffStorage\n"));
 return S_OK;
}
```

Generally speaking, most objects that need the functionality provided by `IPersistStorage` won't be able to use the implementation provided by ATL. They will have to derive directly from `IPersistStorage` and implement all the methods explicitly.

Additional Persistence Implementations

Given what has been discussed so far, I thought it might be interesting to demonstrate an additional persistence implementation built using functionality you've already seen.

IPersistMemory

Let's look at implementing the IPersistMemory interface. It looks like this:

```
interface IPersistMemory : IPersist
{
   HRESULT IsDirty();
   HRESULT Load([in, size_is(cbSize)] LPVOID pvMem,
               [in] ULONG cbSize);
   HRESULT Save([out, size_is(cbSize)] LPVOID pvMem,
               [in] BOOL fClearDirty, [in] ULONG cbSize);
   HRESULT GetSizeMax([out] ULONG* pCbSize);
   HRESULT InitNew();
};
```

The IPersistMemory interface allows a client to request that the object save its state to a fixed-size memory block (identified with a void*). The interface is very similar to IPersistStreamInit, except that it uses a memory block rather than an expandable IStream. The cbSize argument to the Load and Save methods indicates the amount of memory accessible through pvMem. The IsDirty, Get-SizeMax, and InitNew methods are semantically identical to those in IPersist-StreamInit.

Strangely, the header files show that the IPersistStreamInit::GetSize-Max method expects a parameter that is a ULARGE_INTEGER* and the IPersist-Memory::GetSizeMax method expects a parameter that is a ULONG*. However, the documentation claims both methods are syntactically identical and expect a ULARGE_INTEGER*.

Implementing the IPersistMemory Interface

You've seen that ATL provides the IPersistStreamInitImpl class that saves and restores the state of an object to a stream. The COM API CreateStreamOnH-Global returns an IStream implementation that reads and writes to a global memory block. I can use the two together and easily implement IPersistMemory using the functionality provided by IPersistStreamInitImpl.

With the exception of the Load and Save methods, all methods in my IPersistMemory implementation simply delegate to the same named method in ATL's IPersistStreamInit implementation.

```
template <class T, class S = IPersistStreamInit>
class ATL_NO_VTABLE IPersistMemoryImpl : public IPersistMemory
{
public:
    // IPersist
    STDMETHODIMP GetClassID(CLSID *pClassID) {
        ATLTRACE2(atlTraceCOM, 0,
          _T("IPersistMemoryImpl::GetClassID\n"));
        T* pT = static_cast<T*>(this);
        S* psi = static_cast <S*> (pT);
        return psi->GetClassID(pClassID);
    }


    // IPersistMemory
    STDMETHODIMP IsDirty() {
        ATLTRACE2(atlTraceCOM, 0, _T("IPersistMemoryImpl::IsDirty\n"));
        T* pT = static_cast<T*>(this);
        S* psi = static_cast <S*> (pT);
        return psi->IsDirty();
    }

    STDMETHODIMP Load(void* pvMem, ULONG cbSize) {
        ATLTRACE2(atlTraceCOM, 0, _T("IPersistMemoryImpl::Load\n"));
        T* pT = static_cast<T*>(this);

        // Get memory handle
        HGLOBAL h = GlobalAlloc (GMEM_MOVEABLE, cbSize);
        if (NULL == h) return E_OUTOFMEMORY;
        LPVOID pv = GlobalLock (h);
        if (!pv) return E_OUTOFMEMORY;

        // Copy to memory block
        CopyMemory (pv, pvMem, cbSize);
        CComPtr<IStream> spStrm;
        // Create stream on memory
        HRESULT hr = CreateStreamOnHGlobal (h, TRUE, &spStrm);
        if (FAILED (hr)) {
```

```
      GlobalUnlock (h);
      GlobalFree (h);
      return hr;
    }
    // Stream now owns the memory


    // Load from stream
    S* psi = static_cast <S*> (pT);
    hr = psi->Load (spStrm);

    GlobalUnlock (h);
    return hr;
}
STDMETHODIMP Save(void* pvMem, BOOL fClearDirty, ULONG cbSize) {
    ATLTRACE2(atlTraceCOM, 0, _T("IPersistMemoryImpl::Save\n"));
    T* pT = static_cast<T*>(this);

    // Get memory handle
    HGLOBAL h = GlobalAlloc (GMEM_MOVEABLE, cbSize);
    if (NULL == h) return E_OUTOFMEMORY;

    // Create stream on memory
    CComPtr<IStream> spStrm;
    HRESULT hr = CreateStreamOnHGlobal (h, TRUE, &spStrm);
    if (FAILED (hr)) {
      GlobalFree (h);
      return hr;
    }
    // Stream now owns the memory

    // Set logical size of stream to physical size of memory
    // (Global memory block allocation rounding causes differences)
    ULARGE_INTEGER uli;
    uli.QuadPart = cbSize ;
    spStrm->SetSize (uli);

    S* psi = static_cast <S*> (pT);
    hr = psi->Save (spStrm, fClearDirty);
    if (FAILED (hr)) return hr;

    LPVOID pv = GlobalLock (h);
    if (!pv) return E_OUTOFMEMORY;
```

```
                // Copy to memory block
                CopyMemory (pvMem, pv, cbSize);

                return hr;
            }
            STDMETHODIMP GetSizeMax(ULONG* pCbSize) {
                if (NULL == pCbSize) return E_POINTER;
                *pCbSize = 0 ;

                T* pT = static_cast<T*>(this);
                S* psi = static_cast <S*> (pT);
                ULARGE_INTEGER uli ;
                uli.QuadPart = 0;
                HRESULT hr = psi->GetSizeMax (&uli);
                if (SUCCEEDED (hr)) *pCbSize = uli.LowPart;

                return hr;
            }
            STDMETHODIMP InitNew() {
                ATLTRACE2(atlTraceCOM, 0, _T("IPersistMemoryImpl::InitNew\n"));
                T* pT = static_cast<T*>(this);
                S* psi = static_cast <S*> (pT);
                return psi->InitNew();
            }
        };

        // When/if Visual C++ supports partial specialization, this
        // implementation would allow IPersistMemoryImpl to use an
        // IPersistStream implementation.
        #if 0
        template <class T, class S>
        STDMETHODIMP IPersistMemoryImpl<T, IPersistStream>::InitNew()
        {
            ATLTRACE2(atlTraceCOM, 0, _T("IPersistMemoryImpl::InitNew\n"));
            return S_OK;
        }
        #endif
```

Notice the use of static_cast to down-cast the this pointer to the deriving class, then up-cast the resulting pointer to an IPersistStreamInit*. I do this so I get a compile-time error when the class deriving from IPersistMemoryImpl doesn't also derive from IPersistStreamInit. This approach does require that the deriving class not implement `IPersistStreamInit` in an "unusual" way, such as on a tear-off interface or via aggregation.

Alternatively, I could have retrieved the `IPersistStreamInit` interface using `QueryInterface` something like this:

```
T* pT = static_cast<T*>(this);
CComQIPtr<S> psi = pT->GetUnknown() ;
```

However, then I might find out at runtime that there's no `IPersistStreamInit` implementation available, which means my object then ends up saying it implements `IPersistMemory` without the ability to do so. I prefer compile-time errors whenever possible, so I chose the former approach, accepting its limitations.

Using the IPersistMemoryImpl Template Class

An object uses this `IPersistMemory` implementation this way:

```
class ATL_NO_VTABLE CDemagogue :
    . . .
    public IPersistStreamInitImpl2<CDemagogue>,
    public IPersistMemoryImpl<CDemagogue>,
    public CSupportDirtyBit
{
    . . .
BEGIN_COM_MAP(CDemagogue)
    . . .
    COM_INTERFACE_ENTRY2(IPersist, IPersistStreamInit)
    COM_INTERFACE_ENTRY(IPersistStreamInit)
    COM_INTERFACE_ENTRY(IPersistMemory)
END_COM_MAP()
```

The GetSizeMax Method

With the exception of the `IPersistStream[Init]::GetSizeMax` methods and the `IPersistMemory::GetSizeMax` method, all methods of each persistence interface must be fully implemented. And, in fact, ATL's implementation of `IPersistStreamInitImpl::GetSizeMax` takes advantage of this exception and simply returns E_NOTIMPL. However, as you'll see shortly, it would be more useful if `GetSizeMax` actually worked. So let's fix it—at least in common cases.

I could override `GetSizeMax` in my `CDemagogue` class, but then I'd have to do the same in every class that wants a working version of the method. A better approach is to define a new template class that derives from `IPersistStreamInitImpl` and adds an implementation of GetSizeMax. Here's one (partial) implementation. (For the complete listing, see the utility.h source file in the ATL Internals project.)

```cpp
template <class T>
class ATL_NO_VTABLE IPersistStreamInitImpl2 :
  public IPersistStreamInitImpl<T>
{
public:
    STDMETHOD(GetSizeMax)(ULARGE_INTEGER* pcbSize)
    {
        . . .
        // For each persistent property entry in the property map
        for (int i = 0; pMap[i].pclsidPropPage != NULL; i++) {
            if (pMap[i].szDesc == NULL)
                continue;

            // Just use the actual size of a raw data entry
            if (pMap[i].dwSizeData != 0) {
                pcbSize->QuadPart += pMap[i].dwSizeData;
                continue;
            }

            // Fetch the new IDispatch interface when we don't already
            // have it
            . . .

            // Fetch the property described in the property map
            . . .

            // Interface pointers persist as a CLSID
            // followed by the object's persistent stream
            switch (var.vt) {
            case VT_UNKNOWN:    case VT_DISPATCH:
            {
                . . .
            }

            // Scalar types persist as their size
            case VT_UI1:    case VT_I1:
                pcbSize->QuadPart += sizeof(BYTE);
                continue;
        }
```

```
            return S_OK;
        }
    };
```

This code is highly dependent on ATL's implementation of `IPersistStreamInit` and `CComBSTR::WriteToStream`. Should they change significantly, this code could break. However, the code is relatively efficient and straightforward to maintain.

To use this class in your objects, simply replace the `IPersistStream-InitImpl` base class with a reference to the `IPersistStreamInitImpl2` class. This code

```
class ATL_NO_VTABLE CDemagogue :
    . . .
    public IPersistStreamInitImpl<CDemagogue>,
    public CSupportDirtyBit,
{
    . . .
};
```

becomes

```
class ATL_NO_VTABLE CDemagogue :
    . . .
    public IPersistStreamInitImpl2<CDemagogue>,
    public CSupportDirtyBit,
{
    . . .
};
```

Another technique for calculating the size of the stream is to save the object to a temporary stream and then retrieve the size of the stream.[3] For example, the following class provides a minimal `IStream` implementation that only tracks how much an object writes to a stream.

```
class CDummyStream : public IStream
{
public:
  CDummyStream() { m_libSeek.QuadPart = 0; m_libMaxOffset.QuadPart = 0;}
```

---

[3] Axel Heitland originally inspired this dummy stream approach for calculating the size of persistent data.

```
STDMETHODIMP QueryInterface (REFIID riid, void**ppv) {
  if (riid == IID_IStream ||
      riid == IID_ISequentialStream || riid == IID_IUnknown)
    *ppv = static_cast <IStream*> (this);
  return *ppv = NULL, E_NOINTERFACE;
}
STDMETHODIMP_(ULONG) AddRef() { return 2; }
STDMETHODIMP_(ULONG) Release () { return 1; }

STDMETHODIMP Read(void* pv, ULONG cb, ULONG* pcbRead)
  { return E_NOTIMPL; }
STDMETHODIMP Write(const void* pv, ULONG cb, ULONG* pcbWritten) {
  m_libMaxOffset.QuadPart =
    max (m_libMaxOffset.QuadPart, m_libSeek.QuadPart + cb);
  *pcbWritten = cb;
  return S_OK;
}
STDMETHODIMP Seek(LARGE_INTEGER dlibMove, DWORD dwOrigin,
                  ULARGE_INTEGER*plibNewPosition) {
  switch (dwOrigin) {
  case STREAM_SEEK_SET:
    m_libSeek.QuadPart = dlibMove.QuadPart;
    break;
  case STREAM_SEEK_CUR:
    m_libSeek.QuadPart += dlibMove.QuadPart;
    break;
  case STREAM_SEEK_END:
    m_libSeek.QuadPart = m_libMaxOffset.QuadPart-dlibMove.QuadPart;
    if (m_libSeek.QuadPart < 0) m_libSeek.QuadPart = 0;
    break;
  default:
    return E_UNEXPECTED;
  }
  *plibNewPosition = m_libSeek;
  return S_OK;
}
STDMETHODIMP SetSize(ULARGE_INTEGER libNewSize) {
  m_libMaxOffset.QuadPart = libNewSize.QuadPart;
  return S_OK;
}
STDMETHODIMP CopyTo(IStream* pstm, ULARGE_INTEGER cb,
                    ULARGE_INTEGER* pcbRead,
                    ULARGE_INTEGER* pcbWritten)
```

```
     { return E_NOTIMPL; }
  STDMETHODIMP Commit(DWORD grfCommitFlags) { return E_NOTIMPL; }
  STDMETHODIMP Revert() { return E_NOTIMPL; }
  STDMETHODIMP LockRegion(ULARGE_INTEGER libOffset, ULARGE_INTEGER cb,
                          DWORD dwLockType) { return E_NOTIMPL; }
  STDMETHODIMP UnlockRegion(ULARGE_INTEGER libOffset, ULARGE_INTEGER cb,
                          DWORD dwLockType) { return E_NOTIMPL; }
  STDMETHODIMP Stat(STATSTG* pstatstg, DWORD grfStatFlag)
    { return E_NOTIMPL; }
  STDMETHODIMP Clone(IStream**ppstm) { return E_NOTIMPL; }

  ULARGE_INTEGER Size () { return m_libMaxOffset; }
  void Clear() { m_libMaxOffset.QuadPart = 0; }

  ULARGE_INTEGER m_libSeek;
  ULARGE_INTEGER m_libMaxOffset;
};
```

You can use it to implement the GetSizeMax method this way:

```
STDMETHODIMP GetSizeMax(ULARGE_INTEGER* pcbSize)
{
    if (NULL == pcbSize) return E_POINTER;

    pcbSize->QuadPart = 0;

    CDummyStream ds;
    HRESULT hr = Save (&ds, FALSE);
    if (SUCCEEDED (hr))
        *pcbSize = ds.Size();
    return hr;
}
```

I must caution you to use great care when using the dummy stream approach for calculating the size of an object's persistent data. There are significant issues involved when the object marshals an interface pointer into the stream as part of its persistent data. The object might do this to pass the interface pointer by reference rather than recursively persisting the referenced object. The dummy stream approach effectively results in two Save operations (one from the GetSizeMax call and one from the following Save call), which could cause an interface pointer to be marshaled twice. This produces a dangling reference to the stub, which then must be reclaimed by the garbage collection process.

Adding Marshal-by-Value Semantics Using Persistence

When you pass an interface pointer as a parameter to a remote (out of apartment) method call, the default in COM is to pass by reference. In other words, the object stays where it is and only a reference to the object is given to the recipient of the call. This typically means that references to the object involve round-trips back to the object, which can be quite expensive. An object can override this pass-by-reference default by implementing the IMarshal interface.

The primary reason most developers implement IMarshal on an object is to give it pass-by-value semantics. In other words, when you pass an interface pointer to a remote method call, you'd prefer COM to pass a *copy* of the object to the method. All references to the object are then local and do not involve round-trips back to the "original" object. When an object implements IMarshal in a way such that it has pass-by-value semantics, we typically say that the object *marshals by value*.

```
interface IMarshal : public IUnknown
{
   STDMETHOD GetUnmarshalClass([in] REFIID riid,
                               [unique,in] void* pv,
                               [in] DWORD dwDestContext,
                               [unique,in] void* pvDestContext,
                               [in] DWORD mshlflags,
                               [out] CLSID* pCid);
   STDMETHOD GetMarshalSizeMax([in] REFIID riid,
                               [unique,in] void* pv,
                               [in] DWORD dwDestContext,
                               [unique,in] void* pvDestContext,
                               [in] DWORD mshlflags,
                               [out] DWORD* pSize) ;
   STDMETHOD MarshalInterface([unique,in] IStream* pStm,
                              [in] REFIID riid,
                              [unique][in] void* pv,
                              [in] DWORD dwDestContext,
                              [unique,in] void* pvDestContext,
                              [in] DWORD mshlflags);
   STDMETHOD UnmarshalInterface([unique,in] IStream* pStm,
                                [in] REFIID riid, [out] void** ppv);
   STDMETHOD ReleaseMarshalData([unique,in] IStream* pStm);
   STDMETHOD DisconnectObject([in] DWORD dwReserved);
};
```

Given a complete implementation of `IPersistStream` or `IPersistStreamInit`, it's quite easy to build a marshal-by-value implementation of `IMarshal`.

A class typically implements marshal by value by returning its own CLSID as the result of the `GetUnmarshalClass` method. The `IPersistStream::GetClassID` method produces the needed CLSID.

The `GetMarshalSizeMax` method must return the number of bytes needed to save the persistent state of the object into a stream. The `IPersistStream::GetSizeMax` method produces the needed size.

The `MarshalUninterface` and `UnmarshalInterface` methods need to write and read, respectively, the persistent state of the object into the provided stream. Therefore, I can use the `Save` and `Load` methods of `IPersistStream` for this functionality.

`ReleaseMarshalData` and `DisconnectObject` method can simply return S_OK.

Here's a template class that uses an object's `IPersistStreamInit` interface to provide a marshal-by-value implementation.[4] Once again, I decided to down-cast and up-cast using `static_cast` to obtain the `IPersistStreamInit` interface so I receive an error at compile time when the deriving class doesn't implement `IPersistStreamInit`.

```
template <class T>
class ATL_NO_VTABLE IMarshalByValueImpl : public IMarshal
{
    STDMETHODIMP GetUnmarshalClass(REFIID /* riid */,
                                   void* /* pv */,
                                   DWORD /* dwDestContext */,
                                   void* /* pvDestContext */,
                                   DWORD /* mshlflags */, CLSID *pCid)
    {
        T* pT = static_cast<T*>(this);
        IPersistStreamInit* psi = static_cast <IPersistStreamInit*> (pT);
        return psi->GetClassID (pCid);
    }
    STDMETHODIMP GetMarshalSizeMax(REFIID /* riid */,
                                   void* /* pv */,
                                   DWORD /* dwDestContext */,
```

---

[4]This technique has a history, as does most software development. Jonathon Bordan wrote the first `IMarshalByValueImpl` after being inspired by a *Microsoft System Journal* article written by Don Box. Brent Rector then modified Jonathon's example to the present form.

```
                                         void* /* pvDestContext */,
                                         DWORD /* mshlflags */, DWORD* pSize)
   {
      T* pT = static_cast<T*>(this);
      IPersistStreamInit* psi = static_cast <IPersistStreamInit*> (pT);

      ULARGE_INTEGER uli = { 0 };

      HRESULT hr = psi->GetSizeMax(&uli);
      if (SUCCEEDED (hr)) *pSize = uli.LowPart;
      return hr;
   }
   STDMETHODIMP MarshalInterface(IStream *pStm, REFIID /* riid */,
                      void* /* pv */, DWORD /* dwDestContext */,
                      void* /* pvDestCtx */, DWORD /* mshlflags */)
   {
      T* pT = static_cast<T*>(this);
      IPersistStreamInit* psi = static_cast <IPersistStreamInit*> (pT);
      return psi->Save(pStm, FALSE);
   }
   STDMETHODIMP UnmarshalInterface(IStream *pStm,
                             REFIID riid, void **ppv)
   {
      T* pT = static_cast<T*>(this);
      IPersistStreamInit* psi = static_cast <IPersistStreamInit*> (pT);
      HRESULT hr = psi->Load(pStm);
      if (SUCCEEDED (hr)) hr = pT->QueryInterface (riid, ppv);
      return hr;
   }
   STDMETHODIMP ReleaseMarshalData(IStream* /* pStm */){ return S_OK;}
   STDMETHODIMP DisconnectObject(DWORD /* dwReserved */){ return S_OK;}
};
```

You can use this template class to provide a marshal-by-value implementation for your object. You need to derive your class from the prior IMarshalByValueImpl class (to get the IMarshal method implementations) and previously described IPersistStreamInitImpl2 class (to get the GetSizeMax method implementation plus the default implementation of the IPersistStreamInit method provided by ATL). You must also add a COM_INTERFACE_ENTRY for IMarshal to the class's COM map. Here's an example:

```
class ATL_NO_VTABLE CDemagogue :
    . . .
  public IPersistStreamInitImpl2<CDemagogue>,
  public CSupportDirtyBit,
  public IMarshalByValueImpl<CDemagogue>
  {
. . .
 BEGIN_COM_MAP(CDemagogue)
    COM_INTERFACE_ENTRY2(IPersist, IPersistStreamInit)
    COM_INTERFACE_ENTRY(IPersistStreamInit)
    COM_INTERFACE_ENTRY(IMarshal)
 END_COM_MAP()
. . .
};
```

Note that adding marshal-by-value support to your class this way means that all instances of the class use pass-by-value semantics. It is not possible to pass one object instance by reference and another instance by value (assuming both instances have the same marshaling context—inproc, local, or different machine).

Summary

Many objects need some support for persistence, and ATL provides an easily extensible, table-driven implementation of the `IPersistStream[Init]` and the `IPersistPropertyBag` interfaces. These implementations save and load the properties described by the class's property map entries. By overriding the appropriate methods, you can extend this persistence support for data types not supported by property map entries. The ATL implementation of `IPersistStorage` suffices to allow the object to be embedded into an OLE container but doesn't take advantage of many of the capabilities of the `IStorage` medium.

Using and extending the stream persistence support provided by ATL allows an object to provide additional functionality to its clients. For example, you've seen how to implement `IPersistMemory` support to your object (which MFC-based containers prefer). In addition, you can easily add marshal-by-value semantics to your class by reusing the stream persistence functionality.

Collections and Enumerators

Many COM libraries are exposed as sets of objects known as *object models*. A COM object model is a parent object that holds a set of child objects. COM collections and enumerators are the glue that holds the parent and the children together. This chapter examines COM collections and enumerators and how they work together to build object models.

COM Collection and Enumeration Interfaces

STL Containers and Iterators

STL programmers long ago learned to separate their collections into three pieces: the data itself, the container of the data, and an iterator for accessing the data. This separation is useful for building pieces separately from each other. The container's job is to provide the user the ability to affect the contents of the collection. The iterator's job is to allow the user the ability to access the contents of the container. And although the iterator implementation is dependent on how the data is stored by the container, to the client of the container and the iterator, the implementation details are hidden. For example, imagine the following STL code for populating a container and then accessing it via an iterator:

```
void main() {
  // Populate the collection
  vector<long>  rgPrimes;
  for( long n = 0; n != 1000; ++n ) {
    if( IsPrime(n) ) rgPrimes.push_back(n);
  }

  // Count the number of items in the collection
  cout << "Primes: " << rgPrimes.size() << endl;

  // Iterate over the collection using sequential access
  vector<long>::iterator begin = rgPrimes.begin();
  vector<long>::iterator end   = rgPrimes.end();
```

```
for( vector<long>::iterator it = begin; it != end; ++it ) {
 cout << *it << " ";
}
cout << endl;
}
```

Because the container provides a well-known C++ interface, the client is excused from knowing the implementation details. In fact, STL container classes are so uniform that this simple example would work just as well with a list or a deque as it does with a vector. Likewise, because the iterators provided by the container are uniform, the client doesn't need to know the implementation details of the iterator.

For the client to enjoy these benefits, the container and the iterator have certain responsibilities. The responsibilities of the container include the following.

- The container may allow the user to manipulate the data. Most containers are of variable size and are populated by the client. However, some containers may represent a fixed data set or a set of data that is calculated instead of stored.

- The container may allow the user to obtain the count of items. STL containers have a size method for this purpose.

- The container may allow random access. The STL vector allows this using operator[], whereas the STL list does not.

- The container must allow the user to access the data at least sequentially, if not randomly. STL containers provide this facility by exposing iterators.

Likewise, the responsibilities of the iterator entail the following.

- The iterator must be able to access the container's data. That data may be in some shared spot (for example, memory, file, or database) where the collection and iterator can both access the data. Or, the iterator may have its own copy of the data. This would allow one client to access a snapshot of the data while another client modified the data using the container. Finally, the iterator could generate the data on demand, for example, an iterator that generates the next prime number.

- The iterator must keep track of its current position in the collection of data. Every call to the iterator's operator++ means to advance that position. Every call to the iterator's operator* means to hand out the data at the current position.

- The iterator must be able to indicate the end of the container to the client.

While C++ containers and STL-like iterators are handy in your C++ code, neither is useful as a way for communicating data via a COM interface. Instead, we turn to the COM equivalent of containers and iterators: COM collections and enumerators.

COM Collections and Enumerators

A *COM collection* is a COM object that holds a set of data and allows the client to manipulate its contents via a COM interface. In many ways, a COM collection is very similar to an STL container. By convention, a COM collection interface takes a minimum form. This form is shown below, pretending that Interface Definition Language (IDL) supports templates:

```
[ dual ]
template <typename T>
interface ICollection : IDispatch {
  [propget]
  HRESULT Count([out, retval] long* pnCount);

  [id(DISPID_VALUE), propget]
  HRESULT Item([in] long n, [out, retval] T* pnItem);

  [id(DISPID_NEWENUM), propget]
  HRESULT _NewEnum([out, retval] IUnknown** ppEnum);
};
```

There are several features about this interface worth noting, as follows.

- Although this minimal collection interface doesn't show any methods for adding or removing elements from the collection, most collections include such methods.

- Most collection interfaces are dual interfaces. An IDispatch-based interface is required for some convenient language-mapping features that I'll discuss later.

- Most collection interfaces have a read-only Count property that provides a count of the current elements in the collection. Not all collections can calculate a reliable count, however. Examples include a collection of all prime numbers and a collection of rows from a database query that hasn't yet been completed.

- Most collection interfaces have a read-only Item property for random access to a specific element. The first parameter is the index of the element to access, which I've shown as a `long`. It's also common for this to be a `VARIANT`, so that a number index or a string name can be used. If the index is a number, it is often 1-based. Further, the `Item` property should be given the standard DISPID `DISPID_VALUE`. This marks the property as the "default" property, which certain language mappings use to provide more convenient access. I'll show you how this works later.

- What makes a collection interface is exposing an enumerator via the read-only property _NewEnum, which must be assigned the standard DISPID: `DISPID_NEWENUM`. This DISPID is used by Visual Basic to implement its `For-Each` syntax, as I'll show you soon.

A *COM enumerator* is to a COM collection as an STL iterator is to an STL container. The collection holds the data and allows the client to manipulate it, and the enumerator allows the client sequential access. However, instead of providing sequential access one element at a time, like an iterator, an enumerator allows the client to decide how many elements it would like. This gives the client the ability to balance the cost of round-trips with the memory requirements to handle more elements at once. A COM enumerator interface takes the following form (again, pretending that IDL supports templates):

```
template <typename T>>
interface IEnum : IUnknown {
  [local]
  HRESULT Next([in] ULONG celt,
               [out] T* rgelt,
               [out] ULONG *pceltFetched);

  [call_as(Next)] // Later...
  HRESULT RemoteNext([in] ULONG celt,
                     [out, size_is(celt),
                      length_is(*pceltFetched)] T* rgelt,
                     [out] ULONG *pceltFetched);

  HRESULT Skip([in] ULONG celt);
  HRESULT Reset();
  HRESULT Clone([out] IEnum<T> **ppenum);
}
```

A COM enumerator interface has the following properties.

- The enumerator must be able to access the data of the collection as well as maintain a logical pointer to the next element to retrieve. All operations on an enumerator manage this logical pointer in some manner.

- The Next method allows the client to decide how many elements to retrieve in a single round-trip. A result of S_OK indicates that the exact number of elements requested by the celt parameter has been returned in the rgelt array. A result of S_FALSE indicates that the end of the collection has been reached and that the pceltFetched argument holds the number of elements actually retrieved. In addition to retrieving the elements, the Next method implementation must advance the logical pointer internally so that subsequent calls to Next can retrieve additional data.

- The Skip method moves the logical pointer but retrieves no data. Notice that celt is an unsigned long, so there is no skipping backward. You can think of an enumerator as modeling a single-linked list, although, of course, it can be implemented any number of ways.

- The Reset method moves the logical pointer back to the beginning of the collection.

- The Clone method returns a copy of the enumerator object. The copy refers to the same data (although it may have its own copy) and points to the same logical position in the collection. The combination of Skip, Reset, and Clone make up for the lack of a Back method.

Custom Collection and Enumerator Example

For example, let's model a collection of prime numbers as a COM collection:

```
[dual]
interface IPrimeNumbers : IDispatch {
  HRESULT CalcPrimes([in] long min, [in] long max);

  [propget]
  HRESULT Count([out, retval] long* pnCount);

  [propget, id(DISPID_VALUE)]
  HRESULT Item([in] long n, [out, retval] long* pnPrime);

  [propget, id(DISPID_NEWENUM)] // Not quite right...
  HRESULT _NewEnum([out, retval] IEnumPrimes** ppEnumPrimes);
};
```

The corresponding enumerator would look like this:

```
interface IEnumPrimes : IUnknown {
  [local]
  HRESULT Next([in] ULONG celt,
               [out] long* rgelt,
               [out] ULONG *pceltFetched);

  [call_as(Next)]
  HRESULT RemoteNext([in] ULONG celt,
                     [out, size_is(celt),
                      length_is(*pceltFetched)] long* rgelt,
                     [out] ULONG *pceltFetched);

  HRESULT Skip([in] ULONG celt);
  HRESULT Reset();
  HRESULT Clone([out] IEnumPrimes **ppenum);
};
```

Porting the previous STL client to use the collection and enumerator would look like this:

```
void main() {
  CoInitialize(0);

  CComPtr<IPrimeNumbers> spPrimes;
  if( SUCCEEDED(spPrimes.CoCreateInstance(CLSID_PrimeNumbers)) )
  {
    // Populate the collection
    HRESULT hr;
    hr = spPrimes->CalcPrimes(0, 1000);

    // Count the number of items in the collection
    long  nPrimes;
    hr = spPrimes->get_Count(&nPrimes);
    cout << "Primes: " << nPrimes << endl;

    // Enumerate over the collection using sequential access
    CComPtr<IEnumPrimes> spEnum;
    hr = spPrimes->get__NewEnum(&spEnum);
```

```
        const size_t  PRIMES_CHUNK = 64;
        long          rgnPrimes[PRIMES_CHUNK];

    do {
      ULONG celtFetched;
      hr = spEnum->Next(PRIMES_CHUNK, rgnPrimes, &celtFetched);
      if( SUCCEEDED(hr) ) {
        if( hr == S_OK ) celtFetched = PRIMES_CHUNK;
        for( long* pn = &rgnPrimes[0]; pn != &rgnPrimes[celtFetched];
          ++pn ) {
          cout << *pn << " ";
        }
      }
    }
    while( hr == S_OK );
    cout << endl;

    spPrimes.Release();
  }

  CoUninitialize();
}
```

This client code asks the collection object to populate itself via the `CalcPrimes` method instead of adding each prime number one at a time. Of course, this procedure reduces round-trips. The client further reduces round-trips when retrieving the data in chunks of 64 elements. A chunk size of any number greater than 1 reduces round-trips but increases the data requirement of the client. Only profiling can tell you the right number for each client/enumerator pair, but larger numbers are preferred to reduce round-trips.

Dealing with the Enumerator local/call_as Oddity

One thing that's rather odd about the client side of enumeration is the `pceltFetched` parameter filled by the `Next` method. The COM documentation is ambiguous, but it boils down to this: When only a single element is requested, the client doesn't have to provide storage for the number of elements fetched; that is, `pceltFetched` is allowed to be NULL. Normally, however, MIDL doesn't allow an [out] parameter to be NULL. So, to support the documented behavior for enumeration interfaces, all of them are defined with two versions of the `Next` method. The [local] `Next` method is for use by the client and allows the `pceltFetched` parameter

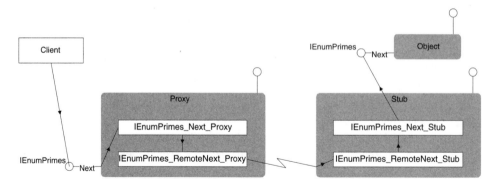

Figure 7.1. The call progression from client, through proxy and stub, to implementation of IEnumPrimes.

to be NULL. The [call_as] RemoteNext method doesn't allow the pceltFetched parameter to be NULL and is the method that performs the marshaling. Although the MIDL compiler will implement the RemoteNext method, since we've marked the Next method as [local] we have to implement Next manually. In fact, we're responsible for implementing two versions of the Next method. One version is called by the client and will in turn call the RemoteNext method implemented by the proxy. The other version is called by the stub and will call the Next method implemented by the object. Figure 7.1 shows the progression of calls from client to object through the proxy, the stub, and our custom code. The canonical implementation is as follows:

```
static HRESULT STDMETHODCALLTYPE
IEnumPrimes_Next_Proxy(
  IEnumPrimes* This, ULONG celt, long* rgelt, ULONG* pceltFetched)
{
  ULONG cFetched;
  if( !pceltFetched && celt != 1 ) return E_INVALIDARG;
  return IEnumPrimes_RemoteNext_Proxy(This, celt, rgelt,
                        pceltFetched ? pceltFetched : &cFetched);
}

static HRESULT STDMETHODCALLTYPE
IEnumPrimes_Next_Stub(
  IEnumPrimes* This, ULONG celt, long* rgelt, ULONG* pceltFetched)
{
  HRESULT hr = This->lpVtbl->Next(This, celt, rgelt, pceltFetched);
```

```
    if( hr == S_OK && celt == 1 ) *pceltFetched = 1;
    return hr;
}
```

Every enumeration interface includes this code in the proxy/stub implementation, including all the standard ones, such as `IEnumUnknown`, `IEnumString`, and `IEnumVARIANT`. The only difference in implementation is the name of the interface and the type of data being enumerated over (as shown in the `IEnumPrimes` example in bold).

When you're building the proxy/stub for your project using the `<project>ps.mk` file generated by the wizard, and you have a custom enumeration interface, it's your job to inject that code into your proxy/stub. One way would be to edit the `<project>_p.c` file, but if you were to recompile the IDL, the implementation would be lost. Another way would be to add another `.c` file to the proxy/stub project, but since this would involve manually editing the makefile (a skill I'd rather not reacquire), this is rather unpleasant. The technique I prefer relies on macro definitions used during the proxy/stub building process and makes heavy use of the `cpp_quote` statement in IDL.[1] Whenever you have a custom enumeration interface, insert code like this at the bottom of the IDL file and all will be right with the world (the bold code changes based on the enumeration interface):

```
cpp_quote("#ifdef __midl_proxy")
cpp_quote("static HRESULT STDMETHODCALLTYPE")
cpp_quote("IEnumPrimes_Next_Proxy")
cpp_quote("(IEnumPrimes* This, ULONG celt, long* rgelt, ULONG*
  pceltFetched)")
cpp_quote("{")
cpp_quote("  ULONG cFetched;")
cpp_quote("  if( !pceltFetched && celt != 1 ) return E_INVALIDARG;")
cpp_quote("  return IEnumPrimes_RemoteNext_Proxy(This, celt, rgelt,")
cpp_quote("                  pceltFetched ? pceltFetched : &cFetched);")
cpp_quote("}")
cpp_quote("")
cpp_quote("static HRESULT STDMETHODCALLTYPE")
cpp_quote("IEnumPrimes_Next_Stub")
cpp_quote("(IEnumPrimes* This, ULONG celt, long* rgelt, ULONG*
  pceltFetched)")
```

---

[1] I learned these tricks from Don Box and his enumeration generation macros. As of the time of this writing, these macros were available at http://www.develop.com/dbox/com/enumgen.h.

```
cpp_quote("{")
cpp_quote("   HRESULT hr = This->lpVtbl->Next(This, celt, rgelt,")
cpp_quote("                                    pceltFetched);")
cpp_quote("   if( hr == S_OK && celt == 1 ) *pceltFetched = 1;")
cpp_quote("   return hr;")
cpp_quote("}")
cpp_quote("#endif // __midl_proxy")
```

All the code within the `cpp_quote` statements will be deposited into the `<proj-ect>.h` file, but, because of the use of the `__midl_proxy` symbol, will only be compiled when building the proxy/stub.

An Enumeration Iterator

One other niggling problem with COM enumerators is their ease of use, or rather, the lack thereof. While it's good that a client has control of the number of elements to retrieve in a single round-trip, logically the client is still processing the data one element at a time. This is obfuscated by the fact that we're using two loops instead of one. Of course, C++ being C++, there's no reason a wrapper can't be built that removes this obfuscation.[2] Such a wrapper is included with the source code examples of this book.[3] It's called the `enum_iterator` and is declared like this:

```
#ifndef ENUM_CHUNK
#define ENUM_CHUNK 64
#endif


template <typename EnumItf, const IID* pIIDEnumItf,
          typename EnumType, typename CopyClass = _Copy<EnumType> >
class enum_iterator {
public:
  enum_iterator(IUnknown* punkEnum = 0, ULONG nChunk = ENUM_CHUNK);
  enum_iterator(const enum_iterator& i);
  ~enum_iterator();

  enum_iterator& operator=(const enum_iterator& rhs);
  bool operator!=(const enum_iterator& rhs);
  bool operator==(const enum_iterator& rhs);
```

---

[2] Or replaces one obfuscation with another, depending on your point of view.
[3] You can download all example source code from the www.wiseowl.com and www.awl.com web sites.

```
   enum_iterator& operator++();
   enum_iterator operator++(int);
   EnumType& operator*();

private:
   ...
};
```

The `enum_iterator` class provides an STL-like forward iterator that wraps a COM enumerator. The type of the enumeration interface and the type of data that it enumerates are specified as template parameters. The buffer size is passed, along with the pointer to the enumeration interface, as a constructor argument. The first constructor allows for the common usage of forward iterators. Instead of asking a container for the beginning and ending iterators, the beginning iterator is created by passing a non-NULL enumeration interface pointer. The ending iterator is created by passing NULL. The copy constructor is used when forming a looping statement. This iterator considerably simplifies the client enumeration code:

```
...
// Enumerate over the collection using sequential access
CComPtr<IEnumPrimes>  spEnum;
hr = spPrimes->get__NewEnum(&spEnum);

// Using an STL-like forward iterator
typedef enum_iterator<IEnumPrimes, &IID_IEnumPrimes, long>
   primes_iterator;
primes_iterator begin(spEnum, 64);
primes_iterator end;
for(primes_iterator it = begin; it != end; ++it ) {
   cout << *it << " ";
 }
cout << endl;
...
```

Or, if you're like to get a little more fancy, you could use the `enum_iterator` with a function object and an STL algorithm, which allows you to avoid writing the looping code altogether. For example:

```
struct OutputPrime {
 void operator()(const long& nPrime) {
```

```
    cout << nPrime << " ";
  }
};


  ...
  // Using an STL algorithm
  typedef primes_iterator<IEnumPrimes, &IID_IEnumPrimes, long>
    enum_primes;
  for_each(primes_iterator(spEnum, 64), primes_iterator(),
    OutputPrime());
  ...
```

Although this example may not be as clear to you as the looping example, it warms the cockles of my STL heart.[4]

Enumeration and Visual Basic

The STL `for_each` algorithm may seem quite like the Visual Basic (VB) `For-Each` statement, and it is. The `For-Each` statement allows a VB programmer to access each element in a collection, whether it's an intrinsic collection built into VB or a custom collection developed using COM. Just as the `for_each` algorithm is implemented using iterators, the `For-Each` syntax is implemented using a COM enumerator, specifically, `IEnumVARIANT`. To support the `For-Each` syntax, the collection interface must be `IDispatch`-based and have the `_NewEnum` property marked with the `DISPID_NEWENUM` DISPID. Because our prime number collection object exposes such a method, you may be tempted to write the following code to exercise the `For-Each` statement:

```
Private Sub Command1_Click()
    Dim primes As IPrimeNumbers
    Set primes = New PrimeNumbers
    primes.CalcPrimes 0, 1000

    MsgBox "Primes: " & primes.Count

    Dim sPrimes As String
    Dim prime As Variant
```

---

[4]I should mention that it warms the cockles of Chris's STL heart. Brent's heart has no such cockles.

```
        For Each prime In primes ' Calls Invoke(DISPID_NEWENUM)
            sPrimes = sPrimes & prime & " "
        Next prime

        MsgBox sPrimes
    End Sub
```

When VB sees the `For-Each` statement, it will invoke the `_NewEnum` property, looking for an enumerator that implements `IEnumVARIANT`. To support this usage, our prime number collection interface must change from exposing `IEnumPrimes` to exposing `IEnumVARIANT`. Here's the twist: The signature of the method is actually `_NewEnum(IUnknown**)`, not `_NewEnum(IEnumVARIANT**)`. VB will take the `IUnknown*` returned from `_NewEnum` and query for `IEnumVARIANT`. It would've been nice for VB to avoid an extra round-trip, but maybe the VB team expects to support other enumeration types in the future.

Modifying `IPrimeNumbers` to support the VB `For-Each` syntax looks like this:

```
[dual]
interface IPrimeNumbers : IDispatch
{
  HRESULT CalcPrimes([in] long min, [in] long max);

  [propget]
  HRESULT Count([out, retval] long* pnCount);

  [propget, id(DISPID_VALUE)]
  HRESULT Item([in] long n, [out, retval] long* pnPrime);

  [propget, id(DISPID_NEWENUM)]
  HRESULT _NewEnum([out, retval] IUnknown** ppunkEnum);
};
```

This brings the `IPrimeNumbers` interface into line with the `ICollection` template form I showed you earlier. In fact, it's fair to say that the `ICollection` template form was defined to work with VB.

The VB Subscript Operator

Using the `Item` method, a VB client can access each individual item in the collection one at a time:

```
...
Dim i As Long
For i = 1 To primes.Count
    sPrimes = sPrimes & primes.Item(i) & " "
Next i
...
```

Because I marked the Item method with DISPID_VALUE, VB allows the following abbreviated syntax that makes a collection seem like an array (if only for a second):

```
...
Dim i As Long
For i = 1 To primes.Count
    sPrimes = sPrimes & primes(i) & " " ' Invoke(DISPID_VALUE)
Next i
...
```

Assigning a property the DISPID_VALUE dispatch identifier makes it the default property as far as VB is concerned. Using this syntax results in VB getting the default property, that is, calling Invoke with DISPID_VALUE. However, because we're dealing with array syntax in VB, we have two problems. The first is knowing where to start the index—1 or 0? A majority of existing code suggests making collections 1-based, but only a slight majority. As a collection implementor, you get to choose. As a collection user, you get to guess.

The other concern with using array-style access is round-trips. Using the Item property puts us smack dab into the middle of what we're trying to avoid by using enumerators: one round-trip per data element. If you think that using the For-Each statement, and therefore enumerators, under VB would solve both of these problems, you're half right. Unfortunately, as of this writing, Visual Basic Enterprise Edition 6.0 continues to access elements one at a time, even though it's using IEnumVARIANT::Next and is perfectly capable of providing a larger buffer. However, using the For-Each syntax does allow you to disregard whether the Item method is 1-based or 0-based.

The Server Side of Enumeration

Of course, because the semantics of enumeration interfaces are loose, you are free to implement them however you like. The data could be pulled from an array, a file, a database result set, or wherever it may be stored. Even better, you might want to calculate the data on demand, saving yourself calculations and storage for elements in which the client isn't interested. Either way, if you're doing it by hand, you have some COM grunge code to write. Or, if you like, ATL is there to help write that grunge code.

Enumerating Arrays

CComEnum

Because enumeration interfaces are all the same except for the actual data being enumerated, their implementation can be standardized, given a couple of assumptions. Depending on how you've stored your data, you can use one of two ATL enumeration interface classes. The most flexible implementation class allows you to provide your data in an STL-like collection. This is called CComEnumOnSTL, which I'll present later. The simplest implementation assumes you've stored your data as an array. It's called CComEnum, and the complete implementation is as follows:

```
template <class Base, const IID* piid, class T, class Copy,
        class ThreadModel = CComObjectThreadModel>
class ATL_NO_VTABLE CComEnum :
    public CComEnumImpl<Base, piid, T, Copy>,
    public CComObjectRootEx< ThreadModel > {
public:
    typedef CComEnum<Base, piid, T, Copy > _CComEnum;
    typedef CComEnumImpl<Base, piid, T, Copy > _CComEnumBase;
    BEGIN_COM_MAP(_CComEnum)
        COM_INTERFACE_ENTRY_IID(*piid, _CComEnumBase)
    END_COM_MAP()
};
```

Although this implementation only comprises a few lines of code, there's quite a lot going on here. The template arguments are as follows:

- Base is the enumeration interface to be implemented, for example, IEnum-Primes.
- piid is a pointer to the interface being implemented, for example, &IID_ IEnumPrimes.
- T is the type of data being enumerated, for example, long.

- Copy is the class responsible for copying the data into the client's buffer as part of the implementation of Next. It may also be used to cache a private copy of the data in the enumerator to guard against simultaneous access and manipulation.

- ThreadModel describes just how thread safe this enumerator needs to be. When you specify nothing, it will use the dominant threading model for objects, as described in Chapter 3. Of course, because a COM enumerator is a COM object like any other, it requires an implementation of IUnknown. Toward that end, CComEnum derives from CComObjectRootEx. You'll see later that I'll further derive CComObject from CComEnum to fill in the vtbl properly.

Really, CComEnum is present simply to bring CComObjectRootEx together with CComEnumImpl, the base class that actually implements Next, Skip, Reset, and Clone. Figure 7.2 shows how these classes fit together.

Copy Policy Classes

The fundamental job of the enumerator is to copy the collection's data into the buffer provided by the client. If the data being enumerated is a pointer or a structure that contains pointers, a simple memcpy or assignment is not going to do the

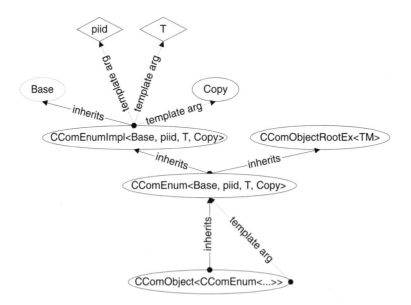

Figure 7.2. The CComEnum inheritance hierarchy

trick. Instead, the client is going to need its own deep copy of each element, which it can release when it has finished with it. Toward that end, ATL enumerators use a class called a *copy policy class*, or often just a *copy policy*, to scope static methods for dealing with deep-copy semantics. The static methods of a copy policy are like the Increment and Decrement methods of the threading model classes, except that instead of incrementing and decrementing a long, copy policies know how to initialize, copy, and destroy data. For simple types, ATL provides a template copy policy class:

```
template <class T>
class _Copy {
public:
  static HRESULT copy(T* p1, T* p2)
    { memcpy(p1, p2, sizeof(T)); return S_OK; }
  static void    init(T*)         {}
  static void    destroy(T*)      {}
};
```

Given an array of a simple type (such as long), this template would work just fine:

```
HRESULT CopyRange(long* dest, long* src, size_t count) {
  for( size_t i = 0; i != count; ++i ) {
    HRESULT hr = _Copy<long>::copy(&dest[i], &src[i]);
    if( FAILED(hr) ) {
      while( i > 0 ) _Copy<long>::destroy(&dest[--i]);
      return hr;
    }
  }
  return S_OK;
}
```

However, given something with trickier semantics, such as a VARIANT or an OLESTR, memcpy is too shallow. For the four most commonly enumerated data types, ATL provides specializations of the _Copy template:

```
template<; > class _Copy<VARIANT>;
template<; > class _Copy<LPOLESTR>;
template<; > class _Copy<OLEVERB>
template<; > class _Copy<CONNECTDATA>;
```

For example, the copy policy for VARIANTs looks like this:

```
template<; > class _Copy<VARIANT> {
public:
 static HRESULT copy(VARIANT* p1, VARIANT* p2) { return
                                       VariantCopy(p1, p2); }
 static void    init(VARIANT* p)          { p->vt = VT_EMPTY; }
 static void    destroy(VARIANT* p)       { VariantClear(p); }
};
```

If you're dealing with interface pointers, again, the _Copy template won't do, but building your own specialization for each interface you'd like to copy is a bit arduous. For interfaces, ATL provides the _CopyInterface copy policy class parameterized on the type of interface you're managing:

```
template <class T> class _CopyInterface {
public:
 static HRESULT copy(T** p1, T** p2) {
   *p1 = *p2;
   if (*p1) (*p1)->AddRef();
   return S_OK;
 }
 static void init(T** )      {}
 static void destroy(T** p) { if (*p) (*p)->Release(); }
};
```

Using copy policies, we now have a generic way to initialize, copy, and delete any kind of data, making it easy to build a generic and safe duplication routine:

```
template <typename T, typename Copy>
HRESULT CopyRange(T* dest, T* src, size_t count) {
  for( size_t i = 0; i != count; ++i ) {
    HRESULT hr = Copy::copy(&dest[i], &src[i]);
    if( FAILED(hr) ) {
      while( i > 0 ) Copy::destroy(&dest[--i]);
      return hr;
    }
  }
  return S_OK;
}
```

CComEnumImpl's implementation of the Next method uses the copy policy passed as the template parameter to initialize the client's buffer and fill it with data from the collection, very much like my sample CopyRange routine. However, before we jump right into the Next method, let's see how CComEnumImpl does its job.

CComEnumImpl

To implement the methods of an enumeration interface, CComEnumImpl maintains five data members:

```
template <class Base, const IID* piid, class T, class Copy>
class ATL_NO_VTABLE CComEnumImpl : public Base {
public:
    CComEnumImpl();
    ~CComEnumImpl();

    STDMETHOD(Next)(ULONG celt, T* rgelt, ULONG* pceltFetched);
    STDMETHOD(Skip)(ULONG celt);
    STDMETHOD(Reset)(void)
    STDMETHOD(Clone)(Base** ppEnum);

    HRESULT Init(T* begin, T* end, IUnknown* pUnk,
                 CComEnumFlags flags = AtlFlagNoCopy);

    T* m_begin;
    T* m_end;
    T* m_iter;
    DWORD m_dwFlags;
    CComPtr<IUnknown> m_spUnk;
    ...
};
```

The m_begin, m_end, and m_iter members are each pointers to the type of data being enumerated, as passed via the T template parameter. Each of these members keeps track of pointers into an array of the data being enumerated. In classic STL style, m_begin points to the beginning of the array, m_end points to one past the end of the array, and m_iter points to the next element to hand out. The m_dwFlags member determines if and when to copy initialization data provided by the creator of the enumerator. The m_spUnk member refers to the owner of the data if the enumerator is sharing it instead of keeping its own copy. The implementations of Next, Skip, Reset, and Clone use these variables to provide their behavior. These variables are set in the Init method of CComEnumImpl.

Initializing CComEnumImpl

Calling the Init method[5] requires that the data has been arranged into an array. Maybe the collection is already maintaining the data as an array, or maybe it's not. Either way, the begin parameter to Init must be a pointer to the beginning of an array of the type being enumerated, and the end parameter must be one past the end of the same array. Where that array comes from and how it's managed by the enumerator depends on the last parameter to Init, the flags parameter, which can take one of three values:

- AtlFlagNoCopy means that the collection already maintains its data in an array of the type being enumerated and is willing to share the data with the enumerator. This is more efficient, because the enumerator doesn't keep its own copy, but merely initializes m_begin, m_end, and m_iter to point at the collection's data. However, this could lead to unpredictable results if a client uses the collection to modify the data while it's being enumerated.

    If you use the AtlFlagNoCopy flag, you should pass an interface pointer to the collection that owns the data as the pUnk parameter to Init. The enumerator will cache this interface pointer, adding to the reference count of the collection. This is necessary to avoid an enumerator outliving the collection and, more important, the data that the collection is maintaining. For each of the other two flags, pUnk will be NULL.

- AtlFlagCopy means that the collection already maintains the data in the appropriate format but would prefer the enumerator to have its own copy of the data. This is less efficient, but will ensure that no manipulation of the collection will affect the data maintained by the enumerator.

- AtlFlagTakeOwnership means that the collection doesn't maintain its data in an array of a type appropriate for use by the enumerator. Instead, the collection has allocated an array of the data type being enumerated using operator new for sole use of the enumerator. When the enumerator is destroyed, it should destroy its copy of the data using operator delete. This is especially handy for the implementation of IEnumVARIANT, because most developers prefer to keep data in types more specific than VARIANT but are willing to provide an array of VARIANTs when creating the enumerator.

---

[5] As of this writing, the Init methods of both CComEnumImpl and CComEnumOnSTLImpl are absolutely essential to using ATL enumerator implementations and are totally undocumented.

CComEnumImpl Implementation

The most interesting part of the CComEnumImpl implementation is the Next method. Recall that Next's job is to copy the client-requested number of elements into the client-provided buffer. CComEnumImpl's implementation of the Next method is identical in concept to the CopyRange function I showed you earlier. Next uses the copy policy to copy the data provided by the collection at initialization into the client's buffer. If anything goes wrong, the copy policy is used to destroy the data already copied. The rest of the logic is argument validation and watching for the end of the data.

```
template <class Base, const IID* piid, class T, class Copy>
STDMETHODIMP
CComEnumImpl<Base, piid, T, Copy>::Next(ULONG celt, T* rgelt,
                                        ULONG* pceltFetched) {
  if (rgelt == NULL || (celt != 1 && pceltFetched == NULL))
    return E_POINTER;
  if (m_begin == NULL || m_end == NULL || m_iter == NULL)
    return E_FAIL;

  ULONG nRem = (ULONG)(m_end-m_iter);
  HRESULT hRes = S_OK;
  if (nRem < celt) hRes = S_FALSE;
  ULONG nMin = min(celt, nRem);
  if (pceltFetched != NULL) *pceltFetched = nMin;

  T* pelt = rgelt;
  while (nMin--) {
    HRESULT hr = Copy::copy(pelt, m_iter);
    if (FAILED(hr)) {
      while (rgelt < pelt)
        Copy::destroy(rgelt++);
      if (pceltFetched != NULL)
        *pceltFetched = 0;
      return hr;
    }
    pelt++;
    m_iter++;
  }
  return hRes;
}
```

The implementations of Skip and Reset are trivial:

```
template <class Base, const IID* piid, class T, class Copy>
STDMETHODIMP CComEnumImpl<Base, piid, T, Copy>::Skip(ULONG celt) {
  m_iter += celt;
  if (m_iter <= m_end) return S_OK;
  m_iter = m_end;
  return S_FALSE;
}

template <class Base, const IID* piid, class T, class Copy>
STDMETHODIMP CComEnumImpl<Base, piid, T, Copy>::Reset()
{ m_iter = m_begin;return S_OK; }
```

The Clone method is responsible for duplicating the current enumerator. This means creating a new enumerator of the same type and initializing it using the Init method. However, the data is never copied again for subsequent enumerators. Instead, if the collection indicated that the data was to be shared, a new enumerator gets the IUnknown* of the original collection, giving the collection another reason to live. Otherwise, if the enumerator is keeping its own copy of the data, the new enumerator is given the IUnknown* of the original enumerator. Since enumerators are read-only, one copy of the data serves for all enumerators.

```
template <class Base, const IID* piid, class T, class Copy>
STDMETHODIMP CComEnumImpl<Base, piid, T, Copy>::Clone(Base** ppEnum) {
  typedef CComObject<CComEnum<Base, piid, T, Copy> > _class;
  HRESULT hRes = E_POINTER;
  if (ppEnum != NULL) {
    *ppEnum = NULL;
    _class* p;
    hRes = _class::CreateInstance(&p);
    if (SUCCEEDED(hRes)) {
      // If the data is a copy then we need to keep "this" object
      // around
      hRes = p->Init(m_begin, m_end, (m_dwFlags & BitCopy) ? this :
        m_spUnk);
      if (SUCCEEDED(hRes)) {
        p->m_iter = m_iter;
        hRes = p->_InternalQueryInterface(*piid, (void**)ppEnum);
      }
```

```
    if (FAILED(hRes)) delete p;
  }
 }
 return hRes;
}
```

CComEnum Usage

As an example of a typical CComEnum usage, let's implement the IPrimeNumbers collection interface:

```
[dual]
interface IPrimeNumbers : IDispatch {
  HRESULT CalcPrimes([in] long min, [in] long max);

  [propget]
  HRESULT Count([out, retval] long* pnCount);

  [propget, id(DISPID_VALUE)]
  HRESULT Item([in] long n, [out, retval] long* pnPrime);

  [propget, id(DISPID_NEWENUM)]
  HRESULT _NewEnum([out, retval] IUnknown** ppunkEnum);
};
```

The collection maintains a list of the prime numbers in an STL vector. The Calc-
Primes method populates the collection:

```
STDMETHODIMP CPrimeNumbers::CalcPrimes(long min, long max) {
  m_rgPrimes.clear();
  for( long n = min; n <= max; ++n ) {
    if( IsPrime(n) ) m_rgPrimes.push_back(n);
  }
  return S_OK;
}
```

The get_Count and get_Item methods use the vector to perform their duties:

```
STDMETHODIMP CPrimeNumbers::get_Count(long* pnCount) {
 *pnCount = m_rgPrimes.size();
 return S_OK;
}
```

```
STDMETHODIMP CPrimeNumbers::get_Item(long n, long* pnPrime) {
  // Oh, let's be 1-based today...
  if( n < 1 || n > m_rgPrimes.size() ) return E_INVALIDARG;
  *pnPrime = m_rgPrimes[n-1];
  return S_OK;
}
```

Because we're going out of our way to support VB with our collection interface, the get_NewEnum method will return an interface on an implementation of
IEnumVARIANT. Since the name of the parameterized enumerator is used more
than once, it's often handy to use a type definition:

```
typedef CComEnum< IEnumVARIANT, &IID_IEnumVARIANT, VARIANT,
  _Copy<VARIANT> > CComEnumVariant;
```

Remember, the CComEnum template parameters are, in order, the interface we'd
like the enumerator to implement, the IID of that interface, the type of data we'd
like to enumerate, and finally, a copy policy class for copying the data from the
enumerator's copy to the client's buffer. To provide an implementation of IUnknown, the CComEnum class is further used as the base class for a new CCom-
Object class. Using this type definition, the implementation of get_NewEnum
entails creating an instance of an enumerator, initializing it with array data, and
filling ppunkEnum with a pointer to the enumerator for use by the client. Because
we're keeping the data as a vector, however, we're going to have to allocate an array of VARIANTs manually, fill the data from the vector, and pass ownership to the
enumeration using AtlFlagTakeOwnership. The following code illustrates this
procedure:

```
STDMETHODIMP CPrimeNumbers::get_NewEnum(IUnknown** ppunkEnum) {
  *ppunkEnum = 0;

  // Create an instance of the enumerator
  CComObject<CComEnumVariant>*  pe = 0;
  HRESULT hr = CComObject<CComEnumVariant>::CreateInstance(&pe);
  if( SUCCEEDED(hr) ) {
    pe->AddRef();

    // Copy data from vector<long> to VARIANT*
    size_t    nPrimes = m_rgPrimes.size();
```

```
      VARIANT*  rgvar = new VARIANT[nPrimes];
      if( rgvar )
      {
        ZeroMemory(rgvar, sizeof(VARIANT) * nPrimes);
        VARIANT*  pvar = &rgvar[0];
        for( vector<long>::iterator it = m_rgPrimes.begin();
             it != m_rgPrimes.end();
             ++pvar, ++it ) {
          pvar->vt = VT_I4;
          pvar->lVal = *it;
        }

        // Initialize enumerator
        hr = pe->Init(&rgvar[0], &rgvar[nPrimes], 0,
          AtlFlagTakeOwnership);
        if( SUCCEEDED(hr) ) {
          // Fill outbound parameter
          hr = pe->QueryInterface(IID_IUnknown, (void**)ppunkEnum);
        }
      }
      else {
        hr = E_OUTOFMEMORY;
      }

      pe->Release();
    }

  return hr;
  }
```

Unfortunately, this code leaves an unpleasant taste in one's mouth. While it would have been considerably simpler if we'd already had an array of VARIANTs holding the data, frankly that's rare. C++ programmers tend to use containers other than the error-prone C++ array. Because of this tendency, we were forced to translate the data from our preferred format to the preferred format of the ATL enumerator implementation. Given the regularity of an STL container's C++ interface, this seems like a waste. In an ideal world, we'd have an enumeration implementation that could handle an STL container instead of an array. In an ideal world, we'd have CComEnumOnSTL. Welcome to my ideal world. . . .

Enumerating STL Collections

CComEnumOnSTL

The declaration of CComEnumOnSTL is similar to CComEnum:

```
template <class Base, const IID* piid, class T, class Copy,
   class CollType, class ThreadModel = CComObjectThreadModel>
class ATL_NO_VTABLE CComEnumOnSTL :
   public IEnumOnSTLImpl<Base, piid, T, Copy, CollType>,
   public CComObjectRootEx< ThreadModel >
{
public:
   typedef CComEnumOnSTL<Base, piid, T, Copy, CollType, ThreadModel >
         _CComEnum;
   typedef IEnumOnSTLImpl<Base, piid, T, Copy, CollType >
         _CComEnumBase;
   BEGIN_COM_MAP(_CComEnum)
      COM_INTERFACE_ENTRY_IID(*piid, _CComEnumBase)
   END_COM_MAP()
};
```

The chief difference between CComEnumOnSTL and CComEnum is the addition of the CollType template parameter. This parameter indicates the type of collection to iterate over. The base class, IEnumOnSTLImpl, uses the collection to implement the Next, Skip, Reset, and Clone methods of the enumeration interface. The type of collection passed as the CollType must expose at least the following C++ interface:

```
template <typename T> class CollType {
public:
  class iterator; // Forward declaration
  iterator begin();
  iterator end();

  class iterator {
  public:
    iterator(const iterator& it); // To support postfix ++
    iterator& operator=(const iterator& it);
    bool      operator!<=(const iterator& rhs);
    T&        operator*();
```

```
        iterator  operator++(int); // Postfix ++
    };
  };
```

All existing STL collections adhere to these minimum requirements. If you wish to make your own collection, it must adhere to this interface as well. I'll show you later how defining your own collection type is useful for enumerating data calculated on demand.

IEnumOnSTLImpl

The base class of CComEnumOnSTL, IEnumOnSTLImpl, uses the STL-like collection passed as the CollType parameter to implement the Next, Skip, Reset, and Clone methods. The following is the declaration of IEnumOnSTLImpl:

```
template <class Base, const IID* piid, class T, class Copy, class
  CollType>
class ATL_NO_VTABLE IEnumOnSTLImpl : public Base {
public:
  HRESULT Init(IUnknown *pUnkForRelease, CollType& collection);

  STDMETHOD(Next)(ULONG celt, T* rgelt, ULONG* pceltFetched);
  STDMETHOD(Skip)(ULONG celt);
  STDMETHOD(Reset)(void);
  STDMETHOD(Clone)(Base** ppEnum);

  //Data
  CComPtr<IUnknown> m_spUnk;
  CollType* m_pcollection;
  CollType::iterator m_iter;
};
```

Just like CComEnumImpl, IEnumOnSTLImpl keeps an m_spUnk pointer. However, unlike CComEnumImpl, the m_spUnk pointer should never be NULL and therefore *the* pUnkForRelease *parameter to* Init *should never be* NULL. Notice that IEnumOnSTLImpl keeps no m_dwFlags member data. It has no option for copying the data from the collection. Instead, it needs to ensure that the collection holding the data outlives the enumerator. Every call to Init assumes the equivalent of the CComEnum's AtlFlagNoCopy flag. While this is more efficient than AtlFlagCopy or the manual copying required for AtlFlagTakeOwnership, if the collection changes while it's being enumerated, the behavior is undefined. If you need ATL's

STL-based enumerator to have its own copy of the data, you'll have to wrap a copy of the data in its own COM object, a technique I'll show you later.

CComEnumOnSTL Usage

If our prime number collection object held an STL collection of VARIANTs, the implementation of get__NewEnum would look like this:

```
STDMETHODIMP CPrimeNumbers::get__NewEnum(IUnknown** ppunkEnum) {
  *ppunkEnum = 0;

  typedef CComEnumOnSTL<IEnumVARIANT, &IID_IEnumVARIANT, VARIANT,
                        _Copy<VARIANT>, vector<VARIANT> >
        CComEnumVariantOnVector;

  CComObject<CComEnumVariantOnVector>* pe = 0;
  HRESULT hr =
    CComObject<CComEnumVariantOnVector>::CreateInstance(&pe);
  if( SUCCEEDED(hr) ) {
    pe->AddRef();

    hr = pe->Init(this->GetUnknown(), m_rgPrimes);
    if( SUCCEEDED(hr) ) {
      hr = pe->QueryInterface(ppunkEnum);
    }

    pe->Release();
  }

  return hr;
}
```

Of course, we'd prefer not to keep a collection of VARIANTs. Instead, we'd like to keep a collection of a type that matches our needs, in this case, longs. Fortunately, unlike CComEnumImpl, IEnumOnSTLImpl allows on-demand data conversion, allowing us to keep our collection in a convenient type but still providing the data in a format required by the enumerator.

On-Demand Data Conversion

The implementations of the Next, Skip, Reset, and Clone methods using an STL collection are almost identical to those of the CComEnumImpl class. The single significant difference is a nifty loophole in the IEnumOnSTLImpl's Next method. The CComEnumImpl class ties the data type being enumerated to the data type held in the array of the enumerator. However, `IEnumOnSTLImpl` has no such limitation. Look at this snippet from `IEnumOnSTLImpl`'s `Next` method:

```
template <class Base, const IID* piid, class T, class Copy, class
  CollType>
STDMETHODIMP
IEnumOnSTLImpl<Base, piid, T, Copy, CollType>::Next(ULONG celt,
                                                    T*rgelt,
                                                    ULONG* pcelt
                                                    Fetched) {
  ...
  T* pelt = rgelt;
  while (SUCCEEDED(hr) && m_iter != m_pcollection->end() &&
    nActual < celt) {
    hr = Copy::copy(pelt, &*m_iter);
    ...
  }
  ...
    return hr;
}
```

The template parameters allow the type of the `*pelt` to be different from the type of the `&*m_iter`. In other words, the type of data that the collection holds can be different from the type of data that the client receives in the call to `Next`. This means that the copy policy class must still be able to initialize and destroy the data of the type being enumerated, but the copy operation could actually be hijacked to convert from one data type to another.

Imagine the following copy policy:

```
struct _CopyVariantFromLong {
    static HRESULT copy(VARIANT* p1, long* p2) {
    p1->vt = VT_I4;
    p1->lVal = *p2;
    return S_OK;
  }

  static void init(VARIANT* p)    { VariantInit(p); }
  static void destroy(VARIANT* p) { VariantClear(p); }
};
```

If the STL collection held `long`s, but the enumerator exposed VARIANTs, the `_CopyVariantFromLong` copy policy could be used to convert that data on demand. For example, if the prime number collection object was keeping an STL collection of longs, the following code would create an enumerator that could convert from long to VARIANT as appropriate during the client's Next call:

```
STDMETHODIMP CPrimeNumbers::get__NewEnum(IUnknown** ppunkEnum) {
  *ppunkEnum = 0;

  typedef CComEnumOnSTL<IEnumVARIANT, &IID_IEnumVARIANT, VARIANT,
                        _CopyVariantFromLong, vector<long> >
      CComEnumVariantOnVectorOflongs;

  CComObject<CComEnumVariantOnVectorOflongs>* pe = 0;
  ... // The rest is the same!
}
```

The only difference between this example and the previous one is the enumerator type definition. Instead of building it using a vector of VARIANTs, we build it using a vector of longs. Since the data type of the collection is different from the data type of the enumerator, we simply provide a copy policy class whose copy method converts appropriately. This is an especially useful technique for mapping between whatever is the most convenient type to hold in your collection object and VARIANTs to support the VB For-Each syntax.

Giving CComEnumOnSTL Its Own Copy

As I mentioned, unlike CComEnum, CComEnumOnSTL doesn't provide an option to copy the data held by the collection. Instead, it assumes it will share the data with the collection. Sometimes this can lead to undefined behavior if the collection is being modified while it is also being enumerated. All is not lost, however. It is possible to give a CComEnumOnSTL object its own copy of the data. The key is to build a COM object whose job it is to hold the STL container for the life of the enumerator. Then, when Init is called, pUnkForRelease is the pointer to this container copy object. Once the enumerator is done, it will release the container copy object, thus destroying the copy of the data. Unfortunately, ATL provides no such class. Fortunately, it's easy to build one. CComContainerCopy is a generic class for holding a copy of an STL container. The complete implementation follows:

```
template <typename CollType, typename ThreadingModel =
  CComObjectThreadModel>
class CComContainerCopy :
  public CComObjectRootEx<ThreadingModel>,
  public IUnknown { // CComEnumOnSTL only needs an IUnknown*
```

```
public:
  HRESULT Copy(const CollType& coll) {
    try {
      m_coll = coll;
      return S_OK;
    }
    catch(...) {
      return E_OUTOFMEMORY;
    }
  }

BEGIN_COM_MAP(CComContainerCopy)
    COM_INTERFACE_ENTRY(IUnknown)
END_COM_MAP()

  CollType  m_coll;
};
```

Notice that the CComContainerCopy class is parameterized by the type of collection it is to hold. This class can be used to copy any STL-like container. The Copy method copies the collection using assignment. Because the CComContainerCopy class derives only from IUnknown, it is ideally suited for one purpose: as the first argument to IEnumOnStlImpl's Init method. The second argument is the public m_coll member. Using the Copy method of the CComContainerCopy class mimics the use of the CComEnum class's AtlFlagCopy. The collection already has the data in the appropriate format, but the enumerator should have its own copy. Populating the m_coll member of the CComContainerCopy directly is like AtlFlag-TakeOwnership. The collection doesn't already have the data in the appropriate format, but the container has converted the data for use by the enumerator. An example usage of CComContainerCopy using the Copy method follows:

```
STDMETHODIMP CPrimeNumbers::get__NewEnum(IUnknown** ppunkEnum) {
  *ppunkEnum = 0;

  typedef CComEnumOnSTL<IEnumVARIANT, &IID_IEnumVARIANT, VARIANT,
                    _Copy<VARIANT>, vector<VARIANT> >
        CComEnumVariantOnVector;

  CComObject<CComEnumVariantOnVector>* pe = 0;
  HRESULT hr =
    CComObject<CComEnumVariantOnVector>::CreateInstance(&pe);
```

```
if( SUCCEEDED(hr) ) {
  pe->AddRef();

  // Create the container copy
  CComObject< CComContainerCopy< vector<VARIANT> > >* pCopy = 0;
  // Use pCopy as a scoping mechanism to bind to the static
  // CreateInstance
  hr = pCopy->CreateInstance(&pCopy);
  if( SUCCEEDED(hr) ) {
    pCopy->AddRef();

    // Copy the STL container to the container copy
    hr = pCopy->Copy(m_rgPrimes);
    if( SUCCEEDED(hr) ) {

      // Init the enumerator with the copy
      hr = pe->Init(pCopy->GetUnknown(), pCopy->m_coll);
      if( SUCCEEDED(hr) ) {
        hr = pe->QueryInterface(ppunkEnum);
      }
    }
    pCopy->Release();
  }
  pe->Release();
}

return hr;
}
```

On-Demand Data Calculation

CComEnum requires initialization with an array of data that is already calculated. CComEnumOnSTL, on the other hand, accesses the data by calling member functions on objects we provide. Therefore, calculating data on demand is a matter of providing implementations of the member functions that perform the calculations instead of accessing precalculated results.

For example, there's no reason the collection of prime numbers needs to precalculate all the results and store them. Instead, we need an STL-like container that looks like what CComEnumOnSTL needs (as I showed you before) but calculates the next prime number on demand. This container has two responsibilities. The first is keeping track of the range of values to iterate over. The second responsibility is exposing an iterator for both the beginning and one past the ending of the data. The beginning and ending iterator must be exposed via `begin` and `end` methods, and each must return a value of type `iterator`, a type nested inside the class. The `PrimesContainer` class lives up to both these responsibilities:

```
class PrimesContainer {
public:
  class iterator; // Forward declaration

  PrimesContainer() : m_min(0), m_max(0) {}

  // For IPrimeNumbers::CalcPrimes
  void SetRange(long min, long max)
  { m_min = min; m_max = max; }

  // For IPrimeNumbers::get_Count
  size_t  size()
  { return CountPrimes(m_min, m_max); }

  // For IPrimeNumbers::get_Item
  long operator[](size_t i)
  { return NthPrime(i + 1, m_min, m_max); }

  // The rest is for CComEnumOnSTL
  iterator begin()
  { return iterator(m_min, m_max); }

  iterator end()
  { return iterator(); }

  class iterator {...};
private:
  long  m_min, m_max;
};
```

Notice that in addition to supporting the minimum interface as required by the implementation of CComEnumOnSTL, the `PrimesContainer` class also provides a `SetRange` method for managing the range of prime numbers, a `size` method for counting the prime numbers in the range, and an `operator[]` method for extracting items in a random-access fashion. These methods make the `PrimesContainer` class suitable for implementing the `IPrimeNumbers` interface.

```
class ATL_NO_VTABLE CPrimeNumbers :
    public CComObjectRootEx<CComSingleThreadModel>,
    public CComCoClass<CPrimeNumbers, &CLSID_PrimeNumbers>,
    public IDispatchImpl<IPrimeNumbers, &IID_IPrimeNumbers> {
public:
...
// IPrimeNumbers
public:
  STDMETHODIMP CalcPrimes(long min, long max)
  { m_rgPrimes.SetRange(min, max); return S_OK; }

  STDMETHODIMP get_Count(long* pnCount)
  { *pnCount = m_rgPrimes.size(); return S_OK; }

  STDMETHODIMP get_Item(long n, long* pnPrime) {
    if( n < 1 || n > m_rgPrimes.size() ) return E_INVALIDARG;
    *pnPrime = m_rgPrimes[n-1];
    return S_OK;
  }

  STDMETHODIMP get__NewEnum(IUnknown** ppunkEnum) {
    *ppunkEnum = 0;

    typedef CComEnumOnSTL<IEnumVARIANT, &IID_IEnumVARIANT, VARIANT,
                          _CopyVariantFromLong, PrimesContainer >
            CComEnumVariantOnPrimesContainer;

    CComObject<CComEnumVariantOnPrimesContainer>* pe = 0;
    HRESULT hr = pe->CreateInstance(&pe);
    if( SUCCEEDED(hr) ) {
      pe->AddRef();

      hr = pe->Init(this->GetUnknown(), m_rgPrimes);
      if( SUCCEEDED(hr) ) {
        hr = pe->QueryInterface(ppunkEnum);
      }
      pe->Release();
    }

    return hr;
  }
```

```
    private:
      PrimesContainer m_rgPrimes;
    };
```

In fact, this code is nearly identical to the code I've already shown you. The difference is that instead of using a container that already has a precalculated set of values, we have one that knows how to calculate them on demand. Specifically, it's the
iterator that does the magic:

```
class PrimesContainer {
...
  iterator begin()
  { return iterator(m_min, m_max); }

  iterator end()
  { return iterator(); }

class iterator {
  public:
    iterator (long min = -1, long max = -1)
    : m_max(max), m_next(NthPrime(1, min, max))
    { if( m_next == -1 ) m_max = -1;  } // Match end()

    bool operator!=(const iterator& rhs)
    { return (m_next != rhs.m_next || m_max != rhs.m_max); }

    long& operator*()
    { return m_next; }

    iterator operator++(int) {
      iterator it(m_next, m_max);
      m_next = NthPrime(1, m_next + 1, m_max);
      if( m_next == -1 ) m_max = -1; // Match end()
      return it;
    }

  private:
    long  m_next, m_max;
  };
...
};
```

The key to understanding the iterator is understanding how CComEnumOnSTL uses it. CComEnumOnSTL keeps a pointer to the collection, called m_pcollection, and an iterator, called m_iter, that marks the current position in the container. The m_iter data member is initialized when the enumerator is constructed or when Reset is called to the result of m_pcollection->begin(). The implementation of begin constructs an iterator that uses the range of possible prime numbers to cache the next prime number and the maximum number to check. As the container is iterated, the next prime number is calculated one ahead of the request. For every element in the container, the following sequence is performed:

1. m_pcollection->end() constructs an iterator that marks the end of the data. This, in turn, creates an iterator with −1 for each of m_min, m_max, and m_next. Special member data values are common for constructing an iterator that marks the end of the data.

2. operator!= compares the current iterator with the ending iterator.

3. operator* pulls out the prime number at the current location of the iterator.

4. The postfix operator++ calculates the next prime number. If there are no more prime numbers, m_min, m_max, and m_next are each set to −1 to indicate the end of the data. The next time through the loop, the comparison with the ending iterator will succeed and CComEnumOnSTL will detect that it has reached the end of the collection.

This behavior can be seen by looking at the main loop in the CComEnumOn-STLImpl::Next implementation:

```
template <class Base, const IID* piid, class T, class Copy, class
  CollType>
STDMETHODIMP
IEnumOnSTLImpl<Base, piid, T, Copy, CollType>::Next(ULONG celt,
                                                    T*rgelt,
                                                    ULONG* pcelt-
                                                    Fetched) {
...

ULONG nActual = 0;
HRESULT hr = S_OK;
T* pelt = rgelt;
while (SUCCEEDED(hr) &&
       m_iter != m_pcollection->end() && nActual < celt) {
```

```
    hr = Copy::copy(pelt, &*m_iter);
    if (FAILED(hr)) {
      while (rgelt < pelt) Copy::destroy(rgelt++);
      nActual = 0;
    }
    else {
      pelt++;
      m_iter++;
      nActual++;
    }
  }
  ...
  return hr;
}
```

If you find occasion to calculate data on demand using a custom container and iterator pair, yours will be called in the same sequence. This gives you an opportunity
to calculate data appropriately for your data set, for example, lines in a file, records
in a database, bytes from a socket. Why go to all this trouble to calculate data on demand? Efficiency in both time and space. There are 9,592 prime numbers between
0 and 100,000. Precalculating and storing the primes as longs costs nearly 38K.
Worse, the client must wait for all primes to be calculated in this range even if it
never gets around to enumerating them all. On the other hand, calculating them on
demand requires the m_min and m_max members of the container and the m_next
and m_max members of the current iterator. That's 16 bytes no matter how many
prime numbers we'd like to calculate, and the cost of calculating them is only realized when the client requests the next chunk.[6]

Collections

ICollectionOnSTLImpl

In addition to parameterized implementations of enumeration interfaces, ATL provides parameterized implementations of collection interfaces, assuming you're willing to keep your data in an STL-like container. The implementation is provided by
the ICollectionOnSTLImpl class:

---

[6]Of course, there are far more efficient ways to store and calculate prime numbers than what I have
shown here. Even so, there are going to be space vs. time trade-offs that make calculating on demand an
attractive option.

```
template <class T, class CollType, class ItemType,
        class CopyItem, class EnumType>
class ICollectionOnSTLImpl : public T {
public:
 STDMETHOD(get_Count)(long* pcount);
 STDMETHOD(get_Item)(long Index, ItemType* pvar);
 STDMETHOD(get__NewEnum)(IUnknown** ppUnk);


 CollType m_coll;
};
```

The ICollectionOnSTLImpl class provides an implementation of the three standard collection properties very much like what I showed you earlier. The chief difference is that the STL container is managed for you in the m_coll member data of the ICollectionOnSTLImpl class. That means that you can't provide a copy of the data to the enumerators, but you can still use a collection that calculates on demand and you can still convert from a convenient type to the type required by the enumerator exposed from get__NewEnum. This is because, although you get to decide the type of the container in a template parameter, you're no longer implementing get__NewEnum.

The template parameters of ICollectionOnSTLImpl are as follows:

- The T parameter indicates the base class, for example, IDispatchImpl <IPrimeNumbers, &IID_IPrimeNumbers>. ICollectionOnSTLImpl will provide the implementation of the standard three properties of this base class, but the deriving class is responsible for the rest.

- The CollType parameter indicates the type of STL-like container to keep, for example, vector<long> or PrimesContainer.

- The ItemType parameter indicates the type of data exposed from the iterator of the collection, for example, long.

- The CopyItem parameter indicates the type of the copy policy class. This copy policy will be used only in the implementation of the get_Item method. The copy policy should be able to copy from a container holding items of type ItemType to a single [out] parameter of type ItemType. If you were managing a container of long numbers, the CopyItem type would be _Copy<long>.

- The EnumType parameter indicates the type of the enumeration implementation class. This enumeration must be able to enumerate over an STL-like container just like CComEnumOnSTL. An example EnumType parameter is CComEnumOnSTLImpl<IEnumVARIANT, &IID_IEnumVARIANT, VARIANT, _Copy<VARIANT>, vector<VARIANT> >.

ICollectionOnSTLImpl Usage

The best way to understand the `ICollectionOnSTLImpl` class is to see it in action. The first STL-based implementation of the `IPrimesCollection` standard collection interface assumed we wanted to manage a precalculated container of VARIANTs. This could be done using `ICollectionOnSTLImpl` like so:

```
// Needed for implementation of get_Item.
// Converts the storage type (VARIANT) to the item type (long).
struct _CopyLongFromVariant {
    static HRESULT copy(long* p1, VARIANT* p2) {
    if( p2->vt == VT_I4 ) {
      *p1 = p2->lVal;
      return S_OK;
    }
    else {
      VARIANT var;
      HRESULT hr = VariantChangeType(&var, p2, 0, VT_I4);
      if( SUCCEEDED(hr) ) *p1 = var.lVal;
      return hr;
    }
 }

 static void init(long* p)    { }
 static void destroy(long* p) { }
};

// Needed for implementation of IDispatch methods
typedef IDispatchImpl<IPrimeNumbers, &IID_IPrimeNumbers>
        IPrimeNumbersDualImpl;

// Needed for implementation of get__NewEnum method
typedef CComEnumOnSTL<IEnumVARIANT, &IID_IEnumVARIANT, VARIANT,
                    _Copy<VARIANT>, vector<VARIANT> >
        CComEnumVariantOnVector;

// Needed for implementation of standard collection methods
typedef ICollectionOnSTLImpl<IPrimeNumbersDualImpl,
                        vector<VARIANT>, long,
                        _CopyLongFromVariant,
                        CComEnumVariantOnVector>
        IPrimeNumbersCollImpl;
```

```
class ATL_NO_VTABLE CPrimeNumbers :
    public CComObjectRootEx<CComSingleThreadModel>,
    public CComCoClass<CPrimeNumbers, &CLSID_PrimeNumbers>,
  public IPrimeNumbersCollImpl
{
public:
...
// IPrimeNumbers
public:
  STDMETHODIMP CalcPrimes(long min, long max) {
    m_coll.clear();
    for( long n = min; n <= max; ++n ) {
      if( IsPrime(n) ) {
        VARIANT var = {VT_I4};
        var.lVal = n;
        m_coll.push_back(var);
      }
    }

    return S_OK;
  }
};
```

If we'd like to precalculate the prime numbers but keep them as a vector of long numbers, this is how we'd use ICollectionOnSTLImpl:

```
// Needed for implementation of get__NewEnum.
// Converts the storage type (long) to the enumeration type (VARIANT).
struct _CopyLongFromVariant {
    static HRESULT copy(long* p1, VARIANT* p2) {
    if( p2->vt == VT_I4 ) {
      *p1 = p2->lVal;
      return S_OK;
    }
    else {
      VARIANT var;
      HRESULT hr = VariantChangeType(&var, p2, 0, VT_I4);
      if( SUCCEEDED(hr) ) *p1 = var.lVal;
      return hr;
    }
  }
```

```
  static void init(long* p)    { }
  static void destroy(long* p) { }
};

// Needed for implementation of IDispatch methods
typedef IDispatchImpl<IPrimeNumbers, &IID_IPrimeNumbers>
        IPrimeNumbersDualImpl;

// Needed for implementation of get__NewEnum method
typedef CComEnumOnSTL<IEnumVARIANT, &IID_IEnumVARIANT, VARIANT,
                    _CopyVariantFromLong, vector<long> >
        CComEnumVariantOnVectorOflongs;

// Needed for implementation of standard collection methods
typedef ICollectionOnSTLImpl<IPrimeNumbersDualImpl,
                            vector<long>, long, _Copy<long>,
                            CComEnumVariantOnVectorOflongs>
        IPrimeNumbersCollImpl;

class ATL_NO_VTABLE CPrimeNumbers :
    public CComObjectRootEx<CComSingleThreadModel>,
    public CComCoClass<CPrimeNumbers, &CLSID_PrimeNumbers>,
    public IPrimeNumbersCollImpl
{
public:
...
// IPrimeNumbers
public:
  STDMETHODIMP CalcPrimes(long min, long max) {
    m_coll.clear();
    for( long n = min; n <= max; ++n ) {
      if( IsPrime(n) ) {
        m_coll.push_back(n);
      }
    }

    return S_OK;
  }
};
```

Finally, if we'd like to have the prime numbers calculated on demand and exposed as `long` numbers, we'd use `ICollectionOnSTLImpl` like so:

```
// Calculates prime numbers on demand
class PrimesContainer;

// Needed for implementation of get_Item.
// Converts the storage type (VARIANT) to the item type (long).
struct _CopyVariantFromLong;

// Needed for implementation of IDispatch methods
typedef IDispatchImpl<IPrimeNumbers, &IID_IPrimeNumbers>
        IPrimeNumbersDualImpl;

// Needed for implementation of get__NewEnum method
typedef CComEnumOnSTL<IEnumVARIANT, &IID_IEnumVARIANT, VARIANT,
                    _CopyVariantFromLong, PrimesContainer >
        CComEnumVariantOnPrimesContainer;

// Needed for implementation of standard collection methods
typedef ICollectionOnSTLImpl<IPrimeNumbersDualImpl,
                        PrimesContainer, long, _Copy<long>,
                        CComEnumVariantOnPrimesContainer>>
        IPrimeNumbersCollImpl;

class ATL_NO_VTABLE CPrimeNumbers :
    public CComObjectRootEx<CComSingleThreadModel>,
    public CComCoClass<CPrimeNumbers, &CLSID_PrimeNumbers>,
  public IPrimeNumbersCollImpl
{
public:
...
// IPrimeNumbers
public:
  STDMETHODIMP CalcPrimes(long min, long max)
  { m_coll.SetRange(min, max); }
};
```

Jim Springfield, the Father of ATL, says "`ICollectionOnSTLImpl` is not for the faint of heart." He's absolutely right. It provides a lot of flexibility, but at the expense of complexity. Still, once you've mastered the complexity, as with any good class library, you can get a lot done with very little code.

STL Collections of ATL Data Types

If you're an STL fan (many modern developers are), you may find yourself wishing to keep some of ATL's smart types (that is, CComBSTR, CComVariant, CComPtr, and CComQIPtr) in an STL container. Many STL containers have a requirement concerning the elements they hold that makes this difficult for STL smart types: operator& must return an address to an instance of the type being held. However, all the smart types except CComVariant overload operator& to return the address of the internal data:

```
BSTR*  CComBSTR:operator&()    { return &m_str; }
T**    CComPtr::operator&()    { ATLASSERT(p==NULL); return &p; }
T**    CComQIPtr::operator&()  { ATLASSERT(p==NULL); return &p; }
```

These overloads mean that CComBSTR, CComPtr, and CComQIPtr cannot be used in many STL containers or with STL algorithms with the same requirement. The classic work-around for this problem is to maintain a container of a type that holds the ATL smart type but that doesn't overload operator&. ATL provides the CAdapt class for this purpose.

ATL Smart-Type Adapter

The CAdapt class is provided for the sole purpose of wrapping ATL smart types for use in STL collections. It's parameterized to accept any of the current or future such types:

```
template <class T> class CAdapt {
public:
  CAdapt() {}

  CAdapt(const T& rSrc)
  { m_T = rSrc; }

  CAdapt(const CAdapt& rSrCA)
  { m_T = rSrCA.m_T; }

  CAdapt& operator=(const T& rSrc)
  { m_T = rSrc; return *this; }
```

```
bool operator<(const T& rSrc) const
{ return m_T < rSrc; }

bool operator==(const T& rSrc) const
{ return m_T == rSrc; }

operator T&()
{ return m_T; }

operator const T&() const
{ return m_T; }

T m_T;
};
```

Notice that CAdapt does not have an operator&, so it will work just fine for STL containers and collections. Also notice that the real data is held in a public member variable called m_T. Typical usage requires using either this data member or a static_cast to obtain the underlying data.

CAdapt Usage

For example, imagine that you wanted to expose prime numbers as words instead of digits. Of course, you'd like the collection to support multiple languages, so you'd like to expose the strings in Unicode. Also, you'd like to support type-challenged COM mappings, so the strings have to be BSTRs. These requirements suggest the following interface:

```
[dual]
interface IPrimeNumberWords : IDispatch {
    HRESULT CalcPrimes([in] long min, [in] long max);

    [propget]
    HRESULT Count([out, retval] long* pnCount);

    [propget, id(DISPID_VALUE)]
    HRESULT Item([in] long n, [out, retval] BSTR* pbstrPrimeWord);

    [propget, id(DISPID_NEWENUM)]
    HRESULT _NewEnum([out, retval] IUnknown** ppunkEnum);
};
```

Notice that the Item property exposes the prime number as a string, not a number. Also keep in mind that although the signature of _NewEnum is unchanged, we will be returning VARIANTs to the client that contain BSTRs, not long numbers.

Because we're dealing with one of the COM data types that's inconvenient for C++ programmers, BSTRs, we'd like to use the CComBSTR smart data type described in Chapter 2. However, the compiler will complain if we try to use a data member like this to maintain the data:

```
vector<CComBSTR> m_rgPrimes;
```

Instead, we'll use CAdapt to hold the data:

```
vector< CAdapt<CComBSTR> > m_rgPrimes;
```

Of course, because we're using strings, our method implementations change. To calculate the data, we'll be changing the prime numbers to strings:

```
STDMETHODIMP CPrimeNumberWords::CalcPrimes(long min, long max) {
  while( min <= max ) {
    if( IsPrime(min) ) {
      char  sz[64];
      CComBSTR  bstr = NumWord(min, sz);
      m_rgPrimes.push_back(bstr);
    }
    ++min;
  }


  return S_OK;
}
```

Notice how we can simply push a CComBSTR onto the vector. The compiler will use the CAdapt<CComBSTR> constructor that takes a const CComBSTR& to construct the appropriate object for the vector to manage. The get_Count method doesn't change, but the get_Item method does:

```
STDMETHODIMP CPrimeNumberWords::get_Item(long n, BSTR* pbstrPrimeWord){
  if( n < 1 || n > m_rgPrimes.size() ) return E_INVALIDARG;

  CComBSTR& bstr = m_rgPrimes[n-1].m_T;
  return bstr.CopyTo(pbstrPrimeWord);
}
```

Notice that we're reaching into the vector and pulling out the appropriate element. Again, remember that the type of element we're holding is CAdapt<CComBSTR>, so I've used the m_T element to access the CComBSTR data inside. However, because the CAdapt<CComBSTR> class has an implicit cast operator to CComBSTR&, using the m_T member explicitly is not necessary.

Finally, the get__NewEnum method must also change. Remember that we're implementing IEnumVARIANT, but instead of holding long numbers, we're holding BSTRs. Therefore, the on-demand data conversion must convert between a CAdapt <CComBSTR> (the data type held in the container) to a VARIANT holding a BSTR. This can be accomplished with another custom copy policy class:

```
struct _CopyVariantFromAdaptBstr {
    static HRESULT copy(VARIANT* p1, CAdapt<CComBSTR>* p2) {
    p1->vt = VT_BSTR;
    p1->bstrVal = p2->m_T.Copy();
    return (p1->bstrVal ? S_OK : E_OUTOFMEMORY);
  }

  static void init(VARIANT* p)    { VariantInit(p); }
  static void destroy(VARIANT* p) { VariantClear(p); }
};
```

The corresponding enumeration type definition looks like this:

```
typedef CComEnumOnSTL<IEnumVARIANT, &IID_IEnumVARIANT, VARIANT,
                    _CopyVariantFromAdaptBstr,
                    vector< CAdapt<CComBSTR> > >
      CComEnumVariantOnVectorOfAdaptBstr;
```

Using these two type definitions, implementing get__NewEnum looks much like it always does:

```
STDMETHODIMP CPrimeNumberWords::get__NewEnum(IUnknown** ppunkEnum) {
  *ppunkEnum = 0;

  CComObject<CComEnumVariantOnVectorOfAdaptBstr>* pe = 0;
  HRESULT hr = pe->CreateInstance(&pe);
  if( SUCCEEDED(hr) ) {
    pe->AddRef();
```

```
    hr = pe->Init(this->GetUnknown(), m_rgPrimes);
    if( SUCCEEDED(hr) ) {
      hr = pe->QueryInterface(ppunkEnum);
    }

    pe->Release();
  }

  return hr;
}
```

Using ICollectionOnSTLImpl with CAdapt

If you'd like to combine the use of ICollectionOnSTLImpl with CAdapt, you already have half the tools, namely, the custom copy policy and the enumeration type definition. You still need another custom copy policy that copies from the vector of CAdapt<CComBSTR> to the BSTR* provided by the client to implement get_Item. This copy policy can be implemented like so:

```
struct _CopyBstrFromAdaptBstr {
    static HRESULT copy(BSTR* p1, CAdapt<CComBSTR>* p2) {
    *p1 = SysAllocString(p2->m_T);
    return (p1 ? S_OK : E_OUTOFMEMORY);
 }

 static void init(BSTR* p)     { }
 static void destroy(BSTR* p) { SysFreeString(*p); }
};
```

Finally, we can use CAdapt with ICollectionOnSTLImpl like so:

```
typedef IDispatchImpl<IPrimeNumberWords, &IID_IPrimeNumberWords>
        IPrimeNumberWordsDualImpl;

typedef ICollectionOnSTLImpl<IPrimeNumberWordsDualImpl,
                             vector< CAdapt<CComBSTR> >,
                             BSTR,
                             _CopyBstrFromAdaptBstr,
                             CComEnumVariantOnVectorOfAdaptBstr>
        IPrimeNumberWordsCollImpl;
```

```
class ATL_NO_VTABLE CPrimeNumberWords :
    public CComObjectRootEx<CComSingleThreadModel>,
    public CComCoClass<CPrimeNumberWords, &CLSID_PrimeNumberWords>,
    public IPrimeNumberWordsCollImpl {
public:
...
// IPrimeNumberWords
public:
  STDMETHODIMP CalcPrimes(long min, long max) {
    while( min <= max ) {
      if( IsPrime(min) ) {
        char  sz[64];
        CComBSTR  bstr = NumWord(min, sz);
        m_coll.push_back(bstr);
      }
      ++min;
    }

    return S_OK;
  }
};
```

Simple Collections

Using STL puts one burden firmly on the shoulders of the developer: exception
handing. Many calls into STL collections and algorithms can cause exceptions that
must be caught before they leave the method boundary.[7] And because C++ exception handling requires the C runtime (CRT), the CRT libraries must be linked
with any ATL project that uses STL. Unfortunately, many ATL servers are built without the CRT, and therefore a replacement for the STL is needed. ATL provides two
simple classes that provide basic array and map functionality that are not unlike the
STL vector and map classes. In the spirit of ATL, neither of these classes throws
exceptions or requires the CRT.

---

[7] Letting a C++ or Win32 structured exception escape a COM method is illegal. All such exceptions must
be caught and turned into appropriate HRESULTs. For more information on this topic, see *Effective COM*,
by Don Box, Keith Brown, Tim Ewald, and Chris Sells (Addison-Wesley, 1998).

CSimpleArray

The simple array class in ATL is named, appropriately enough, CSimpleArray. It's a dynamically sized array that grows on demand. It is a template class, so it can hold any kind of data. Its declaration is as follows:

```
template <class T> class CSimpleArray {
public:
    T* m_aT;
    int m_nSize;
    int m_nAllocSize;

// Construction/destruction
 CSimpleArray();
 ~CSimpleArray();

// Operations
    int  GetSize() const;
    BOOL Add(T& t);
    BOOL Remove(T& t);
    BOOL RemoveAt(int nIndex);
    void RemoveAll();
    T&   operator[] (int nIndex) const;
    T*   GetData() const;
    void SetAtIndex(int nIndex, Tt);
    int  Find(T& t) const;
};
```

The class members manage the memory associated with the m_aT data member, a dynamically sized array of type T. Unfortunately, CSimpleArray isn't too useful for implementing an enumeration interface, even though it could be easily used with CComEnum, because you're not likely to want to hold data in the same type as is being enumerated. Because CComEnum doesn't support conversion on demand like CComEnumOnSTL does, you must manually convert your CSimpleArray data into an array of data appropriate for enumeration. However, that doesn't mean that CSimpleArray can't be used for simpler [*sic*] jobs.

CSimpleValArray

Notice that in CSimpleArray, we're passing around references to data elements. This works fine for user-defined types, but not so well for simple types that have constant values; that is, the compiler frowns on passing 4 by reference. For these simple types, ATL provides `CSimpleValArray`, where arguments are passed by value instead:

```
template <class T> class CSimpleValArray : public CSimpleArray<T> {
public:
 BOOL Add(T t)
 { return CSimpleArray<T>::Add(t); }

 BOOL Remove(T t)
 { return CSimpleArray<T>::Remove(t); }

 T operator[] (int nIndex) const
 { return CSimpleArray<T>::operator[](nIndex); }
};
```

CSimpleMap

If you'd like the functionality of the STL map class without the burden of the CRT, ATL provides `CSimpleMap`:

```
template <class TKey, class TVal> class CSimpleMap {
public:
    TKey* m_aKey;
    TVal* m_aVal;
    int   m_nSize;

// Construction/destruction
    CSimpleMap();
    ~CSimpleMap();

// Operations
    int   GetSize() const;
    BOOL  Add(TKey key, TVal val);
    BOOL  Remove(TKey key);
    void  RemoveAll();
    BOOL  SetAt(TKey key, TVal val);
    TVal  Lookup(TKey key) const;
    TKey  ReverseLookup(TVal val) const;
    TKey& GetKeyAt(int nIndex) const;
    TVal& GetValueAt(int nIndex) const;
    void  SetAtIndex(int nIndex, TKey& key, TVal& val);
    int   FindKey(TKey& key) const;
```

```
    int   FindVal(TVal& val) const;
};
```

CSimpleMap maintains two matching dynamically sized arrays. Each element in the key array matches an element of the value array. CSimpleMap would be useful for implementing collection item lookup by name instead of by index.

Object Models

A COM object model is a hierarchy of objects. Collections allow the subobjects to be manipulated. Enumerators allow these objects to be accessed. Most object models have one top-level object and several noncreateable subobjects. The following stylized IDL shows a minimal object model:

```
library OBJECTMODELLib {
    importlib("stdole32.tlb");
    importlib("stdole2.tlb");

    // Document subobject //////////////////////////////////////
    [ dual ] interface IDocument : IDispatch {
        [propget] HRESULT Data([out, retval] BSTR *pVal);
        [propput] HRESULT Data([in] BSTR newVal);
    };

    coclass Document {
        [default] interface IDocument;
    };

    // Documents collection ////////////////////////////////////
    [ dual ] interface IDocuments : IDispatch {
        HRESULT AddDocument([out, retval] IDocument** ppDocument);
        [propget] HRESULT Count([out, retval] long* pnCount);
        [id(DISPID_VALUE), propget]
          HRESULT Item([in] long n, [out, retval] IDocument** ppdoc);
        [id(DISPID_NEWENUM), propget]
          HRESULT _NewEnum([out, retval] IUnknown** ppEnum);
    };

    coclass Documents {
        [default] interface IDocuments;
    };
```

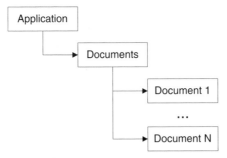

Figure 7.3. Simple object model instance hierarchy

```
// Application top-level object //////////////////////////////////
[ dual ] interface IApplication : IDispatch {
    [propget] HRESULT Documents([out, retval] IDocuments** pVal);
};

coclass Application {
    [default] interface IApplication;
};
};
```

An instance hierarchy of this object model would look like Figure 7.3.

Implementing the Top-Level Object

The top-level object of an object model is createable and will expose any number of properties as well as any number of collection subobjects. The example implementation looks like the following:

```
class ATL_NO_VTABLE CApplication :
    public CComObjectRootEx<CComSingleThreadModel>,
    public CComCoClass<CApplication, &CLSID_Application>,
    public IDispatchImpl<IApplication, &IID_IApplication> {
public:
DECLARE_REGISTRY_RESOURCEID(IDR_APPLICATION)
DECLARE_NOT_AGGREGATABLE(CApplication)
DECLARE_PROTECT_FINAL_CONSTRUCT()

BEGIN_COM_MAP(CApplication)
    COM_INTERFACE_ENTRY(IApplication)
    COM_INTERFACE_ENTRY(IDispatch)
END_COM_MAP()
```

```
   // Create instance of the Documents collection
   HRESULT CApplication::FinalConstruct()
   {  return CDocuments::CreateInstance(&m_spDocuments); }

// IApplication
public:
   // Hand out the Documents collection to interested parties
   STDMETHODIMP CApplication::get_Documents(IDocuments** pVal)
   { return m_spDocuments.CopyTo(pVal); }

private:
   CComPtr<IDocuments> m_spDocuments;
};
```

Implementing the Collection Object

The collection object is the most difficult of the three layers to implement, not because of any difficult code but because of the maze of type definitions. The first set is required to implement the enumerator:

```
template <typename T>
struct _CopyVariantFromAdaptItf {
   static HRESULT copy(VARIANT* p1, CAdapt< CComPtr<T> >* p2) {
   HRESULT hr = p2->m_T->QueryInterface(IID_IDispatch, (void**)&p1-
   >pdispVal);
   if( SUCCEEDED(hr) ) {
     p1->vt = VT_DISPATCH;
   }
   else {
     hr = p2->m_T->QueryInterface(IID_IUnknown, (void**)&p1->punkVal);
     if( SUCCEEDED(hr) ) {
       p1->vt = VT_UNKNOWN;
     }
   }

   return hr;
  }

  static void init(VARIANT* p)    { VariantInit(p); }
  static void destroy(VARIANT* p) { VariantClear(p); }
};
```

```
typedef CComEnumOnSTL<IEnumVARIANT, &IID_IEnumVARIANT, VARIANT,
                      _CopyVariantFromAdaptItf<IDocument>,
                      list< CAdapt< CComPtr<IDocument> > > >
        CComEnumVariantOnListOfDocuments;
```

The _CopyVariantFromAdaptItf class is a reusable class that converts an interface into a VARIANT for use in enumerating a collection of interface pointers. The collection object is expected to hold an STL container of elements of type CAdapt <CComPtr<T>>. Notice how the copy policy is used in the type definition of CComEnumVariantsOnListOfDocuments to obtain the implementation of IEnumVARIANT for the collection object.

The next set of type definitions is for the implementation of the collection methods:

```
template <typename T>
struct _CopyItfFromAdaptItf {
    static HRESULT copy(T** p1, CAdapt< CComPtr<T> >* p2) {
    if( *p1 = p2->m_T ) return (*p1)->AddRef(), S_OK;
    return E_POINTER;
  }

  static void init(T** p)    {}
  static void destroy(T** p) { if( *p ) (*p)->Release(); }
};


typedef ICollectionOnSTLImpl< IDispatchImpl<IDocuments,
  &IID_IDocuments>,
                              list< CAdapt< CComPtr<IDocument> > >,
                              IDocument*,
                              _CopyItfFromAdaptItf<IDocument>,
                              CComEnumVariantOnListOfDocuments>
        IDocumentsCollImpl;
```

The _CopyItfFromAdaptItf is used to implement the Item property, again assuming an STL container holding elements of type CAdapt<CComPtr<T>>. The copy policy is then used to define the collection interface implementation, IDocumentsCollImpl.

Finally, IDocumentsCollImpl is used as the base class of the IDocuments implementation:

```
class ATL_NO_VTABLE CDocuments :
    public CComObjectRootEx<CComSingleThreadModel>,
    public CComCoClass<CDocuments>, // noncreateable
    public IDocumentsCollImpl
{
public:
DECLARE_NO_REGISTRY()
DECLARE_NOT_AGGREGATABLE(CDocuments)
DECLARE_PROTECT_FINAL_CONSTRUCT()

BEGIN_COM_MAP(CDocuments)
    COM_INTERFACE_ENTRY(IDocuments)
    COM_INTERFACE_ENTRY(IDispatch)
END_COM_MAP()

// IDocuments
public:
  STDMETHODIMP AddDocument(IDocument** ppDocument) {
    // Create a document to hand back to the client
    HRESULT hr = CDocument::CreateInstance(ppDocument);
    if( SUCCEEDED(hr) ) {
      // Put the document on the list
      CComPtr<IDocument>  spDoc = *ppDocument;
      m_coll.push_back(spDoc);
    }

    return hr;
  }
};
```

The benefit of all the type definitions is that the standard methods of the collection are implemented for us. We have but to implement the AddDocument method, which creates a new CDocument and adds it to the list maintained by the ICollectionOnSTLImpl base class.

Implementing the Subobjects

The subobjects can do whatever you'd like, including maintaining collections of objects further down the hierarchy. Our example maintains a BSTR, representing its data:

```
STDMETHODIMP CDocument::get_Data(BSTR *pVal) {
  return m_bstrData.CopyTo(pVal);
}

STDMETHODIMP CDocument::put_Data(BSTR newVal) {
  m_bstrData = newVal;
  return (m_bstrData || !newVal ? S_OK : E_OUTOFMEMORY);
}
```

Using the Object Model

You normally design an object model to be used by many language mappings, including scripting environments. Here's an example HTML page that uses this example object model:

```
<html>
<script language=vbscript>
    dim app
    set app = CreateObject("ObjectModel.Application")

    dim docs
    set docs = app.Documents

    dim doc
    set doc = docs.AddDocument
    doc.Data = "Document 1"

    set doc = docs.AddDocument
    doc.Data = "Document 2"

    for each doc in docs
        msgbox doc.data
    next
</script>
</html>
```

Summary

COM has abstractions much like those of STL. Collections maintain lists of things, often objects. Enumerators enable navigation over the list of things maintained in a collection. To standardize access to collections and enumerators, they have a standard protocol. These standards aren't required, but if they are followed, they make an object, model programmer's life easier because the usage will be familiar. Implementing an object model is a matter of defining the higher-level object, the level-level object and the collection that joins the two together. ATL will implement both collection and enumeration interfaces, if you're not afraid of the type definitions required to make it all work.

CHAPTER

8 | Connection Points

A Review of Connection Points

An object implements one or more interfaces to expose its functionality. The term *connection points* refers to a logically inverse mechanism that allows an object to expose its capability to *call* one or more specific interfaces.

Another perspective is that `QueryInterface` allows a client *to retrieve from* an object a pointer to an interface that the object implements. Connection points allow a client *to give* an object a pointer to an interface that the client implements. In the first case, the client uses the retrieved interface pointer to call methods provided by the object. In the second case, the object uses the provided interface pointer to call methods provided by the client.

A slightly closer inspection of the two mechanisms reveals that `QueryInterface` allows a client to retrieve from an object only those interfaces that the client knows how to call. Connection points allow a client to provide to an object only those interfaces that the object knows how to call.

A *connection* has two parts: the object making calls to the methods of a specific interface, called the *source* or, alternatively, the *connection point;* and the object implementing the interface (receiving the calls), called the *sink object* (Figure 8.1). Using my terminology from the prior paragraphs, the object is the source and makes calls to the sink interface methods. The client is the sink and implements the sink interface. One additional complexity is that a particular source object may have connections to multiple sink objects.

The IConnectionPoint Interface

A client uses the source object's implementation of the `IConnectionPoint` interface to establish a connection. Here is the definition of the `IConnectionPoint` interface:

```
interface IConnectionPoint : IUnknown
{
HRESULT GetConnectionInterface ([out] IID* pIID);
HRESULT GetConnectionPointContainer
  ([out] IConnectionPointContainer** ppCPC);
```

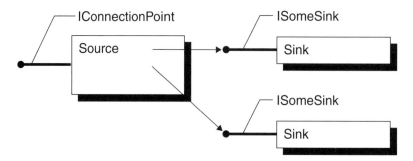

Figure 8.1. A connection to each of two sinks

```
HRESULT Advise ([in] IUnknown* pUnkSink, [out] DWORD* pdwCookie);
HRESULT Unadvise ([in] DWORD dwCookie);
HRESULT EnumConnections ([out] IEnumConnections** ppEnum);
}
```

The GetConnectionInterface method returns the interface identifier (IID) of the sink interface for which a connection point makes calls. Using the prior example, calling GetConnectionInterface would return IID_ISomeSink. A client calls the Advise method to establish a connection. The client provides the appropriate sink interface pointer for the connection point and receives a magic cookie (token) that represents the connection. A client can later call the Unadvise method, specifying the magic cookie to break the connection. The EnumConnections method returns a standard COM enumeration object that a client uses to enumerate all the current connections held by a connection point. The last method is GetConnectionPointContainer, which introduces a new complexity.

So far, this design allows a source object to make calls on only one specific interface. The source object maintains a list of clients that wish to receive calls on that specific interface. When the source object determines that it should call one of the methods of its sink interface, the source iterates through its list of sink objects, calling that method for each sink object. What the design (again, as described so far) doesn't include is the ability for an object to originate calls on multiple different interfaces using this mechanism. Alternatively, to present the question directly, we have a design in which an object can support multiple connections to a single connection point, but how can an object support multiple different connection points?

The solution is to demote the source object to subobject status and have an encapsulating object, called the *connectable object* (Figure 8.2), act as a container of these source subobjects. A client uses the source object's GetConnectionPointContainer method to retrieve a pointer to the connectable object. A connectable object implements the IConnectionPointContainer interface.

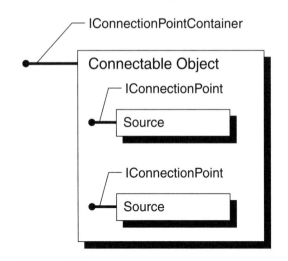

Figure 8.2. A connectable object

Implementing `IConnectionPointContainer` indicates that a COM object supports connection points and, more specifically, that it can provide a connection point (a source subobject) for each sink interface the connectable object knows how to call. Clients then use the connection point as described previously to establish the connection.

The IConnectionPointContainer Interface

Here is the definition of the `IConnectionPointContainer` interface:

```
interface IConnectionPointContainer : IUnknown
{
HRESULT EnumConnectionPoints ([out] IEnumConnectionPoints ** ppEnum);
HRESULT FindConnectionPoint ([in] REFIID riid,
                             [out] IConnectionPoint** ppCP);
}
```

You call the `FindConnectionPoint` method to retrieve an `IConnectionPoint` interface pointer to a source subobject that originates calls on the interface specified by the `riid` parameter. The `EnumConnectionPoints` method returns a standard COM enumerator subobject that implements the `IEnumConnection-Points` interface. You can use this enumerator interface to retrieve an `ICon-nectionPoint` interface pointer for each connection point supported by the connectable object.

Most often, a client that wishes to establish a connection to a connectable object does the following (with error checking removed for clarity):

```
CComPtr<IUnknown> pSource =      /* Set to the source of the events */ ;
CComPtr<_ISpeakerEvents> pSink = /* Sink to receive the events */ ;
DWORD dwCookie ;
CComPtr<IConnectionPointContainer> pcpc;
HRESULT hr = pSource.QueryInterface (&pcpc);

CComPtr<IConnectionPoint> pcp ;
hr = pcpc->FindConnectionPoint (__uuidof(_ISpeakerEvents), &pcp) ;
hr = pcp->Advise (pSink, &dwCookie) ; // Establish connection
                                 // Time goes by, callbacks occur...
hr = pcp->Unadvise (dwCookie) ;       // Break connection
```

In fact, ATL provides two useful functions that make and break the connection between a source and a sink object. The AtlAdvise function makes the connection between a connectable object's connection point (specified by the pUnkCP and iid parameters) and a sink interface implementation (specified by the pUnk parameter) and returns a registration code for the connection in the pdw location. The AtlUnadvise function requests the connectable object's connection point to break the connection identified by the dw parameter.

```
ATLAPI AtlAdvise(IUnknown* pUnkCP, IUnknown* pUnk,
               const IID& iid, LPDWORD pdw);
ATLAPI AtlUnadvise(IUnknown* pUnkCP, const IID& iid, DWORD dw);
```

You would use these functions like this:

```
DWORD dwCookie;
// Make a connection
hr = AtlAdvise (pSource, pSink, __uuidof (_ISpeakerEvents), &dwCookie);
// . . . Receive callbacks . . .
// Break the connection
hr = AtlUnadvise (pSource, __uuidof (_ISpeakerEvents), dwCookie);
```

In summary, to establish a connection, you need an interface pointer for the connectable object, an interface pointer to an object that implements the sink interface, and the sink interface ID.

You will commonly find connection points used by ActiveX controls. An ActiveX control is often a source of events. An event source implements event callbacks as method calls on a specified event sink interface. Typically, an ActiveX control container will implement an event sink interface so that it can receive specific events from its contained controls. Using the connection points protocol, the control container establishes a connection from the source of events in the control (the connection point) to the event sink in the container. When an event occurs, the connection point calls the appropriate method of the sink interface for each sink connected to the connection point.

I should point out that the connection points design is deliberately a very general mechanism, which means using connection points isn't terribly efficient in some cases.[1] Connection points are most useful in the case in which an unknown number of clients may wish to establish callbacks to a variety of different sink interfaces. In addition, the connection points protocol is well known; therefore, objects with no custom knowledge of each other can use it to establish connections. If you are writing both the source and sink objects, you may wish to invent a custom protocol, which is easier to use than the connection point protocol, to trade interface pointers.

Creating an ATL-Based Connectable Object

The Brilliant Example Problem That Produces Blinding Insight

Let's create a Demagogue COM object. It represents a public speaker. The ATL-based **CDemogogue** class will implement the **ISpeaker** interface. When asked to **Speak**, a speaker can whisper, talk, or yell his or her **Speech** depending on the value of **Volume**.

```
interface ISpeaker : IDispatch
{
    [propget, id(1)] HRESULT Volume([out, retval] long *pVal);
    [propput, id(1)] HRESULT Volume([in] long newVal);
    [propget, id(2)] HRESULT Speech([out, retval] BSTR *pVal);
    [propput, id(2)] HRESULT Speech([in] BSTR newVal);
    [id(3)] HRESULT Speak();
};
```

---

[1] For ActiveX controls and other in-process objects, connection points are acceptable, but when round-trips are a concern, they are horrid. Read *Effective COM* by Don Box, Keith Brown, Tim Ewald, and Chris Sells (Addison-Wesley, 1998) for an in-depth discussion of these issues.

Whispering, talking, and yelling generate event notifications on the _ISpeaker-
Events source dispatch interface, and the recipient(s) of the events hear the
speech. Many client components can only receive event notifications when the
source interface is a dispatch interface.

```
dispinterface _ISpeakerEvents
{
properties:
methods:
    [id(1)] HRESULT OnWhisper(BSTR bstrSpeech);
    [id(2)] HRESULT OnTalk(BSTR bstrSpeech);
    [id(3)] HRESULT OnYell(BSTR bstrSpeech);
};
```

The underscore prefix is a naming convention that causes many type library
browsers to not display the interface name. Because an event interface is an implementation detail, typically you won't want such interfaces displayed to the authors
of scripting languages when they use your component.

Note: The Microsoft Interface Definition Language (MIDL) compiler prefixes DIID_ to the
name of a dispinterface when it generates its named globally unique identifier (GUID), so
DIID__ISpeakerEvents is the named GUID for this interface.

Therefore, the following coclass definition describes a Demagogue. I've
added an interface that lets me name a particular Demagogue if I don't like the default, which is Demosthenes.

```
coclass Demagogue
{
    [default]           interface       IUnknown;
                        interface       ISpeaker;
                        interface       INamedObject;
    [default, source] dispinterface _ISpeakerEvents;
};
```

I'll start with the CDemagogue class: an ATL-based, single-threaded-apartment res-
ident, COM-createable object to represent a Demagogue.

```
class ATL_NO_VTABLE CDemagogue :
    public CComObjectRootEx<CComSingleThreadModel>,
    public CComCoClass<CDemagogue, &CLSID_Demagogue>,
    public ISupportErrorInfo,
```

```
    public IDispatchImpl<ISpeaker, &IID_ISpeaker,
       &LIBID_ATLINTERNALSLib>,
    . . .
  { };
```

Seven Steps to a Connectable Object

There are seven steps to creating a connectable object using ATL.

1. You need to implement the `IConnectionPointContainer` interface.
2. `QueryInterface` should respond to requests for `IID_IConnectionPoint-Container`.
3. You need to implement the `IConnectionPoint` interface for each source interface supported by the connectable object.
4. You need to provide a connection map, that is, a table that associates an IID with a connection point implementation.
5. You must update the `coclass` definition for the connectable object class in your IDL file to specify each source interface. Each source interface must have the `[source]` attribute. The primary source interface should have the `[default, source]` attributes.
6. Typically, you will want helper methods that call the sink methods for all connected sinks.
7. You must call the helper methods at the appropriate times.

Adding Required Base Classes to Your Connectable Object

In order for an object to fire events using the connection points protocol, the object must be a connectable object. This means the object must implement the `IConnectionPointContainer` interface. You can use an ATL-provided implementation of `IConnectionPointContainer` and `IConnectionPoint` by deriving the connectable object class from the appropriate base classes.

Step 1. Derive the `CDemagogue` connectable object class from the ATL template class `IConnectionPointContainerImpl`. This template class requires one parameter—the name of your derived class. This derivation provides the connectable object with an implementation of the `IConnectionPointContainer` interface.

```
    class ATL_NO_VTABLE CDemagogue :
       ...
```

```
    public IConnectionPointContainerImpl<CDemagogue>,
    ...
```

Changes to the COM_MAP for a Connectable Object

Step 2. Any time you add a new interface implementation to a class, you should immediately add support for the interface to your `QueryInterface` method. ATL implements `QueryInterface` for an object by searching the object's COM_MAP for an entry matching the requested IID. To indicate that the object supports the `IConnectionPointContainer` interface, add a COM_INTERFACE_ENTRY macro for the interface:

```
BEGIN_COM_MAP(CDemagogue)
...
    COM_INTERFACE_ENTRY(IConnectionPointContainer)
...
END_COM_MAP ()
```

Adding Each Connection Point

A connection point container needs a collection of connection points to contain (otherwise, the container is somewhat boring as well as misleading). For each source interface that the connectable object supports, you need a connection point subobject. A connection point subobject is logically a separate object (that is, its COM object identity is unique) that implements the `IConnectionPoint` interface.

Step 3. To create connection point subobjects, you derive your connectable object class from the template class `IConnectionPointImpl` one or more times—once for each source interface supported by the connectable object. This derivation provides the connectable object with one or more implementations of the `IConnectionPoint` interface on separately reference-counted subobjects. The `IConnectionPointImpl` class requires three template parameters: the name of your connectable object class, the IID of the connection point's source interface, and, optionally, the name of a class that manages the connections.

```
class ATL_NO_VTABLE CDemagogue :
    ...
    public IConnectionPointContainerImpl<CDemagogue>,
    public IConnectionPointImpl<CDemagogue, &DIID__ISpeakerEvents>
    ...
```

Where, Oh Where Are the Connection Points? Where, Oh Where Can They Be?

Any implementation of `IConnectionPointContainer` needs some fundamental information: a list of connection point objects and the IID supported by each connection point object. The ATL implementation uses a table called a *connection point map* in which you provide the required information. You define a connection point map in your connectable object's class declaration using three ATL macros.

The `BEGIN_CONNECTION_POINT_MAP` macro specifies the beginning of the table. The only parameter is the class name of the connectable object. Each CON-NECTION_POINT_ENTRY macro places an entry in the table and represents one connection point. The macro's only parameter is the IID of the interface supported by the connection point.

Note that the `CONNECTION_POINT_ENTRY` macro requires you to specify an IID, whereas the `COM_INTERFACE_ENTRY` macro needs an interface class name. Historically, you could always prepend an `IID_` prefix to an interface class name to produce the name of the GUID for the interface. Prior versions of ATL's COM_ INTERFACE_ENTRY macro actually did this to produce the appropriate IID.

However, source interfaces have no such regular naming convention. Various versions of MFC, MKTYPLIB, and MIDL have generated different prefixes to a `dispinterface`. The `CONNECTION_POINT_ENTRY` macro thus couldn't assume a prefix and therefore required you to specify the IID explicitly.

As of version 3.0, ATL uses, by default, the `__uuidof` keyword to obtain the IID for a class. Unfortunately, changing the CONNECTION_POINT_ENTRY macro to expect a class name would break existing code.

The `END_CONNECTION_MAP` macro generates an end-of-table marker and a static member function that returns the address of the connection map and its size.

Step 4. Here's the connection map for the `CDemagogue` class.

```
BEGIN_CONNECTION_POINT_MAP(CDemagogue)
    CONNECTION_POINT_ENTRY(DIID__ISpeakerEvents)
END_CONNECTION_POINT_MAP()
```

Update the Coclass to Support the Source Interface

Step 5. Clients often read the type library, which describes an object that is a source of events, in order to determine certain implementation details, such as the object's source interface(s). You'll need to ensure that the source object's `coclass` description is up-to-date by adding an entry to describe the source interface.

```
coclass Demagogue
{
    [default]          interface      IUnknown;
                       interface      ISpeaker;
                       interface      INamedObject;
    [default, source] dispinterface _ISpeakerEvents;
};
```

Where There Are Events, There Must Be Fire

So far, we have a Demagogue connectable object that is a container of connection points, and one connection point. The implementation, as presented up to this point, permits a client to register a callback interface with a connection point. All the enumerators will work. The client can even disconnect. However, the connectable object never issues any callbacks. This isn't terribly useful and has been a bit of work for no significant gain, so we'd better continue and finish things off. A connectable object needs to call the sink interface methods, otherwise known as *firing the events.*

To fire an event, you call the appropriate event method of the sink interface for each sink interface pointer registered with a connection point. This task is complex enough that you'll generally find it useful to add event firing helper methods to your connectable object class. You'll have one helper method in your connectable object class for each method in each of your connection points' supported interfaces.

You fire an event by calling the associated event method of a particular sink interface. You do this for each sink interface registered with the connection point. This means you need to iterate through a connection point's list of sink interfaces and call the event method for each interface pointer. "How and where does a connection point maintain this list?" you ask. Good timing—I was about to get to that.

Each IConnectionPointImpl base class object (which means each connection point) contains a member variable m_vec that ATL declares as a vector of IUnknown pointers. It actually is a vector of sink interface pointers of the appropriate type. For example, the vector in the connection point associated with DIID_ISpeakerEvents actually contains _SpeakerEvents pointers. You don't need to call QueryInterface for DIID_ISpeakerEvents after retrieving each sink pointer. ATL's implementation of IConnectionPointImpl::Advise has already performed this query for you.

By default, m_vec is a CComDynamicUnkArray object, which is a dynamically allocated array of IUnknown pointers, each a client sink interface pointer for the connection point. The CComDynamicUnkArray class grows the vector as required, so the default implementation provides an unlimited number of connections.

Alternatively, when you declare the `IConnectionPointImpl` base class you can specify that `m_vec` is a `CComUnkArray` object that holds a fixed number of sink interface pointers. Use the `CComUnkArray` class when you want to support a fixed maximum number of connections. ATL also provides an explicit template, `CComUnkArray<1>`, that is specialized for a single connection.

Step 6. To fire an event, you iterate through the array and, *for each non-*NULL *entry,* call the sink interface method associated with the event you wish to fire. Here's a simple helper method that fires the `OnTalk` event of the `_SpeakerEvents` interface. Note that `m_vec` is only unambiguous when you have a single connection point.

```
HRESULT Fire_OnTalk(BSTR bstrSpeach)
{
    CComVariant arg, varResult;
    int nIndex, nConnections = m_vec.GetSize();

    for (nIndex = 0; nIndex < nConnections; nIndex++) {
        CComPtr<IUnknown> sp = m_vec.GetAt(nIndex);
        IDispatch* pDispatch = reinterpret_cast<IDispatch*>(sp.p);
        if (pDispatch != NULL) {
            VariantClear(&varResult);
            arg = bstrSpeach;
            DISPPARAMS disp = { &arg, NULL, 1, 0 };
            pDispatch->Invoke(0x2, IID_NULL, LOCALE_USER_DEFAULT,
                DISPATCH_METHOD, &disp, &varResult, NULL, NULL);
        }
    }
    return varResult.scode;
}
```

The ATL Connection Point Proxy Generator

Writing the helper methods that call back a connection point interface method is tedious and prone to errors. An additional complexity is that a sink interface can be a custom COM interface or a `dispinterface`. There is considerably more work to making a `dispinterface` callback (such as, using `IDispatch::Invoke`) than making a vtable callback. Unfortunately, the `dispinterface` callback is the most frequent case because it's the only event mechanism supported by scripting languages, Internet Explorer, and most ActiveX control containers.

The Visual C++ IDE, however, provides a source code generation tool that generates a connection point class that contains all the necessary helper methods for making callbacks on a specific connection point interface. In the Visual C++ ClassView pane, right-click on the C++ class that you want to be a source of events. Select the Implement Connection Point menu item from the context menu. The Implement Connection Point dialog appears (Figure 8.3).

The Implement Connection Point dialog creates one or more classes (declared and defined in the specified header file) that represent the specified interface(s) and their methods. To use the code generator, you must have a type library that describes the desired event interface. The code generator reads the type library description of an interface and generates a class, derived from `IConnection-PointImpl`, that contains an event firing helper function for each interface method. You specify the generated class name as one of your connectable object's base classes. This base class implements a specific connection point and contains all necessary event firing helper methods.

The Implement Connection Point Proxy Generated Code

The proxy generator produces a template class with a name in the form `CProxy<SinkInterfaceName>`. This proxy class requires one parameter: your connectable object's class name. The proxy class derives from an `IConnection-`

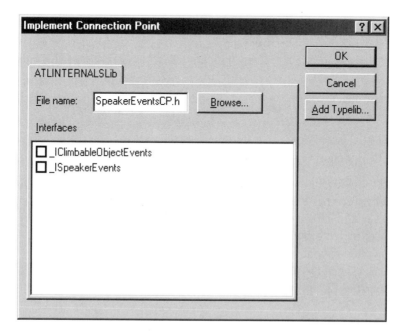

Figure 8.3. The Implement Connection Point dialog

`PointImpl` template instantiation that specifies your source interface ID and the dynamic array connection manager.

Here is the code generated for the previously described `_ISpeakerEvents` interface by the Implement Connection Point proxy generator:

```
#ifndef _SPEAKEREVENTSCP_H_
#define _SPEAKEREVENTSCP_H_

template <class T>
class CProxy_ISpeakerEvents :
 public IConnectionPointImpl<T, &DIID__ISpeakerEvents,
                             CComDynamicUnkArray>
{
//Warning this class may be recreated by the wizard.
public:
HRESULT Fire_OnWhisper(BSTR bstrSpeach)
{
    CComVariant varResult;
    T* pT = static_cast<T*>(this);
    int nConnectionIndex;
    CComVariant* pvars = new CComVariant[1];
    int nConnections = m_vec.GetSize();

    for (nConnectionIndex = 0; nConnectionIndex < nConnections;
         nConnectionIndex++) {
        pT->Lock();
        CComPtr<IUnknown> sp = m_vec.GetAt(nConnectionIndex);
        pT->Unlock();
        IDispatch* pDispatch = reinterpret_cast<IDispatch*>(sp.p);
        if (pDispatch != NULL) {
            VariantClear(&varResult);
            pvars[0] = bstrSpeach;
            DISPPARAMS disp = { pvars, NULL, 1, 0 };
            pDispatch->Invoke(0x1, IID_NULL, LOCALE_USER_DEFAULT,
                DISPATCH_METHOD, &disp, &varResult, NULL, NULL);
        }
    }
    delete[] pvars;
    return varResult.scode;
}
// Other methods similar, deleted for clarity
};
#endif
```

Using the Connection Point Proxy Code

Putting everything together so far, here are the pertinent parts of the CDemagogue connectable object declaration. The only change from previous examples is the use of the generated connection point proxy class, CProxy_ISpeakerEvents<CDemagogue>, as a base class for the connection point instead of the more generic IConnectionPointImpl class.

```
class ATL_NO_VTABLE CDemagogue :
...
    public IConnectionPointContainerImpl<CDemagogue>,
    public CProxy_ISpeakerEvents<CDemagogue>,
...
{

BEGIN_COM_MAP(CDemagogue)
...
    COM_INTERFACE_ENTRY(IConnectionPointContainer)
...
END_COM_MAP()

BEGIN_CONNECTION_POINT_MAP(CDemagogue)
    CONNECTION_POINT_ENTRY(DIID__ISpeakerEvents)
END_CONNECTION_POINT_MAP()
...
};
```

Firing the Events

Step 7. The final step to make everything work is to fire each event at the appropriate time. When to do this is very application specific, but here is one example.

The CDemagogue object makes its speech when a client calls the Speak method. The Speak method, based on the current volume property, either whispers, talks, or yells. It does this by calling the OnWhisper, OnTalk, or OnYell event method, as appropriate, of all clients listening to the demagogue's _Speaker-Events interface.

```
STDMETHODIMP CDemagogue::Speak()
{
    if (m_volume <= -100)
        return Fire_OnWhisper (m_speech) ;
```

```
    if (m_volume >= 100)
        return Fire_OnYell (m_speech) ;

    return Fire_OnTalk (m_speech) ;
}
```

Going the Last Meter/Mile, Adding One Last Bell

The changes described so far provide a complete implementation of the connection point protocol. However, there is one last change that makes your connectable object easier for clients to use. A connectable object should provide convenient client access to information about the interfaces supported by the object.

More specifically, many clients that wish to receive events from a connectable object may ask the object for its `IProvideClassInfo2` interface. Microsoft Internet Explorer, Visual Basic, and ATL-based ActiveX control containers do this, for example. The client calls the `GetGUID` method of this interface with the parameter `GUIDKIND_DEFAULT_SOURCE_DISP_IID` to retrieve the IID of the primary event `dispinterface` supported by the connectable object. This is the IID of the `dispinterface` listed in the connectable object's `coclass` description with the `[default, source]` attributes.

Supporting `IProvideClassInfo2` allows arbitrary clients a convenient mechanism for determining the primary event source IID and then using the IID to establish a connection. Note that the IID returned by this call to `GetGUID` must be a `dispinterface`. It cannot be a standard `IUnknown`-derived (vtable) interface.

When a connectable object fails the query for `IProvideClassInfo2`, some clients will ask for `IProvideClassInfo`. A client can use this interface to retrieve an `ITypeInfo` pointer about the connectable object's class. With a considerable bit of effort, a client can use this `ITypeInfo` pointer and determine the default source interface, supported by the connectable object. The `IProvideClassInfo2` interface derives from the `IProvideClassInfo` interface, so by implementing the first interface, you've already implemented the second one.

Because most connectable objects should implement the `IProvideClass-Info2` interface, ATL provides a template class for the implementation, `IProvide-ClassInfo2Impl`. `IProvideClassInfo2Impl` provides a default implementation of all the `IProvideClassInfo` and `IProvideClassInfo2` methods. The declaration of the class looks like this:

```
template< const CLSID* pcoclsid, const IID* psrcid, const GUID*
  plibid, WORD wMajor = 1, WORD wMinor = 0,
  class tihclass = CComTypeInfoHolder >
class IProvideClassInfo2Impl : public IProvideClassInfo2
```

To use this implementation in your connectable object, you must derive the connectable object class from the `IProvideClassInfo2Impl` class. The last two template parameters in the following example are the major and minor version numbers of the component's type library. They default to 1 and 0, respectively, so I didn't need to list them. However, when you change the type library's version number, you also need to change the numbers in the template invocation. You won't get a compile error if you fail to make the change, but things won't work correctly!

By always listing the version number explicitly, I find I remember to make this change more often.

```
#define LIBRARY_MAJOR    1
#define LIBRARY_MINOR    0

class ATL_NO_VTABLE CDemagogue :
...
    public IConnectionPointContainerImpl<CDemagogue>,
    public CProxy_ISpeakerEvents<CDemagogue>,
    public IProvideClassInfo2Impl<&CLSID_Demagogue,
                            &DIID__ISpeakerEvents,
            &LIBID_ATLINTERNALSLib, LIBRARY_MAJOR, LIBRARY_MINOR> ...
...
};
```

You also need to update the COM_MAP so `QueryInterface` responds to `IProvideClassInfo` and `IProvideClassInfo2`.

```
BEGIN_COM_MAP(CDemagogue)
...
  COM_INTERFACE_ENTRY(IProvideClassInfo2)
  COM_INTERFACE_ENTRY(IProvideClassInfo)
END_COM_MAP()
```

Finally, here are all connectable-object-related changes in one place:

```
#define LIBRARY_MAJOR    1
#define LIBRARY_MINOR    0

// Event dispinterface
dispinterface _ISpeakerEvents
{
properties:
methods:
```

```
    [id(1)] HRESULT OnWhisper(BSTR bstrSpeech);
    [id(2)] HRESULT OnTalk(BSTR bstrSpeech);
    [id(3)] HRESULT OnYell(BSTR bstrSpeech);
};


// Connectable object class
coclass Demagogue
{
    [default]          interface     IUnknown;
                       interface     ISpeaker;
                       interface     INamedObject;
    [default, source] dispinterface _ISpeakerEvents;
};


// Implementation class for coclass Demagogue
class ATL_NO_VTABLE CDemagogue :
...
    public IConnectionPointContainerImpl<CDemagogue>,
    public CProxy_ISpeakerEvents<CDemagogue>,
    public IProvideClassInfo2Impl<&CLSID_Demagogue,
                               &DIID__ISpeakerEvents,
        &LIBID_ATLINTERNALSLib, LIBRARY_MAJOR, LIBRARY_MINOR> ...
    {
public:
BEGIN_COM_MAP(CDemagogue)
    COM_INTERFACE_ENTRY(IConnectionPointContainer)
    COM_INTERFACE_ENTRY(IProvideClassInfo2)
    COM_INTERFACE_ENTRY(IProvideClassInfo)
...
END_COM_MAP()

BEGIN_CONNECTION_POINT_MAP(CDemagogue)
    CONNECTION_POINT_ENTRY(DIID__ISpeakerEvents)
END_CONNECTION_POINT_MAP()
...
};
```

Creating an Object That Is an Event Recipient

It is quite easy, in theory, to implement an object that receives events on a single interface. You define a class that implements the interface and connect the object
to the event source. We have a Demagogue class that generates events on the

_ISpeakerEvents dispatch interface. Let's define an EarPolitic class (clearly one ear of the body politic) that implements _ISpeakerEvents.

```
coclass EarPolitic
{
    [default] dispinterface _ISpeakerEvents;
};
```

Now implement the class using ATL as the CEarPolitic class.

```
class ATL_NO_VTABLE CEarPolitic :
    . . .
    public _ISpeakerEvents,
    . . .
{
public:
    . . .
BEGIN_COM_MAP(CEarPolitic)
    COM_INTERFACE_ENTRY(IDispatch)
    COM_INTERFACE_ENTRY(_ISpeakerEvents)
. . .
END_COM_MAP()

// _ISpeakerEvents
    STDMETHOD(GetTypeInfoCount)(UINT* pctinfo);
    STDMETHOD(GetTypeInfo)(UINT itinfo, LCID lcid, ITypeInfo**
      pptinfo);
    STDMETHOD(GetIDsOfNames)(REFIID riid, LPOLESTR* rgszNames,
      UINT cNames, LCID lcid, DISPID* rgdispid);
    STDMETHOD(Invoke)(DISPID dispidMember, REFIID riid, LCID lcid,
        WORD wFlags, DISPPARAMS* pdispparams, VARIANT* pvarResult,
        EXCEPINFO* pexcepinfo, UINT* puArgErr);
};
```

Unfortunately, an event interface is typically a dispinterface, so this requires that we implement the IDispatch interface and support, at a minimum, the Invoke method. Invoke is a tedious method to write for any nontrivial event interface.

Another alternative is to use the IDispatch interface implementation provided by the IDispatchImpl template class. Unfortunately, the template class requires parameters describing a dual interface, not a dispinterface. To use

`IDispatchImpl`, you need to define a dummy dual interface that has the same dispatch methods, dispatch identifiers, and function signatures as the event `dispinterface`.

This has more implications than are usually apparent. A `dispinterface` is not immutable, unlike a regular COM interface. If you don't control the definition of the `dispinterface`, it might change from release to release. (Yes, it's not that likely to change, but it is possible.) This means your dual interface needs to change as well. This implies that you cannot document the dual interface, because once it is published it is immutable because some client may implement it. Because you shouldn't describe the dual interface in a type library (because that documents it), you cannot use the universal type-library-driven marshaler and need a remoting proxy/stub for the dual interface. These are all theoretical issues because the dual interface in this case is an implementation detail specific to the implementation class, but they give motivation enough to look for another solution.

On a slightly different note, what if you want to receive the same events from more than one event source and you want to know which source fired the event? For example, let's say you want to implement an `EarPolitic` class that acts as a judge listening to `_SpeakerEvents` from both a Defendant object and a Plaintiff object. Each object is a source of `OnWhisper`, `OnTalk`, and `OnYell` events, but the judge needs to keep track of who is saying what.

This requires you to implement the `_SpeakerEvents` interface multiple times —once for each event source. Providing separate implementations of any interface multiple times in a class requires each implementation to be in a different context (that is, in a separate COM identity). Two typical solutions to this problem are member-wise composition (where each implementation is in a nested class) and something similar to tear-off interfaces (where each implementation is in a separate class).

The IDispEventImpl and IDispEventSimpleImpl Classes

ATL provides two template classes, `IDispEventImpl` and `IDispEventSimple-Impl`, that provide an implementation of the `IDispatch` interface for an ATL COM object. Typically, you will use one of these classes in an object that wishes to receive event callbacks. Both classes implement the dispatch interface on a nested class object that maintains a separate COM identity from the deriving class. This means you can derive from these classes multiple times when you need to implement multiple source dispatch interfaces.

The `IDispEventImpl` class requires a type library that describes the dispatch interface. The class uses the `typeinfo` at runtime to map the VARIANT parameters received in the `Invoke` method call to the appropriate types and stack frame layout necessary for calling the event handler member function.

```
template <UINT nID, class T, const IID* pdiid = &IID_NULL,
         const GUID* plibid = &GUID_NULL,
         WORD wMajor = 0, WORD wMinor = 0,
         class tihclass = CComTypeInfoHolder>
class ATL_NO_VTABLE IDispEventImpl :
public IDispEventSimpleImpl<nID, T, pdiid>
```

The `IDispEventSimpleImpl` class doesn't use a type library, so it's a lighter-weight class. You use it when you don't have a type library or when you want to be more efficient at runtime.

```
template <UINT nID, class T, const IID* pdiid>
class ATL_NO_VTABLE IDispEventSimpleImpl :
         public _IDispEventLocator<nID, pdiid>
```

When using the `IDispEventSimpleImpl` class, you must provide an `_ATL_FUNC_INFO` structure containing information that describes the expected parameters for the event handler.

```
struct _ATL_FUNC_INFO
{
    CALLCONV cc;              // Calling convention
    VARTYPE vtReturn;         // VARIANT type for return value
    SHORT nParams;            // Number of parameters
                             // Array of parameter VARIANT type
    VARTYPE pVarTypes[_ATL_MAX_VARTYPES];
};
```

Notice that `IDispEventImpl` derives from the `IDispEventSimpleImpl` class. It's the `IDispEventSimpleImpl` class that calls the event handler based on the information in an `_ATL_FUNC_INFO` structure. You can provide the structure statically (at compile time) by referencing the structure in the sink map (described later in this chapter).

When you provide no structure reference, the `IDispEventSimpleImpl` class calls the virtual method `GetFuncInfoFromId` to get an `_ATL_FUNC_INFO` structure for the event handler associated with the specified `DISPID`. You provide the structure dynamically by overriding `GetFuncInfoFromId` and returning the appropriate structure when called. You must use `GetFuncInfoFromId` when you want to call different event methods based on the locale provided by the event source.

Here's the default implementation provided by the `IDispEventSimpleImpl` class:

```
//Helper for finding the function index for a DISPID
virtual HRESULT GetFuncInfoFromId(const IID& iid,
                                  DISPID dispidMember,
                                  LCID lcid, _ATL_FUNC_INFO& info)
{
    return E_NOTIMPL;
}
```

The `IDispEventImpl` class overrides this virtual method to create the structure from the `typeinfo` in the specified type library.

Implementing an Event Sink

The *easiest* way to implement one or more event sinks in an ATL object is to derive the object one or more times from `IDispEventImpl`—once for each unique event interface coming from each unique event source. Here's the template class specification once more:

```
template <UINT nID, class T, const IID* pdiid = &IID_NULL,
          const GUID* plibid = &GUID_NULL,
          WORD wMajor = 0, WORD wMinor = 0,
          class tihclass = CComTypeInfoHolder>
class ATL_NO_VTABLE IDispEventImpl :
public IDispEventSimpleImpl<nID, T, pdiid>
```

The `nID` parameter specifies an identifier for the event source that is unique to the deriving class T. You'll see in Chapter 10, ActiveX Controls, that when the event source is a contained control and the event recipient is a composite control, the identifier is the contained control's child window identifier.

A composite control can default all other template parameters, but an arbitrary COM object must specify all parameters except the last. The `pdiid` parameter specifies the GUID for the event `dispinterface` that this class implements. The `dispinterface` must be described in the type library specified by the `plibid` parameter and the type library major and minor version numbers, `wMajor` and `wMinor`. The `tihclass` parameter specifies the class to manage the type information for the deriving class T. The default `CComTypeInfoHolder` class is generally acceptable.

The more *efficient* way to implement one or more event sinks in an ATL object uses the `IDispEventSimpleImpl` class and needs no type library at runtime. You must, however, provide the necessary _ATL_FUNC_INFO structure, as described previously. When using the IDispEventSimpleImpl class, you need specify only the nID event source identifier, the deriving class T, and the pdiid GUID for the event dispinterface:

```
template <UINT nID, class T, const IID* pdiid>
class ATL_NO_VTABLE IDispEventSimpleImpl :
        public _IDispEventLocator<nID, pdiid>
```

Let's redefine the CEarPolitic class to implement the _SpeakerEvents dispatch interface twice: once for a Demagogue acting as a Defendant and once for a different Demagogue acting as a Plaintiff. I have a type library, so I'll use the IDispEventImpl class to implement the sink for the Defendant object's _Speaker-Events callbacks. I'll use the IDispEventSimpleImpl class for the Plaintiff object's _SpeakerEvents callbacks so I can demonstrate the alternative implementation. I typically introduce a typedef for each event interface implementation to minimize typing and mistakes.

```
static const int  DEFENDANT_SOURCE_ID = 0 ;
static const int  PLAINTIFF_SOURCE_ID = 1 ;

class CEarPolitic;

typedef IDispEventImpl<DEFENDANT_SOURCE_ID, CEarPolitic,
    &DIID__ISpeakerEvents, &LIBID_ATLINTERNALSLib, LIBRARY_MAJOR,
    LIBRARY_MINOR> DefendantEventImpl;

typedef IDispEventSimpleImpl<PLAINTIFF_SOURCE_ID, CEarPolitic,
    &DIID__ISpeakerEvents> PlaintiffEventImpl;
```

In this example, I arbitrarily chose 0 and 1 for the event source identifiers. The identifiers could have been any numbers.

Now we need to derive the CEarPolitic class from the two event implementation classes:

```
class ATL_NO_VTABLE CEarPolitic :
    . . .
    public DefendantEventImpl,
    public PlaintiffEventImpl
{
// Event sink map required in here
};
```

The Event Sink Map

The IDispEventSimpleImpl class's implementation of the Invoke method receives the event callbacks. The event source, when it calls the Invoke method, specifies the event that has occurred, using the DISPID parameter. The IDispEventSimpleImpl implementation searches an event sink table for the function to call when event DISPID occurs on dispatch interface DIID from event source identifier SOURCE.

You specify the beginning of the event sink map using the BEGIN_SINK_MAP macro within the declaration of the class that derives from IDispEventImpl and/ or IDispEventSimpleImpl. You map each unique SOURCE/DIID/DISPID triple to the proper event handling method using the SINK_ENTRY, the SINK_ENTRY_EX, and the SINK_ENTRY_FUNC macros.

- SINK_ENTRY(SOURCE, DISPID, func): Use this macro in a composite control to name the handler for the specified event in the specified contained control's default source interface. This macro assumes the use of IDispEventImpl and assumes that you call the AtlAdviseSinkMap function to establish the connection. The AtlAdviseSinkMap function assumes that your class is derived from CWindow. All in all, the SINK_ENTRY macro isn't very useful for non-user-interface (UI) objects wishing to receive events.

- SINK_ENTRY_EX(SOURCE, DIID, DISPID, func): Use this macro to indicate the handler for the specified event in the specified object's specified source interface. This macro is most useful for non-UI objects wishing to receive events and for composite controls wishing to receive events from a contained control's nondefault source interface.

- SINK_ENTRY_FUNC(SOURCE, DIID, DISPID, func, info): This macro is similar to the SINK_ENTRY_EX macro with the addition that you can specify the _ATL_FUNC_INFO structure to be used when calling the event handler. You typically use this macro when using the IDispEventSimpleImpl class.

You end the event sink map using the END_SINK_MAP macro.

The general form of the table is as follows:

```
BEGIN_SINK_MAP(CEarPolitic)
  SINK_ENTRY_EX(SOURCE, DIID, DISPID, EventHandlerFunc)
  SINK_ENTRY_INFO(SOURCE, DIID, DISPID, EventHandlerFunc, &info)
  . . .
END_SINK_MAP()
```

In the CEarPolitic example, there are three events, all from the same dispatch interface but coming from two different event sources. Therefore, we need six event sink map entries. I can use the SINK_ENTRY_EX macro to identify the event handlers for the Defendant event source. I don't need to specify the _ATL_FUNC_ INFO structure because the IDispEventImpl base class will use the type library to provide the appropriate structure at runtime. I need to use the SINK_ENTRY_ INFO macro for the Plaintiff object. Because I used the IDispEventSimpleImpl base class, I need to provide the function information structure describing each event method.

Each function information structure describes one event method. The structure contains the calling convention, the VARIANT type of the return value of the method, the number of parameters, and the VARIANT types of each of the parameters. The calling convention should be set to CC_STDCALL because that's what the IDispEventSimpleImpl class expects the event handlers to use.

```
struct _ATL_FUNC_INFO
{
    CALLCONV cc;              // Calling convention
    VARTYPE vtReturn;         // VARIANT type for return value
    SHORT nParams;            // Number of parameters
                              // Array of parameter VARIANT type
    VARTYPE pVarTypes[_ATL_MAX_VARTYPES];
};
```

Here are the function prototypes for the Plaintiff's three event methods and their information structures (all identical in this example). Event handlers typically do not return a value; that is, they are void functions.

Note: The proper vtReturn value in the _ATL_FUNC_INFO structure to represent a void function return is VT_EMPTY, not VT_VOID.

```
void __stdcall OnHearPlaintiffWhisper(BSTR bstrText);
void __stdcall OnHearPlaintiffTalk(BSTR bstrText);
void __stdcall OnHearPlaintiffYell(BSTR bstrText);

static const int  DISPID_WHISPER = 1 ;
static const int  DISPID_TALK    = 2 ;
static const int  DISPID_YELL    = 3 ;

_ATL_FUNC_INFO OnHearWhisperInfo =
              {CC_STDCALL, VT_EMPTY, 1, { VT_BSTR }};
_ATL_FUNC_INFO OnHearTalkInfo    =
              {CC_STDCALL, VT_EMPTY, 1, { VT_BSTR }};
```

```
_ATL_FUNC_INFO OnHearYellInfo     =
                {CC_STDCALL, VT_EMPTY, 1, { VT_BSTR }};
```

Here's the event sink map for the CEarPolitic object:

```
BEGIN_SINK_MAP(CEarPolitic)
  SINK_ENTRY_EX(DEFENDANT_SOURCE_ID, DIID__ISpeakerEvents,
    DISPID_WHISPER, OnHearDefendantWhisper)
  SINK_ENTRY_EX(DEFENDANT_SOURCE_ID, DIID__ISpeakerEvents, DISPID_TALK,
            OnHearDefendantTalk)
  SINK_ENTRY_EX(DEFENDANT_SOURCE_ID, DIID__ISpeakerEvents, DISPID_TALK,
            OnHearDefendantTalk)
  SINK_ENTRY_INFO(PLAINTIFF_SOURCE_ID, DIID__ISpeakerEvents,
    DISPID_WHISPER, OnHearPlaintiffWhisper, &OnHearTalkInfo)
  SINK_ENTRY_INFO(PLAINTIFF_SOURCE_ID, DIID__ISpeakerEvents,
    DISPID_TALK, OnHearPlaintiffTalk, &OnHearTalkInfo)
  SINK_ENTRY_INFO(PLAINTIFF_SOURCE_ID, DIID__ISpeakerEvents,
    DISPID_TALK,
            OnHearPlaintiffTalk, &OnHearTalkInfo)
END_SINK_MAP()
```

One caution: The sink map contains a hard-coded DISPID for each event. This means that the sink map technically is specific to a particular dispinterface version. COM does allow the DISPIDs in a dispinterface to change from version to version. Now, this isn't something that often happens—and a control vendor who does such a thing is just asking for tech support calls and angry customers—but it is allowed.

The only absolutely correct way to obtain a DISPID is to ask the object at startup for the DISPID corresponding to an event or to read the object's type library at runtime. However, ATL doesn't support this. Visual Basic and MFC don't either. They all assume that the DISPIDs in a dispinterface will never change as a questionable performance optimization.

The Callback Methods

The callback method specified by the sink entry macros must use the __stdcall calling convention. The parameters for each callback method specified in the sink map must agree in type and number with the corresponding event method as described in the type library. Here are the Defendant's event methods. They are identical to the Plaintiff's, as expected.

```
void __stdcall OnHearDefendantWhisper(BSTR bstrText);
void __stdcall OnHearDefendantTalk(BSTR bstrText);
void __stdcall OnHearDefendantYell(BSTR bstrText);
```

Two remaining steps and the ear will be complete: Implement the callback methods and establish the connection between a CEarPolitic instance and a Demagogue (which implements _ISpeakerEvents).

I'll use the following simple implementation for each of the event handlers:

```
void __stdcall CEarPolitic::OnHearDefendantTalk(BSTR bstrText)
{
    USES_CONVERSION;

    CComBSTR title ;
    CreateText (title, OLESTR("defendant"), OLESTR("talking"),
      m_defendant);

    MessageBox (NULL, OLE2CT(bstrText), OLE2CT(title), MB_OK);
}

void CEarPolitic::CreateText (CComBSTR& text, LPCOLESTR strRole,
                             LPCOLESTR strAction, LPUNKNOWN punk)
{
    text.Empty ();

    text = m_name;
    text += OLESTR (" hears the ");
    text += strRole;
    text += OLESTR (" (");

    CComQIPtr<INamedObject> pno = punk;
    CComBSTR name;
    HRESULT hr = pno->get_Name (&name) ;

    text.AppendBSTR (name);
    text += OLESTR (") ");

    text += strAction;
}
```

Connecting the Event Sink to an Event Source

When your class is a composite control, you should use the `AtlAdviseSinkMap`
function to establish and remove the connections between all the source interfaces
of the contained controls listed in the sink map and your `IDispEventImpl` imple-
mentation(s). This method uses the event source identifier as a child window
identifier. Using the `CWindow::GetDlgItem` method, `AtlAdviseSinkMap` navi-
gates to a child window handle and from there to the contained control's `IUnknown`
interface. From the `IUnknown` interface, it gets the `IConnectionPointContainer`
interface, then the appropriate connection point, and then calls its `Advise` method.

```
template <class T>
inline HRESULT AtlAdviseSinkMap(T* pT, bool bAdvise);
```

You *must* use the `AtlAdviseSinkMap` function to establish the connections anytime you use the `IDispEventImpl` class and you specify only the first two template
parameters, using default values for the rest. Not specifying the source interface
implies using the default source interface for the event source. It is the `AtlAdvise-
SinkMap` method that determines the default source interface, if unspecified, for
each event source and establishes the connection point to that interface.

When your class isn't a composite control, as in the ongoing example, you
must explicitly call the `DispEventAdvise` method of each of your `IDispEvent-
SimpleImpl` (or derived) base classes to connect each event source to each event
sink implementation. The pUnk parameter to the `DispEventAdvise` method is any
interface on the event source, and the `piid` parameter is the desired source dispatch interface GUID. The `DispEventUnadvise` method breaks the connection.

```
HRESULT DispEventAdvise(IUnknown* pUnk, const IID* piid);
HRESULT DispEventUnadvise(IUnknown* pUnk, const IID* piid);
```

Here is the `IListener` interface. I added it to the `EarPolitic coclass` to
provide a means to determine if a COM object can listen to a Defendant and a Plaintiff. It also provides the `ListenTo` and `StopListening` methods to establish and
break the connection point between a Speaker event source and the Defendant or
Plaintiff event sink.

```
interface IListener : IDispatch
{
    typedef enum SpeakerRole { Defendant, Plaintiff } SpeakerRole ;
```

```
    [id(1)] HRESULT ListenTo(SpeakerRole role, IUnknown* pSpeaker);
    [id(2)] HRESULT StopListening(SpeakerRole role);
};
```

The implementation of these methods is straightforward. `ListenTo` calls the `DispEventAdvise` method on the appropriate event sink to establish the connection.

```
STDMETHODIMP CEarPolitic::ListenTo(SpeakerRole role,
                                   IUnknown *pSpeaker)
{
    HRESULT hr = StopListening (role) ; // Validates role
    if (FAILED (hr)) return hr ;

    switch (role) {
    case Defendant:
      hr =
      DefendantEventImpl::DispEventAdvise (pSpeaker,
                                      &DIID__ISpeakerEvents) ;
      if (SUCCEEDED (hr))
          m_defendant = pSpeaker ;
      else
          Error (OLESTR("The defendant does not support listening"),
                 __uuidof(IListener), hr);
      break;
    case Plaintiff:
      hr =
      PlaintiffEventImpl::DispEventAdvise (pSpeaker,
                                      &DIID__ISpeakerEvents) ;
      if (SUCCEEDED (hr))
          m_plaintiff = pSpeaker ;
      else
          Error (OLESTR("The Plaintiff does not support listening"),
                 __uuidof(IListener), hr);
      break;
    }
    return hr;
}
```

The `StopListening` method calls `DispEventUnadvise` to break the connection.

```
STDMETHODIMP CEarPolitic::StopListening(SpeakerRole role)
{
    HRESULT hr = S_OK ;
    switch (role) {
    case Defendant:
        if (m_defendant)
            hr = DefendantEventImpl::DispEventUnadvise (m_defendant,
                    &DIID__ISpeakerEvents) ;

        if FAILED(hr)
            Error (OLESTR("Unexpected error trying to stop listening to "
                    "the defendant"),
                __uuidof(IListener), hr);

        m_defendant = NULL;
        break;

    case Plaintiff:
        if (m_plaintiff)
            hr = PlaintiffEventImpl::DispEventUnadvise (m_plaintiff,
                    &DIID__ISpeakerEvents) ;

        if FAILED(hr)
            Error (OLESTR("Unexpected error trying to stop listening to "
                    "the Plaintiff"),
                __uuidof(IListener), hr);

        m_plaintiff = NULL;
        break;

    default:
        hr = E_INVALIDARG;
        break;
    }

    return hr;
}
```

In summary, use the `IDispEventImpl` and `IDispEventSimpleImpl` classes to implement an event sink for a dispatch interface. Call the `DispEventAdvise` and `DispEventUnadvise` methods of each class to establish and break the connection.

Derive your class directly from the source interface when the source is a simple COM interface. Call the AtlAdvise and AtlUnadvise global functions to establish and break the connection. When you need to implement the same source interface multiple times, you'll need to use one of the various standard techniques (nested composition, method coloring, separate classes, or intermediate base classes) to avoid name collisions.

How It All Works: The Messy Implementation Details

Classes Used by an Event Source

The IConnectionPointContainerImpl Class

Let's start by examining the IConnectionPointContainerImpl template class implementation of the IConnectionPointContainer interface.

First, the class needs to provide a vtable compatible with the IConnection-PointContainer interface. This vtable must contain five methods: the three IUn-known methods and the two IConnectionPointContainer methods.

```
///////////////////////////////////////////////////////////////////////
// IConnectionPointContainerImpl

template <class T>
class ATL_NO_VTABLE IConnectionPointContainerImpl :
public IConnectionPointContainer
{
typedef CComEnum<IEnumConnectionPoints,
        &IID_IEnumConnectionPoints, IConnectionPoint*,
        _CopyInterface<IConnectionPoint> >
        CComEnumConnectionPoints;
public:
    STDMETHOD(EnumConnectionPoints)(IEnumConnectionPoints** ppEnum)
    {
        if (ppEnum == NULL) return E_POINTER;
        *ppEnum = NULL;
        CComEnumConnectionPoints* pEnum = NULL;
        ATLTRY(pEnum = new CComObject<CComEnumConnectionPoints>)
        if (pEnum == NULL) return E_OUTOFMEMORY;

        int nCPCount;
        const _ATL_CONNMAP_ENTRY* pEntry = T::GetConnMap(&nCPCount);
```

```
    // allocate and initialize a vector of connection point
    // object pointers
    IConnectionPoint** ppCP = (IConnectionPoint**)
    alloca(sizeof(IConnectionPoint*)*nCPCount);


    int i = 0;
    while (pEntry->dwOffset != (DWORD)-1) {
        ppCP[i++] = (IConnectionPoint*)((int)this+pEntry->
          dwOffset);
        pEntry++;
    }


    // copy the pointers: they will AddRef this object
    HRESULT hRes = pEnum->Init(((IConnectionPoint**)&ppCP[0],
                (IConnectionPoint**)&ppCP[nCPCount],
                reinterpret_cast<IConnectionPointContainer*>(this),
                AtlFlagCopy);
    if (FAILED(hRes)) {
        delete pEnum;
                return hRes;
                }
    hRes = pEnum->QueryInterface(IID_IEnumConnectionPoints,
                                (void**)ppEnum);

    if (FAILED(hRes))
        delete pEnum;
    return hRes;
}
STDMETHOD(FindConnectionPoint)(REFIID riid, IConnectionPoint** ppCP)
{
    if (ppCP == NULL) return E_POINTER;
    *ppCP = NULL;
    HRESULT hRes = CONNECT_E_NOCONNECTION;
    const _ATL_CONNMAP_ENTRY* pEntry = T::GetConnMap(NULL);
    IID iid;
    while (pEntry->dwOffset != (DWORD)-1) {
        IConnectionPoint* pCP = (IConnectionPoint*)
            ((int)this+pEntry->dwOffset);
        if (SUCCEEDED(pCP->GetConnectionInterface(&iid)) &&
            InlineIsEqualGUID(riid, iid)) {
            *ppCP = pCP;
            pCP->AddRef();
            hRes = S_OK;
```

```
            break;
        }
        pEntry++;
    }
    return hRes;
  }
};
```

The IUnknown methods are easy. The class doesn't implement them. You bring in the proper implementation of these three methods when you define a CComObject class parameterized on your connectable object class, for example, CComObject<CConnectableObject>.

The CComEnumConnectionPoints typedef declares a class for a standard COM enumerator that implements the IEnumConnectionPoints interface. You use this class of enumerator to enumerate IConnectionPoint interface pointers. A template expansion of the ATL CComEnum class provides the implementation. The implementation of the EnumConnectionPoints method creates and returns an instance of this enumerator.

EnumConnectionPoints begins with some basic error checking, then creates a new instance of a CComEnumConnectionPoints enumerator on the heap. The ATL enumerator implementation requires that, after instantiation, an enumerator must be initialized. ATL enumerators are rather inflexible in that, to initialize an enumerator, you must pass it an array of the items the enumerator enumerates. In this particular case, the enumerator provides IConnectionPoint pointers, so the initialization array must be an array of IConnectionPoint pointers.

A connectable object's connection map contains the information needed to produce the array of IConnectionPoint pointers. Each connection map entry contains the offset in the connectable object from the base of the IConnectionPointContainerImpl instance (that is, the current this pointer value) to the base of an IConnectionPointImpl instance.

EnumConnectionPoints allocates space for the initialization array on the stack, using alloca. It iterates through each entry of the connection map, calculates the IConnectionPoint interface pointer to each IConnectionPointImpl object, and stores the pointer in the array. Note that these pointers are not reference counted because the lifetime of the pointers in a stack-based array is limited to the method lifetime.

The call to the enumerator Init method initializes the instance. It's critical here to use the AtlFlagCopy argument. This informs the enumerator to make a proper copy of the items in the initialization array. For interface pointers, this means to AddRef the pointers when making the copy.

The pEnum pointer is a CComEnumConnectionPoints pointer, though it would be a bit better if it were declared as a CComObject<CComEnumConnection-

Points> pointer because that's what it actually is. Regardless, EnumConnection-Points must return an IEnumConnectionPoints pointer, not pEnum itself, so it queries the enumerator (via pEnum) for the appropriate interface pointer and returns the pointer.

The FindConnectionPoint method is quite straightforward. After the usual initial error checking, FindConnectionPoint uses the connection map to calculate an IConnectionPoint interface pointer to each connection point in the connectable object. Using the interface pointer, it asks each connection point for the IID of its supported interface and compares it with the IID it's trying to find. A match causes it to return the appropriate AddRef'ed interface pointer with status S_OK; otherwise, failure returns the CONNECT_E_NOCONNECTION status code. Most of the real work is left to the connection point implementation, so let's look at it next.

The IConnectionPointImpl Class

The IConnectionPointImpl template class implements the IConnectionPoint interface. To do that, the class needs to provide a vtable compatible with the IConnectionPoint interface. This vtable must contain eight methods: the three IUnknown methods and the five IConnectionPoint methods.

The first item of note is that the IConnectionPointImpl class derives from the _ICPLocator class.

```
template <class T, const IID* piid, class CDV = CComDynamicUnkArray >
class ATL_NO_VTABLE IConnectionPointImpl : public _ICPLocator<piid>
...
```

The _ICPLocator Class. More important, the _ICPLocator class contains the declaration of the virtual method, _LocCPQueryInterface. A virtual method occupies a slot in the vtable, so this declaration states that calls through the first entry in the vtable, the entry used by callers to invoke QueryInterface, will be sent to the method _LocCPQueryInterface. The declaration is pure virtual, so a derived class needs to provide the implementation. This is important because each connection point needs to provide a unique implementation of _LocCPQueryInterface.

```
template <const IID* piid>
class ATL_NO_VTABLE _ICPLocator
{
public:
  //this method needs a different name than QueryInterface
  STDMETHOD(_LocCPQueryInterface)(REFIID riid, void ** ppvObject) = 0;
  virtual ULONG STDMETHODCALLTYPE AddRef(void) = 0;
  virtual ULONG STDMETHODCALLTYPE Release(void) = 0;
};
```

A connection point must maintain a COM object identity separate from its connection point container. A connection point therefore needs its own implementation of `QueryInterface`. If you named the first virtual method in the `_ICPLocator` class "QueryInterface," C++ multiple inheritance rules would see the name as just another reference to a single implementation of `QueryInterface` for the connectable object. Normally, that's exactly what you want. For example, you have a class derived from three interfaces. All three interfaces mention the virtual method `QueryInterface`, but you want a single implementation of the method that all base classes share. Similarly, you want a shared implementation of `AddRef` and `Release` as well. But you don't want this for a connection point in a base class.

The idea here is that we want to expose two different COM identities (the connectable object and the connection point), which requires two separate implementations of `QueryInterface`, but we merge the remaining `IUnknown` implementation (`AddRef` and `Release`) because we don't want to keep a separate reference count for each connection point. ATL uses this "unique" approach to avoid having to delegate `AddRef` and `Release` calls from the connection point object to the connectable object.

The IConnectionPointImpl Class's Methods

The `IUnknown` methods are more complicated in `IConnectionPointImpl` than was the case in `IConnectionPointContainerImpl` so that a connection point can implement its own unique `QueryInterface` method. For a connection point, this is the `_LocCPQueryInterface` virtual method.

```cpp
template <class T, const IID* piid, class CDV = CComDynamicUnkArray >
class ATL_NO_VTABLE IConnectionPointImpl : public _ICPLocator<piid>
{
    typedef CComEnum<IEnumConnections, &IID_IEnumConnections,
        CONNECTDATA, _Copy<CONNECTDATA> > CComEnumConnections;
    typedef CDV _CDV;
public:
    ~IConnectionPointImpl();
    STDMETHOD(_LocCPQueryInterface)(REFIID riid, void ** ppvObject)
    {
        if (InlineIsEqualGUID(riid, IID_IConnectionPoint) ||
            InlineIsEqualUnknown(riid)) {
            if (ppvObject == NULL) return E_POINTER;
            *ppvObject = this;
            AddRef();
#ifdef _ATL_DEBUG_INTERFACES
            _Module.AddThunk((IUnknown**)ppvObject,
                        _T("IConnectionPointImpl"), riid);
```

```
#endif // _ATL_DEBUG_INTERFACES
        return S_OK;
    }
    else
        return E_NOINTERFACE;
}


STDMETHOD(GetConnectionInterface)(IID* piid2)
{
    if (piid2 == NULL) return E_POINTER;
    *piid2 = *piid;
    return S_OK;
}
STDMETHOD(GetConnectionPointContainer)(IConnectionPointContainer**
  ppCPC)
{
    T* pT = static_cast<T*>(this);
    // No need to check ppCPC for NULL since QI will do that for us
    return pT->QueryInterface(IID_IConnectionPointContainer,
(void**)ppCPC);
}
STDMETHOD(Advise)(IUnknown* pUnkSink, DWORD* pdwCookie);
STDMETHOD(Unadvise)(DWORD dwCookie);
STDMETHOD(EnumConnections)(IEnumConnections** ppEnum);
CDV m_vec;
};
```

The _LocCPQueryInterface Method.   The `_LocCPQueryInterface` method has
the same function signature as the COM `QueryInterface` method but only responds to requests for `IID_IUnknown` and `IID_IConnectionPoint` by producing an `AddRef`'-ed pointer to itself. *This makes each base class instance of an*
`IConnectionPointImpl` object a unique COM identity.

The AddRef and Release Methods.   As usual, you bring in the proper implementation of these two methods when you define a `CComObject` class parameterized
on your connectable object class, for example, `CComObject<CConnectable-`
`Object>`.

The GetConnectionInterface and GetConnectionPointContainer Methods.   The
`CComEnumConnections` typedef declares a class for a standard COM enumerator that implements the `IEnumConnections` interface. You use this class of

enumerator to enumerate CONNECTDATA structures, which contain a client sink interface pointer and its associated magic cookie registration token. A template expansion of the ATL CComEnum class provides the implementation. The implementation of the EnumConnections interface method creates and returns an instance of this enumerator.

The GetConnectionInterface interface method simply returns the source interface IID for the connection point, so the implementation is trivial. The Get-ConnectionPointContainer interface method is also simple, but there is some involved type casting required in order to request the correct interface pointer.

The issue is that the current class, this particular IConnectionPointImpl expansion, doesn't support the IConnectionPointContainer interface. But the design of the template classes requires your connectable object class, represented by class T in the template, to implement the IConnectionPointContainer interface.

```
T* pT = static_cast<T*>(this);
return pT->QueryInterface(IID_IConnectionPointContainer,
  (void**)ppCPC);
```

The type cast goes from the connection point subobject down the class hierarchy to the (deriving) connectable object class and calls that class's QueryInterface implementation to obtain the required IConnectionPointContainer interface pointer.

The Advise, Unadvise, and EnumConnections Methods.   The Advise, Unadvise, and EnumConnections methods all need a list of active connections. Advise adds new entries to the list, Unadvise removes entries from the list, and EnumConnections returns an object that enumerates over the list.

This list is of template parameter type CDV. By default, this is type CComDynamicUnkArray, which provides a dynamically growable array implementation of the list. As I described previously, the ATL provides a fixed-size list implementation and a specialized single-entry list implementation. However, it is relatively easy to provide a custom list implementation because the Advise, Unadvise, and EnumConnections implementations always access the list through its well-defined methods, namely, Add, Remove, begin, end, GetCookie, and GetUnknown.[2]

---

[2]One reason for a custom implementation could be to keep separate sink lists—one for each security principal—and only send certain events to certain sinks based on the principal's security clearances.

The Advise Method.   The `Advise` method retrieves the sink interface IID for this connection point and queries the `IUnknown` pointer provided by the client for the sink interface. This ensures that the client passes an interface pointer to an object that actually implements the expected sink interface. Failure to provide the correct interface pointer produces a `CONNECT_E_CANNOTCONNECT` error. You don't want to keep a connection to something that can't receive the callback. Plus, by obtaining the correct interface pointer here, the connection point doesn't have to query for it during each callback.

```
template <class T, const IID* piid, class CDV>
STDMETHODIMP IConnectionPointImpl<T, piid, CDV>::Advise(IUnknown*
  pUnkSink, DWORD* pdwCookie)
{
    T* pT = static_cast<T*>(this);
    IUnknown* p;
    HRESULT hRes = S_OK;
    if (pUnkSink == NULL || pdwCookie == NULL) return E_POINTER;
    IID iid;
    GetConnectionInterface(&iid);
    hRes = pUnkSink->QueryInterface(iid, (void**)&p);
    if (SUCCEEDED(hRes)) {
        pT->Lock();
        *pdwCookie = m_vec.Add(p);
        hRes = (*pdwCookie != NULL) ? S_OK : CONNECT_E_ADVISELIMIT;
        pT->Unlock();
        if (hRes != S_OK)
            p->Release();
    }
    else if (hRes == E_NOINTERFACE) hRes = CONNECT_E_CANNOTCONNECT;
    if (FAILED(hRes)) *pdwCookie = 0;
    return hRes;
}
```

When the query succeeds, the connection point needs to add the connection to the list. So it acquires a lock on the entire connectable object, adds the connection to the list if there's room, and releases the lock.

The Unadvise Method. The `Unadvise` method is relatively simple. It locks the connectable object, asks the list class to translate the provided magic cookie value into the corresponding `IUnknown` pointer, removes the connection identified by the cookie, unlocks the connectable object, and releases the held sink interface pointer.

```
template <class T, const IID* piid, class CDV>
STDMETHODIMP IConnectionPointImpl<T, piid, CDV>::Unadvise(DWORD
    dwCookie)
{
    T* pT = static_cast<T*>(this);
    pT->Lock();
    IUnknown* p = _CDV::GetUnknown(dwCookie);
    HRESULT hRes = m_vec.Remove(dwCookie) ? S_OK :
                                            CONNECT_E_NOCONNECTION;
    pT->Unlock();
    if (hRes == S_OK && p != NULL)
        p->Release();
    return hRes;
}
```

The EnumConnections Method. `EnumConnection` begins with some basic error checking, then creates a new instance of a `CComObject<CComEnumConnections>` enumerator on the heap. As before, the ATL enumerator implementation requires that, after instantiation, an enumerator must be initialized from an array, in this particular case, a contiguous array of `CONNECTDATA` structures.

```
template <class T, const IID* piid, class CDV>
STDMETHODIMP IConnectionPointImpl<T, piid, CDV>::EnumConnections(
    IEnumConnections** ppEnum)
{
    if (ppEnum == NULL) return E_POINTER;
    *ppEnum = NULL;
    CComObject<CComEnumConnections>* pEnum = NULL;
    ATLTRY(pEnum = new CComObject<CComEnumConnections>)
    if (pEnum == NULL) return E_OUTOFMEMORY;
    T* pT = static_cast<T*>(this);
    pT->Lock();
    CONNECTDATA* pcd = NULL;
```

```
ATLTRY(pcd = new CONNECTDATA[m_vec.end()-m_vec.begin()])
if (pcd == NULL) {
    delete pEnum;
    pT->Unlock();
    return E_OUTOFMEMORY;
}
CONNECTDATA* pend = pcd;
// Copy the valid CONNECTDATAs
for (IUnknown** pp = m_vec.begin();pp<m_vec.end();pp++) {
    if (*pp != NULL) {
        (*pp)->AddRef();
            pend->pUnk = *pp;
            pend->dwCookie = _CDV::GetCookie(pp);
            pend++;
    }
}
// don't copy the data, but transfer ownership to it
pEnum->Init(pcd, pend, NULL, AtlFlagTakeOwnership);
pT->Unlock();
HRESULT hRes =
    pEnum->_InternalQueryInterface(IID_IEnumConnections,
        (void**)ppEnum);
if (FAILED(hRes))
    delete pEnum;
return hRes;
}
```

The connection list stores IUnknown pointers. The CONNECTDATA structure contains the interface pointer and its associated magic cookie. EnumConnections allocates space for the initialization array from the heap. It iterates through the connection list entries, copying the interface pointer and its associated cookie to the dynamically allocated CONNECTDATA array. It's important to note that any non-NULL interface pointers are AddRef'ed. This copy of the interface pointers is going to have a lifetime greater than the EnumConnections method.

The call to the enumerator Init method initializes the instance. It's critical here to use the AtlFlagTakeOwnership argument. This informs the enumerator to use the provided array directly, rather than making yet another copy of it. This also means the enumerator is responsible for correctly releasing the elements in the array as well as the array itself.

The `EnumConnections` method now uses `_InternalQueryInterface` to return an `IEnumConnections` interface pointer on the enumerator object, which, at this point, is the only outstanding reference to the enumerator.[3]

Classes Used by an Event Sink

First, you need to understand the big picture about event sinks. Your object class may wish to implement multiple event sink interfaces and/or the same event sink interface multiple times. All event sink interfaces need nearly identical functionality—`IUnknown`, `IDispatch`, `Invoke`, and looking up the `DISPID` in a sink map and delegating the event method call to the appropriate event handler. But each implementation also needs some custom functionality—specifically, each implementation must be a unique COM identity.

ATL defines a class, `_IDispEvent`, that implements the common functionality and, through the use of template parameters and interface coloring, allows each derivation from this one C++ class to maintain a unique COM identity. This means ATL implements all specialized event sink implementations using a single C++ class, `_IDispEvent`.

The _IDispEvent Class

Let's examine the `_IDispEvent` class. The first interesting aspect is that it is intended to be used as an abstract base class. The first three virtual methods are declared using the COM standard calling convention and are all pure virtual. The first method is `_LocDEQueryInterface`, and the following two are the `AddRef` and `Release` methods. This gives the `_IDispEvent` class the vtable of a COM object supporting the `IUnknown` interface. The `_IDispEvent` class cannot simply derive from `IUnknown` because it needs to provide a specialized version of `QueryInterface`. A derived class will need to supply the `_LocDEQueryInterface`, `AddRef`, and `Release` methods.

```
class ATL_NO_VTABLE _IDispEvent
{
public:
 //this method needs a different name than QueryInterface
 STDMETHOD(_LocDEQueryInterface)(REFIID riid, void ** ppvObject) = 0;
 virtual ULONG STDMETHODCALLTYPE AddRef(void) = 0;
 virtual ULONG STDMETHODCALLTYPE Release(void) = 0;
```

---

[3]`EnumConnections` uses `_InternalQueryInterface` rather than `IUnknown::QueryInterface` because the latter results in a virtual function call, whereas the former is a more efficient direct call.

The class maintains five member variables, only one of which is always used, m_dwEventCookie, which is the only member variable initialized by the constructor.

```
_IDispEvent() {m_dwEventCookie = 0xFEFEFEFE;}
```

The m_dwEventCookie variable holds the connection point registration value returned from the source object's IConnectionPoint::Advise method. It's needed to break the connection. The class assumes that no event source will ever use the value 0xFEFEFEFE as the connection cookie because it uses that value as a flag to indicate that no connection is established.[4] While highly unlikely, this event is not impossible.

The m_libid, m_iid, m_wMajorVerNum, and m_wMinorVerNum variables hold the type library GUID, the source interface IID, and the type library major and minor version number, respectively.

```
GUID m_libid;
IID m_iid;
unsigned short m_wMajorVerNum;
unsigned short m_wMinorVerNum;
DWORD m_dwEventCookie;
```

This _IDispEvent class provides the DispEventAdvise and DispEvent-Unadvise methods, which establish and break, respectively, a connection between the specified source object's (pUnk) source interface (piid) and the _DispEvent sink object.

```
HRESULT DispEventAdvise(IUnknown* pUnk, const IID* piid)
{
    ATLASSERT(m_dwEventCookie == 0xFEFEFEFE);
    return AtlAdvise(pUnk, (IUnknown*)this, *piid, &m_dwEventCookie);
}

HRESULT DispEventUnadvise(IUnknown* pUnk, const IID* piid)
{
```

[4]Note that this places a constraint on a connection list implementation (that is, the CDV template parameter class), namely, that it never provide the value 0xFEFEFEFE as a connection cookie.

Of course, the _IDispEvent class could maintain a separate "connection established" flag, but that would increase the size of a class instance. Minimizing instance size doesn't seem to be a concern in the _IDispEvent class, though, because the class contains four other member variables that aren't always used. Typically, the approach in ATL is to factor out into a separate, derived class any member variables that aren't always needed in its base class.

```
    HRESULT hr = AtlUnadvise(pUnk, *piid, m_dwEventCookie);
    m_dwEventCookie = 0xFEFEFEFE;
    return hr;
}
```

You can implement multiple event sinks in a single ATL COM object. In the most general case, this means you need a unique event sink for each different source of events (source identifier). Further, this means you need a unique event sink object for each separate connection (source interface) to a source of events.

The _IDispEventLocator Class

Implementing multiple event sinks requires the sink to derive indirectly from _IDispEvent multiple times. But we need to do so in a way that allows us to find a particular _IDispEvent base class instance, given a source object identifier and the source interface on that object.

ATL uses the template class _IDispEventLocator to do this. Each unique _IDispEventLocator template invocation produces a different, addressable _IDispEvent event sink instance.[5]

```
template <UINT nID, const IID* piid>
class ATL_NO_VTABLE _IDispEventLocator : public _IDispEvent
{
public:
};
```

The _IDispEventSimpleImpl Class

The IDispEventSimpleImpl class implements the IDispatch interface. It derives from the _IDispEventLocator<nID, pdiid> class to inherit the IUnknown vtable, the member variables, and the connection point Advise and Unadvise support provided by the _IDispEvent base class.

```
template <UINT nID, class T, const IID* pdiid>
class ATL_NO_VTABLE IDispEventSimpleImpl :
        public _IDispEventLocator<nID, pdiid>
{
```

---

[5] Keith Brown pointed out that it would have been more appropriate to call these "Locator" classes "COMIdentity" classes, for example, _IDispEventCOMIdentity and IConnectionPointCOMIdentity. Their fundamental purpose is to provide a unique base class instance for each required COM identity. Yes, you need to locate the appropriate base class when needed, but the sole purpose in renaming the QueryInterface method is to implement a separate identity.

```
// Abbreviated for clarity
    STDMETHOD(_LocDEQueryInterface)(REFIID riid, void ** ppvObject);
    virtual ULONG STDMETHODCALLTYPE AddRef();
    virtual ULONG STDMETHODCALLTYPE Release();
    STDMETHOD(GetTypeInfoCount)(UINT* pctinfo);
    STDMETHOD(GetTypeInfo)(UINT itinfo, LCID lcid, ITypeInfo**
        pptinfo);
    STDMETHOD(GetIDsOfNames)(REFIID riid, LPOLESTR* rgszNames, UINT
        cNames, LCID lcid, DISPID* rgdispid);
    STDMETHOD(Invoke)(DISPID dispidMember, REFIID riid, LCID lcid,
        WORD wFlags, DISPPARAMS* pdispparams, VARIANT* pvarResult,
        EXCEPINFO* pexcepinfo, UINT* puArgErr);
};
```

Notice that the `IDispEventSimpleImpl` class provides an implementation of the `_LocDEQueryInterface`, `AddRef`, and `Release` methods that it inherited from its `_IDispEvent` base class. Notice as well that the next four virtual methods are the standard `IDispatch` interface methods. The `IDispEventSimpleImpl` class now has the proper vtable to support `IDispatch`. It cannot simply derive from `IDispatch` to obtain the vtable because the class needs to provide a specialized version of `QueryInterface`.

The `IDispEventSimpleImpl` class implements the `_LocDEQueryInterface` method such that each event sink is a separate COM identity from that of the deriving class. The event sink object is supposed to respond positively to requests for its source dispatch interface ID, the `IUnknown` interface, the `IDispatch` interface, and the GUID contained in the `m_iid` member variable. But the ATL 3.0 version of the code has a few bugs in it.

```
STDMETHOD(_LocDEQueryInterface)(REFIID riid, void ** ppvObject)
{
    if (InlineIsEqualGUID(riid, *pdiid) ||
        InlineIsEqualUnknown(riid) ||
        InlineIsEqualGUID(riid, IID_IDispatch) ||
        InlineIsEqualGUID(riid, m_iid)) {
        if (ppvObject == NULL) return E_POINTER;
        *ppvObject = this;
        AddRef();
#ifdef _ATL_DEBUG_INTERFACES
        _Module.AddThunk((IUnknown**)ppvObject, _T("IDispEventImpl"),
            riid);
```

```
#endif // _ATL_DEBUG_INTERFACES
        return S_OK;
    }
    else
        return E_NOINTERFACE;
}
```

The first problem is that when you are using the `IDispEventSimpleImpl` class directly, the `m_iid` member variable is never initialized. Fortunately, the sink is commonly asked only for its source dispatch interface ID (the `*pdiid` value), its `IUnknown` interface (by the remoting layer), or its `IDispatch` interface (by scripting languages). In these cases the buggy code (the last `InlineIsEqualGUID` call) never gets executed.

However, when a query isn't for one of these three interface GUIDs, the event sink will hand out its interface pointer in response to some random GUID. In Debug builds, uninitialized memory is set, by default, to the bit pattern `0xCD`. For heap allocated instances in debug builds, the `_LocDEQueryInterface` method responds to queries for the GUID {CDCDCDCD-CDCD-CDCD-CDCD-CDCDCDCDCDCD}. In release builds, it responds to a random GUID.

The second problem is that you can use the `IDispEventImpl` class (discussed shortly) without having to specify the source dispatch interface GUID template parameter. The template provides a default value of `IID_NULL`. Composite controls frequently do this. The `m_iid` parameter is then initialized from the type library to the appropriate default source interface GUID. But the code responds to queries for `IID_NULL` (`*pdiid`) when it shouldn't.

The `IDispEventSimpleImpl` class also provides a simple implementation of the `AddRef` and `Release` methods. This permits the class to be used directly as a COM object.

```
virtual ULONG STDMETHODCALLTYPE AddRef()  { return 1; }
virtual ULONG STDMETHODCALLTYPE Release() { return 1; }
```

However, when you compose the class into a more complex ATL-based COM object, the `AddRef` and `Release` methods in the deriving class will be used. In other words, an `AddRef` to the event sink of a typical ATL COM object will call the deriving object's `CComObject::AddRef` method (or whatever your most-derived class is). Watch out for reference-counting cycles due to this. A client holds a reference to the event source, which holds a reference to (nominally) the event sink but which is actually to the client itself.

The `IDispEventSimpleImpl` class implements the `GetTypeInfoCount`, `GetTypeInfo`, and `GetIDsOfNames` methods by returning the error `E_NOTIMPL`.

An event dispatch interface is only required to support the IUnknown methods and the Invoke method.

```
STDMETHOD(GetTypeInfoCount)(UINT* pctinfo)
{return E_NOTIMPL;}

STDMETHOD(GetTypeInfo)(UINT itinfo, LCID lcid, ITypeInfo** pptinfo)
{return E_NOTIMPL;}

STDMETHOD(GetIDsOfNames)(REFIID riid, LPOLESTR* rgszNames,
                         UINT cNames,
                         LCID lcid, DISPID* rgdispid)
{return E_NOTIMPL;}

STDMETHOD(Invoke)(DISPID dispidMember, REFIID riid,
    LCID lcid, WORD wFlags, DISPPARAMS* pdispparams,
    VARIANT* pvar Result, EXCEPINFO* pexcepinfo, UINT* puArgErr);
```

The Invoke method searches the deriving class's event sink map for the appropriate event handler for the current event. It finds the appropriate sink map by calling _GetSinkMap, which is a static member function defined in the deriving class by the BEGIN_SINK_MAP macro (described later in this section). The proper event handler is the entry that has the matching event source ID (nID) as the template invocation, the same source interface IID (pdiid) as the template invocation, and the same DISPID as the argument to Invoke.

When the matching event sink entry specifies an _ATL_FUNC_INFO structure (meaning the event sink entry was defined using the SINK_ENTRY_INFO macro), Invoke uses the structure to call the handler. Otherwise, Invoke calls the Get-FuncInfoFromId virtual function to obtain the required structure. When the Get-FuncInfoFromId function fails, Invoke silently returns S_OK. This is as it should be because an event handler must respond with S_OK to events the handler doesn't recognize.

You must override the GetFuncInfoFromId method when using the SINK_ENTRY_EX macro with the IDispEventSimpleImpl class. The default implementation silently fails:

```
virtual HRESULT GetFuncInfoFromId(const IID& iid,
                                  DISPID dispidMember,
                                  LCID lcid, _ATL_FUNC_INFO& info)
{ return E_NOTIMPL; }
```

But this does mean that if you use the `IDispEventSimpleImpl` class directly, and you specify an event handler using the `SINK_ENTRY_EX` macro, and you forget to override the `GetFuncInfoFromId` method or implement it incorrectly, everything compiles cleanly but *your event handler will never be called.*

The `IDispEventSimpleImpl` class provides some overloaded helper methods for establishing and breaking a connection to an event source. The following two methods establish and break a connection between the current sink and the specified event interface (`piid`) on the specified event source (`pUnk`).

```
//Helpers for sinking events on random IUnknown*
HRESULT DispEventAdvise(IUnknown* pUnk, const IID* piid)
{
    ATLASSERT(m_dwEventCookie == 0xFEFEFEFE);
    return AtlAdvise(pUnk, (IUnknown*)this, *piid, &m_dwEventCookie);
}
HRESULT DispEventUnadvise(IUnknown* pUnk, const IID* piid)
{
    HRESULT hr = AtlUnadvise(pUnk, *piid, m_dwEventCookie);
    m_dwEventCookie = 0xFEFEFEFE;
    return hr;
}
```

The next two methods establish and break a connection between the current sink and the specified event source using the sink's dispatch interface.

```
HRESULT DispEventAdvise(IUnknown* pUnk)
{
    return _IDispEvent::DispEventAdvise(pUnk, pdiid);
}
HRESULT DispEventUnadvise(IUnknown* pUnk)
{
    return _IDispEvent::DispEventUnadvise(pUnk, pdiid);
}
```

The Sink Map: Associated Structure, Macros, and the _GetSinkMap Method

The sink map is an array of _ATL_EVENT_ENTRY structures. The structure contains the following fields:

nControlID   The event source identifier; control ID for contained controls

piid   The source dispatch interface IID

nOffset	The offset of the event sink implementation from the deriving class
dispid	The event callback dispatch ID
pfn	The member function pointer of the event handler to invoke
pInfo	The _ATL_FUNC_INFO structure used for the event handler call

```
template <class T>
struct _ATL_EVENT_ENTRY
{
    UINT nControlID;              //ID identifying object instance
    const IID* piid;             //dispinterface IID
    int nOffset;                 //offset of dispinterface from this pointer
    DISPID dispid;               //DISPID of method/property
    void (__stdcall T::*pfn)();  //method to invoke
    _ATL_FUNC_INFO* pInfo;       //pointer to info structure
};
```

When you use the BEGIN_SINK_MAP macro, you define a static member function in your class called _GetSinkMap. It returns the address of the array of _ATL _EVENT_ENTRY structures.

```
#define BEGIN_SINK_MAP(_class)\
    static const _ATL_EVENT_ENTRY<_class>* _GetSinkMap()\
    {\
        typedef _class _atl_event_classtype;\
        static const _ATL_EVENT_ENTRY<_class> map[] = {
```

Each SINK_ENTRY_INFO macro adds one _ATL_EVENT_ENTRY structure to the array.

```
#define SINK_ENTRY_INFO(id, iid, dispid, fn, info) \
{id, &iid,
(int)(static_cast<_IDispEventLocator<id, &iid>*>
  ((_atl_event_classtype*)8))-8,
dispid, (void (__stdcall _atl_event_classtype::*)())fn, info},
```

Two aspects of the macro are a little unusual. The following expression computes the offset of the _IDispEventLocator<id, &iid> base class with respect to your deriving class (the class containing the sink map). This allows us to find the appropriate event sink referenced by the sink map entry.

```
(int)(static_cast<_IDispEventLocator<id, &iid>*>
                                 (_atl_event_classtype*)8))-8
```

The following cast saves the event handler function address as a pointer to a member function.

```
(void (__stdcall _atl_event_classtype::*)()) fn
```

The SINK_ENTRY_EX macro is the same as the SINK_ENTRY_INFO macro with a NULL pointer for the function information structure. The SINK_ENTRY macro is the same as the SINK_ENTRY_INFO macro with IID_NULL for the dispatch interface and a NULL pointer for the function information structure.

```
#define SINK_ENTRY_EX(id, iid, dispid, fn)\
  SINK_ENTRY_INFO(id, iid, dispid, fn, NULL)
#define SINK_ENTRY(id, dispid, fn)\
  SINK_ENTRY_EX(id, IID_NULL, dispid, fn)
```

The END_SINK_MAP macro ends the array and completes the _GetSinkMap function implementation.

```
#define END_SINK_MAP() {0, NULL, 0, 0, NULL, NULL} }; return map;}
```

The _IDispEventImpl Class

Finally, we come to the IDispEventImpl class. This is the class used by the code generation wizards. It derives from the IDispEventSimpleImpl class and therefore inherits all the functionality previously discussed. The additional template parameters specify a type library that describes the source dispatch interface for the event sink.

```
template <UINT nID, class T, const IID* pdiid = &IID_NULL,
         const GUID* plibid = &GUID_NULL, WORD wMajor = 0,
         WORD wMinor = 0,
         class tihclass = CComTypeInfoHolder>
class ATL_NO_VTABLE IDispEventImpl :
         public IDispEventSimpleImpl<nID, T, pdiid>
```

The main feature of the `IDispEventImpl` class is that it uses the type information to implement functionality missing in the base class. The class implements the `GetTypeInfoCount`, `GetTypeInfo`, and `GetIDsOfNames` methods using the type library via a `CComTypeInfoHolder` object.

```
STDMETHOD(GetTypeInfoCount)(UINT* pctinfo)
  {*pctinfo = 1; return S_OK;}
STDMETHOD(GetTypeInfo)(UINT itinfo, LCID lcid, ITypeInfo** pptinfo)
    {return _tih.GetTypeInfo(itinfo, lcid, pptinfo);}
STDMETHOD(GetIDsOfNames)(REFIID riid, LPOLESTR* rgszNames,
                         UINT cNames,
                         LCID lcid, DISPID* rgdispid)
{return _tih.GetIDsOfNames(riid, rgszNames, cNames, lcid, rgdispid);}
```

It also overrides the `GetFuncInfoFromId` method and initializes an `_ATL_FUNC _INFO` structure using the information provided in the type library.

```
//Helper for finding the function index for a DISPID
HRESULT GetFuncInfoFromId(const IID& /*iid*/, DISPID dispidMember,
                          LCID lcid, _ATL_FUNC_INFO& info);
```

Summary

The connection point protocol defines a mechanism for a client interested in receiving event callbacks to pass its event sink interface pointer to an event source. Neither the client nor the event source needs to be written with knowledge of each other. Objects hosted on a web page or, more generally, objects used by scripting languages, must use the connection points protocol to fire events to the scripting engine. Also, ActiveX controls fire their events using the connection points protocol. While this protocol is acceptable for intra-apartment use, it is inefficient (when considering round-trips) for use across an apartment boundary.

ATL provides the `IDispEvent` and `IDispEventsSimple` classes for a client object to use to receive event callbacks. Additionally, ATL provides the Connection Points Proxy Generator so you can easily generate a class that manages a connection point and contains helper methods to fire the events to all connected clients.

9 | Windowing

ATL is not simply a set of wrapper classes for COM. In the same style, it also wraps the section of the Win32 API relating to creating and manipulating windows, dialogs, and Windows controls. In addition to basic support to remove the drudgery of Windows programming, the ATL windowing classes include such advanced features as subclassing and superclassing. Further, this window support forms the basis for both COM controls and COM control containment, covered in the following chapters.

The Structure of a Windows Application

A standard Windows application consists of several well-known elements, as follows:

- The entry point, `_tWinMain`, which provides the `HINSTANCE` of the application, the command-line arguments, and the flag indicating how to show the main window.
- A call to `RegisterClass` to register the main window class.
- A call to `CreateWindow` to create the main window.
- A call to `ShowWindow` and `UpdateWindow` to show the main window.
- A message loop to dispatch messages.
- A procedure to handle the main window's messages.
- A set of message handlers for messages the window is interested in handling.
- A call to `DefWindowProc` to let Windows handle messages we're not interested in.
- A call to `PostQuitMessage` once the main window has been destroyed.

A bare-bones example follows:

```
#include "stdafx.h" // Includes windows.h and tchar.h
LRESULT CALLBACK WndProc(HWND, UINT, WPARAM, LPARAM);
```

```cpp
// Entry point
int APIENTRY _tWinMain(HINSTANCE hinst,
                       HINSTANCE /*hinstPrev*/,
                       LPTSTR    pszCmdLine,
                       int       nCmdShow)
{
  // Register the main window class
  LPCTSTR      pszMainWndClass = __T("WindowsApp");
  WNDCLASSEX   wc = { sizeof(WNDCLASSEX) };
  wc.style          = CS_HREDRAW | CS_VREDRAW;
  wc.hInstance      = hinst;
  wc.hIcon          = LoadIcon(0, IDI_APPLICATION);
  wc.hCursor        = LoadCursor(0, IDC_ARROW);
  wc.hbrBackground  = (HBRUSH)(COLOR_WINDOW+1);
  wc.lpszClassName  = pszMainWndClass;
  wc.lpfnWndProc    = WndProc;
  if( !RegisterClassEx(&wc) ) return -1;

  // Create the main window
  HWND     hwnd = CreateWindowEx(WS_EX_CLIENTEDGE,
                                 pszMainWndClass,
                                 __T("Windows Application"),
                                 WS_OVERLAPPEDWINDOW,
                                 CW_USEDEFAULT, 0,
                                 CW_USEDEFAULT, 0,
                                 0, 0, hinst, 0);
  if( !hwnd ) return -1;

  // Show the main window
  ShowWindow(hwnd, nCmdShow);
  UpdateWindow(hwnd);

  // Main message loop
  MSG msg;
  while( GetMessage(&msg, 0, 0, 0) ) {
    TranslateMessage(&msg);
    DispatchMessage(&msg);
  }

  return msg.wParam;
}
```

```
// Windows procedure
LRESULT CALLBACK WndProc(HWND hwnd, UINT nMsg,
                        WPARAM wparam, LPARAM lparam)
{
  switch( nMsg )
  {
  // Message handlers for messages we're interested in
  case WM_PAINT: {
    PAINTSTRUCT ps;
    HDC         hdc = BeginPaint(hwnd, &ps);
    RECT        rect; GetClientRect(hwnd, &rect);
    DrawText(hdc, __T("Hello, Windows"), -1, &rect,
             DT_CENTER | DT_VCENTER | DT_SINGLELINE);
    EndPaint(hwnd, &ps);
  }
  break;

  // Post the quit message when main window is destroyed
  case WM_DESTROY:
    PostQuitMessage(0);
  break;

  // Let Windows handle message we don't want
  default:
    return DefWindowProc(hwnd, nMsg, wparam, lparam);
  break;
  }

  return 0;
}
```

All Windows applications have similar requirements. These requirements can be expressed in procedural Win32 calls, as the example just showed. However, when procedural calls model an underlying object model, C++ programmers feel compelled to wrap those calls behind member functions. The windowing part of the Win32 API (often called User32) is clearly modeling an underlying object model consisting of window classes (represented by the WNDCLASSEX structure), window objects (represented by the HWND), and member function invocation (represented by calls to the WndProc). For C++ programmers averse to the schism between their preferred object model and that of User32, ATL provides a small set of windowing classes, as shown in Figure 9.1. The classes in bold, CWindow,

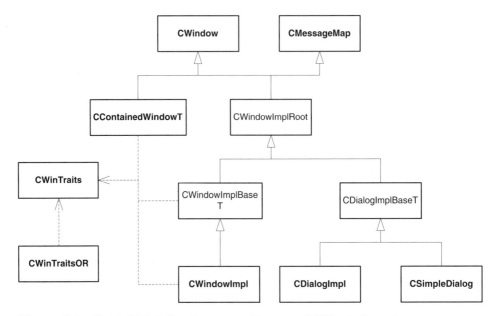

Figure 9.1. Unified Modeling Language diagram of ATL window classes

`CWindowImpl`, `CWinTraits`, `CWinTraitsOR`, `CDialogImpl`, `CSimpleDialog`, and `CContainedWindowT`, are the most important. The others, `CWindowImpl-Root`, `CWindowImplBaseT`, and `CDialogImplBaseT`, are helper classes to separate parameterized code from invariant code. This separation helps to reduce template-related code bloat, but these classes are not a fundamental part of the ATL windowing classes. The former classes will form the discussion for the bulk of the rest of this chapter.

CWindow

An HWND Wrapper

The most basic of the windowing classes in ATL is `CWindow`. Its chief job is to hold an `HWND`, which it can obtain via several member functions:

```
class CWindow {
public:
 CWindow(HWND hWnd = NULL)
 { m_hWnd = hWnd; }

 CWindow& operator=(HWND hWnd)
 { m_hWnd = hWnd; return *this; }
```

```
void Attach(HWND hWndNew)
{ m_hWnd = hWndNew; }

HWND Create(LPCTSTR lpstrWndClass, HWND hWndParent, RECT& rcPos,
            LPCTSTR szWindowName = NULL, DWORD dwStyle = 0,
            DWORD dwExStyle = 0, UINT nID = 0,
            LPVOID lpCreateParam = NULL) {
  // Calls CreateWindowEx and caches result in m_hWnd
  return m_hWnd;
}

HWND Create(LPCTSTR lpstrWndClass, HWND hWndParent,
            LPRECT lpRect = NULL,
            LPCTSTR szWindowName = NULL, DWORD dwStyle = 0,
            DWORD dwExStyle = 0, HMENU hMenu = NULL,
            LPVOID lpCreateParam = NULL) {
  // Calls CreateWindowEx and caches result in m_hWnd
  return m_hWnd;
}
...
};
```

The HWND itself is available either as a public data member or via the HWND type-cast operator:

```
class CWindow {
public:
 HWND m_hWnd;
 operator HWND() const { return m_hWnd; }
...
};
```

If you'd like to clear the HWND, you can set the m_hWnd manually or use the Detach member function:

```
inline HWND CWindow::Detach() {
    HWND hWnd = m_hWnd;
    m_hWnd = NULL;
    return hWnd;
}
```

A `CWindow` object represents a wrapper around the HWND, not the window itself. The `CWindow` destructor will not destroy the underlying window. Hence, there's really no need to ever call `Detach`.

HWND Wrapper Functions

Once the `CWindow` object has an HWND, you can make use of the rest of the `CWindow` class member functions. The purpose of `CWindow` is to act as a wrapper for all the functions of the User32 API. For every function that takes an HWND as the first argument, the `CWindow` class has a corresponding member function that uses the cached `m_hWnd`. For example, instead of calling `SetWindowText`,

```
void SayHello(HWND hwnd) {
  SetWindowText(hwnd, __T("Hello"));
}
```

you would use the `SetWindowText` member function:

```
void SayHello(HWND hwnd) {
  CWindow wnd = hwnd;
  wnd.SetWindowText(__T("Hello"));
}
```

When I said all the User32 functions that take an HWND as a first parameter, I meant *all*. As near as I can tell, with the exception of one function (`SetForegroundWindow`), the entire windowing API is represented as a member function of `CWindow`. The `CWindow` class declaration comments break the wrapped functions down into several categories:

Alert functions	Attributes	Caret functions
Clipboard functions	Coordinate mapping functions	Dialog box item functions
Font functions	Help functions	Hot key functions
Icon functions	Menu functions	Message functions
Miscellaneous operations	Scrolling functions	Timer functions
Update and painting functions	Window access functions	Window size and position functions
Window state functions	Window text functions	Window tree access

HWND Helper Functions

The vast majority of the CWindow member functions are merely inline wrappers on the raw functions. This means you get the syntactic convenience of member functions without any additional runtime overhead. In addition, there are several helper functions that encapsulate common functionality that we often end up writing time and again above and beyond straight wrappers:

```
class CWindow {
...
  DWORD GetStyle() const;
  DWORD GetExStyle() const;
  BOOL  ModifyStyle(DWORD dwRemove, DWORD dwAdd, UINT nFlags = 0);
  BOOL  ModifyStyleEx(DWORD dwRemove, DWORD dwAdd, UINT nFlags = 0);
  BOOL  ResizeClient(int nWidth, int nHeight, BOOL bRedraw = TRUE);
  HWND  GetDescendantWindow(int nID) const;
  BOOL  CenterWindow(HWND hWndCenter = NULL);
  BOOL  GetWindowText(BSTR* pbstrText);
  BOOL  GetWindowText(BSTR& bstrText);
  HWND  GetTopLevelParent() const;
  HWND  GetTopLevelWindow() const;
...
};
```

Likewise, CWindow provides a number of type-safe wrappers for calling Send-Message for common messages, performing the error-prone casting chores for us:

```
class CWindow {
...
  void  SetFont(HFONT hFont, BOOL bRedraw = TRUE);
  HFONT GetFont() const;
  void  Print(HDC hDC, DWORD dwFlags) const;
  void  PrintClient(HDC hDC, DWORD dwFlags) const;
  void  SetRedraw(BOOL bRedraw = TRUE);
  HICON SetIcon(HICON hIcon, BOOL bBigIcon = TRUE);
  HICON GetIcon(BOOL bBigIcon = TRUE) const;
  int   SetHotKey(WORD wVirtualKeyCode, WORD wModifiers);
  DWORD GetHotKey() const;
  void  NextDlgCtrl() const;
  void  PrevDlgCtrl() const;
```

```
void   GotoDlgCtrl(HWND hWndCtrl) const;
void   SendMessageToDescendants(UINT message, WPARAM wParam = 0,
                                LPARAM lParam = 0, BOOL bDeep = TRUE);
...
};
```

Using CWindow

Before we can put the CWindow class to use in our sample Windows application, we have to establish support for the ATL window classes in our Win32 application. The first step is to add the following lines to the precompiled header (called stdafx.h):

```
// Needed to use ATL windowing classes
#include <atlbase.h>
extern CComModule _Module;
#include <atlwin.h>
```

The ATL windowing classes are defined in atlwin.h, but before we can include that, we have two responsibilities. The first is to include atlbase.h, which atl-win.h depends on. The second is to declare an instance of a CComModule called _Module, just like an ATL server. Very much in the same way that all MFC programs have a single global instance of the CWinApp class, all ATL windowing applications must have a single global instance of a module called _Module. The module's job in a windowing application is mostly to hold onto the application's HINSTANCE, which we must remember to provide in a call to the CComModule member function Init. The following modified _tWinMain implementation shows the initialization and termination of the module as well as using a CWindow instead of an HWND:

```
#include "stdafx.h"
LRESULT CALLBACK WndProc(HWND, UINT, WPARAM, LPARAM);

// The single, global ATL module
CComModule _Module;

// Entry point
int APIENTRY _tWinMain(HINSTANCE hinst,
                       HINSTANCE /*hinstPrev*/,
                       LPTSTR    pszCmdLine,
                       int       nCmdShow)
{
```

```
    // Initialize the ATL module
    _Module.Init(0, hinst);

    // Register the main window class
    ...

    // Create the main window
    CWindow wnd;
    wnd.Create(pszMainWndClass, 0, CWindow::rcDefault,
            _T("Windows Application"),
            WS_OVERLAPPEDWINDOW, WS_EX_CLIENTEDGE);
    if( !wnd ) return -1;

    // Show the main window
    wnd.CenterWindow();
    wnd.ShowWindow(nCmdShow);
    wnd.UpdateWindow();

    // Main message loop
    ...

    // Shut down the ATL module
    _Module.Term();

    return msg.wParam;
}
```

Notice that the structure of the program remains the same. The only difference is that we're calling member functions instead of global functions. The WndProc can be similarly updated:

```
LRESULT CALLBACK WndProc(HWND hwnd, UINT nMsg,
                         WPARAM wparam, LPARAM lparam)
{
 switch( nMsg )  {
 // WM_PAINT handler
 case WM_PAINT: {
   PAINTSTRUCT ps;
   CWindow     wnd(hwnd);
   HDC         hdc = wnd.BeginPaint(&ps);
```

```
RECT        rect; wnd.GetClientRect(&rect);
 DrawText(hdc, __T("Hello, Windows"), -1, &rect,
          DT_CENTER | DT_VCENTER | DT_SINGLELINE);
 wnd.EndPaint(&ps);
}
break;

... // The rest is the same
}

return 0;
}
```

CWindow is a step in the right direction. Instead of calling global functions and passing a handle, we're now able to call member functions on an object. However, we're still registering a Windows class instead of creating a C++ class and we're still handling callbacks via a WndProc instead of via member functions. To completely fulfill our desires, we need the next most important class in the ATL windowing hierarchy, CWindowImpl.

CWindowImpl

The Window Class

The CWindowImpl class derives ultimately from CWindow and provides two additional features, window class registration and message handling. I'll discuss message handling after we explore how CWindowImpl manages the window class. First, notice that, unlike CWindow, the CWindowImpl member function Create doesn't take the name of a window class:

```
template <class T, class TBase = CWindow,
         class TWinTraits = CControlWinTraits>
         class ATL_NO_VTABLE CWindowImpl :
  public CWindowImplBaseT < TBase, TWinTraits >
{
public:
     DECLARE_WND_CLASS(NULL)

     HWND Create(HWND hWndParent, RECT& rcPos,
              LPCTSTR szWindowName = NULL,
```

```
                    DWORD dwStyle = 0, DWORD dwExStyle = 0,
                    UINT nID = 0, LPVOID lpCreateParam = NULL);
};
```

Instead of passing the name of the window class, the name of the window class is
provided in the DECLARE_WND_CLASS macro. A value of NULL will cause ATL to
generate a window class of the form ATL<8-digit number>. We could declare
a CWindowImpl-based class using the same window class name we registered using RegisterClass. However, that's not necessary. It's far more convenient to let
ATL register the window class the first time we call Create on an instance of our
CWindowImpl-derived class. This initial window class registration is done in the
implementation of CWindowImpl::Create:

```
HWND CWindowImpl::Create(HWND hWndParent, RECT& rcPos,
                    LPCTSTR szWindowName = NULL,
                    DWORD dwStyle = 0, DWORD dwExStyle = 0,
                    UINT nID = 0, LPVOID lpCreateParam = NULL)
{
   // Generate a class name if one is not provided
   if (T::GetWndClassInfo().m_lpszOrigName == NULL)
    T::GetWndClassInfo().m_lpszOrigName = GetWndClassName();
   // Register the window class if it hasn't already been registered
   ATOM atom = T::GetWndClassInfo().Register(&m_pfnSuperWindowProc);

   ...
}
```

Assuming a class derived from CWindowImpl, our _tWinMain has gotten much
smaller:

```
class CMainWindow : public CWindowImpl<CMainWindow> {...};

// Entry point
int APIENTRY _tWinMain(HINSTANCE hinst,
                    HINSTANCE /*hinstPrev*/,
                    LPTSTR    pszCmdLine,
                    int       nCmdShow)
{
 // Initialize the ATL module
 ...
```

```
// Create the main window
CMainWindow wnd;
wnd.Create(0, CWindow::rcDefault, __T("Windows Application"),
           WS_OVERLAPPEDWINDOW, WS_EX_CLIENTEDGE);
if( !wnd ) return -1;

// Show the main window, run the message look, shut down the module
...

return msg.wParam;
}
```

Modifying the Window Class

Each CWindowImpl class maintains a static data structure called a CWndClass-Info, which is a type definition for either an _ATL_WNDCLASSINFOA or an _ATL _WNDCLASSINFOW structure, depending on whether you're doing a Unicode build or not. The ANSI version is shown here:

```
struct _ATL_WNDCLASSINFOA {
        WNDCLASSEXA m_wc;
        LPCSTR m_lpszOrigName;
        WNDPROC pWndProc;
        LPCSTR m_lpszCursorID;
        BOOL m_bSystemCursor;
        ATOM m_atom;
        CHAR m_szAutoName[13];
        ATOM Register(WNDPROC* p)
        { return AtlModuleRegisterWndClassInfoA(&_Module, this, p); }
};
```

The most important members of this structure are m_wc and m_atom. The m_wc member represents the window class structure, that is, what you would use to register a class if you were doing it by hand. The m_atom member is used to determine if the class has been already been registered or not. This is useful if you'd like to make changes to m_wc before the class has been registered.

Each class derived from CWindowImpl gets an instance of CWndClassInfo in the base class from the use of the DECLARE_WND_CLASS macro, defined as follows:

```
#define DECLARE_WND_CLASS(WndClassName) \
static CWndClassInfo& GetWndClassInfo() { \
  static CWndClassInfo wc = { \
```

```
  { sizeof(WNDCLASSEX), CS_HREDRAW | CS_VREDRAW | CS_DBLCLKS, \
    StartWindowProc, 0, 0, NULL, NULL, NULL, \
    (HBRUSH)(COLOR_WINDOW + 1), NULL, WndClassName, NULL \
  }, \
  NULL, NULL, IDC_ARROW, TRUE, 0, _T("") \
}; \
return wc; \
}
```

This macro defines a function called `GetWndClassInfo` and initializes the values to commonly used defaults. If you'd like to also specify the class style and the background color, you can use another macro called DECLARE_WND_CLASS_EX:

```
#define DECLARE_WND_CLASS_EX(WndClassName, style, bkgnd) \
static CWndClassInfo& GetWndClassInfo() { \
 static CWndClassInfo wc = { \
   { sizeof(WNDCLASSEX), style, StartWindowProc, \
    0, 0, NULL, NULL, NULL, (HBRUSH)(bkgnd + 1), NULL, WndClassName, \
      NULL \
   }, \
   NULL, NULL, IDC_ARROW, TRUE, 0, _T("") \
 }; \
 return wc; \
}
```

However, neither macro provides enough flexibility to set all the window class information you'd like, for example, large and small icons, cursor, or background brush. While it's possible to define an entire set of macros in the same vein as DECLARE_WND_CLASS, the combinations of what you'd like to set and what you'd like to leave as a default value quickly get out of hand. Frankly, it's easier to modify the `CWndClassInfo` structure directly using the `GetWndClassInfo` function. The `CWindowImpl`-derived class's constructor is a good place to do that, using the `m_atom` variable to determine if the window class has already been registered. For example:

```
CMainWindow() {
    // Retrieve the window class information
    CWndClassInfo& wci = GetWndClassInfo();

    // If the wc hasn't already been registered, update it
    if( !wci.m_atom ) {
```

```
            wci.m_wc.hIcon = LoadIcon(_Module.GetResourceInstance(),
                                 MAKEINTRESOURCE(IDI_BAREBONES));
            wci.m_wc.hIconSm = (HICON)::LoadImage(_Module.GetResource-
                                        Instance(),
                                     MAKEINTRESOURCE(IDI_BAREBONES),
                                     IMAGE_ICON, 16, 16,
                                     LR_DEFAULTCOLOR);
            wci.m_wc.hbrBackground = CreateHatchBrush(HS_DIAGCROSS, RGB(0, 0,
                                        255));
        }
    }
```

Setting the WNDCLASSEX member directly will work for most of the members of the m_wc member of CWndClassInfo. However, for some reason, the ATL team decided to treat cursors differently. For cursors, the CWndClassInfo structure has two members, m_lpszCursorID and m_bSystemCursor, that will be used to override whatever is set in the hCursor member of m_wc. For example, to set a cursor from the available system cursors, you must do the following:

```
// Can't do this:
// wci.m_wc.hCursor = LoadCursor(0, MAKEINTRESOURCE(IDC_BAREBONES));

// Must do this:
wci.m_bSystemCursor = TRUE;
wci.m_lpszCursorID = IDC_CROSS;
```

Likewise, to load a custom cursor, the following is required:

```
// Can't do this:
// wci.m_wc.hCursor = LoadCursor(_Module.GetResourceInstance(),
//                          MAKEINTRESOURCE(IDC_BAREBONES));

// Must do this:
wci.m_bSystemCursor = FALSE;
wci.m_lpszCursorID = MAKEINTRESOURCE(IDC_BAREBONES);
```

Remember to keep this special treatment of cursors in mind when creating CWindowImpl-derived classes with custom cursors.

Window Traits

In the same way that an icon and a cursor are coupled with a window class, often it makes sense for the styles and the extended styles to be coupled as well. For example, frame windows have different styles than child windows. When we develop a window class, we typically know how it's going to be used; for example, our CMain-Window class is going to be used as a frame window and WS_OVERLAPPEDWINDOW is going to be part of the styles for every instance of CMainWindow. Unfortunately, there is no way to set default styles for a window class in the Win32 API. Instead, the window styles have to be specified in every call to CreateWindowEx. To allow default styles and extended styles to be coupled with a window class, ATL allows you to group styles together and reuse them in an instance of the CWinTrait class:

```
template <DWORD t_dwStyle = 0, DWORD t_dwExStyle = 0>
class CWinTraits {
public:
 static DWORD GetWndStyle(DWORD dwStyle)
 { return dwStyle == 0 ? t_dwStyle : dwStyle; }
 static DWORD GetWndExStyle(DWORD dwExStyle)
 { return dwExStyle == 0 ? t_dwExStyle : dwExStyle; }
};
```

As you can see, the CWinTrait class holds a set of styles and extended styles. When combined with a style or an extended style DWORD, it will hand out the passed DWORD if it is nonzero; otherwise, it will hand out its own value. For example, to bundle my preferred styles together into a window trait, I would do the following:

```
typedef CWinTraits<WS_OVERLAPPEDWINDOW, WS_EX_CLIENTEDGE>
  CMainWinTraits;
```

A window traits class can be associated with a CWindowImpl by passing it as a template parameter:

```
class CMainWindow : public CWindowImpl<CMainWindow, CWindow,
  CMainWinTraits>
{...};
```

Now, when creating instances of a CWindowImpl-derived class, I can be explicit about what parameters I want, or, by passing 0 for the style and/or the extended style, I can get the window traits style associated with the class. For example:

```
// Use the default value of 0 for the style and the
// extended style to get the window traits for this class.
wnd.Create(0, CWindow::rcDefault, __T("Windows Application"));
```

Because I've used a CWinTrait class to group together related styles and extended styles, if I need to change a style in a trait, the change will be propagated to all instances of any class that uses that trait. This saves me from finding the instances and manually changing them one at a time. For the three most common kinds of windows—frame windows, child windows, and MDI child windows—ATL comes with three built-in window traits classes:

```
typedef
CWinTraits<WS_CHILD | WS_VISIBLE | WS_CLIPCHILDREN | WS_CLIPSIBLINGS,
  0>CControlWinTraits;

typedef
CWinTraits<WS_OVERLAPPEDWINDOW | WS_CLIPCHILDREN | WS_CLIPSIBLINGS,
          WS_EX_APPWINDOW | WS_EX_WINDOWEDGE>
CFrameWinTraits;

typedef
CWinTraits<WS_OVERLAPPEDWINDOW | WS_CHILD | WS_VISIBLE |
  WS_CLIPCHILDREN | WS_CLIPSIBLINGS, WS_EX_MDICHILD>
CMDIChildWinTraits;
```

If you'd like to leverage the styles of an existing window traits class but add styles, you can use the CWindowTraitsOR class:

```
template <DWORD t_dwStyle = 0, DWORD t_dwExStyle = 0,
          class TWinTraits = CControlWinTraits>
class CWinTraitsOR {
public:
 static DWORD GetWndStyle(DWORD dwStyle)
 { return dwStyle | t_dwStyle | TWinTraits::GetWndStyle(dwStyle); }
 static DWORD GetWndExStyle(DWORD dwExStyle)
 { return dwExStyle | t_dwExStyle | TWinTraits::GetWndExStyle
    (dwExStyle); }
};
```

Using CWinTraitsOR, CMainWinTraits can be redefined like so:

```
// Leave CFrameWinTraits styles alone.
// Add the WS_EX_CLIENTEDGE bit to the extended styles.
typedef CWinTraitsOR<0, WS_EX_CLIENTEDGE, CFrameWinTraits>
  CMainWinTraits;
```

The Window Procedure

To handle window messages, every window needs a window procedure. This window procedure is set in the `lpfnWndProc` member of the `WNDCLASSEX` structure used during window registration. You may have noticed that in the expansion of `DECLARE_WND_CLASS` and `DECLARE_WND_CLASS_EX`, the name of the window procedure is `StartWindowProc`. `StartWindowProc` is a static member function of `CWindowImplBase`. Its job is to establish the mapping between the `CWindowImpl`-derived object's `HWND` and the object's `this` pointer. The goal is to handle calls made by Windows to a window procedure global function and map them to a member function of an object. The mapping between `HWND` and an object's `this` pointer is done by the `StartWindowProc` when handling the first window message.[1] After the new `HWND` is cached in the `CWindowImpl`-derived object's member data, the object's real window procedure is substituted for the `StartWindowProc`, as shown here:

```
template <class TBase, class TWinTraits>
LRESULT CALLBACK
CWindowImplBaseT<TBase, TWinTraits>::StartWindowProc(HWND hWnd,
                                                     UINT uMsg,
                                                     WPARAM wParam,
                                                     LPARAM lParam) {
  CWindowImplBaseT< TBase, TWinTraits >* pThis =
    (CWindowImplBaseT<TBase, TWinTraits>*)
    _Module.ExtractCreateWnd Data();
  ATLASSERT(pThis != NULL);
  pThis->m_hWnd = hWnd;
  pThis->m_thunk.Init(pThis->GetWindowProc(), pThis);
  WNDPROC pProc = (WNDPROC)&(pThis->m_thunk.thunk);
  WNDPROC pOldProc =
    (WNDPROC)::SetWindowLong(hWnd, GWL_WNDPROC, (LONG)pProc);
  return pProc(hWnd, uMsg, wParam, lParam);
}
```

---

[1] The first window message is the moment when Windows first communicates the new `HWND` to the application. This happens before `CreateWindow[Ex]` returns with the `HWND`.

The m_thunk member is the interesting part. The ATL team had several different options they could have used to map the HWND associated with each incoming window message to the object's this pointer responsible for handling the message. They could have kept a global table that mapped HWNDs to this pointers, but the lookup time would grow as the number of windows grew. They could have tucked the this pointer into the window data,[2] but then the application/component developer might unwittingly overwrite the data when doing work with window data himself or herself. Plus, empirically, this lookup is not as fast as one might like when handling many messages per second.

Instead, the ATL team used a technique based on a set of assembly (ASM) instructions grouped together into a *thunk*, avoiding any lookup at all. The term *thunk* is overused in Windows, but in this case, the thunk is a group of ASM instructions that keeps track of a CWindowImpl object's this pointer and acts like a function, specifically, a window procedure. Each CWindowImpl object gets its own thunk; that is, each object has its own window procedure. How a thunk can seem like an object (remember, it holds another object's this pointer) and a function at the same time gets to the core of why ATL uses ASM to implement thunks. C++ does not treat a function as a first-class object. For example, you cannot give a function member data nor can you create new instances of functions at runtime. However, most CPUs are perfectly happy to let you compose machine code on the fly and execute it. That's what a thunk is: machine instructions built on the fly, one per window. For example, imagine two windows of the same class created like so:

```
class CMyWindow : public CWindowImpl<CMyWindow> {...};
CMyWindow wnd1; wnd1.Create(...);
CMyWindow wnd2; wnd2.Create(...);
```

Figure 9.2 shows the per-window-class and per-HWND data maintained by Windows, the thunks, and the CWindowImpl objects that would result from this example code.

The thunk's job is to replace the HWND on the stack with the CWindowImpl object's this pointer before calling the CWindowImpl static member function WindowProc to further process the message. The ASM instructions that replace the HWND with the object's this pointer are kept in a data structure called the _WndProcThunk:

```
#if defined(_M_IX86)
#pragma pack(push,1)
```

---

[2]A window may maintain extra information via the cbWndExtra member of the WNDCLASS[EX] structure or via the GetWindowLong/SetWindowLong family of functions.

```
struct _WndProcThunk {
 DWORD  m_mov;      // mov dword ptr [esp+0x4], pThis (esp+0x4 is hWnd)
 DWORD  m_this;     //
 BYTE   m_jmp;      // jmp WndProc
 DWORD  m_relproc;  // relative jmp
};
#pragma pack(pop)
#elif defined (_M_ALPHA)
... // Alpha code elided for clarity
#else
#error Only Alpha and X86 supported
#endif
```

This data structure is kept per CWindowImpl-derived object and is initialized by StartWindowProc with the object's this pointer and the address of the static member function used as the window procedure. The m_thunk member that

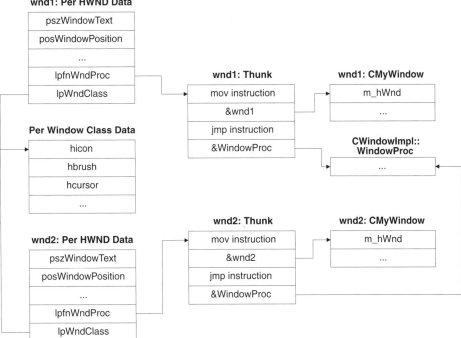

Figure 9.2. One thunk per CWindowImpl object

StartWindowProc initializes and uses as the thunking window procedure is an instance of the CWndProcThunk class:

```
class CWndProcThunk {
public:
    union {
        _AtlCreateWndData cd;
        _WndProcThunk thunk;
    };
    void Init(WNDPROC proc, void* pThis) {
#if defined (_M_IX86)
        thunk.m_mov = 0x042444C7;  //C7 44 24 0C
        thunk.m_this = (DWORD)pThis;
        thunk.m_jmp = 0xe9;
        thunk.m_relproc = (int)proc-((int)this+sizeof
            (_WndProcThunk));
#elif defined (_M_ALPHA)
... // Alpha code elided for clarity
#endif
        // write block from data cache and
        // flush from instruction cache
        FlushInstructionCache(GetCurrentProcess(), &thunk,
            sizeof(thunk));
    }
};
```

Once the thunk has been set up in StartWindowProc, each window message is routed from the CWindowImpl object's thunk to a static member function of CWindowImpl to a member function of the CWindowImpl object itself, as shown in Figure 9.3. On each window message, the thunk removes the HWND as provided by Windows as the first argument and replaces it with the CWindowImpl-derived object's this pointer. Once this first argument has been replaced, the thunk forwards the entire call stack to the actual window procedure. Unless the virtual GetWindowProc function is overridden, the default window procedure is the WindowProc static function shown here:

```
template <class TBase, class TWinTraits>
LRESULT CALLBACK
CWindowImplBaseT< TBase, TWinTraits >::WindowProc(HWND hWnd,
                                                  UINT uMsg,
                                                  WPARAM wParam,
                                                  LPARAM lParam) {
```

```
CWindowImplBaseT< TBase, TWinTraits >* pThis =
 (CWindowImplBaseT< TBase, TWinTraits >*)hWnd;

// set a ptr to this message and save the old value
MSG msg = { pThis->m_hWnd, uMsg, wParam, lParam, 0, { 0, 0 } };
const MSG* pOldMsg = pThis->m_pCurrentMsg;
pThis->m_pCurrentMsg = &msg;

// pass to the message map to process
LRESULT lRes;
BOOL bRet = pThis->ProcessWindowMessage(pThis->m_hWnd, uMsg,
                                        wParam, lParam, lRes, 0);

// restore saved value for the current message
ATLASSERT(pThis->m_pCurrentMsg == &msg);
pThis->m_pCurrentMsg = pOldMsg;

// do the default processing if message was not handled
if(!bRet) {
  if(uMsg != WM_NCDESTROY)
    lRes = pThis->DefWindowProc(uMsg, wParam, lParam);
  else {
```

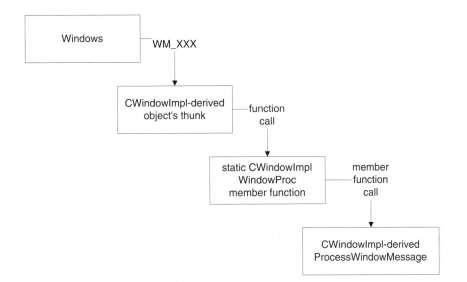

Figure 9.3. Each message is routed through a thunk to map the HWND to the this pointer

```
    // unsubclass, if needed
    LONG pfnWndProc = ::GetWindowLong(pThis->m_hWnd, GWL_WNDPROC);
    lRes = pThis->DefWindowProc(uMsg, wParam, lParam);
    if(pThis->m_pfnSuperWindowProc != ::DefWindowProc &&
        ::GetWindowLong(pThis->m_hWnd, GWL_WNDPROC) == pfnWndProc)
        ::SetWindowLong(pThis->m_hWnd, GWL_WNDPROC,
                        (LONG)pThis->m_pfnSuperWindowProc);

    // clear out window handle
    HWND hWnd = pThis->m_hWnd;
    pThis->m_hWnd = NULL;

    // clean up after window is destroyed
    pThis->OnFinalMessage(hWnd);
    }
  }
  return lRes;
}
```

The first thing WindowProc does is extract the object's this pointer out of the call stack by casting the HWND parameter. Since this HWND parameter has been cached in the object's m_hWnd member, no information is lost. However, if you override GetWindowProc and provide a custom WndProc for use by the window thunk, remember that the HWND is a this pointer, not an HWND.

After obtaining the object's this pointer, WindowProc caches the current message into the m_pCurrentMsg member of the CWindowImpl-derived object. This message is then passed along to the CWindowImpl-derived object's virtual member function ProcessWindowMessage, which must be provided by the deriving class with the following signature:

```
virtual BOOL
ProcessWindowMessage(HWND hWnd, UINT uMsg,
                     WPARAM wParam, LPARAM lParam,
                     LRESULT& lResult, DWORD dwMsgMapID);
```

This is where any message handling is to be done by the object. For example, our CMainWindow could handle window messages like so:

```
class CMainWindow : public CWindowImpl<CMainWindow> {
public:
```

```
    virtual BOOL
    ProcessWindowMessage(HWND hWnd, UINT uMsg,
                         WPARAM wParam, LPARAM lParam,
                         LRESULT& lResult, DWORD /*dwMsgMapID*/) {
    BOOL bHandled = TRUE;
    switch( uMsg ) {
    case WM_PAINT:   lResult = OnPaint(); break;
    case WM_DESTROY: lResult = OnDestroy(); break;
    default:         bHandled = FALSE; break;
    }
    return bHandled;
  }

private:
  LRESULT OnPaint();
  {
    PAINTSTRUCT ps;
    HDC         hdc = BeginPaint(&ps);
    RECT        rect; GetClientRect(&rect);
    DrawText(hdc, __T("Hello, Windows"), -1, &rect,
             DT_CENTER | DT_VCENTER | DT_SINGLELINE);
    EndPaint(&ps);
    return 0;
  }

  LRESULT OnDestroy() {
    PostQuitMessage(0);
    return 0;
  }
};
```

Notice how the message handlers are now member functions instead of global functions. This makes programming a bit more convenient. For example, inside the OnPaint handler, BeginPaint, GetClientRect, and EndPaint all resolve to member functions of the CMainWindow object to which the message has been sent. Also notice that returning FALSE from ProcessWindowMessage is all that is required if the window message is not handled. WindowProc will handle calling DefWindowProc for unhandled messages.

As a further convenience, OnFinalMessage is called by WindowProc after the last message has been handled by the window and after the HWND has been zeroed out. This is handy for shutdown when used on the application's main window. For example, we can remove WM_DESTROY from our switch statement and replace the OnDestroy handler with OnFinalMessage like so:

```
virtual void CMainWindow::OnFinalMessage(HWND /*hwnd*/)
{ PostQuitMessage(0); }
```

As you might imagine, writing the ProcessWindowMessage function is going to be a lot of boilerplate coding, tediously mapping window messages to function names. Soon, I'll show you the message map data structure that will handle this chore for us.

Windows Superclassing

The Windows object model of declaring a window class and creating instances of that class is similar to that of the C++ object model. The WNDCLASSEX structure is to an HWND as a C++ class declaration is to a this pointer. Extending this analogy, Windows *superclassing*[3] is like C++ inheritance. Superclassing is a technique in which the WNDCLASSEX structure for an existing window class is duplicated and given its own name and its own WndProc. When a message is received for that window, it's routed to the new WndProc. If that WndProc decides not to handle that message fully, then, instead of being routed to DefWindowProc, the message is routed to the original WndProc. If you think of the original WndProc as a virtual function, the superclassing window overrides the WndProc and decides on a message-by-message basis whether to let the base class handle the message or not.

The reason for using superclassing is the same reason as for using inheritance of implementation, that is, the base class has some functionality that the deriving class would like to extend. ATL supports superclassing via the DECLARE_WND_SUPERCLASS macro:

```
#define DECLARE_WND_SUPERCLASS(WndClassName, OrigWndClassName) \
static CWndClassInfo& GetWndClassInfo() { \
  static CWndClassInfo wc = { \
    { sizeof(WNDCLASSEX), 0, StartWindowProc, \
      0, 0, NULL, NULL, NULL, NULL, NULL, WndClassName, NULL \
    }, \
    OrigWndClassName, NULL, NULL, TRUE, 0, _T("") \
  }; \
  return wc; \
}
```

---

[3] The theory of Windows superclassing is really beyond the scope of this book. For a more in-depth discussion, see *Win32 Programming*, by Brent Rector and Joe Newcomer (Addison-Wesley, 1997).

The WndClassName is the name of the deriving class's window class. As with DECLARE_WND_CLASS[_EX], to have ATL generate a name, use NULL for this parameter. The OrigWndClassName parameter is the name of the existing window class from which you'd like to "inherit."

For example, the existing edit control uses the ES_NUMBER style to indicate that it should only allow the input of numbers. If you wanted to provide similar functionality but only allow the input of letters, you would have two choices. You could build your own edit control from scratch or you could superclass the existing edit control and handle WM_CHAR messages like so:

```
// Letters-only edit control
class CLetterBox : public CWindowImpl<CLetterBox> {
public:
  DECLARE_WND_SUPERCLASS(0, "EDIT")

  virtual BOOL
  ProcessWindowMessage(HWND hWnd, UINT uMsg,
                       WPARAM wParam, LPARAM lParam,
                       LRESULT& lResult, DWORD /*dwMsgMapID*/) {
    BOOL bHandled = TRUE;
    switch( uMsg ) {
    case WM_CHAR:   lResult = OnChar((TCHAR)wParam, bHandled); break;
    default:        bHandled = FALSE; break;
    }
    return bHandled;
  }

private:
  LRESULT OnChar(TCHAR c, BOOL& bHandled) {
    if( isalpha(c) ) bHandled = FALSE;
    else             MessageBeep(0xFFFFFFFF);
    return 0;
  }
};
```

When an instance of CLetterBox is created, it will look and act just like a built-in Windows edit control, except that it will only accept letters and will beep otherwise.

While powerful, it turns out that superclassing is rarely used. A much more commonly used technique is known as subclassing, which I'll discuss later when I present CContainedWindow.

Handling Messages

Whether it's superclassing, subclassing, or neither, a major part of registering a window class is providing the WndProc. The WndProc determines the behavior of the window by handling the appropriate messages. You've seen how the default WindowProc provided by ATL routes the messages to the ProcessWindowMessage function provided by your CWindowImpl-derived class. You've also seen how tedious it is to route messages from the ProcessWindowMessage function to the individual message handler member functions. Toward that end, ATL provides a set of macros for building a message map that will generate an implementation of ProcessWindowMessage for you. Providing the skeleton of the message map are the BEGIN_MSG_MAP and END_MSG_MAP macros, defined as follows:

```
#define BEGIN_MSG_MAP(theClass) \
public: \
 BOOL ProcessWindowMessage(HWND hWnd, UINT uMsg, WPARAM wParam, \
        LPARAM lParam, LRESULT& lResult, DWORD dwMsgMapID = 0) \
 { \
   BOOL bHandled = TRUE; \
   hWnd; uMsg; wParam; lParam; lResult; bHandled; \
   switch(dwMsgMapID) { \
   case 0:

#define END_MSG_MAP() \
    break; \
   default: \
     ATLTRACE2(atlTraceWindowing, 0,
               _T("Invalid message map ID (%i)\n"),
               dwMsgMapID); \
     ATLASSERT(FALSE); \
     break; \
   } \
   return FALSE; \
 }
```

Notice that the message map is a giant switch statement. However, the switch is not on the message IDs themselves but rather on the message map ID. A single set of message map macros can handle the messages of several windows, typically the parent and several children. The parent window (that is, the window for which we're providing the message map) is identified with the message map ID of 0. Later, I'll discuss segregating message handling into different sections of the same message map, resulting in nonzero message map IDs (known as alternate message map IDs).

Handling General Messages

Each message that the window wishes to handle corresponds to an entry in the message map. The simplest is the MESSAGE_HANDLER macro, which provides a handler for a single message:

```
#define MESSAGE_HANDLER(msg, func) \
 if(uMsg == msg) { \
   bHandled = TRUE; \
   lResult = func(uMsg, wParam, lParam, bHandled); \
   if(bHandled) return TRUE; \
 }
```

If you'd like to use a single message handler for a range of window messages, you can use the MESSAGE_RANGE_HANDLER macro:

```
#define MESSAGE_RANGE_HANDLER(msgFirst, msgLast, func) \
 if(uMsg >= msgFirst && uMsg <= msgLast) { \
   bHandled = TRUE; \
   lResult = func(uMsg, wParam, lParam, bHandled); \
   if(bHandled) return TRUE; \
 }
```

Using the message map macros, we can replace the sample implementation of ProcessWindowMessage with the following message map:

```
BEGIN_MSG_MAP(CMainWindow)
 MESSAGE_HANDLER(WM_PAINT, OnPaint)
END_MSG_MAP()
```

This will expand roughly to the following implementation of ProcessWindow-Message:

```
// BEGIN_MSG_MAP(CMainWindow)
BOOL ProcessWindowMessage(HWND hWnd, UINT uMsg, WPARAM wParam,
                          LPARAM lParam, LRESULT& lResult,
                          DWORD dwMsgMapID = 0) {
```

```
BOOL bHandled = TRUE;
switch (dwMsgMapID) {
case 0:

    // MESSAGE_HANDLER(WM_PAINT, OnPaint)
    if(uMsg == WM_PAINT) {
    bHandled = TRUE;
    lResult = OnPaint(uMsg, wParam, lParam, bHandled);
    if (bHandled) return TRUE;
    }

    // END_MSG_MAP()
    break;
default:
    ATLTRACE2(atlTraceWindowing, 0,
            _T("Invalid message map ID (%i)\n"),
            dwMsgMapID);
    ATLASSERT(FALSE);
    break;
}
return FALSE;
}
```

There are two things of note here. First, if there is an entry in the message map, that message is assumed to be handled; that is, the default window procedure will not be called for that message. However, the BOOL& bHandled is provided to each message handler, so you can change it to FALSE in the message handler if you'd like ATL to keep looking for a handler for this message. In the event that you are subclassing or superclassing, the original window procedure will receive the message only when bHandled is set to FALSE. Also, it's possible that another message handler further down the map will receive the message. This is useful for message map chaining, which I'll discuss soon. Ultimately, if nobody is interested in the message, DefWindowProc will get it.

The second interesting thing to note in this generated code is the member function signature required to handle a message map entry. All general messages are passed to a message handler with the following signature:

```
LRESULT
MessageHandler(UINT nMsg, WPARAM wparam, LPARAM lparam,
                BOOL& bHandled);
```

You can either add the entry and the member function by hand, or, in the ClassView, you can right-click on any class with a message map and choose Add Windows Message Handler (as described in Chapter 1). Unfortunately, however you add the handler, you're still responsible for cracking your own messages. For example, if you're interested in the optional HDC that may accompany the WM_PAINT message, you're responsible for performing the correct cast on the WPARAM. For example:

```
LRESULT OnPaint(UINT nMsg, WPARAM wparam, LPARAM lparam,
                BOOL& bHandled) {
  HWND hdc = (HDC)wparam;
  ...
  return 0;
}
```

Since at last count there were over 300 standard messages, each with their own interpretation of WPARAM and LPARAM, this can be quite a job. Hopefully, a future version of ATL will provide this functionality.

WM_COMMAND and WM_NOTIFY Messages

Of the hundreds of Windows messages, ATL does provide a bit of message cracking assistance for two of them, WM_COMMAND and WM_NOTIFY. A Windows control uses these messages to communicate with its parent. I should point out that Windows controls are not OLE or ActiveX controls. A standard Windows control is a child window whose class is defined by the Windows operating system. Some of these controls have been with us since Windows 1.0. Classic examples of Windows controls include buttons, scrollbars, edit boxes, list boxes, and combo boxes. With the new Windows shell introduced with Windows 95, these controls were expanded to include things like toolbars, status bars, tree views, list views, and rich text edit boxes. Further, with the integration of Internet Explorer with the shell, more Windows controls were introduced to include things like rebars, the date picker, and the IP address control.

Creating a Windows control is a matter of using CreateWindow with the proper window class name, for example, EDIT, just like creating any other kind of window. Communicating with a child Windows control is a matter of calling SendMessage with the appropriate parameters. Communicating the other way, that is, between a child Windows control and a parent, is also done via Windows messages, specifically WM_COMMAND or WM_NOTIFY. These messages provide enough information packed into WPARAM and LPARAM to describe the event of which the control is notifying the parent, as shown here:

WM_COMMAND
```
wNotifyCode  = HIWORD(wParam); // notification code
wID          = LOWORD(wParam); // item, control, or accelerator
                               // identifier
hwndCtl      = (HWND)lParam;   // handle of control
```

WM_NOTIFY
```
idCtrl = (int)wParam;     // control identifier
pnmh   = (LPNMHDR)lParam; // address of NMHDR structure
```

Notice that the WM_NOTIFY message is accompanied by a pointer to an NMHDR, which is defined like this:

```
typedef struct tagNMHDR {
  HWND  hwndFrom; // handle of the control
  UINT  idFrom;   // control identifier
  UINT  code;     // notification code
} NMHDR;
```

For example, an edit box will notify the parent of a change in the text with a WM_COMMAND message using the EN_CHANGE notification code. The parent may or may not wish to handle this particular message, but if it did, it would like to avoid the responsibility of breaking out the individual parts of the command notification. ATL provides several macros for splitting out the parts of WM_COMMAND and WM_NOTIFY messages. All these macros assume the following handler function signatures (one for command messages and one for notify messages):

```
LRESULT
CommandHandler(WORD wNotifyCode, WORD wID, HWND hWndCtl,
               BOOL& bHandled);

LRESULT
NotifyHandler(int idCtrl, LPNMHDR pnmh, BOOL& bHandled);
```

The most basic handler macros are COMMAND_HANDLER and NOTIFY_HANDLER:

```
#define COMMAND_HANDLER(id, code, func) \
 if(uMsg == WM_COMMAND && \
    id == LOWORD(wParam) && \
    code == HIWORD(wParam)) \
 { \
```

```
   bHandled = TRUE; \
   lResult = func(HIWORD(wParam), LOWORD(wParam), (HWND)lParam, \
     bHandled); \
   if(bHandled) return TRUE; \
 }

#define NOTIFY_HANDLER(id, code, func) \
 if(uMsg == WM_NOTIFY && \
    id == ((LPNMHDR)lParam)->idFrom && \
    code == ((LPNMHDR)lParam)->code) \
 { \
   bHandled = TRUE; \
   lResult = func((int)wParam, (LPNMHDR)lParam, bHandled); \
   if(bHandled) return TRUE; \
 }
```

These basic handler macros let you specify both the id of the control and the command/notification code that the control is sending. Using these macros, handling an EN_CHANGE notification from an edit control would look like this:

```
COMMAND_HANDLER(IDC_EDIT1, EN_CHANGE, OnEdit1Change)
```

Likewise, handling a TBN_BEGINDRAG notification from a toolbar control would look like this:

```
NOTIFY_HANDLER(IDC_TOOLBAR1, TBN_BEGINDRAG, OnToolbar1BeginDrag)
```

As a further example, let's add a menu bar to the sample Windows application like so:

```
int APIENTRY _tWinMain(HINSTANCE hinst,
                       HINSTANCE /*hinstPrev*/,
                       LPTSTR    pszCmdLine,
                       int       nCmdShow)
{
 // Initialize the ATL module
 ...

 // Create the main window
 CMainWindow wnd;
```

```
// Load a menu
HMENU hMenu = LoadMenu(_Module.GetResourceInstance(),
                       MAKEINTRESOURCE(IDR_MENU));

// Use the value 0 for the style and the extended style
// to get the window traits for this class.
wnd.Create(0, CWindow::rcDefault, _T("Windows Application"), 0, 0,
           (UINT)hMenu);
if( !wnd ) return -1;

... // The rest is the same
}
```

Assuming standard File|Exit and Help|About items in our menu, handling these menu item selections would look like this:

```
class CMainWindow : public CWindowImpl<CMainWindow, CWindow,
  CMainWinTraits> {
public:
BEGIN_MSG_MAP(CMainWindow)
  MESSAGE_HANDLER(WM_PAINT, OnPaint)
  COMMAND_HANDLER(ID_FILE_EXIT, 0, OnFileExit)
  COMMAND_HANDLER(ID_HELP_ABOUT, 0, OnHelpAbout)
END_MSG_MAP()
...
  LRESULT OnFileExit(WORD wNotifyCode, WORD wID, HWND hWndCtl,
                     BOOL& bHandled);
  LRESULT OnHelpAbout(WORD wNotifyCode, WORD wID, HWND hWndCtl,
                      BOOL& bHandled);
};
```

You may notice that menus are a little different from most Windows controls. Instead of using the ID of a child window as the first parameter, like for an edit control, we use the ID of the menu item. The command code itself is unused. In general, it's not uncommon for the ID or the code to be unimportant when routing a message to a handler. One example we've already seen: handling a menu item doesn't require checking the code. Another example of not worrying about the code would be if we wanted to route all events for one control to a single handler. Since the code is provided as an argument to the handler, further decisions could be made about how to handle a specific code for a control. To route events without regard for the specific code, ATL provides COMMAND_ID_HANDLER and NOTIFY_ID_HANDLER:

```
#define COMMAND_ID_HANDLER(id, func) \
  if(uMsg == WM_COMMAND && id == LOWORD(wParam)) \
  { \
        bHandled = TRUE; \
    lResult = func(HIWORD(wParam), LOWORD(wParam), (HWND)lParam, \
      bHandled); \
    if(bHandled) \
    return TRUE; \
  }

#define NOTIFY_ID_HANDLER(id, func) \
  if(uMsg == WM_NOTIFY && id == ((LPNMHDR)lParam)->idFrom) \
  { \
        bHandled = TRUE; \
    lResult = func((int)wParam, (LPNMHDR)lParam, bHandled); \
    if(bHandled) \
    return TRUE; \
  }
```

Using COMMAND_ID_HANDLER, our menu routing would more conventionally be
written this way:

```
COMMAND_ID_HANDLER(ID_FILE_EXIT, OnFileExit)
COMMAND_ID_HANDLER(ID_HELP_ABOUT, OnHelpAbout)
```

Further, if you'd like to route notifications for a range of controls, ATL provides
COMMAND_RANGE_HANDLER and NOTIFY_RANGE_HANDLER:

```
#define COMMAND_RANGE_HANDLER(idFirst, idLast, func) \
  if(uMsg == WM_COMMAND && LOWORD(wParam) >= idFirst && LOWORD(wParam)\
    <= idLast) \
  { \
        bHandled = TRUE; \
    lResult = func(HIWORD(wParam), LOWORD(wParam), (HWND)lParam, \
      bHandled); \
    if(bHandled) \
    return TRUE; \
  }
```

```
#define NOTIFY_RANGE_HANDLER(idFirst, idLast, func) \
 if(uMsg == WM_NOTIFY && ((LPNMHDR)lParam)->idFrom >= idFirst && \
   ((LPNMHDR)lParam)->idFrom <= idLast) \
 { \
       bHandled = TRUE; \
   lResult = func((int)wParam, (LPNMHDR)lParam, bHandled); \
   if(bHandled) \
   return TRUE; \
 }
```

It's also possible that you want to route messages without regard for their ID. This is useful if you'd like to use a single handler for multiple controls. ATL supports this usage with COMMAND_CODE_HANDLER and NOTIFY_CODE_HANDLER:

```
#define COMMAND_CODE_HANDLER(code, func) \
 if(uMsg == WM_COMMAND && code == HIWORD(wParam)) \
 { \
   bHandled = TRUE; \
   lResult = func(HIWORD(wParam), LOWORD(wParam), (HWND)lParam, \
     bHandled); \
   if(bHandled) \
   return TRUE; \
 }

#define NOTIFY_CODE_HANDLER(cd, func) \
 if(uMsg == WM_NOTIFY && cd == ((LPNMHDR)lParam)->code) \
 { \
   bHandled = TRUE; \
   lResult = func((int)wParam, (LPNMHDR)lParam, bHandled); \
   if(bHandled) \
   return TRUE; \
 }
```

Again, since the ID of the control is available as a parameter to the handler, you can make further decisions based on which control is sending the notification code.

Why WM_NOTIFY?

As an aside, you may be wondering why we have both WM_COMMAND and WM_NOTIFY. After all, WM_COMMAND alone sufficed for Windows 1.0 through Windows 3.x. However, when the new shell team was building the new controls, they really wanted to send along more information than just the ID of the control and the notification code. Unfortunately, all the bits of both WPARAM and LPARAM were already being used in WM_COMMAND. Therefore, they invented a new message—WM_NOTIFY—so that they could send a pointer to a structure as the LPARAM, keeping the ID of the control in the WPARAM. However, if you examine the definition of the NMHDR structure, you'll notice that there is no more information than was available in WM_COMMAND! Actually, there is a difference. Depending on the type of control that is sending the message, the LPARAM could point to something else that has the same layout as an NMHDR but has extra information tacked onto the end. For example, if you receive a TBN_BEGIN_DRAG, the NMHDR pointer will actually point to an NMTOOLBAR structure:

```
typedef struct tagNMTOOLBAR {
    NMHDR     hdr;
    int       iItem;
    TBBUTTON  tbButton;
    int       cchText;
    LPTSTR    pszText;
} NMTOOLBAR, FAR* LPNMTOOLBAR;
```

Since the first member of the NMTOOLBAR structure is an NMDHR, it's safe to cast the LPARAM to an NMHDR, even though it actually points at an NMTOOLBAR. If you like, you can consider this "inheritance" for C programmers.

Message Chaining

If you find yourself handling messages again and again in the same way, you may wish to reuse the message handler implementations. If you're willing to populate the message map entries yourself, there's no reason you can't use normal C++ implementation techniques:

```
template <typename Deriving>
class CFileHandler {
public:
  LRESULT OnFileNew(WORD, WORD, HWND, BOOL&);
  LRESULT OnFileOpen(WORD, WORD, HWND, BOOL&);
  LRESULT OnFileSave(WORD, WORD, HWND, BOOL&);
  LRESULT OnFileSaveAs(WORD, WORD, HWND, BOOL&);
  LRESULT OnFileExit(WORD, WORD, HWND, BOOL&);
};
```

```
class CMainWindow :
    public CWindowImpl<CMainWindow, CWindow, CMainWinTraits>,
    public CFileHandler<CMainWindow>
{
public:
BEGIN_MSG_MAP(CMainWindow)
 MESSAGE_HANDLER(WM_PAINT, OnPaint)
 // Route messages to base class
 COMMAND_ID_HANDLER(ID_FILE_NEW, OnFileNew)
 COMMAND_ID_HANDLER(ID_FILE_OPEN, OnFileOpen)
 COMMAND_ID_HANDLER(ID_FILE_SAVE, OnFileSave)
 COMMAND_ID_HANDLER(ID_FILE_SAVE_AS, OnFileSaveAs)
 COMMAND_ID_HANDLER(ID_FILE_EXIT, OnFileExit)
 COMMAND_ID_HANDLER(ID_HELP_ABOUT, OnHelpAbout)
END_MSG_MAP()
 ...
};
```

This technique is somewhat cumbersome, however. If the base class were to gain a new message handler, for example, OnFileClose, each deriving class would have to manually add an entry to its message map. What we'd really like is the ability to "inherit" a base class's message map as well as a base class's functionality. For this, ATL provides *message chaining*.

Simple Message Chaining

Message chaining is the ability to extend a class's message map by including the message map of a base class or another object altogether. The simplest macro of the message chaining family is CHAIN_MSG_MAP:

```
#define CHAIN_MSG_MAP(theChainClass) { \
  if (theChainClass::ProcessWindowMessage(hWnd, uMsg, wParam, lParam,\
                                          lResult)) \
  return TRUE; \
}
```

This macro allows chaining to the message map of a base class. For example:

```
template <typename Deriving>
class CFileHandler {
public:
// Message map in base class
```

```
BEGIN_MSG_MAP(CMainWindow)
 COMMAND_ID_HANDLER(ID_FILE_NEW, OnFileNew)
 COMMAND_ID_HANDLER(ID_FILE_OPEN, OnFileOpen)
 COMMAND_ID_HANDLER(ID_FILE_SAVE, OnFileSave)
 COMMAND_ID_HANDLER(ID_FILE_SAVE_AS, OnFileSaveAs)
 COMMAND_ID_HANDLER(ID_FILE_EXIT, OnFileExit)
END_MSG_MAP()

 LRESULT OnFileNew(WORD, WORD, HWND, BOOL&);
 LRESULT OnFileOpen(WORD, WORD, HWND, BOOL&);
 LRESULT OnFileSave(WORD, WORD, HWND, BOOL&);
 LRESULT OnFileSaveAs(WORD, WORD, HWND, BOOL&);
 LRESULT OnFileExit(WORD, WORD, HWND, BOOL&);
};

class CMainWindow :
    public CWindowImpl<CMainWindow, CWindow, CMainWinTraits>,
    public CFileHandler<CMainWindow>
{
public:
BEGIN_MSG_MAP(CMainWindow)
 MESSAGE_HANDLER(WM_PAINT, OnPaint)
 COMMAND_ID_HANDLER(ID_HELP_ABOUT, OnHelpAbout)
 // Chain to a base class
 CHAIN_MSG_MAP(CFileHandler<CMainWindow>)
END_MSG_MAP()
...
};
```

Any base class that provides its own implementation of ProcessWindowMessage (for example, with the message map macros) can be used as a chainee. Also notice that CFileHandler is parameterized by the name of the deriving class. This is useful when used with a static cast to obtain a pointer to the more derived class. For example, when implementing OnFileExit, you'll need to destroy the window represented by the deriving class:

```
template <typename Deriving>
LRESULT CFileHandler<Deriving>::OnFileExit(WORD, WORD, HWND, BOOL&) {
    static_cast<Deriving*>(this)->DestroyWindow();
    return 0;
}
```

Message chaining to a base class can be extended for any number of base classes. For example, if you wanted to handle the File, Edit, and Help menus in separate base classes, you would have several chain entries:

```
class CMainWindow :
    public CWindowImpl<CMainWindow, CWindow, CMainWinTraits>,
    public CFileHandler<CMainWindow>,
    public CEditHandler<CMainWinow>,
    public CHelpHandler<CMainWindow>
{
public:
BEGIN_MSG_MAP(CMainWindow)
 MESSAGE_HANDLER(WM_PAINT, OnPaint)
 COMMAND_ID_HANDLER(ID_HELP_ABOUT, OnHelpAbout)
 // Chain to a base class
 CHAIN_MSG_MAP(CFileHandler<CMainWindow>)
 CHAIN_MSG_MAP(CEditHandler<CMainWindow>)
 CHAIN_MSG_MAP(CHelpHandler<CMainWindow>)
END_MSG_MAP()
 ...
};
```

If, instead of chaining to a base class message map, you'd like to chain to the message map of a data member, you can use the CHAIN_MSG_MAP_MEMBER macro:

```
#define CHAIN_MSG_MAP_MEMBER(theChainMember) { \
 if (theChainMember.ProcessWindowMessage(hWnd, uMsg, wParam, lParam,\
                                         lResult)) \
 return TRUE; \
}
```

If a handler is going to be a data member, it's going to need to access a pointer to the actual object differently; that is, a static cast won't work. For example, an updated CFileHandler takes a pointer to the window for which it's handling messages in the constructor:

```
template <typename TWindow>
class CFileHandler {
public:
BEGIN_MSG_MAP(CFileHandler)
 COMMAND_ID_HANDLER(ID_FILE_NEW, OnFileNew)
 COMMAND_ID_HANDLER(ID_FILE_OPEN, OnFileOpen)
```

```
 COMMAND_ID_HANDLER(ID_FILE_SAVE, OnFileSave)
 COMMAND_ID_HANDLER(ID_FILE_SAVE_AS, OnFileSaveAs)
 COMMAND_ID_HANDLER(ID_FILE_EXIT, OnFileExit)
END_MSG_MAP()
 CFileHandler(TWindow* pwnd) : m_pwnd(pwnd) {}

 LRESULT OnFileNew(WORD, WORD, HWND, BOOL&);
 LRESULT OnFileOpen(WORD, WORD, HWND, BOOL&);
 LRESULT OnFileSave(WORD, WORD, HWND, BOOL&);
 LRESULT OnFileSaveAs(WORD, WORD, HWND, BOOL&);
 LRESULT OnFileExit(WORD, WORD, HWND, BOOL&);

private:
 TWindow* m_pwnd;
};
```

An updated implementation would use the cached pointer to access the window instead of a static cast. For example:

```
template <typename TWindow>
LRESULT CFileHandler<TWindow>::OnFileExit(WORD, WORD wID, HWND, BOOL&){
    m_pwnd->DestroyWindow();
    return 0;
}
```

Once we have an updated handler class, using it looks like this:

```
class CMainWindow : public CWindowImpl<CMainWindow, CWindow,
  CMainWinTraits> {
public:
BEGIN_MSG_MAP(CMainWindow)
 MESSAGE_HANDLER(WM_PAINT, OnPaint)
 COMMAND_ID_HANDLER(ID_HELP_ABOUT, OnHelpAbout)
 // Chain to the CFileHandler member
 CHAIN_MSG_MAP_MEMBER(m_handlerFile)
END_MSG_MAP()
...
CMainWindow() : m_handlerFile(this) {}
private:
  CFileHandler<CMainWindow> m_handlerFile;
};
```

Alternate Message Maps

It's possible to break a message map into multiple pieces. Each piece is called an *alternate message map*. Recall that the message map macros expand into a switch statement that switches on the dwMsgMapID parameter to ProcessWindowMessage. The main part of the message map is the first part and is identified with a 0 message map ID. An alternate part of the message map, on the other hand, is distinguished with a nonzero message map ID. As each message comes in, it's routed first by message map ID and then by message. When a window receives its own messages and those messages chained from another window, an alternate part of the message map allows the window to distinguish where the messages are coming from. A message map is broken up into multiple parts using the ALT_MSG_MAP macro:

```
#define ALT_MSG_MAP(msgMapID) \
  break; \
  case msgMapID:
```

For example, imagine a child window that is receiving messages routed to it from the main window:

```
class CView : public CWindowImpl<CView> {
public:
BEGIN_MSG_MAP(CView)
// Handle CView messages
  MESSAGE_HANDLER(WM_PAINT, OnPaint)

// Handle messages chained from the parent window
ALT_MSG_MAP(1)
  COMMAND_HANDLER(ID_EDIT_COPY)
END_MSG_MAP()
...
};
```

Since the message map has been split, the child window (CView) will only receive its own messages in the main part of the message map. However, if the main window were to chain messages using CHAIN_MSG_MAP_MEMBER, the child would receive the messages in the main part of the message map, not the alternate part.

To chain messages to an alternate part of the message map, ATL provides two macros, CHAIN_MSG_MAP_ALT and CHAIN_MSG_MAP_ALT_MEMBER:

```
#define CHAIN_MSG_MAP_ALT(theChainClass, msgMapID) { \
  if (theChainClass::ProcessWindowMessage(hWnd, uMsg, wParam, lParam,\
                                          lResult, msgMapID)) \
    return TRUE; \
}
```

```
#define CHAIN_MSG_MAP_ALT_MEMBER(theChainMember, msgMapID) { \
  if (theChainMember.ProcessWindowMessage(hWnd, uMsg, wParam, lParam,\
                                          lResult, msgMapID)) \
    return TRUE; \
}
```

For example, for the parent window to route unhandled messages to the child, it can use CHAIN_MSG_ALT_MEMBER like so:

```
class CMainWindow : ... {
public:
BEGIN_MSG_MAP(CMainWindow)
  MESSAGE_HANDLER(WM_CREATE, OnCreate)
  ...
  // Route unhandled messages to the child window
  CHAIN_MSG_MAP_ALT_MEMBER(m_view, 1)
END_MSG_MAP()

  LRESULT OnCreate(UINT, WPARAM, LPARAM, BOOL&) {
    return m_view.Create(m_hWnd, CWindow::rcDefault) ? 0 : -1;
  }
  ...
private:
  CView m_view;
};
```

Dynamic Chaining

Message map chaining to a base class or a member variable is useful, but not as flexible as we might like. What if you'd like a looser coupling between the window that sent the message and the handler of the message? For example, the MFC WM_COMMAND message routing depends on just such loose coupling. The view receives all the WM_COMMAND messages initially, but the document handles file-related command messages. If we'd like to construct such a relationship using ATL, we have one more chaining message map macro, CHAIN_MSG_MAP_DYNAMIC:

```
#define CHAIN_MSG_MAP_DYNAMIC(dynaChainID) { \
  if (CDynamicChain::CallChain(dynaChainID, hWnd, uMsg, wParam, \
    lParam, lResult)) \
  return TRUE; \
}
```

Chaining sets up a relationship between two objects that handle messages. If the object that first receives the message doesn't handle it, the second object in line can handle it. The relationship is established using a *dynamic chain ID*. A dynamic chain ID is a number that the primary message processor uses to identify the secondary message processor that wishes to process unhandled messages. To establish the dynamic chaining relationship, two things must happen. First, the secondary message processor must derive from CMessageMap:

```
class ATL_NO_VTABLE CMessageMap {
public:
 virtual BOOL
 ProcessWindowMessage(HWND hWnd, UINT uMsg, WPARAM wParam,
        LPARAM lParam, LRESULT& lResult, DWORD dwMsgMapID) = 0;
};
```

CMessageMap is actually a fairly poorly named class. A better name would be something like CMessageHandler or even CMessageProcessor. All that CMessageMap does is guarantee that every class that derives from it will implement ProcessWindowMessage. In fact, CWindowImpl derives from it as well, making an implementation of ProcessWindowMessage mandatory for CWindowImpl-derived classes. The reason that a secondary message processor must derive from CMessageMap is so that it can be placed in the ATL_CHAIN_ENTRY structure managed by the primary message processor:

```
struct ATL_CHAIN_ENTRY {
  DWORD        m_dwChainID;
  CMessageMap* m_pObject;
  DWORD        m_dwMsgMapID;
};
```

Second, a primary message processor must derive from CDynamicChain, a base class that manages a dynamic array of ATL_CHAIN_ENTRY structures.

CDynamicChain provides two important member functions. The first, SetChain-Entry, is used to add an ATL_CHAIN_ENTRY structure to the list:

```
BOOL
CDynamicChain::SetChainEntry(DWORD dwChainID, CMessageMap* pObject,
                            DWORD dwMsgMapID = 0);
```

The other important function, CallChain, is used by the CHAIN_MSG_MAP_DYNAMIC macro to chain messages to any interested parties:

```
BOOL
CDynamicChain::CallChain(DWORD dwChainID, HWND hWnd, UINT uMsg,
                         WPARAM wParam, LPARAM lParam,
                         LRESULT& lResult);
```

As an example of this technique, imagine an application built using a simplified document/view architecture. The main window acts as the frame, holding the menu bar and two other objects, a document and a view. The view manages the client area of the main window and handles the painting of the data maintained by the document. The view is also responsible for handling view-related menu commands, such as Edit|Copy. The document is responsible for maintaining the current state as well as handling document-related menu commands, such as File|Save. To route command messages to the view, the main window will use alternate-message-map, member function chaining (which we've already seen). However, to continue routing commands from the view to the document, the main window, after creating both the document and the view, will "hook" them together, if you will, using SetChain-Entry. Any messages unhandled by the view will automatically be routed to the document by the CHAIN_MSG_MAP_DYNAMIC entry in the view's message map. The document, finally, will handle any messages it likes, leaving unhandled messages for DefWindowProc.

The main window creates the document and view and hooks them together:

```
class CMainWindow : public CWindowImpl<CMainWindow, CWindow,
CMainWinTraits> {
public:
BEGIN_MSG_MAP(CMainWindow)
 // Handle main window messages
 MESSAGE_HANDLER(WM_CREATE, OnCreate)

 ...
 // Route unhandled messages to the view
 CHAIN_MSG_MAP_ALT_MEMBER(m_view, 1)
```

```
 // Pick up messages the view hasn't handled
 COMMAND_ID_HANDLER(ID_HELP_ABOUT, OnHelpAbout)
END_MSG_MAP()

 CMainWindow() : m_doc(this), m_view(&m_doc) {
   // Hook up the document to receive messages from the view
   m_view.SetChainEntry(1, &m_doc, 1);
  }

private:
 // Create the view to handle the main window's client area
 LRESULT OnCreate(UINT, WPARAM, LPARAM, BOOL&)
 { return (m_view.Create(m_hWnd, CWindow::rcDefault) ? 0 : -1); }

 LRESULT OnHelpAbout(WORD, WORD, HWND, BOOL&);
 virtual void OnFinalMessage(HWND /*hwnd*/);
 ...
private:
 CDocument<CMainWindow>  m_doc;
 CView<CMainWindow>      m_view;
};
```

The view handles the messages it wants and chains the rest to the document:

```
template <typename TMainWindow>
class CView :
 public CWindowImpl<CView>,
 // Derive from CDynamicChain to support dynamic chaining
 public CDynamicChain {
public:
 CView(CDocument<TMainWindow>* pdoc) : m_pdoc(pdoc) {
   // Set the document-managed string
   m_pdoc->SetString(__T("ATL Doc/View"));
  }

BEGIN_MSG_MAP(CView)
 // Handle view messages
 MESSAGE_HANDLER(WM_PAINT, OnPaint)

ALT_MSG_MAP(1) // Handle messages from the main window
 CHAIN_MSG_MAP_DYNAMIC(1) // Route messages to the document
END_MSG_MAP()
```

```
private:
  LRESULT OnPaint(UINT, WPARAM, LPARAM, BOOL&);

private:
  // View caches its own document
  CDocument<TMainWindow>* m_pdoc;
};
```

The document handles any messages it receives from the view:

```
template <typename TMainWindow>
class CDocument :
  // Derive from CMessageMap to receive dynamically chained messages
  public CMessageMap {
public:
BEGIN_MSG_MAP(CDocument)

// Handle messages from the view and the main frame
ALT_MSG_MAP(1)
  COMMAND_ID_HANDLER(ID_FILE_NEW, OnFileNew)
  COMMAND_ID_HANDLER(ID_FILE_OPEN, OnFileOpen)
  COMMAND_ID_HANDLER(ID_FILE_SAVE, OnFileSave)
  COMMAND_ID_HANDLER(ID_FILE_SAVE_AS, OnFileSaveAs)
  COMMAND_ID_HANDLER(ID_FILE_EXIT, OnFileExit)
END_MSG_MAP()

  CDocument(TMainWindow* pwnd) : m_pwnd(pwnd) { *m_sz = 0; }

  void    SetString(LPCTSTR psz);
  LPCTSTR GetString();

// Message handlers
private:
  LRESULT OnFileNew(WORD, WORD, HWND, BOOL&);
  LRESULT OnFileOpen(WORD, WORD, HWND, BOOL&);
  LRESULT OnFileSave(WORD, WORD, HWND, BOOL&);
  LRESULT OnFileSaveAs(WORD, WORD, HWND, BOOL&);
  LRESULT OnFileExit(WORD, WORD, HWND, BOOL&);

private:
  TMainWindow* m_pwnd;
  TCHAR        m_sz[64];
};
```

Filtering Chained Messages

In many ways, ATL's CMessageMap is like MFC's CCmdTarget. However, MFC makes a distinction between command messages and noncommand messages. While it's useful for the view and the document to participate in handling the main window's command messages, the rest (for example, WM_XXX) aren't nearly so useful. The view and the document manage to ignore the rest of the messages using alternate parts of their message maps, but still, it would be nice if every message weren't routed this way. Unfortunately, there's no built-in way to route only command messages using the message chaining macros. However, a custom macro could do the trick:

```
#define CHAIN_COMMAND_DYNAMIC(dynaChainID) { \
 if ((uMsg == WM_COMMAND) && \
     CDynamicChain::CallChain(dynaChainID, hWnd, uMsg, wParam, lParam,\
                              lResult)) \
 return TRUE; \
}
```

This macro would chain only WM_COMMAND messages very much like MFC does. However, you'd still need corresponding equivalents for the nondynamic message chaining macros.

CDialogImpl

Dialogs represent, if you will, a declarative style of user interface development. While normal windows provide all kinds of flexibility (you can put anything you want in the client area of a window), dialogs are more static. Actually, dialogs are just windows whose layout has been predetermined. The built-in dialog box window class knows how to interpret dialog box resources to create and manage the child windows that make up a dialog box. To show a dialog box *modally*—that is, while the dialog is visible the parent is inaccessible—Windows provides the DialogBoxParam[4] function:

```
int DialogBoxParam(
  HINSTANCE  hInstance,     // handle to application instance
  LPCTSTR    lpTemplate,    // identifies dialog box template
  HWND       hWndParent,    // handle to owner window
```

---

[4]The DialogBox function is merely a wrapper around DialogBoxParam, passing 0 for the dwInitParam argument.

```
    DLGPROC     lpDialogFunc, // pointer to dialog box procedure
    LPARAM      dwInitParam); // initialization value
```

The result of the `DialogBoxParam` function is the command that closes the dialog, for example, `IDOK` or `IDCANCEL`. To show the dialog box *modelessly*—that is, the parent window is still accessible while the dialog is visible—the `CreateDialog-Param`[5] function is used instead:

```
HWND CreateDialogParam(
    HINSTANCE   hInstance,    // handle to application instance
    LPCTSTR     lpTemplate,   // identifies dialog box template
    HWND        hWndParent,   // handle to owner window
    DLGPROC     lpDialogFunc, // pointer to dialog box procedure
    LPARAM      dwInitParam); // initialization value
```

Notice that the parameters to `CreateDialogParam` are identical to `DialogBox-Param`, but the return value is different. The return value from `CreateDialog-Param` represents the `HWND` of the new dialog box window, which will live until the dialog box window is destroyed.

Regardless of how a dialog is shown, however, developing a dialog is the same. First, you lay out a dialog resource using your favorite resource editor. Second, you develop a dialog box procedure (DlgProc). The DlgProc will be called by the window procedure of the dialog box class to give you an opportunity to handle each message (although you never have to call `DefWindowProc` in a DlgProc). Third, you call either `DialogBoxParam` or `CreateDialogParam` (or one of the variants) to show the dialog. This is the same kind of grunt work we had to do when we wanted to show a window, namely, register a window class, develop a window procedure, and create the window. And just as ATL lets us work with `CWindow`-derived objects instead of raw windows, ATL also lets us work with `CDialogImpl`-derived classes instead of raw dialogs.

Showing a Dialog

`CDialogImpl` provides a set of wrapper functions around common dialog operations (like `DialogBoxParam` and `CreateDialogParam`):

```
template <class T, class TBase = CWindow>
class ATL_NO_VTABLE CDialogImpl : public CDialogImplBaseT<TBase> {
public:
```

---

[5]Likewise, `CreateDialog` is a wrapper around the `CreateDialogParam` function.

```
// modal dialogs
int DoModal(HWND hWndParent = ::GetActiveWindow(),
            LPARAM dwInitParam = NULL) {
  _Module.AddCreateWndData(&m_thunk.cd,
                           (CDialogImplBaseT<TBase>*) this);

  return ::DialogBoxParam(_Module.GetResourceInstance(),
                          MAKEINTRESOURCE(T::IDD),
                          hWndParent,
                          (DLGPROC)T::StartDialogProc,
                          dwInitParam);
}


BOOL EndDialog(int nRetCode) {
  return ::EndDialog(m_hWnd, nRetCode);
}


// modeless dialogs
HWND Create(HWND hWndParent, LPARAM dwInitParam = NULL) {
  _Module.AddCreateWndData(&m_thunk.cd,
                           (CDialogImplBaseT<TBase>*) this);

  HWND hWnd = ::CreateDialogParam(_Module.GetResourceInstance(),
                                  MAKEINTRESOURCE(T::IDD),
                                  hWndParent,
                                  (DLGPROC)T::StartDialogProc,
                                  dwInitParam);
  return hWnd;
}


BOOL DestroyWindow() {
  return ::DestroyWindow(m_hWnd);
}
...
};
```

There are a couple of interesting things going on in this small class. First, notice the use of the thunk. ATL sets up a thunk between Windows and the `ProcessWindowMessage` member function of your `CDialogImpl`-based objects, just as it does for `CWindowImpl`-based objects. In addition to all the tricks that `WindowProc` performs (see the section The Window Procedure earlier in this chapter), the static member function `CDialogImpl::DialogProc` also manages the weirdness of DWL_MSGRESULT. For some dialog messages, the DlgProc must return the result of the message. For others, the result is set by calling `SetWindowLong` with DWL_MSGRESULT. And while I can never remember which is which, ATL can. Our dialog message handlers need only return the value; if it needs to go into the DWL_MSG-RESULT, ATL will put it there.

Something else interesting to notice is that `CDialogImpl` derives from `CDialogImplBaseT`, which provides some other helper functions:

```
template <class TBase = CWindow>
class ATL_NO_VTABLE CDialogImplBaseT : public CWindowImplRoot<TBase> {
public:
 virtual WNDPROC GetDialogProc() { return DialogProc; }
 static LRESULT CALLBACK StartDialogProc(HWND, UINT, WPARAM, LPARAM);
 static LRESULT CALLBACK DialogProc(HWND, UINT, WPARAM, LPARAM);
 LRESULT DefWindowProc() { return 0; }

 BOOL MapDialogRect(LPRECT pRect)
   { return ::MapDialogRect(m_hWnd, pRect); }
 virtual void OnFinalMessage(HWND /*hWnd*/) {}
};
```

Again, notice the use of the `StartDlgProc` to bootstrap the thunk, and the `DialogProc` function that actually does the mapping to the `ProcessWindowMessage` member function. Also, notice the `DefWindowProc` member function. Remember, for DlgProcs, there's no need to pass an unhandled message to `DefWindowProc`. Since the message handling infrastructure of ATL requires a `DefWindowProc`, the `CDialogImplBaseT` class provides an inline, do-nothing function the compiler is free to toss away.

More useful to the dialog developer are the `CDialogImplBaseT` member functions `MapDialogRect` and `OnFinalMessage`. `MapDialogRect` is a wrapper around the Windows function `::MapDialogRect`, which maps dialog box units to pixels. Finally, `OnFinalMessage` is called after the last dialog message has been processed, just like the `CWindowImpl::OnFinalMessage` member function.

You may wonder how far the inheritance hierarchy goes for `CDialogImpl`. Refer again to Figure 9.1 at the beginning of this chapter. Notice that `CDialogImpl` ultimately derives from `CWindow`, so all of the wrappers and helpers that are available for windows are also available to dialogs.

Before we get too far away from `CDialogImpl`, notice where the dialog resource identifier comes from. The deriving class is required to provide a numeric symbol called IDD indicating the resource identifier.[6] For example, assuming a resource ID of IDD_ABOUTBOX, you would implement a typical About box like so:

```
class CAboutBox : public CDialogImpl<CAboutBox> {
public:
BEGIN_MSG_MAP(CAboutBox)
 MESSAGE_HANDLER(WM_INITDIALOG, OnInitDialog)
 COMMAND_ID_HANDLER(IDOK, OnOK);
END_MSG_MAP()

  enum { IDD = IDD_ABOUTBOX };

private:
 LRESULT OnInitDialog(UINT, WPARAM, LPARAM, BOOL&) {
   CenterWindow();
   return 1;
 }

 LRESULT OnOK(WORD, UINT, HWND, BOOL&) {
   EndDialog(IDOK);
   return 0;
 }
};
```

CAboutBox has all the elements. It derives from CDialogImpl, has a message map, and provides a value for IDD that indicates the resource ID. If you want to use the Dialog object type in the ATL Object Wizard,[7] it will get you started, but it's not difficult to do by hand.

Using a CDialogImpl-derived class is a matter of creating an instance of the class and calling either DoModal or Create. For example:

```
LRESULT CMainWindow::OnHelpAbout(WORD, WORD, HWND, BOOL&) {
 CAboutBox dlg;
 dlg.DoModal();
 return 0;
}
```

---

[6] Why the dialog resource ID isn't just a template parameter, I have no idea.
[7] Assuming you've convinced the ATL Object Wizard to insert an object into your project. See Faking out the ATL Object Wizard in Chapter 1 for some advice.

Simple Dialogs

For simple modal dialogs, like About boxes, that don't have any interaction requirements beyond the standard buttons (such as OK and Cancel), ATL provides CSimpleDialog:

```
template <WORD t_wDlgTemplateID, BOOL t_bCenter = TRUE>
class CSimpleDialog : public CDialogImplBase {
public:
  int DoModal(HWND hWndParent = ::GetActiveWindow()) {
    _Module.AddCreateWndData(&m_thunk.cd, (CDialogImplBase*)this);

    int nRet = ::DialogBox(_Module.GetResourceInstance(),
                           MAKEINTRESOURCE(t_wDlgTemplateID),
                           hWndParent,
                           (DLGPROC)StartDialogProc);
    m_hWnd = NULL;
    return nRet;
  }

BEGIN_MSG_MAP(CSimpleDialog<t_wDlgTemplateID, t_bCenter>)
  MESSAGE_HANDLER(WM_INITDIALOG, OnInitDialog)
  COMMAND_RANGE_HANDLER(IDOK, IDNO, OnCloseCmd)
END_MSG_MAP()

  LRESULT OnInitDialog(UINT, WPARAM, LPARAM, BOOL&) {
    if (t_bCenter) CenterWindow(GetParent());
    return TRUE;
  }

  LRESULT OnCloseCmd(WORD, WORD wID, HWND, BOOL&) {
    ::EndDialog(m_hWnd, wID);
    return 0;
  }
};
```

Notice that the resource ID is passed as a template parameter, as is a flag indicating whether the dialog should be centered. This reduces the definition of the CAboutBox class to the following type definition:

```
typedef CSimpleDialog<IDD_ABOUTBOX> CAboutBox;
```

However, the usage of CAboutBox remains the same.

Data Exchange and Validation

Unfortunately, most dialogs aren't simple. In fact, most are downright complicated. This complication is mostly due to two things: writing data to child controls managed by the dialog and reading data from child controls managed by the dialog. Exchanging data with a modal dialog typically goes like this:

1. Application creates an instance of a `CDialogImpl`-derived class.
2. Application copies some data into the dialog object's data members.
3. Application calls `DoModal`.
4. Dialog handles `WM_INITDIALOG` by copying data members into child controls.
5. Dialog handles the OK button by validating the data held by child controls. When the data is invalid, the dialog complains to the user and makes him or her keep trying until he or she either gets it right or gets frustrated and hits the Cancel button.
6. When the data is valid, the data is copied back into the dialog's data members and the dialog ends.
7. When the application gets `IDOK` from `DoModal`, it copies the data from the dialog data members over its own copy.

   If the dialog is to be shown modelessly, the interaction between the application and the dialog is a little different, but the relationship between the dialog and its child controls is the same. A modeless dialog sequence goes like this (differences from the modal case are shown in italics):

1. Application creates an instance of a `CDialogImpl`-derived class.
2. Application copies some data into the dialog object's data members.
3. Applications calls `Create`.
4. Dialog handles `WM_INITDIALOG` by copying data members into child controls.
5. Dialog handles the *Apply* button by validating the data held by child controls. When the data is invalid, the dialog complains to the user and makes him or her keep trying until he or she either gets it right or gets frustrated and hits the Cancel button.
6. When the data is valid, the data is copied back into the dialog's data members and *the application is notified[8] to read the updated data from the dialog.*
7. *When the application is notified*, it copies the data from the dialog data members over its own copy.

---

[8] A custom window message sent to the dialog's parent is excellent for this duty.

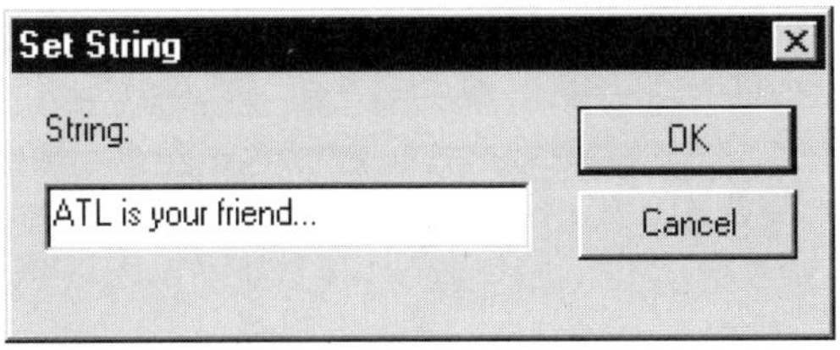

Figure 9.4. A dialog that needs to manage data exchange and validation

Either way, modal or modeless, the dialog's job is to exchange the data back and forth between its data members and the child controls and to validate it along the way. MFC has something called DDX/DDV (Dialog Data Exchange/Dialog Data Validation) for just this purpose. ATL has no such support, but it turns out to be pretty easy to build yourself.

For example, to beef up our standalone Windows application sample, imagine a dialog that allowed one to modify the display string, as shown in Figure 9.4. The CDialogImpl-based class would look like this:

```
class CStringDlg : public CDialogImpl<CStringDlg> {
public:
 CStringDlg() { *m_sz = 0; }

BEGIN_MSG_MAP(CStringDlg)
 MESSAGE_HANDLER(WM_INITDIALOG, OnInitDialog)
 COMMAND_ID_HANDLER(IDOK, OnOK)
 COMMAND_ID_HANDLER(IDCANCEL, OnCancel)
END_MSG_MAP()

 enum { IDD = IDD_SET_STRING };
 TCHAR m_sz[64];

private:
 bool CheckValidString() {
   // Check the length of the string
   int cchString = ::GetWindowTextLength(GetDlgItem(IDC_STRING));
   return cchString ? true : false;
 }

 LRESULT OnInitDialog(UINT, WPARAM, LPARAM, BOOL&) {
   CenterWindow();
```

```
        // Copy the string from the data member to the child control (DDX)
        SetDlgItemText(IDC_STRING, m_sz);

        return 1; // Let dialog manager set initial focus
    }

    LRESULT OnOK(WORD, UINT, HWND, BOOL&) {
        // Complain if the string is of zero length (DDV)
        if( !CheckValidString() ) {
            MessageBox("Please enter a string", "Hey!");
            return 0;
        }

        // Copy the string from the child control to the data member (DDX)
        GetDlgItemText(IDC_STRING, m_sz, lengthof(m_sz));

        EndDialog(IDOK);
        return 0;
    }

    LRESULT OnCancel(WORD, UINT, HWND, BOOL&) {
        EndDialog(IDCANCEL);
        return 0;
    }
};
```

In this example, DDX-like functionality happens in `OnInitDialog` and `OnOK`.
`OnInitDialog` copies the data from the data member into the child edit control.
Likewise, `OnOK` copies the data from the child edit control back to the data member
and ends the dialog, if the data is valid. Checking the validity of the data (DDV-like)
is performed before the call to `EndDialog` in `OnOK` by calling the helper function
`CheckValidString`. I decided that a zero-length string would be too boring, so I
made it invalid. In that case, `OnOK` puts up a message box and doesn't end the dialog. To be fair, MFC would have automated all this with a macro-based table, which
makes handling a lot of DDX/DDV chores easier, but ATL certainly doesn't prohibit
data exchange or validation.

In fact, I can do even better in the data validation area with this example. Although this example, and MFC-based DDX/DDV, only validates when the user
presses the OK button, sometimes it's handy to validate as the user enters the data.
For example, by handling EN_CHANGE notifications from the edit control, I can
check for a zero-length string as the user enters it. If the string ever gets to zero, disabling the OK button would make it impossible for the user to attempt to commit

the data at all, making the complaint dialog unnecessary. The following updated code shows this technique:

```cpp
class CStringDlg : public CDialogImpl<CStringDlg> {
public:
  ...
BEGIN_MSG_MAP(CStringDlg)
  ...
  COMMAND_HANDLER(IDC_STRING, EN_CHANGE, OnStringChange)
END_MSG_MAP()

private:
 void CheckValidString() {
    // Check the length of the string
    int cchString = ::GetWindowTextLength(GetDlgItem(IDC_STRING));

    // Enable the OK button only if the string is of nonzero length
    ::EnableWindow(GetDlgItem(IDOK), cchString ? TRUE : FALSE);
 }

 LRESULT OnInitDialog(UINT, WPARAM, LPARAM, BOOL&) {
    CenterWindow();

    // Copy the string from the data member to the child control (DDX)
    SetDlgItemText(IDC_STRING, m_sz);

    // Check the string length (DDV)
    CheckValidString();

    return 1; // Let dialog manager set initial focus
 }

 LRESULT OnStringChange(WORD, UINT, HWND, BOOL&) {
  // Check the string length each time it changes (DDV)
  CheckValidString();
  return 0;
 }

 ... // The rest is the same
};
```

In this case, notice that OnInitDialog takes on some DDV responsibilities, while OnOK loses some. In OnInitDialog, if the string starts with a zero length, the OK button is immediately disabled. In the `OnStringChange` handler for `EN_CHANGE`, as the text in the edit control changes, we revalidate the data, enabling or disabling the OK button as necessary. Finally, we know that if we reach the `OnOK` handler at all, the OK button must be enabled and the DDV chores must already have been done. Neither ATL nor MFC can help us with this kind of DDV, but then again, neither hinders us from providing a user interface that handles both DDX and DDV in a friendly way.

Windows Control Wrappers

Child Window Management

You may have noticed in the last two examples that whenever I needed to manipulate a child control, such as getting and setting the edit control's text or enabling and disabling the OK button, I used a dialog item function. The ultimate base class of `CDialogImpl`, `CWindow`, provides a number of helper functions to manipulate child controls:

```
class CWindow {
public:
  ...
  // Dialog-Box Item Functions

  BOOL CheckDlgButton(int nIDButton, UINT nCheck);
  BOOL CheckRadioButton(int nIDFirstButton, int nIDLastButton,
                        int nIDCheckButton);

  int DlgDirList(LPTSTR lpPathSpec, int nIDList box,
                 int nIDStaticPath, UINT nFileType);
  int DlgDirListComboBox(LPTSTR lpPathSpec, int nIDComboBox,
                         int nIDStaticPath, UINT nFileType);

  BOOL DlgDirSelect(LPTSTR lpString, int nCount, int nIDList box);
  BOOL DlgDirSelectComboBox(LPTSTR lpString, int nCount,
                            int nIDComboBox);

  UINT GetDlgItemInt(int nID, BOOL* lpTrans = NULL,
                     BOOL bSigned = TRUE) const;
  UINT GetDlgItemText(int nID, LPTSTR lpStr, int nMaxCount) const;
  BOOL GetDlgItemText(int nID, BSTR& bstrText) const;
```

```
HWND GetNextDlgGroupItem(HWND hWndCtl, BOOL bPrevious = FALSE)
  const;
HWND GetNextDlgTabItem(HWND hWndCtl, BOOL bPrevious = FALSE) const;

UINT IsDlgButtonChecked(int nIDButton) const;

LRESULT SendDlgItemMessage(int nID, UINT message, WPARAM wParam = 0,
                           LPARAM lParam = 0);

BOOL SetDlgItemInt(int nID, UINT nValue, BOOL bSigned = TRUE);
BOOL SetDlgItemText(int nID, LPCTSTR lpszString);
};
```

Although ATL adds no overhead to these functions, since they're just inline wrappers of Windows functions, you can just feel that something's not quite as efficient as it could be when you use one of these functions. Every time we pass in a child control ID, the window is probably doing a lookup to figure out the HWND and then calling the actual function on the window. For example, if I ran the zoo, Set-DlgItemText would be implemented as follows:

```
BOOL SetDlgItemText(HWND hwndParent, int nID, LPCTSTR lpszString) {
  HWND hwndChild = GetDlgItem(hwndParent, nID);
  if( !hwndChild ) return FALSE;
  return SetWindowText(hwndChild, lpszString);
}
```

While using that implementation is fine for family, when your friend comes over, it's time to pull out the good dishes. I'd prefer to cache the HWND and use SetWindow-Text. Plus, if I don't want to refer to a dialog or a main window with an HWND, why would I want to refer to my child windows with UINT? Instead, I find it convenient to wrap windows created by the dialog manager with CWindow objects in OnInit-Dialog:

```
LRESULT CStringDlg::OnInitDialog(UINT, WPARAM, LPARAM, BOOL&) {
  CenterWindow();

  // Cache HWNDs
  m_edit.Attach(GetDlgItem(IDC_STRING));
  m_ok.Attach(GetDlgItem(IDOK));
```

```
// Copy the string from the data member to the child control (DDX)
m_edit.SetWindowText(m_sz);

// Check the string length (DDV)
CheckValidString();

return 1; // Let dialog manager set initial focus
}
```

Now the functions that used any of the dialog item family of functions can use CWindow member functions instead:

```
void CStringDlg::CheckValidString() {
// Check the length of the string
int cchString = m_edit.GetWindowTextLength();

// Enable the OK button only if the string is of nonzero length
m_ok.EnableWindow(cchString ? TRUE : FALSE);
}

LRESULT CStringDlg::OnOK(WORD, UINT, HWND, BOOL&) {
// Copy the string from the child control to the data member (DDX)
m_edit.GetWindowText(m_sz, lengthof(m_sz));

EndDialog(IDOK);
return 0;
}
```

A Better Class of Wrappers

Now, my examples have been purposefully simple. A dialog box with a single edit control is not much work, no matter how you build it. However, let's mix things up a little. What if we were to build a dialog with a single list box control instead, as shown in Figure 9.5? This simple change makes the implementation quite a bit more complicated. Instead of being able to use SetWindowText, as we could with an edit control, manipulating a list box control means using special Windows messages. For example, populating the list box and setting the initial selection means using the following code:

```
LRESULT CStringListDlg::OnInitDialog(UINT, WPARAM, LPARAM, BOOL&) {
CenterWindow();
```

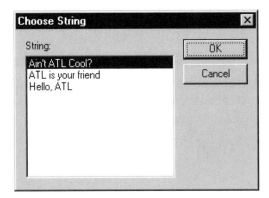

Figure 9.5: A dialog with a list box

```
// Cache list box HWND
m_lb.Attach(GetDlgItem(IDC_LIST));

// Populate the list box
m_lb.SendMessage(LB_ADDSTRING, 0, (LPARAM)__T("Hello, ATL"));
m_lb.SendMessage(LB_ADDSTRING, 0, (LPARAM)__T("Ain't ATL Cool?"));
m_lb.SendMessage(LB_ADDSTRING, 0, (LPARAM)__T("ATL is your friend"));

// Set initial selection
int n = m_lb.SendMessage(LB_FINDSTRING, 0, (LPARAM)m_sz);
if( n == LB_ERR ) n = 0;
m_lb.SendMessage(LB_SETCURSEL, n);

return 1; // Let dialog manager set initial focus
}
```

Likewise, pulling out the final selection in OnOK is just as much fun:

```
LRESULT CStringListDlg::OnOK(WORD, UINT, HWND, BOOL&) {
 // Copy the selected item
 int n = m_lb.SendMessage(LB_GETCURSEL);
 if( n == LB_ERR ) n = 0;
 m_lb.SendMessage(LB_GETTEXT, n, (LPARAM)(LPCTSTR)m_sz);

 EndDialog(IDOK);
 return 0;
}
```

The problem is that, although `CWindow` provides countless wrapper functions common to all windows, it does not provide any wrappers for the built-in Windows controls, such as list boxes. And whereas MFC provides such wrapper classes (for example, `CListBox`), ATL doesn't . . . officially. However, unofficially, buried deep in the `atlcon`[9] sample lives an undocumented and unsupported set of classes that fit the bill nicely. The `atlcontrols.h` file defines the following Windows control wrappers inside the `ATLControls` namespace:

CAnimateCtrl	CButton	CComboBox	CComboBoxEx
CDateTimePickerCtrl	CDragListBox	CEdit	CFlatScrollBar
CHeaderCtrl	CHotKeyCtrl	CImageList	CIPAddressCtrl
CListBox	CListViewCtrl	CMonthCalendarCtrl	CPagerCtrl
CProgressBarCtrl	CReBarCtrl	CRichEditCtrl	CScrollBar
CStatic	CStatusBarCtrl	CTabCtrl	CToolBarCtrl
CToolInfo	CToolTipCtrl	CTrackBarCtrl	CTreeItem
CTreeViewCtrl	CTreeViewCtrlEx	CUpDownCtrl	

For example, the `CListBox` class provides a set of inline wrapper functions, one per LB_XXX message. The ones that would be useful for the example are shown here.

```
template <class Base>
class CListBoxT : public Base {
public:
    ...
    // for single-selection list boxes
    int GetCurSel() const
    { return (int)::SendMessage(m_hWnd, LB_GETCURSEL, 0, OL); }

    int SetCurSel(int nSelect)
    { return (int)::SendMessage(m_hWnd, LB_SETCURSEL, nSelect, OL); }
    ...
    // Operations
    // manipulating list box items
    int AddString(LPCTSTR lpszItem)
    { return (int)::SendMessage(m_hWnd, LB_ADDSTRING, 0, (LPARAM)
                                lpszItem); }
```

---

[9]As of Visual C++, you'll find the `atlcontrols.h` file on the library edition of MSDN, CD-1, in the \samples\vc98\atl\atlcon directory.

```
...
// selection helpers
int FindString(int nStartAfter, LPCTSTR lpszItem) const
{ return (int)::SendMessage(m_hWnd, LB_FINDSTRING, nStartAfter,
                            (LPARAM)lpszItem); }
...
};


typedef CListBoxT<CWindow>  CListBox;
```

Assuming a data member of type ATLControls::CListBox, the updated example
dialog code can now look much more pleasing:

```
LRESULT CStringListDlg::OnInitDialog(UINT, WPARAM, LPARAM, BOOL&) {
   CenterWindow();

   // Cache list box HWND
   m_lb.Attach(GetDlgItem(IDC_LIST));

   // Populate the list box
   m_lb.AddString(_T("Hello, ATL"));
   m_lb.AddString(_T("Ain't ATL Cool?"));
   m_lb.AddString(_T("ATL is your friend"));

   // Set initial selection
   int n = m_lb.FindString(0, m_sz);
   if( n == LB_ERR ) n = 0;
   m_lb.SetCurSel(n);

   return 1; // Let dialog manager set initial focus
}

LRESULT CStringListDlg::OnOK(WORD, UINT, HWND, BOOL&) {
   // Copy the selected item
   int n = m_lb.GetCurSel();
   if( n == LB_ERR ) n = 0;
   m_lb.GetText(n, m_sz);

   EndDialog(IDOK);
   return 0;
}
```

Since the Windows control wrappers are merely a collection of inline functions that call SendMessage for you, the generated code is the same. The good news, of course, is that you don't have to pack the messages yourself. These classes turn out to be so useful that I'd be very surprised if they didn't turn up as supported, documented classes in future versions of ATL. However, because they are unsupported and undocumented, be prepared for the names and/or functionality to change.

CContainedWindow

The Parent Handling the Messages of the Child

A CWindow-based object lets an existing window class handle its messages. This is useful for wrapping child windows. A CWindowImpl-based object handles its own messages via a message map. This is handy for creating parent windows. Objects of another ATL window class, CContainedWindow, let its parent handle the messages, letting an existing window class handle the messages the parent passes through. This is used to centralize message handling in a parent window. The parent window can either create an instance of the child window class or it can let someone else create it, for example, the dialog manager, and subclass it later (I'll discuss subclassing soon). Either way, the messages of the child window will be routed through the message map of the parent window. How does the parent window discern its own messages from those of one or more children? Alternate message maps. Each CContainedWindow will be given a message map ID and its messages will be routed to that alternate part of the parent's message map.

To support both creation of contained windows and subclassing of windows, CContainedWindow is defined as follows:

```
template <class TBase = CWindow, class TWinTraits =
  CControlWinTraits>
class CContainedWindowT : public TBase {
public:
 CWndProcThunk m_thunk;
 LPCTSTR        m_lpszClassName;
 WNDPROC        m_pfnSuperWindowProc;
 CMessageMap*   m_pObject;
 DWORD          m_dwMsgMapID;
 const MSG*     m_pCurrentMsg;

 // If you use this constructor you must supply
 // the Window Class Name, Object* and Message Map ID
```

```
// later to the Create call
CContainedWindowT();

CContainedWindowT(LPTSTR lpszClassName, CMessageMap* pObject,
                  DWORD dwMsgMapID = 0);
CContainedWindowT(CMessageMap* pObject, DWORD dwMsgMapID = 0);

void SwitchMessageMap(DWORD dwMsgMapID);
const MSG* GetCurrentMessage() const;
LRESULT DefWindowProc();
LRESULT DefWindowProc(UINT uMsg, WPARAM wParam, LPARAM lParam);

static LRESULT CALLBACK
  StartWindowProc(HWND hWnd, UINT uMsg, WPARAM wParam,
                  LPARAM lParam);
static LRESULT CALLBACK
  WindowProc(HWND hWnd, UINT uMsg, WPARAM wParam, LPARAM lParam);
ATOM RegisterWndSuperclass();

HWND Create(CMessageMap* pObject, DWORD dwMsgMapID, HWND hWndParent,
            RECT* prcPos, LPCTSTR szWindowName = NULL,
            DWORD dwStyle = 0, DWORD dwExStyle = 0,
            UINT nID = 0, LPVOID lpCreateParam = NULL);

HWND Create(LPCTSTR lpszClassName, CMessageMap* pObject,
            DWORD dwMsgMapID, HWND hWndParent, RECT* prcPos,
            LPCTSTR szWindowName = NULL, DWORD dwStyle = 0,
            DWORD dwExStyle = 0, UINT nID = 0,
            LPVOID lpCreateParam = NULL);

// This function is deprecated; use the version
// that takes a RECT* instead
HWND Create(HWND hWndParent, RECT& rcPos,
            LPCTSTR szWindowName = NULL,
            DWORD dwStyle = 0, DWORD dwExStyle = 0,
            UINT nID = 0, LPVOID lpCreateParam = NULL);

HWND Create(HWND hWndParent, RECT* prcPos,
            LPCTSTR szWindowName = NULL,
            DWORD dwStyle = 0, DWORD dwExStyle = 0,
            UINT nID = 0, LPVOID lpCreateParam = NULL);
```

```
BOOL SubclassWindow(HWND hWnd);
HWND UnsubclassWindow(BOOL bForce = FALSE);
};


typedef CContainedWindowT<CWindow> CContainedWindow;
```

Notice that CContainedWindow does not derive from CWindowImpl, nor does it derive from CMessageMap. CContainedWindow objects do not have their own message map. Instead, the WindowProc static member function of CContained-Window routes messages to the parent window. The specific message map ID is provided either to the constructor or to the Create function.

Creating Contained Windows

Notice also the various constructors and Create functions, some taking the name of the window class and some not. If you're going to create an instance of a CContainedWindow instead of subclassing, you have quite a bit of flexibility. For example, to morph the letter box example to create an edit control that accepts only letters, CContainedWindow would be used like this:

```
class CMainWindow :
 public CWindowImpl<CMainWindow, CWindow, CMainWindowTraits> {
public:
...
BEGIN_MSG_MAP(CMainWindow)
 ...
// Handle the child edit control's messages
ALT_MSG_MAP(1)
 MESSAGE_HANDLER(WM_CHAR, OnEditChar)
END_MSG_MAP()

 LRESULT OnCreate(UINT, WPARAM, LPARAM, BOOL&) {
  // Create the contained window, routing its messages to us
  if( m_edit.Create("edit", this, 1, m_hWnd, &CWindow::rcDefault) ) {
   return 0;
  }
  return -1;
 }

 // Let the child edit control receive only letters
 LRESULT OnEditChar(UINT, WPARAM wparam, LPARAM, BOOL& bHandled) {
  if( isalpha((TCHAR)wparam) ) bHandled = FALSE;
```

```
    else                         MessageBeep(0xFFFFFFFF);
    return 0;
  }
  ...
private:
  CContainedWindow  m_edit;
};
```

When the main window is created, this code associates an HWND with the CContainedWindow object m_edit by creating a new edit control, so identified because of the window class passed as the first parameter to Create. The second parameter is the CMessageMap pointer for where the contained window's messages are going to be routed. This parameter is most often the parent window, but doesn't have to be.

To separate the parent's messages from the child's, the parent's message map is broken up into two parts: the main part and one alternate part. The ID of the alternate part of the message map is passed as the third parameter to Create.

Finally, to filter out all characters but the letters sent to the contained edit control, the WM_CHAR handler only passes through the WM_CHAR messages that contain letters. By setting bHandled to FALSE, the parent window is indicating to the CContainedWindow window procedure that it should keep looking for a handler for this message. Eventually, after the message map has been exhausted (including any chaining that may be going on), the WindowProc passes the message onto the edit control's normal window procedure. For nonletters, the WM_CHAR handler leaves bHandled set to TRUE (the default), which stops the message from going anywhere else and stops the child edit control from seeing any WM_CHAR messages without letters in them. As far as the child edit control is concerned, the user entered only letters.

Subclassing Contained Windows

If you'd like to contain a child control that has already been created (for example, the dialog manager that has already created an edit control), you'll have to *subclass*[10] it. Previously in this chapter, I described superclassing as the Windows version of inheritance for window classes. Subclassing is a much more modest and much more used technique. Instead of creating a whole new window class, with subclassing we merely hijack the messages of a single window. Subclassing is accomplished by creating a window of a certain class and replacing its window procedure with our own using SetWindowLong(GWL_WNDPROC). The replacement window

---

[10] For a more complete dissection of Windows subclassing, see *Win32 Programming*, by Brent Rector and Joe Newcomer (Addison-Wesley, 1997).

procedure gets all the messages first and can decide whether to let the original window procedure handle it as well. If you think of superclassing as specialization of a class, subclassing is specialization of a single instance. Subclassing is usually performed on child windows, for example, an edit box that the dialog wishes to restrict to letters only. The dialog would subclass the child edit control during WM_INIT-DIALOG and handle WM_CHAR messages, throwing out any that weren't suitable.

For example, subclassing an edit control in a dialog would look like this:

```
class CLettersDlg : public CDialogImpl<CLettersDlg> {
public:
 // Set the CMessageMap* and the message map ID
 CLettersDlg() : m_edit(this, 1) {}

BEGIN_MSG_MAP(CLettersDlg)
  ...
ALT_MSG_MAP(1)
 MESSAGE_HANDLER(WM_CHAR, OnEditChar)
END_MSG_MAP()

 enum { IDD = IDD_LETTERS_ONLY };

 LRESULT OnInitDialog(UINT, WPARAM, LPARAM, BOOL&) {
   // Subclass the existing child edit control
   m_edit.SubclassWindow(GetDlgItem(IDC_EDIT));

   return 1; // Let the dialog manager set the initial focus
 }
 ...
private:
 CContainedWindow  m_edit;
};
```

In this case, because the example doesn't call Create, it has to pass the CMessageMap pointer and the message map ID of the child edit control in the constructor using the member initialization list syntax. It would seem that the ATL folks could've had one more version of SubclassWindow, since they had so many versions of Create, but maybe they ran out of bits. Anyway, once the contained window knows to whom to route the messages and to which part of the message map, it only needs to know the HWND of the window to subclass. It gets this in the SubclassWindow call in the WM_INITDIALOG handler.

How subclassing is performed is shown in the CContainedWindow implementation of SubclassWindow:

```
template <class TBase, class TWinTraits>
BOOL CContainedWindowT<TBase, TWinTraits>::SubclassWindow(HWND hWnd){
  m_thunk.Init(WindowProc, this);
  WNDPROC pProc = (WNDPROC)&m_thunk.thunk;
  WNDPROC pfnWndProc = (WNDPROC)::SetWindowLong(hWnd, GWL_WNDPROC,
                                                  (LONG)pProc);

  if (pfnWndProc == NULL) return FALSE;
  m_pfnSuperWindowProc = pfnWndProc;
  m_hWnd = hWnd;
  return TRUE;
}
```

The important part is the call to `SetWindowLong` passing `GWL_WNDPROC`. This replaces the current window object's window procedure with an ATL thunking version that routes messages to the container. It also returns the existing window procedure, which `CContainedWindow` caches to call for any messages the container doesn't handle.

Containing the Windows Control Wrappers

After being introduced to the ATL Windows control wrapper classes (such as `CEdit`, `CListBox`, etc.), you may dread window containment. If `CContainedWindow` derives from `CWindow`, where do all the nifty inline wrapper functions come from? Never fear, ATL is here. As you've already seen, `CContainedWindow` is really just a type definition for the `CContainedWindowT` template class. One of the parameters is a window traits class, which won't help you. The other, however, is the name of the base class. `CContainedWindow` uses `CWindow` as the base for `CContainedWindowT`, but there's no reason you have to. By using one of the ATL Windows control wrapper classes instead, you can have a contained window that also has all the wrapper's functions. For example, we can change the type of the `m_edit` variable like so:

```
CContainedWindowT<ATLControls::CEdit> m_edit;
```

This technique is especially handy when you're using `Create` instead of `SubclassWindow`. With `Create`, you have to provide the name of the window class. If you call `Create` without a window class, the `CContainedWindow` object attempts to acquire a window class by calling the base class function `GetWndClassName`, which is implemented by `CWindow` like so:

```
static LPCTSTR CWindow::GetWndClassName()
{ return NULL; }
```

However, each of the ATL Windows control wrappers overrides this function to provide its window class name. For example:

```
static LPCTSTR CEditT::GetWndClassName()
{ return _T("EDIT"); }
```

Now, when creating an instance of one of the contained window wrapper classes, you don't have to dig through the documentation to figure out what the class name is of your favorite intrinsic window class, you can simply call `Create`:

```
class CMainWindow : public CWindowImpl<...> {
...
  LRESULT OnCreate(UINT, WPARAM, LPARAM, BOOL&) {
    // Window class name provided by base class
    if( m_edit.Create(this, 1, m_hWnd, &CWindow::rcDefault) ) {
       return 0;
    }
    return -1;
  }
...
private:
  CContainedWindowT<ATLControls::CEdit> m_edit;
};
```

Summary

ATL takes the same principles of efficiency and flexibility that were originally developed for COM and applies them to another part of the Windows API, User32. This support takes the form of a small set of windowing classes. CWindow, which forms the root class of the windowing hierarchy, provides a large number of inline wrapper functions for manipulating an existing HWND. To create a new window class or to superclass an existing one and to handle messages from windows of that class, ATL provides CWindowImpl. CDialogImpl provides the same functionality for dialog boxes, both modal and modeless. To subclass child windows and manage messages in the parent, ATL provides CContainedWindow. These classes can be used in standalone applications or in COM servers. For COM servers that expose COM controls, the windowing classes form the core of how input and output are managed, as discussed in the following chapter.

CHAPTER

10 | **ActiveX Controls**

A Review of ActiveX Controls

A complete review of the COM interfaces and interactions between an ActiveX control and a control container is outside the scope of this book. If you are unfamiliar with the various interfaces and interactions described in this chapter, there are various other texts that specifically address these topics. *Inside OLE* by Kraig Brockschmidt (Microsoft Press, 1995) is the original COM text and devotes hundreds of pages to in-place activation and visual interface components.

An ActiveX control is a superset of an in-place activated object, so you'll also need to read the OLE controls specification from Microsoft, which describes the requirements of a control. In addition, the OLE controls 1996 specification, commonly referred to as the OC96 spec, documents optimizations for control activations (such as windowless controls and windowless control containment), two-pass rendering for nonrectangular windows, hit testing for nonrectangular windows, and fast activation protocols between controls and containers, as well as numerous other features.

So, rather than rewording the material available in the references just described, I'm going to show you how to implement such an object. This chapter describes how to implement a feature-complete ActiveX control using ATL.

ActiveX Control Functionality

A control incorporates much of the functionality you've seen in prior chapters. For example, a control is a COM object. Therefore, an ATL control contains all the standard functionality of an ATL-based COM object. A control is a user-interface (UI) component; therefore it has thread affinity and should live in a single-threaded apartment. A control thus derives from the `CComObjectRootEx<CComSingle-ThreadModel>` base class.

A control must be a createable class so its container can instantiate it. Therefore, the control class will also derive from `CComCoClass`. Many controls use the `CComCoClass` default class object's implementation of the `IClassFactory` interface. Licensed controls override this default by specifying the DECLARE_CLASS-FACTORY2 macro, which declares a class object that implements the `IClass-Factory2` interface.

In addition, most controls will support one or more of the following features:

- Stock properties and methods such as ForeColor and Refresh that a container can access via the control's IDispatch implementation.

- Custom properties and methods that a container can access via the control's IDispatch implementation.

- Stock and custom event callback methods using the connection points protocol to a container's dispinterface implementation. This requires the control to implement the IConnectionPointContainer and IProvideClass-Info2 interfaces as well as a connection point that makes calls to the event dispinterface.

- Property change notifications to one or more clients using the connection points protocol to the clients' IPropertyNotifySink interface implementations. Control properties that send such change notifications should be marked in the control's type library using the bindable and/or requestedit attributes, as appropriate.

- On-demand rendering of a view of the object via the IViewObject, IView-Object2, and IViewObjectEx interfaces.

- Standard OLE control functionality as provided by the IOleControl interface and in-place activation using the IOleObject and IOleInPlaceActive-Object interfaces.

- Persistence support for various containers. At a minimum, a control typically provides support so that a container can save the object into a stream using the IPersistStreamInit interface. Many controls will additionally support persistence to a property bag using IPersistPropertyBag because Visual Basic and Internet Explorer prefer this medium. Some controls additionally support IPersistStorage so they can be embedded into OLE documents.

- Fast and efficient windowless activation as provided by the IOleInPlace-ObjectWindowless interface when the control's container supports this optimization.

- Fast and efficient exchange of multiple interfaces during activation between a control and its controls using the IQuickActivate interface.

- Object safety settings either through component category membership or via IObjectSafety.

- Drag-and-drop support as provided by implementations of the IDataObject, IDropSource, and IDropTarget interfaces.

- A graphical user interface that provides a means to edit the control's properties. Typically a control provides one or more COM objects, called *property pages*, each of which displays a user interface that can modify a logically related subset of the control's properties. A container requests the CLSIDs of the property page COM objects using the control's `ISpecifyPropertyPages` interface implementation.

- A container that can access information about the properties of a control that supports property pages by using the `IPerPropertyBrowsing` interface. For example, the container can obtain a text string describing a property, determine which property page contains the user interface to edit the property, and retrieve a list of strings describing the allowed values for the property.

- Support for arranging the control's properties by category in Visual Basic's property view. A control implements the `ICategorizeProperties` interface to provide the list of categories to Visual Basic and to map each property to a category.

- Default keyboard handling for an ActiveX control. This is commonly needed for tabbing, default button press on Enter, arrow keys, and popping up help.

- Setting the `MiscStatus` flags for a control. Special settings are necessary for some controls to operate properly.

Property Page Functionality

Because a control frequently provides one or more property pages, a complete control implementation will also supply one or more property page objects, which each

- Implement (at least) the `IPropertyPage` interface, which provides the main features of a property page object.

- Optionally implement the `IPropertyPage2` interface to support selection of a specific property. Visual Basic uses this support to open the correct property page and set the input focus directly to the specified control when the user wants to edit a property.

- Receive property change notifications from one or more controls using the connection points protocol to the property page's `IPropertyNotifySink` interface implementation.

The BullsEye Control Requirements

This chapter describes the ATL implementation of a feature-rich control called BullsEye. The BullsEye control implements all the previously described features. The BullsEye control draws a bulls-eye. You can configure the number of rings in the bulls-eye (from one to nine) and the color of the center ring as well as the color of the ring adjacent to the center (called the alternate ring color). BullsEye draws additional rings by alternately using the center and alternate colors.

The area around the bulls-eye can be transparent or opaque. When transparent, the background around the bulls-eye shows through. When opaque, the bulls-eye fills the area around the circle using the background color. By default, BullsEye uses the container's ambient background color as the background color. BullsEye also uses the foreground color to draw a line separating each ring.

You can assign score values to each ring. By default, the center ring is worth 512 points and each other ring is worth half the points of its adjacent inner ring. When a user clicks on a ring, the control fires an `OnRingHit` event and an `OnScoreChanged` event. The argument to the `OnRingHit` event method specifies the ring upon which the user clicked. Rings are numbered from 1 to N, where 1 is the centermost ring. The `OnScoreChanged` event specifies the point value of the clicked ring. For example, clicking on ring 2 with default scores fires an `OnScoreChanged` event with an argument of 256 points.

In addition, when you click on one of the bulls-eye rings, the control can provide feedback by playing a sound. By default, you hear the sound of an arrow striking the bulls-eye. The Boolean `Beep` property, when set to TRUE, indicates the control should play its sound on a ring hit.

BullsEye supports all standard control functionality. In addition to windowed activation, BullsEye can be activated as a windowless control when its container supports such functionality.

Many containers ask their controls to save their state using the `IPersistStreamInit` interface and an `IStream` medium. When embedding a control in an OLE document, a container asks a control to save its state using the `IPersistStorage` interface and the `IStorage` medium. A container, such as Internet Explorer and Visual Basic, that prefers to save the state of a control as textual name/value pairs uses the control's `IPersistPropertyBag` interface and the `IPropertyBag` medium. BullsEye supports all three persistence protocols and media—streams, storages, and property bags.

BullsEye also provides two property pages. One property page is custom to the BullsEye control and allows you to set the `Enabled`, `Beep` (sound on ring hit), and `BackStyle` (transparent) properties (Figure 10.1). The other is the standard color selection property page (Figure 10.2). The BullsEye control has four color properties: the center ring color, the alternate ring color, the background color (used to fill the area around the bulls-eye) and the foreground color (used to draw the separator line between rings).

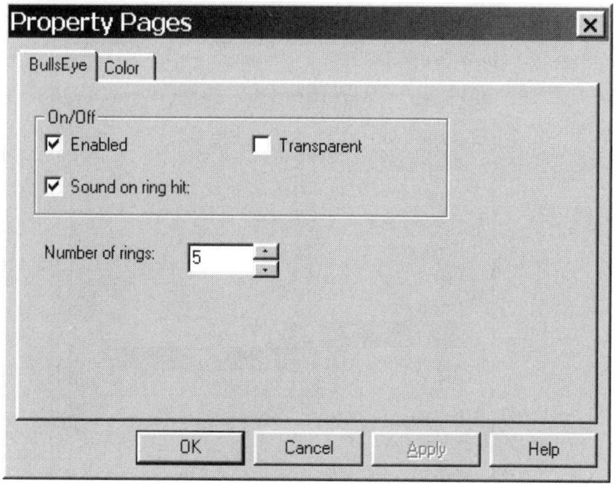

Figure 10.1. BullsEye custom property page

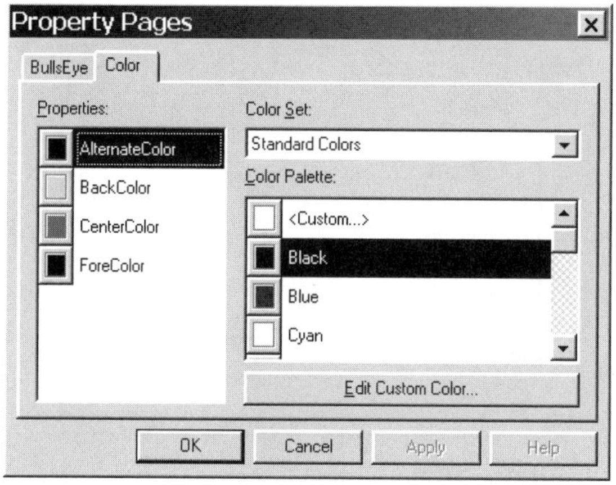

Figure 10.2. BullsEye color property page

The BullsEye control also categorizes its properties for Visual Basic. Visual Basic has a property view window in which you can select a view that sorts the properties by standard and control-defined categories (Figure 10.3). The BullsEye control lists its color properties and the `RingCount` property in the standard Appearance category. The control lists its `Beep` property in the standard Behavior category.

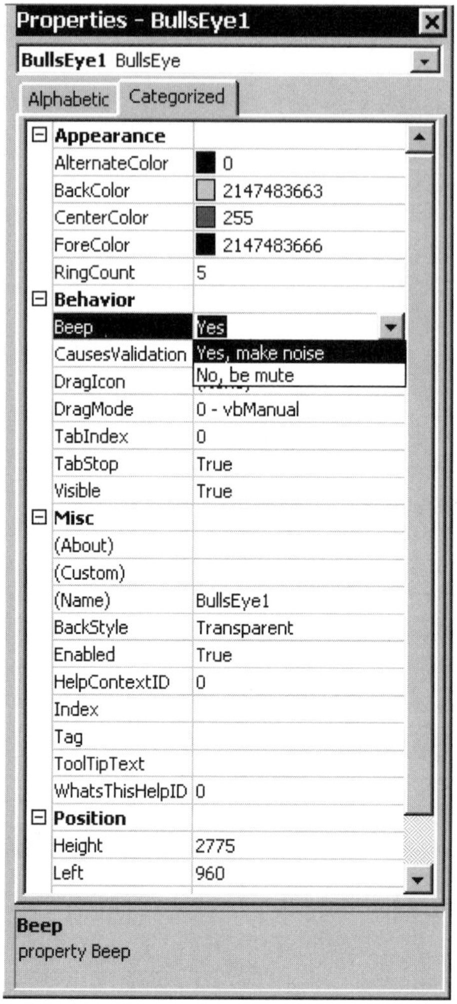

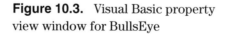

Figure 10.3. Visual Basic property
view window for BullsEye

BullsEye also supports per-property browsing. Per-property browsing allows a control to specify a list of strings that a container should display as the available choices for a property's value. Notice in the example Visual Basic property view window that, in the Behavior category, Visual Basic displays the strings "Yes, make noise" and "No, be mute" as the selections available for the Beep property.

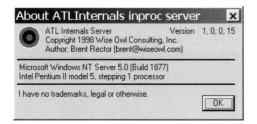

Figure 10.4. BullsEye About box

Also notice that the Misc category contains an entry called (About) that represents the `AboutBox` stock method. BullsEye displays the dialog box shown in Figure 10.4 when the user selects the About entry.

Requirements: The Properties and Methods

BullsEye supports the four stock properties shown in Table 10.1. In addition, BullsEye supports all three stock methods, as shown in Table 10.2. Finally, BullsEye supports the custom properties listed in Table 10.3.

Table 10.1. BullsEye Stock Properties

Property name	Type	Stock DISPID	Description
`BackColor`	`OLE_COLOR`	`DISPID_BACKCOLOR`	Background color
`BackStyle`	`long`	`DISPID_BACKSTYLE`	Background style: transparent or opaque
`Enabled`	`VARIANT_BOOL`	`DISPID_ENABLED`	Enabled status: `TRUE` or `FALSE`
`ForeColor`	`OLE_COLOR`	`DISPID_FORECOLOR`	Foreground color

Table 10.2. BullsEye Stock Methods

Method name	Stock DISPID	Description
`AboutBox`	`DISPID_ABOUTBOX`	Display the control's Help About dialog
`DoClick`	`DISPID_DOCLICK`	Simulate a mouse click on the control
`Refresh`	`DISPID_REFRESH`	Redraw the control

Table 10.3. BullsEye Custom Properties

Property name	Type	Custom DISPID	Description
Application	IDispatch*	DISPID_APPLICATION	Return the IDispatch* for the hosting application
Alternate-Color	OLE_COLOR	DISPID_ALTERNATE-COLOR	Get/set the color of the alternate (even) rings
Beep	VARIANT_BOOL	DISPID_BEEP	Enable/disable sound effects for the control
CenterColor	OLE_COLOR	DISPID_CENTERCOLOR	Get/set the color of the center (odd) rings
Parent	IDispatch*	DISPID_PARENT	Return the IDispatch* for the control's parent
RingCount	short	DISPID_RINGCOUNT	Get/set the number of rings
RingValue	long	DISPID_RINGVALUE	Get/set the value of each ring

Declaring the Properties and Methods in IDL

A control container accesses the properties and methods of a control using the control's IDispatch interface. A control must therefore provide an implementation of IDispatch when it has properties and methods.

ATL-based controls, in general, and the BullsEye control, specifically, implement their properties and methods using a dual interface, not a dispatch interface, even though a *dual* interface is unnecessary because the vtable portion of the dual interface will typically go unused. A custom C++ control container could access the control's properties and methods using the vtable, but no other container currently does. At the time of this writing, even Visual Basic 6 accesses properties and methods of a control using the control's IDispatch interface. Visual Basic only uses the vtable portion of a dual interface for noncontrol objects.

The BullsEye control provides access to its properties and methods on the default IBullsEye dual interface. When you generate a new ATL-based control class, the wizard generates the definition of the default dual interface, but you must populate the definition with the accessor methods for your control's properties and the control's methods. The definition of the IBullsEye interface is given in Listing 10.1.

Listing 10.1. The `IBullsEye` interface

```
[ object, dual, pointer_default(unique),
  uuid(7DC59CC4-36C0-11D2-AC05-00A0C9C8E50D),
  helpstring("IBullsEye Interface"),
]
interface IBullsEye : IDispatch
{
 const int DISPID_ALTERNATECOLOR = 1; const int DISPID_BEEP       = 2;
 const int DISPID_CENTERCOLOR    = 3; const int DISPID_RINGCOUNT   = 4;
 const int DISPID_RINGVALUE      = 5; const int DISPID_APPLICATION = 6;
 const int DISPID_PARE           = 7;
#define PROPGET         propget, bindable, requestedit
#define PROPPUT         propput, bindable, requestedit
 [PROPPUT, id(DISPID_BACKCOLOR)] HRESULT BackColor([in]OLE_COLOR clr);
 [PROPGET, id(DISPID_BACKCOLOR)] HRESULT BackColor
   ([out,retval]OLE_COLOR*pclr);
 [PROPPUT, id(DISPID_BACKSTYLE)] HRESULT BackStyle([in]long style);
 [PROPGET, id(DISPID_BACKSTYLE)] HRESULT BackStyle([out,retval]long*
   style);
 [PROPPUT, id(DISPID_FORECOLOR)] HRESULT ForeColor([in]OLE_COLOR clr);
 [PROPGET, id(DISPID_FORECOLOR)] HRESULT ForeColor
   ([out,retval]OLE_COLOR* pclr);
 [PROPPUT, id(DISPID_ENABLED)] HRESULT Enabled([in]VARIANT_BOOL vbool);
 [PROPGET, id(DISPID_ENABLED)] HRESULT Enabled
   ([out,retval]VARIANT_BOOL* pbool);
 [PROPPUT, id(DISPID_ALTERNATECOLOR)] HRESULT AlternateColor([in]
   OLE_COLOR newVal);
 [PROPGET, id(DISPID_ALTERNATECOLOR)] HRESULT AlternateColor([out,
   retval] OLE_COLOR *pVal);
 [PROPPUT, id(DISPID_BEEP)] HRESULT Beep([in] VARIANT_BOOL newVal);
 [PROPGET, id(DISPID_BEEP)] HRESULT Beep([out, retval] VARIANT_BOOL
   *pVal);
 [PROPPUT, id(DISPID_CENTERCOLOR)] HRESULT CenterColor([in] OLE_COLOR
   newVal);
 [PROPGET, id(DISPID_CENTERCOLOR)] HRESULT CenterColor([out, retval]
   OLE_COLOR *pVal);
 [PROPPUT, id(DISPID_RINGCOUNT)] HRESULT RingCount([in] short newVal);
 [PROPGET, id(DISPID_RINGCOUNT)] HRESULT RingCount([out, retval] short
   *pVal);
```

```
[PROPPUT, id(DISPID_RINGVALUE)] HRESULT RingValue([in] short
  sRingNumber, [in] long newVal);
[PROPGET, id(DISPID_RINGVALUE)] HRESULT RingValue([in] short
  sRingNumber, [out, retval] long *pVal);
[PROPGET, id(DISPID_APPLICATION)] HRESULT Application([out, retval]
  LPDISPATCH *pVal);
[PROPGET, id(DISPID_PARENT)] HRESULT Parent([out, retval] LPDISPATCH
  *pVal);
[id(DISPID_REFRESH)] HRESULT Refresh();
[id(DISPID_DOCLICK)] HRESULT DoClick();
[id(DISPID_ABOUTBOX)] HRESULT AboutBox();
};
```

Requirements: The Events

BullsEye Custom Events

The BullsEye control doesn't support any of the stock events. However, it has two custom events, as detailed in Table 10.4.

An event interface contains only methods and should be a dispatch interface in order for all containers to receive the event callbacks. Some containers, such as Visual Basic, can receive event callbacks on custom IUnknown-derived interfaces. An event interface should never be a dual interface.

Table 10.4. BullsEye Custom Events

Event	Event DISPID	Description
void OnRingHit (short sRingNumber)	DISPID_ONRINGHIT	The user clicked on one of the bulls-eye rings. The argument specifies the ring that the user clicked. Rings are numbered from 1 to N from the center outward.
void OnScoreChanged (long RingValue)	DISPID_ONSCORECHANGED	This event follows the On-RingHit event when the user clicks on a bulls-eye ring. The argument specifies the score value of the ring that the user clicked.

Declaring the Event Dispatch Interface in IDL

The definition of the _IBullsEyeEvents dispatch interface is shown in Listing 10.2. In order for the constants for the DISPIDs to appear in the MIDL-generated C/C++ header file, the definitions of the constants must appear in the IDL file outside of the library block. You must define the dispinterface itself inside the library block.

Listing 10.2. The _IBullsEyeEvents dispatch interface

```
const int DISPID_ONRINGHIT     = 1;
const int DISPID_ONSCORECHANGED = 2;


[
    uuid(19FF9872-36ED-11d2-AC05-00A0C9C8E50D),
    helpstring("Event interface for BullsEye Control")
]
dispinterface _IBullsEyeEvents
{
    properties:
    methods:
    [id(DISPID_ONRINGHIT)] void OnRingHit(short ringNumber);
    [id(DISPID_ONSCORECHANGED)] void OnScoreChanged(long ringValue);
};
```

Requirements: The BullsEye and Property Page Coclasses

Declaring the BullsEye Class and Its Property Page Class in IDL

You must also define the BullsEye coclass in the library block of the IDL file (Listing 10.3). At a minimum, you must specify the default IDispatch interface (IBullsEye), via which a container can access the control's properties and methods, and the default source interface (_IBullsEyeEvents), through which the BullsEye control fires events to its container.

Listing 10.3. The BullsEye coclass

```
[   uuid(7DC59CC5-36C0-11D2-AC05-00A0C9C8E50D),
    helpstring("BullsEye Class")
]
coclass BullsEye
{
```

```
    [default]        interface    IBullsEye;
    [default, source] dispinterface _IBullsEyeEvents;
};
```

Additionally, you should define all the custom property page classes implemented by your control in the library block of the IDL file. BullsEye only has one
custom property page, called BullsEyePropPage (Listing 10.4).

Listing 10.4. The BullsEyePropPage coclass

```
[   uuid(7DC59CC8-36C0-11D2-AC05-00A0C9C8E50D),
    helpstring("BullsEyePropPage Class")
]
coclass BullsEyePropPage
{
    interface IUnknown;
};
```

Creating the Initial Control Using the ATL Wizard

Some people prefer to write all the code for a control by hand. They don't care for
the wizard-generated code because they don't understand what it does and doesn't
do. Occasionally, the wizard-generated code is incorrect, as well. Even if you generate the initial code base using the wizard, you will change it greatly before the
control is complete anyway, so you might as well save some time and effort initially
by using the wizard.

Selecting Options for the CBullsEye Implementation Class

I took the requirements for the BullsEye control, used the new ATL Object Wizard,
and requested a Full Control because it is the option most like my requirements.
Here are my responses to the wizard dialogs.

First I defined the name of my implementation class, CBullsEye, its source file
names, the primary interface name (IBullsEye) and various COM object registration information (Figure 10.5).

Then I specified various COM object options for the control (Figure 10.6).
Controls need thread affinity (because they are UI components and use window
handles, which are associated with a thread). Therefore the wizard correctly only
allows you to request the Single or Apartment threading models for a control.

Containers will access a control's properties and methods using the control's
IDispatch interface. The easiest way to get an IDispatch implementation in your

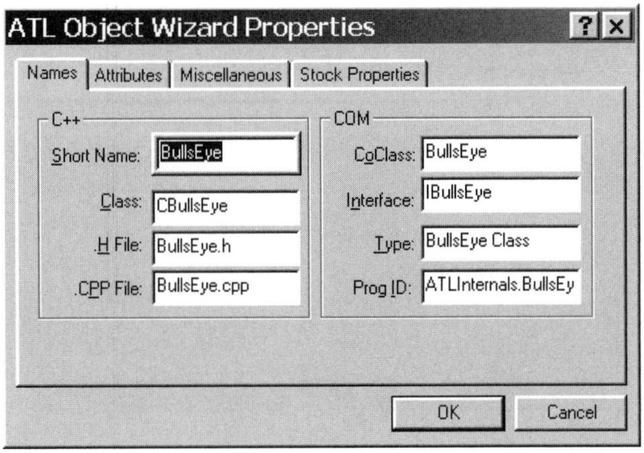

Figure 10.5. BullsEye Names dialog

Figure 10.6. COM object attributes for the BullsEye control

control is to specify that the primary interface be a dual interface. Should you specify the Custom interface option, you'd need to implement IDispatch separately on the control. Controls can be aggregated or not. I've requested that BullsEye support aggregation, even though it increases the size of each instance by eight bytes.

A COM object that implements a dual interface should also support the ISupportErrorInfo interface so it can return rich error messages using the COM error object mechanism. The BullsEye control fires events, and containers expect to receive control events via the connection points protocol, so I asked for connection point support as well. A control should never use the Free-Threaded Marshaler, so be sure to leave that selection unchecked.

Figure 10.7. Miscellaneous control options for
the BullsEye control

The Miscellaneous page allows you to select various control options not available elsewhere. The only options that apply to the BullsEye control are the ones selected in the dialog shown in Figure 10.7. Select the Opaque option when your control is completely opaque and none of the container shows through within the control's boundaries. This helps the container draw the control more quickly. An opaque control can also specify that the background is a solid color, not a patterned brush.

I'll discuss how to implement the BullsEye rendering code so that it supports transparent areas around the bulls-eye, but let's start with an opaque control. The Opaque and Solid Background options simply specify the flags used in the DE-CLARE_VIEW_STATUS macro.

When selected, the Normalize DC (device context) option causes your control to override the OnDraw method for its rendering. When not selected, the control overrides the OnDrawAdvanced method by default. OnDrawAdvanced saves the state of the device context, switches to MM_TEXT mapping mode, calls OnDraw, and then restores the saved device context. Therefore, when you ask for a normalized DC and don't override OnDrawAdvanced, you introduce a little more overhead. BullsEye uses this support, though.

The Insertable option allows the control to be embedded by any application that supports embedded objects through the Insert Object system dialog. Microsoft Word and Excel are two such applications. Selecting this option causes, among other things, your control to support the IPersistStorage and IDataObject interfaces.

Finally, you can have the wizard generate support for any stock properties you want the control to support. BullsEye requires four stock properties, which I've selected in the dialog (Figure 10.8). You'll have to slightly enhance the IDL for the

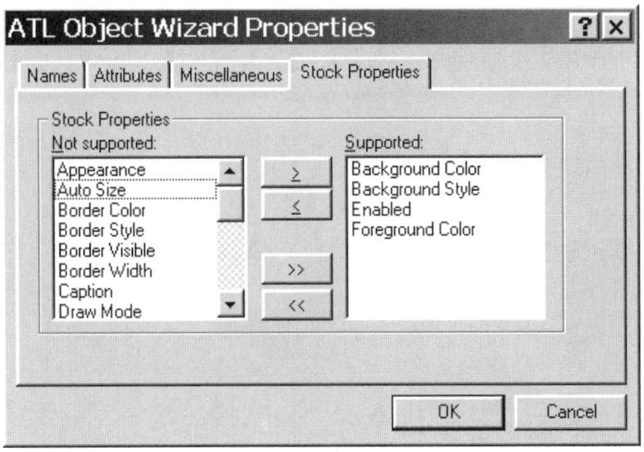

Figure 10.8. Stock properties for the BullsEye control

stock properties, but ATL provides the implementation of the property accessor methods.

There is no wizard support for stock methods, so you'll have to implement them, as well as BullsEye's custom properties, by hand.

Base Classes Used by Wizard-Generated Classes

The ATL wizard generates the initial source code for a control. The control class derives from a number of different base classes, depending on the type of control you ask the wizard to generate. The wizard also adds support for various features based on various selections you make from the ATL Object Wizard Properties dialog pages. Table 10.5 summarizes the base classes used by the different types of wizard-generated controls.

The Initial BullsEye Source Files

The Initial CBullsEye Class Declaration

The initial wizard-generated class declaration for the CBullsEye control class is shown in Listing 10.5. I'll have to make a number of changes to the class before it meets all the requirements described at the beginning of the chapter. For example, I'll need to add a few more base classes to obtain all the required control functionality. Also, presently there are no properties supported by the control except the stock properties I selected via the wizard dialogs. Plus, there is quite of bit of implementation code to write to make the control draw and behave as a bulls-eye. I'll get to all that, but first, let's look at the initial source code.

Table 10.5. Base Classes Used by Various Control Types

Base classes used	Full control	Lite control	Composite control	HTML control	Lite composite control	Lite HTML control
CComObjectRootEx<TM>	✓	✓	✓	✓	✓	✓
CComCoClass	✓	✓	✓	✓	✓	✓
CComControl	✓	✓		✓		✓
CComCompositeControl			✓		✓	
CStockPropImpl	SP	SP	SP	SP	SP	SP
IConnectionPointContainerImpl	CPE	CPE	CPE	CPE	CPE	CPE
IDataObjectImpl	✓	✓	✓	✓		
IDispatchImpl	No SP & Dual	No SP & Dual	No SP & Dual	✓	No SP & Dual	✓
IOleControlImpl	✓	✓	✓	✓	✓	✓
IOleInPlaceActiveObjectImpl	✓	✓	✓	✓	✓	✓
IOleInPlaceObjectWindowlessImpl	✓	✓	✓	✓	✓	✓
IOleObjectImpl	✓	✓	✓	✓	✓	✓
IPersistStorageImpl	✓		✓	✓		
IPersistStreamInitImpl	✓	✓	✓	✓	✓	✓
IPropertyNotifySinkCP	CPE		CPE	CPE	✓	
IProvideClassInfo2Impl	✓		✓	✓		
IQuickActivateImpl	✓		✓	✓		
ISpecifyPropertyPagesImpl	✓		✓	✓		
ISupportErrorInfoImpl	SEI	SEI	SEI	SEI	SEI	SEI
IViewObjectExImpl	✓	✓	✓	✓	✓	✓
Control uses normalized DC	User	User	✓	User	✓	User
Control is windowed only	User	User	✓	✓	✓	✓

SP = Stock properties selected; CPE = Connection points enabled; SEI = SupportErrorInfo enabled; User = User selection on wizard property page.

I've reformatted the source code slightly from the original wizard-generated source code to group related functionality together and to add a few comments.

Listing 10.5. The initial wizard-generated `CBullsEye` class

```
//////////////////////////////////////////////////////////////////////
// CBullsEye
class ATL_NO_VTABLE CBullsEye :
   // COM object support
   public CComObjectRootEx<CComSingleThreadModel>,
   // Class object support
   public CComCoClass<CBullsEye, &CLSID_BullsEye>,
   // Default dual (IDispatch-derived) interface to control
   // Request for properties preprocessed by stock property base class
   public CStockPropImpl<CBullsEye, IBullsEye,
                         &IID_IBullsEye, &LIBID_ATLInternalsLib>,
   // Error info support for default dual interface
   public ISupportErrorInfo,
   // Basic "Lite" control implementation
   public CComControl<CBullsEye>,
   public IOleControlImpl<CBullsEye>,
   public IOleObjectImpl<CBullsEye>,
   public IOleInPlaceActiveObjectImpl<CBullsEye>,
   public IOleInPlaceObjectWindowlessImpl<CBullsEye>,
   public IViewObjectExImpl<CBullsEye>,
   // "Lite" control persistence implementation
   public IPersistStreamInitImpl<CBullsEye>,
   // Full control additional implementations
   // Support for OLE embedding
   public IDataObjectImpl<CBullsEye>,
   public IPersistStorageImpl<CBullsEye>,
   // Support for property pages
   public ISpecifyPropertyPagesImpl<CBullsEye>,
   // Support for fast activation
   public IQuickActivateImpl<CBullsEye>,
   // Connection point implementation
   public IConnectionPointContainerImpl<CBullsEye>,
   public IProvideClassInfo2Impl<&CLSID_BullsEye,
                                 &DIID__IBullsEyeEvents,
                                 &LIBID_ATLInternalsLib>,
```

```
        // Full controls supporting connection points
        // also receive property change notification support
        public IPropertyNotifySinkCP<CBullsEye>
    {
    public:
        CBullsEye() { }

    DECLARE_REGISTRY_RESOURCEID(IDR_BULLSEYE)
    DECLARE_PROTECT_FINAL_CONSTRUCT()

    BEGIN_COM_MAP(CBullsEye)
        // Default dual (IDispatch-derived) interface to control
        COM_INTERFACE_ENTRY(IBullsEye)
        COM_INTERFACE_ENTRY(IDispatch)
        // Error info support for default dual interface
        COM_INTERFACE_ENTRY(ISupportErrorInfo)
        // Basic "Lite" control implementation
        COM_INTERFACE_ENTRY(IOleControl)
        COM_INTERFACE_ENTRY(IOleObject)
        COM_INTERFACE_ENTRY(IOleInPlaceActiveObject)
        COM_INTERFACE_ENTRY(IOleInPlaceObject)
        COM_INTERFACE_ENTRY(IOleInPlaceObjectWindowless)
        COM_INTERFACE_ENTRY2(IOleWindow, IOleInPlaceObjectWindowless)
        COM_INTERFACE_ENTRY(IViewObjectEx)
        COM_INTERFACE_ENTRY(IViewObject2)
        COM_INTERFACE_ENTRY(IViewObject)
        // "Lite" control persistence implementation
        COM_INTERFACE_ENTRY(IPersistStreamInit)
        COM_INTERFACE_ENTRY2(IPersist, IPersistStreamInit)
        // Full control additional implementations
        // Support for OLE embedding
        COM_INTERFACE_ENTRY(IDataObject)
        COM_INTERFACE_ENTRY(IPersistStorage)
        // Support for property pages
        COM_INTERFACE_ENTRY(ISpecifyPropertyPages)
        // Support for fast activation
        COM_INTERFACE_ENTRY(IQuickActivate)
        // Support for connection points
        COM_INTERFACE_ENTRY(IConnectionPointContainer)
        COM_INTERFACE_ENTRY(IProvideClassInfo2)
        COM_INTERFACE_ENTRY(IProvideClassInfo)
    END_COM_MAP()
```

```
// Initially, the control's stock properties are the only
// properties supported via persistence and property pages
BEGIN_PROP_MAP(CBullsEye)
    PROP_DATA_ENTRY("_cx", m_sizeExtent.cx, VT_UI4)
    PROP_DATA_ENTRY("_cy", m_sizeExtent.cy, VT_UI4)
    PROP_ENTRY("BackColor", DISPID_BACKCOLOR, CLSID_StockColorPage)
    PROP_ENTRY("BackStyle", DISPID_BACKSTYLE, CLSID_NULL)
    PROP_ENTRY("Enabled", DISPID_ENABLED, CLSID_NULL)
    PROP_ENTRY("ForeColor", DISPID_FORECOLOR, CLSID_StockColorPage)
END_PROP_MAP()

// Initially, enabling connection point support for a full control
// only supports property change notifications
BEGIN_CONNECTION_POINT_MAP(CBullsEye)
    CONNECTION_POINT_ENTRY(IID_IPropertyNotifySink)
END_CONNECTION_POINT_MAP()

// Initially, the control passes all Windows messages to the base class
BEGIN_MSG_MAP(CBullsEye)
    CHAIN_MSG_MAP(CComControl<CBullsEye>)
    DEFAULT_REFLECTION_HANDLER()
END_MSG_MAP()

// ISupportErrorInfo
    STDMETHOD(InterfaceSupportsErrorInfo)(REFIID riid)
    { // Implementation deleted for clarity. . . }

// IViewObjectEx
    DECLARE_VIEW_STATUS(VIEWSTATUS_SOLIDBKGND | VIEWSTATUS_OPAQUE)

// IBullsEye
public:

    HRESULT OnDraw(ATL_DRAWINFO& di)
    { // . . .  Sample drawing code omitted for clarity }
    // Initially, the only member variables are those for the stock
    // properties
    OLE_COLOR m_clrBackColor;
    LONG m_nBackStyle;
    BOOL m_bEnabled;
    OLE_COLOR m_clrForeColor;
};
```

The Initial IBullsEye Interface

Listing 10.6 is the initial wizard-generated IDL description for the `IBullsEye` interface. The wizard generates the interface containing any stock properties you've specified. I'll need to add all the custom properties for the control as well as any stock and custom methods supported by the control.

Listing 10.6. The initial wizard-generated IDL for the `IBullsEye` interface

```
[ object, dual
    uuid(7DC59CC4-36C0-11D2-AC05-00A0C9C8E50D),
    helpstring("IBullsEye Interface"),
    pointer_default(unique)
]
interface IBullsEye : IDispatch
{
 [propput, id(DISPID_BACKCOLOR)] HRESULT BackColor([in]OLE_COLOR clr);
 [propget, id(DISPID_BACKCOLOR)] HRESULT BackColor
    ([out,retval]OLE_COLOR* pclr);
 [propput, id(DISPID_BACKSTYLE)] HRESULT BackStyle([in]long style);
 [propget, id(DISPID_BACKSTYLE)] HRESULT BackStyle([out,retval]long*
    pstyle);
 [propput, id(DISPID_FORECOLOR)] HRESULT ForeColor([in]OLE_COLOR clr);
 [propget, id(DISPID_FORECOLOR)] HRESULT ForeColor
    ([out,retval]OLE_COLOR* pclr);
 [propput, id(DISPID_ENABLED)] HRESULT Enabled([in]VARIANT_BOOL vbool);
 [propget, id(DISPID_ENABLED)] HRESULT
    Enabled([out,retval]VARIANT_BOOL* pbool);
};
```

The Initial _IBullsEyeEvents Dispatch Interface

The initial `_IBullsEyeEvents` dispatch interface is empty (Listing 10.7). I'll need to add the BullsEye custom events to the `dispinterface`. When a control supports any of the stock events, you'd add them to the event interface as well.

Listing 10.7. The initial wizard-generated IDL for the `_IBullsEyeEvent` dispatch interface

```
[   uuid(19FF9872-36ED-11d2-AC05-00A0C9C8E50D),
    helpstring("Event interface for BullsEye Control")
]
```

```
dispinterface _IBullsEyeEvents
{
    properties:
    methods:
};
```

Developing the BullsEye Control Step by Step

Stock Properties and Methods

Updating Stock Properties and Methods in the IDL

Your IDL file describing the control's default dispatch interface must contain an entry for each stock property accessor method and all stock methods you support. The ATL Object Wizard will generate these method definitions for those stock properties added using the ATL Object Wizard dialogs. Listing 10.6 shows the method definitions for the BullsEye properties.

However, there are a couple of changes you must manually make to the method definitions. First, all stock properties should have the `bindable` and `requestedit` attributes. This is because the stock property put methods fire change notifications to a container before and after changing a property. Therefore, you need to change each method like this:

```
// Original wizard-generated version
[propput, id(DISPID_BACKCOLOR)] HRESULT BackColor([in]OLE_COLOR clr);
[propget, id(DISPID_BACKCOLOR)]
   HRESULT BackColor([out,retval]OLE_COLOR* pclr);

// Corrected version
[propput, bindable, requestedit, id(DISPID_BACKCOLOR)]
   HRESULT BackColor([in]OLE_COLOR clr);
[propget, bindable, requestedit, id(DISPID_BACKCOLOR)]
   HRESULT BackColor([out,retval]OLE_COLOR* pclr);
```

This change has no effect on the way the control actually operates. However, the type library describing the control now more accurately describes the actual behavior of the control.

The ATL Object Wizard currently has no support for stock methods. You'll need to add any stock methods explicitly to the default dispatch interface definition in your IDL file. There are only three stock methods presently defined (AboutBox,

DoClick, and Refresh), and BullsEye supports them all. So I've added the following lines to the IBullsEye interface definition:

```
[id(DISPID_ABOUTBOX)] HRESULT AboutBox();
[id(DISPID_DOCLICK)] HRESULT DoClick();
[id(DISPID_REFRESH)] HRESULT Refresh();
```

Listing 10.1, shown earlier in this chapter, contains the complete definition of the
IBullsEye interface with all the above recommended changes.

Implementing Stock Properties and Methods Using CStockPropImpl

The CStockPropImpl class contains an implementation of every stock property
you can choose from the Stock Properties tab in the ATL Object Wizard. A control
derives from CStockPropImpl when it wants an implementation of any of the
stock properties. The declaration of the template class looks like this:

```
template < class T, class InterfaceName,
        const IID* piid, const GUID* plibid>
class ATL_NO_VTABLE CStockPropImpl :
        public IDispatchImpl< InterfaceName, piid, plibid >
```

The class T parameter is the name of your control class. The InterfaceName parameter is the name of the dual interface defining the stock property propget and
propput methods. The CStockPropImpl class implements these accessor methods. The piid parameter is a pointer to the IID for the InterfaceName interface.
The plibid parameter is a pointer to the GUID of the type library that contains a
description of the InterfaceName interface.
    The CBullsEye class implements its stock properties using CStockPropImpl
like this:

```
class ATL_NO_VTABLE CBullsEye :
    public CStockPropImpl<CBullsEye, IBullsEye, &IID_IBullsEye,
                    &LIBID_ATLINTERNALSLib>,
    . . .
```

The CStockPropImpl class contains an implementation of the property accessor
(get and put) methods for all stock properties. These methods notify and synchronize with the control's container when any stock property changes.
    Most controls don't need support for all the possible stock properties. How-
ever, the CStockPropImpl base class contains supporting code for all stock properties. This code needs a data member for each property. ATL expects your deriving

Table 10.6. Stock Properties Supported by `CStockPropImpl`

Stock property	Data member	Stock property	Data member
APPEARANCE	m_nAppearance	ENABLED	m_bEnabled
AUTOSIZE	m_bAutoSize	FILLCOLOR	m_clrFillColor
BACKCOLOR	m_clrBackColor	FILLSTYLE	m_nFillStyle
BACKSTYLE	m_nBackStyle	FONT	m_pFont
BORDERCOLOR	m_clrBorderColor	FORECOLOR	m_clrForeColor
BORDERSTYLE	m_nBorderStyle	HWND	m_hWnd
BORDERVISIBLE	m_bBorderVisible	MOUSEICON	m_pMouseIcon
BORDERWIDTH	m_nBorderWidth	MOUSEPOINTER	m_nMousePointer
CAPTION	m_bstrCaption	PICTURE	m_pPicture
DRAWMODE	m_nDrawMode	READYSTATE	m_nReadyState
DRAWSTYLE	m_nDrawStyle	TABSTOP	m_bTabStop
DRAWWIDTH	m_nDrawWidth	TEXT	m_bstrText
		VALID	m_bValid

class, the control class, to provide the data members for only the stock properties that your control supports. You must name these data members the exact same variable name as used by the `CStockPropImpl` class. Table 10.6 lists the appropriate name for each supported stock property.

The `CStockPropImpl` class contains references *to all these member variables* because it contains property accessor methods *for all these properties*. In order that a control need not allocate space for all properties when it only needs to support a few properties, the `CComControlBase` class defines a union of all these member variables. `CComControlBase` itself is the base class for `CComControl`, from which `CBullsEye` derives.

```
union
{
    // m_nFreezeEvents is the only one actually used
    int m_nFreezeEvents; // count of freezes versus thaws
    // These are here to make stock properties work
    IPictureDisp* m_pMouseIcon;
    IPictureDisp* m_pPicture;
    IFontDisp* m_pFont;
    OLE_COLOR m_clrBackColor;
```

```
    OLE_COLOR m_clrBorderColor;
    OLE_COLOR m_clrFillColor;
    OLE_COLOR m_clrForeColor;
    BSTR m_bstrText;
    BSTR m_bstrCaption;
    BOOL m_bValid;
    BOOL m_bTabStop;
    BOOL m_bBorderVisible;
    BOOL m_bEnabled;
    LONG m_nBackStyle;
    LONG m_nBorderStyle;
    LONG m_nBorderWidth;
    LONG m_nDrawMode;
    LONG m_nDrawStyle;
    LONG m_nDrawWidth;
    LONG m_nFillStyle;
    SHORT m_nAppearance;
    LONG m_nMousePointer;
    LONG m_nReadyState;
};
```

The net result of this space optimization is this: When you add a member variable to your control class to hold a stock property and you misspell the member variable name, you will receive no compilation errors. The code in CStockPropImpl simply references the field of the above anonymous union contained in your control's base class. Typically, this is not the behavior you want.

The Object Wizard generates the proper member variable(s) in your control's class when you add a stock property initially. For example, here are the member variables generated for the stock properties in the CBullsEye class.

```
    OLE_COLOR m_clrBackColor;
    LONG      m_nBackStyle;
    BOOL      m_bEnabled;
    OLE_COLOR m_clrForeColor;
```

CStockPropImpl implements explicit put and get methods for the stock properties that are interface pointers, including FONT, MOUSEICON, and PICTURE. It also implements a get method for the HWND stock property. For each other stock property, CStockPropImpl invokes one of three macros that expand to a standard put and get method for the property: These macros are IMPLEMENT_STOCKPROP, IMPLEMENT_BOOL_STOCKPROP, and IMPLEMENT_BSTR_STOCKPROP.

The IMPLEMENT_STOCKPROP(type, fname, pname, dispid) macro

- Expects to be used in a template class containing a template parameter named T.

- Expects the class T to contain a declaration of a member variable for a property of the specified type. The macro references the member variable by prefixing m_ to pname. For example, when pname is bEnabled, the macro references m_bEnabled.

- Defines a put method and a get method for the property. The macro creates the put and get method names by prefixing put_ and get_ to fname, respectively. For example, when fname is Enabled, the method names are put_Enabled and get_Enabled. The put method notifies the container when the property changes.

- Associates the DISPID dispid with the property.

The IMPLEMENT_BOOL_STOCKPROP(fname, pname, dispid) macro implements a stock Boolean property's accessor methods. It has the same attributes as listed for the IMPLEMENT_STOCKPROP macro except that the get method tests the value of the data member containing the property and returns VARIANT_TRUE or VARIANT_FALSE rather than returning the value.

The IMPLEMENT_BSTR_STOCKPROP(fname, pname, dispid) macro implements a stock text property's accessor methods using a BSTR.

Note that these macros do not work as presently described in the documentation. They do not allocate the member variable and cannot be used in your control class. Basically, they are only used and only of use within the CStockPropImpl template class.

Let's look at the implementation of the IMPLEMENT_STOCKPROP macro. There are a couple of other issues illustrated by the ATL version 3.0 code that are worth noting and that apply to all stock properties.

```
#define IMPLEMENT_STOCKPROP(type, fname, pname, dispid) \
HRESULT STDMETHODCALLTYPE put_##fname(type pname) \
{ \
    ATLTRACE2(atlTraceControls,2,_T("CStockPropImpl::put_%s\n"), \
             _T(#fname)); \
    T* pT = (T*) this; \
    if (pT->FireOnRequestEdit(dispid) == S_FALSE) return S_FALSE; \
    pT->m_##pname = pname; \
    pT->m_bRequiresSave = TRUE; \
    pT->FireOnChanged(dispid); \
    pT->FireViewChange(); \
```

```
    pT->SendOnDataChange(NULL); \
    return S_OK; \
} \
HRESULT STDMETHODCALLTYPE get_##fname(type* p##pname) \
{ \
    ATLTRACE2(atlTraceControls,2,_T("CStockPropImpl::get_%s\n"), \
             _T(#fname)); \
    T* pT = (T*) this; \
    *p##pname = pT->m_##pname; \
    return S_OK; \
}
```

First, notice that the put method fires an `OnRequestEdit` and an `OnChanged` event notification to the control's container before and after, respectively, changing the value of a stock property. This behavior is why I changed the IDL for the stock properties to add the `bindable` and `requestedit` attributes.

Second, the put method fires the `OnRequestEdit` and `OnChanged` events without regard to a control's freeze event count. When a control's freeze event count (maintained in `CComControlBase` in the `m_nFreezeEvents` member variable) is nonzero, a control should hold off firing events or discard them completely. The failure of the stock property put methods to obey this rule causes some containers to break.

For example, the Test Container application shipped with Visual C++ 6.0 crashes when a control fires change notifications in its `FinalConstruct` method. A control should be able to call `FreezeEvents(TRUE)` in `FinalConstruct` to disable change notifications, initialize its properties using the put methods, and then call `FreezeEvents (FALSE)` to enable change notifications if they were previously enabled.

It's a minor point, but note that changing a stock property sets the `m_bRequiresSave` member variable of your class to TRUE. A control inherits this member variable from the `CComControlBase` class, so you don't explicitly provide it. Theoretically, though, you might want to support stock properties in noncontrols, for example, server-side components. Such an object would have to provide its own definition of this member variable.

Occasionally, you'll decide to support additional stock properties after creating the initial source code. The wizard lacks support for adding features to your class after the initial code generation, so you'll have to make the previously described changes to your code manually.

Finally, often you'll want to do some work over and above that which the stock property put functions perform. For example, the `CBullsEye` class needs to know whenever the background color changes so it can delete the old background brush and schedule the rendering logic to create a new background brush. To do this, you have to override the `put_BackColor` method provided by the `CStockPropImpl` class. Basically, this means you often end up rewriting most, if not all, of the stock property put methods. You can reuse the get methods, but they are, for the most part, trivial.

It would be nice if future versions of the `CStockPropImpl` put methods called a `pT->OnStockPropChanged` member function, for example, `OnBackColor-Changed`, to notify their deriving class that a particular stock property has changed value. `CStockPropImpl` could provide empty inline functions for all the stock properties and, therefore, not incur any overhead for the function when it wasn't overridden.

Custom Properties and Methods

Adding Custom Properties and Methods to the IDL

In addition to any stock properties, your control's default dispatch interface must contain an entry for the property get and put methods for each custom control property as well as all the stock and custom methods you support. The ATL Object Wizard doesn't currently support stock methods, so you'll add them to your class as if they were custom methods, which, in fact, they are except that you don't get to choose the function signatures.

You can use the Visual C++ IDE to add the properties and methods to an interface or you can make the source code changes manually. To use the IDE, right-click on the interface name in the ClassView and select Add Method or Add Property. After you respond to the resulting dialogs, the IDE changes two parts of your project.

First, it updates the IDL for the specified interface and adds the appropriate property or method definition. Second, it updates your control class's declaration (.h file) and adds a skeletal function body for each property accessor function or method. I prefer my methods to reside in the implementation (.cpp) file, so I frequently convert the skeletal function body into a function prototype and place the function body in the class's implementation file.

The BullsEye control supports the stock methods and custom properties listed in Table 10.2 and Table 10.3, respectively. Listing 10.1 contains the complete definition for the `IBullsEye` interface, but here's an excerpt showing the definition of the `CenterColor` custom property and the `AboutBox` stock method.

```
[propput, bindable, requestedit, id(DISPID_CENTERCOLOR)]
    HRESULT CenterColor([in] OLE_COLOR newVal);

[propget, bindable, requestedit, id(DISPID_CENTERCOLOR)]
    HRESULT CenterColor([out, retval] OLE_COLOR *pVal);

[id(DISPID_ABOUTBOX)] HRESULT AboutBox();
```

Implementing Custom Properties and Stock and Custom Methods

You'll need to add a function prototype to your control class for each method added to the IDL in the previous step. When you use the IDE, it adds a skeletal function body for each method. For the above custom property and stock method, I added the following function prototypes to the CBullsEye class.

```
STDMETHODIMP get_CenterColor(/*[out, retval]*/ OLE_COLOR *pVal);
STDMETHODIMP put_CenterColor(/*[in]*/ OLE_COLOR newVal);
STDMETHODIMP AboutBox();
```

Declaring the Function Prototypes

Note that you must declare each interface member function as using the STD-METHODIMP calling convention. A system header file defines this macro to be the appropriate calling convention for COM interface methods on a given operating system. This calling convention does change among various operating systems. By using the macro, rather than explicitly writing its expansion, your code is more portable across operating systems. On Win32 operating systems, the macro expands to HRESULT __stdcall.

The code generated by the ATL wizards incorrectly uses the STDMETHOD macro. On Win32 operating systems, this macro expands as virtual HRESULT __stdcall, which just happens to work. It won't necessarily work on other operating systems that support COM.

Basically, STDMETHOD should only be used in the *original definition* of an interface; for example, this is typically the MIDL-generated header file. (MIDL, however, doesn't use the macro but simply generates its expansion instead.) When implementing an interface method in a class (which we are doing in CBullsEye), you should use the STDMETHODIMP macro.

There are a couple of changes you should manually make to the method definitions. First, all stock properties should have the bindable and requestedit attributes. This is because the stock property put methods fire change notifications to a container before and after changing a property. Therefore, you need to change each method as shown in the following section.

Defining the Functions

The function implementations are all pretty straightforward. The get_Center-Color method validates its argument and returns the value of the CenterColor property.

```
STDMETHODIMP CBullsEye::get_CenterColor(OLE_COLOR *pVal)
{
    if (NULL == pVal) return E_POINTER;
```

```
    *pVal = m_clrCenterColor;
    return S_OK;
}
```

The `put_CenterColor` method, like all property change functions, is a bit more complicated.

```
STDMETHODIMP CBullsEye::put_CenterColor(OLE_COLOR newVal)
{
    if (m_clrCenterColor == newVal) return S_OK;

    if (!m_nFreezeEvents)
        if (FireOnRequestEdit(DISPID_CENTERCOLOR) == S_FALSE)
            return S_FALSE;

    m_clrCenterColor = newVal;              // Save new color
    ::DeleteObject (m_centerBrush);         // Clear old brush color
    m_centerBrush = NULL;

    m_bRequiresSave = TRUE;                 // Set dirty flag
    if (!m_nFreezeEvents)
        FireOnChanged(DISPID_CENTERCOLOR);  // Notify container of change
    FireViewChange();                       // Request redraw
    SendOnDataChange(NULL);                 // Notify advise sinks of
                                            //    change

    return S_OK;
}
```

First, the method checks to see if the new value is the same as the current value of the `CenterColor` property. If so, the value isn't changing, so we exit quickly. Then, unlike the current stock property code, it properly checks to see if the container presently doesn't want to receive events, that is, if the freeze events count is nonzero.

When the container has not frozen events, the `put_CenterColor` method fires the `OnRequestEdit` event to ask the container for permission to change the `CenterColor` property. When the container refuses the change, `put_Center-Color` returns S_FALSE.

When the container grants permission, `put_CenterColor` updates the member variable in the control that contains the color. It also changes some values that cause the control's rendering code to use the new color the next time the control redraws.

After the method changes the property, it sets the control's dirty flag (m_bRequiresSave) to remember that the state of the control now needs to be saved. The various persistence implementations check this flag when executing their IsDirty method.

Next, the method fires the OnChanged event to notify the container of the property change, assuming events are not frozen, of course.

The CenterColor property is a property that affects the visual rendering (view) of the control. When a control changes such properties, the control should notify its container that the control's appearance has changed by calling the FireViewChange function. In response, eventually, the container will ask the control to redraw itself. After that, the method notifies all advise sinks (which typically means the container) that the state (data) of the control has changed by calling SendOnDataChange.

Note that the state of a control changes independently of the control's view. Some control property changes, like changes to CBullsEye's Beep property, have no effect on the appearance of the control. So the put_Beep method doesn't call FireViewChange.

The stock AboutBox method simply displays the Help About (credits) dialog:

```
STDMETHODIMP CBullsEye::AboutBox()
{
    CAboutDlg dlg;
    dlg.DoModal();
    return S_OK;
}
```

Stock and Custom Events

Adding Stock and Custom Events to the IDL

Your IDL file describing the control's *default source interface* must contain an entry for each stock and custom event method you support. As described previously, for maximum compatibility with all control containers, you should implement the default source interface as a dispatch interface. There is no current support in the IDE for adding event methods to a dispinterface.

The BullsEye control needs to support the two custom events described in Table 10.4. Here's the updated IDL describing the event dispatch interface. All dispatch interfaces must be defined within the library block of an IDL file.

```
[  uuid(19FF9872-36ED-11d2-AC05-00A0C9C8E50D),
   helpstring("Event interface for BullsEye Control")
]
```

```
dispinterface _IBullsEyeEvents
{
    properties:
    methods:
    [id(DISPID_ONRINGHIT)] void OnRingHit(short ringNumber);
    [id(DISPID_ONSCORECHANGED)] void OnScoreChanged(long ringValue);
};
```

You'll also want to ensure that the IDL correctly describes the `BullsEye` class itself. The `BullsEye coclass` definition in the library block of the IDL file should define the `IBullsEye` interface as the default interface for the control and the `_IBullsEyeEvents` dispatch interface as the default source interface.

```
[   uuid(7DC59CC5-36C0-11D2-AC05-00A0C9C8E50D),
    helpstring("BullsEye Class")
]
coclass BullsEye
{
    [default]          interface IBullsEye;
    [default, source] dispinterface _IBullsEyeEvents;
};
```

Adding Connection Point Support for the Events

Many containers use the connection points protocol to hand the container's sink interface pointer to the event source (the control). Chapter 8 discusses connection points in detail, so I'll just summarize the steps needed for a control.

To support connection point events, a control must implement the `IConnectionPointContainer` interface as well as one `IConnectionPoint` interface for each outgoing (source) interface. Typically, most controls will support two source interfaces: the control's default source dispatch interface (`_IBullsEyeEvents` for the BullsEye control) and the property change notification source interface (`IPropertyNotifySink`).

Implementing the IConnectionPointContainer Interface

When you initially create the source code for a control and select the Support Connection Points option, the ATL Object Wizard adds the `IConnectionPointContainerImpl` base class to your control class declaration. This is ATL's implementation of the `IConnectionPointContainer` interface. You'll need to add this base class explicitly if you decide to support connection points after creating the initial source code.

```
class ATL_NO_VTABLE CBullsEye :
    . . .
    // Connection point container support
        public IConnectionPointContainerImpl<CBullsEye>,
    . . .
```

You'll also need one connection point for each source interface supported by your control. ATL provides the IConnectionPointImpl class, which is described in depth in Chapter 8, as an implementation of the IConnectionPoint interface. Typically, you will not directly use this class, but will instead derive a new class from IConnectionPointImpl, customizing the class by adding various event firing methods. Your control will inherit from this derived class.

Supporting Property Change Notifications

ATL provides a specialization of IConnectionPointImpl, called IProperty-NotifySinkCP, that implements a connection point for the IPropertyNotify-Sink interface. The IPropertyNotifySinkCP class also defines the type definition _ATL_PROP_NOTIFY_EVENT_CLASS (note the single leading underscore), as an alias for the CFirePropNotifyEvent class.

```
template <class T, class CDV = CComDynamicUnkArray >
class ATL_NO_VTABLE IPropertyNotifySinkCP :
        public IConnectionPointImpl<T, &IID_IPropertyNotifySink, CDV>
{
public:
        typedef CFirePropNotifyEvent _ATL_PROP_NOTIFY_EVENT_CLASS;
};
```

When you use the ATL Object Wizard to create a full control that supports connection points, the wizard adds the IPropertyNotifySinkCP base class to your control. You'll have to add it otherwise.

```
class ATL_NO_VTABLE CBullsEye :
    . . .
    public IPropertyNotifySinkCP<CBullsEye>,
    . . .
```

Recall that a control's property put methods, for both custom and stock properties, call the FireOnRequestEdit and FireOnChanged functions to send property change notifications. These methods are defined in the CComControlBase class like this:

```
template <class T, class WinBase =  CWindowImpl< T > >
class ATL_NO_VTABLE CComControl :  public CComControlBase,
                                   public WinBase
{
public:
  HRESULT FireOnRequestEdit(DISPID dispID)
  {
   T* pT = static_cast<T*>(this);
   return T::__ATL_PROP_NOTIFY_EVENT_CLASS::FireOnRequestEdit
                  (pT->GetUnknown(), dispID);
  }
  HRESULT FireOnChanged(DISPID dispID)
  {
   T* pT = static_cast<T*>(this);
   return T::__ATL_PROP_NOTIFY_EVENT_CLASS::FireOnChanged
                  (pT->GetUnknown(), dispID);
  }
  . . .
};
```

Therefore, the call to FireOnChanged in a property put method of a CComControl-derived class actually is a call to the FireOnChanged of the class __ATL_PROP _NOTIFY_EVENT_CLASS (note the double leading underscore) within your actual control class. When you derive your control class from IPropertyNotifySinkCP, your control class inherits a typedef for _ATL_PROP_NOTIFY_EVENT_CLASS (note the single leading underscore).

```
    typedef CFirePropNotifyEvent _ATL_PROP_NOTIFY_EVENT_CLASS;
```

For some odd reason (unknown to me), it's the property map in your control class that equates the two types. The BEGIN_PROP_MAP macro defines the type __ATL _PROP_NOTIFY_EVENT_CLASS (note the double leading underscore) as equivalent to the type _ATL_PROP_NOTIFY_EVENT_CLASS (note the single leading underscore).

```
#define BEGIN_PROP_MAP(theClass) \
    typedef _ATL_PROP_NOTIFY_EVENT_CLASS \
    __ATL_PROP_NOTIFY_EVENT_CLASS; \
    . . .
```

In the BullsEye control, this means that when your property put method calls FireOnChanged,

- This is actually a call to your CComControl::FireOnChanged base class method.

- FireOnChanged calls CBullsEye::__ATL_PROP_NOTIFY_EVENT_CLASS:: FireOnChanged.

- The property map aliases __ATL_PROP_NOTIFY_EVENT_CLASS to _ATL _PROP_NOTIFY_EVENT_CLASS.

- IPropertyNotifySinkCP aliases _ATL_PROP_NOTIFY_SINK_CLASS to CFirePropNotifyEvent.

- Therefore, you actually call the CBullsEye::CFirePropNotifyEvent:: FireOnChanged function.

The CFirePropNotifyEvent class contains two static methods, FireOn-RequestEdit and FireOnChanged, that use your control's own connection point support to enumerate through all connections for the IPropertyNotifySink interface and call the OnRequestEdit and OnChanged methods, respectively, of each connection.

```
class CFirePropNotifyEvent
{
public:
 static HRESULT FireOnRequestEdit(IUnknown* pUnk, DISPID dispID)
 {
 CComQIPtr<IConnectionPointContainer, &IID_IConnectionPointContainer>
   pCPC(pUnk);
 if (!pCPC) return S_OK;
 CComPtr<IConnectionPoint> pCP;
 pCPC->FindConnectionPoint(IID_IPropertyNotifySink, &pCP);
 if (!pCP) return S_OK;
 CComPtr<IEnumConnections> pEnum;
 if (FAILED(pCP->EnumConnections(&pEnum))) return S_OK;
 CONNECTDATA cd;
```

```
while (pEnum->Next(1, &cd, NULL) == S_OK) {
  if (cd.pUnk) {
    HRESULT hr = S_OK;
    CComQIPtr<IPropertyNotifySink, &IID_IPropertyNotifySink>
      pSink(cd.pUnk);
    if (pSink) hr = pSink->OnRequestEdit(dispID);
    cd.pUnk->Release();
    if (hr == S_FALSE) return S_FALSE;
  }
}
return S_OK;
}


static HRESULT FireOnChanged(IUnknown* pUnk, DISPID dispID)
{
// Code similar to above deleted for clarity
. . .
while (pEnum->Next(1, &cd, NULL) == S_OK) {
  if (cd.pUnk) {
    CComQIPtr<IPropertyNotifySink, &IID_IPropertyNotifySink>
      pSink(cd.pUnk);
    if (pSink) pSink->OnChanged(dispID);
    cd.pUnk->Release();
  }
}
};
```

All this means that you must derive your control class from `IPropertyNotify-SinkCP` in order to get the `typedef` that maps the `FireOnRequestEdit` and `FireOnChanged` methods in `CComControl` to the actual firing functions in `CFirePropNotifyEvent`.

When you don't derive from `IPropertyNotifySinkCP`, you can still call the `FireOnRequestEdit` and `FireOnChanged` methods in `CComControl`. As long as your control class contains a property map, the code compiles without error and the method calls do nothing at runtime.

ATL defines a `typedef` for the symbol `_ATL_PROP_NOTIFY_EVENT_CLASS` at global scope:

```
typedef CFakeFirePropNotifyEvent _ATL_PROP_NOTIFY_EVENT_CLASS;
```

When your control derives from `IPropertyNotifySinkCP`, you inherit a definition for `_ATL_PROP_NOTIFY_EVENT_CLASS` that hides the global definition. When you don't derive from `IPropertyNotifySinkCP`, the compiler uses the global definition just given. The `CFakeFirePropNotifyEvent` class looks like this:

```
class CFakeFirePropNotifyEvent
{
public:
    static HRESULT FireOnRequestEdit(IUnknown* /*pUnk*/, DISPID
                                     /*dispID*/)
    { return S_OK; }
    static HRESULT FireOnChanged(IUnknown* /*pUnk*/, DISPID
                                 /*dispID*/)
    { return S_OK; }
};
```

In the BullsEye control, this means that when you don't derive from `IPropertyNotifySinkCP` and your property put method calls `FireOnChanged`,

- This is actually a call to your `CComControl::FireOnChanged` base class method.
- `FireOnChanged` calls `CBullsEye::__ATL_PROP_NOTIFY_EVENT_CLASS::FireOnChanged`.
- The property map aliases `__ATL_PROP_NOTIFY_EVENT_CLASS` to `_ATL_PROP_NOTIFY_EVENT_CLASS`.
- The global `typedef` aliases `_ATL_PROP_NOTOFY_SINK_CLASS` to `CFakeFirePropNotifyEvent`.
- Therefore, you actually call the `CBullsEye::CFakeFirePropNotifyEvent::FireOnChanged` function, which simply returns S_OK.

Supporting the Control's Event Connection Point

You'll want to use a specialization of `IConnectionPointImpl` for each of your control's event interfaces. Typically, a control implements only one event interface because Visual Basic and scripting languages can only hook up to the default event interface. This is the interface you describe in your object's `coclass` definition with the [`default, source`] attributes. However, a custom C++ client to your control can connect to any of its source interfaces.

The specialized class derives from `IConnectionPointImpl` and adds the appropriate event firing helper methods for your events. Chapter 8 describes the details of creating such a specialized class. The easiest way to create a specialized connection point class is to right-click on the `BullsEye` class in the ClassView and select the Implement Connection Point item.

Here's the specialized connection point class, `CProxy_IBullsEye-Events`, generated by the wizard for the `_IBullsEyeEvents` dispatch interface.

```
template <class T>
class CProxy_IBullsEyeEvents :
    public IConnectionPointImpl<T, &DIID__IBullsEyeEvents,
      CComDynamicUnkArray>
{
    // Warning: this class may be recreated by the wizard.
public:
    VOID Fire_OnRingHit(SHORT ringNumber)
    {
        T* pT = static_cast<T*>(this);

        int nConnectionIndex;
        CComVariant* pvars = new CComVariant[1];
        int nConnections = m_vec.GetSize();

        for (nConnectionIndex = 0;
             nConnectionIndex < nConnections; nConnectionIndex++) {
            pT->Lock();
            CComPtr<IUnknown> sp = m_vec.GetAt(nConnectionIndex);
            pT->Unlock();
            IDispatch* pDispatch = reinterpret_cast<IDispatch*>(sp.p);
            if (pDispatch != NULL) {
                pvars[0] = ringNumber;
                DISPPARAMS disp = { pvars, NULL, 1, 0 };
                pDispatch->Invoke(0x1, IID_NULL, LOCALE_USER_DEFAULT,
                            DISPATCH_METHOD, &disp, NULL, NULL, NULL);
            }
        }
        delete[] pvars;
    }
    VOID Fire_OnScoreChanged(LONG ringValue)
    {
        // Code similar to above deleted for clarity
    }
};
```

You use this class by adding it to the base class list of the control. Therefore, Bulls-Eye now has two connection points in its base class list:

```
class ATL_NO_VTABLE CBullsEye :
    // events and property change notifications
    public CProxy_IBullsEyeEvents<CBullsEye>,
    public IPropertyNotifySinkCP<CBullsEye>,
    . . .
```

Updating the Connection Map

Finally, the `IConnectionPointContainerImpl` class needs a table that associates source interface IIDs with the base class `IConnectionPointImpl` specialization that implements the connection point. You define this table in your control class using the `BEGIN_CONNECTION_POINT_MAP`, `CONNECTION_POINT_ENTRY`, and `END_CONNECTION_POINT_MAP` macros, as described in Chapter 8.

Here's the table for the `CBullsEye` class:

```
BEGIN_CONNECTION_POINT_MAP(CBullsEye)
    CONNECTION_POINT_ENTRY(DIID__IBullsEyeEvents)
    CONNECTION_POINT_ENTRY(IID_IPropertyNotifySink)
END_CONNECTION_POINT_MAP()
```

Supporting IProvideClassInfo2

Many containers, such as Visual Basic and Internet Explorer, use a control's `IProvideClassInfo2` interface to determine the control's event interface. When a control doesn't support `IProvideClassInfo2`, these containers assume that the control doesn't source events and they never establish a connection point to your control. Other containers, such as Test Container, don't use a control's `IProvide-ClassInfo2` interface and browse a control's type information to determine the default source interface.

ATL provides an implementation of this interface in `IProvideClassInfo-2Impl`. To use it, derive your control class from `IProvideClassInfo2Impl`. The `IProvideClassInfo2` interface itself derives from the `IProvideClassInfo` interface, so when you update your control's interface map, you'll need to provide entries for both interfaces.

```
class ATL_NO_VTABLE CBullsEye :
 public IProvideClassInfo2Impl<&CLSID_BullsEye,
                               &DIID__IBullsEyeEvents,
                               &LIBID_ATLInternalsLib>,
    . . .
```

```
   BEGIN_COM_MAP(CBullsEye)
   . . .
   // Support for connection points
   COM_INTERFACE_ENTRY(IConnectionPointContainer)
   COM_INTERFACE_ENTRY(IProvideClassInfo2)
   COM_INTERFACE_ENTRY(IProvideClassInfo)
END_COM_MAP()
```

On-Demand Rendering of Your Control's View

A control must be able to render its image when requested by its container. There are basically three different situations in which a control receives a rendering request:

1. The control has a window and that window receives a WM_PAINT message. A control handles this request in CComControlBase::OnPaint.

2. The control is windowless and the container's window receives a WM_PAINT message encompassing the area occupied by the control. A control handles this request in CComControlBase::IViewObject_Draw.

3. The container requests the control to render its image into a metafile. A control handles this request in CComControlBase::IDataObject_GetData.

Although all three types of rendering requests arrive at the control via different mechanisms, the ATL control implementation classes eventually forward the requests to a control's OnDrawAdvanced method.

```
virtual HRESULT OnDrawAdvanced( ATL_DRAWINFO& di );
```

ATL bundles all parameters to the rendering requests into an ATL_DRAWINFO structure. You need to use the information in this structure when drawing your control. Unfortunately, the structure definition itself is presently all the documentation that is available about the structure. However, most of the fields are simply copies of similar parameters to the IViewObject::Draw method. Here's the structure:

```
struct ATL_DRAWINFO
{
    UINT cbSize;            // Set to sizeof (struct ATL_DRAWINFO)
    DWORD dwDrawAspect;     // Drawing aspect - typically
                            // DVASPECT_CONTENT
    LONG lindex;            // Commonly -1, which specifies all of the
                            // data
```

```
    DVTARGETDEVICE* ptd;       // Render the object for this target device
    HDC hicTargetDev;          // Information context for the target device
    HDC hdcDraw;               // Draw on this device context
    LPCRECTL prcBounds;        // Draw within this rectangle
    LPCRECTL prcWBounds;       // Window extent and origin when rendering a
                               // metafile
    BOOL bOptimize;            // Can control use drawing optimizations?
    BOOL bZoomed;              // Object extent differs from drawing
                               // rectangle?
    BOOL bRectInHimetric;      // Rectangle in HiMetric?
    SIZEL ZoomNum;             // Rectangle size: X zoom = ZoomNum.cx/
                               // ZoomDen.cx
    SIZEL ZoomDen;             // Extent size: Y zoom = ZoomNum.cy/
                               // ZoomDen.cy
};
```

ATL provides the following default implementation of the OnDrawAdvanced method in CComControl.

```
inline HRESULT CComControlBase::OnDrawAdvanced(ATL_DRAWINFO& di)
{
    BOOL bDeleteDC = FALSE;
    if (di.hicTargetDev == NULL) {
        di.hicTargetDev = AtlCreateTargetDC(di.hdcDraw, di.ptd);
        bDeleteDC = (di.hicTargetDev != di.hdcDraw);
    }
    RECTL rectBoundsDP = *di.prcBounds;
    BOOL bMetafile = GetDeviceCaps(di.hdcDraw, TECHNOLOGY) ==
      DT_METAFILE;
    if (!bMetafile) {
        ::LPtoDP(di.hicTargetDev, (LPPOINT)&rectBoundsDP, 2);
        SaveDC(di.hdcDraw);
        SetMapMode(di.hdcDraw, MM_TEXT);
        SetWindowOrgEx(di.hdcDraw, 0, 0, NULL);
        SetViewportOrgEx(di.hdcDraw, 0, 0, NULL);
        di.bOptimize = TRUE; //since we save the DC we can do this
    }
    di.prcBounds = &rectBoundsDP;
    GetZoomInfo(di);
```

```
   HRESULT hRes = OnDraw(di);
   if (bDeleteDC) ::DeleteDC(di.hicTargetDev);
   if (!bMetafile) RestoreDC(di.hdcDraw, -1);
   return hRes;
}
```

CComControl::OnDrawAdvanced prepares a normalized device context for drawing, then calls your control class's OnDraw method. A normalized device context is called that because the device context has (some of) the normal defaults for a device context—specifically, the mapping mode is MM_TEXT, the window origin is 0,0, and the viewport origin is 0,0. Override the OnDrawAdvanced method when you want to use the device context passed by the container as is, without normalizing it. For example, if you don't want these default values, you should override OnDrawAdvanced, rather than OnDraw, for greater efficiency.

When a container asks a control to draw into a device context, the container specifies whether or not the control can use optimized drawing techniques. When the bOptimize flag in the ATL_DRAWINFO structure is TRUE, the control can use drawing optimizations. This allows the control to avoid restoring certain settings of the device context after changing the setting.

- When IDataObject_GetData calls OnDrawAdvanced to retrieve a rendering of the control in a metafile, IDataObject_GetData saves the device context state, calls OnDrawAdvanced, then restores the device context state. Therefore, IDataObject_GetData sets the bOptimize flag to TRUE.

- When OnPaint calls OnDrawAdvanced to have the control render to its window, the bOptimize flag is set to FALSE.

- When IViewObject_Draw calls OnDrawAdvanced to have the control render to the container's window, the bOptimize flag is set to TRUE if and only if the container supports optimized drawing.

Therefore, when you override OnDrawAdvanced, you should always check the value of the bOptimize flag and restore the state of the device context as necessary.

For a nonmetafile device context device, OnDrawAdvanced saves the state of the entire device context and restores it after calling your control's OnDraw method. Because of this, the default OnDrawAdvanced method sets the bOptimize flag to TRUE.

Therefore, when you override OnDraw in ATL's current implementation, the bOptimize flag is always TRUE. This doesn't mean you shouldn't check the flag. It means that you should always go to the effort of supporting optimized drawing when overriding OnDraw because such support will always be used.

Listing 10.8 gives the drawing code for the BullsEye control. There are a few features of note in this code:

- BullsEye supports transparent drawing via the BackStyle stock property. When BackStyle is 1 (opaque), the control uses the background color to fill the area around the bulls-eye. When BackStyle is 0 (transparent), the control doesn't draw to the area outside the circle of the bulls-eye. This leaves the area around the circle transparent, and the underlying window contents will show through.

- BullsEye draws differently into a metafile device context versus another device context. There are some operations you cannot do when drawing to a metafile. Therefore, BullsEye sets up the device context slightly differently in these two cases.

- BullsEye supports optimized drawing.

Listing 10.8. BullsEye `OnDraw` and `DrawBullsEye` methods

```
HRESULT CBullsEye::OnDraw(ATL_DRAWINFO& di)
{
    CRect rc = *(RECT*)di.prcBounds;
    HDC hdc  = di.hdcDraw;

    // Create the background color brush only when necessary
    if (NULL == m_backBrush) {
        OLE_COLOR ocBack;
        HRESULT hr = get_BackColor (&ocBack);  // Get the background
                                                // color
        ATLASSERT (SUCCEEDED (hr));

        COLORREF  crBack;            // Translate the color to a COLORREF
        hr = ::OleTranslateColor (ocBack, NULL, &crBack);
        ATLASSERT (SUCCEEDED (hr));

        m_backBrush = ::CreateSolidBrush (crBack);  // Create the
                                                    // background brush
        ATLASSERT (NULL != m_backBrush);
    }

    // First, fill in background color in invalid area when BackStyle is
       Opaque
```

```
if (1 /* Opaque*/ == m_nBackStyle) {
    int s = ::FillRect (hdc, &rc, m_backBrush);
    ATLASSERT (0 != s);
}


int nPrevMapMode;
POINT   ptWOOrig, ptVOOrig;
SIZE szWEOrig, szVEOrig;

BOOL bMetafile = GetDeviceCaps(di.hdcDraw, TECHNOLOGY) ==
  DT_METAFILE;
if (!bMetafile) {
    // OnDrawAdvanced normalized the device context.
    // We are now using MM_TEXT and the coordinates are in device
    // coordinates.

    // Establish convenient coordinate system
    nPrevMapMode = ::SetMapMode (hdc, MM_ISOTROPIC);
    ATLASSERT (0 != nPrevMapMode);

    // Map logical 0,0 to physical center of rectangle
    BOOL bSuccess = ::SetWindowOrgEx (hdc, 0, 0, &ptWOOrig);
    ATLASSERT (0 != bSuccess);
    bSuccess = ::SetViewportOrgEx (hdc, rc.left + rc.Width () / 2,
                                   rc.top + rc.Height () / 2,
                                   &ptVOOrig);
    ATLASSERT (0 != bSuccess);

    // Map logical extent (LOGWIDTH, LOGWIDTH) to physical extent of
    // rectangle
    bSuccess = ::SetWindowExtEx (hdc, LOGWIDTH, LOGWIDTH,
                                 &szWEOrig);
    ATLASSERT (0 != bSuccess);
    bSuccess = ::SetViewportExtEx (hdc, rc.Width (), -rc.Height (),
                                   &szVEOrig);
    ATLASSERT (0 != bSuccess);
}
else {
    // We will be played back in ANISOTROPIC mapping mode

    // The rectangle will be in device units
    CRect rcBoundsDP (rc) ;
```

```
        // We can't use SetViewportOrg and SetViewportExt in a metafile
        // because the container will want to place the metafile.
        //
        // Find the center coordinate and the shorter side
        CSize size = rcBoundsDP.Size () ;
        int iShortSide = min (size.cx, size.cy) ;
        CPoint ptCenter (rcBoundsDP.left + size.cx / 2,
                         rcBoundsDP.top  + size.cy / 2) ;

        // Compute the ratio of LOGWIDTH / shorter side
        double dRatio = (double) LOGWIDTH / (double) iShortSide ;

        // Set the logical origin of the window and swap coordinate axes
        BOOL bSuccess = SetWindowOrgEx (hdc,
                              -int (ptCenter.x * dRatio),
                              int (ptCenter.y * dRatio), &ptWOOrig) ;
        ATLASSERT (0 != bSuccess);

        // Set the logical extent of the window
        // Compensate for the drawing code which draws from -LOGWIDTH to
        // +LOGWIDTH
        bSuccess = SetWindowExtEx (hdc,  int (size.cx * dRatio),
                              -int (size.cy * dRatio),
                              &szWEOrig) ;
        ATLASSERT (0 != bSuccess);
    }

// Draw the BullsEye
DrawBullsEye (di);

// Note on optimized drawing:
// Even when using optimized drawing, a control cannot
// leave a changed mapping mode, coordinate transformation value,
// selected bitmap, clip region, or metafile in the device context.

if (!bMetafile) {
    ::SetMapMode (hdc, nPrevMapMode);

    ::SetViewportOrgEx (hdc, ptVOOrig.x,  ptVOOrig.y,  NULL);
    ::SetViewportExtEx (hdc, szVEOrig.cx, szVEOrig.cy, NULL);
}
```

```
    ::SetWindowOrgEx (hdc, ptWOOrig.x,  ptWOOrig.y,  NULL);
    ::SetWindowExtEx (hdc, szWEOrig.cx, szWEOrig.cy, NULL);

    return S_OK;
}

void CBullsEye::DrawBullsEye (ATL_DRAWINFO& di)
{
    HDC hdc  = di.hdcDraw;

    // Create the border pen only when necessary
    if (NULL == m_borderPen) {
        OLE_COLOR ocFore;
        HRESULT hr = get_ForeColor (&ocFore);
        ATLASSERT (SUCCEEDED (hr));

        COLORREF crFore;
        hr = ::OleTranslateColor (ocFore, NULL, &crFore);
        ATLASSERT (SUCCEEDED (hr));

        m_borderPen = ::CreatePen (PS_SOLID, 0, crFore);
        ATLASSERT (NULL != m_borderPen);
    }

    // Create the center color brush only when necessary
    if (NULL == m_centerBrush) {
        COLORREF  crCenter;
        HRESULT hr = ::OleTranslateColor (m_clrCenterColor, NULL,
                                          &crCenter);
        ATLASSERT (SUCCEEDED (hr));

        m_centerBrush = ::CreateSolidBrush (crCenter);
        ATLASSERT (NULL != m_centerBrush);
    }

    // Create the alternate color brush only when necessary
    if (NULL == m_alternateBrush) {
        COLORREF  crAlternate;
        HRESULT hr =
            ::OleTranslateColor (m_clrAlternateColor, NULL,
                                 &crAlternate);
```

```
        ATLASSERT (SUCCEEDED (hr));

        m_alternateBrush = ::CreateSolidBrush (crAlternate);
        ATLASSERT (NULL != m_alternateBrush);
    }

    // Compute the width of a ring
    short sRingCount;
    HRESULT hr = get_RingCount (&sRingCount);
    ATLASSERT (SUCCEEDED (hr));

    int ringWidth = LOGWIDTH / (sRingCount * 2-1);

    // Draw the border between rings using the border pen
    HPEN hOldPen = (HPEN) SelectObject (hdc, m_borderPen);

    HBRUSH hOldBrush = NULL;

    // Draw each ring from outermost to innermost
    // This isn't nearly as efficient as it could be
    for (short i = sRingCount-1; i >= 0; i-) {

        // Compute the ring's bounding rectangle
        int ringDiameter = i * 2 * ringWidth + ringWidth;
        int ringRadius   = ringDiameter / 2;
        CRect rcRing (-ringRadius, ringRadius, ringRadius, -ringRadius);

        // Rings are numbered from 1 to N from center to outside.
        // However, the loop iterates from N-1 to 0 from outside to
        // center.
        // Therefore, even-numbered rings should be the center color,
        // which implies odd-numbered rings use the alternate color.
        HBRUSH& ringBrush = i & 1 ? m_alternateBrush : m_centerBrush;

        // Set the correct ring color
        HBRUSH hBrush = (HBRUSH) ::SelectObject (hdc, ringBrush);
        if (NULL == hOldBrush)        // First time through, save the
                                      // original brush
            hOldBrush = hBrush;
```

```
        BOOL bStatus =  // Draw the ring
          ::Ellipse (hdc, rcRing.left, rcRing.right, rcRing.top,
                     rcRing.bottom);
        ATLASSERT (NULL != bStatus);
    }

    // When optimized drawing is not in effect, restore the original pen
    // and brush
    if (!di.bOptimize) {
        ::SelectObject (hdc, hOldPen);
        ::SelectObject (hdc, hOldBrush);
    }
}
```

Property Persistence

A control typically needs to save its state upon request by its container. Various containers prefer different persistence techniques. For example, Internet Explorer and Visual Basic prefer to save a control's state using a property bag, which is an association (or dictionary) of text name/VARIANT value pairs. The dialog editor in Visual C++ prefers to save a control's state in binary form using a stream. Containers of embedded objects save the object(s) into a structured storage.

ATL provides three persistence interface implementations:

IPersistStreamInitImpl	Saves properties in binary form into a stream.
IPersistStorageImpl	Saves properties in binary form in a structured storage.
IPersistPropertyBagImpl	Saves properties as name/VARIANT value pairs.

Most controls should derive from all three persistence implementation classes so that they support the widest variety of containers. The BullsEye control does this:

```
class ATL_NO_VTABLE CBullsEye :
    . . .
    // Persistence
       public IPersistStreamInitImpl<CBullsEye>,
       public IPersistStorageImpl<CBullsEye>,
       public IPersistPropertyBagImpl<CBullsEye>,
};
```

As always, you need to add entries to the COM map for each supported interface. The persistence interfaces all derive from IPersist, so you need to add it to the COM map as well.

```
BEGIN_COM_MAP(CBullsEye)
   . . .
   // Persistence
        COM_INTERFACE_ENTRY(IPersistStreamInit)
        COM_INTERFACE_ENTRY2(IPersist, IPersistStreamInit)
        COM_INTERFACE_ENTRY(IPersistStorage)
        COM_INTERFACE_ENTRY(IPersistPropertyBag)
END_COM_MAP()
```

All three persistence implementations save the properties listed in the control's property map. You define the property map using the BEGIN_PROP_MAP and END_PROP_MAP macros. Here's the CBullsEye class's property map:

```
BEGIN_PROP_MAP(CBullsEye)
  PROP_DATA_ENTRY("_cx", m_sizeExtent.cx, VT_UI4)
  PROP_DATA_ENTRY("_cy", m_sizeExtent.cy, VT_UI4)
  PROP_ENTRY("BackStyle",      DISPID_BACKSTYLE, CLSID_BullsEyePropPage)
  PROP_ENTRY("Beep",           DISPID_BEEP,      CLSID_BullsEyePropPage)
  PROP_ENTRY("Enabled",        DISPID_ENABLED,   CLSID_BullsEyePropPage)
  PROP_ENTRY("RingCount",      DISPID_RINGCOUNT, CLSID_BullsEyePropPage)
PROP_ENTRY("AlternateColor", DISPID_ALTERNATECOLOR, CLSID_StockColorPage)
  PROP_ENTRY("BackColor",      DISPID_BACKCOLOR, CLSID_StockColorPage)
  PROP_ENTRY("CenterColor",    DISPID_CENTERCOLOR, CLSID_StockColorPage)
  PROP_ENTRY("ForeColor",      DISPID_FORECOLOR, CLSID_StockColorPage)
END_PROP_MAP()
```

The ATL Object Wizard adds the first two PROP_DATA_ENTRY macros to a control's property map when it generates the initial source code. These entries cause ATL to save and restore the extent of the control. When you describe a persistent property using a PROP_DATA_ENTRY macro, ATL directly accesses the member variable in the control.

You must explicitly add entries for any additional properties that the control needs to persist. The BullsEye control lists all but one of its persistent properties using the PROP_ENTRY macro. This macro causes ATL to save and restore the specified property by accessing the property using the default dispatch interface for the control. Alternatively, you can use the PROP_ENTRY_EX macro to specify the IID, other than IID_IDispatch, of the dispatch interface that supports the property. You'd use the PROP_ENTRY_EX macro when your control supports multiple dispatch interfaces with various properties accessible via different dispatch interfaces. Supporting multiple dispatch interfaces is, generally speaking, not a good thing to do. One caution: Don't add a PROP_ENTRY macro that has a property name containing an embedded space character. Some relatively popular containers, for example, Visual Basic, provide an implementation of IPropertyBag::Write that cannot handle names with embedded spaces. This is a bug in the current version of Visual Basic, as other containers allow space-separated property names.

For properties described with the PROP_ENTRY and PROP_ENTRY_EX macros, the various persistence implementations query for the appropriate interface and call IDispatch::Invoke, specifying the DISPID from the property map entry to get and put the property.

There is presently a bug in the ATL implementation of property bag persistence for properties described using the PROP_DATA_ENTRY macro. The problem is in the AtlIPersistPropertyBag_Load function. Chapter 6 describes the problem in detail and shows you how to fix it. The summary is: Have the BullsEye control provide an IPersistPropertyBag_Load method that simply calls a fixed version of AtlIPersistPropertyBag_Load.

As it turns out, I need to provide an IPersistPropertyBag_Load method anyway. The BullsEye control has one additional property—the RingValues indexed (array) property. The ATL property map doesn't support indexed properties. In order to persist such properties, you must explicitly implement the IPersistStreamInit_Save, IPersistStreamInit_Load, IPersistPropertyBag_Save, and IPersistPropertyBag_Load methods normally provided by the ATL persistence implementation classes and read/write the indexed property. Here's an example from the BullsEye control. It calls a fixed version of AtlIPersistPropertyBag_Load, then saves the indexed property.

```
HRESULT CBullsEye::IPersistPropertyBag_Load(LPPROPERTYBAG pPropBag,
    LPERRORLOG pErrorLog, ATL_PROPMAP_ENTRY* pMap)
{
   if (NULL == pPropBag) return E_POINTER;

   // Load the properties described in the PROP_MAP
   // Work around ATL 3.0 bug in AtlIPersistPropertyBag_Load
   HRESULT hr = FixedAtlIPersistPropertyBag_Load(pPropBag, pErrorLog,
     pMap, this, GetUnknown());
      if (SUCCEEDED(hr)) m_bRequiresSave = FALSE;
```

```
    if (FAILED (hr)) return hr;

    // Load the indexed property-RingValues
    // Get the number of rings
    short sRingCount;
    get_RingCount (&sRingCount);

    // For each ring, read its value
    for (short nIndex = 1; nIndex <= sRingCount; nIndex++) {

        // Create the base property name
        CComBSTR bstrName = OLESTR("RingValue");

        // Create ring number as a string
        CComVariant vRingNumber = nIndex;
        hr = vRingNumber.ChangeType (VT_BSTR);
        ATLASSERT (SUCCEEDED (hr));

        // Concatenate the two strings to form property name
        bstrName += vRingNumber.bstrVal;

        // Read ring value from the property bag
        CComVariant vValue = 0L;
        hr = pPropBag->Read(bstrName, &vValue, pErrorLog);
        ATLASSERT (SUCCEEDED (hr));
        ATLASSERT (VT_I4 == vValue.vt);

        if (FAILED (hr)) {
           hr = E_UNEXPECTED;
           break;
    }

        // Set the ring value
        put_RingValue (nIndex, vValue.lVal);
          }

    if (SUCCEEDED(hr)) m_bRequiresSave = FALSE;
    return hr;
  }
```

IQuickActivate

Some control containers ask a control for its IQuickActivate interface and use the interface to exchange quickly a number of interfaces between the container and the control during the control's activation process, thus the interface name.

ATL provides an implementation of this interface, IQuickActivateImpl, which, by default, full, composite and HTML controls use. However, a control container also provides a control a few ambient properties during this quick activation process, which the ATL implementation doesn't save. Should your control need these ambient properties—BackColor, ForeColor, and Appearance—it's more efficient to save them during the quick activation process than to incur three more round-trips to the container to fetch them later.

The tricky aspect is that a container might not quick activate your control. Therefore, the control should save the ambient properties when quick activated, or retrieve the ambient properties when the container provides the control's client site, but not both. However, it's easy to add this functionality to your control.

When a container quick activates your control, it calls the control's IQuick-Activate::QuickActivate method, which is present in your control's IQuick-ActivateImpl base class. This method delegates the call to your control class's IQuickActivate_QuickActivate method. By default, a control class doesn't provide the method, so the call invokes a default implementation supplied by CComControlBase. You simply need to provide an implementation of the IQuick-Activate_QuickActivate method that saves the ambient properties and forwards the call to the method in CComControlBase, like so:

```
HRESULT CBullsEye::IQuickActivate_QuickActivate(QACONTAINER *pQACont,
                                                QACONTROL *pQACtrl)
{
    m_clrForeColor = pQACont->colorFore;
    m_clrBackColor = pQACont->colorBack;
    m_nAppearance  = (short) pQACont->dwAppearance;
    m_bAmbientsFetched = true;

    HRESULT hr = CComControlBase::IQuickActivate_QuickActivate(pQACont,
        pQACtrl);
    return hr;
}
```

Note that the function also sets a flag, m_bAmbientsFetched, to remember that it has already obtained the ambient properties and therefore shouldn't fetch them again when the control receives its client site. BullsEye initializes the flag to `false` in its constructor and checks the flag in its `IOleObject_SetClientSite` method like this:

```
HRESULT CBullsEye::IOleObject_SetClientSite(IOleClientSite
                                             *pClientSite)
{
    HRESULT hr = CComControlBase::IOleObject_SetClientSite(pClientSite);
    if (!m_bAmbientsFetched) {
        HRESULT hr = GetAmbientBackColor (m_clrBackColor);
                hr = GetAmbientForeColor (m_clrForeColor);
                hr = GetAmbientAppearance (m_nAppearance);
    }
    return hr;
}
```

Component Categories

Frequently you'll want your control to belong to one or more component categories. For example, the BullsEye control belongs to the "ATL Internals Sample Components" category. Additionally, BullsEye is a member of the "Safe for Initialization" and "Safe for Scripting" categories so that the control may be initialized and accessed by scripts on an HTML page without security warnings. Adding the proper entries to the control's category map registers the class as a member of the specified component categories. BullsEye uses this category map:

```
BEGIN_CATEGORY_MAP(CBullsEye)
IMPLEMENTED_CATEGORY(CATID_ATLINTERNALS_SAMPLES)
IMPLEMENTED_CATEGORY(CATID_SafeForScripting)
IMPLEMENTED_CATEGORY(CATID_SafeForInitializing)
END_CATEGORY_MAP()
```

Registering a control as a member of the Safe for Initialization and/or Safe for Scripting component categories is a static decision. In other words, you're deciding that the control is or is not always safe. A control may prefer to restrict its functionality at runtime when it needs to be safe for initialization or scripting but at other times have its full, potentially unsafe, functionality available.

Such controls must implement the `IObjectSafety` interface. ATL provides a default implementation of this interface in the `IObjectSafetyImpl` class. You specify, as a template parameter, the safety options supported by the control, and a container can use methods of this interface to selectively enable and disable each supported option. A control can determine its current safety level, and potentially disable or enable unsafe functionality, by checking the m_dwCurrentSafety member variable.

You use this implementation class like most of the others, derive your control class from the appropriate template class, and add the proper interface entry to the COM interface map. BullsEye does it like this:

```
class ATL_NO_VTABLE CBullsEye :
    . . .
    // Object safety support
    public IObjectSafetyImpl<CBullsEye,
       INTERFACESAFE_FOR_UNTRUSTED_CALLER |
       INTERFACESAFE_FOR_UNTRUSTED_DATA>,
    . . .

BEGIN_COM_MAP(CBullsEye)
    // Object safety support
    COM_INTERFACE_ENTRY(IObjectSafety)
    . . .
END_COM_MAP()
```

ICategorizeProperties

Visual Basic provides a property view that displays the properties of a control on a form. The property view can display the properties on a control alphabetically or grouped by arbitrary categories. Figure 10.3 shows the categorized list of the Bulls-Eye control's properties when the control is contained on a Visual Basic form.

A control must implement the ICategorizeProperties interface so that Visual Basic can display the control's properties in the appropriate categories in its property view. Unfortunately, this interface isn't presently defined in any system IDL file or any system header file, and ATL provides no implementation class for the interface. So here's what you need to do to support it.

First, here's the IDL for the interface:

```
[
       object, local,
       uuid(4D07FC10-F931-11CE-B001-00AA006884E5),
       helpstring("ICategorizeProperties Interface"),
       pointer_default(unique)
```

```
        ]
        interface ICategorizeProperties : IUnknown
        {
            typedef [public] int PROPCAT;

            const int PROPCAT_Nil        = -1;
            const int PROPCAT_Misc       = -2;
            const int PROPCAT_Font       = -3;
            const int PROPCAT_Position   = -4;
            const int PROPCAT_Appearance = -5;
            const int PROPCAT_Behavior   = -6;
            const int PROPCAT_Data       = -7;
            const int PROPCAT_List       = -8;
            const int PROPCAT_Text       = -9;
            const int PROPCAT_Scale      = -10;
            const int PROPCAT_DDE        = -11;

            HRESULT MapPropertyToCategory([in] DISPID dispid, [out] PROPCAT*
                                          ppropcat);
            HRESULT GetCategoryName([in] PROPCAT propcat, [in] LCID lcid, [out]
                                    BSTR* pbstrName);
        }
```

I keep this IDL in a separate file, `CategorizeProperties.idl`, and import the file into the `BullsEye.idl` file. This way, when Microsoft finally adds the interface to a system IDL file, I can simply remove the import from the `BullsEye.idl` file.

You implement the interface like all interfaces in ATL: Derive your control class from `ICategorizeProperties`, add the interface entry to the control's interface map, and implement the two methods, `MapPropertyToCategory` and `GetCategoryName`. Note that there are eleven predefined property categories with negative values. You can define your own custom categories, but be sure to assign them positive values.

The `MapPropertyToCategory` method returns the appropriate property category value for the specified property.

```
STDMETHODIMP CBullsEye::MapPropertyToCategory(/*[in]*/ DISPID dispid,
  /*[out]*/ PROPCAT* ppropcat)
{
    if (NULL == ppropcat) return E_POINTER;
```

```
    switch (dispid) {
    case DISPID_FORECOLOR:    case DISPID_BACKCOLOR:
    case DISPID_CENTERCOLOR: case DISPID_ALTERNATECOLOR:
    case DISPID_RINGCOUNT:    case DISPID_BACKSTYLE:
        *ppropcat = PROPCAT_Appearance;
        return S_OK;

    case DISPID_BEEP:         case DISPID_ENABLED:
        *ppropcat = PROPCAT_Behavior;
        return S_OK;

    case DISPID_RINGVALUE:
        *ppropcat = PROPCAT_Scoring;
        return S_OK;

    default:
        return E_FAIL;
    }
}
```

The `GetCategoryName` method simply returns a BSTR containing the category name. You only need to support your custom category values, because Visual Basic knows the names of the standard property category values.

```
STDMETHODIMP CBullsEye::GetCategoryName(/*[in]*/ PROPCAT propcat,
                                        /*[in]*/ LCID lcid,
                                        /*[out]*/ BSTR* pbstrName)
{
    if(PROPCAT_Scoring == propcat) {
        *pbstrName = ::SysAllocString(L"Scoring");
        return S_OK;
    }
    return E_FAIL;
}
```

BullsEye supports one custom category, "Scoring," and associates its `Ring-Value` property with the category. Unfortunately, the `RingValue` property is an indexed property and Visual Basic doesn't presently support indexed properties. Thus, the `RingValue` property doesn't appear in Visual Basic's property view, either in the alphabetic list or the categorized list.

Per-Property Browsing

When Visual Basic and similar containers display a control's property in a property view, they can ask the control for a string that better describes the property's current value than the actual value of the property. For example, a particular property may have valid numerical values of 1, 2, and 3, which represent the colors red, blue, and green, respectively. When Visual Basic asks the control for a display string for the property when the property has value 2, the control returns the string "blue."

A container uses the control's IPerPropertyBrowsing interface to retrieve the display strings for a control's properties. When the control doesn't provide a display string for a property, some containers, such as Visual Basic, will provide default formatting if possible.[1] Of course, the container can always simply display the actual property value.

Notice in Figure 10.3 that the Visual Basic property view displays "Yes" for the value of the Beep property (which was set to − 1) and "Transparent" for the Back-Style property (which was set to 0). To provide custom display strings for a property's value, your control must implement IPerPropertyBrowsing and override the GetDisplayString method. You return the appropriate string for the requested property based on the property's current value. Here's the GetDisplay-String method for the CBullsEye class:

```
STDMETHODIMP CBullsEye::GetDisplayString(DISPID dispid,BSTR *pBstr)
{
    ATLTRACE2(atlTraceControls,2,_T("CBullsEye::GetDisplayString\n"));
    switch (dispid) {
    case DISPID_BEEP:
        if (VARIANT_TRUE == m_beep)
          *pBstr = SysAllocString (OLESTR("Yes"));
        else
          *pBstr = SysAllocString (OLESTR("No"));

        return *pBstr ? S_OK : E_OUTOFMEMORY;

    case DISPID_BACKSTYLE:
        if (1 == m_nBackStyle)
          *pBstr = SysAllocString (OLESTR("Opaque"));
```

---

[1] Visual Basic first queries a control for IPerPropertyBrowsing to retrieve the display strings for a property. When that query fails, Visual Basic will load the type library and retrieve the enumerated values that were specified in the IDL for the property, if available. Failing that, Visual Basic displays the actual property value.

```
              else
                *pBstr = SysAllocString (OLESTR("Transparent"));

              return *pBstr ? S_OK : E_OUTOFMEMORY;

       case DISPID_ALTERNATECOLOR:    // Make Visual Basic apply default
                                      // formatting
       case DISPID_BACKCOLOR:         // for these color properties.
       case DISPID_CENTERCOLOR:       // Otherwise it displays color values
                                      // in decimal
       case DISPID_FORECOLOR:         // and doesn't draw the color sample
                                      // correctly.
          return S_FALSE;             // This is an undocumented return
                                      // value that works...
    }

       return IPerPropertyBrowsingImpl<CBullsEye>::
         GetDisplayString(dispid, pBstr);
  }
```

The `IPerPropertyBrowsingImpl<T>::GetDisplayString` implementation fetches the value of the specified property and, if it's not already a BSTR, converts the value into a BSTR using `VariantChangeType`. This produces relatively uninteresting display strings for anything but simple numerical value properties.

Visual Basic will provide default formatting for certain property types, such as `OLE_COLOR` and `VARIANT_BOOL` properties, but only if your `GetDisplayString` method doesn't provide a string for the property. The default implementation fails when the property doesn't exist, or the property exists but cannot be converted into a BSTR, or the BSTR memory allocation fails. This basically means that the default implementation of `GetDisplayString` often provides less than useful strings for many properties.

BullsEye's `GetDisplayString` method lets Visual Basic provide default formatting for all its `OLE_COLOR` properties by returning S_FALSE when asked for those properties. This value isn't documented as a valid return value for `GetDisplayString`, but there are a couple of convincing reasons to use it: The default ATL implementation of `GetDisplayString` returns this value when it cannot provide a display string for a property and . . . it works.

When you let Visual Basic provide the display string for an `OLE_COLOR` property, it displays the color value in hexadecimal and displays a color sample. ATL's default implementation displays the color value in decimal, and the sample image is

typically always black. When you let Visual Basic provide the display string for a
VARIANT_BOOL property, Visual Basic displays "True" and "False." ATL's default implementation displays "−1" and "0," respectively.

Also notice in Figure 10.3, that when you click on a property in Visual Basic's
property view in order to modify the property, a drop-down arrow appears to the
right side of the property value. Clicking on this arrow produces a drop-down list
containing strings representing the valid selections for the property. You provide
this support via the IPerPropertyBrowsing interface too. A container will call
the interface's GetPredefinedStrings method to retrieve the strings the container displays in the drop-down list. For each string, the method also provides a
DWORD value (cookie). When a user selects one of the strings from the drop-down
list, the container calls the interface's GetPredefinedValue method and provides
the cookie. The method returns the property value associated with the selected
string. The container then typically performs a property put IDispatch call to
change the property to the predefined value.

The BullsEye control supports predefined strings and values for the Beep and
BackStyle properties, as shown in the following code.

```
/************************/

/* GetPredefinedStrings */

/************************/

#define DIM(a) (sizeof(a)/sizeof(a[0]))

static const LPCOLESTR    rszBeepStrings [] = { OLESTR("Yes, make
                                                        noise"),
                                              OLESTR("No, be mute") };
static const DWORD        rdwBeepCookies [] = { 0, 1 };
static const VARIANT_BOOL rvbBeepValues  [] = { VARIANT_TRUE,
                                                VARIANT_FALSE };

static const UINT cBeepStrings = DIM(rszBeepStrings);
static const UINT cBeepCookies = DIM(rdwBeepCookies);
static const UINT cBeepValues  = DIM(rvbBeepValues);

static const LPCOLESTR    rszBackStyleStrings [] = { OLESTR("Opaque"),
                                                     OLESTR("Transparent") };
static const DWORD        rdwBackStyleCookies [] = { 0, 1 };
static const long         rvbBackStyleValues  [] = { 1, 0 };
```

```
static const UINT cBackStyleStrings = DIM(rszBackStyleStrings);
static const UINT cBackStyleCookies = DIM(rdwBackStyleCookies);
static const UINT cBackStyleValues  = DIM(rvbBackStyleValues);

STDMETHODIMP CBullsEye::GetPredefinedStrings(/*[in]*/ DISPID dispid,
                                             /*[out]*/ CALPOLESTR
                                              *pcaStringsOut,
                                             /*[out]*/ CADWORD
                                              *pcaCookiesOut)
{
 ATLTRACE2(atlTraceControls,2,_T("CBullsEye::GetPredefinedStrings\n"));
 if (NULL == pcaStringsOut || NULL == pcaCookiesOut) return E_POINTER;

    ATLASSERT (cBeepStrings == cBeepCookies);
    ATLASSERT (cBeepStrings == cBeepValues);

    ATLASSERT (cBackStyleStrings == cBackStyleCookies);
    ATLASSERT (cBackStyleStrings == cBackStyleValues);

    pcaStringsOut->cElems = 0;
    pcaStringsOut->pElems = NULL;
    pcaCookiesOut->cElems = 0;
    pcaCookiesOut->pElems = NULL;

    HRESULT hr = S_OK;
    switch (dispid) {
    case DISPID_BEEP:
        hr = SetStrings (cBeepValues, rszBeepStrings, pcaStringsOut);
        if (FAILED (hr)) return hr;
        return SetCookies (cBeepValues, rdwBeepCookies, pcaCookiesOut);

    case DISPID_BACKSTYLE:
        hr = SetStrings (cBackStyleValues, rszBackStyleStrings,
                        pcaStringsOut);
        if (FAILED (hr)) return hr;
        return SetCookies (cBackStyleValues, rdwBackStyleCookies,
                        pcaCookiesOut);
    }
    return IPerPropertyBrowsingImpl<CBullsEye>::
      GetPredefinedStrings(dispid, pcaStringsOut, pcaCookiesOut);
}
```

```
/**********************/
/* GetPredefinedValue */
/**********************/

STDMETHODIMP CBullsEye::GetPredefinedValue(DISPID dispid,
                                           DWORD dwCookie,
                                           VARIANT* pVarOut)
{
    if (NULL == pVarOut) return E_POINTER;

    ULONG i;
    switch (dispid) {
    case DISPID_BEEP:
        // Walk through cookie array looking for matching value
        for (i = 0; i < cBeepCookies; i++) {
            if (rdwBeepCookies[i] == dwCookie) {
                pVarOut->vt = VT_BOOL;
                pVarOut->boolVal = rvbBeepValues [i];
                return S_OK;
            }
        }
        return E_INVALIDARG;

    case DISPID_BACKSTYLE:
        // Walk through cookie array looking for matching value
        for (i = 0; i < cBackStyleCookies; i++) {
            if (rdwBackStyleCookies[i] == dwCookie) {
                pVarOut->vt = VT_I4;
                pVarOut->lVal = rvbBackStyleValues [i];
                return S_OK;
            }
        }
        return E_INVALIDARG;
    }

    return
        IPerPropertyBrowsingImpl<CBullsEye>::GetPredefinedValue(dispid,
                                                dwCookie, pVarOut);
}
```

Some containers will let you edit a control's property using the appropriate property page for the property. When you click on such a property in Visual Basic's property view, Visual Basic displays a small pushbutton containing "..." to the right of the property value. Clicking on this button displays the control's property page for the property.

A container uses a control's `IPerPropertyBrowsing::MapProperty-ToPage` method to find the property page for a property. Unfortunately, ATL 3.0's `IPerPropertyBrowsingImpl` class has a small bug in its implementation. When it finds a property listed in the property map, it returns the CLSID contained in the map. However, the property map serves two functions. It maps properties to property pages and it also lists properties supported by the persistence interfaces. For a property that you want persisted but for which you have no property page editing support, you add an entry such as the following to the property map:

```
PROP_ENTRY("SomeProperty", DISPID_SOMEPROPERTY, CLSID_NULL)
```

`IPerPropertyBrowsingImpl` finds this entry in the property map and returns `CLSID_NULL` for the property page class. This causes Visual Basic to display the pushbutton, and when you click on it, you receive an error message stating that `CLSID_NULL` is not registered. To correct the problem, override `MapProperty-ToPage` in your control. Invoke `IPerPropertyBrowsingImpl::MapProperty-ToPage` and when it finds the requested property, check for `CLSID_NULL` as the output. In this case, return the proper error status: `PERPROP_E_NOPAGEAVAILABLE`.

```
STDMETHODIMP CBullsEye::MapPropertyToPage(DISPID dispid, CLSID *pClsid)
{
  HRESULT hr =
  IPerPropertyBrowsingImpl<CBullsEye>::MapPropertyToPage(dispid,
    pClsid);
  if (SUCCEEDED(hr) && CLSID_NULL == *pClsid)
    hr = PERPROP_E_NOPAGEAVAILABLE;
  return hr;
}
```

Keyboard Handling for an ActiveX Control

When an ATL-based ActiveX control has the focus on a Visual Basic form, it does not give the focus to the default button on the form (the button with a `Default` property of `True`) when you press Enter. ATL provides implementations of the `IOleControl::GetControlInfo` and the `IOleInPlaceActiveObject::TranslateAccelerator` methods that return `E_NOTIMPL`. A container calls a control's `GetControlInfo` method to get the control's keyboard mnemonics and keyboard behavior, and it calls the control's `TranslateAccelerator` method to process the key presses.

BullsEye overrides the two default implementations provided by ATL with the following code:

```
STDMETHODIMP CBullsEye::GetControlInfo(CONTROLINFO *pci)
{
    if(!pci) return E_POINTER;
    pci->hAccel  = NULL;
    pci->cAccel  = 0;
    pci->dwFlags = 0;
    return S_OK;
}


typedef enum tagKEYMODIFIERS {
    KEYMOD_SHIFT      = 0x00000001,
    KEYMOD_CONTROL    = 0x00000002,
    KEYMOD_ALT        = 0x00000004
} KEYMODIFIERS;


STDMETHODIMP CBullsEye::TranslateAccelerator(MSG *pMsg)
{
    if (((pMsg->message >= WM_KEYFIRST) && (pMsg->message <=
                                            WM_KEYLAST)) &&
        ((VK_TAB == pMsg->wParam) || (VK_RETURN == pMsg->wParam))) {

        CComQIPtr<IOleControlSite, &IID_IOleControlSite>
            spCtrlSite(m_spClientSite);
        if (spCtrlSite) {
            DWORD km = 0;
            km |= GetKeyState (VK_SHIFT)   < 0 ? KEYMOD_SHIFT   : 0;
            km |= GetKeyState (VK_CONTROL) < 0 ? KEYMOD_CONTROL : 0;
            km |= GetKeyState (VK_MENU)    < 0 ? KEYMOD_ALT     : 0;

            return spCtrlSite->TranslateAccelerator (pMsg, km);
        }
    }
    return S_FALSE;
}
```

When the BullsEye control has the input focus, these method implementations pass all Tab and Enter key presses to the container for processing. This implementation allows one to tab into and out of the BullsEye control while the control has the input focus, pressing the Enter key activates the default pushbutton on a Visual Basic form, if any.

Of course, for the BullsEye control it doesn't make much sense to allow a user to tab into the control. You can use the MiscStatus for a control to inform the control's container that the control doesn't wish to be activated by tabbing. A container asks a control for its MiscStatus setting by calling the control's IOleObject::GetMiscStatus method. ATL provides an implementation of this method in the IOleControlImpl class. It looks like this:

```
STDMETHOD(GetMiscStatus)(DWORD dwAspect, DWORD *pdwStatus)
{
  ATLTRACE2(atlTraceControls,2,_T("IOleObjectImpl::GetMiscStatus\n"));
  return OleRegGetMiscStatus(T::GetObjectCLSID(), dwAspect,
                           pdwStatus);
}
```

This code simply delegates the call to the OleRegGetMiscStatus function, which reads the value from the control's registry entry. A control can have multiple MiscStatus values—one for each drawing aspect supported by the control. Most controls support drawing aspect DVASPECT_CONTENT, which has the value of 1. You specify the drawing aspect as a subkey of MiscStatus. The value of the subkey is the string of decimal numbers comprising the sum of the desired OLEMISC enumeration values.

For example, BullsEye uses the following MiscStatus settings:

OLEMISC_SETCLIENTSITEFIRST	131072
OLEMISC_NOUIACTIVATE	16384
OLEMISC_ACTIVATEWHENVISIBLE	256
OLEMISC_INSIDEOUT	128
CANTLINKINSIDE	16
OLEMISC_RECOMPOSEONRESIZE	1

The sum of these values is 147857, so you specify that as the value of the subkey called "1" of your class.

```
ForceRemove {7DC59CC5-36C0-11D2-AC05-00A0C9C8E50D} = s 'BullsEye Class'
{
  . . .
  'MiscStatus' = s '0'
  {
```

```
     '1' = s '147857'
  }
}
```

Alternatively, BullsEye could override the `GetMiscStatus` method and provide the desired value, and the registry entry would not be needed:

```
STDMETHODIMP CBullsEye::GetMiscStatus (DWORD dwAspect, DWORD
                                        *pdwStatus)
{
   if (NULL == pdwStatus) return E_POINTER;

   *pdwStatus =
       OLEMISC_SETCLIENTSITEFIRST |
       OLEMISC_ACTIVATEWHENVISIBLE |
       OLEMISC_INSIDEOUT |
       OLEMISC_CANTLINKINSIDE |
       OLEMISC_RECOMPOSEONRESIZE |
       OLEMISC_NOUIACTIVATE ;

   return S_OK;
}
```

The `OLEMISC_NOUIACTIVATE` setting is the one that prevents Visual Basic from giving the BullsEye control the input focus when a user attempts to tab into the control.

Summary

ActiveX controls use much of the functionality discussed so far. An ATL-based control typically supports properties and methods using ATL's `IDispatchImpl` support. In addition, a control typically fires events; therefore, it often derives from `IConnectionPointContainerImpl` and uses a connection point proxy-generated class (`IConnectionPointImpl`-derived) for each connection point. A control generally requires persistence support, so uses one or more of the persistence implementation classes: `IPersistsStreamInitImpl`, `IPersistProper-tyBagImpl`, and `IPersistsStorageImpl`.

In addition there are numerous other interfaces many controls should implement so they integrate well with various control containers, such as Visual Basic. In the next chapter, you'll learn how ATL supports hosting ActiveX control and how to write a control container using ATL.

11 | Control Containment

Containment of COM controls can take many forms. A window can contain any number of COM controls, as can a dialog or another control (called a composite control). All these containers share common characteristics, which is the subject of this chapter.

How Controls Are Contained

To contain a COM control,[1] a container must do two things:

1. Provide a window to act as the parent for the child COM control. The parent window may be used by a single child COM control or shared between many.

2. Implement a set of COM interfaces that the control uses to communicate with the container. The container must provide at least one object per control, called the site, to implement these interfaces. However, the interfaces may be spread between up to two other container-provided objects, called the document and the frame.

The window provided by the container may be a parent window of the control or, in the case of a windowless control, it may be shared by the control. The control will use the window in its interaction with the user. The interfaces implemented by the container are used for integration with the control and mirror those interfaces implemented by the control. Figure 11.1 shows the major interfaces implemented by the container and how they are mirrored by those implemented by the control.

As with Chapter 10, full coverage of the interaction between controls and containers is beyond the scope of this book. Refer to the sources listed in Chapter 10 for more information.[2] However, this chapter will present those things you need to know to host controls both in standalone applications and inside of COM servers.

---

[1] This chapter doesn't distinguish between OLE controls and ActiveX controls.
[2] You may also want to refer to the MSDN article, "Notes on Implementing an OLE Control Container," for control container-specific information.

**Container Object
Interfaces**

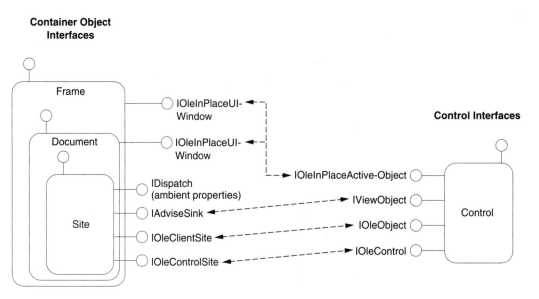

Figure 11.1. Container and control interfaces

Your hosting options include windows, dialogs, and composite controls. Before diving into the details of dialogs or controls hosting other controls, let's start with the basics by examining control containment in a simple frame window.

Basic Control Containment

Control Creation

The control creation process in ATL exposes the core of how ATL hosts controls. Figure 11.2 shows the overall process, and what follows is a detailed look at the relevant bits of code involved.

CAxHostWindow

ATL's implementation of the required container interfaces is called CAxHost-Window:[3]

```
// This class is not cocreateable
class ATL_NO_VTABLE CAxHostWindow :
  public CComCoClass<CAxHostWindow , &CLSID_NULL>,
  public CComObjectRootEx<CComSingleThreadModel>,
```

---

[3]This class is defined in atlhost.h.

```
   public CWindowImpl<CAxHostWindow>,
   public IAxWinHostWindow,
   public IOleClientSite,
   public IOleInPlaceSiteWindowless,
   public IOleControlSite,
   public IOleContainer,
   public IObjectWithSiteImpl<CAxHostWindow>,
   public IServiceProvider,
   public IAdviseSink,
#ifndef _ATL_NO_DOCHOSTUIHANDLER
   public IDocHostUIHandler,
#endif
   public IDispatchImpl<IAxWinAmbientDispatch,
                        &IID_IAxWinAmbient Dispatch,
                        &LIBID_ATLLib>
{...};
```

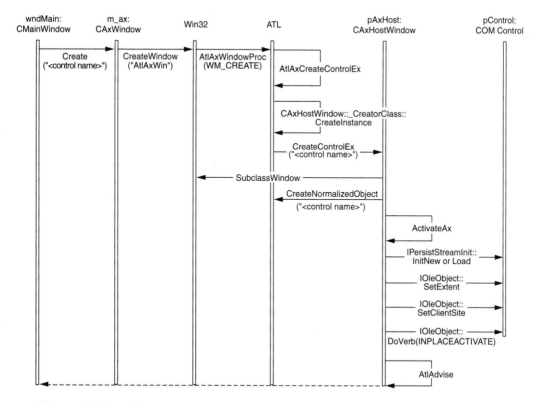

Figure 11.2. A UML sequence diagram of the ATL control creation process

Notice that a CAxHostWindow is two things: a window (from CWindowImpl) and a COM implementation (from CComObjectRootEx). When the container wishes to host a control, it will create an instance of CAxHostWindow, but not directly. Instead, it will create an instance of a window class defined by ATL called AtlAxWin. This window will act as the parent window for the control and will eventually be subclassed by an instance of CAxHostWindow. Before an instance of this window class can be created, the window class must first be registered. ATL provides a function called AtlAxWinInit to register the AtlAxWin window class.

```
// This either registers a global class (if AtlAxWinInit is in
// ATL.DLL)
// or it registers a local class
ATLINLINE ATLAPI_(BOOL) AtlAxWinInit() {
  EnterCriticalSection(&_Module.m_csWindowCreate);
  WM_ATLGETHOST = RegisterWindowMessage(_T("WM_ATLGETHOST"));
  WM_ATLGETCONTROL = RegisterWindowMessage(_T("WM_ATLGETCONTROL"));
  WNDCLASSEX wc;

  // first check if the class is already registered
  wc.cbSize = sizeof(WNDCLASSEX);
  BOOL bRet = ::GetClassInfoEx(_Module.GetModuleInstance(),
                        CAxWindow::GetWndClassName(), &wc);

  // register class if not
  if(!bRet) {
     wc.cbSize = sizeof(WNDCLASSEX);
#ifdef _ATL_DLL_IMPL
     wc.style = CS_GLOBALCLASS;
#else
     wc.style = 0;
#endif
     wc.lpfnWndProc = AtlAxWindowProc;
     wc.cbClsExtra = 0;
     wc.cbWndExtra = 0;
     wc.hInstance = _Module.GetModuleInstance();
     wc.hIcon = NULL;
     wc.hCursor = ::LoadCursor(NULL, IDC_ARROW);
     wc.hbrBackground = (HBRUSH)(COLOR_WINDOW + 1);
     wc.lpszMenuName = NULL;
     wc.lpszClassName = CAxWindow::GetWndClassName(); // "AtlAxWin"
     wc.hIconSm = NULL;
```

```
    bRet = (BOOL)::RegisterClassEx(&wc);
  }
  LeaveCriticalSection(&_Module.m_csWindowCreate);
  return bRet;
}
```

Once the `AtlAxWin` class has been registered, creating an instance of one will also create an instance of `CAxHostWindow`. The `CAxHostWindow` object will then use the title of the window as the name of the control to create and to host. For example, the following code will create a `CAxHostWindow` and cause it to host a new instance of the BullsEye control developed in Chapter 10:

```
class CMainWindow : public CWindowImpl<CMainWindow, ...> {
...
  LRESULT OnCreate(UINT uMsg, WPARAM wParam, LPARAM lParam, BOOL&
                    lResult) {
    // Create the host window, the CAxHostWindow object, and
    // the BullsEye control, and host the control
    RECT    rect; GetClientRect(&rect);
    LPCTSTR pszName = __T("ATLInternals.BullsEye");
    HWND    hwndContainer = m_ax.Create(__T("AtlAxWin"), m_hWnd, rect,
                                        pszName, WS_CHILD | WS_VISIBLE);
    if( !hwndContainer ) return -1;
    return 0;
  }

private:
  CWindow m_ax;
};
```

The creation of the `CAxHostWindow` object and the corresponding control is initiated in the `WM_CREATE` handler of the `AtlAxWin` window procedure, `AtlAxWindowProc`:

```
static LRESULT CALLBACK
AtlAxWindowProc(HWND hWnd, UINT uMsg, WPARAM wParam, LPARAM lParam) {
  switch(uMsg) {
  case WM_CREATE: {
    // create control from a PROGID in the title
    // This is to make sure drag drop works
    ::OleInitialize(NULL);
```

```
CREATESTRUCT* lpCreate = (CREATESTRUCT*)lParam;
int nLen = ::GetWindowTextLength(hWnd);
LPTSTR lpstrName = (LPTSTR)_alloca((nLen + 1) * sizeof(TCHAR));

// Extract window text to be used as name of control to host
::GetWindowText(hWnd, lpstrName, nLen + 1);
::SetWindowText(hWnd, _T(""));

IAxWinHostWindow* pAxWindow = NULL;
...
USES_CONVERSION;
CComPtr<IUnknown> spUnk;

// Create CAxHostWindow instance and host the control
HRESULT hRet = AtlAxCreateControl(T2COLE(lpstrName), hWnd,
                                  spStream, &spUnk);
if(FAILED(hRet)) return -1;  // abort window creation

hRet = spUnk->QueryInterface(IID_IAxWinHostWindow, (void**)
                             &pAxWindow);
if(FAILED(hRet)) return -1;   // abort window creation

// Keep a CAxHostWindow interface in the window's user data
::SetWindowLong(hWnd, GWL_USERDATA, (DWORD)pAxWindow);
...
// continue with DefWindowProc
}
break;

case WM_NCDESTROY: {
  IAxWinHostWindow*
    pAxWindow = (IAxWinHostWindow*)::GetWindowLong(hWnd, GWL_
                                                   USERDATA);

// When window goes away, release the host (and the control)
  if(pAxWindow != NULL) pAxWindow->Release();
  OleUninitialize();
}
break;
}
```

```
    return ::DefWindowProc(hWnd, uMsg, wParam, lParam);
}
```

Notice that the window's text, as passed to the call to `CWindow::Create`, is used as the name of the control to create. The call to `AtlAxCreateControl`, passing the name of the control, forwards to `AtlAxCreateControlEx`, which furthers things by creating a `CAxHostWindow` object and asking it to create and host the control:

```
ATLINLINE ATLAPI
AtlAxCreateControlEx(
  LPCOLESTR    lpszName,
  HWND         hWnd,
  IStream*     pStream,
  IUnknown**   ppUnkContainer,
  IUnknown**   ppUnkControl,
  REFIID       iidSink,
  IUnknown*    punkSink)
{
  AtlAxWinInit();
  HRESULT hr;
  CComPtr<IUnknown> spUnkContainer;
  CComPtr<IUnknown> spUnkControl;

  hr = CAxHostWindow::_CreatorClass::CreateInstance(NULL,
                                        IID_IUnknown,
                                    (void**)&spUnkContainer);
  if (SUCCEEDED(hr)) {
    CComPtr<IAxWinHostWindow> pAxWindow;
    spUnkContainer->QueryInterface(IID_IAxWinHostWindow, (void**)
                               &pAxWindow);
    CComBSTR bstrName(lpszName);
    hr = pAxWindow->CreateControlEx(bstrName, hWnd, pStream,
      &spUnkControl, iidSink, punkSink);
  }
  ...
  return hr;
}
```

IAxWinHostWindow

`AtlAxCreateControlEx` uses the `IAxWinHostWindow` interface to create the control. `IAxWinHostWindow` is one of the few interfaces that ATL defines and one of the interfaces that CAxHostWindow implements. Its job is to allow for management of the control that it's hosting:

```
interface IAxWinHostWindow : IUnknown {
  HRESULT CreateControl([in] LPCOLESTR lpTricsData, [in] HWND hWnd,
                        [in] IStream* pStream);
  HRESULT CreateControlEx([in] LPCOLESTR lpTricsData, [in] HWND hWnd,
                        [in] IStream* pStream, [out] IUnknown** ppUnk,
                  [in] REFIID riidAdvise, [in] IUnknown* punkAdvise);
  HRESULT AttachControl([in] IUnknown* pUnkControl, [in] HWND hWnd);
  HRESULT QueryControl([in] REFIID riid,
                        [out, iid_is(riid)] void **ppvObject);
  HRESULT SetExternalDispatch([in] IDispatch* pDisp);
  HRESULT SetExternalUIHandler([in] IDocHostUIHandlerDispatch* pDisp);
};
```

To create a new control in the CAxHostWindow, IAxWinHostWindow provides CreateControl or CreateControlEx, which is what AtlAxCreateControlEx uses after the CAxHostWindow object is created. The parameters for Create-Control[Ex] are as follows:

- **lpTricsData**. The name of the control to create. Can take the form of a CLSID, a ProgID, a URL, a file name, or raw HTML. I'll discuss more about this later.

- **hWnd**. Parent window in which to host the control. This window will be subclassed by CAxHostWindow.

- **pStream**. Stream that holds object initialization data. The control will be initialized via IPersistStreamInit. If pStream is non-NULL, Load will be called. Otherwise, InitNew will be called.

- **ppUnk**. Will be filled with an interface to the newly created control.

- **riidAdvise**. If not IID_NULL, CAxHostWindow will attempt to set up a connection point connection between the control and the sink object represented by the punkAdvise parameter. CAxHostWindow will manage the resultant cookie and tear down the connection when the control is destroyed.

- **punkAdvise**. An interface to the sink object that implements the sink interface specified by riidAdvise.

The AttachControl method of the IAxWinHostWindow method attaches a control that has already been created and initialized to an existing CAxHostWindow object. The QueryControl method allows access to the control's interfaces being hosted by the CAxHostWindow object. Both SetExternalDispatch and SetExternalUIHandler are for use when hosting the Internet Explorer HTML control and will be discussed at the end of the chapter in the HTML Controls section.

CreateControlEx

CAxHostWindow's implementation of CreateControlEx subclasses the parent window for the new control, creates a new control, and then activates it. If an initial connection point is requested, AtlAdvise is used to establish that connection. If the newly created control is to be initialized from raw HTML or to be navigated to via a URL, CreateControlEx does that, too:

```
STDMETHODIMP CAxHostWindow::CreateControlEx(
LPCOLESTR  lpszTricsData,
HWND       hWnd,
IStream*   pStream,
IUnknown** ppUnk,
REFIID     iidAdvise,
IUnknown*  punkSink)
{
HRESULT hr = S_FALSE;

// Release previously held control
ReleaseAll();
...
if (::IsWindow(hWnd)) {
    // Route all messages to CAxHostWindow object
    SubclassWindow(hWnd);
    ...

    bool bWasHTML;
    // Create control based on lpszTricsData
    hr = CreateNormalizedObject(lpszTricsData, IID_IUnknown,
      (void**)ppUnk,
                                bWasHTML);
    bool bInited = hr == S_FALSE;

    // Activate the control.
    if (SUCCEEDED(hr)) hr = ActivateAx(*ppUnk, bInited, pStream);
```

```
// Try to hook up any sink the user might have given us.
m_iidSink = iidAdvise;
if(SUCCEEDED(hr) && *ppUnk && punkSink)
  AtlAdvise(*ppUnk, punkSink, m_iidSink, &m_dwAdviseSink);

// If raw HTML, give HTML control its HTML
...


// If it's an URL, navigate the Browser control to the URL
...


if (FAILED(hr) || m_spUnknown == NULL) {
  // We don't have a control or something failed, so release
  ReleaseAll();

    ...

  }
 }
return hr;
}
```

How the control name is interpreted depends on another function called `Create-NormalizedObject`. The activation is handled by the `ActivateAx` function.

CreateNormalizedObject

The `CreateNormalizedObject` function will create an instance of a COM object using strings of the form shown in Table 11.1. Because `CAxHostWindow` uses the title of the window to obtain the name passed to `CreateNormalizedObject`, you

Table 11.1. String Formats Understood by `CreateNormalizedObject`

Type	Example(s)	CLSID of created object
HTML	mshtml:<body>Wow!</body>	`CLSID_HTMLDocument`
CLSID	{7DC59CC5-36C0-11D2-AC05-00A0C9C8E50D}	Result of `CLSIDFromString`
ProgID	ATLInternals.BullsEye	Result of `CLSIDFromProgID`
URL	http://www.awl.com	
	res://htmlapp.exe/main.htm	`CLSID_WebBrowser`
Active	D:\Atl Internals\11 Control Containment.doc	
document	file://D:\Atl Internals\10 Controls.doc	`CLSID_WebBrowser`

can use any of these string formats when creating an instance of the `AtlWinInit` window class.

ActivateAx

The `ActivateAx` function is the part of the control creation process that really performs the magic. It takes an interface pointer from the object that `Create-NormalizedObject` creates and activates it as a COM control in the parent window. `ActivateAx` is responsible for the following:

- Setting the client site, that is, the `CAxHostWindow`'s implementation of `IOle-ClientSite`, via the control's implementation of `IOleObject`.
- Calling either `InitNew` or `Load` (depending on whether the `pStream` argument to `AtlAxCreateControlEx` is NULL or non-NULL) via the control's implementation of `IPersistStreamInit`.
- Passing the `CAxHostWindow`'s implementation of `IAdviseSink` to the control's implementation of `IViewObject`.
- Setting the control's size to the size of the parent window, also via the control's implementation of `IOleObject`.
- Finally, to show the control and allow it to handle input and output, calling `DoVerb(OLEIVERB_INPLACEACTIVATE)` via the control's implementation of, again, `IOleObject`.

This process completes the activation of the control. However, creating an instance of `CAxHostWindow` via direct reference to the `AtlAxWin` window class is not typical. The implementation details of `AtlAxWin` and `CAxHostWindow` are meant to be hidden from the average ATL programmer. The usual way a control is hosted under ATL is via an instance of a wrapper class called `CAxWindow`.

CAxWindow

`CAxWindow` simplifies the use of `CAxHostWindow` with a set of wrapper functions. The initial creation part of `CAxWindow` class is defined as follows.

```
template <class TBase = CWindow> class CAxWindowT : public TBase {
public:
// Constructors
CAxWindowT(HWND hWnd = NULL) : TBase(hWnd) {}
CAxWindowT< TBase >& operator=(HWND hWnd)
   { m_hWnd = hWnd; return *this; }
```

```
// Attributes
static LPCTSTR GetWndClassName() { return _T("AtlAxWin"); }

// Operations
HWND Create(HWND hWndParent, RECT& rc, LPCTSTR szName = NULL, ...)
{ return CWindow::Create(GetWndClassName(), hWndParent, rc,
                         szName, ...); }

HWND Create(HWND hWndParent, LPRECT lpr = NULL, LPCTSTR szName =
            NULL...)
{ return CWindow::Create(GetWndClassName(), hWndParent, lpr,
                         szName, ...); }
...
};


typedef CAxWindowT<CWindow> CAxWindow;
```

Notice that both `Create` functions still require the parent window and the name of
the control, but do not require passing the name of the `CAxHostWindow` window
class. Instead, `CAxWindow` knows the name of the appropriate class itself (available
via the static member function `GetWndClassName`) and passes it to the `CWindow`
base class just like we had done manually. Using `CAxWindow` reduces the code required to host a control to the following:

```
class CMainWindow : public CWindowImpl<CMainWindow, ...> {
...
  LRESULT OnCreate(UINT uMsg, WPARAM wParam, LPARAM lParam, BOOL&
                   lResult) {
    // Create the host window, the CAxHostWindow object, and
    // the BullsEye control, and host the control
    RECT    rect; GetClientRect(&rect);
    LPCTSTR pszName = __T("ATLInternals.BullsEye");
    HWND    hwndContainer = m_ax.Create(m_hWnd, rect,
                                        pszName, WS_CHILD | WS_VISIBLE);
     if( !hwndContainer ) return -1;
    return 0;
  }

private:
 CAxWindow m_ax;
};
```

The combination of a custom window class and a CWindow-based wrapper provides exactly the same model as the window control wrappers that I discussed in Chapter 9. For example, EDIT is a window class, and the CEdit class provides the client-side wrapper. The implementation of the EDIT window class happens to use the window text passed via CreateWindow as the text to edit. The AtlAxWin class, on the other hand, uses the window text as the name of the control to create. The job of both wrapper classes is to provide a set of member functions that replace calls to SendMessage. CEdit provides member functions like CanUndo and Get-LineCount, which send the EM_CANUNDO and EM_GETLINECOUNT messages. CAx-Window, on the other hand, provides member functions that also send window messages to the AtlAxWin class (which I'll discuss later). The only real difference between EDIT and AtlAxWin is that EDIT is provided with the operating system, whereas AtlAxWin is only provided with ATL.[4]

Two-Step Control Creation

You may have noticed that AtlAxCreateControlEx takes some interesting parameters, such as an IStream interface pointer and an interface ID/interface pointer pair to specify an initial connection point. However, while the window name can be used to pass the name of the control, there are no extra parameters to CreateWindow for a couple of interface pointers and a globally unique identifier (GUID). Instead, CAxWindow provides a few extra wrapper functions, namely, CreateControl and CreateControlEx:

```
template <class TBase = CWindow> class CAxWindowT : public TBase {
public:
...
 HRESULT CreateControl(LPCOLESTR lpszName, IStream* pStream = NULL,
                      IUnknown** ppUnkContainer = NULL)
 { ATLASSERT(::IsWindow(m_hWnd));
    return AtlAxCreateControl(lpszName, m_hWnd, pStream,
                             ppUnkContainer);
 }

 HRESULT CreateControl(DWORD dwResID, IStream* pStream = NULL,
                      IUnknown** ppUnkContainer = NULL)
 { // bstrURL == URL of the form "res://<module>/<dwResID>"
    ATLASSERT(::IsWindow(m_hWnd));
    return AtlAxCreateControl(bstrURL, m_hWnd, pStream,
                             ppUnkContainer);
 }
```

---

[4] Arguably, a window class whose function is to host COM controls should be part of the OS.

```
HRESULT CreateControlEx(LPCOLESTR lpszName, IStream* pStream = NULL,
                        IUnknown** ppUnkContainer = NULL,
                        IUnknown** ppUnkControl = NULL,
                        REFIID iidSink = IID_NULL,
                        IUnknown* punkSink = NULL)
{ ATLASSERT(::IsWindow(m_hWnd));
  return AtlAxCreateControlEx(lpszName, m_hWnd, pStream,
            ppUnkContainer, ppUnkControl, iidSink, punkSink);
}


HRESULT CreateControlEx(DWORD dwResID,  IStream* pStream = NULL,
                        IUnknown** ppUnkContainer = NULL,
                        IUnknown** ppUnkControl = NULL,
                        REFIID iidSink = IID_NULL,
                        IUnknown* punkSink = NULL)
{ // bstrURL == URL of the form "res://<module>/<dwResID>"
  ATLASSERT(::IsWindow(m_hWnd));
  return AtlAxCreateControlEx(bstrURL, m_hWnd, pStream,
            ppUnkContainer, ppUnkControl, iidSink, punkSink);
}
...
};
```

CreateControl and CreateControlEx allow for the extra parameters that
AtlAxCreateControlEx supports. The extra parameter that the CAxWindow
wrappers support beyond those passed to AtlAxCreateControlEx is the dwRes-
ID parameter, which serves as an ID of an HTML page embedded in the resources
of the module. This parameter will be formatted into a string of the format
res://<module path>>/<dwResID> before being passed to AtlAxCreate-
ControlEx.

These functions are meant to be used in a two-stage construction of first the
host and then its control. For example:

```
LRESULT
CMainWindow::OnCreate(UINT uMsg, WPARAM wParam, LPARAM lParam, BOOL&
                      lResult)
{
 RECT    rect; GetClientRect(&rect);
 // Phase one: Create the container
 HWND    hwndContainer = m_ax.Create(m_hWnd, rect, 0, WS_CHILD |
                                     WS_VISIBLE);
  if( !hwndContainer ) return -1;
```

```
  // Phase two: Create the control
  LPCOLESTR pszName = OLESTR("ATLInternals.BullsEye");
  HRESULT hr = m_ax.CreateControl(pszName); // This leaks, keep
  // reading!
  return (SUCCEEDED(hr) ? 0 : -1);
};
```

I'll show you how to persist a control and how to handle events from a control later in this chapter. If you've already created a control and initialized it, you can still use the hosting functionality of ATL by attaching the existing control to a host window via the AttachControl function:

```
template <class TBase = CWindow> class CAxWindowT : public TBase {
public:
...
  HRESULT AttachControl(IUnknown* pControl, IUnknown** ppUnkContainer){
    ATLASSERT(::IsWindow(m_hWnd));
    return AtlAxAttachControl(pControl, m_hWnd, ppUnkContainer);
  }
...
};
```

AttachControl is meant to be used like so:

```
LRESULT
CMainWindow::OnCreate(UINT uMsg, WPARAM wParam, LPARAM lParam, BOOL&
                      lResult)
{
 RECT    rect; GetClientRect(&rect);
 // Phase one: Create the container
 HWND    hwndContainer = m_ax.Create(m_hWnd, rect, 0, WS_CHILD |
                           WS_VISIBLE);
 if( !hwndContainer ) return -1;

 // Create and initialize a control
 CComPtr<IUnknown> spunkControl; // ...

 // Phase two: Attach an existing control
 HRESULT hr = m_ax.AttachControl(spunkControl); // This also leaks!
 return (SUCCEEDED(hr) ? 0 : -1);
};
```

Avoid CAxWindow Functions CreateControl, CreateControlEx, and AttachControl

As attractive as the `CreateControl`, `CreateControlEx`, and `AttachControl` member functions are, however, as of ATL 3.0, you should avoid using them. They leak. Phase one creates an instance of `CAxHostWindow`, even if the window text is empty. All three of the second-phase control creator functions also create an instance of `CAxHostWindow` and *never destroy the first one*. You're leaking the size of a `CAxHostWindow` object (224 bytes) every time you call one of these three functions.

Luckily, there's a workaround. If you use the `QueryHost` member function of `CAxWindow`, you can obtain the `IAxWinHostWindow` interface on the existing `CAxHostWindow` object:

```
template <class TBase = CWindow> class CAxWindowT : public TBase {
public:

  HRESULT QueryHost(REFIID iid, void** ppUnk) {
    CComPtr<IUnknown> spUnk;
    HRESULT hr = AtlAxGetHost(m_hWnd, &spUnk);
    if (SUCCEEDED(hr)) hr = spUnk->QueryInterface(iid, ppUnk);
    return hr;
  }

  template <class Q> HRESULT QueryHost(Q** ppUnk)
  { return QueryHost(__uuidof(Q), (void**)ppUnk); }
};
```

The `QueryHost` member function uses the `AtlAxGetHost` function to send a custom window message to the `AtlAxWin` window to obtain an interface pointer on the host. Once you have the `IAxWinHostWindow` interface, you can call the interface member functions `CreateControl`, `CreateControlEx`, or `AttachControl` without worry of leaking because now you're reusing the existing `CAxHostWindow` instead of creating a new one. For example:

```
LRESULT
CMainWindow::OnCreate(UINT uMsg, WPARAM wParam, LPARAM lParam, BOOL&
                      lResult)
{
  RECT    rect; GetClientRect(&rect);
  // Phase one: Create the container
  HWND    hwndContainer = m_ax.Create(m_hWnd, rect, 0, WS_CHILD |
                                      WS_VISIBLE);
  if( !hwndContainer ) return -1;
```

```
// Phase two: Create the control in the existing container
CComPtr<IAxWinHostWindow> spAxWindow;
HRESULT hr = m_ax.QueryHost(&spAxWindow);
if( FAILED(hr) ) return -1;

LPCOLESTR pszName = OLESTR("ATLInternals.BullsEye");
hr = spAxWindow->CreateControl(pszName, m_ax.m_hWnd, 0);
if( FAILED(hr) ) return -1;

 return 0;
};
```

Because it's a pain to do this all manually, the source code provided for this book contains a fix for CAxWindow called CAxWindow2.[5] CAxWindow2 derives from CAxWindow and provides implementations of CreateControl, CreateControl-Ex, and AttachControl that reuse the existing CAxHostWindow object, if one is available, instead of creating a new one. On the other hand, if the m_hwnd member of the CAxWindow2 object has not been subclassed by an instance of CAxHost-Window, one will be created using the same techniques that CAxWindow uses. For example, the CreateControlEx function is implemented like so:

```
HRESULT
CAxWindowT2::CreateControlEx(
  LPCOLESTR  lpszName,
  IStream*    pStream = NULL,
  IUnknown** ppUnkContainer = NULL,
  IUnknown** ppUnkControl = NULL,
  REFIID     iidSink = IID_NULL,
  IUnknown*  punkSink = NULL)
{
  ATLASSERT(::IsWindow(m_hWnd));

  HRESULT hr = E_FAIL;
  CComPtr<IAxWinHostWindow> spAxWindow;

  // Reuse existing CAxHostWindow
  hr = QueryHost(&spAxWindow);
  if( SUCCEEDED(hr) ) {
    CComPtr<IUnknown> spunkControl;
```

---

[5]The name of the file that defines CAxWindow2 is axwin2.h.

```
        hr = spAxWindow->CreateControlEx(lpszName, m_hWnd, pStream,
                                          &spunkControl, iidSink, punkSink);
        if( FAILED(hr) ) return hr;

        if( ppUnkControl ) (*ppUnkControl = spunkControl)->AddRef();
        if( ppUnkContainer ) (*ppUnkContainer = spAxWindow)->AddRef();
    }
    // Create a new CAxHostWindow
    else {
      return AtlAxCreateControlEx(lpszName, m_hWnd, pStream,
                                  ppUnkContainer, ppUnkControl, iidSink,
                                  punkSink);
    }

     return S_OK;
    }


    typedef CAxWindowT2<CWindow> CAxWindow2;
```

The CAxWindow2 class allows you to use the CAxWindow member functions CreateControl, CreateControlEx and AttachControl as a replacement for CAx-
Window, but without the leak.

Using the Control

Once you've created the control, it's really two things: a window and a control. The
window is an instance of AtlAxWin and hosts the control, which may or may not
have its own window (CAxHostWindow provides full support for windowless controls). Since CAxWindow derives from CWindow, you can treat it like a window
(such as move it, resize it, hide it); AtlAxWin will handle those messages by trans-
lating them into the appropriate COM calls on the control. For example, if you'd like
the entire client area of a frame window to contain a control, you can handle the
WM_SIZE message like so:

```
class CMainWindow : public CWindowImpl<CMainWindow, ...> {
...
  LRESULT OnSize(UINT, WPARAM, LPARAM lParam, BOOL&) {
    if( m_ax ) { // m_ax will be Created earlier, for example WM_CREATE
      RECT rect = { 0, 0, LOWORD(lParam), HIWORD(lParam) };
      m_ax.MoveWindow(&rect); // Resize the control
    }
    return 0;
  }
```

```
private:
 CAxWindow m_ax;
};
```

However, unlike Windows controls, COM controls do not accept functionality requests via Windows messages (remember, a COM control may not even have a window). Instead, because COM controls are COM objects, they expect to be programmed via their COM interface(s). To obtain an interface on the control, CAx-Window provides the QueryControl method:

```
template <class TBase = CWindow> class CAxWindowT : public TBase {
public:
...
 HRESULT QueryControl(REFIID iid, void** ppUnk) {
   CComPtr<IUnknown> spUnk;
   HRESULT hr = AtlAxGetControl(m_hWnd, &spUnk);
   if (SUCCEEDED(hr)) hr = spUnk->QueryInterface(iid, ppUnk);
   return hr;
 }

 template <class Q> HRESULT QueryControl(Q** ppUnk)
 { return QueryControl(__uuidof(Q), (void**)ppUnk); }
};
```

Like QueryHost, QueryControl uses a global function (AtlAxGetControl in this case) that sends a window message to the AtlAxWin window to retrieve an interface, but this time from the hosted control itself. Once the control has been created, QueryControl can be used to get at the interfaces of the control:

```
// Import interface definitions for BullsEye
#import "D:\ATLBook\src\atlinternals\Debug\BullsEyeCtl.dll" \
       raw_interfaces_only raw_native_types no_namespace named_guids

LRESULT
CMainWindow::OnCreate(UINT uMsg, WPARAM wParam, LPARAM lParam, BOOL&
                      lResult)
{
 // Create the control
 ...

 // Set initial BullsEye properties
 CComPtr<IBullsEye>  spBullsEye;
```

```
HRESULT hr = m_ax.QueryControl(&spBullsEye);
if( SUCCEEDED(hr) ) {
  spBullsEye->put_Beep(VARIANT_TRUE);
  spBullsEye->put_CenterColor(RGB(0, 0, 255));
}

return 0;
};
```

Notice the use of the #import statement to pull in the definitions of the interfaces of the control you're programming against. This is necessary if you only have the control's server DLL and the bundled type library but no original IDL (a common occurrence when programming against controls). Notice also the use of the #import statement attributes, for example, raw_interfaces_only. These attributes are used to mimic as closely as possible the C++ language mapping you would have gotten had you used midl.exe on the server's IDL file. Without these attributes, Visual C++ will create a language mapping that uses the compiler-provided wrapper classes (such as _bstr_t, _variant_t, and _com_ptr_t), which are different from the ATL-provided types (such as CComBSTR, CComVariant, and CComPtr). While the compiler-provided classes have their place, I find it's best not to mix them with the ATL-provided types if I can help it. Apparently the ATL team agrees with me, because the ATL Wizard-generated #import statements also use these attributes. (I'll talk more about the control-containment-related wizards later.)

Sinking Control Events

Not only are you likely to want to program against the interfaces that the control implements, but you're also likely to want to handle events fired by the control. Most controls have an event interface, which, for maximum compatibility with the largest number of clients, is often a dispinterface.[6] For example, the BullsEye control from the last chapter defined the following event interface:

```
const int DISPID_ONRINGHIT     = 1;
const int DISPID_ONSCORECHANGED = 2;

dispinterface _IBullsEyeEvents {
properties:
methods:
  [id(DISPID_ONRINGHIT)]       void OnRingHit(short ringNumber);
  [id(DISPID_ONSCORECHANGED)] void OnScoreChanged(long ringValue);
};
```

---

[6]The scripting engines that Internet Explorer (IE) hosts will only allow you to handle events defined in a dispinterface.

For a control container to handle events fired on a dispinterface would require an implementation of IDispatch. Implementations of IDispatch are easy if the interface is defined as a dual interface, but much harder if it is defined as a raw dispinterface.[7] However, as you recall from Chapter 8, ATL provides a helper class called IDispEventImpl for implementing an event dispinterface:

```
template <UINT nID, class T, const IID* pdiid = &IID_NULL,
          const GUID* plibid = &GUID_NULL, WORD wMajor = 0, WORD
          wMinor = 0,
          class tihclass = CComTypeInfoHolder>
class ATL_NO_VTABLE IDispEventImpl :
 public IDispEventSimpleImpl<nID, T, pdiid> {...};
```

IDispEventImpl uses a data structure called a sink map established via the following macros:

```
#define BEGIN_SINK_MAP(_class) ...
#define SINK_ENTRY_INFO(id, iid, dispid, fn, info) ...
#define SINK_ENTRY_EX(id, iid, dispid, fn) ...
#define SINK_ENTRY(id, dispid, fn) ...
#define END_SINK_MAP() ...
```

The gory details of these macros are explained in Chapter 8, but the gist is that the sink map provides a mapping between a specific object/iid/dispid that defines an event and a member function to handle that event. If the object is a nonvisual one, the usage of the sink map can be a bit involved. However, if the object is a COM control, usage of IDispEventImpl and the sink map are quite simple, as you're about to see.

To handle events, the container of the controls will derive from one instance of IDispEventImpl per control. Notice that the first template parameter of IDispEventImpl is an ID. This ID will match to the contained control via the child window ID, that is, the nID parameter to Create. This same ID will be used in the sink map to route events from a specific control to the appropriate event handler. The child window ID is what makes IDispEventImpl so simple in the control case. Nonvisual objects have no child window ID and the mapping is somewhat more difficult (although, as Chapter 8 described, is still entirely possible).

So, handling the events of the BullsEye control merely requires an IDispEventImpl base class and an appropriately constructed sink map:

---

[7] ATL's IDispatchImpl can only be used to implement dual interfaces.

```
const UINT ID_BULLSEYE = 1;

class CMainWindow :
 public CWindowImpl<CMainWindow, CWindow, CMainWindowTraits>,
 public IDispEventImpl<ID_BULLSEYE,
                       CMainWindow,
                       &DIID__IBullsEyeEvents,
                       &LIBID_BullsEyeLib, 1, 0>
{
public:
...
 LRESULT OnCreate(...) {
   RECT rect; GetClientRect(&rect);
   m_ax.Create(m_hWnd, rect, __T("AtlInternals.BullsEye"),
               WS_CHILD | WS_VISIBLE, 0, ID_BULLSEYE);
   ...
   return (m_ax.m_hWnd ? 0 : -1);
 }

BEGIN_SINK_MAP(CMainWindow)
 SINK_ENTRY_EX(ID_BULLSEYE, DIID__IBullsEyeEvents, 1, OnRingHit)
 SINK_ENTRY_EX(ID_BULLSEYE, DIID__IBullsEyeEvents, 2, OnScoreChanged)
END_SINK_MAP()

 void __stdcall OnRingHit(short nRingNumber);
 void __stdcall OnScoreChanged(LONG ringValue);

private:
 CAxWindow m_ax;
};
```

Notice that the child window control ID (ID_BULLSEYE) is used in four places. The first is the IDispEventImpl base class. The second is the call to Create, marking the control as the same one that will be sourcing events. The last two uses of ID_BULLSEYE are the entries in the sink map, which route events from the ID_BULLS-EYE control to their appropriate handlers.

Notice also that the event handlers are marked __stdcall. Remember that we're using IDispEventImpl to implement IDispatch for a specific event interface (as defined by the DIID_IBullsEyeEvents interface identifier). That means that IDispEventImpl must unpack the array of VARIANTs passed to Invoke, push them on the stack, and call our event handler. It does this using type information at runtime, but, as mentioned in Chapter 8, it still has to know about the calling convention, that is, in what order the parameters should be passed on the stack and who's responsible for cleaning them up. To alleviate any confusion, IDisp-EventImpl requires that all event handlers have the same calling convention, which __stdcall defines.

Once we have IDispEventImpl and the sink map set up, we're not done. Unlike Windows controls, COM controls have no real sense of their "parent." This means that instead of implicitly knowing to whom to send events, like an edit control does, a COM control must be told who wants the events. Because events are established between controls and containers with the connection point protocol, somebody has to call QueryInterface for IConnectionPointContainer, call FindConnectionPoint to obtain the IConnectionPoint interface, and finally call Advise to establish the container as the sink for events fired by the control. For one control, that's not so much work, and ATL even provides a function called Atl-Advise to help. However, for multiple controls, it can become a chore to manage the communication with each of them. And since we have a list of all the controls with which we'd like to establish communications in the sink map, it makes sense to leverage that knowledge to automate the chore. Luckily, we don't even have to do this much, because ATL's already done it for us with AtlAdviseSinkMap:

```
template <class T> inline HRESULT AtlAdviseSinkMap(T* pT, bool
                                                   bAdvise)
```

The first argument to AtlAdviseSinkMap is a pointer to the object wishing to set up the connection points with the objects listed in the sink map. The second parameter is a Boolean determining if we are setting up or tearing down communication. Because AtlAdviseSinkMap depends on the child window ID to map to a window that already contains a control, both setting up and tearing down connection points must occur when the child windows are still living and contain controls. Handlers for the WM_CREATE and WM_DESTROY messages are excellent for this purpose:

```
LRESULT CMainWindow::OnCreate(...) {
  ... // Create the controls
  AtlAdviseSinkMap(this, true); // Establish connection points
  return 0;
}

LRESULT CMainWindow::OnDestroy(...) {
  // Controls still live
  AtlAdviseSinkMap(this, false); // Tear down connection points
  return 0;
}
```

The combination of IDispEventImpl, the sink map, and the AtlAdvise-SinkMap function are all that is needed to sink events from a COM control. However, we can further simplify things. Most controls implement only a single event interface and publish this fact in one of two places. The default source interface can be provided by an implementation of IProvideClassInfo2[8] and can be published in the coclass statement in the IDL (and, therefore, as part of the type library). For example:

```
coclass BullsEye {
  [default]           interface IBullsEye;
  [default, source]   dispinterface _IBullsEyeEvents;
};
```

In the event that IDispEventImpl is used with IID_NULL as the template parameter (which is the default value) describing the sink interface, ATL will do its best to establish communications with the default source interface via a function called AtlGetObjectSourceInterface. This function will attempt to obtain the object's default source interface, using the type information obtained via the Get-TypeInfo member function of IDispatch. It first attempts the use of IProvide-ClassInfo2; if that's not available, it will dig through the coclass looking for the [default, source] interface. The upshot is that if you want to source the default interface of a control, the parameters to IDispEventImpl are fewer and you can use the simpler SINK_ENTRY. For example, the following is the complete code necessary to sink events from the BullsEye control:

```
#import "D:\ATLBook\src\atlinternals\Debug\BullsEyeCtl.dll" \
        raw_interfaces_only raw_native_types no_namespace named_guids

#define ID_BULLSEYE 1

class CMainWindow :
  public CWindowImpl<CMainWindow, CWindow, CMainWindowTraits>,
  // Sink the default source interface
  public IDispEventImpl< ID_BULLSEYE, CMainWindow>
{
...
  LRESULT OnCreate(...) {
    RECT rect; GetClientRect(&rect);
```

---

[8]The scripting engines that Internet Explorer hosts will only allow you to handle events on the default source interface as reported by IProvideClassInfo2.

```
    m_ax.Create(m_hWnd, rect, __T("AtlInternals.BullsEye"),
            WS_CHILD | WS_VISIBLE, 0, ID_BULLSEYE);
    AtlAdviseSinkMap(this, true);
    return (m_ax.m_hWnd ? 0 : -1);
  }


  LRESULT CMainWindow::OnDestroy(...)
  { AtlAdviseSinkMap(this, false); return 0; }

BEGIN_SINK_MAP(CMainWindow)
  // Sink events from the default BullsEye event interface
  SINK_ENTRY(ID_BULLSEYE, 1, OnRingHit)
  SINK_ENTRY(ID_BULLSEYE, 2, OnScoreChanged)
END_SINK_MAP()


  void __stdcall OnRingHit(short nRingNumber);
  void __stdcall OnScoreChanged(LONG ringValue);

private:
  CAxWindow m_ax;
};
```

Property Changes

In addition to a custom event interface, controls will often source events on the
IPropertyNotifySink interface:

```
interface IPropertyNotifySink : IUnknown {
  HRESULT OnChanged([in] DISPID dispID);
  HRESULT OnRequestEdit([in] DISPID dispID);
}
```

A control uses the IPropertyNotifySink interface to ask the container if it's
OK to change a property (OnRequestEdit) and to notify the container that a property has been changed (OnChanged). OnRequestEdit is used for data binding,
which is beyond the scope of this book, but OnChanged can be a handy notification, especially if the container expects to persist the control and wants to use
OnChanged as an is-dirty notification. Even though IPropertyNotifySink is a
connection point interface, it's not a dispinterface, so neither IDispEventImpl

nor a sink map is required. Normal C++ inheritance and `AtlAdvise` will do. For example:

```
class CMainWindow :
 public CWindowImpl<CMainWindow, ...>,
 public IPropertyNotifySink {
public:
...
  // IUnknown, assuming an instance on the stack
  STDMETHODIMP QueryInterface(REFIID riid, void** ppv) {
    if( riid == IID_IUnknown || riid == IID_IPropertyNotifySink )
      *ppv = static_cast<IPropertyNotifySink*>(this);
    else return *ppv = 0, E_NOINTERFACE;
    return reinterpret_cast<IUnknown*>(*ppv)->AddRef(), S_OK;
  }

  STDMETHODIMP_(ULONG) AddRef() { return 2; }
  STDMETHODIMP_(ULONG) Release() { return 1; }

  // IPropertyNotifySink
  STDMETHODIMP OnRequestEdit(DISPID dispID) { return S_OK; }
  STDMETHODIMP OnChanged(DISPID dispID)        { m_bDirty = true; return
                                                 S_OK; }

private:
 CAxControl m_ax;
 bool       m_bDirty;
};
```

You have two choices when setting up and tearing down the IProperty-NotifySink connection point with the control. You could use `AtlAdvise` after the control is successfully created and `AtlUnadvise` just before it is destroyed. This requires management of the connection point cookie yourself. For example:

```
LRESULT CMainWindow::OnCreate(...) {
  ... // Create the control
  // Set up IPropertyNotifySink connection point
  CComPtr<IUnknown> spunkControl;
  m_ax.QueryControl(spunkControl);
  AtlAdvise(spunkControl, this, IID_IPropertyNotifySink, &m_dwCookie);
  return 0;
}
```

```
LRESULT CMainWindow::OnDestroy(...) {
  // Tear down IPropertyNotifySink connection point
  CComPtr<IUnknown> spunkControl;
  m_ax.QueryControl(spunkControl);
  AtlUnadvise(spunkControl, IID_IPropertyNotifySink, &m_dwCookie);
  return 0;
}
```

Choice number two is to use the CAxWindow member function CreateControlEx, which allows for a single connection point interface to be established and the cookie to be managed by the CAxHostWindow object. This simplifies the code considerably:

```
LRESULT CMainWindow::OnCreate(...) {
  ... // Create the control host
  // Create the control and set up IPropertyNotifySink connection point
  m_ax.CreateControlEx(OLESTR("AtlInternals.BullsEye"), 0, 0, 0,
                       IID_IPropertyNotifySink, this);
  return 0;
}
```

The connection point cookie for IPropertyNotifySink will be managed by the CAxHostWindow object, and when the control is destroyed, the connection will be torn down automatically. While this trick only works for one connection point interface, this technique combined with the sink map are likely all you'll ever need when handling events from controls.

Ambient Properties

In addition to programming the properties of the control, you may wish to program the properties of the control's environment, known as ambient properties. For this purpose, CAxHostWindow implements the IAxWinAmbientDispatch interface:

```
interface IAxWinAmbientDispatch : IDispatch {
 [propput]
 HRESULT AllowWindowlessActivation([in]VARIANT_BOOL b);
 [propget]
 HRESULT AllowWindowlessActivation([out,retval]VARIANT_BOOL* pb);

 // DISPID_AMBIENT_BACKCOLOR
 [propput, id(DISPID_AMBIENT_BACKCOLOR)]
 HRESULT BackColor([in]OLE_COLOR clrBackground);
 [propget, id(DISPID_AMBIENT_BACKCOLOR)]
 HRESULT BackColor([out,retval]OLE_COLOR* pclrBackground);
```

```
// DISPID_AMBIENT_FORECOLOR
[propput, id(DISPID_AMBIENT_FORECOLOR)]
HRESULT ForeColor([in]OLE_COLOR clrForeground);
[propget, id(DISPID_AMBIENT_FORECOLOR)]
HRESULT ForeColor([out,retval]OLE_COLOR* pclrForeground);

// DISPID_AMBIENT_LOCALEID
[propput, id(DISPID_AMBIENT_LOCALEID)]
HRESULT LocaleID([in]LCID lcidLocaleID);
[propget, id(DISPID_AMBIENT_LOCALEID)]
HRESULT LocaleID([out,retval]LCID* plcidLocaleID);

// DISPID_AMBIENT_USERMODE
[propput, id(DISPID_AMBIENT_USERMODE)]
HRESULT UserMode([in]VARIANT_BOOL bUserMode);
[propget, id(DISPID_AMBIENT_USERMODE)]
HRESULT UserMode([out,retval]VARIANT_BOOL* pbUserMode);

// DISPID_AMBIENT_DISPLAYASDEFAULT
[propput, id(DISPID_AMBIENT_DISPLAYASDEFAULT)]
HRESULT DisplayAsDefault([in]VARIANT_BOOL bDisplayAsDefault);
[propget, id(DISPID_AMBIENT_DISPLAYASDEFAULT)]
HRESULT DisplayAsDefault([out,retval]VARIANT_BOOL*
                         pbDisplayAsDefault);

// DISPID_AMBIENT_FONT
[propput, id(DISPID_AMBIENT_FONT)]
HRESULT Font([in]IFontDisp* pFont);
[propget, id(DISPID_AMBIENT_FONT)]
HRESULT Font([out,retval]IFontDisp** pFont);

// DISPID_AMBIENT_MESSAGEREFLECT
[propput, id(DISPID_AMBIENT_MESSAGEREFLECT)]
HRESULT MessageReflect([in]VARIANT_BOOL bMsgReflect);
[propget, id(DISPID_AMBIENT_MESSAGEREFLECT)]
HRESULT MessageReflect([out,retval]VARIANT_BOOL* pbMsgReflect);

// DISPID_AMBIENT_SHOWGRABHANDLES
[propget, id(DISPID_AMBIENT_SHOWGRABHANDLES)]
HRESULT ShowGrabHandles(VARIANT_BOOL* pbShowGrabHandles);
```

```
// DISPID_AMBIENT_SHOWHATCHING
[propget, id(DISPID_AMBIENT_SHOWHATCHING)]
HRESULT ShowHatching(VARIANT_BOOL* pbShowHatching);


// IDocHostUIHandler Defaults
...
};
```

QueryHost can be used on a CAxWindow to obtain the IWinAmbientDispatch interface so that these ambient properties can be changed. For example:

```
LRESULT CMainWindow::OnSetGreenBackground(...) {
  // Set up green ambient background
  CComPtr<IAxWinAmbientDispatch> spAmbient;
  hr = m_ax.QueryHost(&spAmbient);
  if( SUCCEEDED(hr) ) {
    spAmbient->put_BackColor(RGB(0, 255, 0));
  }
    return 0;
}
```

Whenever an ambient property is changed, the control is notified via its implementation of the IOleControl member function OnAmbientPropertyChange. The control can then QueryInterface any of its container interfaces for IDispatch to obtain the interface for retrieving the ambient properties (which is why IWinAmbientDispatch is a dual interface).

Hosting Property Pages

If your container is a development environment, it's possible that you'd like to allow the user to show the control's property pages. This can be accomplished by calling the IOleObject member function DoVerb, passing in the OLEIVERB_PROPERTIES verb ID:

```
LRESULT CMainWindow::OnEditProperties(...) {
  CComPtr<IOleObject> spoo;
  HRESULT hr = m_ax.QueryControl(&spoo);
  if( SUCCEEDED(hr) ) {
    CComPtr<IOleClientSite> spcs; m_ax.QueryHost(&spcs);
    RECT rect; m_ax.GetClientRect(&rect);
```

```
        hr = spoo->DoVerb(OLEIVERB_PROPERTIES, 0, spcs, -1, m_ax.m_hWnd,
                            &rect);
        if( FAILED(hr) ) MessageBox(__T("Properties unavailable"),
                                    __T("Error"));
    }
    return 0;
}
```

In the event that you'd like to add your own property pages to those of the control or you'd like to show the property pages of a control that doesn't support the OLEIVERB_PROPERTIES verb, you can take matters into your own hands with a custom property sheet. First, you'll need to ask the control for its property pages via the ISpecifyPropertyPages member function GetPages. Second, you may want to augment the control's property pages with your own. Finally, you'll show the property pages (each a COM object with its own CLSID) via the COM global function OleCreatePropertyFrame, as demonstrated in the ShowProperties function I developed for this purpose:

```
HRESULT ShowProperties(IUnknown* punkControl, HWND hwndParent) {
  HRESULT hr = E_FAIL;

  // Ask the control to specify its property pages
  CComQIPtr<ISpecifyPropertyPages> spPages = punkControl;
  if (spPages) {

    CAUUID  pages;
    hr = spPages->GetPages(&pages);
    if( SUCCEEDED(hr) ) {
      // TO DO: Add your custom property pages here

      CComQIPtr<IOleObject> spObj = punkControl;
      if( spObj ) {
        LPOLESTR pszTitle = 0;
        spObj->GetUserType(USERCLASSTYPE_SHORT, &pszTitle);

        // Show the property pages
        hr = OleCreatePropertyFrame(hwndParent, 10, 10, pszTitle,
                                    1, &punkControl, pages.cElems,
                                    pages.pElems, LOCALE_USER_DEFAULT,
                                    0, 0);
```

```
      CoTaskMemFree(pszTitle);
    }
    CoTaskMemFree(pages.pElems);
  }
}

return hr;
}
```

The `ShowProperties` function can be used instead of the call to `DoVerb`. For example:

```
LRESULT CMainWindow::OnEditProperties(...) {
 CComPtr<IUnknown> spunk;
 if( SUCCEEDED(m_ax.QueryControl(&spunk)) ) {
   if( FAILED(ShowProperties(spunk, m_hWnd)) ) {
     MessageBox(__T("Properties unavailable"), __T("Error"));
   }
 }
 return 0;
}
```

Either way, if the control's property pages are shown and the Apply or OK button is pressed, your container should receive `IPropertyNotifySink` calls, one per property that has changed.

Persisting a Control

It may be that the control's state is something that you'd like to persist between application sessions. As discussed in Chapter 6, this can be done with any number of persistence interfaces, of which most controls implement `IPersistStreamInit` (although `IPersistStream` is a common fallback). For example, saving a control to a file can be done with a stream in a structured storage document:

```
bool CMainWindow::Save(LPCOLESTR pszFileName) {
 // Make sure object can be saved
 // Note: Our IPersistStream interface pointer could end up holding an
 //       IPersistStreamInit interface. This is OK since IPersistStream
 //       is a layout-compatible subset of IPersistStreamInit.
 CComQIPtr<IPersistStream> spPersistStream;
```

```
        HRESULT hr = m_ax.QueryControl(&spPersistStream);
        if( FAILED(hr) ) {
          hr = m_ax.QueryControl(IID_IPersistStreamInit,
                                 (void**)&spPersistStream);
          if( FAILED(hr) ) return false;
        }

        // Save object to stream in a storage
        CComPtr<IStorage>   spStorage;
        hr = StgCreateDocfile(pszFileName,
                              STGM_DIRECT | STGM_WRITE |
                              STGM_SHARE_EXCLUSIVE | STGM_CREATE,
                              0, &spStorage);
        if( SUCCEEDED(hr) ) {
          CComPtr<IStream>    spStream;
          hr = spStorage->CreateStream(OLESTR("Contents"),
                                       STGM_DIRECT | STGM_WRITE |
                                       STGM_SHARE_EXCLUSIVE | STGM_CREATE,
                                       0, 0, &spStream);
          if( SUCCEEDED(hr) ) {
            // Get and store the CLSID
            CLSID clsid;
            hr = spPersistStream->GetClassID(&clsid);
            if( SUCCEEDED(hr) ) {
              hr = spStream->Write(&clsid, sizeof(clsid), 0);

              // Save the object
              hr = spPersistStream->Save(spStream, TRUE);
            }
          }
        }

      if( FAILED(hr) ) return false;
      return true;
    }
```

Restoring a control from a file is somewhat easier because both the Create-Control and the CreateControlEx member functions of CAxWindow take an IStream interface pointer to use for persistence. For example:

```
bool CMainWindow::Open(LPCOLESTR pszFileName) {
// Open object a stream in the storage
CComPtr<IStorage>   spStorage;
CComPtr<IStream>    spStream;
HRESULT             hr;
hr = StgOpenStorage(pszFileName, 0,
                    STGM_DIRECT | STGM_READ | STGM_SHARE_EXCLUSIVE,
                    0, 0, &spStorage);
if( SUCCEEDED(hr) ) {
  hr = spStorage->OpenStream(OLESTR("Contents"), 0,
                             STGM_DIRECT | STGM_READ |
                             STGM_SHARE_EXCLUSIVE,
                             0, &spStream);
}

if( FAILED(hr) ) return false;

// Read a CLSID from the stream
CLSID   clsid;
hr = spStream->Read(&clsid, sizeof(clsid), 0);
if( FAILED(hr) ) return false;

RECT    rect; GetClientRect(&rect);
OLECHAR szClsid[40]; StringFromGUID2(clsid, szClsid,
                                     lengthof(szClsid));

// Create the control's host window
if( !m_ax.Create(m_hWnd, rect, 0, WS_CHILD | WS_VISIBLE, 0,
                 ID_CHILD_CONTROL) {
  return false;
}

// Create the control, persisting from the stream
hr = m_ax.CreateControl(szClsid, spStream);
if( FAILED(hr) ) return false;
return true;
}
```

When a NULL IStream interface pointer is provided to either CreateControl or CreateControlEx, ATL will attempt to call the IPersistStreamInit

member function `InitNew` to make sure that either `InitNew` or `Load` is called, as appropriate.

Accelerator Translations

It's common for contained controls to contain other controls. In order for keyboard accelerators (such as the tab key) to provide for navigation between controls, the main message loop must be augmented with a call to each window hosting a control to allow it to pretranslate the message as a possible accelerator. This functionality must ask the host of the control with focus if it wants to handle the message. If the control does handle the message, no more handling need be done on that message. Otherwise, the message processing can proceed as normal. A typical implementation of a function to attempt to route messages from the container window to the control itself (whether it's a windowed or a windowless control) is shown here:

```
BOOL CMainWnd:: PreTranslateAccelerator(MSG* pMsg) {
    // Accelerators are only keyboard or mouse messages
    if ((pMsg->message < WM_KEYFIRST || pMsg->message > WM_KEYLAST) &&
        (pMsg->message < WM_MOUSEFIRST || pMsg->message > WM_MOUSELAST))
        return FALSE;

        // Find a direct child of this window from the window that has
        // focus.
        // This will be AxAtlWin window for the hosted control.
        HWND hWndCtl = ::GetFocus();
        if( IsChild(hWndCtl) && ::GetParent(hWndCtl) != m_hWnd ) {
            do hWndCtl = ::GetParent(hWndCtl);
            while( ::GetParent(hWndCtl) != m_hWnd );
        }

        // Give the control (via the AtlAxWin) a chance to translate
        // this message
        if (::SendMessage(hWndCtl, WM_FORWARDMSG, 0, (LPARAM)pMsg) )
            return TRUE;

    // Check for dialog-type navigation accelerators
    return IsDialogMessage(pMsg);
}
```

The crux of this function forwards the message to the `AtlAxWin` via the `WM_FORWARDMSG` message. This message is interpreted by the host window as an attempt to let the control handle the message if it so desires. This message will be forwarded to the control via a call to the `IOleInPlaceActiveObject` member function `TranslateAccelerator`. The `PreTranslateAccelerator` function should be called from the application's main message pump like so:

```
int WINAPI WinMain(...) {
...
CMainWindow wndMain;
...
HACCEL  haccel = LoadAccelerators(_Module.GetResourceInstance(),
                                  MAKEINTRESOURCE(IDC_MYACCELS));
MSG msg;
while( GetMessage(&msg, 0, 0, 0) ) {
  if( !TranslateAccelerator(msg.hwnd, haccel, &msg) &&
      !wndMain.PreTranslateAccelerator(&msg) ) {
    TranslateMessage(&msg);
    DispatchMessage(&msg);
  }
}
...
}
```

The use of a `PreTranslateAccelerator` function on every window that contains a control will give the keyboard navigation keys a much greater chance of working, although the individual controls have to cooperate too.

Hosting a Control in a Dialog

Inserting a Control into a Dialog Resource

So far, I've discussed the basics of control containment using a frame window as a control container. An even more common place to contain controls is the ever-popular dialog. For quite a while, the Visual C++ resource editor has allowed a control to be inserted into a dialog resource by right-clicking on a dialog resource and choosing Insert ActiveX Control. As of Visual C++ 6.0, ATL supports creating dialogs that host the controls inserted into dialog resources. The Insert ActiveX Control dialog is shown in Figure 11.3.

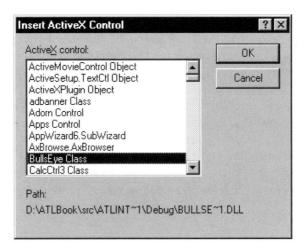

Figure 11.3. Insert ActiveX Control dialog

The container example provided as part of this chapter has a simple dialog box with a BullsEye control inserted, along with a couple of static controls and a button. This is what that dialog resource looks like in the `.rc` file:

```
IDD_BULLSEYE DIALOG DISCARDABLE  0, 0, 342, 238
STYLE DS_MODALFRAME | WS_POPUP | WS_CAPTION | WS_SYSMENU
CAPTION "BullsEye"
FONT 8, "MS Sans Serif"
BEGIN
    CONTROL         "",IDC_BULLSEYE,"{7DC59CC5-36C0-11D2-AC05-
                                     00A0C9C8E50D}",
                    WS_TABSTOP,7,7,269,224
    LTEXT           "&Score:",IDC_STATIC,289,7,22,8
    CTEXT           "Static",IDC_SCORE,278,18,46,14,SS_CENTERIMAGE |
                    SS_SUNKEN
    PUSHBUTTON      "Close",IDCANCEL,276,41,50,14
END
```

Control Initialization

Notice that the window text part of the CONTROL resource is a CLSID, specifically, the CLSID of the BullsEye control. This window text will be passed to an instance of the `AtlAxWin` window class to determine the type of the control to create. In addition, another part of the `.rc` file maintains a separate resource called a `DLGINIT` resource, which is identified with the same ID as the BullsEye control on the dialog, that is, IDC_BULLSEYE. This resource contains the persistence information, converted to text format, that will be handed to the BullsEye control at creation time (via IPersistStreamInit):

```
IDD_BULLSEYE DLGINIT
BEGIN
    IDC_BULLSEYE, 0x376, 154, 0
0x0026, 0x0000, 0x007b, 0x0039, 0x0035, 0x0036, 0x0046, 0x0043, 0x0032,
...
0x0000, 0x0040, 0x0000, 0x0020, 0x0000,
    0
END
```

Because most folks prefer not to enter this information directly, right-clicking on a COM control and choosing Properties will show the control's property pages, along with the custom property pages of the resource editor. Figure 11.4 shows the Bulls-Eye properties dialog.

The DLGINIT resource for each control is constructed by asking each control for IPersistStreamInit, calling Save, converting the result to a text format, and dumping it into the .rc file. In this way, all information set at design time will be automatically restored at runtime.

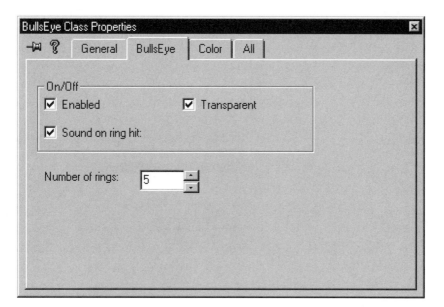

Figure 11.4. BullsEye properties dialog

Sinking Control Events in a Dialog

Recall that sinking control events requires adding one `IDispEventImpl` per control to the list of base classes of your dialog class and populating the sink map. Although this has to be done by hand if a window is the container, it can be performed automatically if a dialog is to be the container. By right-clicking on the control and choosing Events, you can choose the events to handle, and the `IDispEventImpl` and sink map entries will be added for you. Figure 11.5 shows the Event Handlers dialog.

However, although the wizard will add the `IDispEventImpl` classes and manage the sink map, it will not insert code to call `AtlAdviseSinkMap`, either in `WM_INITDIALOG` to establish connection points with the controls or in `WM_DESTROY` to tear down the connection points. You have to remember to do this yourself.

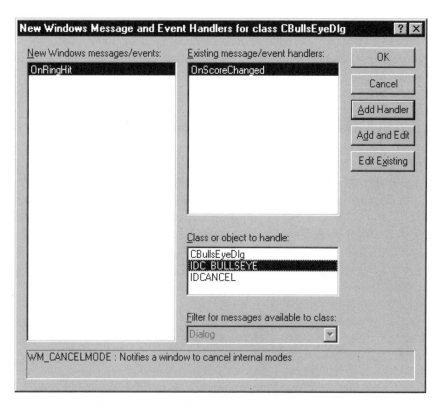

Figure 11.5. BullsEye Event Handlers dialog

CAxDialogImpl

In Chapter 9, I discussed the `CDialogImpl` class, which, unfortunately, is not able to host controls. Recall that the member function wrappers `DoModal` and `Create` merely call the Win32 functions `DialogBoxParam` and `CreateDialogParam`. Since the built-in dialog box manager window class has no idea how to host controls, ATL has to perform some magic on the dialog resource. Specifically, it must preprocess the dialog box resource looking for `CONTROL` entries and replacing them with entries that will create an instance of an `AtlAxWin` window. Once this is done, the `AtlAxWin` uses the name of the window to create the control and the `DLGINIT` data to initialize it, providing all the control hosting functionality we've spend most of this chapter dissecting. To hook up this preprocessing step when hosting controls in dialogs, we use the `CAxDialogImpl` base class:

```
template <class T, class TBase = CWindow>
class ATL_NO_VTABLE CAxDialogImpl : public CDialogImplBaseT< TBase >{
public:
 // modal dialogs
 int DoModal(HWND hWndParent = ::GetActiveWindow(),
          LPARAM dwInitParam = NULL) {
   _Module.AddCreateWndData(&m_thunk.cd, (CDialogImplBaseT< TBase
                       >*)this);
   return AtlAxDialogBox(_Module.GetResourceInstance(),
                   MAKEINTRESOURCE(T::IDD), hWndParent,
                   (DLGPROC)T::StartDialogProc, dwInitParam);
 }

 BOOL EndDialog(int nRetCode)
 { return ::EndDialog(m_hWnd, nRetCode); }

 // modeless dialogs
 HWND Create(HWND hWndParent, LPARAM dwInitParam = NULL) {
   _Module.AddCreateWndData(&m_thunk.cd, (CDialogImplBaseT< TBase
                       >*)this);
   HWND hWnd = AtlAxCreateDialog(_Module.GetResourceInstance(),
                        MAKEINTRESOURCE(T::IDD), hWndParent,
                        (DLGPROC)T::StartDialogProc,
                        dwInitParam);

   return hWnd;
 }
```

```
// for CComControl
HWND Create(HWND hWndParent, RECT&, LPARAM dwInitParam = NULL)
{ return Create(hWndParent, dwInitParam); }


BOOL DestroyWindow()
{ return ::DestroyWindow(m_hWnd); }
};
```

Notice that the DoModal and Create wrapper functions call AtlAxDialogBox and AtlAxCreateDialog instead of DialogBoxParam and CreateDialog-Param, respectively. These functions perform the preprocessing necessary to add swap instances of AtlAxWin for each CONTROL entry in the dialog resource.

Using CAxDialogImpl as the base class, we can have a dialog that hosts COM controls like so:

```
class CBullsEyeDlg :
 public CAxDialogImpl<CBullsEyeDlg>,
 public IDispEventImpl<IDC_BULLSEYE, CBullsEyeDlg> {
public:
BEGIN_MSG_MAP(CBullsEyeDlg)
 MESSAGE_HANDLER(WM_DESTROY, OnDestroy)
 MESSAGE_HANDLER(WM_INITDIALOG, OnInitDialog)
 COMMAND_ID_HANDLER(IDCANCEL, OnCancel)
END_MSG_MAP()

BEGIN_SINK_MAP(CBullsEyeDlg)
 SINK_ENTRY(IDC_BULLSEYE, 0x2, OnScoreChanged)
END_SINK_MAP()

// Map this clas to a specific dialog resource
enum { IDD = IDD_BULLSEYE };

// Hook up connection points
LRESULT OnInitDialog(...)
{ AtlAdviseSinkMap(this, true); return 0; }

// Tear down connection points
LRESULT OnDestroy(UINT uMsg, WPARAM wParam, LPARAM lParam, BOOL&
                  bHandled)
{ AtlAdviseSinkMap(this, false); return 0; }
```

```
  // Window control event handlers
  LRESULT OnCancel(WORD, UINT, HWND, BOOL&);

  // COM control event handlers
  VOID __stdcall OnScoreChanged(LONG ringValue);
};
```

Notice that, just like a normal dialog, the message map handles messages for the dialog itself (such as WM_INITDIALOG and WM_DESTROY) as well as provides a mapping between the class and the dialog resource ID (via the IDD symbol). The only thing new is that, because we've used CAxDialogImpl as the base class, the COM controls will be created as the dialog is created.

Attaching a CAxWindow

During the life of the dialog, you will likely need to program against the interfaces of the contained COM controls, which means you'll need some way to obtain an interface on a specific control. One way to do this is with an instance of CAxWindow. Since ATL has created an instance of the AtlAxWin window class for each of the COM controls on the dialog, you use the Attach member function of a CAxWindow to attach to a COM control, and thereafter use the CAxWindow object to manipulate the host window. This is very much like you'd use the Attach member function of the window wrapper classes discussed in Chapter 9 to manipulate an edit control. Once you've attached a CAxWindow object to an AtlAxWin window, you can use the member functions of CAxWindow to communicate with the control host window. Recall the QueryControl member function to obtain an interface from a control, as shown here:

```
class CBullsEyeDlg :
 public CAxDialogImpl<CBullsEyeDlg>,
 public IDispEventImpl<IDC_BULLSEYE, CBullsEyeDlg> {
public:
...
 LRESULT OnInitDialog(...) {
   // Attach to the BullsEye control
   m_axBullsEye.Attach(GetDlgItem(IDC_BULLSEYE));

   // Cache BullsEye interface
   m_axBullsEye.QueryControl(&m_spBullsEye);
   ...
   return 0;
 }
```

```
...
private:
 CAxWindow               m_axBullsEye;
 CComPtr<IBullsEye>      m_spBullsEye;
};
```

In this example, I've cached both the HWND to the AtlAxWin, for continued communication with the control host window, and one of the control's interfaces, for communication with the control itself. If you don't need the HWND, but only an interface, you may want to consider using GetDlgControl instead.

GetDlgControl

The CDialogImpl class, because it derives from CWindow, provides the GetDlg-Item function to retrieve the HWND of a child window given the ID of the child. Likewise, CWindow also provides a GetDlgControl member function, but to retrieve an interface pointer instead of an HWND:

```
HRESULT CWindow::GetDlgControl(int nID, REFIID iid, void** ppUnk) {
 HRESULT hr = E_FAIL;
 HWND hWndCtrl = GetDlgItem(nID);
 if (hWndCtrl != NULL) {
   *ppUnk = NULL;
   CComPtr<IUnknown> spUnk;
   hr = AtlAxGetControl(hWndCtrl, &spUnk);
   if (SUCCEEDED(hr)) hr = spUnk->QueryInterface(iid, ppUnk);
 }
 return hr;
}
```

The GetDlgControl member function calls the AtlAxGetControl function, which uses the HWND of the child window to retrieve an IUnknown interface. AtlAx-GetControl does this by sending the WM_GETCONTROL window message that windows of the class AtlAxWin understand. In the event that the child window is not an instance of the AtlAxWin window class, or if the control does not support the interface being requested, GetDlgControl will return a failed HRESULT. Using GetDlg-Control simplifies the code to cache an interface on a control considerably:

```
LRESULT OnInitDialog(...) {
 // Cache BullsEye interface
 GetDlgControl(IDC_BULLSEYE, IID_IBullsEye, (void**)&m_spBullsEye);
 ...
 return 0;
}
```

The combination of the CAxDialogImpl class, the control containment wizards in Visual C++, and the GetDlgControl member function makes managing COM controls in a dialog much like managing Windows controls.

Composite Controls

Declarative User Interfaces for Controls

There's beauty in using a dialog resource for managing the user interface (UI) of a window. Instead of writing pages of code to create, initialize, and place controls on a rectangle of gray, we can use the resource editor to do it for us. At design time we lay out the size and location of the elements of the UI, and the ATL-augmented dialog manager is responsible for the heavy lifting. This is an extremely useful mode of UI development, and it's not limited to dialogs. It can also be used for *composite controls*. A composite control is a COM control that uses a dialog resource to lay out its UI elements. These UI elements can be Windows controls or other COM controls.

To a Windows control, a composite control appears as a parent window. To a COM control, the composite control appears as a control container. To a control container, the composite control appears as a control itself. To the developer of the control, a composite control is all three. In fact, take all the programming techniques from Chapter 10, combine them with the techniques I've shown you thus far in this chapter, and you have a composite control.

CComCompositeControl

ATL provides support for composite controls via the CComCompositeControl base class:

```
template <class T>
class CComCompositeControl : public CComControl< T,
  CAxDialogImpl< T > > {...};
```

Notice that CComCompositeControl derives both from CComControl and CAx-DialogImpl, combining the functionality of a control and the drawing of the dialog manager, augmented with the COM control hosting capabilities of AtlAxWin. Both of the Wizard-generated composite control types (composite control and lite composite control) derive from CComCompositeControl instead of CComControl and provide an IDD symbol mapping to the control's dialog resource:

```
class ATL_NO_VTABLE CDartBoard :
  public CComObjectRootEx<CComSingleThreadModel>,
  public IDispatchImpl<IDartBoard, &IID_IDartBoard,
                  &LIBID_CONTROLSLib>,
```

```
public CComCompositeControl<CDartBoard>,
...
public CComCoClass<CDartBoard, &CLSID_DartBoard> {
public:
...
enum { IDD = IDD_DARTBOARD };

CDartBoard() {
    // Composites can't be windowless
    m_bWindowOnly = TRUE;

    // Calculate natural extent based on dialog resource size
    CalcExtent(m_sizeExtent);
}
...
};
```

Notice that the construction of the composite control sets the m_bWindowOnly flag, disabling windowless operation. The control's window needs to be of the same class as that managed by the dialog manager. Also notice that the m_sizeExtent member variable is set by a call to CalcExtent, a helper function provided in CComCompositeControl. CalcExtent is used to set the initial preferred size of the control to be exactly that of the dialog box resource.

Composite-Control Drawing

Since a composite control is based on a dialog resource, and its drawing will be managed by the dialog manager and the child controls, no real drawing chores have to be performed. Instead, setting the state of the child controls, which will cause them to redraw, is all that's required to update the visual state of a control.

For example, the DartBoard example available with the source code of this book uses a dialog resource to lay out its elements, as shown in Figure 11.6. This dialog resource holds a BullsEye control, two static controls, and a button. When the user clicks on a ring of the target, the score is incremented. When the Reset button is pressed, the score is cleared. The composite control takes care of all the logic, but the dialog manager performs the drawing.

However, in the case in which a composite control is shown but not activated, the composite control's window will not be created and the drawing must be done manually. For example, a composite control must perform its own drawing when hosted in a dialog resource during the design mode of the Visual C++ resource

Figure 11.6. DartBoard composite control dialog resource

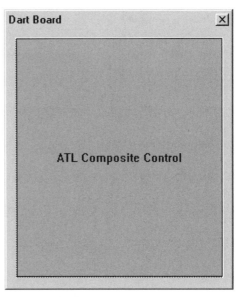

Figure 11.7. Default CComCompositeControl's inactive OnDraw implementation

editor. The ATL Object Wizard will generate an implementation of OnDraw that handles this case, as shown in Figure 11.7. I find this implementation somewhat inconvenient, because it doesn't show the dialog resource as I'm using the control. Specifically, it doesn't show the size of the resource. Toward that end, I've provided another implementation that is a bit more helpful, as shown in Figure 11.8.

This implementation shows the light gray area as the recommended size of the control based on the current dialog resource. The dark gray area is the part of the control that is still managed by the control, but is outside the area managed by the dialog manager. The updated OnDraw implementation is shown here:

```
// Draw an inactive composite control
virtual HRESULT OnDraw(ATL_DRAWINFO& di) {
 if( m_bInPlaceActive ) return S_OK;

 // Draw background rectangle
 SelectObject(di.hdcDraw, GetStockObject(BLACK_PEN));
 SelectObject(di.hdcDraw, GetStockObject(GRAY_BRUSH));
 Rectangle(di.hdcDraw, di.prcBounds->left, di.prcBounds->top,
         di.prcBounds->right, di.prcBounds->bottom);
```

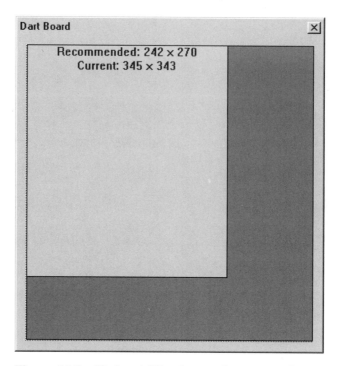

Figure 11.8. Updated CComCompositeControl's inactive OnDraw implementation

```
// Draw proposed dialog rectangle
SIZE  sizeMetric; CalcExtent(sizeMetric);
SIZE  sizeDialog; AtlHiMetricToPixel(&sizeMetric, &sizeDialog);
SIZE  sizeBounds = { di.prcBounds->right-di.prcBounds->left,
                     di.prcBounds->bottom-di.prcBounds->top };
SIZE  sizeDialogBounds = { min(sizeDialog.cx, sizeBounds.cx),
                           min(sizeDialog.cy, sizeBounds.cy) };
RECT  rectDialogBounds = { di.prcBounds->left, di.prcBounds->top,
                           di.prcBounds->left + sizeDialogBounds.cx,
                           di.prcBounds->top + sizeDialogBounds.cy };
SelectObject(di.hdcDraw, GetStockObject(LTGRAY_BRUSH));
Rectangle(di.hdcDraw, rectDialogBounds.left, rectDialogBounds.top,
        rectDialogBounds.right, rectDialogBounds.bottom);

// Report natural and current size of dialog resource
SetTextColor(di.hdcDraw, ::GetSysColor(COLOR_WINDOWTEXT));
SetBkMode(di.hdcDraw, TRANSPARENT);
```

```
TCHAR sz[256];
wsprintf(sz, __T("Recommended: %d x %d\r\nCurrent: %d x %d"),
        sizeDialog.cx, sizeDialog.cy, sizeBounds.cx, sizeBounds.cy);

DrawText(di.hdcDraw, sz, -1, &rectDialogBounds, DT_CENTER);

return S_OK;
}
```

Using a dialog resource and deriving from `CComCompositeControl` are the only differences between a control that manages its own UI elements and one that leans on the dialog manager. A composite control is a powerful way to lay out a control's UI elements at design time. However, if you really want to wield the full power of a declarative UI when building a control, you need an HTML control.

HTML Controls

Generating an HTML Control

The HTML control is available from the ATL Object Wizard in the Controls category as either an HTML Control or a Lite HTML Control. The wizard-generated code will create a control that derives from `CComControl`, sets `m_bWindowOnly` to `TRUE`, and provides a resource for the layout of the UI elements of your control. This is very similar to the resource resulting from running the Object Wizard for a composite control, except that instead of using a dialog resource, an HTML control will use an HTML resource. The same WebBrowser control that provides the UI for Internet Explorer 4.0+ will provide the parsing for the HTML resource at runtime. This allows a control to use a declarative style of UI development, but with all the capabilities of the HTML engine in Internet Explorer. The following are a few of the advantages that HTML provides over a dialog resource:

- Support for resizing via `height` and `width` attributes, both in absolute pixels and percentages.

- Support for scripting when using top-level initialization code, defining functions, and handling events.

- Support for extending the object model of the HTML document via an "external" object.

- Support for flowing of mixed text and graphics.

- Support for multiple font families, colors, sizes, and styles.

In fact, pretty much everything you've ever seen on a web site can be performed using the HTML control.

HTML Control Creation

The magic of hooking up the WebBrowser control is performed in the `OnCreate` handler generated by the ATL Object Wizard:

```
LRESULT CSmartDartBoard::OnCreate(UINT, WPARAM, LPARAM, BOOL&) {
  // Wrap the control's window to use it to host control
  // (not an AtlAxWin, so no CAxHostWindow yet created)
  CAxWindow wnd(m_hWnd);

  // Create a CAxWinHost: It will subclass this window and
  // create a control based on an HTML resource.
  HRESULT hr = wnd.CreateControl(IDH_SMARTDARTBOARD);
  ...
  return SUCCEEDED(hr) ? 0 : -1;
}
```

Because `m_bWindowedOnly` is set to `true`, activation of the HTML control will cause a window to be created. To give this window control containment capabilities so that it may host an instance of the WebBrowser control, the HTML control's window must be subclassed and sent through the message map provided by `CAx-HostWindow`, just like every other control container. However, because the HTML control's window is not an instance of the `AtlAxWin` class, the subclassing must be handled manually. Notice that the first thing that the wizard-generated `OnCreate` function does is wrap an instance of `CAxWindow` around the control's HWND. The call to `CreateControl` creates an instance of `CAxHostWindow`. The `CAxHostWindow` object subclasses the HTML control's window, creates an instance of the Web-Browser control, and feeds it a URL of the form `res://<modulename>/<resource ID>`, using `CreateNormalizedControl`. In effect, the HWND of the HTML control is an instance of the WebBrowser control, which then uses the HTML resource to manage the UI elements of the control. This is exactly analogous to the composite control, in which the HWND of the control was an instance of the dialog manager that used a dialog resource to manage the elements of the UI.

Element Layout

For example, the SmartDartBoard HTML control that is available with the source code of this book uses HTML to lay out its UI, just like the DartBoard composite control. However, in HTML, I can use the auto layout capabilities of a `<table>`

element to auto-size the HTML control to whatever size the user wishes, instead of limiting myself to a single size, as with the dialog resource. The following shows how the SmartDartBoard control's HTML resource lays out its elements:

```
<!-Use all of the control's area->
<table width=100% height=100%>
<tr>
    <td colspan=2>
    <object id=objBullsEye width=100% height=100%
            classid<="clsid:7DC59CC5-36C0-11D2-AC05-00A0C9C8E50D">
    </object>
    </td>
</tr>
<tr height=1>
    <td>Score: <span id=spanScore>0</td>
    <td align=right><input type=button id=cmdReset value="Reset"></td>
</tr>
</table>
```

To test the UI of the HTML control without compiling, you can right-click on the HTML file and choose Preview, which will show the HTML in Internet Explorer. For example, Figures 11.9 and 11.10 show the control's UI resizing itself properly to fit into the space that it's given.

Figure 11.9. Small SmartDartBoard UI

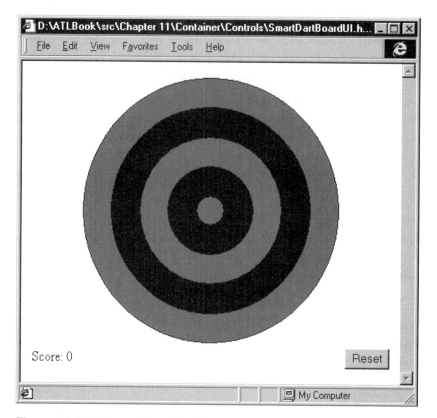

Figure 11.10. Large SmartDartBoard UI

Accessing the HTML from the Control

When you create an instance of the WebBrowser control, you're actually creating two things: a WebBrowser control, which knows about URLs, and an HTML Document control, which knows about parsing and displaying HTML. The WebBrowser control forms the core of the logic of Internet Explorer and lives in shdocvw.dll. The WebBrowser control implements the IWebBrowser2 interface, with methods like Navigate, GoBack, GoForward, and Stop. Since the CAxWindow object is merely used to bootstrap hosting the WebBrowser control, and you'd need to be able to access the WebBrowser control in other parts of your code, the OnCreate code generated by the Wizard uses QueryControl to cache the IWebBrowser2 interface:

```
LRESULT CSmartDartBoard::OnCreate(UINT, WPARAM, LPARAM, BOOL&) {
...
// Cache the IWebBrowser2 interface
if (SUCCEEDED(hr))
  hr = wnd.QueryControl(IID_IWebBrowser2, (void**)&m_spBrowser);
...
}
```

To display the HTML, the WebBrowser control creates an instance of the HTML Document control, which is implemented in `mshtml.dll`. The HTML Document represents the implementation of the Dynamic HTML object model (DHTML). This object model exposes each named element on a page of HTML as a COM object, each of which implements one or more COM interfaces and many of which fire events. While the full scope and power of DHTML is beyond the scope of this book, the rest of this chapter is dedicated to showing you just the tip of the iceberg of functionality that DHTML provides.

The HTML Document object implements the `IHTMLDocument2` interface, whose most important property is the `all` property. Getting from the WebBrowser control to the HTML Document control is a matter of retrieving the `IWebBrowser2 Document` property and querying for the `IHTMLDocument2` interface. Accessing any named object on the HTML page, that is, any tag with an `id` attribute, is done via the `all` property of the `IHTMLDocument2` interface. Retrieving a named object on an HTML page in C++ can be accomplished with a helper function like the `GetHTMLElement` helper shown here:

```
HRESULT CSmartDartBoard::GetHTMLElement(
LPCOLESTR        pszElementID,
IHTMLElement**  ppElement) {
ATLASSERT(ppElement);
*ppElement = 0;

// Get the document from the browser
HRESULT hr = E_FAIL;
CComPtr<IDispatch> spdispDoc;
hr = m_spBrowser->get_Document(&spdispDoc);
if( FAILED(hr) ) return hr;

CComQIPtr<IHTMLDocument2> spDoc = spdispDoc;
if( !spDoc ) return E_NOINTERFACE;
```

```
// Get the All collection from the document
CComPtr<IHTMLElementCollection> spAll;
hr = spDoc->get_all(&spAll);
if( FAILED(hr) ) return hr;

// Get the element from the All collection
CComVariant          varID = pszElementID;
CComPtr<IDispatch>   spdispItem;
hr = spAll->item(varID, CComVariant(0), &spdispItem);

// Return the IHTMLElement interface
return spdispItem->QueryInterface(ppElement);
}
```

Once you have the IHTMLElement interface, you can change just about anything about that element. For example, notice the <span> tag named spanScore in the SmartDartBoard HTML resource:

```
...
<td>Score: <span id=spanScore>0</span></td>
...
```

A span is just a range of HTML with a name so that it can be programmed against. As far as we're concerned, every named object in the HTML is a COM object that we can access from our control's C++ code. This span's job is to hold the control's current score, so when the WebBrowser control has been created, we need to set the span to the m_nScore property of the control. The SetScoreSpan helper function in the SmartDartBoard HTML control uses the GetHTMLElement helper and the IHTMLElement interface to set the innerText property of the span:

```
HRESULT CSmartDartBoard::SetScoreSpan() {
  // Convert score to VARIANT
  CComVariant varScore = m_nScore;
  HRESULT hr = varScore.ChangeType(VT_BSTR);
  if( FAILED(hr) ) return hr;

  // Find score span element
  CComPtr<IHTMLElement> speScore;
  hr = GetHTMLElement(OLESTR("spanScore"), &speScore);
  if( FAILED(hr) ) return hr;
```

```
    // Set the element's inner text
    return speScore->put_innerText(varScore.bstrVal);
}
```

Whenever the score changes, this function is used to update the contents of the HTML span object from the control's C++ code.

Sinking WebBrowser Events

You may be tempted to use the `SetScoreSpan` function right from the `OnCreate` handler to set the initial score value when the control is activated. Unfortunately, the architecture of the HTML Document object dictates that we wait for the document to be completely processed before the object model is exposed to us. To detect when that happens, we need to sink events on the `DWebBrowserEvents2` interface. Specifically, we need to know about the `OnDocumentComplete` event. Once we receive this event, we can access all the named objects on the page. Since `DWebBrowserEvents2` is a `dispinterface`, sinking the events can be accomplished with `IDispEventImpl` and an entry in the sink map:

```
typedef IDispEventImpl<1, CSmartDartBoard, &DIID_DWebBrowserEvents2,
                    &LIBID_SHDocVw, 1, 0>
    BrowserEvents;

class ATL_NO_VTABLE CSmartDartBoard :
    public CComObjectRootEx<CComSingleThreadModel>,
...
// Sink browser events
 public BrowserEvents {
...
BEGIN_SINK_MAP(CSmartDartBoard)
  SINK_ENTRY_EX(1, DIID_DWebBrowserEvents2, 0x00000103,
                OnDocumentComplete)
END_SINK_MAP()
void __stdcall OnDocumentComplete(IDispatch*, VARIANT*);

...
};
```

The `OnCreate` handler and the `OnDestroy` handler are good places to establish and shut down the `DWebBrowserEvent2` connection point:

```
LRESULT CSmartDartBoard::OnCreate(UINT, WPARAM, LPARAM, BOOL&) {
  ...
  // Set up connection point w/ the browser
  if( SUCCEEDED(hr) )
    hr = BrowserEvents::DispEventAdvise(m_spBrowser);
  ...
  return SUCCEEDED(hr) ? 0 : -1;
}


LRESULT CSmartDartBoard::OnDestroy(UINT, WPARAM, LPARAM, BOOL&) {
  DispEventUnadvise(m_spBrowser);
  return 0;
}
```

In the implementation of the OnDocumentComplete event handler, we can
finally access the HTML object:

```
void __stdcall CSmartDartBoard::OnDocumentComplete(IDispatch*,
                                                   VARIANT*) {
  // Set the spanScore object's inner HTML
  SetScoreSpan();
}
```

Accessing the Control from the HTML

In addition to accessing the named HTML objects from the control, you may find
yourself wishing to access the control from the HTML. For this to happen, the HTML
must have some hook into the control. This is provided with the window.external
property. The script can expect this to be another dispinterface of the control
itself. In fact, the ATL Object Wizard generates two dual interfaces on an HTML control. The first, I<ControlName>, is the default interface available to the control's
clients. The second, I<ControlName>UI, is an interface given to the WebBrowser
control via the SetExternalDispatch function on the CAxWindow object:

```
HRESULT CAxWindow::SetExternalDispatch(IDispatch* pDisp);
```

The wizard-generated implementation of OnCreate sets this interface as part of the
initialization procedure:

```
LRESULT CSmartDartBoard::OnCreate(UINT, WPARAM, LPARAM, BOOL&) {
...
  if (SUCCEEDED(hr))
   hr = wnd.SetExternalDispatch
     (static_cast<ISmartDartBoardUI*>(this));
...
 return SUCCEEDED(hr) ? 0 : -1;
}
```

In the SmartDartBoard example, the interface used by control containers is
ISmartDartBoard:

```
[dual] interface ISmartDartBoard : IDispatch {
 [propget] HRESULT Score([out, retval] long *pVal);
 [propput] HRESULT Score([in] long newVal);
 HRESULT ResetScore();
};
```

On the other hand, the interface used by the HTML script code is ISmart-
DartBoardUI:

```
[dual] interface ISmartDartBoardUI : IDispatch {
 HRESULT AddToScore([in] long ringValue);
 HRESULT ResetScore();
};
```

This interface represents a bidirectional communication channel. A script block in
the HTML can use this interface for whatever it likes. For example:

```
<table width=100% height=100%>
...
</table>

<script language=vbscript>
    sub objBullsEye_OnScoreChanged(ringValue)
        ' Access the ISmartDartBoardUI interface
        window.external.AddToScore(ringValue)
    end sub
```

```
sub cmdReset_onClick
    ' Access the ISmartDartBoardUI interface
    window.external.ResetScore
end sub
</script>
```

In this example, we're using the `ISmartDartBoardUI` interface as a way to raise events to the control from the HTML, but instead of using connection points, we're using the window's external interface, which is far easier to set up.

Sinking HTML Element Events in C++

Notice that the previous HTML code handled events from the objects in the HTML itself. We're using the `object_event` syntax of VBScript; for example, `cmdReset _onClick` is called when the `cmdReset` button is clicked. It probably doesn't surprise you to learn that all the HTML objects fire events on an interface established via the connection point protocol. There's no reason we can't sink the events from the HTML objects in our control directly instead of using the `window.external` interface to forward the events. For example, the `cmdReset` button will fire events on the `HTMLInputTextElementEvents` dispinterface. Handling these events is, again, a matter of deriving from `IDispEventImpl` and adding entries to the sink map:

```
typedef IDispEventImpl<2, CSmartDartBoard, &DIID
  _HTMLInputTextElementEvents, &LIBID_MSHTML, 4, 0>
        ButtonEvents;

class ATL_NO_VTABLE CSmartDartBoard :
        public CComObjectRootEx<CComSingleThreadModel>,
    ...
    // Sink events on the DHTML Reset button
    public ButtonEvents {
    ...
BEGIN_SINK_MAP(CSmartDartBoard)
    ...
    SINK_ENTRY_EX(2, DIID_HTMLInputTextElementEvents, DISPID_CLICK,
                OnClickReset)
END_SINK_MAP()
    VARIANT_BOOL __stdcall OnClickReset();
    ...
};
```

Since we need to have an interface on the `cmdReset` button, we need to wait until the `OnDocumentComplete` event to establish a connection point with the button:

```
void __stdcall CSmartDartBoard::OnDocumentComplete(IDispatch*,
                                                   VARIANT*) {
// Set the spanScore object's inner HTML
SetScoreSpan();

// Retrieve the Reset button
HRESULT hr;
CComPtr<IHTMLElement> speReset;
hr = GetHtmlElement(OLESTR("cmdReset"), &speReset);
if( FAILED(hr) ) return;

// Set up the connection point w/ the button
ButtonEvents::DispEventAdvise(speReset);
}
```

Once we've established the connection with the Reset button, every time the user clicks on it we'll get a callback in our `OnClickReset` event handler. This means that we no longer need the `cmdReset_onClick` handler in the script. However, from a larger perspective, since we program and handle events back and forth between the C++ and the HTML code, we have the flexibility to use whichever is more convenient when writing the code. This is quite a contrast from a dialog resource, where the resource was good for laying out the elements of the UI (as long as the UI was a fixed size), but only our C++ code could provide any behavior.

Extended UI Handling

It turns out that the external dispatch is but one setting you can set on the `CAxHostWindow` that affects the HTML Document control. Several more options can be set via the `IAxWinAmbientDispatch` interface implemented by `CAxHostWindow`:

```
typedef enum tagDocHostUIFlagDispatch {
  docHostUIFlagDIALOG                 = 1,
  docHostUIFlagDISABLE_HELP_MENU      = 2,
  docHostUIFlagNO3DBORDER             = 4,
  docHostUIFlagSCROLL_NO              = 8,
  docHostUIFlagDISABLE_SCRIPT_INACTIVE = 16,
  docHostUIFlagOPENNEWWIN             = 32,
```

```
  docHostUIFlagDISABLE_OFFSCREEN = 64,
  docHostUIFlagFLAT_SCROLLBAR = 128,
  docHostUIFlagDIV_BLOCKDEFAULT = 256,
  docHostUIFlagACTIVATE_CLIENTHIT_ONLY = 512,
} DocHostUIFlagDispatch;

typedef enum tagDOCHOSTUIDBLCLKDispatch {
  docHostUIDblClkDEFAULT         = 0,
  docHostUIDblClkSHOWPROPERTIES  = 1,
  docHostUIDblClkSHOWCODE        = 2,
} DOCHOSTUIDBLCLKDispatch;

interface IAxWinAmbientDispatch : IDispatch {
...
// IDocHostUIHandler Defaults
[propput, helpstring("Set the DOCHOSTUIFLAG flags")]
HRESULT DocHostFlags([in]DWORD dwDocHostFlags);
[propget, helpstring("Get the DOCHOSTUIFLAG flags")]
HRESULT DocHostFlags([out,retval]DWORD* pdwDocHostFlags);

[propput, helpstring("Set the DOCHOSTUIDBLCLK flags")]
HRESULT DocHostDoubleClickFlags([in]DWORD dwFlags);
[propget, helpstring("Get the DOCHOSTUIDBLCLK flags")]
HRESULT DocHostDoubleClickFlags([out,retval]DWORD* pdwFlags);

[propput, helpstring("Enable or disable context menus")]
HRESULT AllowContextMenu([in]VARIANT_BOOL bAllowContextMenu);
[propget, helpstring("Are context menus enabled")]
HRESULT AllowContextMenu([out,retval]VARIANT_BOOL*
                         pbAllowContextMenu);

[propput, helpstring("Enable or disable UI")]
HRESULT AllowShowUI([in]VARIANT_BOOL bAllowShowUI);
[propget, helpstring("Is UI enabled")]
HRESULT AllowShowUI([out,retval]VARIANT_BOOL* pbAllowShowUI);

[propput, helpstring("Set the option key path")]
HRESULT OptionKeyPath([in]BSTR bstrOptionKeyPath);
[propget, helpstring("Get the option key path")]
HRESULT OptionKeyPath([out,retval]BSTR* pbstrOptionKeyPath);
};
```

The `DocHostFlags` property can be any combination of `DocHostUIFlag-Dispatch` flags. The `DocHostDoubleClickFlags` property can be any one of the `DOCHOSTUIDBLCLKDispatch` flags. The `AllowContextMenu` property allows you to shut off the context menu when the user right-clicks on the HTML control.[9] The `AllowShowUI` property controls whether the host will be replacing the IE menus and toolbars. The `OptionKeyPath` property tells the HTML Document where in the registry to read and write its settings.

All these settings affect the `CAxWindowHost` object's implementation of `IDocHostUIHandler`, an interface the HTML Document control expects from its host to fine-tune its behavior. If you'd like to fine-tune this interaction even more, `CAxWindowHost` allows you to set your own `IDocHostUIHandlerDispatch` interface[10] via the `CAxWindow` member function `SetExternalUIHandler`:

```
HRESULT CAxWindow::SetExternalUIHandler(IDocHostUIHandlerDispatch*
                                        pHandler);
```

The `IDocHostUIHandlerDispatch` interface is pretty much a one-to-one mapping to `IDocHostUIHandler`, but in dual interface form. When a `CAxHostWindow` object gets a call from the HTML Document control on `IDocHostUIHandler`, the call will be forwarded if there is an implementation of `IDocHostUIHandlerDispatch` set. For example, if you'd like to replace the context menu of the HTML control rather than just turn it off, you will have to expose the `IDocHostUIHandlerDispatch` interface, call `SetExternalUIHandler` during the `OnCreate` handler, and implement the `ShowContextMenu` member function. When there is no implementation of `IDocHostUIHandlerDispatch` set, the `CAxHostWindow` object will use the properties set via the `IWinAmbientDispatch` interface.

Hosting HTML Is Not Limited to the HTML Control

By hosting the WebBrowser control and/or the HTML Document control, you've given yourself a lot more than just hosting HTML. The HTML Document control represents a flexible COM UI framework called Dynamic HTML. The combination of declarative statements to lay out the UI elements with the ability to control each element's behavior, presentation style, and events at runtime gives you a great deal of flexibility.

Nor is this functionality limited to an HTML control. You can achieve the same effect by creating a `CAxWindow` object that hosts either the WebBrowser or the HTML Document control in a window, a dialog, or a composite control as well as in an HTML control. If fact, you could build entire applications using ATL as the glue

---

[9]There's no reason for the user to know you're just bootlegging IE functionality, is there?
[10]This interface is defined by ATL in `atliface.idl`.

code that initialized a first-tier thin client built entirely from HTML. Unfortunately, the DHTML object model is beyond the scope of this book, but you could do a lot worse things with your time than finding a good resource on DHTML and seeing if it meets your front-end UI goals.

ATL's Control Containment Limitations

Version 3.0 marked ATL's first support for COM control containment. While there's a lot of functionality packed in, it's not quite all you might like. There are several problems with the way that ATL implements control containment:

- All interfaces are implemented by a single class, CAxHostWindow which acts as the site, as well as the document and the frame. If you contain multiple controls, you get duplicate implementation of interfaces that could have been shared. This is particularly cumbersome if the control asks for the HWND for the document or the frame. Instead of allowing the client application programmer to designate their own document and/or frame window, ATL creates a new window, resulting in potentially three container windows per control. If the control creates its own window, that's four windows instead of just one, to host a single control.

- Each control must have its own window on the container side for the CAx-HostWindow object to work with. Even a windowless controls will have one window associated with it. Not exactly the windowless-ness one for which one would hope.

- The implementations of the interfaces are less than complete. Several of the control containment member functions return E_NOTIMPL or S_OK without doing anything. This is especially troublesome in the keyboard accelerator handling methods, but shows itself in many areas.

- Finally, unlike the rest of ATL, the control containment architecture is not well factored. You can't easily reach in and change how one piece works without also changing the other pieces. If, for example, you'd like to have a shared frame between all of the control sites, you have to replace CAxHostWindow (probably by deriving from it) as well as changing how CAxWindow hooks up the control site so that it uses your new class. Ideally one would like to override some CAxHostWindow members, but still be able to use the rest of the containment framework as is.

What do these limitations mean to you? For a lot of the work you're likely to do with control containment, not much. This chapter has shown you the considerable use to which you can put ATL's control containment framework. However, if you're looking for the C++ equivalent of a general-purpose, full-featured control containment like Visual Basic, ATL isn't quite there yet.

Summary

ATL provides the ability to host controls in windows, dialogs, or other controls. Control containment under ATL is based on a new window class, `AtlAxWin`. As a wrapper around this window class, ATL provides the `CAxWindow` class. Once a control-hosting window has been created, it can be treated as a window, using the functionality of the `CWindow` base class. It can also be used as a COM object, using the interfaces available with the `QueryControl` member function of the `CAxWindow` class. The interfaces of the control can be used to sink events, persist the control's state, or program against the control's custom interface(s).

Many objects in ATL can make use of the `AtlAxWin` window class to host controls. Windows can use them manually via the `CAxWindow` class. Dialogs can use them automatically when using the `CAxDialogImpl` class. Controls can contain other controls in ATL when derived from `CComCompositeControl`. Finally, HTML controls can host the WebBrowser control, combining the best of the dialog resource declarative model and a full-featured COM UI framework model.

A | C++ Templates by Example

This appendix is meant to be a brief introduction to the basics of C++ templates using examples. It will also show some of the advanced template features that ATL uses, but without any ATL code cluttering things up. For a more thorough introduction to templates, see Stan Lippman's *C++ Primer*, published by Addison-Wesley.

The Need for Templates

Imagine a simple bounds-checked array class:

```
#define MAX_ELEMS 8

class Array {
public:
 long& operator[](size_t n) {
   if( n < 0 || n >= MAX_ELEMS ) throw "out of bounds!";
   return m_rg[n];
 }

protected:
 long  m_rg[MAX_ELEMS];
};
```

This class makes quiet, hard-to-find errors loud and easy to find:

```
int main(int argc, char* argv[]) {
 long rg[8]; // Built-in array type
 rg[8] = 1;  // will corrupt the stack, but quietly

 Array array;  // Bounds-checked array type
 array[8] = 1; // will complain loudly

 return 0;
}
```

The bounds-checking part of the `Array` class really has nothing to do with the data being managed. In fact, using a little bit of C++ trickery, this is even easier to spot:

```
typedef long T;
class Array {
public:
 T& operator[](size_t n) {
   if( n < 0 || n >= MAX_ELEMS ) throw "out of bounds!";
   return m_rg[n];
 }

protected:
 T m_rg[MAX_ELEMS];
};
```

Notice that we've replaced the use of `long` with a generic type T. Unfortunately, this trick doesn't allow us to reuse the `Array` class with different types T. Once the compiler sees the `Array` class, it won't let us change T and compile it again with another type T. To get any reuse out of the `Array` class as it is, we'd have to do some cut and paste work and create different `Array` classes, one for each type we're interested in managing. For example:

```
class ArrayOfChar {
public:
 char& operator[](size_t n);

protected:
 char m_rg[MAX_ELEMS];
};

class ArrayOflong {
public:
 long& operator[](size_t n);

protected:
 long m_rg[MAX_ELEMS];
};
```

Besides the tedium involved with this technique, the developer of the `Array` family of classes would have to build an `Array` class for every type that the user of the class may want to manage. Since some of these types may be defined *after* the `Array` class is built, this is an especially difficult task. We'd really like the compiler to step in and help us here. And so it will, with templates.

Template Basics

Using template syntax, we can create an `Array` class that is parameterized on any number of parameters, including the type of data to manage and how large the internal buffer should be:

```
template <typename¹ T, size_t MAX_ELEMS>
class Array {
public:
 T& operator[](size_t n) {
    if( n < 0 || n >= MAX_ELEMS ) throw "out of bounds!";
    return m_rg[n];
 }

protected:
 T m_rg[MAX_ELEMS];
};
```

Notice that the only difference in this code is the use of the `template` statement before the class declaration. When the compiler sees a template, it knows to store the class declaration in its internal data structures but to not generate any code. The compiler can't generate the code until it sees how the client would like to use it. For example:

```
struct Point { long x; long y; };

int main(int argc, char* argv[]) {
 Array<long, 8>    a1; // Array of 8 longs
 Array<char, 256> a2; // Array of 256 chars
 Array<Point, 16> a3; // Array of 16 Points
 ...
 return 0;
}
```

---

[1]The ANSI C++ standard allows the use of the keyword `class` instead of the keyword `typename`, but the use of `class` is deprecated.

The compiler will use the client's template parameters to generate the code for the class on demand, effectively creating a new member of the `Array` family of classes with each usage.[2] Because the compiler is using the template parameters to generate the code, only parameters whose value is known at compile time are allowed. However, that includes built-in types, user-defined types, constants, and even function pointers. To make the template even more convenient for the client to use, you're allowed to declare default values for template parameters, just like you would for functions:

```
template <typename T, size_t MAX_ELEMS = 8>
class Array {...};

int main(int argc, char* argv[]) {
 Array<long>      a1; // Array of 8 longs
 Array<char, 256> a2; // Array of 256 chars
 ...
 return 0;
}
```

Template Specialization

You may decide that for a specific combination of template parameters, the generic template expansion isn't good enough. For example, if you decide that an `Array` of 256 characters should have an equality operator, you may decide to override the `Array` general template using the template specialization syntax. For example:

```
template < > // No template arguments here
class Array<char, 256> { // Template argument values here
public:
 // You are not required to provide the same functionality
 // as the general template (although it's a good idea)
 char& operator[](size_t n) {
   if( n < 0 || n >= 256 ) throw "out of bounds!";
   return m_sz[n];
 }

 // You may add functionality not in the general template
 bool operator==(const Array<char, 256>& rhs) {
   return strcmp(m_sz, rhs.m_sz);
 }
```

---

[2] The linker will make sure that only one expansion per set of template parameters actually makes it into the final image.

```
protected:
 char m_sz[256];
};
```

The client doesn't have to do anything new to use the specialized version of the template. When the compiler sees `Array<char, 256>`, the client will automatically get the specialized version.

Templates as Base Classes

Template specialization allows the addition of new functionality and optimized implementations based on specific template parameters. However, although the C++ standard defines something called "partial" specialization, as of this writing, no compilers I'm aware of support it. Luckily, it's fairly easy to simulate using inheritance. For example, the specialization I just showed specializes on all the parameters, both the type and the size of the array. It would probably be more useful to be able to specialize on the type of data held, but to expose additional functionality for character strings of any size. This can be accomplished by using the `Array` as a base class:

```
template <size_t MAX_LEN>
class String : public Array<char, MAX_LEN+1> {
public:
 // Additional functionality
 bool operator==(const String<MAX_LEN>& rhs) {
   return strcmp(m_rg, rhs.m_rg);
 }
};
```

Notice that the `String` is still parameterized on length, and note how it passes arguments to the base `Array` class. The type is fixed, because we're building a string, but the number of elements to store is based on the `String` template argument. In effect, this achieves a partial specialization, although the client code will have to use the `String` template instead of the `Array` template to make use of it.

A Different Kind of Polymorphism

Templates give us a different kind of reuse mechanism than inheritance. Inheritance means that we'd like to reuse the implementation and signature of a base class and extend it in a derived class. Inheritance is type-centric. The derived class is *type compatible* with the base class. Type compatibility means that an instance of the derived class can be used where an instance of the base class is required.

On the other hand, templates allow us to reuse the behavior of a class, but to divorce it from the types involved. As long as the type can fit where it's being used, the compiler doesn't care about the type. For example, all that was required of the type being passed to the `Array` template was that it had a default constructor so that it could be created in arrays. If the type couldn't live up to that requirement, the compiler would complain.

Because of the way the compiler generates code using template arguments, templates really give us a different kind of polymorphism. Instead of polymorphism based on type compatibility, we have polymorphism based on *signature compatibility*. As long as the type has the appropriate function signatures available, the compiler is perfectly happy. This kind of polymorphism has some interesting properties, of which ATL makes heavy use.

Using Behavior Classes

Imagine modifying the `Array` class so that it would only do bounds checking if you so desired:

```
template <typename T, size_t MAX_ELEMS = 8, bool bCheckBounds = true>
class Array {
public:
 T& operator[](size_t n) {
   if( bCheckBounds && (n < 0 || n >= MAX_ELEMS) )
     throw "out of bounds!";
   return m_rg[n];
 }

protected:
 T m_rg[MAX_ELEMS];
};
```

This allows a client to turn bounds checking on or off based on its own requirements:

```
int main(int argc, char* argv[]) {
#ifdef _DEBUG
 bool bCheckBounds = true;
#else
 bool bCheckBounds = false;
#endif
```

```
 Array<long, 256, bCheckBounds>  array;
 array[256] = 1;
 return 0;
}
```

The intent here is that we'll skip the bounds checks in release mode because we hope we have caught the out-of-bounds errors during development. However, we're still doing a check against `bCheckBounds` every time through the `operator[]` member function. We could hope for a good compiler that would optimize away the line because `bCheckBounds` is known at compile time, or we could remove all doubt and make use of a *behavior class*.

A behavior class (also known as a *trait class* or a *trait*) is a class containing some static member functions and/or some type definitions. Behavior classes are never meant to be created. Instead, by putting the functions and type definitions into a class, we've grouped them together and can refer to them as a unit.

To solve our bounds-checking problem, imagine two behavior classes, one that checks the bounds and one that does not:

```
struct DebugBoundsChecker {
 static void CheckBounds(size_t n, size_t nMax) {
   if( n < 0 || n >= nMax ) throw "out of bounds!";
 }
};

struct ReleaseBoundsChecker {
 static void CheckBounds(size_t n, size_t nMax) {}
};
```

Notice that both of the behavior classes have the same function with the same signature. The debug version does the bounds checking, and the release version doesn't do anything. And because both implementations are inline functions, the compiler can optimize easily. Given only the knowledge of the signature of the bounds-checking function, I can rewrite the `Array` class to use the `CheckBounds` function scoped by a type name passed as a template parameter:

```
template <typename T, size_t MAX_ELEMS = 8,
          typename BoundsChecker = DebugBoundsChecker>
class Array {
public:
 T& operator[](size_t n) {
```

```
        BoundsChecker::CheckBounds(n, MAX_ELEMS);
        return m_rg[n];
    }

  protected:
    T m_rg[MAX_ELEMS];
    };
```

The client can now take advantage of the bounds checking or not, as decided at compile time:

```
    int main(int argc, char* argv[]) {
#ifdef _DEBUG
    typedef DebugBoundsChecker BoundsChecker;
#else
    typedef ReleaseBoundsChecker BoundsChecker;
#endif

    Array<long, 256, BoundsChecker> array;
    array[256] = 1;
    return 0;
    }
```

In this case, I've used signature compatibility to make my decisions at compile time, resulting in simpler and more efficient code. If I wanted to add another kind of bounds-checking behavior class in the future, I could do so as long as it had a CheckBounds function that lived up to the signature requirements of the caller.

Simulating Dynamic Binding

One of the benefits of inheritance is the idea of dynamic binding. A virtual function in the base class can be overridden in the derived class to extend or replace base class functionality. One especially powerful expression of this idea is the *pure virtual member function*. A pure virtual member function is a virtual member function that *must* be overridden in the deriving class. In fact, any class with a pure virtual member function is thought of as an *abstract base class* (ABC), and no instance of that class can be created. To use the functionality of an ABC, it must be used as a base class and the deriving class must implement all the pure virtual member functions. This is useful because it allows the base class to define functionality required by the deriving class. For example:

```
template <typename T>
class Array {
public:
 ...
 virtual int Compare(const Array<T>& rhs) =0;

 bool operator< (const Array<T>& rhs)
 { return this->Compare(rhs) < 0; }

 bool operator> (const Array<T>& rhs)
 { return this->Compare(rhs) > 0; }

 bool operator== (const Array<T>& rhs)
 { return this->Compare(rhs) == 0; }

 T m_rg[1024];
};
```

By defining the `Compare` function as pure virtual, the `Array` class designer has decreed that `Array` may only be used as a base class and that the deriving class must provide some way of comparing two arrays of the same type so that the comparison operators can be implemented. For example, a `String` class must implement the `Compare` function:

```
class String : public Array<char> {
public:
 int Compare(const Array<char>& rhs)
 { return strcmp(m_rg, rhs.m_rg); }
};
```

The compiler uses the implementation of the pure virtual member function provided in the derived class to fill in the virtual function table entry for that member function (as it does with all virtual member function pointers). Using function pointers to invoke member functions is how C++ provides dynamic binding, that is, binding to the specific implementation at runtime based on the type of the variable.

However, we're paying the price of dynamic binding for our `String` class. The price of dynamic binding is a virtual function table, shared between all instances, an extra four-byte virtual function pointer per object, and at least two extra pointer indirections to invoke the appropriate implementation. This seems a high price to pay given perfect knowledge at compile time. We know how to compare two `String` objects. Why not make the compiler do the work and save us the overhead of dynamic binding? We can do that by using *simulated dynamic binding.*

Simulated dynamic binding allows us to provide the name of the deriving class to the base class. The base class casts itself to the deriving class to call the required function. Revising the `Array` class to use simulated dynamic binding looks like this:

```
template <typename T, typename Deriving>
class Array {
public:
 ...
 bool operator< (const Array<T, Deriving>& rhs)
 { return static_cast<Deriving*>(this)->Compare(rhs) < 0; }

 bool operator> (const Array<T, Deriving>& rhs)
 { return static_cast<Deriving*>(this)->Compare(rhs) > 0; }

 bool operator== (const Array<T, Deriving>& rhs)
 { return static_cast<Deriving*>(this)->Compare(rhs) == 0; }

 T m_rg[1024];
};
```

Notice that the `Array` template takes an additional parameter—the name of the deriving class. It uses that class name to perform a static cast on itself. Because the compiler will expand the code of the base class while instantiating the deriving class, the static cast performs a perfectly safe downcast (normally a contradiction in terms). The compiler uses the member functions of the deriving cast to resolve the address of the required function at compile time, saving us the cost of dynamic binding. The deriving class must implement the appropriate member function and pass its own name as a parameter to the base class template:

```
class String : public Array<char, String> {
public:
 int Compare(const Array<char, String>& rhs)
 { return strcmp(m_rg, rhs.m_rg); }
};
```

This technique gives us the look and feel of dynamic binding without using virtual member functions. The base class can require functionality of the deriving class. The base class cannot be instantiated by itself. The major difference is that because no virtual functions are required, we don't have the overhead of dynamic binding.

It's my understanding that the ATL team discovered simulated dynamic binding accidentally. When they did, they went immediately to the compiler team, who claimed that the C++ standard does not mandate or prohibit such behavior, but they promised to keep it working for ATL. Does that mean you should use simulated dynamic binding when you're writing your most portable code? Probably not. Should you still understand it because ATL is rife with it? Absolutely. Should you sneak it into your own bag of tricks? Why not? It's in mine.

Function Templates

Classes are not the only thing that can be parameterized; functions can be, too. The canonical example is the `min` function:

```
inline long min(long a, long b) { return (a < b ? a : b); }
inline float min(float a, float b) { return (a < b ? a : b); }
```

Since the code is the same for both overloaded `min` implementations, there's no reason not to make it into a template:

```
template <typename T>
inline T min(T a, T b) { return (a < b ? a : b); }
```

When the template is instantiated, the compiler generates the code on demand based on the usage. For example:

```
void main() {
  long a = 1, b = 2, c = min(a, b);
  float x = 1.1, y = 2.2, z = min(x, y);
  char *r = "hello", *s = "world", *t = min(r, s);
}
```

Notice that the compiler can figure out how to instantiate the `min` template implementation without any fancy angle brackets. However, also notice that sometimes, just as with class templates, function templates don't expand the way we'd like. For example, the `min` that takes two `char*`s will compare two pointer values, not the contents of the strings. A function template can be specialized by merely providing an implementation that takes the types involved. For example:

```
inline char* min(const char* a, const char* b) {
  return (strcmp(a, b) < 0 ? a : b);
}
```

In this case, because a version of the function already exists that takes two character pointers, the compiler will bind to that one instead of generating another implementation based on the `min` function template.

Member Function Templates

The fun of templates doesn't stop at global functions. Oh no. You can create member function templates as well. In fact, as of Visual C++ 6.0, the definition of `IUnknown` has been augmented with a member function template for `QueryInterface`:

```
struct IUnknown {
...
  template <class Q>
  HRESULT STDMETHODCALLTYPE QueryInterface(Q** pp)
  { return QueryInterface(__uuidof(Q), (void**)pp); }
}
```

Before the member function template, all calls to `QueryInterface` had to be sure to match up the interface type and the interface identifier. For example:

```
void Fly(IUnknown* punk) {
 IBird* pbird = 0;
 punk->QueryInterface(IID_ICat, (void**)&pbird); // Oops!
 punk->QueryInterface(IID_IBird, (void**)pbird); // Double oops!
 punk->QueryInterface(IID_IBird, (void**)&pbird); // OK
 pbird->Fly();
 }
```

On the other hand, with the `QueryInterface` member function template, the type of the interface suffices:

```
void Fly(IUnknown* punk) {
 IBird* pbird = 0;
 punk->QueryInterface(&pbird); // __uuidof used to determine IID
 pbird->Fly();
 }
```

In effect, member function templates add new member functions of a class based on usage, just like function templates add new global functions.

Summary

Templates provide two services. The first is code reuse, but in a different way than inheritance. Inheritance requires a certain type relationship. Templates require only that the compiler be able to find the functionality required of the specified type. Inheritance makes type requirements, whereas templates take what types we give them.

The other service that templates provide is efficiency. By mixing in types at compile time, we can use static binding to make decisions at runtime instead of at compile time. This is the key to the promise of smaller, faster code that templates make.

B | ATL Classes and Headers

Assuming the default installation directory for Visual C++, ATL 3.0 source code is installed in the `c:\program files\microsoft visual studio\vc98\atl\include` directory. The following table lists the names of the ATL classes and the header files in which they are declared (and often implemented).

ATL class	Header file
_Copy	ATLCOM.H
_Copy<CONNECTDATA>	ATLCOM.H
_Copy<LPOLESTR>	ATLCOM.H
_Copy<OLEVERB>	ATLCOM.H
_Copy<VARIANT>	ATLCOM.H
_CopyInterface	ATLCOM.H
_ICPLocator	ATLCOM.H
_IDispEvent	ATLCOM.H
_IDispEventLocator	ATLCOM.H
CAccessor	ATLDBCLI.H
CAccessorBase	ATLDBCLI.H
CAccessorRowset	ATLDBCLI.H
CAdapt	ATLBASE.H
CArrayRowset	ATLDBCLI.H
CAssertionInfo	ATLDBSCH.H
CAutoMemRelease	ATLDB.H
CAxDialogImpl	ATLWIN.H
CAxFrameWindow	ATLHOST.H
CAxHostWindow	ATLHOST.H
CAxUIWindow	ATLHOST.H
CAxWindowT	ATLWIN.H
CBindStatusCallback	ATLCTL.H

ATL class	Header file
CBitFieldOps	ATLDB.H
CBookmark	ATLDBCLI.H
CBookmarkBase	ATLDBCLI.H
CBulkRowset	ATLDBCLI.H
CCatalogInfo	ATLDBSCH.H
CCharacterSetInfo	ATLDBSCH.H
CCheckConstraintInfo	ATLDBSCH.H
CCollationInfo	ATLDBSCH.H
CColumnDomainUsageInfo	ATLDBSCH.H
CColumnIds	ATLDB.H
CColumnPrivilegeInfo	ATLDBSCH.H
CColumnsInfo	ATLDBSCH.H
CCOLUMNSRow	ATLDB.H
CComAggObject	ATLCOM.H
CComAggregateCreator	ATLCOM.H
CComApartment	ATLBASE.H
CComAutoCriticalSection	ATLBASE.H
CComAutoThreadModule	ATLBASE.H
CComBSTR	ATLBASE.H
CComCachedTearOffObject	ATLCOM.H
CComClassFactory	ATLCOM.H
CComClassFactory2	ATLCOM.H
CComClassFactoryAutoThread	ATLCOM.H
CComClassFactorySingleton	ATLCOM.H
CComCoClass	ATLCOM.H
CComCompositeControl	ATLCTL.H
CComContainedObject	ATLCOM.H
CComControl	ATLCTL.H
CComControlBase	ATLCTL.H
CComCreator	ATLCOM.H
CComCreator2	ATLCOM.H
CComCriticalSection	ATLBASE.H

ATL class	Header file
CComDispatchDriver	ATLCOM.H
CComDynamicUnkArray	ATLCOM.H
CComEnum	ATLCOM.H
CComEnumImpl	ATLCOM.H
CComEnumOnSTL	ATLCOM.H
CComFailCreator	ATLCOM.H
CComFakeCriticalSection	ATLBASE.H
CComFree	ATLDB.H
CComIEnum	ATLCOM.H
CComInternalCreator	ATLCOM.H
CCommand	ATLDBCLI.H
CCommandBase	ATLDBCLI.H
CComModule	ATLBASE.H
CComMultiThreadModel	ATLBASE.H
CComMultiThreadModelNoCS	ATLBASE.H
CComObject	ATLCOM.H
CComObjectCached	ATLCOM.H
CComObjectGlobal	ATLCOM.H
CComObjectLockT	ATLCOM.H
CComObjectNoLock	ATLCOM.H
CComObjectRootBase	ATLCOM.H
CComObjectRootEx	ATLCOM.H
CComObjectStack	ATLCOM.H
CComPolyObject	ATLCOM.H
CComPtr	ATLBASE.H
CComQIPtr	ATLBASE.H
CComSimpleThreadAllocator	ATLBASE.H
CComSingleThreadModel	ATLBASE.H
CComTearOffObject	ATLCOM.H
CComTearOffObjectBase	ATLCOM.H
CComTypeInfoHolder	ATLCOM.H
CComUnkArray	ATLCOM.H

ATL class	Header file
CComVariant	ATLBASE.H
CConstraintColumnUsageInfo	ATLDBSCH.H
CConstraintTableUsageInfo	ATLDBSCH.H
CContainedWindowT	ATLWIN.H
CConvertHelper	ATLDB.H
CDataSource	ATLDBCLI.H
CDBErrorInfo	ATLDBCLI.H
CDBIDOps	ATLDB.H
CDBPropIDSet	ATLDBCLI.H
CDBPropSet	ATLDBCLI.H
CDialogImpl	ATLWIN.H
CDialogImplBaseT	ATLWIN.H
CDynamicAccessor	ATLDBCLI.H
CDynamicChain	ATLWIN.H
CDynamicParameterAccessor	ATLDBCLI.H
CEnumerator	ATLDBCLI.H
CEnumeratorAccessor	ATLDBCLI.H
CEnumRowsetImpl	ATLDB.H
CExpansionVector	STATREG.H
CFakeFirePropNotifyEvent	ATLCOM.H
CFirePropNotifyEvent	ATLCTL.H
CForeignKeysInfo	ATLDBSCH.H
CIndexesInfo	ATLDBSCH.H
CKeyColumnUsageInfo	ATLDBSCH.H
CManualAccessor	ATLDBCLI.H
CMessageMap	ATLWIN.H
CMultipleResults	ATLDBCLI.H
CNoAccessor	ATLDBCLI.H
CNoMultipleResults	ATLDBCLI.H
CNoRowset	ATLDBCLI.H
CObjectData	ATLSNAP.H
CPrimaryKeyInfo	ATLDBSCH.H

ATL class	Header file
CProcedureColumnInfo	ATLDBSCH.H
CProcedureInfo	ATLDBSCH.H
CProcedureParameterInfo	ATLDBSCH.H
CPropColID	ATLDB.H
CPROVIDER_TYPERow	ATLDB.H
CProviderTypeInfo	ATLDBSCH.H
CReferentialConstraintInfo	ATLDBSCH.H
CRegKey	ATLBASE.H
CRegObject	STATREG.H
CRegParser	STATREG.H
CRestrictions	ATLDBSCH.H
CRowset	ATLDBCLI.H
CRowsetImpl	ATLDB.H
CRunTimeFree	ATLDB.H
CSchemaRowset	ATLDBSCH.H
CSchemas	ATLDBSCH.H
CSchemataInfo	ATLDBSCH.H
CSecurityDescriptor	ATLCOM.H
CSession	ATLDBCLI.H
CSimpleArray	ATLBASE.H
CSimpleDialog	ATLWIN.H
CSimpleMap	ATLBASE.H
CSimpleRow	ATLDB.H
CSimpleValArray	ATLBASE.H
CSnapInDataObjectImpl	ATLSNAP.H
CSnapInItem	ATLSNAP.H
CSnapInItem	ATLSNAP.H
CSnapInItemImpl	ATLSNAP.H
CSnapInObjectRoot	ATLSNAP.H
CSnapInObjectRootBase	ATLSNAP.H
CSnapInPropertyPageImpl	ATLSNAP.H
CSnapInToolbarInfo	ATLSNAP.H

ATL class	Header file
CSQLLanguageInfo	ATLDBSCH.H
CStatisticInfo	ATLDBSCH.H
CStockPropImpl	ATLCTL.H
CTable	ATLDBCLI.H
CTableConstraintInfo	ATLDBSCH.H
CTableInfo	ATLDBSCH.H
CTablePrivilegeInfo	ATLDBSCH.H
CTABLESRow	ATLDB.H
CTranslationInfo	ATLDBSCH.H
CUsagePrivilegeInfo	ATLDBSCH.H
CUtlPropInfo	ATLDB.H
CUtlProps	ATLDB.H
CUtlPropsBase	ATLDB.H
CVBufHelper	ATLBASE.H
CViewColumnUsageInfo	ATLDBSCH.H
CViewInfo	ATLDBSCH.H
CViewTableUsageInfo	ATLDBSCH.H
CVirtualBuffer	ATLBASE.H
CWindow	ATLWIN.H
CWindowImpl	ATLWIN.H
CWindowImplBaseT	ATLWIN.H
CWindowImplRoot	ATLWIN.H
CWinTraits	ATLWIN.H
CWinTraitsOR	ATLWIN.H
CWndProcThunk	ATLWIN.H
IAccessorImpl	ATLDB.H
IAccessorImplBase	ATLDB.H
ICollectionOnSTLImpl	ATLCOM.H
IColumnsInfoImpl	ATLDB.H
ICommandImpl	ATLDB.H
ICommandPropertiesImpl	ATLDB.H
ICommandTextImpl	ATLDB.H

ATL class	Header file
IComponentDataImpl	ATLSNAP.H
IComponentImpl	ATLSNAP.H
IConnectionPointContainerImpl	ATLCOM.H
IConnectionPointImpl	ATLCOM.H
IConvertTypeImpl	ATLDB.H
IDataObjectImpl	ATLCTL.H
IDBCreateCommandImpl	ATLDB.H
IDBCreateSessionImpl	ATLDB.H
IDBInitializeImpl	ATLDB.H
IDBPropertiesImpl	ATLDB.H
IDBSchemaRowsetImpl	ATLDB.H
IDispatchImpl	ATLCOM.H
IDispEventImpl	ATLCOM.H
IDispEventSimpleImpl	ATLCOM.H
IEnumOnSTLImpl	ATLCOM.H
IExtendContextMenuImpl	ATLSNAP.H
IExtendControlbarImpl	ATLSNAP.H
IExtendPropertySheetImpl	ATLSNAP.H
IGetDataSourceImpl	ATLDB.H
IInternalConnectionImpl	ATLDB.H
IObjectSafetyImpl	ATLCTL.H
IObjectWithSiteImpl	ATLCOM.H
IObjectWithSiteSessionImpl	ATLDB.H
IOleControlImpl	ATLCTL.H
IOleInPlaceActiveObjectImpl	ATLCTL.H
IOleInPlaceObjectWindowlessImpl	ATLCTL.H
IOleLinkImpl	ATLCTL.H
IOleObjectImpl	ATLCTL.H
IOpenRowsetImpl	ATLDB.H
IPerPropertyBrowsingImpl	ATLCTL.H
IPersistImpl	ATLCOM.H
IPersistPropertyBagImpl	ATLCOM.H

ATL class	Header file
IPersistStorageImpl	ATLCOM.H
IPersistStreamInitImpl	ATLCOM.H
IPointerInactiveImpl	ATLCTL.H
IPropertyNotifySinkCP	ATLCTL.H
IPropertyPage2Impl	ATLCTL.H
IPropertyPageImpl	ATLCTL.H
IProvideClassInfo2Impl	ATLCOM.H
IProvideClassInfoImpl	ATLCOM.H
IQuickActivateImpl	ATLCTL.H
IResultDataCompareImpl	ATLSNAP.H
IRowsetCreatorImpl	ATLDB.H
IRowsetIdentityImpl	ATLDB.H
IRowsetImpl	ATLDB.H
IRowsetInfoImpl	ATLDB.H
IRowsetNotifyImpl	ATLDBCLI.H
IRunnableObjectImpl	ATLCTL.H
IServiceProviderImpl	ATLCOM.H
ISessionPropertiesImpl	ATLDB.H
ISpecifyPropertyPagesImpl	ATLCOM.H
ISupportErrorInfoImpl	ATLCOM.H
IViewObjectExImpl	ATLCTL.H

Index

Addison-Wesley Computer and Engineering Publishing Group

How to Interact *with Us*

1. Visit our Web site

http://www.awl.com/cseng

When you think you've read enough, there's always more content for you at Addison-Wesley's web site. Our web site contains a directory of complete product information including:

- Chapters
- Exclusive author interviews
- Links to authors' pages
- Tables of contents
- Source code

You can also discover what tradeshows and conferences Addison-Wesley will be attending, read what others are saying about our titles, and find out where and when you can meet our authors and have them sign your book.

2. Subscribe to Our Email Mailing Lists

Subscribe to our electronic mailing lists and be the first to know when new books are publishing. Here's how it works: Sign up for our electronic mailing at http://www.awl.com/cseng/mailinglists.html. Just select the subject areas that interest you and you will receive notification via email when we publish a book in that area.

3. Contact Us via Email

cepubprof@awl.com

Ask general questions about our books.
Sign up for our electronic mailing lists.
Submit corrections for our web site.

bexpress@awl.com

Request an Addison-Wesley catalog.
Get answers to questions regarding your order or our products.

innovations@awl.com

Request a current Innovations Newsletter.

webmaster@awl.com

Send comments about our web site.

jcs@awl.com

Submit a book proposal.
Send errata for an Addison-Wesley book.

cepubpublicity@awl.com

Request a review copy for a member of the media interested in reviewing new Addison-Wesley titles.

We encourage you to patronize the many fine retailers who stock Addison-Wesley titles. Visit our online directory to find stores near you or visit our online store:
http://store.awl.com/ or call 800-824-7799.

Addison Wesley Longman
Computer and Engineering Publishing Group
One Jacob Way, Reading, Massachusetts 01867 USA
TEL 781-944-3700 • FAX 781-942-3076